Clinical Epidemiology

Principles, Methods, and Applications for Clinical Research

SECOND EDITION

Diederick E. Grobbee, MD, PhD
Professor of Clinical Epidemiology
Julius Center for Health Sciences and Primary Care
University Medical Center Utrecht
Utrecht, The Netherlands

Arno W. Hoes, MD, PhD
Professor of Clinical Epidemiology
Julius Center for Health Sciences and Primary Care
University Medical Center Utrecht
Utrecht, The Netherlands

JONES & BARTLETT
LEARNING

World Headquarters
Jones & Bartlett Learning
5 Wall Street
Burlington, MA 01803
978-443-5000
info@jblearning.com
www.jblearning.com

Jones & Bartlett Learning books and products are available through most bookstores and online booksellers. To contact Jones & Bartlett Learning directly, call 800-832-0034, fax 978-443-8000, or visit our website, www.jblearning.com.

Substantial discounts on bulk quantities of Jones & Bartlett Learning publications are available to corporations, professional associations, and other qualified organizations. For details and specific discount information, contact the special sales department at Jones & Bartlett Learning via the above contact information or send an email to specialsales@jblearning.com.

Production Credits

Executive Publisher: William Brottmiller
Publisher: Michael Brown
Associate Editor: Chloe Falivene
Editorial Assistant: Nicholas Alakel
Associate Production Editor: Rebekah Linga
Senior Marketing Manager: Sophie Fleck Teague
Manufacturing and Inventory Control Supervisor:
  Amy Bacus
Composition: Cenveo Publisher Services
Cover Design: Scott Moden
Photo Research and Permissions Associate:
  Ashley Dos Santos
Cover Image: © Volta_ontwerpers, Utrecht
Printing and Binding: Edwards Brothers Malloy
Cover Printing: Edwards Brothers Malloy

Library of Congress Cataloging-in-Publication Data
Grobbee, D. E., author.
  Clinical Epidemiology: Principles, Methods, and Applications for Clinical Research /
Diederick E. Grobbee and Arno W. Hoes.—Second edition.
    p. ; cm.
  Includes bibliographical references and index.
  ISBN 978-1-4496-7432-8 (pbk.)   ISBN 1-4496-7432-1 (pbk.)
  I. Hoes, Arno W., author.   II. Title. [DNLM: 1. Epidemiologic Methods.   2. Epidemiologic Factors.
3. Prognosis. WA 950]
  RA652.2.C55
  614.4—dc23
                                                            2013030779

6048
Printed in the United States of America
18 17 16 15 14   10 9 8 7 6 5 4 3 2

DEDICATION

To Sjoukje and Carin

CONTENTS

PREFACE

In the current era of evidence-based medicine, with an abundance of published information and a clear need for relevant applied clinical research, clinical epidemiology is increasingly being recognized as an important tool in the critical appraisal of available evidence and the design of new studies.

This text is intended for those who are currently practicing medicine and related disciplines (such as pharmacy, health sciences, nursing sciences, veterinary medicine, and dentistry) as well as those involved in the design and conduct of applied clinical research. Apart from these "users," "doers" of applied clinical research, notably undergraduate students and PhD fellows in medicine and related disciplines, will also benefit from the information provided. Clinical epidemiology instructors will find the text to be a valuable resource for their classes.

The purpose of the text is to teach both the "users" and "doers" of quantitative clinical research. Principles and methods of clinical epidemiology are used to obtain quantitative evidence on diagnosis, etiology, and prognosis of disease and on the effects of interventions. The content of this text reflects our teaching experience on the methodology of applied clinical research over the last 25 years. It was the ever-advancing development of clinical epidemiologic methodology, the increasing discrepancies between our teaching material and existing textbooks of epidemiology, and the many requests from students and practicing physicians for a concise text reflecting our courses that fueled our decision to prepare this novel text.

We hope that our text will contribute to a better understanding of the strengths of clinical epidemiology as well as help both researchers and users of quantitative clinical research in their endeavors to further improve patient care in daily clinical practice.

This edition has been revised and updated extensively. In doing so we benefited enormously from the comments given to us by many readers, specifically the PhD fellows and staff members at the Julius Center for Health Sciences and Primary Care, University Medical Center Utrecht, and in the Department of Epidemiology, Radboud University Medical Center Nijmegen.

As more than three thousand copies of the first edition and reprints have found their way to readers across the globe, we are confident that this text is well appreciated by all those engaged in clinical epidemiologic research or using the results of such studies in clinical practice. We hope this new edition will be similarly appreciated and welcome any comments or suggestions for further improvement.

Diederick E. Grobbee and Arno W. Hoes

FOREWORD

Clinicians often think of epidemiology as distinct from clinical research. As a consequence, epidemiologic methods, disease causation, and preventive medicine, as well as strategic public health issues, have been taught chiefly in epidemiology departments and at schools of public health. Many of these institutions, however, have become too isolated from the practice of medicine and the conduct of clinical research. And both camps—epidemiologic research and clinical research—have suffered from this mutual isolation. Epidemiology would be fertilized by close interaction with clinical medicine, while offering a powerful toolbox derived from advanced methodologic developments to clinical researchers. Epidemiologic principles and methods are not only integral to public health, but also highly relevant to clinical research. However, this fundamental fact is still not adequately appreciated by many clinical investigators.

Could epidemiologic methods and clinical epidemiology indeed revolutionize clinical research? Would methodologic rigor, adequate sample size, and skilled statistical analyses allow more rapid progress and quicker implementation of important discoveries? This bold and perhaps naïve idea came to my mind some 30 years ago and my initial hunch that it is true has grown ever since. Still a practicing surgeon at the time, my own research forced and encouraged some familiarity with the fundamental principles of epidemiology. And this familiarity truly changed my perspective on my professional performance in the operating room, clinical ward, outpatient departments, emergency units, and in the classroom where I lectured to medical students.

Foremost, my slowly growing familiarity with epidemiologic methodology helped me understand the fundamental prerequisites for causal inference—after all, a successful treatment is little more than a cause of a good outcome. This insight made me increasingly uncertain about the real benefit of our therapeutic, chiefly surgical, interventions and the performance of our diagnostic technologies. This was a time when hip replacement, coronary bypass surgery, breast-conserving surgery, laparoscopic cholecystectomy, kidney transplantation, vascular reconstruction, and radical prostatectomy (just to mention a few examples) transformed our work in the operating room—often without the support of benefit of new technologies from randomized trials. At the same time, computerized tomography, ultrasound, PET scans, and, subsequently, magnetic resonance revolutionized our ability to visualize organs and assess bodily functions. Today, the flow of novel therapeutic and diagnostic techniques is even more intense.

As a practitioner, I navigated through these years with two competing feelings. One was a growing frustration with how haphazardly clinical methods were used and combined; that novel surgical procedures—unlike the strictly regulated approval of new drugs—could be introduced over-night, often with no strategy to quantify risks versus benefits. As a corollary, decisions influencing the life and health of our patients were based on little scientific evidence. But another feeling grew too—a fascination with epide-miologic theory and methodology as directly relevant to advancing the evidence base for clinical practice. After 17 years, I left the operating room peacefully, permanently, and with no subsequent regret to become a full-time epidemiologist.

Persuading clinicians that methods of extraordinary relevance for their research are readily available in the epidemiologic toolbox can be challeng-ing. But it is trickier still to provide an accessible text that helps them see the light and the opportunities. It is in this context that *Clinical Epidemiol-ogy: Principles, Methods, and Applications for Clinical Research, Second Edition* becomes such a tremendously useful addition to the existing literature. I wish that this text had been available to me 30 years ago. I congratulate all those younger colleagues who now receive a firm and stable helping hand in their necessary endeavor to study a wide variety of clinical phenomena in human populations. And I hope that the text will also be read by the growing number of practitioners who need to understand the sophisticated methods used in cutting-edge clinical research.

Hans-Olov Adami

Hans-Olov Adami, MD, PhD, is Adjunct Professor of Epidemiology and former Chairman of the Department of Epidemiology at the Harvard School of Public Health, Associate Director of Populations Sciences at the Dana Farber/Harvard Cancer Center, and Professor Emeritus of Cancer Epidemiology at the Karolinska Institute, Stockholm, Sweden.

THE JULIUS CENTER

The Julius Center for Health Sciences and Primary Care (http://www.julius center.nl) was established at the University Medical Center Utrecht in December 1996. The Julius Center was built upon previously existing small departments of epidemiology, public health, and clinical epidemiology, and was subsequently expanded to include primary care, biostatistics, and medical humanities.

The name was chosen to serve as a symbol for innovative health sciences rather than to specify the disciplines assembled in the center. Hendrik Willem Julius (1901–1971) was a professor of health sciences and hygiene at Utrecht University during the first half of the 20th century and an early advocate of the clinical trial. Julius was not affiliated with the center, but we are honored to use his name with the consent of his children and grandchildren.

Since its start, the Julius Center has continuously grown in its main domains of research, education, and patient care. A few principles have guided the decisions that shaped the center. One is that epidemiology is a basic medical discipline. This is reflected in the research agenda of the center and the background of its staff, who comprise a fair number of physicians working in productive harmony with epidemiologists from many other biomedical backgrounds. A second principle is the view that clinical epidemiology flourishes best in close approximation and interaction with clinical medicine. Consequently, the center is located in a hospital environment and provides clinical care in primary healthcare centers within a large, newly built area of the city of Utrecht, while joint appointments of staff further support the continuous interaction with other clinical departments. Finally, a leading principle is that the quality of research by junior fellows as well as by experienced staff is determined by the level of understanding of the principles and methods of epidemiology. To achieve this goal, good education is essential.

When the center had just opened and was still small in size, we began with the development of a common theoretical basis through teaching each other, harmonizing, and updating our views along the way. This has formed the basis for the current epidemiologic curriculum in Utrecht, including the content of the international Master of Science in Epidemiology program offered at Utrecht University (http://www.mscepidemiology.eu) and of our teaching of clinical epidemiology to medical students, clinicians, and other health professionals in the Netherlands and abroad.

We believe that a common and consistent set of principles and methods are the strongest assets of epidemiology and the true value clinical epidemiology has to offer to today's applied clinical research.

Much of the content of this text reflects our teaching to numerous students. We and our staff continue to provide courses on a wide range of topics in epidemiology and health sciences. Online versions of these courses may be found at Elevate (www.elevatehealth.eu), an academic educational e-learning platform.

ABOUT THE AUTHORS

Diederick (Rick) E. Grobbee, MD, PhD (1957) was trained in medicine in Utrecht and, after doing a residency in internal medicine, he obtained a PhD in epidemiology at Erasmus University in Rotterdam. His education was continued at McGill University in Montreal and as a visiting Associate Professor at the Harvard University School of Public Health. He spent nearly a decade at Erasmus, where he headed the cardiovascular epidemiology group and was appointed Professor of Clinical Epidemiology. He subsequently moved to the University Medical Center in Utrecht to become Professor of Clinical Epidemiology. Here he founded the Julius Center for Health Sciences and Primary Care in 1996. He served as Chairman for the Center for the next 14 years. He holds honorary appointments at Sydney University and the University of Malaya in Kuala Lumpur. In 2010, he was appointed Distinguished University Professor of International Health Sciences and Global Health at Utrecht University, where he is also Program Director of the international MSc and PhD Epidemiology Program. He is a fellow of the Royal Netherlands Academy of Sciences and chairs its Medical Section and Medical Advisory Council. He is Editor-in-Chief of the *European Journal of Preventive Cardiology*. His teaching experience includes courses on clinical epidemiology and clinical research methods to various audiences in several countries.

Arno W. Hoes, MD, PhD (1958) studied medicine at the Radboud University in Nijmegen. He obtained his PhD degree in clinical epidemiology at the Erasmus Medical Center in Rotterdam. He was further trained in clinical epidemiology at the London School of Hygiene and Tropical Medicine. In 1991, he was appointed Assistant Professor of Clinical Epidemiology and General Practice in the Department of Epidemiology and the Department of General Practice at the Erasmus Medical Center. In the latter department, he headed the research line, "cardiovascular disease in primary care." In 1996, he moved to the Julius Center for Health Sciences and Primary Care of the University Medical Center in Utrecht, where he was appointed Professor of Clinical Epidemiology and Primary Care in 1998. Since 2010, he has been the Chair of the Julius Center. Most of his current research activities focus on the (early) diagnosis, prognosis, and therapy of common cardiovascular diseases. His teaching experience includes courses on clinical epidemiology, diagnostic research, case-control studies, drug risk assessment, and cardiovascular disease. He is a member of the Dutch Medicines Evaluation Board, the Health Council of the Netherlands, and is on the editorial boards of several medical journals.

CONTRIBUTORS

We thank the following colleagues and friends for their invaluable contributions and critical comments on several of the chapters of this text.

Ale Algra, MD, PhD
Professor of Clinical Epidemiology
Julius Center for Health Sciences and Department of Neurology
University Medical Center Utrecht
Department of Clinical Epidemiology
Leiden University Medical Center
The Netherlands

Ale Algra has extensive experience with the design, conduct, and analysis of randomized clinical trials in neurovascular disease. His experience and attention to detail shaped Chapter 10.

Huibert Burger, MD, PhD
Associate Professor of Clinical Epidemiology
Departments of General Practice and Epidemiology
University of Groningen Medical Center
The Netherlands

Huibert Burger has a strong interest in the theoretical basis of prediction research. He made important contributions to Chapter 4 on prognostic research.

Yolanda van der Graaf, MD, PhD
Professor of Clinical Epidemiology
Julius Center for Health Sciences and Primary Care
Department of Radiology
University Medical Center Utrecht
The Netherlands

Yolanda van der Graaf is one of the most experienced "hands-on" clinical epidemiologists in our group and therefore the best equipped to address data analysis from a practical perspective, as is demonstrated in Chapter 12.

Rolf H.H. Groenwold, MD, PhD
Assistant Professor of Clinical Epidemiology
Julius Center for Health Sciences and Primary Care
University Medical Center Utrecht
The Netherlands
Rolf Groenwold is a talented clinical epidemiologist who specializes in confounding adjustment. He contributed significantly to Chapters 3 and 11.

Geert J.M.G. van der Heijden, PhD
Professor of Social Dentistry
Free University
Amsterdam, The Netherlands
Geert van der Heijden is an evidence-based medicine aficionado and a literature search expert. His knowledge is shared in Chapter 11 on meta-analysis.

Jacobus Lubsen, PhD
Professor Emeritus of Clinical Epidemiology
Erasmus University Medical School
Rotterdam, The Netherlands
Jacobus 'Koos' Lubsen is a longtime teacher and friend. Some of his provocative and lucid ideas can be found in Chapter 11.

Carl G.M. Moons, PhD
Professor of Clinical Epidemiology
Julius Center for Health Sciences
Primary Care and Department of Anesthesiology
University Medical Center Utrecht
The Netherlands
Carl Moons is an expert on prediction research, as he explores the conceptual and theoretical foundations utilizing his extensive practical experience. His views are expressed in Chapter 2 on diagnostic research and he has further contributed to Chapter 4 on prognostic research.

Yvonne T. van der Schouw, PhD
Professor of Chronic Disease Epidemiology
Julius Center for Health Sciences and Primary Care
University Medical Center Utrecht
The Netherlands
Yvonne van der Schouw has a strong track record in etiologic epidemiologic research. Her work includes cohort studies and randomized trials on the effects of various nutritional factors on health. She provided the examples in Chapter 3.

ACKNOWLEDGMENTS

We are indebted to all current and former members of the scientific staff of the Julius Center for their crucial role in advancing the center's conceptual ideas of clinical epidemiology and the conduct of applied clinical research. The development of a joint teaching program shortly after the founding of the Julius Center marked an important first step in the process that eventually resulted in this text. Many staff members contributed to specific sections of this text, and their expertise, devotion, and hard work are greatly appreciated.

We thank our former colleagues at the Department of Epidemiology at Erasmus Medical Center Rotterdam for their role in the development of our epidemiologic thinking through many stimulating discussions (even when we disagreed).

We thank the many students, PhD fellows, clinicians, and participants in our teaching programs in the Netherlands and abroad for their criticism, discussions, and wit that continues to encourage us to further develop our understanding of clinical epidemiology and improve our teaching methods.

Our thinking about clinical epidemiology was influenced by many scientists. We would like to mention three in particular.

Hans A. Valkenburg laid the foundation for clinical epidemiology in the Netherlands by combining his clinical expertise and knowledge of epidemiology with his entrepreneurship, designing large-scale studies and laboratory facilities in close collaboration with clinical departments. We are proud that we were trained in clinical epidemiology at his department in Rotterdam. His ideas still serve as a role model for the Julius Center and other clinical epidemiology departments in the Netherlands.

We were profoundly influenced by the wealth of ideas on clinical epidemiology articulated by Olli S. Miettinen. Our many provocative discussions shared with him around the globe not only encouraged us to remain modest about our own contributions to the discipline, but strongly stimulated us to further explore the foundations of clinical epidemiology and their application in clinical research. We have no doubt that his reading of our text will induce further stimulating interaction and future adaptations.

We are grateful to Albert Hofman for his friendship and support in a crucial phase of our scientific development. He is at least partly "guilty" for our choice to pursue a career in clinical epidemiology. His contagious enthusiasm about epidemiology and dedication to scientific excellence had a major impact on our work.

Without the relentless efforts of Monique den Hartog and Giene de Vries in the preparation of the manuscript, this text would never have been published. We truly thank them for their important secretarial contributions.

QUICK START

Throughout this text, we explore the challenges clinicians face in daily practice and the quantitative knowledge required to practice medicine. To serve both readers who mainly use clinical research findings as well as (inexperienced or more advanced) clinical researchers, the text is divided into three parts.

Part One (Overview) provides an introduction to the principles and theoretical background of clinical epidemiologic research and its interplay with clinical practice. In Part Two (Principles of Clinical Research), the four major types of clinical research (diagnostic research, etiologic research, prognostic research, and intervention research) are discussed in much more detail. In Part Three (Tools for Clinical Research), several methods that are often applied in clinical research are presented to assist the reader in the design, conduct, and understanding of specific studies.

The text starts with a theoretical and philosophical overview of the origins and nature of clinical epidemiology (Chapter 1). You may wish to read that at a later stage if your immediate interest is a specific type of research question or study.

The second part of the text emphasizes the design of clinical research, with major emphasis on the type of research question and theoretical design. In each of the chapters we gave ample attention to phrasing the research question. The question should be clear, unequivocal, and relevant in view of the clinical problem. Clinically relevant research questions are categorized with a view to the four types of challenges clinicians are faced with in daily practice and in the hierarchical order in which they occur naturally: (1) diagnostic questions, dealing with the challenge of efficiently setting the diagnosis underlying the patient's signs and symptoms (Chapter 2); (2) etiologic questions, dealing with the challenge of determining the cause(s) of disease (Chapter 3); (3) prognostic questions, dealing with the challenge of efficiently predicting the natural history of disease in a patient, answering the question: "What would happen if I do not intervene?" (Chapter 4); and (4) questions about the beneficial ("intended") and adverse ("unintended") effects of interventions on the course of a disease, dealing with the challenge of determining the effects of a particular therapy on a patient's prognosis (Chapters 5 and 6). We find this distinction between the four clinical domains very useful, both in our teaching of evidence-based medicine and clinical epidemiology and in our clinical research activities. This approach can be summarized as the DEPTh model, where D stands for Diagnosis, E for Etiology, P for Prognosis, and Th for Therapy (or intervention).

A clinically relevant research question, stemming from a problem encountered in clinical practice in one of the 4 DEPTh areas, is leading in the research design. The design of a study should always start with the theoretical design. By theoretical design we mean the formulation of the occurrence relation as it follows from the research question and the subsequent conceptual definition of outcome, determinants, and possible extraneous determinants (confounders). In the theoretical design, a distinction is made between research that addresses causality (etiologic research), and descriptive research that does not address causality (diagnostic and prognostic research). Research on the benefits and risks of interventions is discussed as a separate case because it primarily deals with causality but also has noncausal aspects.

We find the distinction between causal and descriptive research extremely useful to arrive at the best results of a study. We realize that these terms have also been used with different meanings. In our use of the terms, *causal research* is research in which a causal question is addressed. *Descriptive research* is research where causality is not important, such as in diagnostic studies where the value of laboratory measurements to set a diagnosis is studied. While, for example, high blood glucose identifies a patient with diabetes, elevated glucose is a consequence and not a cause of the disease. Consequently, the research is descriptive and not causal. We do not claim that our use of terminology is right. We do believe, however, that our use of terminology provides a model that will help readers better understand the principles of research. Our terminology provides the reader with a consistent and robust framework to design, interpret, and apply clinical research.

The third part of the text is really about the practicalities of empirical clinical research. Data can be collected (Chapter 7) and analyzed (Chapter 12) in a number of ways. Chapters on cohort studies (Chapter 8), case-control studies (Chapter 9), clinical trials (Chapter 10), and meta-analyses (Chapter 11) should prepare the reader to be involved in setting up and carrying out applied clinical research with confidence and will help the reader in critically appraising the work of other researchers. In each chapter, the principles of the design are discussed as well as operational aspects. Worked-out examples should help the reader to understand how the research is actually conducted, analyzed, and interpreted.

In the text we have tried to be as consistent as possible in using epidemiologic terminology. There are different schools of thought and views on common epidemiologic terms. Some will call case-control studies retrospective studies, but we argue that in both cohort and case-control studies the outlook is typically longitudinal and in both types of studies data can be collected retrospectively. In general, we explain why we prefer certain terms. For example, we use the term *extraneous determinant* when speaking about a confounder because it immediately tells us that the determinant is extraneous to the occurrence relationship of interest. The text is essentially self-contained. Extensive knowledge on epidemiology or statistics is not needed to benefit from its contents. References are given to more detailed and advanced texts.

This can be viewed as a comprehensive text covering everything you always wanted to know about clinical epidemiologic research. Alternatively, the reader can immediately zoom in on a topic that has acute relevance in view of the research he or she is engaged in. The chapter titles clearly indicate the content of the chapters and the extensive index at the end of the text should enable a reader to quickly find a topic or method of interest. We had several types of readers in mind when writing the text: students working on their master's or PhD degree should learn the background methodology for the studies they conduct, readers of research papers should be able to distinguish between studies that are relevant and valid and those that are flawed, and clinicians will find tools to assess whether certain findings from clinical research are applicable to their patients. Seasoned investigators should find food for thought and feel challenged to further refine their research approach. We are always eager to receive critical comments and suggestions for improvement that will help to further sharpen our thinking about clinical research.

Part 1

Overview

Chapter 1

Introduction to Clinical Epidemiology

INTRODUCTION

Epidemiology is essentially occurrence research [Miettinen, 1985]. The object of epidemiologic research is to study the occurrence of illness and its relationship to determinants. Epidemiologic research deals with a wide variety of topics. A few examples include the causal role of measles virus infection in the development of inflammatory bowel disease in children, the added value of a novel B-type natriuretic peptide serum bedside test in patients presenting with symptoms suggestive of heart failure, the prognostic implications of the severity of bacterial meningitis on future school performance, and the effect of antibiotics in children with acute otitis media on the duration of complaints. What binds all of these examples is the study and, more precisely, the quantification of the relationship of the determinants (in these cases, measles infection, the novel bedside test, the severity of bacterial meningitis, and antibiotic therapy) with the occurrence of an illness or other clinically relevant outcome (that is, inflammatory bowel disease, heart failure, school performance, and duration of otitis media complaints). Central to epidemiologic studies in such diverse fields is the emphasis on occurrence relations as objects of research.

The origins of epidemiology lie in unraveling the causes of infectious disease epidemics and the emergence of public health as an empirical discipline. Every student of epidemiology will enjoy reading the pioneer works of John Snow on the mode of the transmission of cholera in 19th century London, including the famous words: "In consequence of what I said, the handle of the pump was removed on the following day" [Snow, 1855]. Subsequently, the methods of epidemiology were successfully applied to identifying causes of chronic diseases, such as cardiovascular disease and cancer, and now encompass virtually all fields of medicine.

In recent decades, it has increasingly been acknowledged that the principles and methods of epidemiology may be fruitfully employed in applied clinical research. In parallel with a growing emphasis in medicine on using quantitative evidence to guide patient care and to judge its performance, epidemiology has become one of the fundamental disciplines for patient-oriented research and a cornerstone for evidence-based medicine. Clinical epidemiology deals with questions relevant to clinical practice: questions about diagnosis, causes, prognosis, and treatment of disease. To serve clinical practice best, research should be *relevant* (i.e., deal with problems encountered in clinical practice), *valid* (i.e., the results are true and, thus, not biased), and *precise* (i.e., the results lie within a limited range of uncertainty). (See **Box 1–1.**) These prerequisites are crucial for research results eventually to be applied with confidence in daily practice.

CLINICAL EPIDEMIOLOGY

Clinical epidemiology is epidemiology [Grobbee & Miettinen, 1995]. It is a descriptive label that denotes the application of epidemiologic methods to questions relevant to patient care. Then why use a different term? Clinical epidemiology does not indicate a different discipline or refer to specific aspects of epidemiologic research, such as research on iatrogenic disease. Traditionally, practitioners of epidemiology predominantly have been found in public health or community medicine, which can be well understood from the perspective of its history. Epidemiologic research results have unique value in shaping preventive medicine as well as in the search for causes of infectious and chronic disease that affect large numbers of people in our societies. Yet, with the growing recognition of the importance of probabilistic inference in matters of diagnosis and treatment of individual patients, an obvious interest has grown in the approaches epidemiologic research has to offer in clinical medicine. Use of the term *clinical epidemiology* therefore refers to its relevance in "applied" clinical science; conversely it helps to remind us that the priority in the clinical research agenda must be set with a keen appreciation of what is relevant for patient care. Clinical epidemiology provides a highly useful set of principles and methods for the design and conduct of quantitative clinical research.

Traditionally, epidemiologic research has largely been devoted to etiologic research. Investigators have built careers and departments' reputations on epidemiologic research into the causes of infectious or chronic diseases, while for patient care the ability to establish an individual's diagnosis and prognosis is commonly held to be of greater importance. Still, the work of most master's and doctoral fellows in epidemiology, in particular those working outside of a medical environment, is concentrated on etiology.

BOX 1–1   Valid and Precise

---

valid

Main Entry: **val·id**
Pronunciation: ˈva-ləd
Function: *adjective*
Etymology: Middle French or Medieval Latin; Middle French *valide*, from Medieval Latin *validus*, from Latin, strong, potent, from *ValEre*

1 : having legal efficacy or force; especially : executed with the proper legal authority and formalities <a *valid* contract>

2a : well-grounded or justifiable : being at once relevant and meaningful <a *valid* theory> **b** : logically correct <a *valid* argument> <*valid* inference>

3 : appropriate to the end in view : effective <every craft has its own *valid* methods>

4 *of a taxon* : conforming to accepted principles of sound biological classification

precise

Main Entry: **pre-cise**
Pronunciation: pri-ˈsīs
Function: *adjective*
Etymology: Middle English, from Middle French *precis*, from Latin *praecisus*, past participate of *praecidere* to cut off, from *prae-* + *caedere* to cut

1 : exactly or sharply defined or stated

2 : minutely exact

3 : strictly conforming to a pattern, standard, or convention

4 : distinguished from every other <at just that *precise* moment>

Adapted from the Merriam-Webster online dictionary, © 2013 by Merriam-Webster, Incorporated (*http://www.merriam-webster.com/dictionary/valid* and *http://www.merriam-webster.com/dictionary/precise*. Accessed July 2, 2013.)

Perhaps they do not realize that this focus actually restricts the value of epidemiologic research for medical care.

Clearly, causal knowledge is relevant, because it may help to prevent disease and find new treatments. In clinical practice, however, an adequate diagnosis, prediction of the natural course of an illness, and the setting of appropriate indications and contraindications for action are major concerns. These are often established without knowledge of the causes of the illness. If there is a message in clinical epidemiology today that needs reinforcement, it is that more work is needed in diagnostic and prognostic research that, as will be explained later, is descriptive rather than causal.

RESEARCH RELEVANT TO PATIENT CARE

The motive in applied clinical research should be to obtain knowledge relevant to clinical practice. Consequently, understanding the challenges in clinical practice is essential for understanding the objectives of clinical research. Consider a patient consulting a physician. Most often the reason for consultation is a complaint or symptom suggestive of some illness. For example, a 60-year-old male patient with problems with micturition is referred by his general practitioner to a urologist. For all subsequent action, the point of departure is the patient profile. This patient profile has two components: (1) the clinical profile comprising (among other things) the patient's symptoms, signs, and results of diagnostic tests; and (2) the nonclinical profile that includes characteristics such as age, gender, and socioeconomic status. Of these two sets of facts, the clinical profile is temporary and relates to the illness, whereas the nonclinical profile is present in the absence of illness and thus relates directly to the bearer of the illness, the patient. The two sets are complementary. Starting from the patient profile, the physician faces a number of challenges. In temporal order these are: (1) interpretation of the clinical profile, (2) explanation of the illness, (3) prediction of the course, (4) decision about treatment, and (5) execution of treatment.

The first, diagnostic, challenge is to interpret the patient profile and establish a diagnosis. The question to be answered is: "What is the most likely illness, given this patient's profile?" In this process, the doctor identifies the presence of a particular illness in the patient. Commonly, at some point following the diagnosis, an explanation for the illness may be requested (the second, etiologic, challenge). However, while it seems obvious to pose the etiologic question of why this illness has occurred in this patient at this time, an answer may be impossible to give and quite often is not even necessary for the patient to receive adequate care. For example, appendicitis may be effectively treated by surgery without any understanding of the reasons for its occurrence. Consequently, this step is often skipped in daily practice. Prediction of the course of disease (the third, prognostic, challenge) is usually a much more important task for the physician than a full understanding of its etiology. Certainly, the predicted course is of greatest importance to the patient. The question to be answered here is this: "Given the patient's illness, its possible etiology, and the clinical and nonclinical profiles of the patient, what will be the future course of the illness in this patient?" The prognosis comprises both the prediction of the illness's course, given the diagnosis and other patient characteristics (i.e., the predicted course assuming no intervention takes place, which can be considered the prognostic, or third, challenge), as well as the presumed beneficial or adverse effects on that course by appropriate interventions (which also incorporates the fourth, therapeutic, challenge). Note that this ideally includes a comprehensive prediction, given all legitimate clinical actions as well as interventions induced by the patient himself [Hilden & Habbema, 1987]. Clearly, in contemporary medicine the expected course of disease is likely to depend heavily on the availability and choice of treatment. Once this choice has been made (the fourth challenge), execution of treatment naturally follows (the fifth challenge). The first four consecutive challenges in clinical practice can be summarized with the acronym DEPTh (*D*iagnosis, *E*tiology, *P*rognosis and *Th*erapy/intervention). The DEPTh model is not only useful in designing and understanding clinical research, but also in recognizing clinical problems in daily practice and searching for the evidence to deal with these (see **Figure 1–1**).

FIGURE 1–1   Prognosis.

A modern physician is a scientific physician. In the era of evidence-based medicine, a physician is taught to base his or her actions on scientific evidence and to develop a scientific attitude even in those (alas) frequent circumstances where data are lacking, incomplete, or may never become available with sufficient precision to guide individual patient care. The mission for clinical epidemiologic research is to add to the knowledge base from which practitioners of medicine may draw. This mission inherently calls for a multidisciplinary approach with epidemiology providing a well-established complementary set of principles and methods to the general knowledge base and practical expertise. For a physician to meet the challenges of everyday patient care (see **Table 1–1**), knowledge is essential: diagnostic knowledge for the first challenge, etiologic knowledge for the second, and prognostic knowledge (including knowledge about the effects of interventions) for the third and fourth. As in applied clinical research in general, the role of clinical epidemiology is to assist in providing scientifically valid quantitative knowledge on diagnosis, etiology, and prognosis of illnesses, including the effects of interventions on their course. This inferential, probabilistic knowledge offers a rational basis for decision making in patient care. To make treatment decisions, providers require quantitative knowledge about the prognosis, considering

TABLE 1–1   Challenges of Daily Patient Care

Challenge	Question	Needs
Interpret the clinical profile: predict the presence of the illness	What illness best explains the symptoms and signs of the patient?	Diagnostic knowledge
Explanation of the illness	Why did this illness occur in this patient?	Etiologic knowledge
Predict the course of disease	1. What will the future bring for this patient, assuming no intervention takes place? 2. To what extent may the course of disease be affected by treatment?	Prognostic knowledge (including therapeutic knowledge)
Decision about medical action	Which treatment, if any, should be chosen for this particular patient?	Balancing benefits and risks of available options
Execution of medical action	Initiation of treatment	Skills

various treatment options combined with an evaluation of the benefits and risks of these options for a particular type of patient. The practicing physician will need to combine this knowledge with his or her experience and skills, as well as the patient's point of view, to arrive at a balanced decision on the best treatment strategy. These decisions also may be formally addressed in algorithms that are the domain of clinical decision analysis. In clinical decision analyses, results from quantitative applied clinical research serve as the input, with estimates of patient outcomes (utilities) and costs of various possible management alternatives as the output. Execution of treatments (challenge 5) requires skill and falls beyond the scope of epidemiologic research.

When designing applied clinical research, the principal objective should be to provide knowledge that is applicable in the practice of medicine. To achieve this, the research question should be clearly formulated and an answer should be given in a way that it is both valid and sufficiently precise. First comes validity, the extent to which a research result is true and free from bias. Valid research results must be sufficiently precise to allow adequate predictions for individual patients or groups of subjects. For example, knowing that the 5-year mortality rate after a diagnosis of cancer is validly estimated at 50% is one thing, but when the precision of the estimate ranges between 5% and 80%, the utility of this knowledge is limited for patient care. The design of studies focused on diagnosis, etiology, prognosis, and treatment needs to meet these goals. General and specific design characteristics of clinical epidemiologic research will be discussed in some detail in the next section.

EPIDEMIOLOGIC STUDY DESIGN

Study design in clinical epidemiology has three components: (1) the theoretical design, (2) the design of data collection, and (3) the design of data analysis (see **Box 1–2**). For some reason, many discussions about study designs seem to concentrate largely on issues of data collection: "Are we going to do a cohort study or a case-control study?" Also, the way the data will be analyzed is often more heavily emphasized than the theoretical design, despite the latter's overriding importance.

Theoretical Design

The theoretical design of a study starts from a research question. Formulating the research question is of critical importance as it guides the theoretical

BOX 1–2   Epidemiologic Study Design

- Theoretical design
  Design of the occurrence relation

- Design of data collection
  Design of the conceptual and operational collection of data to document the empirical occurrence relationship in a study population

- Design of data analysis
  This includes a description of the data and quantitative estimates of associations

design and ensures that, eventually, the study produces an answer that fits the needs of the investigator. Therefore, a research question should be expressed as a question and not as a vague ambition. All too often, investigators set out to "examine the association between *X* and *Y*." This is far from a research question and will not lead to a clinically useful answer.

For starters, a research question should end with a question mark. An example of a useful research question is: "Does 5-day treatment with penicillin in children with acute otitis media reduce the duration of complaints?" This research question combines three crucial elements: (1) one or more determinants (in this case 5-day treatment with penicillin), (2) an outcome (the duration of the complaints), and (3) the domain. The domain refers to the population (or set of patients) to whom the results can be applied. The definition of the domain (in this case, children with acute otitis media) is typically much broader than the selection criteria for the patient population included in the study (e.g., children enlisted in 25 primary care practices located in the central region of the Netherlands during the year 2000 who were diagnosed with acute otitis media). Similarly, the domain of the famous British study in the 1940s addressing the causal role of cigarette smoking in lung cancer was man and not restricted in place or time. The domain for a study is like a pharmaceutical package insert. It specifies the type of patients to whom the results can be applied. It guides patient selection for the research, but this selection is usually further restricted for practical or other reasons. When an appropriate research question is formulated, the design of the occurrence relation is relatively easy.

The occurrence relation is central to the theoretical design of a clinical epidemiologic study. The *occurrence relation* is the object of research and relates one or multiple determinants to an outcome. In subsequent phases of the study, the "true" nature and strength of the occurrence relation is documented and quantitatively estimated using empirical data. Occurrence relations in diagnostic, etiologic, prognostic, and intervention research each have particular characteristics, but all have a major impact on the other two components of epidemiologic study design: design of data collection and design of data analysis. To facilitate the theoretical design of a study and determine the (elements of the) occurrence relation, a distinction should be made between descriptive and causal research.

Causal Versus Descriptive Research

By definition, *causal research* aims to explain a relationship in etiologic terms. This is the case in typical etiologic research (such as studies on the causal association between cigarette smoking and lung cancer risk) and also in studies that address questions of treatment efficacy and safety (i.e., the beneficial and adverse effects caused by the intervention). The essence of causal research is that it aims to explain the occurrence of an illness or other outcome. It asks the question, "Does this factor actually cause this outcome?" One could imagine the researcher acting as a judge in the courtroom deciding whether the determinants (factors in the case) are guilty of the crime (outcome). If the verdict is "guilty," this implies that the occurrence of the outcome could not be explained by some other, extraneous, reason.

Extraneous determinants are factors that are not part of the object of research; they are outside of the occurrence relation, but they may have to be considered in view of validity. A more common term for an extraneous determinant is *confounder*. When extraneous determinants are not taken into account, the observed relationship between determinant and outcome may not reflect the true relationship. The observed relationship can be said to be confounded and the results of the study will be biased (i.e., invalid). Consequently, the relationship between determinant and outcome need to be quantified conditional on the confounding factors—the extraneous determinants—in order for the results to be true. Confounding must be excluded to obtain a valid estimate of the causal relationship between the determinant of interest and the outcome. When, for example, the aim is to assess the causal relationship between alcohol intake and the risk of lung cancer, it is evident that an observed positive association may be confounded by smoking. Smoking is an extraneous determinant, because alcohol drinkers smoke more often, smoking is causally related to lung cancer, and smoking is not part of the causal pathway relating alcohol to lung cancer (i.e., it is extraneous). A more elaborate discussion on confounding and ways to exclude it is provided in Chapters 3 and 6.

In *descriptive research*, the aim is to predict rather than explain; this includes diagnostic and prognostic research. In *diagnostic research*, the determinants typically include elements of the clinical profile, which are signs, symptoms, and test results, with the outcome being the diagnosis of the disease that fits the profile. In *prognostic research*, determinants similarly comprise the clinical profile, including any relevant diagnostic information, with the outcome being the prognosis, for example, expressed by survival, cure, or recurrence of disease.

An essential difference between causal and descriptive research is that in descriptive research no causal relationship between determinant and outcome is assumed. In diagnostic research, determinants that result from the disease are often used to predict its presence. For example, to establish a diagnosis of rheumatoid arthritis, the sedimentation rate may be useful, but its elevation clearly results from the disease. Because causal explanation is not necessary, confounding plays no role in descriptive research. It is the rule rather than the exception that multiple determinants are considered at the same time in descriptive research. Yet, none of these determinants is extraneous to the occurrence relation. All determinant information is used to lead to the best prediction of diagnosis or prognosis.

Elements of the Occurrence Relation

The *occurrence relation* has a standard set of elements: the outcome, one or multiple determinants (D), and, when causality is studied, one or multiple extraneous determinants (ED) or confounders. The number of determinants and the need to include extraneous factors depends on the research question and whether the research is descriptive or causal. In descriptive research, typically multiple determinants are studied. If causal, the relationship between a determinant and an outcome must be quantified conditional on extraneous determinants. That is, for the relationship to be truly causal, it needs to be present irrespective of the presence or absence of confounding variables.

The relationship between outcome and determinants is quantified by some mathematical function (f). Mathematically, the occurrence relation can be summarized as follows:

Outcome = $f(D \mid ED)$ for causal occurrence relations and
Outcome = $f(D_1, D_2, D_n)$ for descriptive occurrence relations.

In the theoretical design, outcome and (extraneous) determinants are first defined conceptually. For example, to answer the question of whether depression is causally related to the occurrence of heart disease, the occurrence relation is defined as,

Heart disease = f (depression | ED)

where ED could include lifestyle factors such as smoking and alcohol but also treatments for depression that might lead to heart disease, such as tricyclic antidepressants.

To allow the collection of empirical data for the study, typically the conceptual definitions of outcome and determinants need to be operationalized to measurable variables. In this example, depression could be measured using the Zung depression scale and heart disease could be operationalized by a record of admission to a hospital with an acute myocardial infarction. Often, this step leads to simplification or to measures that do not fully capture the conceptual definitions. For example, we may wish to measure quality of life but may need to settle for a crude approximation using a simple 36-item questionnaire. To appreciate the results of a study, it is important to realize that such compromises may have been made.

DESIGN OF DATA COLLECTION

Now that the overall structure of the research is in place, it is time to design how the data will be collected. Clinical epidemiologic research is empirical research, which means that the theoretical occurrence relations are observed after analyzing empirical data collected from individuals. The true (scientific) nature of the occurrence relation is estimated from the observations. Consequently, an important aspect of the conduct of research is the collection of data that capture the occurrence relation.

There are several ways in which data for a particular study can be collected. The choice will be determined both by the need to obtain a valid estimate of the nature of the occurrence relation and by practical considerations. The former, for example, includes the need to collect full confounder data in causal research. The latter may include restrictions in time or funding that limit the number of options for collecting data. The need to find the truth, and thus the need to never compromise validity, is an essential starting point. Yet, for a given level of validity there may still be several options for the collection of data.

An inventory of ways to collect data in clinical epidemiologic research and their similarities and distinctions can be found in Chapter 7. In brief, the choices to be made for data collection include the time scale (i.e., follow-up time is zero or larger than zero), the nature of the study population (i.e., everyone, the census, is studied or only a sample from the study base), and the option of conducting a study experimentally or nonexperimentally. In a cross-sectional study, the follow-up time for a population is zero. But in a longitudinal study, the follow-up time is greater than zero. In a cohort study, a full population sample is studied (census), while in a case-control study, only cases and a sample of controls are studied. In a randomized trial, subjects are experimentally exposed to a particular determinant, for example a drug. In an observational cohort study, determinants are studied that are present without any experimental manipulation by the investigator. Aspects of the design of data collection will be discussed in the various chapters on diagnostic, etiologic, prognostic, and intervention research and are presented in more detail in the chapters on cohorts, case-control studies, and randomized trials.

DESIGN OF DATA ANALYSIS

The most difficult parts of designing clinical epidemiologic research are completed when the occurrence relation and the data collection have been designed. In the data analysis, the data of the study are summarized and the relationships between determinants and outcome are quantified using statistical methods. Design of data analysis is important because it will determine the utility of the result, so it should maintain the relevance and validity achieved so far. However, in general there are only a few appropriate and feasible ways to analyze data of a given study. Ideally, the design of data analysis follows naturally from the research question, the form of the occurrence relation, and the type of data collected. Some details of the approaches to the design of data analysis can be found in the various chapters on diagnostic, prognostic, and etiologic research, and a summary is presented in Chapter 12.

DIAGNOSTIC, ETIOLOGIC, PROGNOSTIC, AND INTERVENTION RESEARCH

The major types of clinical epidemiologic research are introduced in **Table 1–2** and their distinctions and shared aspects will be emphasized in the sections that follow.

TABLE 1–2   Major Types of Clinical Epidemiologic Research

Type of Research Question	Descriptive/ Causal	Aim (Clinical Challenge)	Relevance
Diagnostic research	Descriptive	To predict the probability of presence of target disease from clinical and nonclinical profile	Relevance for patient and physician to establish diagnosis and guide management
Etiologic research	Causal	To causally explain occurrence of target disease from determinant	Research relevance, may indicate means of prevention and causal intervention
Prognostic research	Descriptive	To predict the course of disease from clinical and nonclinical profile	Relevance for patient and physician to learn about the future and guide management
Intervention research	Causal and descriptive	1. To causally explain the course of disease as influenced by treatment 2. To predict the course of disease given treatment (options) and clinical and nonclinical profile	1. Relevance for research and drug development/ registration 2. Relevance for patient and physician to decide on optimal management

Diagnostic Research

Each day, physicians are faced with multiple diagnostic challenges. For any patient presenting with complaints, the aim is to interpret the signs, symptoms, and results of (other) diagnostic tests so that a diagnosis can be established. This diagnostic process is complicated and involves multiple determinants incorporating the clinical profile as well as the nonclinical profile (e.g., age, sex, socioeconomic status). Although the physician often considers more than one diagnosis, the typical question to be answered in clinical practice is whether a certain patient profile is indicative of a particular illness (the outcome). Empirical evidence that can guide the clinician in choosing the most efficient diagnostic strategy in relevant patient domains is relatively rare, and clearly more diagnostic research is needed. Diagnostic research typically aims to quantify the value of combinations of determinants in diagnosing a particular illness and includes studies assessing the value of novel diagnostic tests in addition to readily available tests (such as signs and symptoms).

Consider a 75-year-old man visiting his primary care physician because of increased dyspnea. The patient had a myocardial infarction 7 years ago, and his frequent efforts to quit smoking have been unsuccessful. In view of the significant smoking history, his physician considers the possibility of chronic obstructive pulmonary disease; however, the most likely diagnosis appears to be heart failure. Recently, a rapid bedside test to determine the level of B-type natriuretic peptide (BNP), a marker known to be increased in most heart failure patients, has become available and the primary care physician wonders whether such a rapid BNP test has diagnostic value in this patient's domain.

The research question addressing this issue can be phrased as follows:

What is the value of the novel rapid BNP test in addition to signs and symptoms when diagnosing heart failure in patients presenting with dyspnea in primary care?

The multiple determinants include the novel BNP test, the findings from history taking (including known comorbidity), and physical examination, which are available in daily practice anyway; the outcome is a diagnosis of heart failure. The domain should not be too narrow and could be defined as patients presenting to primary care with dyspnea or, alternatively, all patients presenting to primary care with symptoms suggestive of heart failure in the view of the physician. The corresponding occurrence relation can be summarized as the presence of heart failure as a function of multiple determinants, including the novel BNP test:

Heart failure = f(BNP, age, sex, prior MI, symptoms, signs . . .)

Chapter 2 examines the specifics of diagnostic research.

Etiologic Research

Clinicians and epidemiologists alike tend to be most familiar with etiologic research, despite its limited direct relevance to patient care and its methodologic complexities. As in all epidemiologic studies, and starting from the research question, the first step is the design of the occurrence relation. For etiologic research, this includes consideration of a determinant as well as one or multiple extraneous determinants.

Consider, for example, the causes of childhood inflammatory bowel disease (IBD), particularly to what extent a certain factor (e.g., a measles virus infection) may be responsible for its occurrence. The research question could be formulated as follows:

Does measles virus infection cause IBD in children?

Measles infection and IBD represent the determinant and outcome, respectively, and children are the domain. Suppose that a study is designed to answer this research question. The object of such a study would be an occurrence relation in which the incidence of IBD is related to the presence or absence of a preceding measles viral infection.

However, the description of the occurrence relation is not complete unless it includes one or multiple extraneous determinants of the occurrence of childhood IBD. In this example, these could include nutritional status, socioeconomic factors, and so forth. The reason to consider these as extraneous determinants is because they may be related to the disease as well as to the likelihood of measles infection and therefore could suggest a relationship between infection and disease that in reality does not exist.

The occurrence relation can be depicted as:

$$\text{IBD} = f(\text{measles infection} \mid \text{ED})$$

A more detailed discussion about etiologic research can be found in Chapter 3.

Prognostic Research

To be able to set a prognosis is an essential feature of daily clinical practice. The process of estimating an individual patient's prognosis is illustrated by the following question often asked by practicing physicians: "What will happen to this patient with this illness if I do not intervene?" In essence, prognostication implies predicting the future, a difficult task at best. As in the diagnostic process, estimating a patient's prognosis means taking into account multiple potential determinants, some of which pertain to the clinical profile (e.g., markers of the severity of the illness) and some of which refer to the nonclinical profile (e.g., age and sex). Ideally, prognostic evidence should help the clinician to adequately and efficiently predict a clinically relevant prognostic outcome in an individual patient. More general prognostic information, such as 5-year survival of types of cancer and 1-year recurrence rates in stroke patients is typically not sufficiently informative to guide patient management. Moreover, several prognostic outcome parameters can be of interest. Apart from survival or specific complications, quality of life indices can also be extremely relevant.

Imagine a 10-year-old child who experienced a recent episode of bacterial meningitis. The parents ask the clinical psychologists about the possible longer-term sequelae of their son's illness. They are particularly worried about their child's future school performance. To predict the child's school performance, in this example, in 5 years' time, the psychologist will consider both nonclinical (such as age and previous school performance) and clinical parameters, notably indices of the severity of the meningitis. The clinical psychologist is uncertain which combination of these latter parameters best predicts future school performance.

An example of a research question of prognostic research addressing this topic is:

> Which combination of measures of disease severity (e.g., duration of symptoms prior to admission because of meningitis, leukocyte count in cerebral spinal fluid, dexamethasone use during admission) best predicts future school performance in children with a recent history of bacterial meningitis?

The determinants include parameters measured during the meningitis episode, the outcome is school performance measured after a certain period (e.g., 5 years) after the illness, and children with recent bacterial meningitis represent the domain.

The occurrence relation is:

School performance = f (duration of symptoms, leukocyte count, pathogen involved, etc.)

Possibly, other nonclinical potential determinants should be considered in the occurrence relation as well, such as the child's age, previous school performance, and parents' education. Thus, the research question could be rephrased as: "Which combination of parameters best predicts future school performance in children with recent bacterial meningitis?"

Chapter 4 includes a thorough presentation of prognostic research.

Intervention Research

An intervention is any action taken in medicine to improve the prognosis of a patient. This can include treatment or advice as well as preventive actions. The most common form of intervention research in medicine is research on the effects of drug treatment. Research into the benefits and risks of interventions merits particular attention. The design of intervention research generally requires the design of an occurrence relation that serves both the estimation of the prognosis of a particular patient when the intervention is initiated and a valid estimation of the causal role of the intervention in that prognosis. In other words, intervention research aims to both predict prognosis following the intervention and understand the effect caused by the intervention.

From the perspective of the patient, the change in prognosis brought about by treatment is of the greatest interest. However, from the perspective of, for example, the drug manufacturer or regulator, the question is whether it is the pharmacologic action of the drug and nothing else that improved the prognosis. The question is about the causality of the treatment effect. Consequently, the object, data collection, and analysis should comply with the specific requirements of both causal and descriptive research. Typically the requirements of being able to draw causal conclusions and the exclusion of confounding factors drive the design. Importantly, intervention research, particularly its most appreciated form, the randomized trial, can serve as a role model for causal research at large because trials are designed to remove major sources of confounding [see Chapter 10 and Miettinen, 1989].

One may question whether causal research that does not take prognostic implications into account has value for clinical medicine. In intervention studies, principles of both causal and descriptive or, according to Miettinen, "intervention-prognostic" research apply [Miettinen, 2004]. Because the design of data collection and data analysis of causal research calls for a strict control of confounding factors, the causal outlook of intervention research commonly dominates in intervention studies. However, the challenge for the investigator is not only to provide an answer on causality but also to produce a meaningful estimate of the effect on the prognosis of individual patients. Consider an 18-month-old toddler visiting a primary care physician because of acute otitis media. According to her mother, this is the second episode of otitis; the first episode occurred some 9 months ago and lasted 10 days. The mother is afraid of continued prolonged periods of complaints and asks for an antibiotic prescription. First, the clinician will estimate the prognosis of the child, taking into account the child's prior medical history, current clinical features (e.g., fever, uni/bilateral ear infection), and other prognostic markers such as age. Then the effects of antibiotic therapy on the prognosis will be estimated. To this end, the causal (i.e., true) effects of antibiotic therapy in young children should be known. The research question of an intervention study providing this evidence is: "Does antibiotic therapy reduce the duration of complaints in young children with acute otitis media?" Here, antibiotic therapy is the determinant and the number of days until resolution of symptoms is the outcome. The domain is young children (younger than 2 years) with acute otitis media. Although one could argue that the domain may be as large as all children with otitis, the prognosis in young children is considered to be relatively poor and the effects of antibiotics could be different in this subgroup of children. The occurrence relation can be summarized as:

Duration of complaints = f (antibiotic therapy | ED)

In a typical intervention study, randomization and blinding will minimize any influence of extraneous determinants. This will be explained in detail in Chapter 5.

Comparison of Diagnostic and Prognostic Research

Diagnostic and prognostic research share several characteristics. First and foremost, they are both descriptive research [Moons & Grobbee, 2002a]. This has important implications for theoretical design, design of data collection, and design of analysis. As a prelude to a more comprehensive discussion of this research, which will be done in subsequent chapters, a few distinctive features should be mentioned. The occurrence relation in diagnostic and prognostic research is given by the presence or future presence (i.e., incidence) of the outcome in relation to and as a function of one or multiple determinants. It is exceedingly rare for both diagnostic and prognostic research questions to be restricted to single determinants. In medical practice, a diagnosis or prognosis is hardly ever based on a single indicator. Arguably, certain instances of screening may be exceptions, but more commonly multiple nonclinical and clinical patient characteristics, including results from diagnostic testing, are used to decide upon the presence of the disease and its prognostic consequences. Unfortunately, one often finds studies addressing the diagnostic capacities of a single test [Moons et al., 1999]. The relevance of research on tests in isolation is markedly limited by the notion that, in the clinical application, it is the added or alternative value of a test that matters rather than its individual merit. For diagnostic or prognostic research to be relevant, all of the putative predictors that are available and considered in a clinical setting need to be included as determinants in the occurrence relation. It is important to realize that theoretically all these determinants have a similar importance. If they predict the outcome in the presence of the other factors they are useful, but if they do not, they are not useful. Consequently, there are no extraneous determinants (confounders); confounding is not an issue in descriptive research. Still, it may be relevant to address the value of a test that is conditional on other determinants. For example, the aim of the investigator may be to determine whether a specific new diagnostic tool has added value or if a less invasive procedure may replace a more invasive one and still maintain the same diagnostic capacity.

Diagnostic and prognostic research both aim for an optimal prediction. In many ways, a prognosis can be viewed as a diagnosis "yet to be made." Where in diagnostic research we attempt to predict the presence of a particular disease, in prognostic research, we attempt to predict the occurrence of a particular disease outcome in the future. The focus of descriptive research could be single or multiple determinants, with the latter being more common. When a prognostic or diagnostic study addresses multiple determinants, there is no inherent determinant hierarchy. Often, however, determinants that are readily available in daily practice (e.g., signs and symptoms) will be studied first, before additional value is sought from more expensive, invasive, and patient-burdening determinants. The aim usually is to reduce a range of available determinants to a subset with the same prognostic or diagnostic value as the full set, or to compare the predictive capacity of a set of determinants inclusive and exclusive of a determinant of particular interest. Inclusion of a larger or smaller number of determinants has no implications for validity as long as the study is large enough to obtain results with sufficient precision. Selection of determinants for inclusion, however, may affect the study's generalizability and thus the relevance of the research. Consider a hospital where magnetic resonance imaging (MRI) scanning is not routinely available in patients admitted to the intensive care unit with head trauma. A study designed to determine which clinical and nonclinical factors may be useful in the diagnostic workup or prognostication of head trauma patients, which does not include the results of MRI scanning, will provide results that are relevant to similar hospitals despite the potential importance of MRI findings when available.

In addition to shared aspects of the theoretical design of diagnostic and prognostic studies, they have similarities in the design of data collection. Collection of determinant information has a particular feature that differentiates diagnostic and prognostic research from etiologic and intervention research. Etiologic research data on the determinant and confounders must be collected in a strict protocol with high precision to maximize the opportunity to obtain valid and precise estimates of the true quantitative association with the outcome. Descriptive research data should be collected in agreement with the quality of data collection in practice. Suppose, for example, that particular diagnostic data in a given study are obtained by the most specialized and experienced senior physician available to the researchers; the importance of the diagnostic indicator is likely to be overestimated relative to the eventual application where, in a routine care setting, average doctors with average capabilities will establish a diagnosis. Note that this makes the use of data collected as part of randomized trials of questionable value in the valid estimation of prognostic factors; data collected in routine care are generally highly suitable for use in descriptive research.

The general approach in prognostic and diagnostic research is to first design the occurrence relation in theoretical and operational terms. Then the data collection is designed, including a choice from different options according to which a study population can be chosen and data collected. The prevalence of the outcome (in diagnostic research) or the incidence of the outcome (in prognostic research) is recorded in a group of patients reflecting the type of patients for which the results of the research are intended to be used. Finally, in the data analysis, the nature and strength of the occurrence relation are calculated by estimating the (regression) coefficients and narrowing the set of determinants to the most informative subset of minimal size.

There are also differences between diagnostic and prognostic research. Diagnostic research is cross-sectional and prognostic research longitudinal. In a diagnostic study, the outcome is the frequency of the presence of the diagnosis of interest. Prognostic research has no simple single outcome. Rather, the outcome of relevance to the patient is the expected future course of the disease expressed by the expected utility or nonutility. The full prognosis is determined by the utilities of the various possible outcomes together with their respective probabilities. These possible outcomes also include all those resulting from treatment options. Consequently, a prognosis is generally not the probability of a single outcome. However, if only for reasons of feasibility, prognostic research is commonly restricted to a particular outcome.

Comparison of Etiologic and Prognostic Research

In etiologic and prognostic research, the temporal dimension of the occurrence relation is longitudinal. Prognostic and etiologic occurrence relation address the future occurrence of an outcome in relation to either prognostic or etiologic factors. However, when the incidence of a state or event is studied as a function of an etiologic factor, the assumed relationship of this determinant to the outcome is causative by definition, while in the case of prognosis, the prognostic determinants may or may not be causally related to the outcome. For example, Oostenbrink and coworkers [2002] determined predictors of the occurrence of permanent neurologic sequelae after childhood bacterial meningitis. Among the predictors was low body temperature at admission to the hospital. The low temperature is likely to be a marker of severity of the disease rather than causally related to the outcome. Research into the effects of interventions is both causal research and descriptive (here it is prognostic) research. In randomized clinical trials—the gold standard for assessment of treatment effects—a prognostic factor (the intervention) is manipulated with the aim of quantifying the causal impact of this factor and estimating its contribution to a change in prognosis.

Because causal explanation has a distinctly different role in etiologic and prognostic research (being absent in the latter), confounding is a critically important concept in etiologic studies and a non-issue in prognostic research, as long as obtaining a causal explanation of the effects of the intervention is not part of the objective. Etiologic studies typically focus on a single determinant. While in a single study more than one possible causal determinant may be of interest, for each causal determinant there is in principle a unique occurrence relation with a tailored set of confounders to be considered. In the simplest data analytic approach, the disease outcome is assessed in groups of subjects classified in an index category where the determinant is present and a reference category where the determinant is absent. Then the interest is in comparative rates of occurrence of disease across the determinant categories. To infer the true causal difference in the rate of occurrence of a disease, this should be estimated while making distributions of extraneous determinants the same across the determinant categories, that is, estimating the parameters that are conditional on confounders.

In contrast to etiologic studies, where a single determinant is of interest, prognostic studies usually emphasize multiple determinants. This does not imply that the investigator may not have a specific interest in a particular determinant. Yet "science" demands arriving at the best prediction possible and if the investigator's favorite prognostic indicator drops out along the way, so be it. In case the focus is more on a specific new or otherwise interesting putative prognostic determinant, given a set of a priori defined codeterminants, the question will be what the predictive capacity is of the selected prognostic indicator beyond these codeterminants, for example, the added predictive information. A prognostic study by Ingenito et al. [1998] prespecified an added value of measuring preoperative inspiratory lung resistance in predicting the outcome of lung-volume reduction surgery. Here, the occurrence relation was the incidence of increase in forced expiratory volume in one second (FEV_1) after surgery as a function of preoperative inspiratory resistance, conditional on other clinical and nonclinical patient characteristics. Note that "conditionality" refers to the added value here and not to conditionality on confounding. The range of clinical and nonclinical characteristics included in the study was determined by what was commonly available in that particular clinical setting and therefore relevant in prediction. None of these determinants was extraneous; potentially they all could contribute and no extraneous determinant could be "forgotten" without incurring the risk of producing an invalid result, as could happen in causal research.

In case of the absence of preference for a particular prognostic indicator, the task entailed in the analysis of prognostic studies is to obtain the maximal predictive capacity of a minimal number of predictors without any inherent hierarchy. For example, to assess the risk of death in patients with burn injuries, a group of U.S. investigators had a simple qualitative concern: to reduce a set of potential prognostic codeterminants to a subset with information about prognosis similar to the initial full set. The occurrence relation of this study was the incidence of mortality as a function of clinical and nonclinical characteristics. Again, there were no extraneous determinants [Ryan et al., 1998].

MOVING FROM RESEARCH TO PRACTICE: VALIDITY, RELEVANCE, AND GENERALIZABILITY

Similar to other research, the motive for applied clinical studies is to learn about an object. Eventually, knowledge produced by the research needs to be incorporated into a knowledge base that guides daily medical care. Whether the results from clinical research are eventually applied in daily practice depends on many circumstances, some of which can be rather subjective, such as the prior beliefs of the clinician. No doubt, however, both the validity and the generalizability of the study findings play a crucial role in the their potential for implementation.

Validity refers to the lack of bias (i.e., lack of systematic error) in the results. Study findings are valid when the quantification of the determinant(s)–outcome relationship is true. In other words, the measure of association (e.g., a relative risk of 2.0 in a study on the causal relationship between the use of oral contraceptives and the risk of breast cancer or an increase in diagnostic accuracy from a ROC area of 0.70 to 0.90 when a C-reactive protein test is added to findings from history taking and physical examination in suspected pneumonia) that is observed is correct. For the causal study, this obviously means that this relative risk of 2.0 is not biased by extraneous determinants (confounding) or other flaws in the design of data collection or data analysis, and for the diagnostic study (where confounding is not an issue) this means that the ROC area represents the unbiased truth for the study population included in the study. The epidemiology literature is "blessed" with a plethora of different types of biases that may endanger the validity of studies. The distinction of so many types of bias and the inconsistent use of the related terms only distracts from the real question that needs to be answered when judging the validity of a study, namely, "Is there bias—yes or no?" To simplify things, we only distinguish between two "types" of bias in our text: (1) confounding (because of its central role in causal studies) and (2) other bias. When study findings are valid, the generalizability of the results (i.e., their applicability to another, larger group of patients) is a major driver for the implementation of the results (and when the results are biased, generalizability is zero). Unfortunately, generalizability is sometimes named "external validity," although it has no bearing on the validity of the findings and contrasts with "internal validity"; the latter is what we designate as validity.

During the design and conduct of research, it is important to be aware of the effects that choices in the design of the study may have on the applicability and implementation of the results. In the critical theoretical, initial phase of study design, the occurrence relation is laid out with all of its elements. Following the theoretical design, a plan is made for how to obtain and summarize knowledge on the nature and strength of the occurrence relation from available or induced experience, such as from empirical data collected in groups of subjects. Here, many decisions need to be made that are separate from the actual way the data are collected. To be able to move from theoretical design to data collection, the occurrence relation needs to be rephrased in both theoretical and operational terms. This will not only point the way to measurement techniques in data collection but also indicate compromises that need to be made to match the ideal format of information on outcome and determinants to what can practically be achieved. For example, suppose we wish to precisely quantify the relationship between the presence of heart failure and subsequent loss of patient autonomy and quality of life. In the data collection, we may then have to choose dyspnea to classify heart failure and the Euroqol questionnaire to assess quality of life [Rasanen et al., 2006]. This need not be a problem, but it is important that these choices are made explicit and recognized in the interpretation of the research. Both the measure of the outcome and the determinant are mere proxies for what we really aim to evaluate. In applied clinical research, it is important to stay close to what matters to patients when deciding on measures of disease outcomes. This is not necessarily intuitive to all clinical investigators.

Investigators frequently rely most on what can be quantified in solid measures rather than on what has the biggest impact for patients. We reviewed studies on new positive inotropic drugs in heart failure [Feenstra et al., 1999]. The profound impacts that congestive heart failure has on life expectancy and quality of life have been a continuous stimulus for the development of new drugs to treat this condition. Despite favorable effects on (aspects of) quality of life in short-term studies, several new agents have been shown to reduce survival rates in mortality trials. However, patients with severe congestive heart failure may experience such incapacitating symptoms that the question should be raised about whether an improvement in quality of life makes the increased risk of mortality associated with these new agents acceptable. Drugs that improve quality of life at the expense of an increased risk of mortality may be valuable in the treatment of patients with severe congestive heart failure. However, this is only the case if the probability of improvement in quality of life and prolongation of life expectancy for those using the drug exceeds the probability of improvement in quality of life and prolongation of life expectancy for those not using the drug. Unfortunately, most clinical trials in which both mortality and quality of life are evaluated fail to provide information on this composite probability. In clinical research, there is a justified growing emphasis on measures of disease that matter to patients, the importance of which was underlined by the outcomes movement and summarized in a seminal article in *The New England Journal of Medicine* [Elwood, 1988].

Questions that trigger applied clinical research result from problems and lack of perceived knowledge in patient care. Certain questions are relevant for particular groups of patients and not to others. Consequently, research findings may be relevant to smaller or larger groups of patients. The essence of scientific research, in contrast to other forms of systematic gathering of data, is that its results can be generalized. The type of knowledge provided by clinical epidemiologic research is inferential, probabilistic knowledge. Scientific knowledge contrasts with factual knowledge because it is not time and place specific. It is true for any patient or group of patients as long as the findings on which the knowledge is based permit scientific generalization to those patients. The patient is a special case of a category of patients to whom the occurrence relation applies. In the initial theoretical phase of study design, a careful appreciation of the type of patients for which the research needs to be relevant is important. As outlined earlier, the (theoretical) population of patients to which the findings apply is called the domain of the study. When choosing a population for empirical data collection (i.e., the study population), the domain should be kept in mind.

Members of the study population should represent the (virtual) population of the domain. Apart from criteria for selecting a study population that follow from the chosen domain, such as the severity of disease or a certain indication for diagnostic work-up, other restrictions may be necessary for recruiting participants in a study that result from logistic or other circumstances. Many of these additional restrictions, such as the need to live near the research institution, to master the local language, and availability of time for additional diagnostic assessments, will not have an impact on the eventual applicability of the results and therefore will not limit the domain. It is important to appreciate which characteristics of a study population are determined because of the intended domain and as such form part of the design, and which characteristics result from factors beyond the theoretical design. With a view to the study domain, those characteristics of the study population require particular consideration that bears on the generalizability of the empirical relation (see **Box 1–3**). The generalizability of research results is the extent to which knowledge obtained in a particular type of patient may be applied to another larger, theoretical, abstract group of patients. Suppose that a study is conducted to determine the value of a certain novel type of surgery in patients with a particular gastrointestinal disease. The results of the study could be that recovery in operated patients of type T is more common than in patients who were not operated on, conditional on all extraneous determinants (confounders) of recovery. The conclusion is that operating enhances recovery in patients of type T, without reference to time or place. The results are generalized from the group of patients on which the empirical data were collected to a larger group of theoretical patients representing the domain of the research.

Generalizability is not an objective process that can be framed in simple statistical terms. Moving from time- and place-specific findings to scientific knowledge requires judgment about the potential of other characteristics

BOX 1–3   Quotation About Generalization

The essence of knowledge is generalization. That fire can be produced by rubbing wood a certain way is a knowledge derived from individual experiences; the statement means that rubbing wood in this way will always produce fire. The art of discovery is therefore the art of generalization. What is irrelevant, such as the particular shape or size of the piece of wood used is to be excluded from the generalization: what is relevant, for example, the dryness of the wood, is to be included in it. The meaning of the term relevant can thus be defined: that is relevant which must be mentioned for the generalization to be valid. The separation of relevant from irrelevant factors is the beginning of knowledge.

Reproduced from Reichenbach H in: The rise of scientific philosophy. New York: Harper and Row. 1965.

inherent to the research setting and study population to modify the nature and strength of the relationship between determinant(s) and outcomes as estimated in the study. A discussion of the concept of modification is included in Chapter 3.

Appreciation of generalizability is essential for scientific inference. Defining the domain of a study as part of the occurrence relation is important because the domain of a relationship provides the basis for generalization. As a rule, the utility of research is greater if the domain of the research findings, to which to generalize the estimated relationships between outcome and determinants, is broader. Consequently, while the design of the occurrence relation needs to be precise and comprehensive, the domain is generally implicitly or explicitly kept broad. In diagnostic research, the domain is defined by the patient profile, representing those subjects for whom a particular diagnostic question is relevant. In etiologic research, the domain is formed by people at risk for the illness at issue and with variability of the causal factor at issue. For example, the domain for research on the etiologic role of smoking in lung cancer is all human beings with lungs who could possibly smoke. In prognostic research, again, the domain is defined by the patient profile of those whom prognostic statements based on the determinants included in the research are considered. For research into treatment effects, the domain is those who may need the treatment. Where most elements of scientific research require maximal specificity, the domain, in general, is loosely defined. Apart from smaller or larger restrictions in the empirical data of a study, either by design or by circumstances, differences will persist among those using the results of research with respect to their willingness to generalize to larger groups. For example, in the absence of results from randomized trials specifically demonstrating the clinical benefits of use of statins in women with elevated cholesterol levels, some people did not accept an indication for use of these drugs in women despite ample evidence of reductions of risk in men with similar risk profiles.

Part 2

Principles of Clinical Research

Chapter 2

Diagnostic Research

INTRODUCTION

A 55-year-old man visits his general practitioner (GP) complaining of dyspepsia. He has had these complaints for more than 3 months, but their frequency and severity have increased over the last 4 weeks. The patient has a history of angina but has not required sublingual nitroglycerin for more than 2 years. He is known to the GP as having been unsuccessful in quiting smoking despite frequent attempts to do so. The GP asks several additional questions related to the nature and severity of the dyspepsia to estimate the chance that the patient suffers from a peptic ulcer. The GP also asks about possible anginal complaints. A short physical examination reveals nothing except some epigastric discomfort during palpation of the abdomen. The GP considers a peptic ulcer the most likely diagnosis. The probability of a coronary origin of the complaints is deemed very low. The GP decides to test for *Helicobacter pylori* serology, to further increase (rule in) or decrease (rule out) the probability of (*H. pylori*-related) peptic ulcer. The *H. pylori* test is negative. The GP prescribes an acid-suppressing agent and asks the patient to visit again in a week. When the man visits the GP again, his complaints have virtually disappeared.

DIAGNOSIS IN CLINICAL PRACTICE

Doctors devote much of their time to diagnosing diseases in patients presenting with particular symptoms or signs. Determining a diagnosis for a patient is important because it provides insight into the prognosis of the patient and directs the physician in making decisions for appropriate patient management (see **Box 2–1**).

The diagnostic process in daily practice typically starts with a patient presenting a certain complaint—symptom or sign—that makes the practitioner suspicious of him or her having a particular disorder (*target disease*)

BOX 2-1   Quotation About Clinical Judgment

Knowing how to live with uncertainty is a central feature of clinical judgment: the skilled physician has learned when to take risks to increase certainty and when to simply tolerate uncertainty.

—**Riegelman, 1990**

Reproduced from: Riegelman, R. Studying a study and testing a test. Boston: Little, Brown, 1990.

out of a series of possible disorders (*differential diagnosis*) [Sackett et al., 1985]. The target disease can best be viewed as the disorder at which the diagnostic process is initially targeted, either because it is the most serious of the possible diagnoses ("the one not to miss") or, a priori, the most probable one. During the diagnostic process, the physician first estimates the probability, or likelihood, of the presence of the target disease in view of the alternative diagnoses (including the absence of any disease) based on information obtained through history taking, including knowledge about a patient's individual and family medical history, and physical examination. This diagnostic probability estimation is typically an implicit and subjective process (see **Box 2–2**).

In addition to *clinical* data about the patient, *nonclinical* data such as age, gender, and working conditions also may be considered. The estimated probability of the target disease will guide the doctor in choosing the most appropriate action. The physician may perform additional diagnostic tests, initiate therapeutic interventions, or, perhaps most importantly, may decide to refrain from further diagnostic or therapeutic actions for that disease (e.g., when the probability of that disease is considered low enough) and possibly search for other underlying diseases [Ferrante di Ruffano et al., 2012]. The diagnostic workup is a continuing process of updating the probability of the target disease presence given all available documented information on the patient. The goal of this workup is to achieve a relatively high or a relatively low probability of a certain diagnosis, that is, the threshold probability beyond or below which a doctor is confident enough about the presence or absence of a certain diagnosis to guide clinical decisions. *Threshold probabilities* are determined by the consequences of a false-positive or false-negative diagnosis. These critically depend on the anticipated course or prognosis of the diagnosis considered and the potential beneficial and adverse effects of possible additional diagnostic procedures or treatments. Importantly, these two thresholds, A and B, are commonly implicitly defined in daily practice and will often vary between doctors. Often, history taking and physical examination already provide important and sufficient diagnostic

BOX 2–2   Diagnosis

διάγνωσις

The term *diagnosis* is a compound of the Greek words διά (dia), which means apart or distinction and γνωσις (gnosis), which means knowledge. Diagnosis in medicine can be defined as "the art of distinguishing one disease from the other." (Dorland WAN. *The American Illustrated Medical Dictionary*, 20th ed. Philadelphia, London: WB Saunders Company; 1944). In clinical practice a diagnosis does not necessarily imply a well-defined, pathophysiologically distinct, disease entity, such as acute myelocyte leukemia; many diagnoses are set on a much more aggregate level, notably in the beginning of the diagnostic process. For example, a physician on weekend call who speaks to a patient with dyspnea or their family member will first try to set or rule out the diagnosis, "a condition requiring immediate action," before a more precise diagnosis can be made, usually at a later stage. The precision of the diagnosis also depends on the clinical setting. In primary care there often is no need for a very specific diagnosis to decide on the next step (for example, an antibiotic prescription for a patient with the diagnosis of "probable pneumonia" based on signs and symptoms only), whereas in an intensive care setting in a tertiary care hospital, with more virulent bacteria, more antibiotic resistance, and more immunocompromised and seriously ill patients, a more specific diagnosis may be required ("vancomycin-resistant pneumococcal ventilator-associated pneumonia") involving imaging techniques, serology, cultures, and resistance patterns.

---

information to rule in or rule out a disease with enough confidence so that the estimated probability of presence of the disease is below A or above B (see **Figure 2–1**).

But when the probability of the disease is estimated to lie in the grey middle area (between A and B), additional diagnostic tests are commonly ordered to decrease the remaining uncertainty about the presence or absence of the disease. Typically, this additional testing first includes simple, easily available tests such as blood and urine markers or simple imaging techniques like chest x-ray. If after these tests are conducted doubt remains (i.e., the probability of disease presence has not yet crossed the thresholds A or B), more invasive and costly diagnostic procedures are applied such as magnetic resonance imaging (MRI), computed tomography (CT), or positron emission tomography (PET) scanning, arthroscopy, and/or biopsy. This process of diagnostic testing ends when the estimated probability of the target disease becomes sufficiently higher or lower than the A or B threshold to guide medical action.

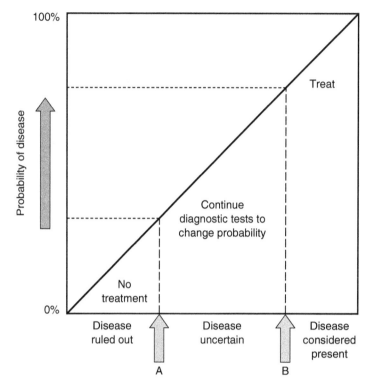

FIGURE 2–1   Diagnostic Testing.

In the example of our patient with complaints of dyspepsia, history taking and physical examination apparently did not provide the doctor with enough information to decide about the initiation of therapeutic interventions, for example, symptomatic treatment with acid-suppressing agents or, alternatively, triple therapy to treat an underlying *H. pylori* infection. In view of the patient burden of invasive *H. pylori* testing (i.e., gastroscopy with biopsy) in combination with the relatively mild complaints and potential benefits of *H. pylori*–targeted therapy, the physician decided to perform a noninvasive serology test, although this test is considered less accurate than the gastroscopy. Apparently, the negative test results indeed convinced the physician that the probability of *H. pylori* ulcer disease was lower than the clinically relevant threshold (e.g., 10 or 20%) because triple therapy targeted at *H. pylori* was not initiated. Instead, symptomatic treatment, an acid-suppressing drug, was prescribed. The probability of coronary heart disease—one of the differential diagnoses of a patient with these complaints—as the underlying cause of the complaints also was considered to be very low from the start (far below threshold A for this disease), such that no additional tests for that diagnosis were ordered.

This example may seem subjective, not quantitative and not evidence based, but the diagnostic process in clinical practice is often just like that. In contrast to many therapeutic interventions, quantitative evidence of the value of diagnostic tests and certainly of the added value of a test beyond previous, more simple test results, is often lacking [Linnet et al., 2012; Moons et al., 2012c]. Given the importance of diagnosis in everyday practice, there is an urgent need for research providing such quantitative knowledge [Grobbee, 2004; Knottnerus, 2002b].

The diagnostic process thus is a multivariable concern. It typically involves the documentation and interpretation of multiple test results (or diagnostic determinants), including nonclinical patient information [Moons et al., 1999]. In practice, hardly any diagnoses are based on a single diagnostic test. The number of diagnostic tests applied in everyday practice may differ considerably and depends, for example, on the targeted disease, patient characteristics, and the diagnostic certainty required to decide on patient management (see **Box 2–3**). Importantly, a natural hierarchy of testing exists. Almost without exception, any diagnostic workup starts with

BOX 2–3   Primum Non Nocere

Primum non nocere (first do no harm) refers to the principle that doctors should always take into account the possible harm of their actions to patients, and that an intervention with an obvious potential for harm should not be initiated, notably when the benefits of the intervention are small or uncertain.

Although this Hippocratic principle is most often applied to discussions on the effects of therapeutic interventions, it is equally applicable to diagnostic tests, especially for the more invasive and burdensome ones. When the course of management for a patient has been determined, additional diagnostic tests obviously have no benefit and can therefore only be harmful, albeit sometimes to the healthcare budget only. In daily practice many diagnostic tests are being performed that have no potential helpful consequences for patient management. Especially when additional test ordering is relatively easy, for example, serum parameters and imaging such as x-rays, the potential consequences for patient management, as well as possible harm, are not always taken into account. In a patient with a rib contusion as a result of a fall, an x-ray to rule out a rib fracture is useless, because the test result will not influence treatment (i.e., rest and painkillers). The challenge to the physician in any diagnostic process thus not only lies in choosing the optimal diagnostic tests and in what order, but also in knowing when to stop testing.

nonintrusive tests such as history taking and physical examination. Although one could argue about whether these should be considered "tests," we will treat them as such here, as each consecutive finding will influence the probability of disease, just as a blood test would. This is followed by simple laboratory or imaging tests, and eventually more burdensome and expensive tests, such as imaging techniques requiring contrast fluids or biopsies. Subsequent test results are always interpreted in the context of previous diagnostic information [Moons et al., 1999; Moons & Grobbee, 2002a]. For example, the test result "presence of chest pain" is obviously interpreted differently in a healthy 5-year-old girl than in a 60-year-old man with a history of myocardial infarction. The challenge to the physician lies in predicting the probability of the absence or presence of a certain target disease based on all documented test results. This requires knowledge about the contribution of each test result to the probability estimation. The diagnostic value of the *H. pylori* test in the earlier example is negligible if it adds nothing to the findings offered by the few minutes of history taking and physical examination, information that is always acquired by physicians anyway. More technically, the *H. pylori* test is worthless if the test result does not change (increase or decrease) the probability of presence of peptic ulcer disease as based on the results from history taking and physical examination. Importantly, in case the next step in clinical management is already decided upon (when the disease probability is below A or above B in Figure 2–1), one may, and perhaps should, refrain from additional testing.

The works of the 18th century Scottish pastor and mathematician, Thomas Bayes, have been instrumental in the development of a more scientific approach toward the diagnostic process in clinical practice. He established a mathematical basis for diagnostic inference. Bayes recognized the sequential and probabilistic nature of the diagnostic process. He emphasized the importance of *prior* probabilities, that is, the probability of the presence of a target diagnosis before any tests are performed. He also recognized that, based on subsequent test results, doctors will update this prior probability to a *posterior* probability. The well-known Bayes' rule formally quantifies this posterior probability of disease presence given the test result, based on the prior probability of that disease and the so-called diagnostic accuracy estimates (such as sensitivity and specificity or likelihood ratio) of that test (see **Box 2–4**). Although it has repeatedly been shown that this mathematical rule often does not hold—because the underlying assumption of constant sensitivity and specificity or likelihood ratio across patient subgroups is not realistic in most situations [Detrano et al., 1988; Diamond, 1992; Hlatky et al., 1984; Moons et al., 1997]—the rule has been crucial in understanding the probabilistic and stepwise nature of diagnostic reasoning in clinical practice.

We should emphasize that setting a diagnosis is not itself a therapeutic intervention. It is a vehicle to inform patients and guide patient management [Biesheuvel et al., 2006; Bossuyt et al., 2012]. An established diagnosis is a label that, despite being highly valued by medical professionals, is of no direct consequence to a patient other than to obtain a first estimate of the expected course of the complaints and to set the optimal management strategy. Accordingly, a diagnostic test commonly has no direct therapeutic effects and therefore does not directly influence a patient's prognosis. Once a diagnosis, or rather the probability of the most likely diagnosis, is established and an assessment of the probable course of disease in the light of different treatment alternatives (including no treatment) has been made, the optimal treatment strategy will be chosen to eventually improve the patient's prognosis. There are also other pathways through which a diagnostic test may affect a patient's health [Ferrante di Ruffano et al., 2012]. Knowledge of specific test results or disease presence may change the patient's (and the physician's) expectations and perceptions, and test results may shorten the time between symptom onset and treatment initiation, as well as improve treatment adherence. Finally, a diagnostic test may have direct therapeutic properties and change patient outcomes. Such procedures are rare, but salpingography to determine patency of the uteral tubes is an example.

Finally, the difference between diagnosing and screening for a disease should be recognized. The former starts with a patient presenting with a particular symptom and sign suspected of a particular disease and is inherently multivariable. Screening for a disease typically starts with asymptomatic individuals and is commonly univariable. Examples include phenylketonuria screening in newborns and breast cancer screening in middle-aged women, where a single diagnostic test is performed in all subjects irrespective of symptoms or signs. In this chapter, we will deal with diagnosing exclusively.

FROM DIAGNOSIS IN CLINICAL PRACTICE TO DIAGNOSTIC RESEARCH

Diagnostic research should be aimed at improving the diagnostic process in clinical practice. Typically it focuses on identifying combination(s) of tests that have the largest diagnostic yield. In clinical epidemiologic terms, the occurrence relation of diagnostic research predicts the probability of the

BOX 2-4 Example of a Two-by-Two Table with Test Results and Bayes' Rule

Test characteristics of test (T) N-terminal pro B-type natriuretic peptide (NT-proBNP; cut-off 36 pmol/L) in the detection of heart failure in primary care patients with conditions known to be associated with a high prevalence of heart failure.

	NT-proBNP positive (T+)	NT-proBNP negative (T−)	Total
Heart failure present (D+)	9	0	9
Heart failure absent (D−)	69	55	124
	78	55	133

where positive predictive value = P(D+ | T+) = 9/78 = 12%; negative predictive value = P(D− | T−) = 55/55 = 100%; sensitivity = P(T+ | D+) = 9/9 = 100%; specificity = P(T− | D−) = 55/124 = 44%; likelihood ratio positive test (LR+) = P(T+ | D+)/[1 − P(T− | D−)] = (9/9)/(69/124) = 1.8; likelihood ratio negative test (LR−) = [(1 − P(T+ | D+)]/ [P(T− | D−)] = (0/9)/(55/124) = 0.

Bayes' rule:

$$P(D+ | T+) = \frac{P(D+) * P(T+ | D+)}{P(D+) * [P(T+ | D+)] + P(D−) * P(T+ | D−)} =$$

$$= \frac{P(D+) * \text{sensitivity}}{P(D+) * \text{sensitivity} + [1 − (P(D+)] * (1 − \text{specificity})} = \frac{9/133 * 1}{9/133 * 1 + 124/133 * 0.56} = 0.12 = 12\% \qquad \text{(Eq. 1)}$$

and

$$P(D− | T+) = \frac{P(D−) * P(T+ | D−)}{P(D+) * [P(T+ | D+) + P(D−) * P(T+ | D−)]} =$$

$$= \frac{P(D−) * (1 − \text{specificity})}{P(D+) * \text{sensitivity} + [1 − (P(D+)] * (1 − \text{specificity})} = \frac{124/133 * 0.56}{9/133 * 1 + 124/133 * 0.56} = 0.88 = 88\% \qquad \text{(Eq. 2)}$$

Alternative (so-called odds) notation of Bayes' rule → (1) divided by (2):

$$\frac{P(D+|T+)}{P(D-|T+)} = \frac{P(D+)}{P(D-)} * \frac{P(T+|D+)}{P(T+|D-)} = \frac{P(D+)}{P(D-)} * LR+ \rightarrow$$

Posterior odds (D+|T+) = prior odds (D+) * LR+

Note: Odds(D+) = P(D+)/[1 – P(D+)]

For sequential diagnostic tests, Bayes' rule theoretically can be simply extended:

$$\frac{P(D+|T_1+, T_2+, T_3+)}{P(D-|T_1+, T_2+, T_3+)} = LR(T_1+) * LR(T_2+) * LR(T_3+)$$

Note that this form of Bayes' rule assumes that the results of test 1 to test 3 are independent of each other. However, it has been shown that this assumption in practice typically does not hold, as test results are often mutually related simply because they are reflections of the same underlying disease (see text).

presence of the disease of interest as a function of multiple diagnostic determinants in the relevant domain. The domain is defined by patients suspected of having that particular disease. Diagnostic determinants are the diagnostic tests under study (so-called index tests) and typically include findings from history taking (including age, gender, symptoms, and known comorbidity) and physical examination (signs), and if applicable and necessary, the findings from more advanced diagnostic testing.

The diagnostic process and thus diagnostic research is predictive or descriptive by nature, as its object is prediction of the presence of the yet unknown underlying disease. The goal is not to explain the cause of the disease under study. Consequently, confounding variables (i.e., factors that may distort a causal relationship between a particular causal determinant and an outcome) do not play a role in diagnostic research and are not part of the occurrence relation. This is in sharp contrast to causal research, where confounders are of critical importance. In diagnostic research, all other determinants merely serve as additional diagnostic test results that may be helpful in further distinguishing between those with and without the disease. Importantly, diagnostic research should be performed in close adherence to daily clinical practice to ensure the applicability of the findings. Thus, the typical features of the diagnostic process outlined previously should be taken into account in the design of the study. This has important consequences for the choice of, for example, the study population, the diagnostic determinants to be evaluated, their hierarchy and temporal sequence of measurement, and the data analysis.

DIAGNOSTIC RESEARCH VERSUS TEST RESEARCH

Alas, many published diagnostic studies are better characterized as *test research* than as *diagnostic research*. The objective of test research is to assess whether a single diagnostic test (index test) adequately can show the presence or absence of a particular disease [Linnet et al., 2012]. Often these studies include a group of patients with the target disease and a group of patients without this disease in whom the results of the index test are also measured. Typically, the results of the index test are categorized as positive or negative and the study results are summarized in a 2×2 contingency table (Box 2–4). The table allows for calculation of the four classic measures to estimate diagnostic accuracy in test research. These are:

1. Positive predictive value $[P(D+|T+)]$; probability (P) of the presence of disease in those with a positive test result

2. Negative predictive value [P(D–|T–)]; probability of absence of disease in those with a negative test result.
3. Sensitivity [P(T+|D+)]; probability of a positive test given presence of the disease (the true positive rate)
4. Specificity [P(T–|D–)]; probability of a negative test in those without disease (the true negative rate)

Other—though less often applied—parameters include the likelihood ratio of a positive test (i.e., the probability of a positive test in the diseased divided by the probability of a positive test in the nondiseased), the likelihood ratio of a negative test (i.e., the probability of a negative test in the diseased divided by the probability of a negative test in the nondiseased), or the odds ratio (which can be calculated as the ratio of the former two). The latter is seldom applied, but it is occasionally used in diagnostic meta-analyses [Reitsma et al., 2012]. If the index test results are not dichotomous but measured on a continuous scale, receiver operating characteristic (ROC) curves can be produced, based on sensitivity and specificity of the different cut-off values of the diagnostic test to be evaluated [Hanley and McNeil, 1982; Harrell et al., 1982].

Test research as described here often deviates from the main principle of clinically relevant diagnostic research in that clinical practice is not followed, first and foremost because the diagnostic process by definition involves multiple tests and a natural hierarchy of diagnostic testing. Second, test research often does not include representatives of the relevant patient domain, that is, patients presenting with symptoms and signs suggestive of the target disease. Rather, a group of patients with evident disease is selected and compared to a group of nondiseased patients, sometimes even healthy individuals who are obviously not suspected of the disease under study. Such selection of study subjects, however, will lead to biased estimates of the test's performance.

There is a clear difference in the occurrence relation between test research and diagnostic research. The occurrence relation of test research can be described as:

$$P(T) = f(D)$$

where P(T), that is, the probability (0–100%) of the test result of the single index test T, is studied as a function of the presence or absence of the target disease D.

In the case of a dichotomous test, this occurrence relation can be rewritten for the estimation of sensitivity as:

$$P(T+) = f(D+),$$

and for estimation of the specificity as:

$$P(T-) = f(D-),$$

where T+ and T– indicate a positive and negative index test result, respectively, and D+ and D– the presence or absence of the target disease.

The occurrence relation of test research that focuses on predictive values of a single test can be summarized as:

$$P(D) = f(T)$$

where the probability of the presence of disease (P[D]); range (0–100%) is studied as a function of the test result.

In case of a dichotomous test, this occurrence relation can be rewritten for the estimation of the positive predictive value as:

$$P(D+) = f(T+),$$

and for estimation of the negative predictive value as:

$$P(D-) = f(T-).$$

The occurrence relation of diagnostic research (i.e., clinically relevant diagnostic studies including multiple diagnostic tests) can be summarized as:

$$P(D) = f(T_1, T_2, T_3, \ldots T_n)$$

where T_1 to T_n are the consecutive multiple diagnostic index tests (or determinants) being studied.

A study to determine the value of plasma N-terminal pro B-type natriuretic peptide (NT-proBNP) levels in diagnosing heart failure serves as an example of a diagnostic study primarily presented as test research. NT-proBNP, a neuropeptide produced in the human cardiac ventricle as a result of increasing pressure, was assessed in a sample of 133 primary care patients [Hobbs et al., 2002]. Selection of these patients was based on the presence of a condition known to be associated with a higher prevalence of heart failure (i.e., a history of myocardial infarction, angina, hypertension, or diabetes), and the study was not restricted to the clinically more relevant group of patients presenting with complaints (e.g., fatigue or dyspnea) suggestive of heart failure.

Box 2–4 summarizes the main results. In addition, Bayes' rule, calculating the post-test probability (or odds) of disease as the product of the pre-test probability (or odds) of the disease, and the test's likelihood ratio are illustrated using the data derived from this study.

It was concluded from the study that NT-proBNP has value in the diagnosis of heart failure. Its main use would be to rule out heart failure in patients with suspected heart failure in whom normal concentrations of NT-proBNP are found. Several critical remarks can be made about this study, most of which were recognized by the authors. First, the focus of this study on the NT-proBNP test as a single test to diagnose or rule out heart failure does not reflect the diagnostic approach in clinical practice. NT-proBNP will never be applied as the sole diagnostic test in diagnosing heart failure. Simpler diagnostic tools inevitably are used first, notably information on age, sex, comorbidity, and symptoms and signs, before additional tests, such as NT-proBNP and perhaps electrocardiography, or even echocardiography, are applied [Rutten et al., 2005b]. The clinically more relevant research aim would thus be to assess whether NT-proBNP appreciably *adds* to the diagnostic information (such as signs and symptoms) that is readily available in clinical care.

This can only be achieved by comparing the diagnostic performance of two diagnostic strategies: one including all diagnostic information available to the physician before NT-proBNP measurement is executed, and one including the same information plus the NT-proBNP levels. In doing so, the multivariable nature of the diagnostic process in clinical practice is taken into account as well as the inherent hierarchy of diagnostic testing. The authors indeed performed a multivariable logistic regression analysis to determine whether a model including sex, history of myocardial infarction or diabetes, Q waves, or bundle branch block pattern on the electrocardiogram, and NT-proBNP performed better in diagnosing heart failure than a similar model excluding NT-proBNP. Nonetheless, the added diagnostic value of NT-proBNP was not emphasized in the presentation of the results or in the conclusion, nor were symptoms and signs included as possible diagnostic tests in the multivariable analysis. In addition, the study population can be criticized. The ability of a diagnostic test or combination of tests to distinguish between diseased and nondiseased should be studied in those patients in whom the diagnostic problem truly exists. In other words, the patients should be representatives of the domain of patients suspected of having that disease and in whom the physician will consider diagnostic testing. This is crucial because the value of diagnostic tests critically depends on the patient mix (see **Box 2–5**) [Lijmer et al., 1999; Rutjes et al., 2006]. Most patients included in the NT-proBNP study (i.e., mainly patients with conditions known to be associated with a high prevalence of heart failure) were not representative of the clinically relevant domain of patients visiting their primary care physician with symptoms and signs suggestive of

BOX 2–5   Sensitivity and Specificity Are Not Constant

Are sensitivity and specificity given properties of a diagnostic test, and do predictive values critically depend on the prevalence of the disease?

The common emphasis on sensitivity and specificity in the presentation of diagnostic studies is at least partly attributable to the notion that predictive values critically depend on the population studied, whereas sensitivity and specificity are considered by many to be constant [Moons & Harrell, 2003]. There is no doubt that predictive values of diagnostic tests are influenced by the patient domain. This may be best illustrated by comparing the performance of a test in primary and secondary care. Because of the inherent higher prevalence of the relevant disease in suspected patients in secondary care compared to primary care (because of the selection of patients with a higher probability of disease for referral), positive predictive values are commonly higher in secondary care (i.e., fewer false-positives) than in primary care (more false-positives), while negative predictive values are usually higher in primary care (fewer false-negatives). Sensitivity, specificity, and likelihood ratios indeed are not directly influenced by the prevalence of the disease because these parameters are conditional upon the presence or absence of disease. It has been shown extensively, however, that they do vary according to differences in the severity of disease [Hlatky et al., 1984; Detrano et al., 1988; Diamond, 1992]. In secondary care, for example, where more severely ill patients will be presented than in primary care, higher levels of diagnostic markers of a particular disease (and thus more test positives) can be expected among those with the disease than in primary care. This will result in a higher sensitivity in secondary care than in primary care and a higher specificity in primary care [Knottnerus, 2002a]. That sensitivity and specificity are not constant is illustrated in two studies by the same researchers on the value of near patient testing for *Helicobacter Pylori* infection in dyspepsia patients. The sensitivity and specificity in the primary care setting were 67% and 98%, respectively, while these values were 92% and 90% in secondary care [Duggan et al., 1999; Duggan et al., 1996].

heart failure. Thus, the applicability of the findings to patients encountered in daily practice is limited.

The focus on the quantification of the value of a single test to diagnose or rule out a disease and the common preoccupation of such research with a test's sensitivity and specificity are typical of prevailing diagnostic research [Moons et al., 2004a; Moons et al., 2012c]. This is also illustrated by the following statements found in classic textbooks in clinical epidemiology or biostatistics:

> *Identify the sensitivity and specificity of the sign, symptom, or diagnostic test you plan to use. Many are already published and sub specialists worth their salt ought either to know them from their field or be able to track them down* [Sackett et al., 1985].

and

> *For every laboratory test or diagnostic procedure there is a set of fundamental questions that should be asked. Firstly, if the disease is present, what is the probability that the test result will be positive? This leads to the notion of the sensitivity of the test. Secondly, if the disease is absent, what is the probability that the test result will be negative? This question refers to the specificity of the test* [Campbell & Machin, 1990].

As the goal of determining a diagnosis for patients is to estimate the probability of disease *given* the diagnostic test results, the parameters of interest undoubtedly are the posterior probabilities or predictive values, which directly reflect the diagnostic probabilities needed for decision making in clinical practice. Indeed, patients do not enter a physician's office saying, "I have been diagnosed with this particular disease and would like to know the probability that the available tests are positive." For the doctor, this probability (i.e., sensitivity) is similarly uninformative. A focus on probabilities of test results given the presence or absence of disease—sensitivity and specificity—is unjustified from a clinical point of view. It should be emphasized that in the NT-proBNP study example, the authors stated that their main conclusion (that heart failure can be excluded in those with normal NT-proBNP values) was indeed based on the excellent negative predictive value. In our experience, researchers as well as journal editors are reluctant to dismiss the sensitivity and specificity as the most important parameters in diagnostic research, as is also reflected in guidelines on the reporting [Bossuyt et al., 2003a, 2003b] and critical appraisal of diagnostic studies [Whiting et al., 2011], although more recently methods focusing on predictive values have been advocated [Leeflang et al., 2012; Reitsma et al., 2012].

A first step to de-emphasize these measures when judging the value of diagnostic tests is to change the order in which the traditional parameters are presented and to present predictive values first [Moons & Harrell, 2003; Rutten et al., 2006]. Diagnostic knowledge is not provided by answering the question, "How good is this test?" Diagnostic knowledge is the information needed to answer the question, "What is the probability of the presence or absence of a specific disease given these test results?"

Notwithstanding its limitations, test research—focusing on estimating the accuracy of a single test—may offer relevant information. Most notably, it is helpful in the developmental phase of a new diagnostic test, when the accuracy of the test is yet unknown. One will often first assess whether the test provides different results in those with overt disease and those without disease, sometimes even using healthy control subjects [Fryback & Thornbury, 1991; Linnet et al., 2012]. Furthermore, test research can be valuable in the realm of screening for a particular disorder in asymptomatic individuals. In this context, no test results other than the single screening test are considered. Depending on the type of screening not even age and gender may need to be accounted for [Moons et al., 2004a].

DIAGNOSTIC RESEARCH

Because the object of diagnosis in practice is to predict the probability of the presence of disease from multiple diagnostic test results, the design of diagnostic research is very much determined by the understanding, if not mimicking, of everyday practice [Moons & Grobbee, 2005]. In the following sections, the three components of clinical epidemiologic diagnostic study design will be discussed: theoretical design, design of data collection, and design of data analysis.

Theoretical Design

As mentioned earlier, the occurrence relation of diagnostic research is:

$$P(D) = f(T_1, T_2, T_3, \ldots T_n)$$

The domain of the occurrence relation in diagnostic research typically includes patients suspected of a particular disease, usually defined by the presence (or combination) of particular symptom(s) and/or sign(s) that have led to consultation of a physician. In this context, the research objective can be to assess the optimal diagnostic strategy; that is, to determine which combination of diagnostic determinants in what order most adequately estimate the probability of disease presence. The goal can also be to assess whether a certain, often newly developed, diagnostic test provides additional diagnostic value in clinical practice. *Added value* means in addition to currently available or previously applied diagnostic tests. This implies a comparison of two occurrence relations: one excluding and one including the new test in the list of determinants studied. Furthermore, one could aim to compare two tests or different combinations of tests, for example, when a new less burdensome or more inexpensive test serves as an alternative to another established diagnostic test. This implies a comparison of an occurrence relation with the routinely available test(s) (including this established test) and a second occurrence relation including the same tests, except that this established test is substituted by the alternative or new test.

For most diagnostic studies, showing that a particular diagnostic test, combination of tests, or test strategy improves estimation (prediction) of the presence of a disease is enough from a clinical point of view, because the clinical consequences (i.e., targeted therapy) and the effects of such therapy are well established [Bossuyt et al., 2012]. Showing that NT-proBNP clearly improves the ability to diagnose or exclude heart failure in suspected patients may suffice to apply such a test in daily practice as there is an impressive body of evidence showing that targeted treatment in heart failure improves survival and quality of life [Kelder et al., 2011]. Sometimes, however, the therapeutic consequences of a diagnosis may not be clear, such as when a new test provides truly novel disease information that potentially calls for other treatment choices compared to the currently available test. An example is functional imaging with PET in diagnosing pancreatic cancer, for which CT is the widely accepted reference standard. Compared to CT, PET may be especially helpful in detecting smaller lesions and distant metastases. Application of PET may lead to other diagnostic classifications that would require initiating other treatment options that potentially have different patient outcomes than the use of CT [Lord et al., 2006; Moons, 2010]. In such a situation, studies may be conducted to estimate the additional benefit of a new diagnostic test or strategy on the patient's *prognosis* (e.g., in terms of morbidity, mortality, or quality of life), rather than doing a study comparing the diagnostic accuracy of PET with CT as the reference standard. Although inspired by a diagnostic question, such studies are not simply predictive. They become analogous to studies assessing the effects of therapeutic interventions on patient outcome and, consequently, carry the characteristics of intervention research. In intervention research the aim is to explain ("Does addition of this test cause an improvement in patients' prognoses?") rather than to predict ("Does this test improve the estimation of the probability of the presence of a certain disease?"). Thus, confounding becomes an issue, because one wishes to ensure that the observed effects are indeed attributable to the diagnostic test or strategy. All of this has important consequences for the theoretical design (notably for the outcome definition), the design of data collection (where randomized trials with a relevant time horizon may be an attractive option), and the data analysis (see **Box 2–6**). For the purpose of understanding the principles of clinical

BOX 2–6   Diagnostic Research Versus Diagnostic Intervention Research

Illustration of the difference between (typical) *diagnostic research*, assessing the contribution of multiple diagnostic determinants to the estimation (prediction) of the presence of a certain disease and diagnostic intervention research aimed at estimating (in this case explaining) the effect of diagnostic tests (plus subsequent interventions) on the patient's prognosis. The latter type of research becomes *intervention research*, and requires taking extraneous determinants (i.e., confounders) into account.

Diagnostic Research

$P(\text{Diagnosis}) = f(T_1, T_2, T_3, \ldots T_n)$

Where P(D) is the probability of the presence (i.e., prevalence) of the disease of interest and $T_1 \ldots T_n$ represent the diagnostic determinants to be assessed

The occurrence relation of diagnostic research covers the bold part of this scheme:

Diagnostic problem → **diagnostic strategy** → **diagnosis** → intervention → outcome

Diagnostic Intervention Study

Prognostic outcome $= f[(T_1, T_2, T_3, \ldots T_n) + (I|ED)]$

Where the prognostic outcome could be any clinically relevant patient outcome, such as survival, incidence of a specific outcome, duration of the complaints or quality of life; $T_1 \ldots T_n$ represent the diagnostic determinants to be assessed; I is intervention following diagnosis and ED are extraneous determinants (or confounders) that should be taken into account in this causal study.

The occurrence relation of a diagnostic intervention study covers this entire scheme:

Diagnostic problem → **diagnostic strategy** → **diagnosis** → **intervention** → **outcome**

epidemiologic study design in typical diagnostic research (where index tests are compared to a reference standard in the relevant patient domain) this category of diagnostic intervention studies is not addressed in detail in this chapter; some other texts discuss the principles of diagnostic intervention studies [Biesheuvel et al., 2006; Bossuyt et al., 2000; Bossuyt et al., 2012; Lijmer & Bossuyt, 2009].

Design of Data Collection

Time

The object of the diagnostic process is cross-sectional by definition. In diagnostic research the probability of the presence of a disease (prevalence) is estimated, not its future occurrence. Accordingly, the data for diagnostic studies are collected cross-sectionally. The determinant(s) (the diagnostic test results) and the outcome (the presence or absence of the target disease as determined by the so-called reference standard) are theoretically determined at the same time. This is the moment that the patient presents with the symptoms or signs suggestive of the disease ($t = 0$). Even when the assessment of all diagnostic determinants to be studied takes some time and when it takes several days or weeks before the definitive diagnosis becomes known, this time period is used to determine whether at $t = 0$ the disease was present. Also, when a "wait and see" period of several months (e.g., to see whether an underlying disease, such as cancer, becomes manifest or whether targeted therapy has a beneficial effect) is used to set the final diagnosis, these additional findings are used to establish the diagnosis present at the time the patient presented the symptoms (i.e., at $t = 0$) [Reitsma et al., 2009], Thus, in our view, diagnostic research is cross-sectional research (time is zero). It should be noted, however, that others consider time to be larger than zero when it takes some time to set the final diagnosis and, as a consequence, they characterize the design of data collection as a follow-up or cohort study.

Census or Sampling

Generally, diagnostic research takes a census approach in which consecutive patients suspected of a certain disease and who fulfill the predefined inclusion criteria are included. The potentially relevant diagnostic determinants as well as the "true" presence or absence of the target disease are measured in all patients.

Sometimes, however, a sampling approach (i.e., a case-control study; see the later chapter on case-control studies) can offer a valid and efficient alternative. In a diagnostic case-control study (which is a cross-sectional case-control study), all patients suspected of the target disease who are eventually diagnosed with the disease ("cases") are studied in detail, together with a sample of those suspected of the disease who turn out to be free from the target disease ("controls"). This implies that the outcome (reference standard) has to be assessed in all patients suspected of the target disease (otherwise the cases cannot be identified and the controls cannot be sampled), but that the diagnostic determinants only have to be measured in cases and controls. As in diagnostic research using a census approach, the goal is to obtain absolute probabilities of disease presence given the determinants. Consequently, in the data analysis of a diagnostic case-control study, the sampling fraction of the controls should always be accounted for. A diagnostic case-control study offers a particularly attractive option when the measurement or documentation of one or more of the diagnostic tests under study are time consuming, burdensome to the patient, or expensive, such as certain imaging tests [Rutjes et al., 2005]. Diagnostic case-control studies are still relatively rare, despite their efficiency [Biesheuvel et al., 2008a]. In the example in **Box 2–7**, a case-control approach was chosen to assess the added value of cardiac magnetic resonance (CMR) imaging in diagnosing heart failure in patients known to have chronic obstructive pulmonary disease. Because of the costs, time, and patient burden involved, CMR measurements were performed in all patients with heart failure (cases) but in only a sample of the remainder of the participants (controls) [Rutten et al., 2008].

Confusingly, diagnostic studies comparing test results in a group of patients with the disease under study—often those in an advanced stage of disease—with test results in a group of patients without this disease, often a group of healthy individuals from the population at large, tend to be referred to as diagnostic case-control studies [Rutjes et al., 2005]. Many of these studies are not case-control studies, however, as there is no sampling of controls from the study base [Biesheuvel et al., 2008a]. In addition, as discussed earlier, such studies will bias the estimates of diagnostic accuracy of the tests being studied and compromise the generalizability of the study results. This is because the cases and certainly the healthy controls do not reflect the relevant patient domain, which is all those suspected of having the disease for whom the tests are intended.

Experimental or Observational

Diagnostic research is typically *observational* research. In patients suspected of the disease in daily practice, the diagnostic determinants of interest (most of which will be measured in clinical practice anyway), including

BOX 2–7   Example of a Diagnostic Case-Control Study

BACKGROUND: Although cardiovascular magnetic resonance (CMR) imaging is well established, its diagnostic accuracy in identifying chronic heart failure (CHF) in patients with chronic obstructive pulmonary disease (COPD) has not yet been quantified.

METHODS: Participants were recruited from a cohort of 405 patients aged 65 years or older with mild to moderate and stable COPD. In this population, 83 (20.5%) patients had a new diagnosis of CHF, all left-sided, established by an expert panel using all available diagnostic information, including echocardiography. In a nested case-control study design, 37 consecutive COPD patients with newly detected CHF (cases) and a random sample of 41 of the remaining COPD patients (controls) received additional CMR measurements. The value of CMR in diagnosing heart failure was quantified using univariable and multivariable logistic modeling in combination with area under the receiver operating characteristic curves (ROC area).

RESULTS: The combination of CMR measurements of left-ventricular ejection fraction, indexed left- and right-atrial volume, and left-ventricular end-systolic dimensions provided high added diagnostic value beyond clinical items (ROC area = 0.91) for identifying CHF. Left-sided measurements of CMR and echocardiography correlated well, including ejection fraction. Right-ventricular mass divided by right-ventricular end-diastolic volume was higher in COPD patients with CHF than in those without concomitant CHF.

CONCLUSIONS: Easily assessable morphologic and volume-based CMR measurements have excellent capacities to identify previously unknown left-sided chronic heart failure in mild to moderate COPD patients. There seems to be an adaptive tendency to concentric right-ventricular hypertrophy in COPD patients with left-sided CHF.

Reproduced with permission of MOSBY, INC, from: Rutten FH, Vonken EJ, Cramer MJ, Moons KG, Velthuis BB, Prakken NH, Lammers JW, Grobbee DE, Mali WP, Hoes AW. Cardiovascular magnetic resonance imaging to identify left-sided chronic heart failure in stable patients with chronic obstructive pulmonary disease. *Am Heart J.* 2008;156:506–512.

possible new tests, will be measured and the presence of disease will be determined using the reference standard. Such a cross-sectional study will be able to show which combination of tests best predicts the presence of disease or whether a new test improves diagnostic accuracy.

As discussed, setting a diagnosis is not an aim in itself, but rather a vehicle to guide patient management and treatment in particular. The ultimate goal of diagnostic testing is to improve patient outcomes. Hence, it has widely been advocated that when establishing the accuracy of a diagnostic test or strategy, its impact on patient outcomes also must be quantified. Consequently, it has been proposed that *experimental* studies (diagnostic intervention studies comparing two diagnostic strategies) be used to answer diagnostic research questions [Bossuyt et al., 2012; Lord et al., 2006].

If a cross-sectional diagnostic study has indicated that the diagnostic test or strategy improves estimation of the presence of the disease, the effect on patient outcome can usually be validly established without the need for a diagnostic intervention study [Koffijberg et al., 2013]. After all, earlier studies often adequately quantified the effects on patient outcome of the available treatment(s) for that disease. Using simple statistical or decision modeling techniques, one can combine the results of the cross-sectional diagnostic accuracy study and those of randomized therapeutic intervention studies. Hence, the effect on patient outcome can be quantified if (1) diagnostic research has shown that the diagnostic test or strategy improves diagnostic accuracy and (2) the effects of available therapeutic interventions in that disease on patient outcome are known, preferably from randomized trials. An example in which a randomized study was not necessary to quantify the effect of the new test on patient outcome is a study assessing whether an immunoassay test for the detection of *H. pylori* infection can replace the established but more costly and invasive reference test (a combination of rapid urease test, urea breath test, and histology) [Weijnen et al., 2001]. The new test indeed provided similar diagnostic accuracy. As consensus exists about the therapeutic management of patients infected with *H. pylori* (based on randomized controlled trials establishing the efficacy of treatment [McColl, 2002]), a subsequent diagnostic intervention study to quantify the effects of using the new immunoassay test on patient outcome was not needed.

There are situations, however, in which diagnostic intervention studies are needed to properly quantify the consequences of a novel diagnostic test or strategy on patient outcome [Biesheuvel et al., 2006; Bossuyt et al., 2000; Lord et al., 2006]. Notably, when a new diagnostic technology under study might be "better," to the extent that it provides new information potentially leading to other treatment choices, than the existing tests or strategy, a randomized trial may be useful. As described previously, functional imaging with PET in diagnosing pancreatic cancer, for which CT is the current reference, is an example. Also, when there is no direct link between the result of the new diagnostic test under study and an established treatment indication, such as the finding of uncalcified small nodules (less than 5.0 mm) when screening for lung cancer with low-dose spiral CT scanning, an experimental approach quantifying the effect on patient outcome may be required. When an acceptable reference standard for a disease is lacking, for instance, in a diagnostic study in suspected migraine or benign prostatic hyperplasia, a diagnostic intervention may also be the best option. Finally, as mentioned earlier, the index test itself (e.g., salpingography in suspected tubal blockage) may have direct therapeutic effects.

When performing a diagnostic intervention study to determine the impact of a diagnostic test or strategy on patient outcome, an initial diagnostic research question is transformed into a therapeutic research question (with the goal of establishing causality) with corresponding consequences for the design of the study. A disadvantage of a randomized approach to directly quantifying the contribution of a diagnostic test and treatment to the patient's outcome is that it often addresses diagnosis and treatment as a single combined strategy, a "package deal." This makes it impossible to determine afterward whether a positive effect on patient outcome can be attributed solely to the improved diagnostic accuracy or to the new subsequent treatment strategies.

Study Population

A diagnostic test or strategy should be able to distinguish between those with the target disease and those without, among subjects representing the relevant clinical domain. The domain is thus defined by patients suspected of having a particular disease. Consequently, patients in whom the presence of disease has already been established or in whom the probability of the disease is considered high enough to initiate adequate therapeutic actions fall outside the domain, similar to when the probability of disease is deemed sufficiently low to exclude the diagnosis (see also Figure 2–1). Furthermore, we recommend that investigators restrict domain definitions, and thus the study population, to the setting or level of care (e.g., primary or secondary care), as the diagnostic accuracy and combinations of these tests usually vary across care settings [Knottnerus, 2002a; Oudega et al., 2005a]. This is a consequence of differences in the distribution of severity of the disease across the different settings.

The population of a study could be defined as all consecutive patients suspected of the disease of interest that present themselves to one of the participating centers during a defined period and in whom the additional diagnostic tests under investigation are considered. Exclusion criteria should be few to ensure wide applicability of the findings. They would typically include alarm symptoms requiring immediate action or referral (e.g., melena in the dyspepsia example in the beginning of this chapter) and contraindications for one of the major diagnostic determinants (tests) involved (e.g., claustrophobia when MRI assessments are involved). One could argue that "patients suspected of the disease" as an inclusion criterion is too subjective. In many studies the definition, therefore, includes symptoms and signs often accompanying the disease. For example, a study to address the added value of a novel test to diagnose or exclude myocardial infarction in the primary care setting could include "patients with symptoms suggestive of myocardial infarction in primary care." Alternatively, the study population can be defined as "patients with chest pain or discomfort in primary care" or a combination of the two: "patients with chest pain of discomfort or other symptoms and signs compatible with a myocardial infarction in primary care" [Bruins Slot et al., 2013].

Diagnostic Determinants

As the diagnosis in practice is typically made on the basis of multiple *diagnostic determinants*, all test results that are (potentially) used in practice should be considered and measured. In the earlier example of the *H. pylori* test to diagnose peptic ulcer, the main signs and symptoms as well as the *H. pylori* test have to be included as potential determinants. There is, however, a limit to the number of tests that can be included in a study, because of logistics and the larger sample size required with each additional test that is considered (see the following discussion). Hence, the choice of the determinants to be included should be based on both the available literature and a thorough understanding of clinical practice.

To optimize the applicability of the findings of diagnostic research, the assessment of the diagnostic determinants should resemble the quality of this information in daily clinical practice. Consequently, one could argue that all determinant information should be collected according to usual care, without efforts to standardize or improve the diagnostic assessment. In a study involving multiple sites and physicians, this may significantly increase inter-observer variability in diagnostic testing, which means the potential diagnostic value of test results could be underestimated, although the study would indicate the current average diagnostic value of the tests in clinical practice. This effect is likely to be larger for more subjective tests, such as auscultation of the lungs. An alternative would be to train the physicians to apply a standardized diagnostic assessment. One may also ask experts in the field to do the diagnostic tests under study. This, however, has the disadvantage that it will likely overestimate the diagnostic accuracy of the tests in daily practice and reduce the applicability of the study results. For a multicenter, multi-doctor study, we recommend a pragmatic approach where all diagnostic determinants are assessed as much as possible according to daily practice and by the practicing physicians involved, with some efforts to standardize measurements.

Outcome

The *outcome* in diagnostic research is typically dichotomous: the presence or absence of the disease of interest (e.g., myocardial infarction or pneumonia). As discussed, in clinical practice commonly more than one disease is considered in a patient presenting with particular symptoms and signs, that is, the so-called differential diagnosis [Sackett et al., 1985]. Thus, the outcome should be polytomous rather than dichotomous, although in daily practice sequential dichotomous steps are often taken; the most likely (or most severe) disease in the differential diagnosis is diagnosed or excluded before the next diagnosis is considered. Diagnostic research with polytomous or even ordinal outcomes is relatively rare and the data analysis is more complicated [Harrell, 2001]. Current methodologic developments in this field no doubt will increase the use of polytomous outcomes in diagnostic research [Biesheuvel et al., 2008b; Roukema et al., 2008; Van Calster et al., 2012].

In diagnostic research, as in each epidemiologic study, adequate assessment of the outcome is crucial. The outcome should be measured as accurately as possible and with the best available methods. The term most often applied to indicate the ideal diagnostic outcome is *gold standard*, referring to the virtually nonexistent situation where measuring the disease is devoid of false-negatives and false-positives [Reitsma et al., 2009]. More recently, the more appropriate term *reference standard* was introduced to indicate the "non-golden" properties of almost all diagnostic procedures in today's practice, including procedures like biopsy combined with histologic confirmation for cancer diagnoses. Very few diagnostic procedures do not require human interpretation. Deciding on the reference standard is a crucial but difficult task in diagnostic research. The reference standard is the best procedure(s) that exists at the time of study initiation to determine the presence or absence of the target disease. The word *best* in this context means the measurement of disease that best guides subsequent medical action. Hence, the reference method to be used in a diagnostic study may very well include one or a combination of expensive and complicated tests that are not routinely available or applied in everyday clinical practice. Note that this contrasts with the assessment of the diagnostic determinants of interest, which should more or less mimic daily practice to enhance generalizability of study results to daily practice.

Preferably, the final diagnosis should be established independent of the results of the diagnostic tests under study. Commonly, the observer who assesses the final diagnosis using the reference method is blinded for all of the test results under study. If this blinding is not guaranteed, the information provided by the preceding tests may implicitly or explicitly be used in the assessment of the final diagnosis. Consequently, the two information sources cannot be distinguished and the estimates of accuracy of the tests being studied may be biased. Although theoretically this bias can lead to both an under- and overestimation of the accuracy of the evaluated tests, it commonly results in an overestimation; the final diagnosis may be guided to some extent by the results of the test under evaluation, artificially decreasing the number of false-positive and false-negative results. This kind of bias is often referred to as *diagnostic review* or *incorporation bias* [Begg & Metz, 1990; Ransohoff & Feinstein, 1978; Sackett et al., 1985; Swets, 1988].

The possibility of blinding the outcome assessors for the results of the tests under study depends on the type of reference standard applied. It is surely feasible if the reference standard consists of a completely separate test, for example, imaging techniques or serum levels of a marker. Because this kind of reference test is not available for many diseases (e.g., psychiatric disorders), or is infeasible or even unethical to apply in all cases (notably when the test is invasive and patient burdening), next best solutions are often sought. In particular, an approach involving a so-called consensus diagnosis determined by an outcome panel often is applied; this often is combined with a clinical follow-up period to further promote an adequate assessment of the presence of the disease [Begg, 1990; Reitsma et al., 2009; Swets, 1988]. Outcome panels consist of a usually unequal number of experts on the clinical problem. During consensus meetings, the panel establishes the final diagnosis in each study patient based on as much patient information as possible. This includes information from patient history, physical examination, and all additional tests. Often, any clinically relevant information (e.g., future diagnoses, response to treatment targeted at the outcome disease) from each patient during a prespecified follow-up period is also forwarded to the outcome panel in order to allow for a better judgment on whether the target disease was present at the time of (initial) presentation [Moons & Grobbee, 2002b]. When using a consensus diagnosis based on all available information as the reference standard, the test results studied as potential diagnostic determinants are usually also included ("incorporated") in the outcome assessment, leading to a risk of *incorporation bias*. To fully prevent incorporation bias, the outcome panel should decide on the final diagnosis without knowledge of the results of the particular test(s) under study. This may seem an attractive solution, but limiting the information forwarded to the panel may increase misclassification in the outcome assessment. There are no set solutions to this dilemma that is inherent to using a consensus diagnosis as the reference standard. The pros and cons of excluding or including the results from all or some of the tests under study in the assessment of the final diagnosis by the outcome panel should be weighed in each particular study. Consider a study that aims to assess the diagnostic value of NT-proBNP serum levels or echocardiography in addition to signs and symptoms in patients suspected of heart failure. As in several earlier studies on suspected heart failure, an outcome panel can determine the "true" presence or absence of heart failure [Moons & Grobbee, 2002b; Rutten et al., 2005b]. When studying the accuracy of a test known to receive much weight in the consensus judgment (in this example echocardiography and to a lesser extent NT-proBNP levels), it is preferable not to use these tests in the assessment of the final diagnosis. Doing so requires that the remaining diagnostic information, including clinical follow-up data, enable the panel to accurately diagnose patients. Lack of availability of the NT-proBNP levels will probably not pose a major problem, but withholding the echocardiographic findings, a key element in the diagnosis of heart failure, from the outcome panel may seriously endanger the validity of the outcome assessment. Consequently, we may be able to quantify the added value of NT-proBNP levels but not the added value of the echocardiogram [Kelder et al., 2011]. Alternatively, the outcome panel could judge the presence or absence of heart failure first without considering the echocardiographic findings and then subsequently with the echocardiography results. Comparing the outcome classification according to both approaches may provide some insight into the effect of incorporation bias on the (boundaries of the) accuracy of the test under study, in this case echocardiography.

As mentioned earlier, in certain situations it is not feasible and may even be unethical to apply the best available reference method in all study patients at the time of presentation, in particular when the reference test is invasive and may lead to complications (such as pulmonary angiography in suspected pulmonary embolism). Also in studies in suspected malignancies, it is often difficult to establish or rule out a malignancy at t = 0, even when multiple tests, including sophisticated imaging techniques, are performed. Under such circumstances, a clinical follow-up period may offer useful information. It should be emphasized here that a clinical follow-up period is applied to assess whether the disease of interest was indeed present at the time of presentation of the complaints (t = 0). It is then assumed that the natural history of the (untreated) target disease implies that the target disease was present but unrecognized at t = 0. A clinical follow-up period to establish a diagnosis has been successfully applied in studies on the accuracy of diagnostic tests for a variety of diseases, including pulmonary embolism, bacterial meningitis, and certain types of cancer. For example, Fijten et al. [1995] studied which signs and symptoms were helpful in ruling out colorectal cancer in patients presenting with fecal blood loss in primary care. It was impossible to perform colonoscopies and additional imaging or surgery in all participants to rule in or out a malignancy at t = 0. Therefore, all patients were followed for an additional period of at least 12 months after inclusion in the study, assuming that colorectal cancer detected during the follow-up period would indicate presence of the cancer at baseline. Obviously, the follow-up period should be limited in length, especially in diseases with a relatively high incidence, to prevent new cases from being counted as prevalent ones. The acceptable clinical follow-up period varies and depends on the natural history and incidence of the disease studied. A 6- to 12-month period is often encountered in the literature for cancer studies. For venous thromboembolism this is usually 3 months, and in a study of bacterial meningitis it was 1 week.

Besides documenting the natural history of a disease during such a clinical follow-up period, one may also document the response to treatment targeted at the outcome diagnosis and use this information to determine whether the target disease was present at t = 0. Response to therapy may be helpful in excluding (in the case of no response) or confirming (in the case of a beneficial effect on symptoms) the target disease. In these situations, one should be aware that response following therapy provides no definite proof of the disease, because the response could result from other factors. Similarly, lack of response does not preclude the presence of the disease at t = 0. Examples of using the response to empirical treatment to confirm a diagnosis are studies in suspected heart failure [Kelder et al., 2011].

Partial and differential outcome verification.   Ideally, the index tests and reference standard are determined in all study participants and in a standardized manner. For various reasons, however, the reference standard may not have been performed in all patients. Such partial outcome verification might be attributable to ethical concerns or patient or physician preferences (e.g., when the reference test is considered unnecessary or too burdening, or because it is simply impossible to perform in all patients; for example, biopsy and histology as the reference standard in diagnosing cancer can only be performed in subjects with detected nodes or hot spots based on previous testing [de Groot et al., 2011a ; Reitsma et al., 2009]). Partial outcome verification (i.e., partially missing outcome data) often occurs not completely at random but selectively. The reason for performing the reference standard is typically related to the test results of preceding index tests. Such partial verification may lead to biased estimates of the accuracy of the index tests if only the selective subsample of patients in whom the reference test was executed are included in the analysis. This is known as *partial verification bias, work-up bias,* or *referral bias* [Rutjes et al., 2007]. Often researchers use a different, second best, reference test to verify the target disease presence in those subjects for whom the first, preferred reference test cannot be used [de Groot et al., 2011b]. Such differential verification will lead to bias when the results of the two reference tests are treated in the analysis as interchangeable, while both are of different quality in classifying the target disease or may even define the target disease differently. Hence, simply combining all disease outcome data in a single analysis as if both reference tests yield the same disease status does not reflect the "true" pattern of disease presence. Such an estimation of disease prevalence thus differs from what one would have obtained if all subjects had undergone the preferred reference standard. Consequently, all estimated measures of the accuracy of the diagnostic index tests will be biased; this is called *differential verification bias* [de Groot et al., 2011b; Reitsma et al., 2009]. Several solutions to deal with partial and differential outcome verification and its consequential bias have been proposed [de Groot et al., 2011b, 2001c]. One solution is multiple imputation of missing outcomes.

Design of Data Analysis

Objective of the Analysis

Analysis of data from multivariable diagnostic accuracy research (as opposed to test research) may serve a number of purposes: (1) to show *which* potential diagnostic determinants independently contribute to the estimation of the probability of disease presence (i.e., which determinants change the probability of disease presence); (2) to quantify *to what extent* these contributing determinants change the probability of disease presence (i.e., to estimate the relative accuracy or weights of these determinants); (3) to develop and/or validate a diagnostic model or rule to facilitate the estimation of the probability of disease given the combination of test results in individual patients in clinical practice [Moons et al., 2004a; Moons et al., 2012a].

Whether all three goals can or should be pursued depends on the motive of the study. If the aim is only to determine whether a particular test has added value or may replace another existing test, then the third goal may not be relevant. Furthermore, prior knowledge and the amount and type of study data determine whether the second and third goals should be addressed, as we will discuss next. We do not intend to provide full details on the statistical analysis of diagnostic data. For this we refer to the statistical literature.

Required Number of Subjects

The multivariable character of diagnostic research creates problems for the estimation of the required number of study subjects. Power calculations do exist for test research, that is, studies aiming to estimate the diagnostic value (e.g., sensitivity, specificity, predictive values, likelihood ratios, or ROC area) of a single test or to compare the properties of two single tests [Hanley & McNeil, 1983; Simel et al., 1991]. For multivariable studies that aim to quantify the independent contribution of each test with sufficient precision, no straightforward methods to estimate the required patient number are available. Several authors have stipulated, however, that in multivariable prediction research, including diagnostic studies, for each determinant (or diagnostic test) studied at least 10 subjects are needed *in the smallest category* of the outcome variable to allow proper statistical modeling. In case of the typical dichotomous outcome, that is, those with or without the disease, this usually implies 10 individuals with the disease [Harrell et al., 1996; Peduzzi et al., 1996]. If the number of potential determinants is much larger than 10% of the number of diseased, the analysis tends to overestimate the accuracy of the diagnostic strategy or model. The expected number of patients with the target disease thus limits the number of determinants to be analyzed and what might be inferred from a study.

Univariable Analysis

Before proceeding to multivariable analyses, we recommend first performing a univariable analysis in which each individual potential determinant is related to the outcome. Biostatisticians often refer to this type of analysis as a *bivariate analysis* because the association between two variables (determinant and outcome) is studied. In diagnostic research, categorical determinants with more than two categories and continuous determinants are often dichotomized by introducing a threshold. This commonly leads to loss of information [Royston et al., 2006]. For example, dichotomizing the body temperature > 37.5° Celsius (C) as test-positive and ≤ 37.5° Celsius as test-negative implies that the diagnostic implications for a person with a temperature of 38.0°C are the same as for a person with a temperature of 41°C. Second, the resulting association heavily depends on the threshold applied. This may explain why different studies of the same diagnostic test yield different associations. The aim of univariable analysis is to obtain insight into the association of each potential determinant and the presence or absence of the disease. Although it is common to only include in the multivariable analysis the determinants that show statistical significance (P-value < 0.05), in univariable analysis this may lead to optimistic estimates of the accuracy of a diagnostic model [Harrell, 2001; Steyerberg et al., 2000; Sun et al., 1996]. This chance of "optimism" increases when the number of potential determinants clearly exceeds the "1 to 10 rule" described earlier. It is therefore recommended to use a more liberal selection criterion, for example, P < 0.20, 0.25, or an even higher threshold [Steyerberg, 2009]. The downside to this is that more determinants will qualify for multivariable analysis, requiring the need for so-called internal validation and penalization or shrinkage methods that we will discuss later in this chapter. Alternatively, univariable analyses may guide combination and clustering of determinants, ideally influenced by prior knowledge of the most important determinants. Methods have been developed to incorporate prior knowledge into the selection of predictors [Harrell, 2001; Steyerberg et al., 2004]. Finally, univariable analysis is useful to determine the number of missing values for each determinant and for the outcome, and whether these missing values are missing completely at random (MCAR), missing at random (MAR), or missing not at random (MNAR).

Multivariable Analysis

Diagnostic practice is probabilistic, multivariable, and sequential. Consequently, a multivariable approach is the main component of the data analysis in diagnostic research. In the multivariable analysis, the probability of disease is related to combinations of multiple diagnostic determinants, in various orders. Multivariable analysis can accommodate the order in which tests are used in practice and will show which combination of tests truly contributes to the diagnostic probability estimation. To address the chronology and sequence of testing in clinical practice, the accuracy of combinations of easily obtainable determinants should be estimated first and subsequently the added value of the more burdensome and costly tests [Moons et al., 1999].

Logistic regression modeling is the generally accepted statistical method for multivariable diagnostic studies with a dichotomous outcome [Harrell, 2001; Hosmer & Lemeshow, 1989]. Other statistical methods, such as neural networks and classification and regression trees (CART), have been advocated, but these received much criticism as both often result in overly optimistic results [Harrell, 2001; Tu, 1996]. Therefore, we will focus on the use of logistic regression models for multivariable diagnostic research.

The determinants included in the first multivariable logistic regression model are usually selected on the basis of both prior knowledge and the results of univariable analysis. Also, the first model tends to concentrate on determinants that are easy to obtain in practice. Hence, this model typically includes test results from history taking and physical examination [Moons et al., 2004a; Moons et al., 1999]. A logistic regression model estimates the log odds (logit) of the disease probability as a function of one or more predictors:

$$\log [\text{probability (outcome event)}/\text{probability (nonevent)}] = \beta_0 + \beta_1 * T_1 + \ldots \beta_n * T_n = \text{linear predictor} \quad \text{(Eq. 1)}$$

in which β_0 is the intercept and β_1 to β_n are regression coefficients of T_1 to T_n. T_1 to T_n are the results of the diagnostic determinants (tests) obtained from patient history and physical examination. The sum of the intercept and the regression coefficients multiplied by the measured values of the determinants is called the linear predictor (*lp*) [Harrell et al., 1996]. A regression coefficient can be interpreted as the log odds of the outcome event relative to a nonevent per unit increase in a specific test, or in the case of a dichotomous test, the log odds of the outcome event for a positive relative to a negative test. The odds ratio can be computed as the antilog of the regression coefficient [exp(β)]. Equation 1 can be rewritten to estimate the probability of the outcome event for an individual patient:

$$\text{Probability (disease presence)} = \exp(\beta_0 + \beta_1 * T_1 + \ldots \beta_n * T_n)/[1 + \exp(\beta_0 + \beta_1 * T_1 + \ldots \beta_n * T_n)] \quad \text{(Eq. 2)} = 1/\{1 + \exp[- (lp)]\}$$

The probability of absence of disease can be estimated as:

$$\text{Probability (disease absence)} = 1 - \text{probability (disease presence)} \quad \text{(Eq. 3)}$$

The next step is to remove the noncontributing determinants to obtain a reduced model with a similar diagnostic performance as the full multivariable model. Noncontributing tests are manually (one by one) excluded using the log likelihood ratio test, again at a liberal level; for example, diagnostic tests could be excluded if the significance level (P-value) exceeds, say 0.10 or 0.15. This leads to a so-called *reduced model* that includes only those history and physical determinants that independently contribute to the probability estimation. The regression coefficient of each determinant reflects its independent contribution (weight) to the outcome probability (see Equation 1).

The next step is to estimate the diagnostic accuracy of this reduced multivariable model. The accuracy of a model is commonly estimated by two parameters: the *calibration* (reliability or goodness of fit) and the *discrimination* [Harrell, 2001; Hosmer & Lemeshow, 1989; Steyerberg, 2009]. Calibration is measured by the level of agreement between the disease probabilities (ranging from 0–100%) estimated by the model versus the observed disease frequencies. This is usually quantified by constructing equally large patient subgroups (say 20) after ordering of the estimated disease probabilities of all individual participants (from 0–100%) and by comparing the calculated frequency of the disease in each subgroup (in this case from those at the lowest to those at the highest 5% end of the distribution) to the number of diseased observed in each category. Good calibration means that the estimated probability of disease presence in the subgroups is similar to the observed disease frequency. The best way to examine this is by a graphical comparison. **Figure 2–2** shows a calibration plot of a "reduced diagnostic history and physical model" for the diagnosis of deep vein thrombosis

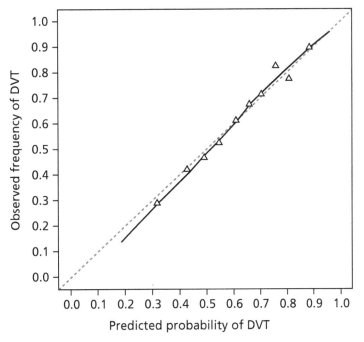

FIGURE 2–2   Calibration plot of a reduced multivariable logistic regression model, including six determinants from patient history and physical examination to estimate the probability of the presence of DVT in 400 patients suspected of DVT. The dotted line represents the line of identity, that is, perfect model calibration. All triangles represent 10% of the patients. The triangle on the left end represents the 10% with the lowest predicted probability of disease, with the mean predicted probability (32%) on the x-axis and a somewhat lower observed prevalence of DVT (28%) in the same patients on the y-axis.

(DVT) estimated from 400 primary care patients suspected of DVT. Ideally, the slope of the calibration plot is 1 and the intercept 0. The presented model includes six patient history and physical examination determinants, taking the form of Equation 1. The calibration of this model was very good, as the predicted probabilities are very similar to the observed disease prevalence across the entire distribution. Figure 2–2 shows a slight overestimation by the model in those patients in the lower estimated disease probability range.

A common statistic used to assess whether a multivariable model shows good calibration is the *goodness-of-fit test*. A statistically significant ($P < 0.05$) test indicates marked differences between predicted and observed probabilities and thus poor calibration [Hosmer & Lemeshow, 1989]. This test, however, often lacks statistical power to determine important deviations from good calibration because the P-value is seldom less than 0.05 [Harrell, 2001; Hosmer & Lemeshow, 1989]. We therefore recommend that the investigator closely examines the calibration plot to determine a model's calibration.

The discrimination of a multivariable model refers to the model's ability to discriminate between subjects with and without the disease. This is estimated with the area under the ROC curve or the c-index (index of concordance) of the model [Hanley & McNeil, 1982; Harrell et al., 1982]. **Figure 2–3** shows the ROC curve of the "reduced multivariable history and physical examination model." A multivariable model in fact can be considered a "single" test, existing of several component tests, with the model's estimated probability of disease presence (using Equation 2) as the "single" test result. The ROC curve exhibits the sensitivity ("true-positive rate") and 1 – specificity ("false-positive rate") of the model for each possible threshold in the range of "estimated probabilities." The area under the ROC curve reflects the overall discriminative value of the model, irrespective of the chosen threshold. It exhibits the extent to which the model can discriminate between subjects with and without the target disease. The diagonal line reflects the worst model or test; for each threshold, the number of correctly diagnosed patients equals the number of false diagnoses, that is, no discriminating value and an ROC area of 0.5 ("half of the square"). In other words, the probability of a false and true diagnosis is both 50% and such a model is no better than flipping a coin. The best model is reflected by the "curve" that runs from the lower left to the upper left and upper right corners, yielding an ROC area of 1.0 ("the entire square"). Hence, the more the ROC curve is in the left upper corner—the higher the area under the curve (the closer to 1.0)—the higher the discriminative value of the model. More exactly defined, the ROC area is the probability that for each (randomly) chosen pair of one diseased and one nondiseased subject, the model estimates a higher probability for the diseased than for the

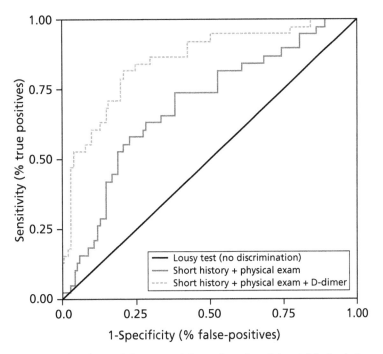

FIGURE 2–3   Example of an ROC curve of the reduced multivariable logistic regression model, including the same six determinants as in Figure 2.2. The ROC area of the "reduced history + physical model" was 0.70 (95% confidence interval [CI], 0.66–0.74) and of the same model added with the D-dimer assay 0.84 (95% CI, 0.80–0.88).

nondiseased individual [Hanley & McNeil, 1982; Harrell et al., 1982]. In our example, the ROC area of the "reduced history + physical model" was 0.70.

The next step is to extend this model by the subsequent test from the workup in our example study on DVT; this was the D-dimer assay. This allows estimation of the assay's diagnostic value in addition to the items from history taking and physical examination. In this analysis, the same statistical procedures as just described are used. Whether the D-dimer test is a truly independent predictor is estimated again by the log likelihood ratio test [Harrell, 2001; Hosmer & Lemeshow, 1989]. Next, the calibration and discrimination of the extended model (including the "reduced history + physical model" items plus the D-dimer assay) are examined. The calibration of this extended model was good (data not shown), and the discriminatory value was high (ROC area = 0.84; Figure 2–3). Methods have been proposed to formally estimate the precision of differences between ROC areas, in this case 0.84–0.70 = 0.14, by calculating the 95% confidence interval (CI) or

P-value of this difference. In this calculation, one needs to account for the correlation between both models ("tests") as they are based on the same subjects [Hanley & McNeil, 1983]. In our example study, the CIs did not overlap, indicating a significant added value of the D-dimer assay at the 0.05 level.

This process of model extension can be repeated for each subsequent test. Moreover, all of these analytic techniques can be used to compare the difference in the added diagnostic value of two tests separately when the aim is to choose between the two or to compare the diagnostic accuracy of various test orders. We should emphasize that the ROC area of a multivariable diagnostic model or even a single diagnostic test has no direct clinical meaning. It estimates and can compare the overall discriminative value of diagnostic models or strategies.

The DVT example exemplifies the need for multivariable diagnostic research. A comparison between models including fewer or additional tests enables the investigator to learn not only about the added value of tests but also about the relevance of moving from simple to more advanced testing in practice. It should be noted that the data analysis as outlined here only quantifies which subsequent tests have independent or incremental value in the diagnostic probability estimation and thus should be included in the final diagnostic model from an accuracy point of view. It might still be relevant to judge whether the increase in accuracy of the test outweighs its costs and patient burden. This weighing can be done formally, including a full cost-effectiveness or cost-minimization analysis accounting for the consequences and utilities of false-positive and false-negative diagnoses [Moons et al., 2012b; Vickers & Elkin, 2006]. This enters the realm of medical decision making and medical technology assessment and is not covered here.

The multivariable analysis can be used to create a clinical prediction rule that can be used in clinical practice to estimate the probability that an individual patient has the target disease given his or her documented test results. There are various examples of such multivariable diagnostic rules: a rule for diagnosing the presence or absence of DVT [Oudega et al., 2005b; Wells et al., 1997], pulmonary embolism [Wells et al., 1997], conjunctivitis [Rietveld et al., 2004], and bacterial meningitis [Oostenbrink et al., 2001]. How to derive a diagnostic rule, the ways to present it in a publication and how to enhance its use in clinical practice will be described next.

Internal Validation and Shrinkage of the Diagnostic Model

An initial prediction model commonly shows a too optimistic discrimination (ROC area relatively high, closer to 1.0) and calibration (slope close to 1.0 and intercept close to 0) when it is applied to the data from which it is derived (i.e., the derivation or development data set). The model is so-called *overfitted* [Harrel, 2001; van Houwelingen, 2001]. This means that the model's predicted probabilities will be too extreme (too high for the diseased and too low for the nondiseased) when the model is applied to new patients; calibration will be poorer and discrimination lower in daily practice [Altman et al., 2009; Moons et al., 2012b]. The amount of optimism (overfitting) in both calibration and discrimination can be estimated using so-called *internal validation methods*. Here internal means that no new data are used, just data from the derivation set.

The most widely used internal validation methods are the *split-sample*, *cross-validation*, and *bootstrapping* methods [Harrell, 2001; Steyerberg, 2009]. In the first two, part of the derivation data set (e.g., a random sample of 75% or a sample based on the time of inclusion in the study) is used for model development. The remainder (25%) is applied for estimating the model's accuracy. With bootstrapping, first a model is developed (fitted) on the full sample as described earlier. Then, multiple random samples (e.g., 100) are drawn from the full sample. On each bootstrap sample, the model is redeveloped. The calibration (slope and intercept of the calibration plot) and discrimination (ROC area) of each bootstrap model are then compared to the corresponding estimates of the bootstrap models when applied (tested) in the original full sample. These differences can be averaged, and they provide an indication of the average optimism of the bootstrap models. This average optimism in discrimination and calibration can be used to adjust the original model estimated in the full sample, that is, adjusting or shrinking the regression coefficients and ROC area. Application of the shrunken model (regression coefficients) in new patients will generally yield better (less optimistic) calibration, and the adjusted discrimination (ROC area) better approximates the discrimination that can be expected in clinical practice [Harrell, 2001; Steyerberg et al., 2001]. Bootstrapping is preferred over split-sample or cross-validation as an internal validation tool as it is more efficient; bootstrapping uses all patient data for model development and for the model validation. Importantly, all steps in the model's development, including decisions on the transformation, clustering, and re-coding of variables as well as on the selection of variables (both in the univariable and multivariable analysis) can and should be redone in every bootstrap sample [Harrell, 2001; Steyerberg et al., 2003]. Bootstrapping techniques have become widely available in standard statistical software packages, such as STATA, SAS, and S-plus. Alternative methods for shrinkage or penalizing a model for potential overfitting are the use of a heuristic shrinkage factor [Copas, 1983; van Houwelingen & LeCessie, 1990] and the use of penalized estimation methods [Harrell, 2001; van Houwelingen, 2001; Moons et al., 2004b].

Inferences from Multivariable Analysis

The lower the number of study patients and the higher the number of candidate determinants, the larger the chance of optimism of the final diagnostic model and the need for bootstrapping and shrinkage. Under certain extreme circumstances, even bootstrapping and shrinkage techniques cannot account for all optimism [Bleeker et al., 2003; Steyerberg et al., 2003]. The analysis and inferences then should be more cautious. Preferably one should then not try to achieve the third goal described previously, but rather restrict the analysis to identifying independent predictors of the presence or absence of the disease (first goal) and estimate their shrunken relative weights (second goal). If after bootstrapping and shrinkage a full model is still reported, we advise investigators to stress the need for future studies focused on confirming the observed predictor–outcome associations, and to estimate the calibration and discrimination of these predictors in new patient samples.

Prediction Rules and Scores

A diagnostic model developed to assist in setting a diagnosis in individual patients can be presented (or reported) in three ways. The most precise method is to report the original (untransformed) logistic model with the shrunken regression coefficients and corresponding discrimination and calibration of the model. This model presentation has the form of Equation 1. Readers may apply this model directly to estimate an individual patient's probability of the disease by multiplying the patient's test results by the corresponding coefficients, summing these up, and taking the antilog of the sum using Equation 2. This, however, requires a calculator or computerized patient record, which are not always available in clinical practice. To improve the applicability of a multivariable model in practice, one can use the (shrunken) regression coefficients to create a nomogram, as shown in **Figure 2–4**. This is rarely done, although the creation of a nomogram has become easy with the statistical package S-plus.

A final method to present a prediction model and to facilitate its implementation is a so-called *simplified risk score* or *scoring rule*. The original (shrunken) regression coefficients (first method, Equation 1) are then transformed to rounded numbers that are easily added together. This is commonly done by dividing each regression coefficient by the smallest regression coefficient, multiplying it by 10, and rounding this to the nearest integer. The reporting of a simplified rule must be accompanied by the observed disease frequencies across score categories, as we will show in the example that follows. This simplification of a risk score will lead to some loss of information and thus some loss in diagnostic accuracy, because the original regression coefficients are simplified and rounded. However, this

FIGURE 2–4 Nomogram of a diagnostic model used to estimate the probability of DVT in suspected patients. To use this nomogram, a man (corresponding with 7 points from the "Points" scale at the top of the figure), who (obviously) does not use oral contraception (0 points), has no leg trauma (6 points), and no recent malignancy (0 points), underwent surgery in the past 3 months (4 points), has a difference in calf circumference more than 3 cm (11 points), no vein distention (0 points), and a D-dimer concentration of ≥ 500 μg/L (20 points), receives a "Total Points" score of 48. The lower two scales of the graphic show that this score corresponds to a probability of DVT of about 0.55 (or 55%).

loss in precision usually does not affect clinical relevance. Ideally, the loss in precision should be minimal, with the simplified risk score as accurate as the original model but more easy to use. To allow readers to choose, we recommend that the report includes both the original untransformed model and the simplified risk score with the ROC areas.

The multivariable analysis presented earlier shows which combination of tests best predicts the presence of disease (or whether a new or alternative test improves prediction) and provides a tool to estimate an individual patient's probability of having a specific disease. It does not quantify in what proportion of suspected patients the use of a diagnostic model or the addition of a new or alternative test will change patient management. Such a change in patient management can best be illustrated in Figure 2–1.

Patients suspected of having a disease can be categorized as those with a probability of the disease low enough to exclude the diagnosis (i.e., below threshold A), those with a probability high enough to consider the disease to be present (i.e., beyond threshold B), and those in the grey area in between, where additional testing may be considered. For a new or alternative diagnostic strategy or test to have an impact on patient management, the proportion of patients that is correctly reclassified from one category to another (thus those with the disease to a higher category and those without to a lower category) should be high enough. When, for example, the addition of a new test increases the estimated probability of disease in some patients with the target disease from, for example, 80–90%, while both proportions lie above the B threshold for this particular disease, the impact in daily practice will be limited. When, however a new test correctly reclassifies many patients from the gray area to either the area below the A or above the B threshold, its impact will be much higher. Such a quantification of the reclassification of patients (through, for example, the net reclassification improvement) is increasingly being applied in prediction research [Pencina et al., 2008; Steyerberg et al., 2012]. This requires, however, definition of the thresholds A and B. This may be quite a challenge, as it typically requires reaching consensus about something rather subjective. Methods to formally quantify the optimal probability thresholds are available, but they fall beyond the scope of this text.

External Validation

As explained earlier, the possible optimism of a diagnostic model may be addressed by internal validation. However, external validation, using new data, is generally necessary before a model can be used in practice with confidence [Altman & Royston, 2000a; Justice et al., 1999; Reilly & Evans, 2006]. External validation is the application and testing of the model in new patients. The term *external* refers to the use of data from subjects who were not included in the study in which the prediction model was developed. So defined, external validation can be performed, for example, in patients from the same centers but from a later period than that during which the derivation study was conducted, or in patients from other centers or even another country [Justice et al., 1999; Reilly & Evans, 2006]. External validation studies are clearly warranted when one aims to apply a model in another setting (e.g., transporting a model from secondary to primary care) or in patient subgroups that were not included in the development study (e.g., transporting a model from adults to children) [Knottnerus, 2002a; Oudega et al., 2005a].

Too often, researchers use their data only to develop their own diagnostic model, without even mentioning—let alone validating—previous models.

This is unfortunate as prior knowledge is not optimally used. Moreover, recent insights show that in the case where a prediction (diagnostic or prognostic) model performs less accurately in a validation population, the model can easily be adjusted based on the new data to improve its accuracy in that population [Moons et al., 2012b; Steyerberg et al., 2004]. For example, the original Framingham coronary risk prediction model and the Gail breast cancer model were adjusted based on later findings and validation studies [Costantino et al., 1999; Grundy et al., 1998]. An adjusted model will then be based on both the development and the validation data set, which will further improve its stability and applicability to other populations. The adjustments may vary from parsimonious techniques such as updating the intercept of the model for differences in outcome frequency, via adjusting the originally estimated regression coefficients of the determinants in the model, to even adding new determinants to the model. It has been shown, however, that simple updating methods are often sufficient and thus preferable to the more extensive model adjustments [Janssen et al., 2008 & 2009; Steyerberg et al., 2004].

With these advances, the future may be one in which prediction models—provided that they are correctly developed—are continuously validated and updated if needed. This resembles cumulative meta-analyses in therapeutic research. Obviously, the more diverse the settings in which a model is validated and updated, the more likely it will generalize to new settings. The question arises about how many validations and adjustments are needed before it is justifiable to implement a prediction model in daily practice. Currently there is no simple answer. "Stopping rules" for validating and updating prediction models should be developed for this purpose.

APPLICATION OF STUDY RESULTS IN PRACTICE

Why are prediction models constantly used in, for example, weather forecasting and economics (albeit with varying success), while they still have limited application in medicine? There are several potential explanations. First, prediction models are often too complex for daily use in clinical settings that are not supported by computer technology. This may improve with the introduction of computerized patient records but also may require a change in attitude by practicing physicians. Second, because diagnostic (and prognostic) models often are not routinely validated in other populations, clinicians may not—and perhaps should not—trust the probabilities provided by these models. External validation studies as described earlier in the chapter are still scarce. Even less frequently are models validated or tested for their ability to change clinicians' decisions, not to mention their ability to improve a patient's prognosis [Reilly & Evans, 2006; Stiell et al., 1995]. There are no formal criteria to judge the generalizability of diagnostic study results, but a few rules of thumb can be given. Generalizability of a diagnostic model is first and foremost determined by its use in the appropriate domain of patients suspected of having the target disease. Second, it is commonly determined by the setting (primary, secondary, tertiary care) in which the model was developed and perhaps validated. For example, particular symptoms or signs presented by patients in an academic hospital may be less relevant in patient populations from a general hospital or from primary care and vice versa [Knottnerus, 2002a]. This has been shown, for example, for extrapolation of a diagnostic rule for DVT developed in secondary care patients to primary care patients [Oudega et al., 2005a]. Third, generalizability is determined by the tests included in the final model. For example, the inclusion of particular advanced tests, such as spiral CT scanning, may lead to a limited applicability of the model to other patient populations or settings.

A final reason why diagnostic models are often not applied in daily practice is that clinicians may find it difficult to include explicit predicted probabilities in their decision making; many doctors are reluctant to accept that a simplified mathematical formula replace their clinical experience, skills, and complicated diagnostic reasoning in everyday patient care. The latter opinion clearly is a misunderstanding. Diagnostic rules are tools that should be used to aid physicians in their daily tasks, indeed, to help them cope with their complicated diagnostic challenges. Such tools are not meant to be a substitute for clinical experience and skills, but to strengthen them.

WORKED-OUT EXAMPLE

Recognition and ruling out of DVT is difficult based on history taking and physical examination alone. An adequate diagnosis in patients presenting with symptoms suggestive of DVT (usually a painful, swollen leg) is crucial because of the risk of potentially fatal pulmonary embolism when DVT is not adequately treated with anticoagulants. False-positive diagnoses also should be avoided because of the bleeding risk associated with anticoagulant therapy. The serum D-dimer test clearly improves the accuracy of diagnosing and ruling out DVT in suspected patients. Algorithms, including clinical assessment (i.e., signs and symptoms) and D-dimer testing are available that are widely applied in clinical practice and recommended in current guidelines. The most famous of these, the Wells rule, was developed and validated in secondary care settings [Wells et al., 1997]. Research

BOX 2–8   Ruling Out Deep Venous Thrombosis in Primary Care: A Simple Diagnostic
Algorithm Including D-dimer Testing

In primary care, the physician has to decide which patients have to be referred
for further diagnostic work-up. At present, only in 20% to 30% of the referred
patients the diagnosis DVT is confirmed. This puts a burden on both patients and
health care budgets. The question arises whether the diagnostic work-up and
referral of patients suspected of DVT in primary care could be more efficient. A
simple diagnostic decision rule developed in primary care is required to safely
exclude the presence of DVT in patients suspected of DVT, without the need for
referral. In a cross-sectional study, we investigated the data of 1295 consecutive
patients consulting their primary care physician with symptoms suggestive of
DVT, to develop and validate a simple diagnostic decision rule to safely exclude
the presence of DVT. Independent diagnostic indicators of the presence of DVT
were male gender, oral contraceptive use, presence of malignancy, recent surgery,
absence of leg trauma, vein distension, calf difference and D-dimer test result.
Application of this rule could reduce the number of referrals by at least 23%
while only 0.7% of the patients with a DVT would not be referred. We conclude
that by using eight simple diagnostic indicators from patient history, physical
examination and the result of D-dimer testing, it is possible to safely rule out
DVT in a large number of patients in primary care, reducing unnecessary patient
burden and health care costs.

Reproduced from: Oudega R, Moons KGM, Hoes AW. Ruling out deep venous thrombosis in primary
care: A simple diagnostic algorithm including D-dimer testing. *Thromb Haemost* 2005b;94:200–5.

demonstrated that the Wells rule cannot adequately rule out DVT in patients suspected of DVT in primary care as too many (16%) patients in the
low-risk category (Wells score below 1) still had DVT [Oudega et al., 2005a].
The goal of the study presented here (see **Box 2–8**), was to develop the
optimal diagnostic strategy, preferably by way of a diagnostic rule, to be
applied in the primary care setting [Oudega et al., 2005b].

Theoretical Design

The research question was: "Which combination of diagnostic determinants best estimates the probability of DVT in patients suspected of having
DVT in primary care?"

Determinants considered included findings from history taking and
physical examination as well as the D-dimer test result. The occurrence relation can be summarized as:

$$P (DVT) = f (T_1, T_2, T_3, \ldots T_n)$$

where $T_1 \ldots T_n$ refer to all potential diagnostic determinants studied (in total 17).

The domain of the study consisted of patients presenting to primary care with symptoms suggestive of DVT.

Design of Data Collection

Data were collected cross-sectionally. Participating primary care physicians were asked to include all patients in whom the presence of DVT was suspected during an inclusion period of 17 months. All 17 diagnostic determinants and the reference standard were assessed in all included patients. Thus, the time dimension of data collection was zero, a census (and no sampling) approach was taken, and the study was observational (and not experimental).

The inclusion criterion was phrased as "all patients aged 18 years or older in whom the primary care physician suspected deep vein thrombosis," while in the information forwarded to the primary care physician, suspicion of DVT was explicitly defined as at least one of the following symptoms or signs of the lower extremities: swelling, redness, and/or pain. Exclusion criteria included a duration of the symptoms exceeding 30 days and suspicion of pulmonary embolism. In total, 110 primary care physicians in three regions in the central part of the Netherlands, each served by one hospital, were involved.

All items from history and physical examination were recorded in the case record form by the patient's primary care physician. The D-dimer test and the reference standard (real time B-mode compression ultrasonography) were performed in the adherent hospital. In patients with a normal compression ultrasonography, the procedure was repeated after 7 days to definitely rule out DVT. The diagnostic determinants under study and the result from the reference standard were recorded in all 1,295 included patients.

Design of Data Analysis

After univariable analysis, a multivariable logistic regression analysis was done including all 16 findings from history taking and physical examination in the model to determine which of these independently contributed to the presence or absence of DVT. Model reduction was performed by excluding variables from the model with a P-value > 0.10 based on the log likelihood ratio test. Subsequently, the D-dimer test was added to the reduced "history + physical" model to quantify its incremental value, which resulted in the final model. The calibration and ROC area of both models (with and without D-dimer) were estimated. Bootstrapping techniques, repeating the entire modeling process, were used to internally validate the final model and to adjust the estimated performance of the model for optimism. The model's performance obtained after bootstrapping was considered to approximate the expected performance in similar future patients. To construct an easily applicable diagnostic rule, the regression coefficients of the variables in the final model were transformed to integers according to their relative contributions (quantified through the regression coefficients) to the probability estimation. Finally, after estimating the score for each patient, the absolute percentages of correctly diagnosed patients across score categories were estimated. One hundred and twenty-seven subjects had missing values for one or more tests under study. Per predictor, on average, 2–3% of the values were missing. As data were not MCAR, deleting subjects with a missing value would lead not only to a loss of statistical power but also to biased results. To decrease bias and increase statistical efficiency, the missing values were imputed.

Results and Implications

Of the 1,295 patients included, 289 had DVT (prevalence 22%). An abnormal D-dimer level was by far the strongest determinant of the presence of DVT (univariable odds ratio of 35.7; 95% CI, 13.3–100.0). In multivariable analysis, 7 of the history and physical examination items were independent predictors of DVT: male gender, use of oral contraceptives, presence of malignancy, recent surgery, absence of leg trauma, vein distension, and a difference in calf circumference between the two legs of 3 cm or more. The ROC of this model was 0.68 (95% CI, 0.65–0.71). The multivariable model including these 7 determinants plus the D-dimer test had an ROC area of 0.80 before and 0.78 (95% CI, 0.75–0.81) after bootstrapping and shrinkage. This indicates a substantial added value. The odds ratio of the D-dimer assay (after shrinkage) was 20.3 (8.3–49.9). The calibration plot—after bootstrapping—of the final model showed good calibration; the P-value of the goodness of fit test was 0.56.

The final, untransformed model after shrinkage was:

Probability of DVT = 1/[1 + exp– (–5.47 + 0.59*male gender + 0.75*OC use + 0.42*presence of malignancy + 0.38*recent surgery + 0.60*absence of leg trauma + 0.48*vein distension + 1.13*calf difference ≥ 3cm + 3.01*abnormal D-dimer)]

TABLE 2–1   Probability of Deep Vein Thrombosis (DVT) by Risk Score

Risk	Score Range	Number of Patients (%)	Number of Patients with DVT Present (%)
Very low	0–3	293 (23%)	2 (0.7%)
Low	4–6	66 (5%)	3 (4.5%)
Moderate	7–9	663 (51%)	144 (21.7%)
High	10–13	273 (21%)	140 (51.3%)
Total	0–13	1,295	289 (22.0%)

To facilitate application of this model in daily practice, the following simplified scoring rule was derived:

Score = 1*male gender + 1*oral contraceptive use + 1*presence of malignancy + 1*recent surgery + 1*absence of leg trauma + 1*vein distension + 2*difference in calf circumference ≥ 3 cm + 6*abnormal D-dimer test

The score ranged from 0–13 points, and the ROC area of the simplified rule was also 0.78. **Table 2–1** shows the number of participants and probability of DVT in different categories of the risk score.

As an example, a woman using oral contraceptives who was without a leg trauma but had vein distension and a negative D-dimer test would receive a score of 3 (0 + 1 + 0 + 0 + 1 + 1 + 0 + 0), corresponding with a very low estimated probability of DVT of 0.7%.

It was concluded from the study that a simple diagnostic algorithm based on history taking, physical examination, and D-dimer testing can be helpful in safely ruling out DVT in primary care and thus would reduce the number of unnecessary referrals for suspected DVT.

Later, the accuracy of this simplified rule was externally validated in three regions in the Netherlands [Büller et al., 2009]. This study showed that among DVT-suspected patients not referred for ultrasonography in daily practice because of a risk score of ≤ 3, the proportion with a diagnosis of DVT or pulmonary embolism within 3 months was indeed low (1.4%). The rule has been included in the current primary care clinical guideline on suspected DVT in the Netherlands.

Chapter 3

Etiologic Research

█ INTRODUCTION

A 57-year-old female had a heart attack. She had no prior symptoms of vascular disease, is not obese, is a nonsmoker and has normal blood pressure and lipid levels. However, she has several family members who experienced a myocardial infarction at a relatively young age. At the time of her cardiac event, she was quickly transported to the hospital and had immediate coronary angioplasty with placement of a drug-eluting stent. The attending cardiologist subsequently put her on a regimen of aspirin, beta-blockers, and an angiotensin-converting enzyme (ACE) inhibitor.

She visits you to ask what she can do to prevent a future cardiac event. Is there an explanation for her disease? Might it be genetic? Is it because of reaching menopause? Is there anything she should change in her lifestyle? You promise her that you will look at the literature, and soon you come across an intriguing report by Sullivan [1981] suggesting that one protective mechanism for heart disease in women before menopause is actually monthly periods. In some women, the loss of blood compensates for excessive iron storage. Excessive iron storage can make the heart more vulnerable to ischemia or promote atherosclerosis. Another paper by Roest et al. [1999] shows that a relatively common heterozygous form of the gene that also codes for hemochromatosis may lead to subclinical cardiac tissue iron accumulation and thereby increase the risk of cardiac events. Apart from a genetic tendency to accumulate iron, it also has been suggested that excess iron storage may result from an inappropriately high intake of iron through the diet. This raises the question of whether a high dietary iron intake may be involved in cardiac risk in otherwise low-risk individuals.

ETIOLOGIC RESEARCH IN EPIDEMIOLOGY

The origins of today's clinical epidemiology can be found in early research on the causes of common diseases in the population. Initially, the focus was on communicable diseases with classic discoveries like the one by John Snow, who unmasked the Broad Street pump as a source of a cholera epidemic in London even before the notion of germs as a cause of infectious diseases became firmly established (see **Figure 3–1**). Gradually the scope has broadened, with virtually all chronic and acute diseases now being addressed by epidemiologic research. Although there seems to be a common belief that epidemiologic studies alone cannot clarify causal associations, the generally accepted relationships between smoking and lung cancer, cholesterol and

FIGURE 3–1   Cover of John Snow's report, *On the Mode of Communication of Cholera,* published in 1855 by John Churchill, London. Snow's observations on the method of transfer of this disease virtually ended a London cholera epidemic and laid the foundation for the new science of clinical epidemiology.

Reproduced from Snow (1855). *On the Mode of Communication of Cholera*. London: John Churchill, New Burlington Street, England.

cardiovascular disease, and the occurrence of vaginal cancer in daughters of diethylstilbestrol (DES) users provide compelling examples to the contrary.

This chapter discusses the principles and methods of etiologic epidemiologic research in a clinical setting and is exemplified by a clinical epidemiologic study on the causal effect of excessive iron storage on coronary heart disease risk in women (see **Box 3–1**). This cohort study examined a large group of women for baseline iron metabolism values and other relevant factors who subsequently were followed over time, with the occurrence of myocardial infarction and other manifestations of cardiovascular disease being recorded. As the baseline assessments included measurements of dietary intake, the data allowed the relationship between varying levels of dietary iron intake with the probability of future cardiovascular events to be established.

BOX 3–1   Dietary Haem Iron and Coronary Heart Disease in Women

DAPHNE L. VAN DER A
PETRA H.M. PEETERS
DIEDERICK E. GROBBEE

JOANNES J.M. MARX
YVONNE T. VAN DER SCHOUW

AIMS: A role for iron in the risk of ischaemic heart disease has been supported by in vitro and in vivo studies. We investigated whether dietary haem iron intake is associated with coronary heart disease (CHD) risk in a large population-based cohort of middle-aged women.

METHODS AND RESULTS: We used data of 16,136 women aged 49–70 years at recruitment between 1993 and 1997. Follow-up was complete until 1 January 2000 and 252 newly diagnosed CHD cases were documented. Cox proportional hazards analysis was used to estimate hazard ratios of CHD for quartiles of haem iron intake, adjusted for cardiovascular and nutritional risk factors. We stratified by the presence of additional cardiovascular risk factors, menstrual periods, and antioxidant intake to investigate the possibility of effect modification. High dietary haem iron intake was associated with a 65% increase in CHD risk [hazard ratio (HR) = 1.65; 95% confidence interval (CI): 1.07–2.53], after adjustment for cardiovascular and nutritional risk factors. This risk was not modified by additional risk factors, menstruation, or antioxidant intake.

CONCLUSION: The results indicate that middle-aged women with a relatively high haem iron intake have an increased risk of CHD.

Reproduced from Van der A DL, Peeters PHM, Grobbee DE, Marx JJM, Van der Schouw Y. Dietary haem iron and coronary heart disease in women. *European Heart Journal* 2005;26:257–262.

THEORETICAL DESIGN

Etiologic epidemiologic research explores the causes of a health outcome. Its aim is to demonstrate or exclude the relationship between a potential cause and the occurrence of a disease or other health outcome. To achieve this goal, alternative explanations for an apparent link between determinant and outcome need to be excluded in the research. These alternative explanations are offered by relationships due to extraneous determinants (confounders). The form of the etiologic occurrence relation, the object of research, is therefore outcome as a function of a determinant, conditional on confounders. The domain, the type of subjects for whom the relation is relevant, is defined by all those capable of having the outcome and who are at risk of being exposed to the determinant. Thus the domain for a study on the role of boxing in causing memory deficits is all human beings who could possibly engage in boxing, which is essentially everyone. The domain for the study in Box 3–1 on risks of coronary disease due to excessive iron intake is all women, and possibly all men too. The perspective on whether men should be a subset in the domain rests on the degree to which the investigator believes that a risk associated with high iron exposure is something particular to women or is a general feature of *Homo sapiens*.

Typically, etiologic research focuses on a single determinant at a time. In the example in Box 3–1, the emphasis was on haem iron intake operationalized by estimating intake from a food frequency questionnaire. All variables potentially related to both the risk of coronary disease and the levels of iron intake were treated as possible confounders; an elaborate discussion of the definition of confounders is given later in this chapter. In this study on iron intake and heart disease risk, the confounders were age, total energy intake, body mass index (BMI), smoking, physical activity, hypertension, diabetes, hypercholesterolemia, energy-adjusted intakes of saturated fat and carbohydrates, fiber, alcohol, beta-carotene, vitamin E, and vitamin C intake. All were measured at the time of inclusion in the cohort. When each was taken into account, however, none changed the risk estimate of iron intake materially, suggesting that none had a major impact in the association.

In another study addressing the importance of lifestyle in the occurrence of breast cancer, a particular research question might focus on the putative causal role of a high alcohol intake in the occurrence of breast cancer. The occurrence relation would then be breast cancer as a function of alcohol use, conditional on confounders. The domain would be all women. Among the confounders, smoking would most likely be important. In a second analysis of the same study, the question could be about the causal role of smoking in breast cancer. Now smoking would be the single causal determinant of interest and alcohol presumably among the confounders. (The importance of making clear distinctions between determinants and confounders in a given analysis for a given research question is outlined next.) Disregarding confounders or having incomplete or suboptimal confounder information may lead to results that are not true and thus invalid. The overriding importance of the need to exclude confounding makes etiologic epidemiologic research particularly difficult.

Courtroom Perspective

If you are doing etiologic research, pretend that you are in a courtroom. You are the prosecutor and your task is to show beyond reasonable doubt that the defendant, and not someone else, is to blame for the criminal act. Etiologic research is about accusation. As an investigator (author of the study), you must convince the jury (your peers and readers) that the determinant is causally involved in the occurrence of the disease. It is common for an initial report on a causal factor in disease to be superseded by newer research contradicting the initial finding because of evidence on confounders. One report in 1981 [MacMahon et al.] suggested a strong relationship between coffee use and pancreatic cancer. Since then, however, most studies could not confirm a substantial association when more confounding factors were considered, and the overall evidence suggests that coffee consumption is not related to pancreatic cancer risk.

CONFOUNDING

Assessment of confounding by detecting the presence of possible extraneous determinants is critical to obtaining valid results in etiologic studies. A first step is to clearly decide which determinant is the assumed causal factor of interest. Commonly, diseases are caused by multiple factors, which can act in concert or separately. In subsequent studies, multiple possible causative agents may be addressed consecutively. At each instant, however, there is typically one determinant of primary etiologic interest, while other determinants of the outcome are extraneous to that particular occurrence relation. Confounders can be very specific to a particular determinant–outcome relationship. Potential confounders may or may not distort the relationship between the determinant of interest and the outcome in the data, depending on the presence or absence of associations between these variables.

Frequently, assessment of confounding is proposed by simply determining the links of possible extraneous determinants between both the outcome and the causal determinant of interest. The prevailing view is that if a factor X is known to be related to both the determinant and outcome in an occurrence relation, then X is a confounder. Clearly, if a confounder is not related to both outcome and determinant, confounding will never result. However, even when a perceived extraneous determinant is simultaneously associated with the outcome and determinant, this does not invariably imply confounding. An example is when the variable is somewhere in the causal pathway and thus not extraneous.

For a third variable to act as a confounder in etiologic research, it should be (1) related to the occurrence of the outcome and thus be a determinant of the outcome by itself, (2) associated with the exposure determinant of interest, and (3) extraneous to the occurrence relation. By extraneous, we mean that this variable is not an inevitable part of the causal relationship or causal chain between the determinant of interest and the outcome variable (e.g., because it is part of the causal pathway; see the discussion that follows). The terms *confounder* and *extraneous determinant* can be used interchangeably; although less commonly used, the use of the term *extraneous determinant* indicates more clearly the type of determinant.

Assume that you are interested in the causal relationship between body weight and the occurrence of diabetes mellitus (see **Figure 3–2**). In a study designed to shed light on the causal role of obesity in diabetes, age is extraneous to the occurrence relation. Because age is known to be related to both body weight and the occurrence of diabetes (note the two arrows in the figure), any estimate of a causal effect of excessive body weight in the occurrence of diabetes is likely to be distorted by the effect of age. To validly estimate the true effect of obesity, differences in distributions of age across groups of patients with different body weights should be taken into account, either in the design of the data collection or in the design of data analysis. To return to the courtroom analogy, you should not blame body weight for the occurrence of diabetes when in fact age is "guilty." Extraneous to the

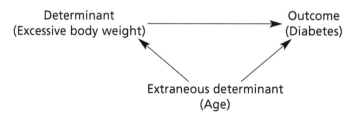

FIGURE 3–2   A simple causal pathway showing the influence of an extraneous determinant on the determinant and outcome.

occurrence relation also means that the third variable should not be part of the causal chain. If it is part of the causal chain, the variable is an *intermediate factor* rather than an extraneous variable. Such an intermediate factor may induce changes in other factors, which then serve to change the outcome.

An example of the intermediate factor situation is the role of high-density lipoprotein (HDL) cholesterol levels in the presumed cardio-protective effects of moderate alcohol use. Alcohol use may increase serum HDL cholesterol, which has anti-atherogenic and cardio-protective properties. In a study of the link between alcohol and heart disease, when adjustments are made for differences in serum HDL cholesterol levels between those who do or do not drink alcoholic beverages, an underestimation of the true cardio-protective effect of alcohol will result. Adjustments for intermediate factors are inappropriate, because the variable is in the causal chain between the determinant and the outcome and over-adjustment will result. "In the causal chain" often implies that the causal determinant influences a certain variable that follows the determinant and forms a true intermediate between determinant and outcome.

Alcohol consumption $\uparrow \rightarrow$ HDL cholesterol $\uparrow \rightarrow$ heart disease $\downarrow$

Alternatively, a variable could be a precursor to the causal determinant of interest and, thus, also part of the causal chain (although not an intermediate in the strict sense) and not extraneous to the occurrence relation. For example, when studying the occurrence of heart disease as a function of HDL cholesterol levels conditional on confounders, alcohol intake should not be treated as an extraneous determinant in view of the causal pathway depicted in the given equation. Increases in alcohol intake may induce ("precuse") increases in HDL cholesterol. The investigator may, however, make use of the change in risk estimate when alcohol is included in the model to address another research question: "To what extent is the protective effect of increased HDL levels explained by alcohol use?" In this way a "static" data set becomes almost a living laboratory where the investigator can insert or remove certain exposures to learn more about possible pathways and mechanisms.

Note that the relationships between the intermediate factor, the determinant of interest, and the outcome need not necessarily be directly causal. For example, in many circumstances social and economic factors are considered possible confounders of associations between putative causes of disease and disease outcome. However, social and economic status commonly act as indicators of one, multiple, or even unknown causal factors, such as diet or healthcare access, rather than being directly causally implicated.

A classic example of a variable that is not a confounder although it is noncausally associated with both the causal determinant under study and the outcome is possession of a lighter or matches in the study of smoking as a cause of lung cancer. Clearly, possession of a lighter is related to both the determinant (cigarette smoking) and the outcome (i.e., those carrying a lighter are more likely to develop lung cancer, although, obviously, a lighter or matches will not cause the cancer). The two arrows from Figure 3–2 exist, but the third prerequisite to be a confounder is not met because carrying a lighter is not extraneous to the occurrence relation. Possession of the lighter is a noncausal intermediate factor in the causal relationship between cigarette smoking and lung cancer, but it is not a confounder (see the equation that follows). Consequently, adjustment for carrying a lighter is inappropriate and would artificially dilute the existing association between smoking cigarettes and lung cancer.

Cigarette smoking → carrying a lighter → lung cancer

A study on the risk of congenital malformations as a causal consequence of using certain anti-epileptic drugs serves as another example of the role of confounding. Specific anti-epileptic drugs are not selected by chance by treating physicians. Rather they tend to be given for certain indications that are related to the type of epilepsy of the mother and her age of onset. These maternal characteristics may themselves constitute risk factors for congenital malformations irrespective of drug use and therefore act as confounders. Consequently, these characteristics are related to both the potentially causal determinant (a specific anti-epileptic drug, for example, phenobarbital) and the outcome (see **Figure 3–3**), and are possible confounders because they are also extraneous to the occurrence relation under study (and not an intermediate factor).

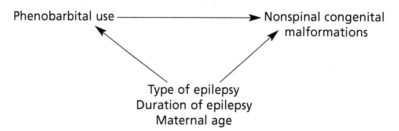

FIGURE 3–3   A specific example of a causal pathway showing several extraneous determinants.

In this example, the simple ("crude") increased risk for nonspinal malformations in offspring of women using phenobarbital (relative risk 2.0; 95% confidence interval [CI] 1.7–7.1) disappears once maternal characteristics were adjusted for in the analyses (adjusted relative risk 1.2; 95% CI 0.5–2.1), indicating that these extraneous determinants indeed confounded the relationship between phenobarbital and nonspinal malformations in offspring.

A major problem in the assessment and handling of confounding in etiologic research is the need for knowledge, or lack thereof, about extraneous determinants either conceptually or with regard to their availability in the data. When it is known from the literature that certain extraneous determinants exist for a specific outcome and information on these putative confounding factors is available in the data, it is generally recommended to remove the influence of these confounders in the design of data collection or data analysis, irrespective of whether the data obtained in the study actually show that these possible confounders are indeed correlated with both the determinant and the outcome. It should be emphasized that when a correlation analysis shows that there is no correlation between the causal determinant and a potential extraneous determinant, this variable may in certain circumstances still act as a confounder [Groenwold et al., 2011]. Also, when no correlation between the extraneous determinant and the outcome is revealed in the data, confounding by these determinants can sometimes not be excluded. Nevertheless, such a correlation analysis can be useful to illustrate the potential for confounding and other associations relevant to the occurrence relation. **Table 3–1** shows the results of a correlation analysis of several variables from a cohort study to determine the causal impact of BMI on blood pressure level. As age is known to be associated with these two variables and this association is confirmed in the table, it may act as a confounder. Heart rate is also known to be related to blood pressure and BMI (as also shown in the table) but is judged to be an intermediate factor. Number of cigarettes per day is not related to blood pressure or BMI (neither in the literature nor in the table) and is not considered a confounder.

In this example, systolic blood pressure increased 2 mm Hg per one unit of BMI without an adjustment for age ($P < 0.001$), and 1.2 mm Hg per unit after adjustment for age ($P < 0.001$; results are from linear regression analysis). As expected, the magnitude of the relationship between blood pressure and BMI became smaller when age was taken into account.

More difficult than assessing correlations in the data is achieving the necessary comprehensive inventory of possible extraneous determinants in the design phase of a study. This requires a good understanding of the nature

TABLE 3–1   Correlation of Variables from a Cohort Study

	Systolic Blood Pressure (mm Hg)	Heart Rate (bmp)	Cigarettes (n)	Age (years)	BMI (K/m²)
Systolic blood pressure	1.0000	–	–	–	–
Heart rate	0.1427*	1.0000	–	–	–
Cigarettes	–0.0122	0.1349*	1.0000	–	–
Age	0.2879*	–0.0090	–0.1102*	1.0000	–
Body mass index	0.2529*	0.0892*	–0.0411	0.1065*	1.0000

Data are from 1,265 individuals. Pairwise correlations are between blood pressure, heart rate, cigarette smoking, age, and body mass index.

$* P < 0.05.$

of the clinical problem and the likely operational mechanisms. Potential confounders need to be identified up front, because when neglected and otherwise missing in the total data collected, they may be impossible to resolve when the data are analyzed. Eventually, it is the investigator's task to completely remove confounding before arriving at any conclusions regarding causality. As an investigator, you can be assured that following the publication in which you, for example, blame sodium intake for causing cardiovascular events, other researchers ("lawyers in the same court room") will challenge such a supposition because of the potential for confounding.

The ongoing debate about the possible increased risk of myocardial infarction in subjects with a high coffee intake serves as an example. In the mid-1970s, reports were published suggesting that coffee users were at a twofold increased risk of myocardial infarction compared to nonusers. The increased risk remained after adjustment for possible confounding factors. Hennekens and coworkers [1976] published a case-control study in which they compared the effects of adjustment for a limited set of extraneous determinants; these included restricted adjustment as in other published reports at the time and adjustment for a more extensive set of possible confounders that included several dietary variables. Cases were male patients who had a fatal myocardial infarction, and controls were sampled from neighbors who remained free from coronary heart disease during the same time period. Information on coffee use and a range of confounders was obtained by interviewing the wives of the myocardial infarction victims and their neighbors (controls). First, an analysis was performed that replicated previous reports with adjustment for a limited set of 10 confounders.

In this analysis, the relative risk of myocardial infarction for coffee users compared to those who did not drink coffee was 1.8 (95% CI 1.2–2.5). However, when nine additional confounders were taken into account in the analyses, the relative risk was reduced to 1.1 (95% CI 0.8–1.6), which showed an insignificant 10% risk, rather than an 80% increased risk. Apparently, in previous work the "adjusted" association was still suffering from "residual" confounding. Subsequent studies with larger numbers of patients and even more extensive adjustment for potential confounders have further reduced the likelihood of a clinically meaningful increased risk of heart disease due to drinking coffee [Grobbee et al., 1990]. A possible exception is the use of so-called "boiled" coffee, in the past quite normal in Scandinavia, which has been shown to raise cholesterol and thus increase the risk of atherosclerosis and cardiovascular events [Bak & Grobbee, 1989]. In the latter example, cholesterol elevation is an intermediate variable.

One way to invalidate findings in etiologic research is to fail to consider relevant extraneous factors, and an alternative way to produce invalid results is to measure such confounding factors poorly. Adjustment is incomplete when confounders are not taken into account in the data analyses, but the adjustment for confounders in the analysis may be similarly inadequate if the measurement of confounders is not sufficiently comprehensive and precise.

Example: Estrogen and Bone Density

Let us consider a study that assessed whether postmenopausal circulating estrogen levels determine actual bone density [Van Berkum et al., unpublished data]. To this end, subjects were recruited from a large population study in which plasma estrogen levels were known for all participants. Two groups of participants were selected, one group of women with low circulating estrone levels and one group with high circulating estrone (one of the three estrogen hormones) levels. These two groups were matched for age, age at menopause, and body height. This means that for each woman in the low-estrone group, a women in the high-estrone group was selected who had a comparable age, age at menopause, and height. When baseline characteristics were compared, the matching variables were expectedly similarly distributed within the two groups. However, body weight and BMI appeared significantly lower in the low-estrone group. Consequently, in a simple correlation matrix, obesity would be disclosed as determinant of bone mass as well as being related to estrogen level. Does this make obesity a confounder? The answer has a major impact on the results and inferences from the study.

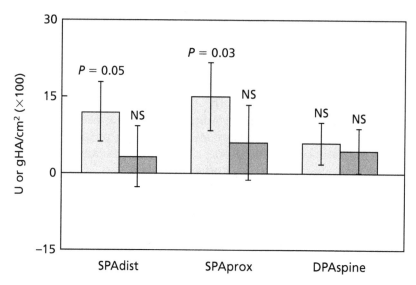

FIGURE 3–4   Do postmenopausal circulating estrogen levels affect bone density? Differences in bone density between high- and low-estone groups, with and without adjustment for differences in BMI are shown above. Measurements were made using dual-photon absorptiometry of the spine (DPAspine) and single-photon absorptiometry of the distal and proximal forearm (SPAdist and SPAprox, repectively). Light gray bars = crude distances between groups; dark gray bars ("NS") = differences after adjustment.

When adjustments are made in the analyses of differences between the two estrone groups in the BMI, the results look materially different compared to the crude unadjusted analysis (see **Figure 3–4**).

After an adjustment for BMI, none of the initial differences in bone density between low- and high-estrone women remains. However, the question arises about whether this adjustment is appropriate. Rather, you could argue that differences in circulating estrone levels between women largely reflect differences in body fat, which is the prime site for estrogen production through conversion of androgens in postmenopausal women. While BMI is correlated to both the determinant and the outcome, it does not qualify as an extraneous determinant because it is not extraneous to the occurrence relation of interest. In contrast, the likely mechanism for increased bone density in post-menopause is:

Obesity → higher estrogen production → higher bone density

Obesity precedes higher estrogen production and thus is in the causal chain relating estrogen to bone density. The example illustrates the notion that classification of a factor related to both outcome and determinant as a confounder assumes this factor to be extraneous. Rather than being extraneous, a certain factor may lead to a changed physiology that in turn affects the determinant under study and subsequently the outcome (see **Figure 3–5**).

An important message from this and the alcohol → HDL cholesterol → heart disease example is that judgment of the potential for confounding requires knowledge of possible etiologic mechanisms involved. This may well create a "catch 22" situation in which an absence of etiologic insight creates confounding that in turn invalidates subsequent observations. Frequently

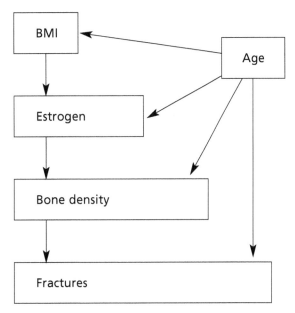

FIGURE 3–5   Determining confounders. Suppose that the objective of your study is to determine the causal role of variation in circulating estrogen levels in the occurrence of bone fractures. You gather a cohort of women and establish a baseline BMI, estrogen levels, and bone density for each. They are followed up for 10 years, as you record the occurence of fractures (outcome) as a function of circulating estrogen levels (determinant), conditional on confounders. Because of the etiologic nature of your research, confounding factors need to be excluded. Age is related with risk of fractures as well as with estrogen levels (and is not in the causal chain) and thus is a confounder. While BMI and bone density both are related to the outcome, they are in the causal chain (fat tissue is a source of estrogen production and bone density is increased by higher circulating estrogen levels). BMI is a precursor and bone density is an intermediate of the association. Consequently, they are not confounding the relationship and their effects should not be removed from the association by adjustments.

in etiologic epidemiologic research, initial observations subsequently must be corrected because of expanding knowledge and adjustment for newly recognized confounders [Taubes, 1995]. While assessment of correlations in the data may be useful to detect possibilities for confounding, statistical software is not sufficiently sophisticated to determine the actual confounder. It remains the responsibility of the investigator to exclude confounding in the design of data collection and the design of data analysis of a study. To decide upon the presence of confounding with confidence, insight into mechanisms involved is required. If a particular determinant is not the putative causal determinant of interest but is a precursor or intermediary in a causal chain, there is no confounding and making an adjustment in the analysis will lead to over-adjustment. This generally results in an underestimation of the true association between the determinant and the outcome.

Handling of Confounding

Once confounding is suspected, there are several approaches to removing it from the observed association. As previously indicated, confounding may occur when a variable is associated with both the determinant of interest and the outcome and it is not part of the causal chain. *Being associated with* implies that the confounder is related to the outcome and that the distribution of the confounder varies across levels of the determinant. To remove confounding requires that the distribution of the confounder is made the same across levels of the determinant. When distributions of the confounder are made the same across levels of the determinant, and the determinant–outcome relationship persists, we conclude that the relationship is conditional on the confounder. Removal of confounding may be achieved in the design of data collection, in the design of data analysis, or the combination of both. For example, suppose that in a particular study age is thought to be a confounder of the relationship between sex and stroke risk, implying that age distributions for men and women are different (and age is associated with stroke risk). In order to remove the confounding effect of age, age distributions need to be made similar for men and women. This can be done in a number of ways. First, confounding may be removed in the design of data collection by means of *restriction*. If only men and women within a small age range are included in the study, the distribution of age across gender is the same and age will not be a confounder. Similarly, men and women may be *matched* for age. Matching can be done on an individual basis (individual matching), where each individual with the determinant (male in this example) is closely matched with someone without the determinant (female in this example) according to the confounder (age in this example). Alternatively, the age distributions among those with and without the determinant are made using approximately the same methods, such as stratified sampling; this is called *frequency matching*. In this example, matching ensures that, although the distributions of age may be wide, they are the same (mean, median, standard deviation) for men and women. One can also remove confounding in the design of data analysis. One approach is to perform a *stratified* analysis. The association between gender and stroke risk is then analyzed in separate age strata, each of which cover a small age range. Within age strata, males and females are similar regarding age, and age will not be a confounder. Next, the estimates for the strata are pooled using some statistical method that weights the information by stratum, such as the Mantel-Haenszel procedure. Essentially the same can be achieved in a *multivariable regression analysis* where age is added to the multivariable model next to the determinant (male/female) and possibly other confounders.

More recently, certain new approaches such as the use of propensity scores and instrumental variables (both can be applied in the design of data analysis and in the design of data collection) have been introduced into clinical epidemiology to remove confounding. These methods have primarily been used in assessing causal treatment effects in observational studies (for a review of classic and new methods to remove confounding see Klungel, 2004). In the assessment of treatment effects without the use of randomization, confounding by indication is a major problem, but the principles of adjustment apply similarly to causal research where the determinant (exposure) is not a drug given for a particular indication, but, for example, is related to lifestyle characteristics such as level of physical activity.

As a summary variable for several confounders, *propensity scores* may be used for statistical adjustment (in the design of data analysis), matching, or restriction (in the design of data collection). Propensity may be defined as an individual's probability of being exposed to the determinant of interest, for example, receiving a specific treatment, given the complete set of all information about that individual. The propensity score provides a single variable that summarizes all the information from potential confounding variables such as disease severity and comorbidity; it estimates the probability of a subject being exposed to the intervention of interest given his or her clinical and nonclinical status. In case of a binary treatment, the propensity score may be estimated for each subject from a logistic regression model in which treatment assignment is the dependent variable. The prognosis in the absence of treatment is assumed to be the same (balanced) across groups of subjects with the same propensity score. When treated and untreated subjects are then matched according to propensity score or the analysis is restricted to those within a limited range of the propensity score, treated and untreated subjects will have on average the same prognosis in the absence of treatment. Alternatively, the propensity score can be included as a covariate in a multivariable regression model relating the treatment to the outcome. An example is a study showing that treatment with beta-blockers may reduce the risk of exacerbations and improve survival in patients with chronic obstructive pulmonary disease [Rutten et al., 2010]. Physicians typically avoid using beta-blockers in patients with chronic obstructive pulmonary disease and concurrent cardiovascular disease because of concerns about adverse pulmonary effects. Therefore, in this observational study, those with chronic obstructive pulmonary disease treated with beta-blockers very likely have a different cardiovascular prognosis then those not treated with them. Adjustments for confounding were made using conventional logistic regression and propensity score analyses. Both methods showed a reduced mortality risk for beta-blocker use, with the propensity score analyses showing larger reductions, suggesting that propensity score analysis more thoroughly deals with confounding in this example. Note, however, that confounding may remain even after propensity score adjustment, if relevant subject characteristics were not measured or were only measured imprecisely [Nicholas, 2008].

The use of *instrumental variables*, originating from econometrics where randomized comparisons are largely impossible, has been suggested for use in epidemiologic analyses with the same objective as propensity scores but with the potential to also adjust for unmeasured confounders [Martens et al., 2006]. The key assumptions for an instrumental variable (IV) are that (1) the IV is strongly associated with the exposure (often treatment assignment), (2) the IV is unrelated to confounders of the occurrence relation, and (3) the IV is independent of the outcome through factors other than the exposure. These three assumptions are shown in **Figure 3–6**.

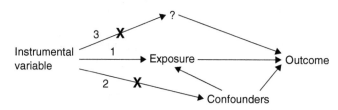

FIGURE 3–6 Assumptions of an instrumental variable applied to remove confounding in a study assessing the causal relationship between an exposure and an outcome. The numbers 1–3 refer to the three assumptions that are explained in the text.

Thus, instrumental variables have no effect on the outcome, other than through their relationship with the exposure. In the setting of drug treatment, instrumental variables may, for example, be regional differences in prescribing patterns, physician preference, patient financial situation, distance to a hospital or facility, or calendar time. Whether all three assumptions hold, however, is difficult to prove and finding an instrumental variable can therefore be a true challenge, if not often impossible [Groenwold et al., 2010]. There are several methods to estimate the strength of the causal association once an IV is used [Martens et al., 2006]. IV estimation is typically done in two regression steps. In a first analysis, exposure status is estimated from the instrumental variable with or without the inclusion of other variables related to prognosis (i.e., potential confounders). Next, the predicted exposure states replace the actual treatment in a regression of the outcome on treatment, usually with confounders as covariates.

While most commonly used in observational research on drug side effects, propensity scores and instrumental variables can also effectively be applied in etiologic research with nondrug exposures. In a particular format of an instrumental variable is a gene determining the level of a putative causal factor, such as the elevation of a circulating risk factor. As genes are randomly distributed in large populations, the gene can be used as an instrumental variable, because it is related to the exposure of interest (the risk factor level), independent of other risk factors for the outcome (because the gene is randomly distributed), and related to the outcome only through the risk factor. Because this approach mimics randomized allocation in an observational setting, it is called *Mendelian randomization* [Smith et al., 2008]. An example is a case-control study on the role of low-density lipoprotein (LDL) and HDL cholesterol levels on myocardial infarction involving a large pooled dataset comprising 12,482 cases of myocardial infarction and 41,331 controls [Voight et al., 2012]. As instrumental variable with a genetic score consisting of 14 common single nucleotide polymorphisms (SNPs) could be used, because this genetic score exclusively associates with HDL cholesterol, is unrelated to confounders of the occurrence relation, and is not associated with cardiovascular disease through any other mechanism. The same was done for a genetic score exclusively predicting LDL cholesterol levels. Previous research in long-term follow-up studies has shown that an increase of one standard deviation in HDL cholesterol is associated with an approximately 40% reduced risk of myocardial infarction. However, a one standard deviation increase in HDL cholesterol due to the genetic score was not associated with the risk of myocardial infarction (OR 0.93, 95% CI 0.68–1.26). For LDL cholesterol, the estimate from previous research (a one standard deviation increase in LDL cholesterol is associated with an approximately 50–60% increased risk) was concordant with that from the genetic score (OR 2.13, 95% CI 1.69–2.69). Consequently, genetic mechanisms that raise plasma HDL cholesterol do not lower risk of myocardial infarction, further fueling the doubts about the causal role of HDL levels in determining the risk of cardiac events. These data seriously challenge the concept that raising plasma HDL cholesterol will uniformly translate into reductions in risk of myocardial infarction.

CAUSALITY

Etiologic research aims to find causal associations. A determinant is believed to be causally related to an outcome if the association remains when confounding is excluded. Other requirements are necessary, however, in order to conclude that the association is indeed causal and to exclude both residual confounding by some unidentified factors and the mere play of chance.

Many criteria have been proposed to make a causal association more probable. These include a large number of independent studies with consistent results, a temporal relationship where the cause precedes the outcome, a strong association, a dose–response relationship, and biologic plausibility. These criteria stem from the work of Hill [1965] and others, but each of the criteria has been challenged and none provides definitive proof. Even a temporal relationship in which the determinant follows the outcome does not rule out the possibility that in other circumstances the determinant could lead to the outcome.

Probably the most limiting factor in disclosing causal relationships in epidemiologic studies is the general focus on single determinant outcome relationships. Very few diseases are caused by a single factor. For example, many people are exposed to methicillin-resistant *Staphylococcus aureus*. Some bacteria will be colonized and still fewer people will suffer from serious infection. It is likely that the genotype modifies the risk of colonization after exposure. The interplay between different factors, possibly through different mechanisms, is the rule rather than the exception in the etiology of the disease. Yet other factors, such as the quality of the immune response, will modify the risk of serious infection. The genetic disorder phenylketonuria (PKU) convincingly shows that the interaction of genes and environment cause a disease commonly thought to be purely genetic. Dietary exposure to a particular amino acid gives rise to mental retardation in children with mutations in the phenylalanine hydroxylase gene on chromosome 12q23.2 encoding the L-phenylalanine hydroxylase enzyme, resulting in PKU. Because exposure to both factors is necessary for PKU to occur, infants with the genetic defect are put on a lifelong restricted diet to prevent the development of the disease. Rothman and Greenland [2005] have made important contributions to our understanding of multicausality in epidemiologic research. (A full discussion goes beyond the scope of this text, however.) The central principle is that a disease can be caused by more than one causal mechanism, and every causal mechanism involves the joint action of a multitude of component causes (see **Figure 3–7**). As a consequence, particular causal determinants of disease may be neither necessary nor sufficient to produce disease. Nevertheless, a cause need not be necessary or sufficient for its removal to be useful in prevention. For example, alcohol use when driving is neither necessary nor sufficient to lead to car accidents, yet prevention of drunk driving will decrease a fair number of casualties. That the cause is not necessary implies that some disease may still occur after the cause is blocked, but a component cause will nevertheless be a necessary cause for some of the cases that occur. When the strength of a causal effect of a certain determinant depends on or is modified by the presence or absence of another factor, there is causal, or biologic, interaction or modification. Although modification of a causal association may be very relevant, it may best be viewed as secondary to the main determinant–outcome relationship. It adds detail to it, albeit sometimes extremely important detail.

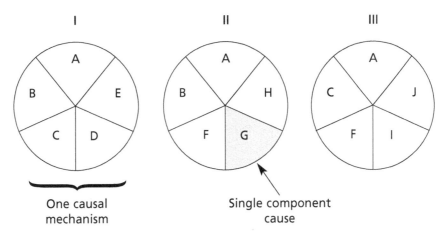

FIGURE 3–7   Three sufficient causes of disease.

Reproduced from Rothman KJ, Greenland S. Causation and causal inference in epidemiolgy. *Am J Public Health* 2005;95 Suppl 1:S144–150.

MODIFICATION AND INTERACTION

There is a fair degree of confusion about the terms *modification, effect modification*, and *interaction*; their roles in epidemiologic research; and the importance of interaction between two or more determinants in research of disease mechanisms.

We consider modification to be present when the measure of association between a given determinant and outcome is not constant across categories of another characteristic [Miettinen, 1985]. This modifier changes the strength of the determinant–outcome relationship. In the literature, such a modifier is often referred to as an *effect modifier* because it changes the effect a determinant has on a certain outcome. We prefer the term *modifier*, because it implies a causal mechanism underlying the modification. In fact, modification is often studied without the aim of explaining the mechanism underlying the modification. We propose the term *descriptive modification* in those instances and the term *causal modification* when the objective is indeed to explain the observed modification of the determinant–outcome association (see discussion that follows).

In statistics, the term *interaction* is merely used to indicate departure from the form of the chosen statistical model. For example, if a multiplicative model explains the data better than a linear model, this is interpreted as the presence of interaction without further causal or other explanation or inference. In epidemiology, the terms *interaction* and *modification* are used rather loosely and interchangeably.

Descriptive Modification

We propose restricting the term *descriptive modification* to the analysis of the extent to which the strength of a causal or noncausal determinant–outcome association varies across another factor without the need to explain the nature of that modification. The extent to which the effectiveness of vaccination varies across age groups serves as an example [Hak et al., 2005]. The only intention here is to determine whether it should be recommended to target the intervention at particular age groups from the perspective of cost-effectiveness. There is no need to understand the modification in causal terms. The causal association addressed here concentrates on the effect of the intervention (i.e., influenza vaccination) on the outcome (e.g., survival) only. Modification is examined to learn about differential effects of vaccination across relevant population subgroups such as those defined by age. The assessment of modification by age adds detail to the research on the causal association between vaccination and the outcome parameter with a view toward practical application of the result.

Descriptive modification may easily occur due to differences in the prevalence of the disease across populations or population subgroups. For example, the effectiveness of screening for HIV will be modified by the proportions of hetero- and homosexual individuals in the populations because this will reflect different prevalence rates of the disease. In other words, while the fraction of cases detected will be the same (90%), the absolute number of HIV-infected subjects detected will be modified by the prevalence of homosexual subjects in the population studies. The latter example illustrates that modification may occur both on a relative scale (as in modification by age of the effect of influenza vaccination on survival) and on an absolute scale (the absolute number of newly detected HIV-infected individuals), further adding to the complexity of the issue.

Descriptive modification can be equally addressed in causal and descriptive studies. An example in descriptive studies is when the question is asked about whether signs and symptoms of heart failure have a different diagnostic value in patients who suffer from chronic lung disease than in patients without this concomitant disease [Rutten et al., 2005a; Rutten & Hoes, 2012].

Causal Modification

The interest in causal modification of a determinant–disease association is of an entirely different nature. Garcia-Closas and colleagues' 2005 study on the extent to which the presence of a particular genotype increases the risk of bladder cancer resulting from cigarette smoking is an example. Here, two causal questions were addressed. Primarily, the causal association between cigarette smoking and bladder cancer occurrence was assessed, but the authors also examined the possible increased sensitivity to cigarette smoke in the presence of the genotype. Garcia-Closas and coworkers [2005] found that persons who were current smokers or had smoked cigarettes in the past had a higher risk of developing bladder cancer. However, the relative risk related to smoking was 2.9-fold increased in those who had the NAT2 slow acetylator genotype and 5.1-fold increased among those with the intermediate or rapid acetylator genotype. In researching the benefits and risks of treatment, causal as well as descriptive modifications are often, albeit sometimes implicitly, addressed when subgroups show a higher or lower response to the intervention.

When to Address Modification

Whether modification is examined for a particular occurrence relation depends on the interest and objectives of the investigator. When the appropriate determinant, outcome, and all confounders are considered, the result is valid plus and minus a chance variation, whether or not modifiers are studied. As mentioned, modifiers add detail that can be either causal or descriptive. For any given determinant–outcome relationship, there is an infinite number of potential modifiers. If modification is to be studied, modifiers need to be selected, preferably a priori, based on clinical relevance and, in the case of causal modification, plausibility. If many potential modifiers are examined without clear a priori views on their relevance or plausibility, there are likely to be several false-positive instances of modification. Frequently, investigators are disappointed in their initial negative (overall) findings and start looking for modifiers. Effectively, they are looking for subgroups of the population characterized by the presence of a modifier in which the determinant–outcome association may still be found. This typically means a search for descriptive modification in the absence of a real view on causal modification. In such cases, any interpretation is risky, but a causal interpretation is particularly elusive. For example, surprisingly, an association is present in women but not in men. What does that mean? If no clear explanation can be given and no previous data have suggested similar gender-specific effects, the result should be considered with great caution, especially when explained in causal terms. Even when the aim is to search for clinically relevant subgroups where the association between the determinant and outcome may be stronger without any causal inference of such modification (refer to the influenza example introduced earlier), a priori determination of a limited number of clinically relevant modifiers is crucial to preclude false-positive identification of modifiers.

A bizarre example of modification detected by unplanned extensive analyses of the data has been reported for the second International Study of Infarct Survival (ISIS) trial (see **Box 3–2**). The ISIS trial examined the benefits and risks of intravenous streptokinase, oral aspirin, both, or neither among 17,187 cases of suspected acute myocardial infarction [ISIS-2, 1988]. All ISIS patients had their date of birth entered as an important "identifier." While the overall benefit for aspirin was highly convincing, the subgroup of patients with the astrological star signs Gemini and Libra showed a 9% increased mortality risk for aspirin. Astrological sign actually seemed to modify the effect of aspirin! Confounding was unlikely to produce this result because the trial was large and patients were randomly allocated to the treatment groups. Given the number of subgroup analyses in this trial, the

BOX 3–2   Astrological Daily Prediction Taking the ISIS Trial Findings on Aspirin into
Account

A loan will be easy to obtain tomorrow, but you must have a list of items you
own so that you will have something to show as collateral. This loan could be to
improve the home or to purchase a car. Things are happening, and your career
or path depends on your own ambition and drive, as well as your ability to be
patient and bide your time. You are able to use good common sense to guide you,
and you can feel the trends and make the right moves. The time is coming soon to
take action and get ahead. You may contemplate a career move and next week is a
most positive one as you make yourself known. You are advised to use no aspirin.

finding is most likely the result of chance. Perhaps even more important,
the finding is theoretically highly implausible.

The presence or absence of modification—descriptive or causal—has a
bearing on the generalizability of research findings. Modifiers point to sub-
domains, which implies that generalizations of study results should be different for populations with or without the particular level of the modifier.
Conversely, when the domain is chosen for a certain occurrence relation
and results from a study performed in a subset of that domain are generalized to the full domain, the assumption is that the study population does
not differ from the domain with regard to determinant–outcome association. Frequently, this is assumed rather than studied and therefore views
between investigators may vary. For example, in the early days of statin
trials for the treatment of elevated serum cholesterol to reduce the risk of
cardiovascular disease, the results were largely obtained for men only. As
cholesterol is a risk factor for heart disease in men as well as in women, does
it follow that women will benefit from statins to the same extent as men?
Some investigators argued that there is no reason to suspect that statins do
not work in women. They implicitly assumed that gender is not a causal
modifier of the relationship between statins, cholesterol reduction, and reduction of heart disease risk. Others were hesitant because they did not
believe that the effects are similar; they demanded the formal assessment of
the modification by conducting separate trials in women. Currently, it is
well established that statins reduce the risk of heart disease in men as well
as women with elevated cholesterol levels. Similarly, it has been well established that the benefits of blood pressure reduction are not causally modified
by age. This means that across a wide range of ages, the rate of cardiovascular

TABLE 3-2   A Meta-Analysis of 24 Blood Pressure Trials Involving 68,099
Randomized Patients[1]

Age	Treated Rate/ 1,000/Year	Control Rate/ 1,000/Year	Rate Ratio	Rate Difference/ 1,000/Year
> 60	26.0	34.8	0.75	8.8
< 60	8.8	11.2	0.79	2.4

"Rate" means rate of cardiovascular disease.

[1]Unpublished results.

disease is reduced by 20–25% if hypertensive patients are treated with anti-hypertensive agents. However, there is a descriptive modification, in this case on an absolute scale. Because background rates of cardiovascular disease increase markedly with age, the rate difference (i.e., the reduction in the absolute risk, for example, a 5-year incidence of cardiovascular disease) resulting from treatment is much higher in older (above 60 years) compared to younger (below 60 years) patients (see **Table 3–2**).

Measurement of Modification

Measurement of modification is conceptually straightforward. Suppose we study the risk of gastric bleeding for those using aspirin therapy by comparing bleeding rates across users and nonusers of aspirin, with adjustments for extraneous determinants related to both aspirin use and the baseline (before use) risk of bleeding (such as age, comorbidity, and the severity of the disease for which the aspirin was prescribed). If an overall increased risk of bleeding caused by aspirin use is established, a next concern may be to determine which patients treated with high-dose aspirin are at a particularly high risk. Certain patients on the same dose of aspirin may be more likely to experience gastric bleeding than others. For example, concurrent use of corticosteroids might enhance the bleeding risk. In other words, steroid use modifies the risk of high-dose aspirin as it makes the risk even higher. In this occurrence relation, corticosteroids are causal modifiers of the risk of bleeding associated with high-dose aspirin use. The modifier changes the magnitude of the association between determinant and outcome; the effect estimate depends on the value of the modifier. In this example, suppose that the overall relative risk of bleeding for those taking high-dose aspirin compared to low-dose aspirin was 2; for those taking a corticosteroid that relative risk became 4. The modification becomes visible when the association of interest is compared across strata of the modifier.

In etiologic research, analysis of modifiers may help the investigator to understand the complexity of multicausality and causally explain why a particular disease may be more common in certain individuals despite an apparent similar exposure to a determinant. After the unconfounded measurement of an overall association between a determinant and an outcome, putative modification may be estimated by comparing the strength of the exposure–outcome association across categories of the modifier. Causal modification also can be studied experimentally. Activated factor VII (FVIIa) is a very potent coagulant and may be a key determinant in the outcome of a cardiovascular event. FVIIa increases in response to dietary fat intake. Mennen and coworkers [1999] studied whether the response of FVIIa to fat intake is modified (in this case reduced) by the genetic R353Q polymorphism. A fat-rich test breakfast and a control meal were given to 35 women carrying the Q allele and 56 women without the Q allele genotype. At 8 AM (after an overnight fast), the first blood sample was taken, and within 30 minutes the subjects ate their breakfasts. Additional blood samples were taken at 1 PM and 3 PM. The mean absolute response of FVIIa was 37.0 U/L in the group with the RR genotype and 16.1 U/L ($P < 0.001$) in those carrying the Q allele (see **Figure 3–8**).

FIGURE 3–8   Comparison of activated factor VII (FVIIa) in women carrying the Q allele and those carrying the RR genotype before and after a meal.

Reproduced from Mennen LI, de Maat MP, Zock P, Grobbee DE, Kok FJ, Kluft C, Schouten EG. Postprandial response of activated factor VII in elderly women depends on the R353Q polymorphism. *Am J Clin Nutr* 1999;70:435–8.

Good examples of causal modification can be found in genetic epidemiology. Arguably, pharmacogenetics is all about causal modification. The typical research question in pharmacogenetics is whether a certain genotype modifies the response of individuals to a particular drug. A classic example of pharmacogenetic modification is the observation that certain patients show a prolonged respiratory muscular paralysis after receiving succinylcholine (a muscle relaxant) during surgery [Kalow & Staron, 1957]. Subsequently, the genetic basis of the effect was discovered to be a mutation that resulted in impaired metabolism by serum cholinesterase in some individuals. In another example, 2,735 individuals on statin therapy—half on atorvastatin and the other half divided among fluvastatin, lovastatin, pravastatin, and simvastatin—were genotyped for 43 SNPs in 16 genes that were previously reported to modify the lipid response to statin treatment. Statistically significant associations with LDL cholesterol (LDL-C) lowering were found for apolipoprotein E2 (apoE2), in which carriers of the rare allele who took atorvastatin lowered their LDL-C by 3.5% more than those homozygous for the common allele, and for rs2032582 (S893A in ABCB1) in which the two groups of homozygotes differed by 3% in LDL-C lowering [Thompson et al., 2005]. Now that increasingly large numbers of mutations can be measured relatively easily, with often little a priori biologic basis for plausibility, pharmacogenetics also offers ample demonstration of the problem of false-positives [Marsh et al., 2002]. The approach to detect modification is to take the modifier into account in the analyses. Typically, modification is addressed by separate analyses among those with and without the modifier. Alternative, so-called interaction terms may be included in regression models in the analyses.

Modification may act differently depending on the measure of risk, for example, whether relative or absolute measures of the risk association are used. Consider the following example: A disease risk per 100,000 is 1 for those who are unexposed to two risk factors A and B (R_{A-B-}); it is 2 for those exposed to risk factor A but not to B (R_{A+B-}), and it is 5 per 100,000 for those unexposed to A but who are exposed to B (R_{A-B+}). You now may ask what the disease risk would be for those who are exposed to both risk factors (R_{A+B+}) and whether the risk factors do not interact and, thus, are independent. Because an absence of interaction (or independence) implies that the disease risks are additive, the absolute risk for the jointly exposed (R_{A+B+}) would, in the case of independence, be: $(2 - 1) + (5 - 1) + 1 = 6$ per 100,000 $(R_{A+B} - R_{A-B-}) + (R_{A-B+} - R_{A-B-}) + (R_{A-B-}) = R_{A+B-} + R_{A-B+} - R_{A-B-}$. Therefore, if the absolute risk for the jointly exposed was, for example, 10, you would conclude that the two risk factors are not independent, or in other words, that modification is present. The modification, or interaction, is visible on an additive scale because: $(2 - 1) + (5 - 1) + 1 = 6 \neq 10$. However, there is no interaction on a multiplicative scale because: $2/1 \times 5/1 = 10$ per 100,000 $(R_{A+B-} / R_{A-B-}) \times (R_{A-B+} / R_{A-B-}) = (R_{A+B+} - R_{A-B-})$; thus, it is the same as the product of the two absolute risks of disease of the individual risk factors [Ahlbom & Alfredsson, 2005].

In etiologic research, investigators often explore effect modification studies on more than one statistical scale, an approach that is likely to increase the rate of false-positive findings. For example, effect modification is examined by using both a multiplicative interaction term in a logistic regression model and a measure of interaction on the additive scale such as the interaction coefficient from an additive relative risk regression model. Starr and McKnight [2004] performed computer simulations to investigate the risk of false-positives when statistical interactions are evaluated by using both type of models. The overall false-positive rate was often greater than 5% when both tests were performed simultaneously. These results provide empiric evidence of the limited validity of a common approach to assess modification.

When the modifiers to be examined as well as the scale on which modification is to be explored have not been specified before the data analysis, the presence of effect modification should be interpreted particularly cautiously. The choice of the scale depends on the aim at which modification is addressed and preferably an a priori view of the nature of the modification, additive or multiplicative, and causal or descriptive. In view of the popularity of logistic regression modeling in etiologic epidemiologic research it is quite common to see modification addressed in a multiplicative manner. For example, Hung and coworkers [2006] studied whether polymorphisms in cell cycle control genes are associated with the risk of lung cancer and if they can alter the effect of ionizing radiation (through x-ray) on lung cancer risk. Cell cycle control is important in the repair of DNA damage. It can trigger cell arrest to allow for DNA lesions (e.g., caused by ionizing radiation) to be repaired before the cell continues its normal processes. TP53 plays a key role in cell cycle control. The effect of this polymorphism on lung cancer risk was examined in a multicenter case-control study including 2,238 incident lung cancer cases and 2,289 controls. The data were analyzed using logistic regression models that included a multiplicative interaction term. Persons with the TP53 intron 3 A2A2 genotype (and a low number of x-ray exposures) had a slightly increased risk of lung cancer compared to those with one or two copies of the A1 genotype (OR = 1.28; 95% CI, 0.67–2.45). Those with a high number of x-ray examinations (> 20, and one or two copies of the A1 genotype) had a 1.3 times higher risk than those with a lower number of x-ray examinations (OR = 1.29; 95% CI, 1.07–1.56). The A2A2 genotype in combination with a high number of x-ray examinations raised lung cancer risk significantly (OR = 9.47; 95% CI, 2.59–34.6). This odds ratio is significantly higher than the product of the two risk factors of the individual risk factors. The OR for interaction was 9.47 ÷ (1.28 × 1.29) = 5.67 (95% CI, 1.33–24.3). The results of this study suggest that sequence variants in TP53 increase the risk of lung cancer and modify the risk conferred by multiple x-ray exposures.

Rothman [2002] has argued that causal modification should be linked to the original scale on which risks are measured. Multiplicative models typically involve logarithmic transformations. Therefore, in his view, causal modification should be examined by studying the presence or absence of additivity of risks. This approach was followed by Patino and coworkers [2005], who examined the extent to which the presence of family dysfunction modifies the risk of psychosis associated with migration (see **Table 3–3**). To quantify the interaction between family dysfunction and migration, relative risks were calculated for exposure to both migration history and family dysfunction, to family dysfunction only, and to migration only, with exposure to neither migration nor family dysfunction as the reference category. The effect when both variables were present

TABLE 3–3   Migration, Familiar Dysfunction, and Risk of Psychosis

	Odds Ratio for Psychotic Symptoms	
	Crude (95% CI)	*Adjusted[1] (95% CI)*
Migration history[2]	1.8 (1.1–3.2)	2.4 (1.3–4.3)
Migration history and no family dysfunction[3]	1.2 (0.5–3.2)	1.5 (0.6–3.9)
Family dysfunction and no migration history[3]	1.5 (0.9–2.5)	1.3 (0.7–2.1)
Migration history and family dysfunction[3]	4.0 (2.0–8.2)	4.1 (1.9–8.5)
AP interaction[4]	0.59 (0.02–0.93)	0.58 (0.05–0.91)

CI, confidence interval.

[1]Adjusted for age, gender, psychiatric illness of a parent, and education level of breadwinner.
[2]Reference category is no migration history.
[3]Reference category is no migration history and no family dysfunction.
[4]Attributable proportion (AP) of cases owing to the interaction of migration history and family dysfunction.

Reproduced from Patino LR, Selten JP, Van Engeland H, Duyx JH, Kahn RS, Burger H. Migration, family dysfunction and psychotic symptoms in children and adolescents. *Br J Psychiatry* 2005;186:442–3.

was larger than the sum of their independent effects, indicating, in this case, causal interaction.

As long as it is well understood that the choice of the scale on which modification is measured and the selection of the statistical model have an impact on the detection and magnitude of modification, and as long as it is clear why the modification is addressed, there is room for additive as well as multiplicative models.

MODIFIERS AND CONFOUNDERS

Modification is an altogether different issue than confounding in etiologic research. Confounders are inherently and exclusively linked to determinant–outcome relationships and need to be adequately and completely removed during the design and analysis of an etiologic study to ensure validity of the findings. In the same study, however, for a given occurrence relation, confounders may also be modifiers. This holds true for both causal and descriptive modifiers. For example, in a nonexperimental study on the risk of hemorrhagic stroke in patients receiving warfarin [Fang et al., 2006], age is a confounder when patients using warfarin are generally older and therefore already at a higher risk of stroke (the outcome). At the same time, however, in older patients, the risk of hemorrhagic stroke associated with warfarin (the relative risk, the risk difference, or both) is higher than in younger patients. Thus, age in this study is both a confounder and a modifier. To fully address confounding and modification of a third variable, the analysis should assess the effect of the determinant both with adjustment for the third variable and across the strata of that variable.

An example of a variable that is a modifier but not a confounder is given in **Box 3–3**. This study addressed the causal role of diet in the occurrence of colon cancer and the modifying potential of lifestyle (in this example physical activity). The association between diet and colon cancer appeared not to be confounded by physical activity. The causal impact of a so-called "high-risk dietary pattern," however, was dependent on the level of physical activity. Physical activity level, therefore, acted as a causal modifier established on a multiplicative scale.

When causal modification is studied, it should be appreciated that the same principles of etiologic research apply as in typical etiologic studies where a determinant is causally related to an outcome. In other words, alternative explanations that could confound the apparent modification by a particular characteristic should be considered.

BOX 3–3   Physical Activity and Colon Cancer: Confounding or Interaction?

SLATTERY ML, POTTER JD

PURPOSE: Although physical activity has been consistently inversely associated with colon cancer incidence, the association of physical activity with other diet and lifestyle factors that may influence this association is less well understood. Confounding and effect modification are examined to better understand the physical activity and colon cancer association.

METHODS: Based on hypothesized biological mechanisms whereby physical activity may alter risk of colon cancer, we evaluated confounding and effect modification using data collected as part of a case-control study of colon cancer (N = 1993 cases and 2410 controls). We examined associations between total energy intake, fiber, calcium, fruit and vegetables, red meat, whole grains as well as dietary patterns along with cigarette smoking, alcohol consumption, BMI, and use of aspirin and/or NSAIDs and physical activity.

RESULTS: No confounding was observed for the physical activity and colon cancer association. However, differences in effects of diet and lifestyle factors were identified depending on level of physical activity. Most striking were statistically significant interactions between physical activity and high-risk dietary pattern and vegetable intake, in that the relative importance of diet was dependent on level of physical activity. The predictive model of colon cancer risk was improved by using an interaction term for physical activity and other variables, including BMI, cigarette smoking, energy intake, dietary fiber, dietary calcium, glycemic index, lutein, folate, vegetable intake, and high-risk diet rather than using models that included these variables as independent predictors with physical activity. In populations where activity levels are high, the estimate of risk associated with high vegetable intake was 0.9 (95% CI 0.6–1.3), whereas in more sedentary populations the estimate of risk associated with high vegetable intake was 0.6 (95% CI 0.5–0.9).

CONCLUSIONS: Physical activity plays an important role in the etiology of colon cancer. Its significance is seen by its consistent association as an independent predictor of colon cancer as well as by its impact on the odds ratios associated with other factors. Given these observations, it is most probable that physical activity operates through multiple biological mechanisms that influence the carcinogenic process.

Reproduced from Slattery ML, Potter JD. Physical activity and colon cancer: Confounding or interaction? *Med Sci Sports Exerc.* 2002 Jun;34(6):913–9.

DESIGN OF DATA COLLECTION

Time

Typically, etiologic studies are longitudinal because the goal is to relate a potentially causal determinant to the future occurrence, for example, the incidence of a disease. This temporal relationship should be incorporated in the design of data collection to ensure that the determinant indeed precedes the development of disease, for example, by means of a cohort study. Consequently, a cross-sectional design, where determinant and outcome are measured at the same point in time, is generally not the preferred approach in etiologic research. Several examples illustrate this point. In studies on dietary habits as a possible cause for cancer, a cross-sectional study design may reveal a positive association between low fat intake and cancer, while in fact the preclinical cancer itself may have caused a change in dietary habits. Such a "which comes first, the chicken or the egg" phenomenon constitutes less of a problem when the etiologic factor cannot change over time (e.g., gender or a genetic trait).

Census or Sampling

The classic approach to collecting data in etiologic epidemiologic research is a *cohort study*, where a group of subjects exposed to the causal factor under study and a group of unexposed subjects are followed over time to compare the incidence of the outcome of interest. Such a study takes a census approach in that in all study participants the determinant, outcome, and potential confounders (and, if the aim is to study modification, modifiers) are measured. Alternatively, and often more efficiently, information on the determinant and confounders (and possibly modifiers) can be collected in patients with the outcome of interest (the cases) and a *sample* (controls) from the population in which these cases arise. The latter approach is called a *case-control study*.

Experimental or Observationally

Etiologic research can be conducted experimentally or observationally (i.e. nonexperimentally). Experimental means that an investigator manipulates the determinant with the goal of learning about its causal effects. Case-control studies are nonexperimental by definition, but cohort studies can either be experimental or nonexperimental. The best known type of experimental cohort study is a randomized trial. Randomized trials are particularly suited to study effects of interventions.

The study in Box 3–1, which addressed the cardiac risks associated with a high haem iron intake, was a cohort study where determinant, confounder, and outcome data were collected on all members of the cohort. From our discussion, it is obvious that in an etiologic study data need not only be collected for the determinant and outcome under study, but also for potential confounders and, in case modification is of interest, the effect modifiers.

There are several ways of collecting this information. Participants can be interviewed, face to face or by telephone; they can answer questionnaires at home or under supervision; they can keep diaries; and physical measurements can take place. The chosen method depends on the reliability of the different ways of collecting the data, the feasibility, and affordability. Determinant, confounder, and modifier data are usually collected at the start of the study, that is, at baseline. It also is possible for information to be collected from the past. In the cohort study in Box 3–1, dietary information was collected for the year prior to enrollment. Another example is when information about reproductive characteristics of women is needed from postmenopausal women. Milestones in their reproductive history such as menarche, menstrual cycles, childbirth, and lactation all happened in the past.

Measurement error is one of the most important problems in the data collection of epidemiologic studies and can lead to considerable bias. Measurement error occurs when the measurement is not valid or when the measurement is not sufficiently precise. Invalid measurements occur when the method used does not measure what the investigator intends to measure. An example is an uncalibrated blood pressure device that systematically measures the blood pressures 10 mm Hg too high. Such an error will impair inference for absolute blood pressure levels. If the measurement is sufficiently precise (i.e., there is little random variation), however, there is no problem with ranking each study participant correctly in the population distribution. In the example in Box 3–1, when the haem iron content is unknown for many foods, this will lead to underestimation of the haem iron intake of essentially all individuals and hence to misclassification of persons with a truly higher intake in categories of lower intake. When this occurs to the same extent for persons who develop coronary heart disease as for persons who do not (this is called *nondifferential misclassification*), it will lead to an underestimation of the association. Suppose that particular foods are missed exclusively for those who subsequently experience heart disease. In this situation the underestimation of intake becomes related to the outcome of interest (this is called *differential misclassification*) and the observed association will become severely biased.

Measurement is as important for the determinant as for the confounders. When there is measurement error for the confounders, the effect of the extraneous determinant cannot be fully adjusted for and this leads to what is called *residual confounding*. Residual confounding leads to biased estimation of the determinant–outcome relationship.

Design of Data Analysis: Measures of Association

In cohort studies, participants are followed over time. In the example in Box 3–1, we collected information on haem iron intake at baseline and then followed our participants for a mean of 4.2 years. During that time, we collected information on the occurrence of coronary heart disease. In the analysis of this type of data, typically the incidence of the outcome is compared between participants with and without the determinant, and usually a relative risk (or incidence rate ratio) is given as the measure of effect. In our example, we defined four categories of haem iron intake, based on the quartiles of the haem iron distribution in the entire population. Women with a daily haem iron intake of less than 1.28 mg were categorized in the lowest quartile, while women whose daily intake was greater than 2.27 mg were placed in the highest quartile (see **Table 3–4**). Next, we calculated incidences of coronary heart disease for each quartile. When follow-up of the cohort is 100% complete, cumulative incidences can be calculated. Often this is not the case, so incidence densities are calculated, where all individuals contribute observation time (person-years) for as long as they participated in the study. People withdraw from a study for many reasons, and investigators generally do not wait until all participants reach the prespecified endpoint. Under these circumstances, it is more meaningful to calculate incidence densities and conduct a time-to-event analysis. The Cox proportional hazards analysis is the most widely used technique for time-to-event data. This method allows for censoring of survival time for those

TABLE 3–4   Incidence Densities of Coronary Heart Disease for Haem Iron Intake Quartiles

	Range (mg/day)	*Cases/Person-Years*
Haem iron intake[c]		
Quartile 1	< 1.28	54/17,413
Quartile 2	1.28–1.76	53/17,384
Quartile 3	1.76–2.27	57/17,334
Quartile 4	> 2.27	88/17,469

Reproduced from Van der A DL, Peeters PHM, Grobbee DE, Marx JJM, van der Schouw YT. Dietary haem iron and coronary heart disease in women. European Heart Journal 2005;26:257-262.

persons who do not reach the endpoint during the study, for example, because they are lost to follow-up after they move to another area or because they do not develop the outcome before the study ends. The uncensored "survival" times are usually referred to as event times; these result from persons who experience the prespecified endpoint. The Cox proportional hazards analysis estimates the effect of a determinant on the baseline hazard distribution, that is, the survival distribution of completely average persons for whom each variable (determinant and confounders) is equal to the average value of that variable for the entire set of subjects in the study. This baseline survival curve does not need to have a particular form. It can have any shape as long as it starts at 1.0 (or 100%) at time 0 and descends steadily with time. The model estimates hazard ratios, which can be interpreted as risk ratios.

To summarize the risk involved with increasing amounts of haem iron intake, we calculated the hazard ratios, which is the risk of higher intakes compared to a reference level of intake (see **Table 3–5**). Usually persons with no exposure, or with the lowest or highest category of exposure, are considered to be the reference group. The choice of the reference group depends on the study question. In our example, we considered those with the lowest intake of haem iron to be hypothetically the best, and therefore we took the lowest quartile as the reference category. Sometimes, when, for example, numbers in the extreme category are very low, other strata are

TABLE 3–5 Hazard Ratios of Coronary Heart Disease for Increasing Haem Iron Intake

Crude Model		Basic Model[a]		Multivariate Model[b]	
Heart Rate	95% CI	Heart Rate	95% CI	Heart Rate	95% CI
1.00	—	1.00	—	1.00	—
0.98	0.67–1.44	1.01	0.68–1.51	1.06	0.71–1.59
1.06	0.73–1.54	1.05	0.71–1.56	1.12	0.74–1.71
1.62	1.16–2.28	1.52	1.06–2.19	1.65	1.07–2.53

[a]Adjusted for age at intake (continuous), BMI (continuous), smoking (current/past/never), physical activity (continuous), hypertension (yes/no), diabetes (yes/no), hypercholesterolemia (yes/no).

[b]Adjusted for age at intake (continuous), total energy intake (continuous), BMI (continuous), smoking (current/past/never), physical activity (continuous), hypertension (yes/no), diabetes (yes/no), hypercholesterolemia (yes/no), energy-adjusted saturated fat intake (continuous), energy-adjusted carbohydrate intake (continuous), energy-adjusted fiber intake (continuous), energy-adjusted alcohol intake (quintiles), energy-adjusted β-carotene intake (continuous), energy-adjusted vitamin E intake (continuous), energy-adjusted vitamin C intake (continuous).

Reproduced from Van der A DL, Peeters PHM, Grobbee DE, Marx JJM, van der Schouw YT. Dietary haem iron and coronary heart disease in women. European Heart Journal 2005;26:257-262.

taken as a reference category. This does not change the inference, but it does affect the relative risk estimates across the strata and should therefore clearly be indicated. Table 3–5 shows the estimates of relative risk, displayed with various degrees of confounder adjustment.

Our study showed that women with the highest haem iron intake had a 1.65 times higher risk of coronary heart disease than women with the lowest intake. This effect is statistically significant, as the 95% confidence interval for the hazard ratio (1.07–2.53) does not include 1. While the hazard ratio or the relative risk represents the likelihood of disease in individuals with the determinant relative to those without, there is also a measure providing information on the absolute effect of the determinant, or the excess risk of disease in those compared to those without the determinant. This is the risk difference (or the attributable risk) and is calculated as the difference of cumulative incidences or incidence densities. In our example, we could calculate the attributable risk as [(88/17,469) – (54/17,413)] = 1.9 per thousand women. From a practical or preventive perspective, it may be useful to estimate the proportion of the incidence of the outcome that is attributable to the determinant (in this case the highest quartile of intake): the attributable risk proportion. It is calculated as [(1.9/1,000)/(88/17,469)] × 100 = 37.7%. It also can be interesting to estimate the excess rate of the outcome in the total study population that might be attributed to the determinant. This measure is called the *population attributable risk* (PAR), and it illustrates the importance of a specific determinant in the causation of a disease or outcome. The PAR is calculated as the rate of disease in the population minus the rate of disease in the subpopulation without the determinant, or alternatively, as the attributable risk multiplied by the proportion of individuals with the determinant in the population. In our example, the PAR is 0.0019 × 0.25 = 4.8 per 10,000 women.

COMMON ETIOLOGIC QUESTIONS IN CLINICAL EPIDEMIOLOGY

Despite the overwhelming number of etiologic epidemiologic studies in the literature, the immediate relevance of etiologic information in patient care is often limited. From the perspective of the patient as well as the physician, two questions are most important: "Given the patient profile, what is the patient's illness?" and "Given the patient's illness, its etiology, the clinical and nonclinical profile, and other factors, what will be the future course of the illness or its manifestations in the presence or absence of treatment?" Often it is not necessary to know the cause of the disease to establish its diagnosis or determine its prognosis. In the case of appendicitis, for example, the cause is not of interest in determining the clinical management. Etiologic knowledge, however, can sometimes be of help in determining subsequent medical actions. For example, in a patient with abdominal complaints, it is important to know that the diagnosis is early colon cancer and subsequently act to improve prognosis by adequate treatment. Yet, etiologic information could help to prevent future occurrences and, in the case of colon cancer, may warrant screening for polyps in family members. Similarly, establishing the cause of allergic rhinitis can be useful to take preventive measures. Still, many of the most urgent questions that need answering in clinical care are those about optimal diagnostic strategies, better prediction of prognosis, and means to improve the course of the disease. There is, however, a slight subtlety in the nature of questions about means to improve prognoses. While the extent to which a certain intervention improves prognosis and is safe is essentially a prognostic question from the viewpoint of patient care, in research on the benefits and risks of treatment it is often also a causal question, and research assessing causal association of an intervention with an outcome shares many features with etiologic research. For example, when a pharmaceutical company launches a research program for a new drug used to treat chronic headache, two questions must be answered. First, "Does the drug help to relieve headache?" and, second, "Is it the drug that causes the benefit or are there alternative explanations?" Thus, in designing an intervention study many principles of etiologic research apply, including the need to fully exclude confounding. Because confounding, and in particular confounding by indication, is a serious problem in intervention research when using data collected from routine care or in nonexperimental cohort studies, definitive conclusions about the benefits of drug treatment and other interventions can often only be obtained by studying these effects in randomized trials. For unintended effects of interventions, similar types of study designs are often applied as in etiologic research (e.g., cohort and case-control studies).

WORKED-OUT EXAMPLE

The beneficial effects of moderate alcohol intake on coronary heart disease risk have been clearly established. Whether there is a similar effect of alcohol intake on risk of type 2 diabetes is not yet clear. For the study in **Box 3–4**, data on alcohol intake as well as information on the occurrence

BOX 3–4 Alcohol Consumption and Risk of Type 2 Diabetes Among Older Women

JOLINE W.J. BEULENS, MSC   DIEDERICK E. GROBBEE, MD
RONALD P. STOLK, MD   HENK F.J. HENDRIKS, PHD
YVONNE T. VAN DER SCHOUW, PHD   MICHIEL L. BOTS, MD

OBJECTIVE: This study aimed to investigate the relation between alcohol consumption and type 2 diabetes among older women.

RESEARCH DESIGN AND METHODS: Between 1993 and 1997, 16,330 women aged 49–70 years and free from diabetes were enrolled in one of the Dutch Prospect-EPIC (European Prospective Study Into Cancer and Nutrition) cohorts and followed for 6.2 years (range 0.1–10.1). At enrollment, women filled in questionnaires and blood samples were collected.

RESULTS: During follow-up, 760 cases of type 2 diabetes were documented. A linear inverse association ($P = 0.007$) between alcohol consumption and type 2 diabetes risk was observed, adjusting for potential confounders. Compared with abstainers, the hazard ratio for type 2 diabetes was 0.86 (95% CI 0.66–1.12) for women consuming 5–30 g alcohol per week, 0.66 (0.48–0.91) for 30–70 g per week, 0.91 (0.67–1.24) for 70–140 g per week, 0.64 (0.44–0.93) for 140–210 g per week, and 0.69 (0.47–1.02) for > 210 g alcohol per week. Beverage type did not influence this association. Lifetime alcohol consumption was associated with type 2 diabetes in a U-shaped fashion.

CONCLUSIONS: Our findings support the evidence of a decreased risk of type 2 diabetes with moderate alcohol consumption and expand this to a population of older women.

of type 2 diabetes were collected as part of a large cohort study initially designed to study the role of diet in cancer occurrence.

Theoretical Design

The research question was, "Does moderate alcohol consumption protect against the development of type 2 diabetes?" This translates into the following occurrence relation:

Incidence of type 2 diabetes = f (alcohol intake | extraneous determinants)

Consideration of confounding is necessary because an etiologic occurrence relation is addressed. The operational definition of the outcome was a first

clinical diagnosis of type 2 diabetes as determined using various information sources during follow-up. The measurement of determinant and confounders was operationalized by recording all relevant information on past
and current alcohol intake, other lifestyle factors, medication use in a questionnaire, and by taking anthropometric measures of the participant during
regular visits to the study center.

Design of Data Collection

Data were collected on a cohort of middle-aged and elderly women. Between 1993 and 1997, a total of 50,313 women aged 49 to 70 years who
were living in and around Utrecht, the Netherlands, were invited to participate in the study during their routine visit for a screening program for
breast cancer. In total, 17,357 women were enrolled in the cohort. At baseline, a general questionnaire containing questions about smoking behavior,
physical activity, reproductive history, medical history, family history, medication use, and a food frequency questionnaire about their normal intake
during the year prior to enrollment, were administered (see **Table 3–6**).
Height, weight, waist, and hip circumference, and systolic and diastolic
blood pressure were measured. For the present analysis, the follow-up period ended on January 1, 2002, after a mean of 6.2 years. During follow-up,
questionnaires were sent out at 5-year intervals to inquire about the occurrence of disease, and these contained seven questions about diabetes. A
new event of type 2 diabetes during follow-up was defined as a report of this
disease in one of two follow-up questionnaires, or a positive urine dipstick
sent out with the first follow-up questionnaire, or a diagnosis of type 2

TABLE 3–6 Baseline Characteristics* by Alcohol Consumption Categories in
16,330 Dutch Women

	Alcohol Consumption (g/week)						
	Teetotaler	0–4.9	5–29.9	30–69.9	70–139.9	140–209.9	≥ 210
Participants (n)	1,513	3,115	3,787	2,586	2,384	1,629	1,316
Age (years)†	59 ± 6	59 ± 6	58 ± 6	57 ± 6	57 ± 6	57 ± 6	56 ± 6
BMI (kg/m²)†	26.9	26.6	26.2	25.8	25.1	25.3	25.3

Data are means ± SD.

*All characteristics are age-adjusted except age.

†P value ≤ 0.001 between alcohol intake categories.

Reproduced from Beulens JW, Stolk RP, van der Schouw YT, Grobbee DE, Hendriks HF, Bots
ML. Alcohol consumption and risk of type 2 diabetes among older women. Diabetes Care
2005;28:2933-2938.

diabetes in the national hospital discharge diagnosis database with which the cohort is linked on an annual basis.

Design of Data Analysis

The principal analysis was performed on the cohort excluding the women who reported diabetes at baseline. Although the follow-up was almost complete, it was not possible to keep track of all enrolled women until January 1, 2002, because some of them moved outside of the Netherlands, and a few of them died. Therefore, the follow-up time was calculated individually for every woman. Because the main interest was the causal association between alcohol intake and type 2 diabetes risk, baseline alcohol intake and lifetime alcohol intake were considered to be potential determinants of the outcome. First, the crude incidence density of type 2 diabetes was calculated for four categories of alcohol intake: teetotalers, and those drinking 0 to 4.9 g/day, 5 to 29.9 g/day, and 30 to 69.9 g/day. Univariate risk ratios with 95% confidence intervals were calculated with Cox proportional hazard analysis, with teetotalers as the reference group. Next, lifestyle factors and medical information were considered as potential confounders of the observed crude association, because they are known to be other determinants of type 2 diabetes risk and often are associated with alcohol intake. Table 3–6 presents the baseline characteristics of the study population, showing that two important determinants of type 2 diabetes, age and BMI, are also related to baseline alcohol intake. A section of these data are presented in **Table 3–7**. The younger and leaner the participants, the more they drink. Although these associations were tested formally, the presence of confounding is best judged by the changes in the risk estimates rather than by statistical significance. To examine the level of confounding, potential confounders were included in the Cox proportional hazards model, and the extent to which adding these variables to the model materially changed the estimates of the risk ratios was judged. There is no universal definition for a material change in risk ratio, leaving this an arbitrary decision of the investigator. However, commonly 5–10% changes in risk ratios are considered large enough to justify adjustment.

Although not displayed in the published article, from Table 3–7 the crude incidence rates and risk ratios for the three categories of alcohol intake compared to teetotalers can easily be calculated to be 1.00 for women drinking 0 to 4.9 g alcohol/day, 0.68 for women drinking 5.0 to 29.9 g alcohol/day, and 0.51 for women drinking 30.0 to 69.9 g alcohol/day. Table 3–7 further shows that adjusting for age and BMI does change the risk estimates quite dramatically, whereas adding additional potential confounders does not result in important changes anymore.

TABLE 3–7   Baseline Alcohol Consumption and Risk of Type 2 Diabetes Among 16,330 Dutch Women

	Alcohol Consumption			
Baseline alcohol consumption (g/day)	0 (teetotaler)	0–4.9	5–29.9	30–69.9
Cases (n)	100	211	174	87
Person-years	9,927	19,533	23,755	16,015
Age and BMI adjusted	1.0	1.05 (0.83–1.33)	0.79 (0.61–1.01)	0.65 (0.49–0.87)
Multivariate adjusted*	1.0	1.04 (0.80–1.34)	0.86 (0.66–1.12)	0.66 (0.48–0.91)
Multivariate adjusted[†]	1.0	1.02 (0.79–1.32)	0.85 (0.65–1.11)	0.64 (0.46–0.89)

Data are means ± SD.

*All characteristics are age-adjusted except age.
[†]P value ≤ 0.001 between alcohol intake categories.

Reproduced from Beulens JW, Stolk RP, van der Schouw YT, Grobbee DE, Hendriks HF, Bots ML. Alcohol consumption and risk of type 2 diabetes among older women. Diabetes Care 2005;28:2933-2938.

Implications and Relevance

The results of this study show that moderate alcohol intake protects against development of type 2 diabetes, which was true for baseline alcohol intake as well as lifetime alcohol intake. The type of alcoholic beverage did not make a difference, which strongly suggests a protective effect of alcohol itself.

A protective effect of moderate alcohol consumption for cardiovascular disease risk is already well established, just as the close relationship between cardiovascular disease and diabetes and other morbidity is well established. You could argue that residual confounding from other comorbidities, notably cardiovascular disease, may be present. However, when excluding cases with cardiovascular disease from the analysis, similar results were obtained.

This study did not specifically address the pathophysiologic mechanism. In a random sample of the population, the relationship between alcohol intake and HDL-C levels was determined, and the expected increasing effect of alcohol was found. Therefore, beneficial effects of alcohol on HDL-C could be part of the mechanism for the protection against type 2 diabetes. However, increases in insulin sensitivity and anti-inflammatory effects also have been associated with moderate alcohol intake, and this might explain the risk reduction of type 2 diabetes [Sierksma et al., 2002].

Chapter 4

Prognostic Research

INTRODUCTION

A 40-year-old woman diagnosed with rheumatoid arthritis contacts her rheumatologist for a routine follow-up visit. This woman is well informed about her disorder, and she has recently learned that patients suffering from rheumatoid arthritis may be at an elevated risk for infections [Doran et al., 2002]. She asks her rheumatologist if there is any reason to worry about infection currently. Her doctor responds by stating that this is indeed a relevant issue, because the patient has been using corticosteroids since her last visit a couple of months ago and these medications may well increase infection risk.

To become better informed about her patient's risk of contracting an infection, the rheumatologist searches for extra-articular manifestations of rheumatoid arthritis, such as skin abnormalities (cutaneous vasculitis), which are also associated with a higher infection risk. She observes none. Still, the rheumatologist feels uncertain about the probability that future infections will occur in her patient. She decides to draw blood and send it to the lab for a leukocyte count. No leukopenia is found. Now the rheumatologist feels confident enough to reassure her patient and does not schedule more frequent follow-up visits than those initially planned.

PROGNOSIS IN CLINICAL PRACTICE

In clinical epidemiology, research questions arise from clinical practice and the answers must serve that practice. Therefore, a discussion of the motive, aim, and process of setting a prognosis in practice is essential before discussing the particulars of prognostic research.

The Motive and Aim of Prognosis

Prognoses are made to inform patients and physicians [Asch, 1990]. Like all humans, patients have a natural interest in their future health. This not only reflects a basic need for certainty, but it also enables people to anticipate the future and thus make informed plans. Consequently, many patients expect a statement from their doctor about their prognosis. In the context of medical practice, a *prognosis* may refer to all elements of future health These include not only direct manifestations of disease such as mortality, pain, or other direct physical or psychological sequelae, but also adverse effects of treatment, treatment response, or failure; limitations in psychosocial or societal functioning; disease recurrence; future need for invasive diagnostic procedures; and other concerns. For physicians, a patient's prognosis is of key clinical importance; prognostication is a core activity [Moons & Grobbee, 2005]. The prognosis of a patient with a given diagnosis forms the point of departure for all subsequent aspects of patient management. Prognosis guides subsequent medical actions such as monitoring the course of disease and planning future interventions or making the decision to refrain from interventions (see **Box 4–1**).

One of the motives for a physician to be interested in a patient's prognosis is that many treatments tend to become more cost-effective as the prognosis

BOX 4–1   Definition

Prognosis in clinical practice can be defined as a prediction of the course or outcome of a certain illness, in a certain patient. It combines the ancient Greek word προ, meaning beforehand, and γνωσις, meaning knowledge. Although prognoses are all around us, such as weather forecasts and corporate finance projections, the word has a medical connotation. After setting a diagnosis, and perhaps making a statement on the surmised etiology of the patient's illness, making a prognosis ("prognostication") is the next challenge a physician faces. Accurate prognostic knowledge is of critical importance to both patients and physicians. Although perhaps obvious, it must be stressed that a person does not require an established illness or disease to have a prognosis. For instance, life expectancy typically is a prognosis relevant to all human beings, diseased and nondiseased. Preventive medicine is concerned with intervening on those who are still free of disease yet have a higher risk of developing a particular disease, that is, those with a poor prognosis. In the medical context and context of clinical epidemiology, however, prognosis is commonly defined as the course and outcome of a given illness in an individual patient.

worsens, which means that patients with a poor prognosis have more to gain. For instance, in patients diagnosed with myocardial infarction that have a low mortality risk (defined as a 1-year risk below 10%), the benefit of reperfusion therapy expressed as the reduction in the absolute risk of mortality has been shown to be less than 3%. For those with a poorer prognosis, for example, a mortality risk of 25%, the mortality risk reduction is much higher, about 15% (ranging from 10–25%) [Boersma & Simons, 1997]. In other instances, a poor prognosis may call for withholding a certain treatment, a relatively common situation in surgery and intensive care medicine. Also, the acceptability of a therapy with serious adverse effects often depends on a patient's prognosis. In women diagnosed with breast cancer, the risk of recurrence of a cancerous tumor determines whether or not systemic adjuvant therapy is initiated [Joensuu et al., 2004]. If the prognosis is favorable, where the recurrence risk is low, the burden of systemic therapy may not outweigh its benefits.

Thus, prognostication often implies answering the question, "What is the predicted course of the disease in this patient if I do not intervene?" [Moons & Grobbee, 2005]. The answer is crucial in the decision to initiate or refrain from therapeutic interventions. Predicting an individual patient's response to a certain therapy also involves prognostication, because the typical aim of the intervention is to improve prognosis [Dorresteijn et al., 2011]. Denys et al. [2003] developed a risk score to estimate the response to pharmacotherapy in patients being treated for obsessive-compulsive disorders. A combination of patient characteristics available at treatment initiation adequately predicted a patient's drug response. This type of score enables the physician to selectively treat those most likely to benefit from treatment, which yields increased treatment efficiency and limits unnecessary drug use.

In practice, patient management is hardly ever based on the expected probability that a patient will develop a single prognostic outcome. Instead, physicians commonly base their decision to start a certain treatment in a given patient on several prognostic outcomes. In fact, for adequate actions, a physician is faced with the considerable challenge of making reliable predictions for virtually all relevant patient outcomes, to assess their utilities (i.e., hazards and benefits), and to weigh and combine these outcomes in discussions with the patient [Braitman & Davidoff, 1996; Dorresteijn et al., 2011]. For instance, in a patient suffering from multiple sclerosis, adequate medical action will be based not only on the predicted mortality risk, but also on the risk of future urinary incontinence, dysarthria, visual acuity, and impairments in activities of daily life, among other contraindications. It also should be emphasized that prognostication is not a "once in the course of illness activity." It is commonly repeated in order to monitor a patient's condition in consideration of eventual treatment alterations, and, of course, to regularly inform the patient. After all, the word *doctor* stems from the Latin word *doctrina*, meaning teacher.

Comprehensive, precise, and repeated evidence-based prognostication is the ultimate aim. However, this often may be unattainable in daily practice, primarily due to a lack of adequate evidence from scientific prognostic research. In addition, there are practical obstacles; multiple or complex risk calculations at the bedside are often incompatible with time constraints in medical practice.

The Format of Prognoses

As the future cannot be predicted with 100% certainty, a prognosis is inherently probabilistic. Therefore, prognoses are formulated in terms reflecting uncertainty, that is, risks or probabilities. For example, short-term mortality in a patient with a recent diagnosis of severe heart failure may be expressed as likely, uncertain, or unlikely. Preferably, a prognosis is expressed in exact quantitative terms, such as a period-specific absolute risk. For instance, the 10-year survival rate for a woman between 50 and 70 years of age with node-negative breast cancer with a tumor diameter less than 10 millimeters is 93% [Joensuu et al., 2004].

Clinically relevant prognoses are to be expressed as absolute risks, or absolute risk categories. Relative risks have no relevance to patients or physicians without reference to absolute probabilities. For instance, the knowledge that a certain patient characteristic is associated with a two-fold risk (i.e., relative risk of two) of a certain outcome has no meaning, unless the probability of the outcome in patients without the characteristic is known. Clearly, doubling of this probability will have a different impact on patient management when it is very low, for example 0.1%, than when it is much higher, for example 10%. Therefore, the preferred format of a prognosis is an absolute risk. Sometimes it is not the probability of the occurrence of a certain event that is to be predicted but rather the absolute level of a future continuous outcome, for instance, pain or quality of life.

APPROACHES TO PROGNOSTICATION

There are at least three different approaches to making a prognosis. The first is to base prognosis on mechanistic and pathophysiologic insight, an approach that fits the educational experience of most doctors. Although mechanistic and pathophysiologic knowledge may be useful in prognostication, it rarely enables a doctor to effectively differentiate patients who have a high risk from those with a low risk of developing a certain outcome. This is because disease outcomes are generally determined by multiple, interrelated, complex, and largely unknown biologic factors and processes with high variability between subjects. In addition, knowledge about underlying mechanisms is not always available and if available is often difficult to measure. In many instances accurate prognostic predictions may, however, be obtained by combining several easy to assess clinical and nonclinical characteristics of the patient, characteristics that are not necessarily causally linked to the course of disease. For example, hip fracture can be accurately predicted from age, gender, height, use of a walking aid, cigarette smoking, and body weight [Burger et al., 1999]. It is likely that these predictors correlate with parameters involved in the causal mechanism underlying fracture risk, that is, low bone density, impaired bone quality, impact on the hip bone from a fall, and postural instability.

Second, clinical experience is a frequently used source of prognostic knowledge [Feinstein, 1994]. Suppose that a cardiologist observes that women diagnosed with heart failure return to the hospital less frequently than men. Obviously, this observation may result from a truly worse prognosis in men than in women. Several other phenomena, however, may have led to a similar observation. Alternative explanations are (1) that survival in women with heart failure actually may be worse than in men, leading to fewer readmissions; (2) women with similar symptoms of worsening heart failure are less likely to be referred to a hospital; or (3) the observation may be wrong. Although clinical experience is of paramount importance in prognostication in daily practice, prognostic research may be useful to confirm or refute and, preferably, quantify prognostic associations.

The third approach is an example of prognostication based on empirical prognostic research: the use of an explicit risk score or prediction model or rule containing multiple prognostic determinants, representing the values of the predictors and their quantitative relationship to a certain prognostically relevant outcome. A good example of an explicit prognostic model is the Apgar score for estimating the probability of neonatal mortality [Apgar, 1953; Casey et al., 2001]. It formally describes how several characteristics of the newborn relate to the probability of dying during the first 28 days after birth. Each characteristic is assigned a score of 0 for absent, a score of 1 for doubtful, and a score of 2 for definitely present. As there are five characteristics, the total score ranges from 0 to 10. Interestingly, the Apgar score (see **Table 4–1**) was already used worldwide decades before its

TABLE 4–1   Apgar Score

Signs	0	1	2
Heartbeat per minute	Absent	Slow (< 100)	> 100
Respiratory effort	Absent	Slow, irregular	Good, crying
Muscle tone	Limp	Some flexion of extremities	Active motion
Reflex irritability	No response	Grimace	Cry or cough
Color	Blue or pale	Body pink, extremities blue	Completely pink

Reproduced from: Finster, Mieczyslaw M.D. and Wood, Margaret M.D.; The Apgar Source Has Survived the Test of Time. Anesthesiology. April 2005. Volume 102. Issue 4. pp 855–857. © 2005 American Society of Anesthesiologists, Inc. Reprinted with permission from Wolters Kluwer Health.

high predictive power for neonatal mortality was confirmed in a formal prognostic study.

In practice, the three approaches discussed in this section are often used implicitly and even simultaneously. It is unlikely that a physician estimates a prognosis based on a prediction model only. The aim of a prediction model in any medical field is not to take over the job of the physician. The intention rather is to guide physicians in their decision making based on more objectively estimated probabilities as a supplement to any other relevant information, including clinical experience and pathophysiologic knowledge [Christensen, 2004; Concato et al., 1993; Feinstein, 1994; Moons et al., 2009a; Moons et al., 2012a].

PROGNOSTICATION IS A MULTIVARIABLE PROCESS

It is common practice in the medical literature as well as during clinical rounds to refer to the prognosis of a disease rather than to the prognosis of a patient: "The prognosis of pancreatic cancer is poor"; "Concussion most often leaves no lasting neurologic problems"; or, more quantitatively, "Five-year survival in osteosarcoma approximates 40%." These so-called textbook prognoses are not individualized prognoses but merely average ones. They are imprecise because many patients will deviate substantially from the average, and they are clinically of limited value because the aim of prognostication—individual risk prediction—cannot be attained. Typically, the prognosis of an individual patient, for example, for 5-year survival is determined by a variety of patient characteristics, not just by a single element such as a diagnosis of osteosarcoma. A combination of prognostic determinants is often referred to as a *risk profile*. This profile usually comprises both nonclinical characteristics such as age and gender, and clinical characteristics such as the diagnosis, symptoms, signs, possible etiology, blood or urine tests, and other tests such as imaging or pathology. Thus, prognosis is rarely adequately estimated by a single prognostic predictor. Physicians—implicitly or explicitly—use multiple predictors to estimate a patient's prognosis [Braitman & Davidoff, 1996; Concato, 2001; Moons et al., 2009a; Moons et al., 2012a]. Adequate prognostication thus requires knowledge about the occurrence of future outcomes given combinations of prognostic predictors. This knowledge in turn requires prognostic studies that follow a multivariable approach in design and analysis to determine which predictors are associated, and to what extent, with clinically meaningful outcomes. The results provide outcome probabilities for different predictor combinations and allow development of tools to estimate these outcome probabilities in daily practice. These tools, often referred to as *clinical prediction models*, *predictions rules*, *prognostic indices*, or *risk scores* enable physicians to explicitly transform combinations of values of prognostic determinants documented in an individual patient to an absolute probability of developing the disease-related event in the future. [Laupacis et al., 1997; Moons et al., 2009a; Randolph et al., 1998; Royston et al., 2009; Steyerberg, 2009]. Similar tools based on multiple determinants are also applied in diagnosis.

ADDED PROGNOSTIC VALUE

As in diagnosis, a logical hierarchy in all available prognostic determinants exists based on everyday practice. Preferably, a doctor will first try to estimate a patient's prognosis based on a combination of a limited number of nonpatient-burdening, easily measurable variables, typically obtained by history taking (including known comorbidity) and physical examination. Before using more cumbersome or costly prognostic markers (e.g., blood tests and imaging), a doctor should be convinced that the additional test indeed has added predictive value beyond the more easily obtained prognostic predictors [Hlatky et al., 2009; Moons et al., 2010]. Unfortunately, recent overviews have shown that in most prognostic studies, single rather than multiple predictors are investigated [Altman et al., 2012; Burton & Altman, 2004; Kyzas et al., 2007; Riley et al., 2003] and that the added value of a novel, potentially valuable prognostic marker is not quantified [Peters et al., 2012; Tzoulaki et al., 2009]. Yet, medical practice slowly shifts from implicit to explicit prognostication, including appreciation of multivariable prediction models, and allowing for quantification of an individual patient's probability of developing a certain outcome within a defined time period. A recent example is the indication for cholesterol-lowering drug therapy in men or women without prior cardiovascular disease. Formerly based on cholesterol level only, recent international guidelines include a cardiovascular risk score (e.g., those based on the Framingham Heart study [Wilson et al., 1998] or the European variant SCORE [Conroy et al., 2003] to predict a person's probability to develop cardiovascular disease during the next 10 years, based on parameters such as age, gender, blood pressure level, smoking habits, glucose tolerance, and, as only one of the prognostic markers, cholesterol level. Other examples of prognostic models in medicine are the previously mentioned breast cancer model [Galea et al., 1992] and the Apgar score, the Acute Physiology and Chronic Health Evaluation (APACHE) score [Knaus et al., 1991], the Simplified Acute Physiology Score (SAPS) [Le Gall et al., 1993], and rules for predicting the occurrence of postoperative nausea and vomiting [Van den Bosch et al., 2005].

Kalkman and colleagues developed an algorithm for predicting the probability of severe early postoperative pain [Kalkman et al., 2003]. Predictors included age, preoperative pain, anxiety level, and the type of surgery. As shown in **Table 4–2**, the lowest total score (0) yields an estimated probability of postoperative pain of 3%, while a high score of 73 corresponds to an 80% probability of postoperative pain.

FROM PROGNOSIS IN CLINICAL PRACTICE TO PROGNOSTIC RESEARCH

In setting a prognosis, the estimation of the likelihood of a certain medical condition does not address the present, but rather the future. A prognosis therefore may be viewed as a future diagnosis. Consequently, it is not surprising that prognostic research shares many characteristics with diagnostic research. However, prognostic research is inherently longitudinal and more often deals with continuous outcomes, such as measures of pain or quality of life, and multiple outcomes, for example, survival and quality of life. Also, as prognostic outcomes inherently involve time, prognostic predictions are generally less accurate than diagnostic

TABLE 4–2 Prognostic Score for Preoperatively Predicting the Probability of Severe Early Postoperative Pain

Sex	Points
Male	0
Female	3

Age (years)	Points
15–19	17
20–24	16
25–29	15
30–34	13
35–39	12
40–44	11
45–49	10
50–54	9
55–59	8
60–64	7
65–69	6
70–74	4
75–79	3
80–84	2
85–89	1
≥ 90	0

Pain Score	Points
0	0
1	2
2	4
3	6
4	8
5	10
6	12
7	14
8	16
9	18
10	20

Surgery Type	Points
Ophthamology	0
Laporoscopy	5
Ear/nose/throat	8
Orthopedic	14
Abdominal	18
Other	7

Incision Size	Points
Small	0
Medium-large	3

Anxiety Level of Patients (APAIS)	Points
4–5	0
6–7	2
8–9	3
10–11	5
12–13	6
14–15	8
16–17	9
18–19	11
12	

Information Seeking Behavior of Patients (APAIS)	Points
2	9
3	8
4	7
5	6
6	5
7	3
8	2
9	1
10	0

Total Points	Probability of Postoperative Pain
0	0.03
11	0.05
22	0.10
34	0.20
41	0.30
48	0.40
53	0.50
59	0.60
65	0.70
73	0.80

BOX 4–2   Application of Prognostic Scores: Hospital Audits

Prognostic information is not only used to guide individual decisions but also to make proper adjustments for "case mix" when comparing the performances of different hospitals. The aim of these comparisons is to make causal inferences about the care given, that is, to assess whether differences in performance are due to differences in quality of care. This can only be accomplished if the analyses are adequately adjusted for the confounding effect of initial prognosis. Prognostic models that are themselves the results of descriptive research can be helpful in achieving this.

A good example comes from a study by the International Neonatal Network. In this study, a scoring system to predict mortality in preterm neonates with low birth weight admitted to neonatal intensive care units was developed [International Neonatal Network, 1993]. The scoring system, denoted as the CRIB score, included birth weight, duration of gestation, congenital malformations, and several physiologic parameters measured during the first 12 hours of life. It showed excellent predictive accuracy with an area under the receiver operating characteristic (ROC) curve of 0.9. Apart from developing this score for the purpose of helping doctors to make mortality predictions in individual neonates, the authors aimed to compare the performance of the intensive care units of tertiary hospitals with those of nontertiary hospitals, as reflected by their relative neonatal mortality rates.

Because the initial prognosis of neonates admitted to tertiary hospitals may be different from that of neonates referred to nontertiary hospitals, these causal analyses were performed adjusting for the confounding effect of initial mortality risk as indicated by the CRIB score. It appeared that only after adjustment for CRIB score did tertiary hospitals showed convincingly less mortality than the nontertiary hospitals. This example illustrates that adjustment for initial prognosis or "case mix" is essential when performance audits are carried out. Yet the validity of this approach is highly dependent on the degree to which the prognostic scores used to adjust for confounding adequately capture prognosis.

predictions, particularly if they predict outcomes occurring a few years later (See **Box 4–2**).

THE PREDICTIVE NATURE OF PROGNOSTIC RESEARCH

The purpose of prognostic research is to assist the physician in the prediction of the future occurrence of a certain health outcome, thereby guiding patient management. This research goal is predictive or descriptive (i.e., noncausal), and fundamentally distinguishing prognostic research from causal research, that is, etiologic and intervention research [Grobbee, 2004; Moons & Grobbee, 2005]. The purely predictive aim of prognostic research is shared with diagnostic research and has major implications for the design, conduct, and reporting of research.

In etiologic research, we assess whether an outcome occurrence can be causally attributed to a particular risk factor, which typically requires adjustment for confounders. The physician aims to explain the occurrence of a certain outcome. For instance, in a study assessing whether unfavorable coping style and low social support in patients with HIV-1 infection are causally related to progression to AIDS, adjustments were made for race and antiviral medications because they were considered potential confounders [Leserman et al., 2000]. Adjustment for confounders is essential to prove causality. Often, etiologic research is motivated by the prospect of new (preventive) interventions. This was explicitly expressed in the conclusion section of Leserman et al.'s study: "Further research is needed to determine if treatments based on these findings might alter the clinical course of HIV-1 infection." Prognostic research aims to predict as accurately as possible the probability or risk of future occurrence of a certain outcome as a function of multiple predictors. The aim is not to explain the outcome.

In prognostic research there is no central factor or determinant whose causal effect must be isolated from the effects of other variables. In addition to the predictive aim, the requirement of practical applicability of prognostic study results is shared with diagnostic research. To this end, the domain is usually comprised of patients presenting with a certain disorder in a certain setting. Prognostic determinants are characteristics typically assessed during history taking, physical examination, blood tests, imaging, and other test results. But they also may include treatments currently used (or used in the past) by the patient. Furthermore, to increase the likelihood that prognostic study results can be translated to everyday practice, the study should be performed in and mimic routine clinical practice, a feature shared with diagnostic research. Finally, results should be expressed as absolute risks in order to be informative for patients and doctors in deciding about patient management. In the HIV example, instead of an etiologic research question, one could also imagine a prognostic research question. For example, "Does coping style in addition to other prognostic items, such as age, gender, and leukocyte counts, predict the development of AIDS?" In this example, all variables would be considered prognostic determinants.

APPRAISAL OF PREVAILING PROGNOSTIC RESEARCH

Many studies labeled as prognostic studies are not actually prognostic as defined earlier in the chapter, but rather are truly etiologic. The researcher is interested in the causal association between a particular determinant and an outcome in patients with a certain disease, rather than in the combined predictive accuracy of multiple determinants in predicting the future development of that disease. This is also reflected in a recent appraisal of the quality of individual studies in systematic reviews of prognostic studies in which "adequate adjustment for confounders" was considered an important item [Hayden et al., 2006]. However, as mentioned earlier, confounding—defined as the undesired influence of other risk factors on the causal association between the determinant and outcome—is a hallmark of causal research, but it is not relevant in prognostic research. Thus, in appraising a study designated as a prognostic study, it is essential that the aim of the study is completely clear: to predict or to explain (i.e., address the causality of) an outcome. In the following sections, the term *prognostic study* is reserved for a study with a purely predictive aim.

Commonly, studies on prognosis, although valuable in themselves, do not produce results that directly establish accurate individualized prognoses in future patients in daily practice. This relates to several issues [Moons et al., 2009a; Moons et al., 2012a]. First, it is not always recognized that for the results to be relevant to individual patient management, period-specific absolute risks based on a combination of prognostic markers should be obtainable from the published report of the prognostic study. As an example, El-Metwally and colleagues [2005] studied the short- and long-term prognosis of preadolescent lower limb pain and assessed factors that contributed to pain persistence. While they did report period-specific absolute risks ("of the baseline students with lower limb pain, 32% reported pain persistence at one year follow-up and 31% reported pain recurrence at four year follow-up"), these risks are average risks that do not allow for individual prognosis. They did study the association of specific prognostic factors with pain recurrence during the 4-year follow-up period, but only relative risks were reported (e.g., a twofold risk in the presence compared to the absence of the factor); absolute risks are clearly more relevant.

Another study concluded that symptomatic deep vein thrombosis carries a high risk of recurrent thromboembolism, especially for patients without transient risk factors, and that this observation challenges the widely adopted short course of anticoagulant therapy. This typically suggests a prognostic (thus, predictive) aim [Prandoni et al., 1997]. Yet, similar to the study on limb pain, only average absolute risks and adjusted relative risks were presented, rather than absolute outcome probabilities within a defined time period for different predictor combinations. A somewhat adapted data analysis strategy (see the later section, Design of Data Analysis) would have provided absolute risks more relevant to both patient and doctor.

In **Box 4–3**, the abstract of a paper presenting a "prognostic study" on the value of gene-expression profiles in predicting distant metastasis in patients with lymph-node-negative primary breast cancer is shown [Whang et al.,

BOX 4–3 Study on the Prognostic Value of Gene-Expression Profiles in Predicting Distant Metastasis in Patients with Lymph-Node-Negative Primary Breast Cancer

Summary

Background: Genome-wide measures of gene expression can identify patterns of gene activity that subclassify tumors and might provide a better means than is currently available for individual risk assessment in patients with lymph-node-negative breast cancer.

Methods: We analyzed, with Affymetrix Human Ul33a GeneChips, the expression of 22,000 transcripts from total RNA of frozen tumor samples from 286 lymph-node-negative patients who had not received adjuvant systemic treatments.

Findings: In a training set of 115 tumors, we identified a 76-gene signature consisting of 60 genes for patients positive for estrogen receptors (ER) and 16 genes for ER-negative patients. This signature showed 93% sensitivity and 48% specificity in a subsequent independent testing set of 171 lymph-node-negative patients. The gene profile was highly informative in identifying patients who developed distant metastases within 5 years (hazard ratio 5.67 [95% CI 2.46–12.4]), even when corrected for traditional prognostic factors in multivariate analysis (5.55 [2.46–12.15]). The 76-gene profile also represented a strong prognostic factor for the development of metastasis in the subgroups of 84 premenopausal patients (9.60 [2.28–40.5]), 87 postmenopausal patients (4.04 [1.57–10.4]), and 79 patients with tumors of 10–12 mm (14.1 [3.34–59.2]), a group of patients for whom prediction of prognosis is especially difficult.

Interpretation: The identified signature provides a power tool for identification of patients at high risk of distant recurrence. The ability to identify patients who have a favorable prognosis could, after independent confirmation, allow clinicians to avoid adjuvant systemic therapy or to choose less aggressive therapeutic options.

2005]. The study was, however, primarily designed and analyzed as an etio-logic study. For example, the authors adjusted for potential confounders, and hazard ratios (instead of absolute risks) were presented as the main finding. In a true prognostic study, the added value of these gene-expression profiles in estimating the absolute probability of developing distant metas-tasis should be determined without considering confounding. Instead of treating, for example, age as a potential confounder, this characteristic should be considered as one of the potentially useful prognostic determi-nants. Whether the 76-gene signature has any prognostic value in addition to age and other easily measurable prognostic factors is of primary interest, but such an analysis was not presented.

A second problem of many prognostic studies is that prognostic vari-ables are often included based on measurements that are not feasible in everyday practice. As a consequence, the practical application of the resulting prognostic model may be hampered. An example is the use of an extensive questionnaire to assess personality trait neuroticism in the prognostication of depression [O'Leary & Costello, 2001].

Third, in cases where the interest of prognostic research lies in the prog-nostic value of a particular new marker, researchers often fail to assess the marker's added predictive value [Hlatky et al., 2009; Moons et al., 2010]. For example, Leslie and colleagues [2007] aimed to predict future osteoporotic fractures with dual-energy x-ray absorptiometry (DXA) in a large clinical cohort. While a valuable study, unfortunately it did not address the key clinical question in this context: whether DXA measurement has prognos-tic value in addition to more conventional and easy to assess predictors such as age, gender, smoking habits, and body weight. Furthermore, this study also only presented age-adjusted hazard ratios (relative risks) for frac-ture rather than absolute risks.

Finally, prognostic studies that do develop a multivariable prediction model or rule seldom validate the model internally (that is, within their own data) or externally by testing the accuracy of the model in another population reflecting the same domain [Altman et al., 2009; Bouwmeester et al., 2012; Dieren et al., 2011; Moons et al., 2012b].

Fortunately, an increasing number of well-designed and reported prog-nostic studies is being published that do enable physicians to reliably esti-mate an individual patient's absolute risk of developing a particular outcome within a defined time period in a practical manner [Steyerberg, 2009]. An example is a study by Steyerberg et al. [2006]. The rationale for this study was the fact that surgery for esophageal cancer has curative potential, but that the procedure is also associated with considerable perioperative risks. Patients with very high perioperative mortality risks as estimated before surgery therefore may not be eligible for this operation. Analyses in this study focused on optimizing predictive accuracy and the presentation of the results were in line with the objective of determining individual absolute risk predictions facilitating patient selection and thus more targeted management. In this study, a chart with the estimated risks according to the presence of several prognostic predictors was combined into a single score. Another study from Hong Kong, in which a prognostic model for patients with severe acute respiratory syndrome (SARS) was developed and validated, also yielded results that can be directly applied in medical practice [Cowling et al., 2006].

PROGNOSTIC RESEARCH

Once it is recognized that the aim of prognostication is to stratify patients according to their absolute risk of a certain future relevant health event, based on their clinical and nonclinical profile, the three components of epidemiologic study design (theoretical design, design of data collection, and design of data analysis) follow logically.

Theoretical Design

The object of medical prognostication is to predict the future occurrence of a health-related outcome based on the patient's clinical and nonclinical profile. Outcomes may include a particular event such as death, disease recurrence, or complication, and also continuous or quantitative outcomes such as pain or quality of life. As noted already, the architecture of prognostic research strongly resembles that of diagnostic research. The major difference is that time or follow-up is elementary to prognostic research, whereas diagnostic research is inherently cross-sectional. The occurrence relation of prognostic research is given by:

Incidence $O = f(d1, d2, d3, \ldots dn)$

where O signifies the outcome (occurrence of an event or realization of a quantitative disease parameter) at a future time point t, and d1 ... dn represent the potential prognostic determinants measured at one or more time point(s) before t. Note that no extraneous determinants (confounders) are included in the occurrence relation, as causality is not at stake.

The domain of a prognostic occurrence relation includes individuals who are at risk of developing the outcome of interest and is usually defined by the presence of a particular condition. This "condition" could be an illness, but it could also be a need for surgery, those who are pregnant, or even newborns. Consequently, patients with a zero or 100% probability of developing the outcome are not part of the domain. An example of individuals that were at a 100% risk of developing the outcome and thus did not belong to the study domain is the group newborns with inevitably lethal conditions in a study evaluating a risk score for the prediction of "in-hospital mortality" in newborns [International Neonatal Network, 1993]. Generalization of the risk score to these children is invalid and clearly irrelevant, because application of the risk score in these newborns will not have any bearing on patient management.

The typical research objective of prognostic research is to assess which combination of potential prognostic determinants under study indeed best predicts the future outcome. As described earlier, the aim also can be to assess whether a new prognostic marker provides additional predictive value beyond other available predictors. Furthermore, it may include comparison of the predictive accuracy of two (new) markers. Both require a comparison of the predictive accuracy of two occurrence relations: one with the new predictor and one without, and one with marker one and one with marker two, respectively [Moons et al., 2012a].

Design of Data Collection

The main objective of a prognostic study is to provide quantitative knowledge about the occurrence of a health outcome in a predefined time period as a function of multiple predictors. The following sections discuss the most important aspects of designing the data collection.

Time

The object of the prognostic process is inherently longitudinal ($t > 0$). Accordingly, prognostic research follows a longitudinal design in which the determinants or prognostic predictors are measured before the outcome is observed. The time period needed to observe the outcome occurrence or outcome development may vary from as short as several hours (e.g., in the case of early postoperative complications) to as long as days, weeks, months, or years.

Census or Sampling

As the outcomes of prognostic studies are generally expressed in absolute terms, the design most suitable to address prognostic questions is a cohort study in which all patients with a certain condition are followed for some time to monitor the development of the outcome; this uses a census approach. Preferably, the data are collected prospectively rather than retrospectively because this allows for optimal measurement of predictors and outcome, as well as adequate (complete) follow-up. Typically, all consecutive patients with a particular condition who are at risk for developing the outcome of interest (i.e., who are part of the domain) are included. The potential prognostic determinants and the outcome are measured in all patients.

As in diagnostic research, sometimes a case-control design (and thus a sampling rather than a census approach) is used in prognostic research [Ganna et al., 2012; Iglesias de Sol et al., 2001;]. This is done for efficiency reasons, for example, when measurement of one or more of the prognostic determinants is burdensome to patients or is expensive, or when the prognostic outcome is rare. This design does not allow for an estimation of absolute risks of an outcome when cases and controls are obtained from a source population of unknown size. When, however, the sampling fraction of the controls (i.e., the proportion of the population experience of the entire cohort that is sampled in the controls) is known, the true denominators, and thus absolute risks, can be estimated by reconstructing the 2×2 table [Biesheuvel et al., 2008; Moons et al., 2009a; Moons et al., 2012a]. The case-cohort design, a specific type of case-control study performed within a cohort study, is increasingly being used in prognostic research because of its efficiency and because it yields absolute probabilities [Ganna et al., 2012].

Experimental or Observational

Almost all prognostic studies outside the realm of intervention research are observational, where a well-defined group of patients with a certain condition are followed for a period of time to monitor the occurrence of the outcome. The researcher observes and measures the nonclinical and clinical parameters anticipated to be of prognostic significance. These potential prognostic determinants are not influenced (let alone randomly allocated) by the researcher. However, as in diagnostic research, one could imagine that prognostic studies involve experimentation, for example, when comparing the impact on a certain outcome (e.g., mortality) of the use of two prognostic risk scores by randomly allocating the two rules to individual physicians or patients [Moons et al., 2012b; Reilly & Evans, 2006].

Alternatively, however, randomized trials can serve as a vehicle for prognostic research. Then the study population of the trial is taken as a plain cohort where the prognostic determinants of interest are just observed and not influenced by the researcher. Consequently, a prognostic study within a trial bears a greater resemblance to an observational study than to a typical experimental study. The issue up for debate is whether one should limit the prognostic analysis to the trial participants in the reference (or

control) group, that is, to those who did not undergo the randomly allocated prognosis-modifying intervention and perhaps were given a placebo
[Moons et al., 2012a]. In the case of an ineffective intervention, most researchers will include both the intervention and reference cohort in the
prognostic study, whereas when the intervention is beneficial or harmful,
only the reference group is included. Is should be emphasized, however,
that even in cases of no observed overall difference in effect of the randomly allocated intervention, the intervention can modify the association
of the prognostic determinants with the outcome. To study such effect
modification, one could perform separate prognostic analyses in the two
comparison groups of the trial, guided by tests for interaction between the
intervention and the other prognostic predictors. Certainly, both analyses
may provide clinically useful information: The prognostic study within the
placebo group of a trial will help physicians to accurately estimate the prognosis in a patient with a certain condition if no intervention is initiated
(i.e., the natural history of a disease or condition) and can be instrumental
in deciding about treatment initiation [Dorresteijn et al., 2011]. A prognostic analysis within the treated patient group will facilitate quantification of
the expected course (in terms of absolute risks) in an individual patient following treatment. An example of a prognostic study performed within a
trial is shown in **Box 4–4**, which attempted to help physicians to identify
those children with acute otitis media prone to experience prolonged complaints (and thus possibly requiring closer monitoring or antibiotic treatment). Rovers et al. [2007] performed a prognostic analysis in a data set
including the placebo groups of all available randomized trials assessing the
effect of antibiotic treatment in children with acute otitis media. An obvious advantage of such an analysis of a trial is the availability of high-quality
data. On the other hand, however, the findings may have restricted generalizability due to the strict inclusion and exclusion criteria applied in the
trials [Kiemeney et al., 1994; Marsoni & Valsecchi, 1991; Moons et al.,
2012a]. Moreover, the high-quality data on prognostic determinants may
be a blessing in disguise, because in the real-life application the available
clinical information may be of lower quality and the predictors thus will
show reduced prognostic performance.

Study Population

The study population in prognostic research should be representative of the
domain. Prognostic predictors, models, or strategies are investigated for
their ability to predict a future health outcome as accurately as possible.
Accordingly, and as noted before, the domain of a prognostic study is

BOX 4–4   Predictors of a Prolonged Course in Children with Acute Otitis Media: An Individual Patient Meta-Analysis

Background: Currently there are no tools to discriminate between children with mild, self-limiting episodes of acute otitis media (AOM) and those at risk of a prolonged course.

Methods: In an individual patient data meta-analysis with the control groups of 6 randomised controlled trials ($n = 824$ children with acute otitis media, aged 6 months to 12 years), we determined the predictors of poor short term outcome in children with AOM. The primary outcome was a prolonged course of AOM, which was defined as fever and/or pain at 3–7 days.

Main findings: Of the 824 included children, 303 (37%) had pain and/or fever at 3–7 days. Independent predictors for a prolonged course were age < 2 years and bilateral AOM. The absolute risks of pain and/or fever at 3–7 days in children aged less than 2 years with bilateral AOM (20% of all children) was 55%, and in children aged 2 years or older with unilateral AOM 25% (47% of all children).

Interpretation: The risk of a prolonged course was two times higher in children aged less than 2 years with bilateral AOM than in children aged 2 years or older with unilateral AOM. Clinicians can use these features to advise parents and to follow these children more actively.

comprised of individuals who are at risk for developing that outcome. Patients who have already developed the outcome or in whom the probability is considered so low ("zero") that the physician does not even consider estimating this probability fall outside the domain, because subsequent patient management (e.g., to initiate or refrain from therapeutic actions) is evident. Furthermore, as in diagnostic research, we recommend restricting domain definitions and thus study populations in prognostic research to the setting of care (notably primary or secondary care) of interest, due to known differences in predictive accuracy of determinants across care settings [Knottnerus, 2002a; Oudega et al., 2005a; Moons et al., 2009b; Toll et al., 2008]. Finally, the selection or recruitment of any study population is often further restricted by logistical circumstances, such as the necessity for patients to live near the research center or the availability of their time to participate in the study. These characteristics are often unlikely to influence the applicability and generalization of study findings. It may be challenging to appreciate which characteristics truly affect the generalizability of results obtained from a particular study population. This appreciation usually requires knowledge of those characteristics (effect modifiers) that may modify the nature and strength of the estimated associations between the prognostic determinants and outcome. Therefore, generalizability from study population to the relevant domain is not an objective process that can be framed in statistical terms. Generalizability is a matter of reasoning, requiring external knowledge and subjective judgment. The question to be answered is whether in other types of subjects from the domain who were not represented in the study population the same prognostic predictors would be found with the same predictive values [Moons & Grobbee, 2005].

Prognostic Determinants (Predictors)

As in diagnostic studies, prognostic studies should mirror real-life situations and consider multiple predictors. Predictors under study can be obtained from patient history (each question is a potential predictor), physical examination, additional testing such as imaging results and biologic markers, characteristics of the severity of the disease, and potentially any interventions that the patient has received [Brotman et al., 2005; Moons et al., 2012a]. Determinants included in a prognostic study should be clearly defined, and their measurement should be sufficiently reproducible to enhance application of study results to daily practice. This notably applies to treatments that are studied as potential predictors [Simon & Altman, 1994], but also to predictors that require subjective interpretation, such as imaging test results, to avoid studying the predictive ability of the observer rather than of the predictors. Predictors should preferably be measured using methods applicable—or potentially applicable—to daily practice, again to enhance generalizability and to prevent too optimistic predictive accuracy of predictors than can be expected in real-life situations. In itself, specialized measurement of predictors is not necessarily a limitation of prediction research. This argument may even be turned around: If substantially better predictions are obtained with specialized or more elaborate measurements, this may call for such measurements, if feasible, in everyday clinical practice. Feasibility plays an important role in choosing determinants to be included in prognostic research. One could decide to study proxy or surrogate predictors if the underlying predictor is too cumbersome to measure; for example, the color of the newborn rather than oxygen saturation is included in the Apgar score.

All potential predictors are usually measured and analyzed in each subject of the study population. This can be done with a view to chronological hierarchy in clinical practice, starting with history and physical examination tests. Subsequent predictors will be measured in each subject if the aim is to determine the added predictive value. However, we do warn against the inclusion of large numbers of determinants in prognostic research. Hence, the choice of the predictors under study should be based on both available literature and a thorough understanding of clinical practice [Harrell et al., 1996; Harrell, 2001; Steyerberg et al., 2000; Steyerberg, 2009].

Outcome

The outcome in prognostic research is typically dichotomous: the occurrence, in this case the incidence (yes/no) of the event or disease course of interest. In addition, prognostic outcomes may comprise continuous variables such as tumor growth, pain, or quality of life, rather than incidence or nonoccurrence of a particular event. In both instances, we recommend that the researcher studies outcomes that really matter to patients, such as remission of disease, survival, complications, pain, or quality of life. One preferably should not study so-called proxy or intermediate outcomes such as joint space in patients with osteoarthritis of the knee (instead of pain, the ability to walk, or quality of life), unless a clear relationship between such an intermediate outcome and outcomes more relevant for patients has been established. The latter may apply for the use of CD4 count as a prognostic outcome (rather than the occurrence of AIDS or even death) in HIV studies.

As in all research, criteria defining the absence or presence of the outcome as well as the measurement tools used should be described in detail. Importantly, the outcome occurrence is assessed as accurately as possible, with the best available methods to prevent misclassification, even if this requires measures that are never taken in clinical practice.

The time period during which the outcome occurrence is measured requires special attention. Predicting an outcome occurrence over a 3-month period typically yields different predictors or different predictor–outcome associations than prediction of the same outcome after 5 years. As with weather and stock value forecasting, prediction over a shorter period is commonly less problematic than prediction over a longer time period.

Finally, as in most research, outcomes should ideally be measured without knowledge of the value of the predictors under study to prevent self-fulfilling prophecies, particularly if the outcome measurement requires observer interpretation. For example, the presence of those determinants believed to be associated with the prognostic outcome may influence the decision to consider the outcome to have occurred. This bias can cause under- or overestimation of the accuracy of predictors, but it more commonly leads to overestimation; it can be prevented by blinding the assessors of the outcome to the values of the prognostic determinants [Loy & Irwig, 2004; Moons et al., 2002c; Moons et al., 2009a]. Blinding is not necessary for mortality or other outcomes that can be measured without misclassification.

BIAS IN PROGNOSTIC RESEARCH

Confounding Bias

In prognostic research, the interest is in the joint predictive accuracy of multiple predictors. As stated earlier, there is no central determinant for which the relationship to the outcome should be causally isolated from other outcome predictors, as in causal research. Confounding thus is not an issue in prognostic research, as in all types of prediction research.

Other Biases

While confounding does not play a role in prediction research, other biases certainly do. Bias that may occur when the outcome assessor is aware of the determinants was discussed in the last paragraph. In addition, loss to follow-up, and thus nonassessment and missing of the outcomes that is not completely at random (MCAR) but rather selectively missing likely leads to biased estimates of the prognostic or predictive value of the predictors under study, if the analysis is reserved to only those individuals in whom the outcome was assessed. Selectively missing outcomes means that the subsample of the original study population with the observed outcomes are different from the subsample with the missing outcomes [de Groot et al., 2011a]. This bias can be addressed or minimized using several methods [de Groot et al., 2008; de Groot et al., 2011b, de Groot et al., 2011c], including the use of multiple imputation techniques [Groenwold et al., 2012]. Bias due to selective loss to follow-up may also occur [Groenwold et al., 2012; Little et al., 2012].

DESIGN OF DATA ANALYSIS

Analysis Objective

The aims of the data analysis in multivariable prognostic research are similar to multivariable diagnostic research, except for the dimension of time: to provide knowledge about which potential predictors independently contribute to the outcome prediction, and to what extent. Also, one may aim to develop and validate a multivariable prediction model or rule to predict the outcome given the values of a combination of predictors. The methods to determine the required number of subjects and the data analysis steps of prognostic studies are similar to diagnostic studies. For example, to guide decision making in individual patients, the analysis and reporting of prognostic studies concentrates on absolute risk estimates (in prognostic studies on incidence and in diagnostic studies on prevalence) of an outcome given combinations of predictors and their values. In view of the large similarities between the analysis of prognostic and diagnostic studies, we will concentrate on the differences that exist between the two types of studies.

Different Outcomes

In contrast to diagnostic research where the outcome is largely dichotomous, prognostic research can distinguish between various types of outcomes. The first and most frequently encountered type of outcome is the occurrence (yes/no) of an event within a specific, preferably short, period of time [Moons et al., 2012a; Steyerberg, 2009]. For example, one might study the occurrence of a certain complication within 3 months, where ideally each included patient has been followed for at least this period. The cumulative incidence, expressed as a probability between 0% and 100%, of the dichotomous outcome at a certain time point (t) is to be predicted using predictors measured before t. For these outcomes, the analysis is identical to the analysis in diagnostic research. The second most common outcome in prognostic research is the occurrence of a particular outcome event over a (usually) longer period of time, where the follow-up time may differ substantially between study participants. Here, the time to occurrence of the event can be predicted using the Kaplan-Meier method or Cox proportional hazard modeling. It is also possible to predict the absolute risk of a certain outcome within multiple time frames (e.g., 3 months, 6 months, 1 year, and 3 years), although the maximum time period is determined by the maximum follow-up period of the included patients (see also the Worked-Out Example at the end of this chapter). Other, less regular outcomes in prognostic prediction studies are continuous variables [Harrell, 2001], such as the level of pain or tumor size at t, and—as in diagnostic research—polytomous (nominal) outcomes [Biesheuvel et al., 2008] or ordinal outcomes [Harrell et al., 1998]. An example of the latter is the Glascow Outcome Scale collapsed into three ordinal levels: death, survival with major disability, and functional recovery [Cremer et al., 2006].

Required Number of Subjects

As for diagnostic research, the multivariable character of prognostic research creates problems for estimating the required number of study subjects; there are no straightforward commonly accepted methods. Ideally, prognostic studies include several hundreds of patients that develop the outcome event [Harrell, 2001; Moons et al., 2009a; Simon & Altman, 1994]. As with all dichotomous outcomes analyzed with multivariable logistic regression analysis, experience has shown that for the analysis of time to event outcomes using Cox proportional hazard modeling, at least 10 subjects in the smallest of the outcome categories (i.e., either with or without the event during the study period) are needed for proper statistical modeling [Concato et al., 1995; Peduzzi et al., 1995]. Such rules are largely lacking for ordinal and polytomous outcomes [Harrell, 2001].

For continuous outcomes, the required number of subjects may be estimated crudely by performing a sample size calculation for the t-test situation where the two groups are characterized by the most important dichotomous predictor. Another approach, more directed at the use of multiple linear regression modeling, is to define the allowable limit in the number of covariates (or rather, degrees of freedom) for the model by dividing the total number of study subjects by 15 [Harrell, 2001]. For more sophisticated approaches, we refer readers to an article by Dupont and Plummer [1998].

Statistical Analysis

Modeling of the cumulative incidence of a dichotomous outcome at a specific time t using logistic regression is discussed elsewhere in the text. For time to event outcomes, also denoted as survival-type outcomes, the univariable analysis can be performed using the Kaplan-Meier method. Similar to the analysis of dichotomous outcomes, the observed probabilities depend on the threshold values of the predictor. Unfortunately, the construction of a receiver operating characteristic (ROC) curve is not straightforward because the outcomes of the censored patients are unknown. The so-called concordance-statistic (c-statistic or c-index), however, can be easily calculated and its value has the same interpretation as the area under the ROC curve [Harrell, 2001]. For the multivariable analysis of time to event data using Cox proportional hazard modeling, we refer to the Worked-Out Example at the end of the chapter.

When the outcome is continuous (for example, tumor size), univariable and multivariable analyses are usually carried out using linear regression modeling. The discriminatory power of a linear regression model can be assessed from the squared multiple correlation coefficient (R^2), also known as the explained variance [Harrell et al., 1996; Harrell, 2001]. This measure unfortunately is not intuitively understood. Detailed information on the analysis of continuous as well as ordinal and polytomous outcomes is available in the literature [Biesheuvel et al., 2008; Harrell, 2001; Roukema et al., 2008].

Internal Validation and Shrinkage of the Developed Prognostic Model

If the number of potential predictors in multivariable logistic regression modeling is much larger than the number of outcomes or subjects, any fitted model will result in overly optimistic predictive accuracy. The internal validation and shrinkage of a multivariable logistic, Cox proportional hazard, and linear, ordinal, and polytomous models are similar [Harrell, 2001; Moons et al., 2012a; Royston et al., 2009; Steyerberg, 2009].

Estimating Added Value

Prognostic factors, tests, and biomarkers differ in predictive accuracy, invasiveness, and cost. Accordingly, tests or markers, especially those whose collection requires more burdensome and costly measurement, should not be evaluated on their individual predictive abilities but rather on the incremental predictive value beyond established, and easier to obtain, predictors [Moons et al., 2012a]. Measures of discrimination such as the c-statistic are not able to detect small improvements in model performance when a new marker is added to a model that already includes important predictors. Recently, new metrics that estimate the added value of predictors have been proposed. These quantify the extent to which an extended model (with addition of a subsequent predictor or marker) improves the classification of participants with and without the outcome compared with the basic model without that predictor. For example, the *net reclassification improvement* (NRI) does this by quantifying the number of individuals that are correctly reclassified into clinically meaningful higher or lower risk categories with the addition of a new predictor, using pre-specified risk groups [Pencina et al., 2008]. Correct reclassifications are shifts to a higher risk category in those who develop the prognostic outcome and shifts to a lower risk category in those who do not. Definition of these risk groups, however, is often arbitrary and differs across studies, which may compromise comparisons of NRIs from different studies. To circumvent this problem, a version of the NRI that does not require stratification of the population into risk groups may be used [Pencina et al., 2011]. Alternatively, the *integrated discrimination improvement* (IDI) may be useful. In contrast to the NRI, the IDI does not require subjectively predefined risk thresholds. The IDI is the estimated improvement in the average sensitivity of the basic model with addition of the new predictor minus the estimated decrease in the mean specificity, summarized over all possible risk thresholds. **Table 4–3** and **Table 4–4** give examples from the USE-IMT pooled analysis of data on the added value of

TABLE 4–3 Reclassification of Cardiovascular Risk with Carotid Artery Intima-Media Thickness Added to Framingham Risk Score: Findings from the USE-IMT Consortium

A Distribution of 45,828 individuals without and with events in USE-IMT across risk categories

Without events

Framingham Risk	Framingham Risk with CIMT		
	< 5%	5–20%	> 20%
< 5%	20271→	867	–
5–20%	1115	←17280→	362
> 20%		315	←1611

Total without events, No. (%)

39162 (93.6%)	No change
1229 (2.9%)	Up classification
1430 (3.4%)	Down classification

With events

Framingham Risk	Framingham Risk with CIMT		
	< 5%	5–20%	> 20%
< 5%	537→	67	–
5–20%	69	←2410→	102
> 20%		85	←737

Total with events, No. (%)

3684 (91.9%)	No change
169 (4.2%)	Up classification
154 (3.8%)	Down classification

B Observed Kaplan-Meier estimates in risk categories

Framingham Risk	Framingham Risk with CIMT		
	< 5%	5–20%	> 20%
< 5%	2.2 (2.0–2.4)	6.2 (4.5–7.9)	–
5–20%	4.6 (3.3–5.9)	10.4 (10.0–10.9)	20.6 (16.4–24.6)
> 20%		19.0 (14.6–23.1)	28.7 (26.7–30.6)

All individuals, No. (%)

42,846 (93.5%)	No change
1398 (3.1%)	Up classification
1584 (3.5%)	Down classification

A, Individuals without and with events classified according to their 10-year absolute risk to develop a myocardial infarction or stroke predicted with the Framingham Risk Score variables or classified according to their 10-year absolute risk to develop a first-time myocardial infarction or stroke predicted with the Framingham Risk Score and a common carotid intima-media thickness (CIMT) measurement. B, Observed Kaplan-Meier absolute risk estimates for all individuals (with and without events). The observed risk in reclassified individuals is significantly different from the observed risk of the individuals in the gray cells.

Reproduced from den Ruijter H et al. Common carotid intima-media thickness measurements in cardiovascular risk prediction. A meta-analysis. *JAMA.* 2012;308(8):796–803.

TABLE 4–4   Summary of the Indices of Added Value in the Total USE-IMT Cohort and in the Intermediate Risk Categories, by Sex: Findings from the USE-IMT Consortium

	ALL	MEN	WOMEN
USE-IMT			
NRI, % (95% CI)	0.8 (0.1 to 1.6)	0.9 (–0.2 to 1.9)	0.8 (– 0.2 to 1.6)
IDI (95% CI)	0.0024 (0.0012 to 0.0036)	0.0024 (0.0004 to 0.0041)	0.0025 (0.0009 to 0.0040)
Relative IDI, %	3.6	3.6	3.7
USE-IMT, Intermediate Risk Group (5% to < 20%)			
NRI, % (95% CI)	3.6 (2.7 to 4.6)	3.2 (2.3 to 4.4)	3.9 (2.7 to 4.9)
IDI (95% CI)	0.0024 (0.0012 to 0.0036)	0.0019 (0.0003 to 0.0034)	0.0031 (0.0013 to 0.0048)
Relative IDI, %	3.6	2.7	4.6

CI, confidence interval; IDI, integrated discrimination improvement; NRI, net reclassification improvement; USE-IMT, USE Intima-Media Thickness collaboration.

Reproduced from den Ruijter H et al. Common carotid intima-media thickness measurements in cardiovascular risk prediction. A meta-analysis. *JAMA*. 2012;308(8):796-803.

carotid artery intima-media thickness measurements for cardiovascular risk prediction based on 14 population-based cohorts contributing data for 45,828 individuals [den Ruijter et al., 2012].

Other Relevant Data Analysis Issues

A summary of issues in the analysis of prognostic data is given in **Box 4–5.** Note that the relevant issues pertaining to reporting of study results, external validation of the developed model, and application of a final model in clinical practice are similar for prognostic and diagnostic research [Altman et al., 2009; Moons et al., 2009b; Moons et al., 2012b; Reilly & Evans 2006].

WORKED-OUT EXAMPLE

This example is based on a study conducted by Spijker and colleagues [2006]. It illustrates the design of data analysis in the case of time to event data, which includes how to obtain absolute risks from a Cox proportional hazard model, how to shrink coefficients, how to assess discriminatory power, and how to calculate theoretical sensitivity and specificity using the predictive values. Useful methodologic considerations underlying this example can be found in the literature [Altman & Andersen, 1989; Harrell, 2001;

BOX 4–5 Guide to the Main Design and Analysis Issues for Prognostic Studies

Design
- *Objective*: To develop a model/tool to enable objective estimation of outcome probabilities (risks) according to different combinations of predictor values.
- *Study participants*: Individuals with the same characteristic, for example, individuals with a particular symptom or sign suspected of a particular disease or with a particular diagnosis, at risk of having (diagnostic prediction model) or developing (prognostic prediction model) a specific health outcome.
- *Sampling design*: Cohort, preferably prospective to allow for optimal documentation of predictors or outcomes, including a cohort of individuals that participate in a randomized therapeutic trial. Case-control studies are not suitable, except nested case-control or case-cohort studies.
- *Outcomes*: Relevant to individuals and preferably measured without knowledge of the measured predictor values. Methods for outcome ascertainment, blinding for the studied predictors, and duration of follow-up (if applicable) should be clearly defined.
- *Candidate predictors*: Theoretically, all potential and not necessarily causal correlates of the outcome of interest. Commonly, however, preselection based on subject matter knowledge is recommended. Similar to the outcomes, candidate predictors are clearly defined and measured in a standard and reproducible way.

Analysis
- *Missing values*: Analysis of individuals with only completely observed data may lead to biased results. Imputation, preferably multiple imputation, of missing values often yields less biased results.
- *Continuous predictors*: Should not be turned into dichotomies and linearity should not be assumed. Simple predictor transformation can be implemented to detect and model nonlinearity, increasing the predictive accuracy of the prediction model.
- *Predictor selection in the multivariable modeling*: Selection based on univariable analysis (single predictor–outcome associations) is discouraged. Preferably, if needed, backward selection or a full model approach should be used, depending on a priori knowledge.
- *Model performance measures*: Discrimination (e.g., c-index), calibration (plots), and (re)classification measures.
- *Internal validation*: Bootstrapping techniques can quantify the model's potential for overfitting, its optimism in estimated model performance measures, and a shrinkage factor to adjust for this optimism.
- *Added value of predictor/test/marker*: Should be pursued for subsequent (or new) predictors, certainly if their measurement is burdensome and costly. Because overall performance measures (e.g., c-index) are often insensitive to small improvements, reclassification measures may be used for this purpose.

Reproduced from Moons KGM, et al. Risk prediction models: I. Development, internal validation, and assessing the incremental value of a new (bio)marker. *Heart.* BMJ (2012), with permission from BMJ Publishing Group Ltd.

Moons et al., 2012b; Steyerberg, 2009; Steyerberg et al., 2000; Steyerberg et al., 2001; Van Houwelingen & Le Cessie, 1990; Vergouwe et al., 2002].

Rationale for the Study

Persistence of a major depressive episode (MDE) is a common and serious problem. If the persistence risk can be estimated accurately, treatment may be tailored to an individual patient's needs. If the risk of persistence is small, a policy of watchful waiting might be adopted, while a high risk of persistence may call for immediate and possibly more aggressive treatment (e.g., antidepressant drug therapy in combination with psychotherapy). Setting a prognosis in individual cases with MDE, however, is notoriously difficult and lacks a sound empirical basis. Although many studies of depressed patients identified predictors of depression persistence, the analyses and presentation of the results do not allow prediction of the absolute risk in individual patients in daily practice [Sargeant et al., 1990].

Theoretical Design

The study objective was to construct a score that allows prediction of MDE persistence over 12 months in individuals with MDE, using potential determinants of persistence identified in previous research. The prognostic determinants considered were measures of social support, somatic disorders, depression severity and recurrence, and duration of previous episodes.

The occurrence relation can be represented as follows:

Persistence after 12 months = $f(d_{1-6})$

The domain in this study was confined to those individuals from the general population with MDE.

Design of Data Collection

A cohort study was performed using data collected between 1996 and 1999 in a general population survey, the Netherlands Mental Health Survey and Incidence Study (NEMESIS)] [Ten Have et al., 2005]. Two hundred and fifty patients diagnosed with MDE according to the *Diagnostic and Statistical Manual of Mental Disorders*, Third Edition revised (DSM-III-R) criteria, as assessed with the Composite International Diagnostic Interview, were identified. For these patients, all information on the six predictors under study was recorded. In an interview conducted 2 weeks to 24 months after the diagnosis (this variability was due to logistic reasons), the duration of depression was assessed using the Life Chart Interview.

Design of Data Analysis

First, a univariable analysis for each predictor was carried out to "keep in touch with the data." Then a multivariable Cox proportional hazards regression model with time to recovery (i.e., no more persistence) as the outcome variable and the six predefined predictors as the independent variables was run. The Cox model, instead of the usual logistic regression model, was applied to account for the varying follow-up times across patients.

The aim of the analysis was to calculate the absolute 12-month risk of not having recovered, that is, the probability of depression persistence 12 months after the diagnosis for individual patients. This appears to be not straightforward, as the Cox regression procedure yields actual survival estimates [$S(t)$] only. These estimates represent the predicted risks of depression persistence for each patient given the patient's follow-up time and values of the prognostic determinants.

Actual survival estimates are defined as:

$$S(t) = S_0(t)^{\exp(LP)}$$

where the linear predictor (LP) is $b_1 \times X_1 + b_2 \times X_2 + \ldots b_n \times X_n$, with the Xs denoting the predictor values of a specific patient and the b's denoting the regression coefficients.

The baseline survival function $S_0(t)$ is the time-dependent cumulative risk of persistence of depression for a person with none of the predictors present, that is, the LP being zero and thus $S_0(t) = S(t)$.

The baseline survival function [$S_0(t)$] can be calculated by remolding the given formula as follows: $S_0(t) = S(t)^{1/\exp(LP)}$. This calculation allowed us to calculate the cumulative 12-month baseline risk from the database for those patients who actually had 12 months of follow-up ($S_0[12 \text{ months}]$). In our study, this value appeared to be 0.2029 (20.3%). The final step is to calculate the 12-month risk for all patients using this S_0(12 months) and an individual's LP, the latter thus representing the individual patient's part of the risk.

In the formula, $S(12 \text{ months}) = S_0(12 \text{ months})^{\exp(LP)} = 0.2029^{\exp(LP)}$.

The 12-month time span was primarily chosen on clinical grounds but also because at that follow-up time, the number of patients at risk of relapse was still sufficiently large. To evaluate the calibration of the model, that is, to assess the extent to which the model predictions are in agreement with the observed probabilities, we calculated the Kaplan-Meier estimate of the 12-month risk of depression persistence for each decile of predicted risk and compared these using a scatter diagram.

As a next step, the discriminatory power of the model was quantified. Because the outcomes of the censored patients are unknown, the construction of a ROC curve for the evaluation of discriminatory power, such as those cal-culated for logistic regression models, is impossible. However, the c-statistic can be calculated. It is numerical and, with regard to interpretation, equal to the area under the ROC curve; it reflects the probability that for a random pair of patients, the one who has the outcome event first has the highest predicted probability. The concordance statistic (as the area under the ROC curve) is an overall measure of discriminatory power. A value of 0.5 indicates no discrimi-nation and a value of 1.0 indicates perfect discrimination between those developing and not developing the study outcome, in this case depression persistence during the defined time period [Altman & Royston, 2000a]. Both the regression coefficients and therefore also the hazard ratios (the regression coefficient, which is interpreted as a relative risk) with their 95% confidence intervals, as well as the c-statistic, were adjusted for overfitting or over-optimism using bootstrapping techniques [Efron & Tibshirani, 1993]. To this end, 100 random bootstrap samples with replacement were drawn from the data set with complete data on all predictors ($N = 250$). The model's predictive performance after bootstrapping is the performance that can be expected when the model is applied to future similar populations.

To construct an easily applicable "persistence of depression score," each coefficient from the model was transformed to a rounded number. As the coefficients reflect the relative weight of each variable in the prediction, they were transformed to a number of points in a uniform way; that is, each coefficient was divided by the coefficient closest to zero, in this case –.107. The number of points was subsequently rounded to the nearest integer. The total score for each individual patient was determined by assigning the points for each variable present and adding them up.

The predicted probability of persistence of depression at 12 months fol-low-up was presented according to four broad categories of the risk score for reasons of statistical stability and practical applicability. The categories were arbitrarily chosen with a view to reasonable size of each category as well as clinical sensibility. Next, the score was transformed to a dichotomous "prog-nostic test," allowing each patient to be classified as at high or low risk of depression persistence. Sensitivity, specificity, and the positive and negative predictive value of categorized values of the score were calculated for the same cut-offs of the score as those used to delineate the scoring categories. Data were analyzed using SPSS 12.0 and S-plus 2000 software programs.

Results

Follow-up time ranged from 2 weeks to 24 months and 187 subjects out of the total population ($N = 250$) recovered. The final proportional hazards

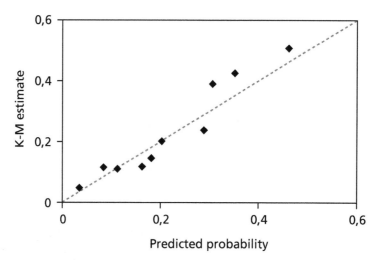

FIGURE 4–1   Calibration plot of the Cox proportional hazards model for the prediction of depression persistence at 12 months of follow-up. The dotted line represents the line of identity, that is, perfect calibration model.

Reproduced with permission from Spijker J, de Graaf R, Ormel J, Nolen WA, Grobbee DE, Burger H. The persistence of depression score. *Acta Psychiatr Scand* 2006;114:411–6.

regression model appeared to be reasonably calibrated as the predicted and observed probabilities were similar over the entire range (see **Figure 4–1**).

The shrinkage factor for the coefficients that was obtained from the bootstrap process was 0.91. The results presented are based on the findings after shrinkage. Coefficients from the model as well as the hazard ratios as measures of relative risk are displayed in **Table 4–5**, together with the risk points per predictor.

Table 4–6 shows the relationship between categories of the score, the observed risk, and the predicted risk of MDE persistence after 1 year. The mean risk was 23% and the predicted risks increased from 7–40% with increasing score categories and were generally in agreement with the observed risk. From Table 4–4, it can also be seen that the patient introduced earlier has a 29% risk of persistence of depression. The overall discriminatory power of the score was fair, with a c-statistic of 0.68. For specific cut-offs, the sensitivity, specificity, and predictive values are also shown.

If, for instance, a cut-off ≥ 5 is chosen as the threshold for a high risk of persistence and thus requires more intense treatment, 69% (sensitivity) of those who would still suffer depression after 1 year will have received this treatment, however, 12% (1-NPV) of those who did not undergo the more intense treatment because their test was negative will have persisting MDE.

TABLE 4–5   Multivariable Predictors of Recovery from Depression at 12 Months

Predictor	Coefficient	Hazard Ratio (95% Confidence Interval)	Contribution to Risk Score
Somatic disorder	–0,319	0.73 (0.54–0.97)	3
Medium social support	–0,107	0.90 (0.64–1.27)	1
Low social support	–0,420	0.66 (0.46–0.95)	4
Severe depression	–0,314	0.73 (0.53–1.01)	3
Recurrent depression	0,392	1.48 (1.10–1.99)	–4
Long duration previous episodes	–0,426	0.65 (0.48–0.89)	4

Total risk score = physical illness*3 + medium social support + low social support*4 + severe depression*3 – recurrent depression*4 + long duration previous episodes*4.

The total risk score was calculated using the formula at the bottom of the table. For instance, a subject with a severe and recurrent MDE, with a comorbid somatic disorder and low social support, has a score of + 3 – 4 + 3 + 4 = 6 points.

Reproduced from Spijker J, de Graaf R, Ormel J, Nolan WA, Grobbee DE, Burger H. The persistence of depression score. *Acta Psychiatr Scand.* 2006;114:411-16.

TABLE 4–6   Prognostic Test Characteristics for 12-month Depression Persistence

Cut-off Score	N (%)	Sensitivity	Specificity	PPV	1-NPV
≥ 2	184 (74%)	93%	32%	27%	7%
≥ 5	109 (44%)	69%	63%	34%	12%
≥ 8	49 (20%)	36%	85%	40%	17%

Reproduced from Spijker J, de Graaf R, Ormel J, Nolan WA, Grobbee DE, Burger H. The persistence of depression score. *Acta Psychiatr Scand.* 2006;114:411–16.

It should be noted that the discriminatory power of the resulting score is modest with a c-statistic of 0.68, in particular when compared with c-statistics or, equivalently, areas under the curve of the ROC curve obtained in many diagnostic studies. However, it must be kept in mind that by nature of the close temporal relationship between predictors and outcome, measures of discrimination generally achieve higher values in diagnostic than in prognostic settings.

It was concluded that the study yielded a risk score for the prediction of persistence of MDE in the general population with depression with reasonable performance. The score may be of value to clinical practice in providing a rational basis for treatment decisions, but external validation in that setting is required before the score is applied in daily practice.

CONCLUSION

Prognostic research shows great similarity to diagnostic research; in fact, prognoses can be seen as diagnoses in the future. Most importantly, they are both variants of prediction research. To ensure applicability of prognostic (and diagnostic) research in clinical practice, several prerequisites should be met:

1. Assemble a patient population that reflects a carefully determined domain in clinical practice.
2. Measure all potential predictors using similar methods as in clinical practice.
3. Measure a clinically relevant outcome as accurately as possible, and in all study subjects.
4. In the analysis, use absolute rather than relative risk estimates.
5. Do not worry about confounding, as it is a non-issue in prediction research.
6. Do not start with too many predictors relative to the number of outcome events or subjects.
7. Include predictors in the model that add to the predictive power of the model, but beware of data-driven selection of predictors. This is an argument against stepwise regression models.
8. Take care that in the presentation the absolute risks can be calculated for (all) predictor combinations in a practical way, for instance, using a risk score or nomogram.
9. Assess the discriminatory power and the calibration of the prediction model.
10. Take care that the model is internally validated and corrected (shrunk) for over-optimism, for example, by bootstrapping, heuristic shrinkage methods, or penalized regression modeling.
11. Apply the model to a different population representing the same domain for external validation before applying the score in daily practice.

Implementation of well-conducted prognostic research may greatly contribute to the efficiency of medical practice and reduce the suffering from disease. Undoubtedly, the introduction of computerized patient records will further increase the interest in multivariable prediction models as described here, because their development, validation, and application in research settings as well as in routine care becomes much more feasible.

Chapter 5

Intervention Research: Intended Effects

INTRODUCTION

Effective treatment is the stronghold of modern medicine. Despite all other types of care clinical medicine has to offer, patients and physicians alike expect first and foremost that diseases can be cured and symptoms relieved by appropriate interventions. Evidence-based treatment—or prevention for that matter—demands the unequivocal demonstration by empirical research of the efficacy and safety of the intervention. In general, all interventions are characterized by intended and unintended effects, where the intended effects (main effects) are those for which the treatments are given. However, interventions also have unintended effects. These may range from relatively trivial discipline required by the patient to adhere to the intervention to potentially life-threatening adverse effects. Ideally, intended effects should be highly common, predictable, and large, and unintended effects rare and mild. Drugs and other interventions vary markedly with regard to the relative frequency and severity of unintended effects, just as they vary in effectiveness with regard to their intended effects. Intervention research aims to quantify the full spectrum of relevant effects of intervention. However, the approaches used for demonstrating the intended or primary effects generally differ from those for demonstrating safety. This chapter concentrates on intended effects.

Research on the benefits and risks of interventions is central to current clinical epidemiologic research. For centuries, the field of medicine was very limited in terms of what it had to offer for adequate treatment. This has dramatically changed in recent decades. Rapidly expanding pharmacopeias and advances in surgical techniques are both progressing, with an increasing emphasis on less invasive techniques. In medicine, *intervention* is a general term for a deliberate action intended to change the prognosis in a patient and includes drug treatment, surgery, physiotherapy, lifestyle interventions such as physical exercise, and preventive actions such as vaccination. To treat a patient with confidence, the physician needs to know about the potential benefit of the treatment (i.e., the intended or main effects of the intervention), which must be weighed against possible risks (i.e., the unintended or side effects of the intervention). The deliberate decision not to treat or to postpone treatment can be viewed as an intervention itself. Increasingly, cost considerations also play a role when choices are made between different treatment options. Money is not only an issue from the perspective of the fair and efficient use of available resources; it is also an important driving force for the development and marketing of new treatments. Pharmaceutical companies and manufacturers producing medical devices increasingly emphasize their compassion for patients as a motive for their search for new compounds, but they typically—and understandably—are primarily focused on their shareholders and profits. This elevates research on treatment effects to an arena in which huge interests play a role. As a consequence, much more than in any other area of medical research, the quality and reliability of intervention research has been the topic of major interest and development. The result is a highly sophisticated set of principles and methods that guides intervention research.

In intervention research, the principles of causal and descriptive research combine. Intervention research is commonly causal research, because it is the true effect of the intervention (i.e., *caused* by the intervention) that needs to be estimated free from confounding variables. Intervention research commonly is also prognostic; in order to use an intervention in medical practice, it is important to know as precisely as possible both the beneficial and untoward impact the intervention may have on an individual patient's prognosis. For example, for a given drug, 1-year mortality may be expected to decrease from 30% to 10% (intended or main effect), while the risk of developing orthostatic hypotension (unintended or side effect) is 10%.

To serve clinical decisions of treatment best, intervention research in general and clinical trials in particular should be viewed as the means to measure the effects of interventions on prognosis. It is generally not sufficient to know whether a treatment works. What is needed is a valid estimate of the size of the effects. In clinical epidemiologic intervention research, randomized controlled trials (RCTs) play an essential role, not only because they are often considered the only approach to definitively demonstrate the magnitude of benefits of treatment, but also because RCTs offer a role model for causal research. The principles of the design of randomized trials are quite straightforward. When appropriately understood, they also will greatly help to improve causal research under those circumstances where a randomized trial cannot be conducted. To understand the nature of randomized trials is to understand unconfounded observation.

INTERVENTION EFFECTS

The challenges of measuring the effects of an intervention can be illustrated by a simple example in which a physician is considering using a new drug to treat high blood pressure in a group of his patients. The drug has been handed to him by a sales representative, who promised a rapid decline in blood pressure for most patients, with excellent tolerability. Let us assume that the physician decides to try out the drug on the next 20 or so patients who visit his office with a first diagnosis of hypertension. He carefully records each patient's baseline blood pressure level and asks them to return a number of times for re-measurement in the next weeks. His experience with these patients is summarized in **Figure 5–1**.

The physician is satisfied. A gradual decline in systolic blood pressure is shown in his patients. Moreover, most were very pleased with the drug because the treatment had few side effects; one patient mentioned the development of mild sleeping disturbances. Would it be wise to conclude that the drug works, is well tolerated, and can now become part of routine treatment with confidence? Clearly not. There are a number of reasons why the observed response may not adequately reflect the effect caused by the drug. In order to use the drug in similar future patients, it is necessary to ensure that the response in fact resulted from the pharmacologic agent and does not reflect other mechanisms. Although a patient may not care why the reduction occurred as long as the hypertension was treated, from a sensible medical viewpoint it is necessary to know whether the effect can be attributed to

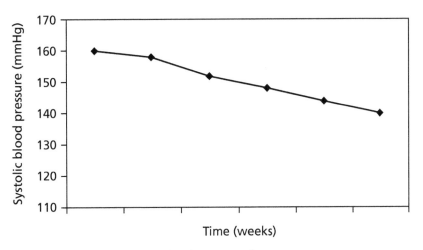

FIGURE 5–1   Hypothetical patient blood pressure data.

the drug. If it is not, then additional costs are generated, the patients is *medicalized*, and side effects may be induced without a sound scientific justification. Let us examine alternative explanations for the observation made by the physician.

Natural History and Regression Toward the Mean

The first question to be answered is whether the same blood pressure response would have been observed if no treatment was given. In other words, is it possible that the natural history of the disease would explain the change over time? *Natural history* is the variability in symptoms and signs of a disease not explained by treatment, which is the prognosis of the disease in the absence of treatment. Many factors can cause changes in the presence or manifestations of disease, and many mechanisms that lead to changes in an individual's course of disease are not understood. Still, the force of natural history can be very powerful. In a study of over a 1,000 women in Sweden with symptoms suggestive of urinary tract infection, confirmed with urine cultures, the spontaneous cure rate of symptoms was 28% after the first week, and 37% had neither symptoms nor bacteria after 5–7 weeks [Ferry et al., 2004]. Spontaneous remission or cure of symptoms or conditions may occur in many diseases. In research aimed at quantifying treatment effects, there is no exception to the rule that the effect of treatment needs to be separated from the natural course of the disease.

An important component of natural history is created by *regression toward the mean*. Regression toward the mean occurs for any measure of disease (severity) or other patient variable and can be explained by a combination of intra-individual variability and selection. The way regression toward the mean works is simple. If patients are selected according to their relatively high or low values of a characteristic that shows intra-individual variability, the value of that variable on re-measurement will be lower or higher, respectively. The cause of the intra-individual variability is irrelevant. It can be a reflection of variation in the measurement, circadian patterns, or some other unknown, biologic mechanism. The magnitude of the effect depends on the magnitude of variability and the level of selection.

This can be illustrated by the classification of individuals as hypertensive and the subsequent re-measurement of blood pressure in the selected group (see **Figure 5–2**). Suppose that all individuals are selected with an initial systolic blood pressure at or above 140 mm Hg. Because blood pressure shows a certain degree of variability in all subjects, some of these individuals will have blood pressure levels above their average level at the time

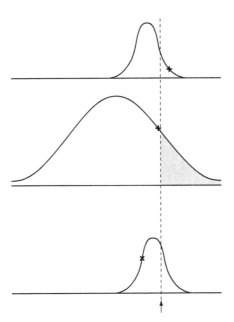

FIGURE 5–2   Mechanism of regression to the mean.

of the measurement. These individuals are more likely to have lower than higher blood pressure levels at a subsequent measurement. Individuals who had a blood pressure below their usual average level and below the cut-off point at the time of the first measurement were classified too low relative to their usual blood pressure and they will not be re-measured, while those individuals in whom the observed value was too high relative to their usual blood pressure level will be re-measured along with all those whose measured blood pressure above 140 mm Hg adequately reflected their usual pressure. Because the selected population subgroup includes more subjects whose blood pressure will be lower on re-measurement than subjects whose blood pressure will be higher at the time of re-measurement, the average blood pressure of the selected population will fall. Regression toward the mean is the inevitable consequence of selection based on a variable that shows variation. Virtually all variables that are measured in clinical research show some degree of intra-individual variability. Also, variables that appear stone solid, such as height or bone density, show some variability when measured in groups, if only because measurement errors can never be completely excluded and these will lead to some degree of variability. Clearly, the issue is more prominent for measures that are inherently variable such as blood pressure, temperature, or measures of pain. The first report of regression toward the mean dates back to the work of Francis Galton [1886], who authored the paper entitled, "Regression Towards Mediocrity in Hereditary Stature." Galton related the heights of children to the average height of their parents, which he called the mid-parent height (see **Figure 5–3**).

Children and parents had the same mean height of 68.2 inches. The ranges differed, however, because the mid-parent height was an average of two observations and thus had a smaller range. Now, consider those parents with a relatively high mid-height between 70 and 71 inches. The mean height of their children was 69.5 inches, which was closer to the mean height of all children than the mean height of their parents was to the mean height of all parents. Galton called this phenomenon *regression toward mediocrity*. The term was coined with this report, but the observation is different from what is currently considered regression toward the mean because this concerned the full population without selection. The principle, however, is the same.

Regression toward the mean is not an exclusive phenomenon in epidemiologic research. Consider, for example, students who take a clinical

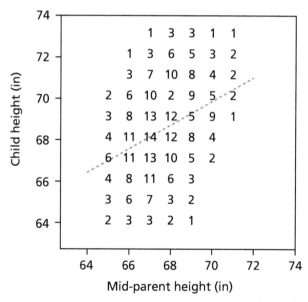

FIGURE 5–3 Comparison of the heights of children to their parents made by Francis Galton (1822–1911). Diagonal line shows the average height.

Reproduced from Bland JM, Altman DG. Statistic notes: regression towards the mean. *BMJ* 1994:308:1499 with permission from BMJ Publishing Group Ltd.

epidemiology exam. Students who receive an unexpected, extremely low score will probably get a better score when they repeat the exam, even when they put no further effort into understanding the topic. It is likely that some bad luck was involved in getting the exceptional score, and this bad luck is unlikely to occur for a second time in a row, given the usual higher score in this student. It is a common mistake in everyday life to assign a causal role to something apparently related to the observed effect that in reality is likely due to regression toward the mean. Take, for example, the case of the poor badminton champion from Kuala Lumpur (see **Box 5–1**). Some of this champion's predecessors very likely achieved greater than their usual level of performances because of a lucky play of chance, and their subsequent downfall was attributed to the "spoiling" by gifts of appreciation.

In medicine, regression toward the mean is also known as "the doctors' friend." General practitioners (GPs) use time as one of their main tools in differentiating between serious and less serious problems. Worried mothers call their GP when they measure a high temperature in their sick child. When the doctor arrives or the parents and child arrive at the emergency room, the temperature often has fallen. People tend to self-select themselves at peak levels of symptoms, such as temperature, cough, depressive symptoms, and pain. Many will show "spontaneous" decline because of regression toward the mean and natural history. The solution in practice is to wait and re-measure. Similarly, in research the approach to removing regression toward the mean is to re-measure and select only those who show stable levels of, for example, elevated blood pressure before entering into a study.

BOX 5–1   Depression Toward the Mean in Badminton

KUALA LUMPUR: Prime Minister Datuk Seri Dr. Mahathir Mohamad congratulated Malaysian shuttler Mohd Hafiz Hashim for his achievement but warned that he should not be "spoilt" with gifts like previous champions.

Dr. Mahathir said people should remember what had happened to previous champions when they were spoilt with gifts of land, money and other items.

"I hope the states will not start giving acres of land and money in the millions, because they all seem not to be able to play badminton after that," he said after taking part in the last dry run and dress rehearsal for the 13th NAM Summit at the PWTC yesterday.

Modified from "Mahathir asks states not to 'spoil' Hafiz," The Star Online, 2/18/2003.

Regression toward the mean is but one component of natural history and it is an entirely statistical phenomenon. There are many other factors that may influence natural history that are linked to the outcome by some pathophysiologic mechanism. When this is known, we may try to adjust our observation based on this knowledge. Typically, however, determinants of natural history are unknown and cannot simply be subtracted from the observed effect.

Extraneous Effects

A second reason why the physician observed a response following drug treatment (but one that is not a result of drug treatment) may be that other determinants of blood pressure changed concomitantly. The patients were told that they had high blood pressure and that this is a risk factor for stroke and myocardial infarction that should be treated. This information could motivate patients to try to adjust their lifestyle. They may have improved their diet, started exercising, or reduced alcohol intake. All of these actions also may have reduced the blood pressure. These effects are called extraneous because they are outside of the effect of interest, namely the drug effect. In a study, we may attempt to measure extraneous effects and take these into account in the observation, but this requires that the effects be known and measurable.

There is one particularly well-known extraneous effect that is so closely linked to the intervention that it generally cannot be directly measured or separated from the drug effect: the *placebo effect*. Placebo effects can result simply from contact with physicians when a diagnosis or simple attention from a respected professional alleviates anxiety. As Hróbjartsson [1996] put it, "Any therapeutic meeting between a conscious patient and a doctor has the potential of initiating a placebo effect." In research, obtaining informed consent has been shown to induce a placebo effect. There is a wealth of literature on placebo effects and considerable dispute on the mechanism of action. Clearly, psychological mechanisms are likely to play a role, and certain personality characteristics have been particularly related to strong placebo responses [Swartzman & Burkell, 1998]. In addition, other, seemingly pharmacologic phenomena are related to placebo responses. For example, the placebo response to placebo-induced analgesia can be reversed by naloxone, an opioid antagonist [Fields & Price, 1997]. Obviously, the type of outcome that is being studied is related to the presence and magnitude of a placebo response. Outcomes that are more subjective, such as anxiety or mood, will be more prone to placebo effects. Expectation also powerfully influences how subjects respond to either an inert or active substance. In a study where subjects were given sugar water but were told that it was an emetic, 80% of patients responded by vomiting [Hahn, 1997].

Placebo effects are, to a greater or lesser extent, an inherent component of interventions and they will obscure the measurement of the intervention effect of interest, such as the pharmacologic action of a drug. This may or may not be a problem in intervention research. Again, from the perspective of the patient, it does not really matter whether the relief results in part from a placebo effect of the drug. Cure is cure. Similarly, from the viewpoint of the physician, the placebo effect may be a welcome additional benefit of an intervention. Even for an investigator studying the benefits of treatment, the placebo effect can be accepted as something that is inseparable from the drug effect and therefore should be included in the overall estimate of the benefit of one treatment compared to another (e.g., non-drug) treatment strategy. Different treatments may have different placebo effects and this will also explain differences in benefits when employed in real life. In other words, the need to exclude placebo effects in research on benefits and risks of interventions is not a given and depends on the objectives of the investigator. Although many believe that the best evidence for treatment effects comes from trials in which a placebo effect has been ruled out by comparing treatment to placebo treatment, there are good examples of research where potential placebo effects were included in the measured treatment effect that provide a more meaningful result than when placebo effects were removed. The motives and consequences of research that does or does not separate the pharmacologic from the placebo effects were well outlined in a classic paper by Schwarz and Lellouch [1967] on pragmatic and explanatory trials. Their article gives an example from a real case in which a decision needed to be made between different options to determine the benefits of a drug aimed at sensitizing cancer patients for required radiotherapy. The assumption was that when patients were pretreated with the drug, the effect of the radiotherapy was enhanced. The investigators decided to do a randomized comparison between usual therapy and the new treatment scheme. For the usual therapy arm of the study, there were two options (see **Figure 5–4**, taken from the original report by Schwarz and Lellouch). One option was to just treat the patients as usual, which implied the immediate treatment with radiotherapy. The alternative option was to first give a placebo drug and then start radiotherapy. In the second option, placebo effects from the drug would be removed from the comparison. However, radiotherapy would be put at a disadvantage because compared to the approach in daily practice the installment of radiotherapy would be delayed. In contrast, in the first option the new approach would be compared to the optimal way of delivering radiotherapy without the sensitizing

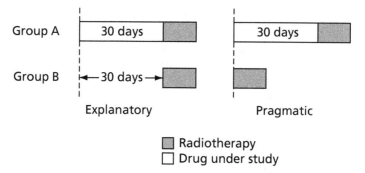

FIGURE 5–4   Trial arms where placebo effects are removed (explanatory) and where the placebo effect was considered to be part of the overall treatment (pragmatic).

Reproduced from Schwartz D, Lellouch J. Explanatory and pragmatic attitudes in therapeutic trials. *J Chron Dis* 1967:20:637–4, with permission from Elsevier.

drug, but placebo effects could not be ruled out. Given that the new drug was not without side effects, a distinction between the pharmacologic and placebo benefits seemed important. There is no single best solution to this problem. Probably, when little is known about a drug, first a comparison with placebo is necessary to determine the true pharmacologic action devoid from placebo effects. Next, the researcher can establish its value in real life as compared with the best standard treatment, in this case immediate radiotherapy. The result of either comparison also determines the relevance of the answer.

Suppose that in the blinded comparison radiotherapy (without the new drug) still is shown to be superior. Now, a comparison with immediate radiotherapy is not needed because, if anything, the effect would be even more beneficial than when combined with the new strategy. In their article, the authors propose the term *explanatory* for a trial in which placebo effects are removed and the term *pragmatic* for a study in which placebo and other extraneous effects are taken as part of the overall treatment response of interest. There are many circumstances in which the true effects, without placebo effects, of a drug are well established and where a pragmatic trial will deliver a result that better reflects the anticipated effect in real life than an explanatory trial. In some cases, the apparent "main" intervention is not even the most important part of the strategy. For example, in a pragmatic randomized trial comparing the effect of minimally invasive coronary bypass surgery to conventional bypass grafting on postsurgery cognitive decline, the assumption was that the necessary use of a cardiopulmonary pump during conventional surgery was the most important component of the intervention with regard to adverse effects on cognitive function [Van Dijk et al., 2002].

Unfortunately, the term *pragmatic* sounds somewhat less scientific and rigorous, and some investigators are hesitant to refrain from rigorous placebo control in their research. In doing so, they may eventually produce results that do not adequately address the question that medical practitioners need to have answered. It is important to understand that removal of placebo and other extraneous effects is a deliberate decision that an investigator needs to make in the design of a study; in some cases pragmatic studies may be the preferred option. There is ample confusion about the nature of pragmatic intervention research. For example, some authors propose that explanatory studies "recruit as homogeneous a population as possible and aim primarily to further scientific knowledge" or that "in a pragmatic trial it is neither necessary nor always desirable for all subjects to complete the trial in the group to which they were allocated" [Roland & Torgerson, 1998]. These views are erroneous. The homogeneity of the study population may affect the generalizability and relates to the domain of a study irrespective of whether a trial is pragmatic or explanatory. In both explanatory and pragmatic trials, patients sometimes complete the study in the group to which they were not randomized; for example, they may need the treatment originally allocated to the other group and thus "cross-over" from one treatment arm to the other. This is common and not a problem as long as the patients are analyzed according to allocated treatment, that is, by *intention to treat*. "Pragmatic" and "explanatory" do not refer to the methodologic rigor or the scientific value of the knowledge that is generated. The distinction between pragmatic and explanatory trials reflects the nature of the comparison that is being made. In pragmatic studies, the treatment response is the total difference between two treatments (i.e., treatment strategies), including treatment and associated placebo or other extraneous effects, and this will often better reflect the likely response in practice.

Observation Effects

The third, and last, reason for an observed response to treatment that is not attributable to the treatment lies in the influence of the observer/researcher or the observed (participant) on the measurement of the outcome (see **Figure 5–5**).

Without deliberate intention, the observer may favorably interpret the report of a patient or adjust (round up or down) measurement results to better values. The observation effect is that which an observer or the observed participant has on the particular observations made. *Observer bias* is a systematic effect that moves the observed effect from the true effect.

FIGURE 5–5   Observer-observee difference in perceived response to treatment.

Observation effects may well reflect an interaction between observer and patient. For example, a physician has just received a sample of a new drug that is reputed to work exceptionally well in cases of chronic sleeping problems. When Mrs. Jones visits his surgery again with a long-lasting complaint of sleeping problems so far resistant to any medication, the doctor proposes this new miracle drug, which may offer a last resort. At the next visit, Mrs. Jones may be inclined not to disappoint her doctor again and gives a somewhat positively colored account of her sleeping history in the last couple of weeks. At the same time, the physician is reluctant to accept yet another failure of treatment in this patient. Together they create a biased observation of an otherwise unchanged problem. Just as with placebo effects, the magnitude of the potential for observation effects will depend on the type of observation that is being made. The "softer" the outcome, the more room for observation effects. In a study on the benefits of a drug in patients with ischemic cardiac disease, measures of quality of life and angina will be more susceptible to observer bias than vital status or myocardial infarction, although the latter is also sufficiently subjective to be affected. For example, disagreement in the determination of electrocardiographic ST-segment elevation by emergency physicians occurs frequently and is related to the amount of ST-segment elevation present on the electrocardiogram.

TREATMENT EFFECT

Despite all of the reasons why an observed treatment response need not necessarily show the benefit of the treatment per se, obviously there is the possibility that the effect being observed is entirely or in part the result of the treatment. In intervention research, the mission is to extract from the observation the component in which we are interested. This can only be achieved by comparing a group of patients who are being treated to a group of patients who are not treated or who are treated differently. There is no way in which a valid estimate of the effect of a drug or other treatment can be obtained from observing treated patients only. Consequently, in the example of the physician trying out a new antihypertensive drug, there is no way that the true effect of the new drug can be determined from the overall observation. A comparative study is needed. The treatment effect and the three alternative explanations for the observed treatment response (natural history, extraneous effects, and observation effects), as well as the handling of the latter three in research, can be illustrated by a simple equation. In a comparative study where a treatment, for example a drug named "R_x," is compared to no treatment at all, the responses in the index (i.e., treated) group can be summarized as follows [Lubsen & de Lang, 1987]:

$$OE_i = R_x + NH_i + EF_i + OB_i$$

where OE_i is the observed effect in the index group, R_x is the treatment effect, NH_i is the effect of natural history, EF_i is the effect of extraneous factors including placebo effects, and OB_i is the observation effect in the index group.

The corresponding equation in the reference (r) group not receiving the intervention is:

$$OE_r = NH_r + EF_r + OB_r$$

The difference between the effects observed in the two comparison groups can be written as:

$$OE_i - OE_r = R_x + (NH_i - NH_r) + (EF_i - EF_r) + (OB_i - OB_r)$$

If the interest is in the treatment effect per se, in this example the single pharmacologic effect of the drug, R_x, $OE_i - OE_r$ needs to equal R_x. To achieve this, the other terms need to cancel out. Consequently, NH_i needs to equal NH_r, EF_i needs to equal EF_r, and OB_i needs to equal OB_r. The equation for a comparison between two treatments (an index treatment R_{xi} and reference treatment R_{xr}) is the same except that after cancelling out the other terms, $OE_i - OE_r$ now equals $R_{xi} - R_{xr}$, that is, the net benefit of the index treatment over the other.

The principles of intervention research can be summarized as ways to make all terms in the equation in the two groups the same, except for the treatment term. This means that natural history, extraneous effects, and observation effects are made the same in the groups that are compared. Note that an alternative way to achieve comparability of natural history, extraneous effects, and observation effects is by removing them completely from the study. However, this is generally impossible to achieve. Rather, by accepting these effects and ensuring that they are cancelled out in the observation, a valid estimate of the treatment effect is obtained.

COMPARABILITY OF NATURAL HISTORY

Comparability of natural history is a *conditio sine qua non* (Latin legal term meaning "without which it could not be") in intervention research. Because natural history may be highly variable between individuals, an intervention effect estimated from research that includes effects from natural history cannot be generalized to what can be expected in practice. Consequently, it is of critical importance that in a comparison between two or more groups to estimate the effect of an intervention, the effects of natural history are the same in all groups.

There are several ways in which this can be achieved. First, a quasi-experimental study can be conducted where the participants in the groups are carefully selected in such a way that each group represents the same distribution of natural histories. For example, in a comparison of two anticancer drugs for treatment of leukemia, patients in the two groups can be deliberately selected so that they have a similar age, proportion of males, severity of the disease, and so on. One could even go as far as to closely match each individual in the index group to an individual from the reference group according to characteristics expected to be related to prognostic characteristics expected to determine natural history. This would improve the probability that, in the absence of treatment, the two groups would show the same natural history and, therefore, an observed difference in response would not reflect a difference in natural history. A related approach would be to restrict the entire study population to a highly homogeneous group of patients who, because of their similarity, are expected to all have a highly similar prognosis (natural history). Alternatively, there could be no preselection made and patients could receive treatment as deemed by the physician, but prognostic indicators would be recorded in detail. Clearly, initiation of a specific intervention in daily practice is everything but random because physicians tend to treat those patients with a relatively poor prognosis more often. Therefore, in the statistical analysis of the data from the study, multivariate adjustments should be made to remove the effect of differences in natural history from the comparison.

A necessary requirement for either of these approaches to ensure comparability of natural history is that all relevant prognostic factors that could be different between the groups are known and can be measured validly. In addition, the source population of patients should be large enough to make preselection and matching possible. Similarly, for multivariate analysis, the size of the study population should be large enough to allow for statistical adjustments. The overriding problem, however, is that comprehensive knowledge of all relevant prognostic factors is typically lacking. A variable that is not known or measured cannot be taken into account in preselecting study groups, nor can it be controlled for in the analysis. This holds true for any causal research where the effect of an exposure needs to be separated from other related but confounding determinants of the outcome. However, the problem in intervention research is accentuated because of the complexity of the decision to treat patients. In setting an indication for prescribing a drug to a patient, the treating physician will take many factors into consideration such as the severity of the disease, the likelihood of good tolerance and compliance, the experience in this patient with previous treatments, the patient's preference, and so forth. When groups of patients with the same disease but with and without a prescription for treatment by a physician are compared, they are probably different in many ways, some of which can be measured while others are very implicit and neither reflected in the patient file nor measurable through additional efforts. The indication for treatment (i.e., the composite of all reasons to initiate it) is a very strong prognostic indicator. If a patient is judged to have an indication to use a drug, this patient probably has a more severe untreated prognosis than a patient with the same diagnosis in which the physician decides to

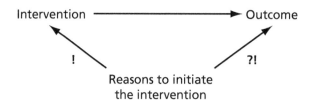

FIGURE 5–6   Reasons underlying the decision to intitiate treatment are important potential confounders.

wait before deciding on drug treatment. The effect on natural history of the presence or absence of a pertinent indication in patients with the same disease who are or are not treated is termed *confounding by indication* [Grobbee & Hoes, 1997].

Figure 5–6 shows that the reasons underlying the decision to initiate treatment are important potential confounders. These reasons, often re-lated to patient characteristics such as severity of disease, by definition are associated with the probability of receiving the intervention (illustrated by the exclamation mark). If these reasons are also related to the probability of developing the outcome, which is the case where patients with more severe disease are more prone (or less prone for that matter) to receive the inter-vention, then the right arrow also exists. Consequently, confounding will occur.

Although many drugs can affect the course of a disease positively, the outcome in people with that disease compared to those who do not have it or who have a less severe form may be worse or, at best, similar. Confound-ing by indication can completely obscure an intervention effect when treated and untreated patients are compared who do or do not receive the intervention in routine care. To illustrate this effect, **Table 5–1** shows the risks for cardiovascular mortality in women with hypertension who partici-pated in a population-based cohort study and were either treated or not treated by their physicians.

The crude rate ratio for mortality was 1, suggesting that the treatment had no effect because the treated and untreated hypertensive groups had the same cardiovascular mortality risk. However, when adjustments were made for a number of factors that were expected to be related to both the indication for treatment and cardiovascular mortality, and thus possibly were confounding the comparison, the rate ratio dropped in a way that was compatible with the rate for a benefit of treatment.

Whether the adjusted rate ratio reflects the true treatment effect de-pends on whether an adjustment was made for all of the differences in

TABLE 5-1   Crude and Adjusted Rate Ratios for Death from Cardiovascular Causes in Untreated and Drug Treated Women that Were All Hypertensive According to Common Criteria

	Rate Ratio (95% Confidence Interval)
Crude value	1.0 (0.6 to 1.5)
Adjusted for:	
Age	0.7 (0.4 to 1.1)
+ Body mass index, pulse rate	0.6 (0.4 to 1.0)
+ Smoking, lipid concentrations	0.6 (0.4 to 0.9)
+ Diabetes	0.5 (0.3 to 0.9)

Reproduced from Grobbee DE, Hoes AW. Confounding and indication for treatment in evaluation of drug treatment for hypertension. BMJ 1997;315:1151-1154.

confounding variables between the treated and untreated groups. This conclusion is very difficult to draw. Confounding by indication commonly creates insurmountable problems for nonrandomized research on intended effects of treatment. Valid inferences can much more likely be drawn under those rare circumstances in which (1) groups of patients with the same indications but different treatments can be compared and (2) residual dissimilarities in characteristics in patients receiving different treatments for the same indications are known, adequately measured, and can be adjusted for. For example, Psaty et al. [1995] compared the effects of several antihypertensive drugs on the risk of angina and myocardial infarction. In a case-control study, they selected patients who all shared the indication for drug treatment for hypertension. Consequently, both cases and controls had this indication. In addition, they took ample measures to exclude residual confounding by indication, notably in the design of data analysis.

Apart from the reasons to start an intervention (i.e., the indication), reasons to refrain from initiating the intervention may act as confounding variables. This is sometimes referred to as *confounding by contraindication*. Just as with confounding by indication (see Figure 5–6), these reasons (e.g., patient characteristics known to increase the risk of developing unintended or side effects of the intervention) will be associated with the probability of receiving the intervention, albeit here the association represented by the left arrow will be inverse. If these reasons not to start the intervention are also associated with the probability of developing the outcome of interest, (i.e., the right arrow exists), then confounding is very likely to occur. Such confounding by contraindication is illustrated in a study on the putative association between the use of the drug ibopamine and mortality, after its use was restricted in 1995 [Feenstra et al., 2001]. In a comparison between patients using the drug before and after September 8, 1995, the relative risk for death associated with the use of ibopamine was 3.02 (95% confidence interval [CI], 2.12–4.30) for the period before and 0.71 (CI, 0.53–0.96) for the period after September 2008. The marked inversion of the relative risk estimate is very likely the result of a changed practice in the use of (relative) contraindications in these patients. Apparently, ibopamide was preferentially prescribed to patients with a much lower mortality risk after 1995 than in the preceding period. Consequently, the observed mortality risk in users of ibopamide was reduced. We will only use the term confounding by indication (where indication is then defined as reasons to initiate or refrain from a certain intervention) to indicate circumstances when the reasons to start or not to initiate the intervention are also related to the beneficial or unfavorable outcome of interest, and, thus, confounding may occur.

RANDOMIZATION

The most effective way to resolve the problem of confounding by indication and other confounding effects of differences in natural history in a comparative study is by randomization (**Figure 5–7**). *Randomization* means that the treatment is allocated at random to individual participants in a study. Indication for drug use is thus set randomly. Any resulting difference in prognosis in the absence of treatment between randomized groups is the sole result of random imbalances. The risk of remaining prognostic differences is thus inversely related to the size of the population that is randomized.

Figure 5–7 shows the major strength of random allocation of patients to an intervention. Because of randomization, the distribution of all known and unknown reasons to start or not to start an intervention that would apply in daily practice (and that may be related to the occurrence of the outcome) are made similar in the two comparison groups. Consequently, there will be no association between (contra)indications and the probability of receiving the intervention: The left arrow does not exist and there will be no confounding. Obviously, patients with an unequivocal indication or

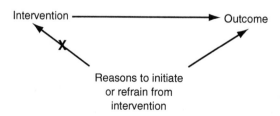

FIGURE 5–7 Major strength of a random allocation of patients to an intervention.

clear contraindication cannot be randomized and would in any event not reflect the domain of a study to determine the effects of an intervention.

Typically, randomizing groups of 50 or more subjects to two treatment arms effectively makes the groups comparable in prognosis. The most attractive feature of randomization is that it makes groups comparable for known as well as unknown variables affecting natural history. The first account on randomization as a preferred allocation scheme in the design of experiments came from Sir Ronald A. Fisher [1935]. One of his books describes how to test the claim, using the example of a woman who said that she could distinguish by the flavor of her tea alone whether the milk or the tea was placed in the cup first. By randomizing the order in which the tea was made, Fisher was able to test if she could actually distinguish between the teas. To test the woman, eight cups of different teas were prepared, four with the tea poured into the cup first, and four with milk added first, and they were presented in random order. She correctly identified the full order, which led to a P value of 0.01 (had she made one error, the P value would have been 0.24). Note that this example also illustrates the first use of the so-called $n = 1$ *trial*, which is a randomized trial in a single subject.

The problems of confounding by natural history in treated and untreated patients and the prospects of randomization led Hill and co-workers [Medical Research Council, 1948] to be among the first to use randomized allocation to treatment in medical research in the Medical Research Council investigation into streptomycin treatment of pulmonary tuberculosis published in the *British Medical Journal*. Randomization rapidly became popular and soon became the standard for treatment allocation in experimental comparisons of treatment effects. A randomized study, better known as a randomized trial, is a prospective and experimental study by definition. Allocation to treatment is not based on a clinical indication motivated by care for the patient, but rather on a random process in patients that all share the indication and are free from contraindications, with the aim to learn about the effects of the intervention.

There are added benefits from randomization in a comparative study. One is that it provides the basis for statistical testing [Fisher, 1925]. A second consequence of randomization is that it enables blinding of participants and investigators for treatment status because the result from the allocation is unpredictable. But by far the most important reason to randomize is that it ensures comparability of natural history. It should be noted that randomization provides no guarantee that important differences in prognostic factors between randomized groups cannot occur. You may just have bad luck as randomization is by nature a random process. Or groups may just be too small. The likelihood of randomly creating groups with the same distribution of men and women when only two males and six females are randomized is clearly small. Several techniques (apart from including more subjects) can prevent randomly occurring differences in important prognostic factors across randomized groups. For example, first separate the study population into subgroups that share similar characteristics, such as a group of male and female participants; next randomize within each of the groups, and then combine the individual patients again in the eventual treatment arms. Using this so-called *stratified randomization scheme* reduces the chance that marked differences in, for example, the proportion of males and females occurs by chance during randomization.

A consequence of randomization is that statistical tests can theoretically not be used to judge eventual imbalances between groups after randomization [Knol et al., 2012]. In a baseline table of a trial, when summarizing the relevant patient characteristics at the start of the study ($t = 0$), judgment is needed to decide whether differences between groups are large enough to create problems in the comparison. There, P values to "test" whether observed differences are attributable to chance (given the "null hypothesis" of no difference between the groups) have no meaning and should not be reported. This is because any difference by definition results from chance, as long as the randomization has been carried out without manipulation. If major differences in prognostically relevant baseline characteristics are present despite adequate randomization, the potential impact on the results is often estimated by comparing the results with and without adjustment for these baseline differences. The choice of whether to adjust for baseline differences at $t = 0$ is difficult. Adjustments only can be made for observed differences in measured baseline variables, while no differences may exist in relevant variables that were not measured at baseline. Then, an adjustment could even induce dissimilarities in some prognostic variables. Any adjustment for baseline differences has an arbitrary component and may thus reduce the credibility of the results.

COMPARABILITY OF EXTRANEOUS EFFECTS

While comparability of natural history is mandatory in a comparative study on treatment effect, the extent to which extraneous effects should be the same in the comparison groups is a matter of choice. As discussed, in an explanatory trial, every effort should be made to exclude extraneous effects, including placebo effects. In a nonexperimental study, this is difficult to achieve. There, placebo effects only can be conquered when two or more treatments are compared that have similar placebo effects. In a randomized trial, placebo treatment and blinding are the two tools that ensure comparability of extraneous effects. Treatment can be compared with placebo treatment without disclosure of the allocation to the patient on the one hand and/or the investigator and healthcare professionals involved on the other. This makes the study blinded, either single- (patient) or double- (patient and observer/healthcare professional) blinded, depending on how many parties remain ignorant about the allocation. In an explanatory trial blinding is crucial to yield explanatory results, while in pragmatic studies extraneous effects are accepted as being inherently part of the intervention strategy and the use of placebo and blinding is not indicated (see **Figure 5–8**).

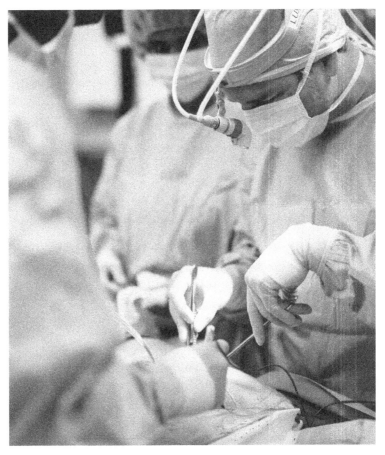

FIGURE 5–8   Tim O'Dogerty, M.D., supervises a placebo transplantation.

© Photos.com

Sometimes a choice can be made between an explanatory and a pragmatic trial for the same intervention. This choice will depend on the research question and the relevance for either type of answer in view of the aim of the investigator. For certain types of interventions, however, the obvious choice is a pragmatic study. This applies, for example, for research in which very different interventions are compared. When the question is addressed of whether the preferred mode of treatment for patients with coronary artery disease is by drugs or surgery, two different *strategies* are compared. The investigator will accept that surgery comes along with anesthesia and hospitalization while drug treatment does not. Although it cannot be excluded that aspects of the surgical procedure beyond the mere creation of an arterial bypass may have an effect on prognosis, this is accepted as an inseparable component of the strategy. Although perhaps conceptually extraneous, these components should not be considered as such in the comparison of the two strategies. This is very common in clinical research where different strategies are compared, such as physiotherapy versus watchful waiting in low back pain, psychotherapy or drug treatment in anxiety disorders, surgery or bed rest in hernia, or lifestyle intervention in diabetes.

COMPARABILITY OF OBSERVATIONS

There are a number of ways to prevent or limit observation effects. First, hard outcomes may be studied. When hard outcomes are used that can be measured objectively, such as mortality, incomparability of observations will be limited. Often, however, softer and more subjective outcomes may be more relevant for the research. Alternatively, the measurement can be highly standardized with strict protocols, which will limit the room for subjective interpretation. This will help but is not foolproof.

A more rigorous way to prevent observation effects is to separate the observation from knowledge of the intervention. By blinding the observer for the assigned treatment, the observation will not be systematically different according to treatment status even if the measurement is sensitive to subjective interpretation. To further reduce the impact of the observer, the patient also can be blinded for the intervention. Another way to separate observation from intervention knowledge is to have an observer who plays no role in the treatment. For example, in a study on the effects of different drugs on glucose control in diabetic patients, the laboratory technician measuring HbA1C need not be informed about which intervention the patients receive. Similarly, a radiologist can judge the presence of vertebral fractures in osteoporotic women participating in a trial on a new anti-osteoporotic treatment without being informed about the mode of treatment the women receive. Note that even in a trial that should preferably be pragmatic, one may still decide to conduct a blinded trial because of the type of outcome involved, with the aim to achieve comparability of observations.

TRIAL LIMITATIONS

The principles of RCTs can be fully understood by appreciation of the comparability requirements. Randomization ensures comparability of natural history ($NH_i = NH_r$). Blinding and use of placebo ensure comparability for extraneous effects ($EF_i = EF_r$). Blinding also prevents observer bias due to differential observations or measurements in either group ($OB_i = OB_r$). While comparability for natural history is always needed for a valid estimation of the treatment effect, the need for blinding varies according to the objective of the trial and the nature of the outcome that is measured. In the case of a pragmatic study, extraneous effects are included in the treatment comparison and placebo treatment is not needed. Still, blinding may be desirable to ensure unbiased outcome assessment. With very solid outcome measures, observation effects may be negligible, making blinding unnecessary.

For a trial that needs to be blinded because of the outcome measure, but has the goal of providing pragmatic knowledge (which calls for an unblinded study), one option is to make the trial only partially blinded. For example, it could be open for the patients but blind for the observers. Because confounding by differences in natural history, in particular confounding by indication, is a major problem in nonrandomized comparisons (where allocation of treatment is done by the doctor in daily practice), the use of nonexperimental studies to assess the benefits of treatment has major disadvantages. The RCT is generally the preferred option to quantify intended treatment effects.

However, there are many reasons why randomized trials, although preferred, cannot always be conducted and an alternative nonexperimental approach needs to be sought. First, the necessary number of participants needed in a particular trial may be too large to be feasible. This applies to studies where the outcome, although important, occurs at a low rate; an example is when preventive treatments are studied in low-risk populations. Low outcome rates are a particular problem in research on side effects of treatments. Take, for example, the relationship between the drug diethylstilbestrol (DES) and vaginal cancer in daughters of users. Vaginal cancer, even in the exposed group, is extremely rare. Alternatively, the expected difference in the rate of events between two interventions that are being compared may be very small, for example, when two active treatments are compared but one is only slightly better than the other. The latter situation is increasingly common for research on new treatments for an indication where an effective intervention already exists. For example, when two effective antihypertensive drugs are compared in a hypertensive population, it may take a very big study to demonstrate a small, albeit meaningful, difference in efficacy. Apart from practical restrictions, a randomized trial simply might be too expensive or time consuming. Randomized trials need considerable budgets, particularly when they are large and of long duration, which is quite common for so-called Phase 3 drug research required as part of the Food and Drug Administration (FDA) or European Medicines Agency (EMA) approval process before marketing. Time may be a problem in itself, for example, when an answer to a question about the effect of a treatment needs to be obtained quickly and there is not enough time for a long-term trial to be completed. This is more often the case in research on side effects than on main effects. If, for example, a life-threatening side effect is suspected, adequate and timely action may be warranted and nonexperimental studies may be necessary to provide the relevant scientific evidence. Another problem with the duration of trials is that they are less suited for outcomes that take many years or even generations to occur. Randomized trials usually run a couple of years at maximum. Longer trials become too expensive, and also with time the number of people who drop out of the study (attrition rate) may become unacceptably high. Recall the DES example; even if vaginal cancer in the daughters of users of this drug is a common outcome, it would be difficult to perform a trial because the follow-up period spans an entire generation.

In circumstances where the sample size, money, or the duration of follow-up poses no insurmountable problems, random allocation of patients may be problematic. For example, random allocation of a lifestyle intervention, such as heavy alcohol use or smoking, is generally impossible. Moreover, "true" blinding in a trial may be difficult to achieve. A trial can be nicely blinded on the surface, but in reality participants or investigators may well be able to recognize the allocated treatment. In the large, three-armed Women's Health Initiative (WHI) trial, examining the effect of long-term postmenopausal hormone therapy on cardiovascular and other outcomes, over 40% of participants correctly identified the allocated treatment. Knowledge of randomized treatment may affect the likelihood of noticing or diagnosing an outcome event and may thus severely invalidate the comparison (see **Table 5–2**), as has been worked out by Garbe and Suissa [2004].

TABLE 5–2 Illustration of Detection Bias for the Ratio of AMI Stratified by Blinding Status of Exposure, Assuming the Unblinded Subjects were 1.2, 1.5, and 1.8 Times More Likely to be Diagnosed than the Blinded Study Subjects

	Estrogen + Progestin			Placebo			Rate ratio
	Cases	n	Rate[a]	Cases	n	Rate[a]	
All subjects	164	8,506	19.3	122	8,102	15.1	1.28
First stratification by exposure blinding (assuming 20% unrecognized myocardial infarction [MI][b])							
Blinded	89	5,062	17.6	112	7,554	14.8	1.19
Unblinded	75	3,444	21.8	10	548	18.2	1.19
Ratio of diagnostic likelihood			1.2			1.2	
Second stratification by exposure blinding (assuming 33% unrecognized MI[b])							
Blinded	81	5,062	16.0	110	7,554	14.6	1.10
Unblinded	83	3,444	24.1	12	548	21.9	1.10
Ratio of diagnostic likelihood			1.5			1.5	
Third stratification by exposure blinding (assuming 44% unrecognized MI[b])							
Blinded	74	5,062	14.6	108	7,554	14.3	1.02
Unblinded	90	3,444	26.1	14	548	25.5	1.02
Ratio of diagnostic likelihood			1.8			1.8	

[a]Rate as cumulative incidence of acute MI per 1,000.

[b]The detection rates of 22–44% relate to the proportion of incident MIs that remain clinically unrecognized at the time they occur but can be detected by ECG (Sheifer et al., 2001).

Reproduced from Garbe E, Suissa S. Issues to debate on the Women's Health Initiative (*WHI) study: Hormone replacement therapy and acute coronary outcomes: methodological issues between randomized and observational studies. Hum Reprod 2004;19:8–13.

Despite randomization, the reported small increase in risk in the WHI study could be spurious because of differential unblinding of hormone replacement therapy users, which could have resulted in higher detection rates of otherwise clinically unrecognized acute myocardial infarction in these women. Altering diagnostic patterns because of unblinding could lower the crude rate ratio of 1.28 to 1.02.

Another possible limitation of trials is that they tend to include highly selected patients and not those patients who are most likely to receive the intervention in daily practice. Typically, randomized trials include younger, healthier patients who have less comorbidity and take fewer medications, and who are more compliant than real-life patients. Evidently, this has no bearing on the validity of the results of the study itself (it can actually be helpful to include a homogeneous population) but may limit the generalizability of the findings to the relevant clinical domain. This only occurs, however, when the differences in characteristics of trial populations and patients in daily practice modify the effect of the intervention. For example, the earlier trials on drug therapy in heart failure included mostly relatively young patients with little comorbidity, whereas the typical heart failure patients are older and have multiple comorbidities. Generalizability of the findings of the earlier studies to the elderly has long been debated. Currently, trials are being conducted among the very old to provide evidence of the efficacy of heart failure therapy in this large group of patients.

Finally, a trial involving randomized allocation and possibly blinding may be deemed to be unethical. An example is when there are highly suggestive data to support the marked superiority of a new treatment, particularly in a situation where no alternative treatments are available for a very serious disease. Unfortunately, the presence of weak data from flawed research sometimes prohibits a decent trial, leaving medical practitioners without a sound basis for treatment decisions. Sir Austin Bradford-Hill [1951] succinctly summarized the problem of publication of questionable but suggestive data on treatment benefits:

> *If a treatment cannot ethically be withheld then clearly no controlled trial can be instituted. All the more important is it, therefore, that a trial should be begun at the earliest opportunity, before there is inconclusive though suggestive evidence of the value of treatment. Not infrequently, however, clinical workers publish favorable results on three or four cases and conclude their article by suggesting that this is the mode of choice, or that what now is required is a trial on an adequate scale. They do not seem to realize that by their very publication they have vastly increased difficulties of the trial or, indeed, made it impossible.*

Random allocation can only be justified if there is a sufficient uncertainty about the superiority and safety of one treatment over another, the so-called principle of *equipoise*. For a discussion of current controversies around the principles of equipoise, see van der Graaf and van Delden [2011].

When no randomized trial can be conducted, the effects of an intervention need to be studied using nonexperimental studies, usually cohort or case-control studies. The results of nonexperimental intervention studies are not inherently less valid than the results of RCTs. However, it is much more difficult to adhere to the comparability requirements in nonexperimental research. This already has been discussed for the problem of confounding by indication that will prohibit nonexperimental studies for many interventions. However, the impossibility of using a placebo and blind participants in a nonexperimental study may make the outcome assessment problematic and leave room for observer bias. Absence of blinding also leads to research in which it is impossible to distinguish between the "true" effect of an intervention (e.g., the pharmacologic effect) and extraneous effects. This may not pose a problem when a pragmatic approach is taken in the study.

To overcome the problem of incomparability of natural history for a concurrent comparison of treated and untreated subjects, sometimes the use of a *historic control group* may offer a solution. This is acceptable if there is assurance that the historic group of patients who were all untreated (e.g., because the treatment has only recently become available) is comparable with regard to all characteristics that determine the severity and thus the natural history of the disease. In other words, the historic cohort and the current cohort of patients would have shown the same prognosis if treatment were not given.

Jones and coworkers [1982] decided to study the benefits of isoprinosine therapy in patients with subacute sclerosing panencephalitis (SSPE), a very rare dementing and fatal illness possibly related to a slow viral infection. Power calculations suggested that close to 100 patients would be needed in each arm of a randomized trial, a number that was unlikely to be recruited in a reasonable time period. Consequently, a multicenter nonrandomized study was conducted that included all 98 patients admitted to 28 medical centers in the United States and Canada between 1971 and 1980. As a reference, three groups of historical untreated control patients were selected who were drawn from medical registries in the preceding time period during which no effective treatment was available. The results were highly suggestive of a marked effect of the treatment (see **Figure 5–9**). To judge the validity of the conclusion, however, assurance is needed that the groups were comparable with regard to natural history, extraneous effects, and observation effects. The natural history may well have changed over several decades. Also,

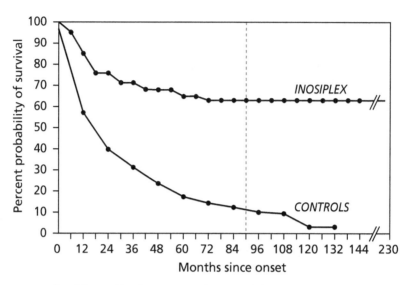

FIGURE 5–9   Life table profiles for 98 inosiplex-treated SSPE patients and for 333 composite SSPE controls (Israeli, Lebanese, and U.S. registry patients).

Reproduced from *The Lancet*, Vol. 319, Jones CE, Dyken PR, Hutten Locher PR, Jabour JT, Maxwell KW. Inosiplex therapy in subacute sclerosing panencephalitis. 1035; © 1982, reprinted with permission from Elsevier.

extraneous factors may be different for the historic and current cohorts. The quality of care and supporting treatments may have changed survival patterns over the years even when the true natural history remained unchanged. Even observation effects cannot be ruled out. It is possible that in the registries only patients with a severe prognosis were listed while milder cases remained undetected. In the current cohort, every effort was made to include all patients with a diagnosis. Selective mortality follow-up could well explain a marked difference in survival rates. For a more detailed discussion of the limitations and implications of this study, see Hoehler et al. [1984].

When the prognosis of patients is very stable or highly predictable, a *before–after study* can be conducted as an alternative to randomized parallel comparisons. This is a cohort study where the patients form their own historic comparison group. For example, to determine the effect of hip replacement surgery in patients with a highly compromised functional status due to severe hip arthritis, it is reasonable to assume that, in the absence of treatment, the functional status would not improve. If a clear improvement after surgery is observed, this may safely be attributed to the intervention. Similarly, antagonism of opioid intoxication in a comatose patient with naloxone does not require a concurrent randomized comparison to allow estimation of the effect of the treatment. When something is obvious, this needs no randomized demonstration; this is clearly underlined by the failed attempt to summarize randomized trial data on the benefits of parachute use to prevent death and major trauma related to gravitational challenge [Smith & Pell, 2003].

THE RANDOMIZED TRIAL AS A PARADIGM FOR ETIOLOGIC RESEARCH

The principles of randomized trials are governed by the need to determine the causal role of the intervention in changing the prognosis of patients. Causal explanation requires the exclusion of confounding and other types of bias. Bias in comparing treatment effects across treated and untreated or differently treated patients may arise from different distributions of prognostic factors, differences in extraneous effects, and differences in observations of outcomes across the comparative groups. In an RCT, problems of confounding are effectively handled by randomization and blinding. The same confounders obviously are relevant in any etiologic study. It may help the investigator, as a mental experiment, to imagine the way a trial would be conducted even in cases where a randomized trial is infeasible. Using the randomized trial as a paradigm for nonexperimental causal research may be particularly helpful to detect problems of confounding and to indicate ways for their control [Miettinen, 1989].

There is more that can be learned from randomized trials when designing nonexperimental studies. There is a common lack of appreciation of the relationship between the way a study population is selected and the extent to which findings in the research can be generalized to other populations. In theory, findings in one population can be generalized to other populations as long as differences between populations do not modify the nature of the determinant–outcome relationship. The finding of the causal relationship between certain genetic sequences and retina pigmentation observed in a population of children can be generalized to elderly subjects without problems because despite the vast difference in characteristics of the two populations, these are judged not to modify the relationship between genes and eye color [Rudakis et al., 2003].

The randomized trial typically uses a highly selective population that is eventually randomized. The Multiple Risk Factor Intervention Trial (MRFIT) was a randomized primary prevention trial designed to test the effect of multifactor intervention on mortality from coronary heart disease [Neaton et al., 1987]. Before randomization, men were seen at three screening visits to establish eligibility. A total of 361,662 men were screened and 12,866 men were randomized. While less than 10% of all those screened were included, the results were judged to be relevant for all men (and even for women) who need risk factor intervention. Indeed, selection may or may not affect generalizability, depending on the effect of the selection on the distribution of variables that have an impact on the relationship between intervention and outcome, and thus are modifiers of the intervention–outcome relationship. In other words, whether a highly selected trial population limits the applicability of the findings is determined by the extent to which the trial population and the population to whom the findings are generalized differ in modifiers of the intervention effect. In a nonexperimental causal study, just like in a trial, the study population should be expressly defined and selected to enable generalization to the domain.

Study populations in causal research can be highly selective. Moreover, selectivity can make causal research much more effective. There is a persistent view that the ideal study population is a random sample from a population. This view is deeply rooted in statistics, where estimates of the mean value of a population, such as height in Japanese males, are best obtained from a random sample of that population. The objective of such estimation, however, is altogether different from an epidemiologic study that aims to find the genetic basis for differences in height among Japanese males. Here, rather than a random sample, it would probably be much more effective to select males at the extremes of the height distribution for genetic analyses. Again, the randomized trial serves as a role model. In a trial, the determinant distribution is deliberately chosen by random allocation. There is clearly no complete representation of the source population in the determinant distribution. Similarly, in a trial the determinant contrast is created by design and does not depend upon a given distribution in a sample. In a trial on the benefits of cholesterol reduction, cholesterol is reduced in one arm of the trial by allocation to, for example, statins while in the other arm the natural history of the cholesterol levels is followed. Then why study a random population sample, with the full cholesterol distribution, in a cohort study to determine the relationship between elevated cholesterol and heart disease risk? The middle part of the distribution adds little information to the research. In a trial, the reference category is explicitly defined and large contrasts are generally created to make the study efficient. The only requirement is that exposure is contrasted to nonexposure, while taking into account the potential for bias, notably confounding. There is no reason not to apply the same principles in nonexperimental research.

Chapter 6

Intervention Research: Unintended Effects

INTRODUCTION

A 75-year-old woman who has had rheumatoid arthritis for more than 25 years visits her doctor because of increasing joint pain. She has been taking nonsteroidal anti-inflammatory drugs (NSAIDs) for many years. In the past, she stopped several NSAIDs and replaced them with others because she suffered from dyspepsia attributed to the drugs. Three years ago she developed a peptic ulcer. Currently, she takes ibuprofen on a daily basis in conjunction with a proton-pump inhibitor to prevent NSAID-induced gastrointestinal side effects. Because of the current severity of the complaints, the doctor decides to switch her to Metoo-coxib, a novel cyclooxygenase (COX)-2 inhibitor, with powerful analgesic properties that is believed to cause less gastrointestinal side effects than classic NSAIDs. COX-2 selective inhibitors were developed as an alternative to classic (nonselective) NSAIDs because COX-1 inhibition exerted by the latter drugs decreases the natural protective mucus lining of the stomach. Indeed, within a month the patient's pain decreases considerably and no gastrointestinal side effects are encountered. Consequently, the proton-pump inhibitor is withdrawn. After 3 months, however, the woman suffers from a myocardial infarction. This certainly comes as a surprise, because apart from advanced age, no cardiovascular risk factors were present. Doctor and patient wonder whether the myocardial infarction was caused by Metoo-coxib.

Interventions (treatments) in clinical practice are meant to improve a patient's prognosis. After careful consideration of the expected natural course of a patient's complaint or disease (prognostication), a physician has to decide whether, and to what extent, a particular intervention is likely to improve this prognosis. To make this decision, it is essential to know the anticipated intended (main) effects of the intervention.

In the rheumatoid arthritis example, the doctor presumably believed that the joint pain of the patient would increase or last an unacceptably long time and thus warranted prescription of a different, novel, and apparently stronger painkiller. The alleged stronger analgesic properties of the novel

BOX 6–1   Side Effects of Interventions: Terminology

Multiple terms for side effects of interventions are used in the literature. A short list is provided here. These include:

- Unintended effects
- Side effects
- Harm
- Adverse effects
- Risks
- Adverse drug reactions (ADRs) or adverse drug events (in the case of pharmaceutical interventions)

In our view, the term *unintended effects* (as opposed to *intended effects*), best reflects the essence of these intervention effects [Miettinen, 1983]. *Pharmaco-vigilance* is the term increasingly being applied to indicate the methodology or discipline or, if one wishes, art, of assessing side effects of pharmacologic interventions. Alternatively, *drug risk assessment, post marketing surveillance,* and *pharmacoepidemiology* are terms often applied, although the latter often also encompasses nonexperimental research on the use of drugs in daily practice (drug utilization) and on intended effects [Strom, 2005].

drug should be based on evidence from valid research on the intended effect. Apart from the primary (intended) effect of an intervention, however, unintended (side) effects could, and in fact should, factor into the decision to initiate or refrain from this or any other intervention (see **Box 6–1**).

Only when the expected benefits are likely to outweigh the anticipated harmful effects is initiation of an intervention justifiable. In the case of the elderly woman with arthritis, the impressive history of gastrointestinal effects that occurred during the use of previous NSAIDs presumably also contributed to the initiation of Metoo-coxib as an intervention, as it was believed to confer fewer gastrointestinal side effects. This decision should have been based on solid evidence that the incidence of these unintended effects is lower with Metoo-coxib than with classic NSAIDs.

RESEARCH ON UNINTENDED EFFECTS OF INTERVENTIONS

With the emergence of multiple interventions in clinical medicine, particularly pharmaceutical interventions, the need to prove their effects greatly increased. Simultaneously, federal regulation passed in the 19th and first

BOX 6–2   Side Effect of Cannabis

Napoleon Bonaparte presumably was among the first to ban a drug (in this case, herbal) because of serious side effects. While in Egypt around 1800 the French occupying forces indulged in the use of cannabis, either through smoking or consumption of hashish-containing beverages.

He prohibited the use of cannabis in 1800: "It is forbidden in all of Egypt to use certain Moslem beverages made with hashish or likewise to inhale the smoke from seeds of hashish. Habitual drinkers and smokers of this plant lose their reason and are victims of violent delirium which is the lot of those who give themselves full to excesses of all sorts" [Allain, 1973].

Although Napoleon undoubtedly interpreted the observed effects of cannabis as side effects, the question remains whether the effects were indeed considered "unintended" by the consumers. The fact that consumption of hashish was reported by some to increase after the official prohibition illustrates that the effects may, to some extent at least, have been "intended."

half of the 20th century to ensure the health interests of the consumers of drugs and foods has facilitated quality assurance for pharmaceuticals and, at a later stage, the methodologic development of studies assessing the intended and unintended effects of interventions (see **Box 6–2**). It took several disasters before drug risk assessment became a mandatory step to obtain marketing authorization for a drug. Research became an important tool to determine the safety of drug interventions, both before and after market authorization.

The thalidomide tragedy dramatically changed the way a drug's primary and side effects are assessed. In 1954, the small German firm Chemie Grünenthal patented the sedative thalidomide. The alleged absence of side effects, even at very high dosages, fueled the impression that the drug was harmless [Silverman, 2002]. The potential hypnotic effect of the drug was revealed after free samples of the, at the time unlicensed, drug were distributed. The drug was licensed in Germany in 1957 and sold as a nonprescription drug because of its presumed safety. Within a few years, the drug was by far the most often used sedative. Sold in more than 40 countries around the world, thalidomide was quick to be marketed as the anti-emetic drug of choice for pregnant women with morning sickness. About a year after its release, however, a neurologist noticed peripheral neuritis in patients who received the drug. Even as reports of this side effect were accumulating rapidly, the company denied any association between thalidomide and this possible unintended effect. In 1960, marketing authorization was sought in the United States. Interestingly, at that time only proof of safety (rather than clinical trials to demonstrate efficacy) of a drug was required for approval by the Federal Drug Administration (FDA). By the end of 1961, the first reports of increasing numbers of children with birth defects were published. These defects included phocomelia, a very rare malformation characterized by severe stunting of the limbs; children had flippers instead of limbs. In that same year, the pediatrician Lenz presented a series of 161 phocomelia cases linked with thalidomide, and the firm withdrew thalidomide from the German market. In **Box 6–3** an extract of a lecture delivered by Dr. Lenz in 1992 is presented, illustrating the way this dramatic unintended effect was discovered. Exact statistics are unknown, but it has been estimated that more than 10,000 infants developed phocomelia because of their mother's use of thalidomide during pregnancy.

Despite its dramatic past, thalidomide received marketing authorization in the late 1990s, with the caveat that it only could be applied under strict conditions and its use in pregnant women was absolutely contraindicated. The drug is currently used for several disorders, including multiple

BOX 6–3   Extract from a Lecture Given by Dr. Widukind Lenz at the 1992 UNITH Congress

Though the first child afflicted by thalidomide damage to the ears was born on December 25, 1956, it took about four and a half years before an Australian gynaecologist, Dr. McBride of Sydney, suspected that thalidomide was the cause of limb and bowel malformations in three children he had seen at Crown Street Women's Hospital. There are only conflicting reports unsubstantiated by documents on the reaction of his colleagues and the Australian representatives of Distillers Company, producers of the British product Distaval between June and December 16, 1961, when a short letter of McBride was published in *The Lancet*. Distillers Company in Liverpool had received the news from Australia on November 21, 1961, almost exactly at the same time as similar news from Germany.

I had suspected thalidomide to be the cause of an outbreak of limb and ear malformation in Western Germany for the first time on November 11, 1961, and by November 16, I felt sufficiently certain from continuing investigations to warn Chemie Gruenenthal by a phone call. It took ten more days of intensive discussions with representatives of the producer firm, of health authorities, and of experts before the drug was withdrawn, largely due to reports in the press.

Reproduced from the lecture "The History of Thalidomide," delivered at the 1992 United International Thalidomide Society Congress. Available at: www.thalidomidesociety.co.uk/publications. htm. Accessed May 9, 2013.

myeloma and erythema nodosum leprosum, a severe complication of leprosy. The beneficial effects of thalidomide have been attributed to its tumor necrosis factor-alpha (TNF-a) lowering properties.

The thalidomide tragedy and other tragedies from pharmaceutical use clearly show the importance of weighing the risks and benefits of interventions before bringing drugs to marketing (i.e., widespread use) as well as in the physician's decision, after licensing, to initiate the intervention in individual patients in daily practice. This requires empirical evidence of the expected intended and unintended effects of the intervention and, thus, valid studies. Naturally, researchers and those employed by the manufacturers of the interventions are more likely to direct their research efforts at the intended effects of interventions than at possible unintended effects. In addition, quantifying unintended effects of interventions is often more complicated than estimating their benefits, because the research paradigm to determine effects of intervention—the randomized trial—is less suited to evaluate unintended effects. In this chapter, the methods available to assess unintended effects of interventions are presented. Most examples in this chapter are drawn from studies on the unintended effects of drug interventions, but the same principles also hold for surgical, lifestyle, and other healthcare interventions.

STUDIES ON UNINTENDED EFFECTS OF INTERVENTIONS: CAUSAL RESEARCH

When the goal is to quantify the association of a specific intervention with the occurrence of an unintended outcome, the main challenge for the researcher lies in establishing causality. As in research on intended effects of interventions, the causal influence of the intervention on a patient's prognosis is the object of study. Although such studies also bear characteristics of prediction (in this case prognostic) research, because the intervention is one of the potential predictors of the probability (ranging from 0–100%) of developing a specific (here, untoward) event, their primary aim is to prove or repudiate causality. In designing studies to quantify the causal association of an intervention with an unintended effect, the analogy of a court room is even more appropriate than in the study of intended effects. Here the researcher, who is analogous to the prosecutor, has to prove beyond a reasonable doubt that the intervention caused the side effect and that the observed "crime" (unintended effect) was not committed by other factors. Be assured that, in the case of a

FIGURE 6–1   The "confounding triangle" in research on unintended effects. The reasons to initiate or refrain from a specific intervention are important potential confounders.

major blockbuster drug from a large pharmaceutical company, there will be a well-selected group of real-life lawyers carefully scrutinizing your study. Consequently, achieving comparability of natural history, extraneous factors, and observation is essential. In particular, the influence of potential confounders should be prevented or accounted for in the investigation. In this process, consideration of the confounding triangle may be helpful (see **Figure 6–1**).

Critical evaluation of the two arrows in Figure 6–1, that is, the association of potential confounders with both the exposure to the intervention and the unintended effect, is essential. In daily practice, as in the study of intended effects of interventions, the reasons an intervention is initiated in or withheld from patients (i.e., relative or absolute indications or contraindications) are by definition associated with exposure to the intervention [Grobbee & Hoes, 1997]. Consequently, the left arrow in Figure 6–1 exists unless allocation of the intervention is a random process. This typically only occurs when the researcher ensures comparability of natural history in those who do or do not receive the intervention through randomization, that is, by performing a randomized controlled trial. The presence or absence of a relationship between the reasons to initiate the intervention (the indication) and the unintended effect (the arrow on the right) determines the potential for confounding. Because the indication then acts as a confounder, this is sometimes termed *confounding by indication*. When drugs are particularly used by ("indicated for") patients at a higher or lower risk of developing the unintended effect of interest than patients not receiving the intervention, failure to take this confounding into account will bias the study findings. When, for example, COX-2 inhibitors are for some reason preferentially prescribed to patients with an unfavorable cardiovascular risk profile, comparison of the incidence of myocardial infarction of patients receiving the drug (such as the 75-year-old woman in the earlier example) with

BOX 6–4   Merck Found Liable in Vioxx Case

Texas Jury Awards Widow $253 Million

by Mark Kaufman
Washington Post Staff Writer
Saturday, August 20, 2005; Page A01

After less than 11 hours of deliberation, a Texas jury yesterday found Merck & Co. responsible for the death of a 59-year-old triathlete who was taking the company's once-popular painkiller, Vioxx.

The jury hearing the first Vioxx case to go to trial awarded the man's widow $253.4 million in punitive and compensatory damages—a sharp rebuke to an industry leader that enjoyed an unusually favorable public image before the Vioxx debacle began to unfold one year ago.

those not using the drug in daily practice may reveal an increased risk of this side effect. At least part of this increased risk will be attributable to confounding by indication.

Box 6–4 is an excerpt from a *Washington Post* article published August 20, 2005. Apparently, the judge considered the causal relationship between the use of rofecoxib (Vioxx), a COX-2 inhibitor, and the untimely death of the athlete proven. Rofecoxib was withdrawn from the market by the manufacturer in September 2004, after a randomized trial showed an increased risk of cardiovascular disease among rofecoxib users [Bresalier et al., 2005].

The importance of taking confounding into account in research on unintended effects of interventions and possible bias attributable to initiation of drug interventions in high-risk patients is clearly exemplified by the following quote from John Urquhart, emeritus professor of pharmacoepidemiology: "Did the drug bring the problem to the patient or did the patient bring the problem to the drug?" (Urquhart, 2001).

As in all types of research aimed at quantifying causal associations, confounding in the assessment of unintended effects of interventions can be accounted for either in the design of data collection or in the design of data analysis. The potential for confounding, however, critically depends on the type of unintended effect involved: type A or type B [Rawlins & Thompson, 1977].

TYPE A AND TYPE B UNINTENDED EFFECTS

Type A Unintended Effects

Type A unintended effects result from the primary action of the intervention and can be considered an exaggerated intended effect. Type A unintended effects are usually common, dose dependent, occur gradually (from a very mild to—often with increasing dosages—more serious presentation), and are in principle predictable. Lowering of the intervention's dosage will usually take the side effect away. Type A unintended effects also may occur at recommended dosages of the intervention, for example, when the drug metabolizes at a lower rate.

A classic example of a type A unintended effect is bleeding resulting from anticoagulant therapy. The unintended effect results from the intended effect of the drug (i.e., its anticoagulant property), is fairly common, usually occurs in a mild form such as bruises (but sometimes fatal hemorrhage may develop), and is to a certain extent predictable because many factors related to bleeding risk during anticoagulant use are known. These include age, dosage, alcohol use, tendency to fall, and relevant comorbidity. Whether the unintended effect is predictable or not is important, because knowledge about the predictors will cause physicians to refrain from prescribing the intervention in high-risk patients. This "good clinical practice" will, on the one hand, prevent the unintended effect from occurring in some patients. However, on the other hand, such preferential nonprescribing should be taken into account when estimating the association between the intervention and such an unintended effect. Uncritical comparison of the incidence of the unintended effect among those receiving the drug and a group of patients not receiving the drug will then dilute the association. Obviously such confounding (often referred to as *confounding by contraindication*) should be accounted for in the design of the study.

Because type A unintended effects are closely related to the intended effects of an intervention, patient characteristics associated with the initiation of an intervention may be predictive of the probability of developing both intended and unintended effects. Consequently, confounding by indication threatens the validity of any study assessing type A unintended effects. This is illustrated in **Figure 6–2**.

Because in Figure 6–2 the left arrow exists by definition (see exclamation mark), any association between one of the determinants of prescribing anticoagulants with the unintended effect of interest may induce confounding. Multiple patient characteristics will influence the decision to

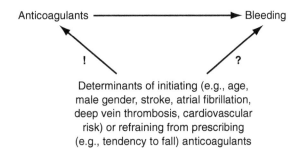

Anticoagulants ⎯⎯⎯⎯⎯⎯⎯⎯→ Bleeding

!   ?

Determinants of initiating (e.g., age,
male gender, stroke, atrial fibrillation,
deep vein thrombosis, cardiovascular
risk) or refraining from prescribing
(e.g., tendency to fall) anticoagulants

FIGURE 6–2   Potential confounding in the study of type A unintended effects of an intervention with the example of anticoagulants and bleeding.

start an intervention in clinical practice (e.g., elderly, men, those at increased cardiovascular risk, and those with clear indications such as atrial fibrillation are more likely to receive anticoagulants), so it seems justified to consider confounding by indication as a given. At least one of these determinants (here, for example, age) is apt to be associated with the probability of developing the unintended effect [Roldán et al., 2013]. Thus, one should always take measures to prevent or adjust for confounding in the assessment of type A unintended effects.

Type B Unintended Effects

In contrast to type A unintended effects, type B unintended effects do not result from the primary action of an intervention. In fact, often the mechanism underlying a type B unintended effect remains unknown. Type B unintended effects typically are rare, not dose dependent, are an "all or nothing" phenomenon, and cannot be predicted. Classic examples of type B unintended effects are anaphylactic shock, aplasia, or other idiosyncratic reactions following the administration of certain drugs. The "all or nothing" phenomenon refers to the fact that type B unintended effects either do not occur or present themselves as a full-blown event, irrespective of the dosage. The unpredictability of such unintended effects is crucial in the understanding of the potential of confounding in research directed at these effects. Consider a study quantifying the association between the use of an antihypertensive drug enalapril (one of the first angiotensin-converting-enzyme [ACE] inhibitors) and the occurrence of angioedema (see **Figure 6–3**).

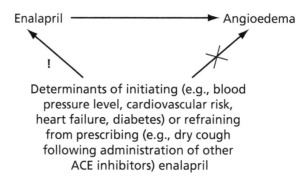

FIGURE 6–3   Potential confounding in the study of type B unintended effects of an intervention with the example of enalapril and angioedema.

This is a rare event characterized by swelling around the eyes and lips, which in severe cases also may involve the throat, a side effect that is potentially fatal.

Again, determinants of enalapril prescription (blood pressure level, levels of other cardiovascular risk factors, and relevant comorbidity such as heart failure or diabetes) will influence the use of the drug in clinical practice (left arrow in Figure 6–3). In contrast to type A unintended effects, these patient characteristics are very unlikely to be associated with the outcome. For example, blood pressure, cholesterol levels, and diabetes are not related to the risk of developing angioedema. Consequently, the arrow on the right in Figure 6–3 is nonexistent and confounding is not a problem in such type B unintended effects [Miettinen, 1982; Vandenbroucke, 2006].

Measures to prevent confounding are therefore generally not necessary in type B unintended effects, although one has to be absolutely sure that characteristics of recipients of the intervention are indeed not related to the unintended event under study.

OTHER UNINTENDED EFFECTS

Unfortunately, many unintended effects are neither typical type A nor typical type B. For example, for gynacomastia as a side effect of the use of cimetidine, an anti-ulcer drug, a type A mechanism related to the action of the drug (although not to the primary action of the drug) has been identified and the effect seems to be dose related [Garcia Rodriguez & Jick, 1994]. The dose-related effect, typically a type A phenomenon, is

BOX 6–5   Example of a Type A Unintended Effect of a Drug Intervention that was First Considered a Type B Effect

Transmural Myocardial Infarction with Sumatriptan

For sumatriptan, tightness in the chest caused by an unknown mechanism has been reported in 3%–5% of users. We describe a 47-year-old woman with an acute myocardial infarction after administration of sumatriptan 6 mg subcutaneously for cluster headache. The patient had no history of underlying ischaemic heart disease or Prinzmetal's angina. She recovered without complications.

Reproduced from *The Lancet,* Vol. 341; Ottervanger JP, Paalman HJA, Boxma GL, Stricker BHCh. Transmural myocardial infarction with sumatriptan. 861–2. © 1993, reprinted with permission from Elsevier.

counterbalanced by the unpredictability of the side effect, a type B characteristic. In addition, some unintended effects that were first considered clear type B may develop into type A unintended effects at a later stage, for example, when the underlying mechanism and predictors of the effect become known.

An example is the abstract in **Box 6–5**. With the first reports of angina pectoris or myocardial infarction in recipients of sumatriptan, a then novel antimigraine drug, these rare events were primarily considered type B unintended effects (see also the wording "unknown" in the abstract) [Ottervanger et al., 1993]. With accumulating evidence, however, the effect was shown to be related to the primary action of the drug, that is, its vasoconstrictive properties, and also the predictability of the effect increased. Currently this adverse drug reaction is primarily considered a type A effect, although it remains, fortunately, rare.

Myocardial infarction is also a possible consequence of Metoo-coxib, the drug introduced in the beginning of this chapter; this is more characteristics of a type A than a type B unintended effect. COX-2 inhibition promotes platelet aggregation because of inhibition of endothelial prostacyclin, while COX-1 inhibition inhibits aggregation because of inhibition of platelet thromboxane synthesis. Thus, selective COX-2 inhibition was expected to increase platelet aggregation, which may indeed promote thrombus formation and eventually cause myocardial infarction. The observed dose–response relationship further illustrates that myocardial infarction may be a type A effect [Andersohn et al., 2006]. Consequently, confounding by indication may pose an important threat to the validity of research on this potential side effect of Metoo-coxib or other COX-2 inhibitors.

THEORETICAL DESIGN

The occurrence relation of research on the unintended effects of an intervention closely resembles that of research on the intended effects of interventions:

Unintended effect $= f$ (intervention | EF)

Because the primary goal is to assess causality, the occurrence relation should be estimated conditional on confounders (external factors, or EF).

The domain usually includes patients with an indication for the intervention (e.g., a specific disease), or defined more broadly, patients in whom a physician considers initiating the intervention.

In the Metoo-coxib example, the occurrence relation would be,

Myocardial infarction $= f$ (Metoo-coxib | EF)

and the domain is defined as a patient with osteoarthritis (or perhaps other diseases) requiring analgesics.

DESIGN OF DATA COLLECTION

Time

As for studies assessing intended effects of interventions, the time dimension for research on unintended effects is larger than zero. The aim is to establish whether a specific intervention is related to the future occurrence of a certain effect. In principle, therefore, research on unintended effects is longitudinal.

Census or Sampling

In contrast to diagnostic studies and research on the intended effects of interventions, studies addressing unintended effects of interventions relatively often take a sampling instead of a census approach. There are several reasons why sampling (and, thus, a case-control study) is attractive here. First, sampling is efficient when the unintended effect is rare, as is typically the case in type B unintended effects. A census approach would imply following in time very large numbers of patients receiving or not receiving the treatment. For the example at the beginning of the chapter, this would entail following a large group of patients with rheumatoid arthritis receiving Metoo-coxib and a large group receiving no or other analgesics. Alternatively, one may hypothetically define and follow a study base, consisting in this example of patients with rheumatoid arthritis, and only study in detail those developing the unintended effect (i.e., cases) during the study period and a sample representative of that study base (i.e., controls). Obviously, the definition of the study base critically depends on the domain of the study. Case-control studies are efficient also when the measurement of the determinant and other relevant characteristics, such as potential confounders and effect modifiers, is expensive, time consuming, or burdensome to the patient. For example, when detailed information, including dosage, duration of use, compliance to medications (including Metoo-coxib), and relevant comorbidity is difficult to obtain, a case-control study should be considered. In addition, when unintended effects take a long time to develop or when the time from exposure to the intervention until the occurrence of the effect are unknown, a case-control approach is attractive.

The classic example of a case-control study establishing the causal association between the use of the estrogen diethylstilboestrol (DES) in mothers and the occurrence of clear-cell adenocarcinoma of the vagina in their daughters illustrates the strengths of case-control studies; a census approach would require an unrealistic follow-up time lasting one generation and a huge study population because vaginal carcinoma is extremely rare. The results of the original case-control study from 1971 on this topic are shown in **Table 6–1** [Herbst et al., 1971].

In that study, eight cases were compared with 32 matched controls. The mothers of seven of the eight daughters with vaginal carcinoma had received DES (a drug primarily prescribed for women with habitual abortion to prevent future fetal loss) during pregnancy, whereas none of the mothers of the 32 control daughters had used DES. Although no quantitative measure of association was reported (in fact the odds ratio cannot be calculated because its numerator includes 0 and the odds ratio reaches infinity), it was not difficult to conclude that DES increases the risk of vaginal carcinoma in daughters. When assuming that the mother of one control received DES during pregnancy, the odds ratio would be $(7 \times 31)/(1 \times 1) = 217$, still indicating a more than 200-fold risk.

Experimental or Observational

The main challenge of research on unintended effects of interventions lies in proving beyond a reasonable doubt that the intervention is causally involved in the occurrence of the outcome. An experimental approach (i.e., a randomized controlled trial) best ensures that the outcome is indeed attributable to the intervention, mainly because randomization will achieve comparability of natural history of those who do and do not receive the

TABLE 6–1 Results of the Original Case-Control Study (with 8 Cases and 32 Controls) on the Association between DES use in Mothers and Vaginal Carcinoma in their Daughters

Case No.	Maternal Age (yr) Case	Maternal Age (yr) Mean of 4 controls	Maternal Smoking Case	Maternal Smoking Control	Bleeding in This Pregnancy Case	Bleeding in This Pregnancy Control	Any Prior Pregnancy Loss Case	Any Prior Pregnancy Loss Control	Estrogen Given in This Pregnancy Case	Estrogen Given in This Pregnancy Control	Breast-feeding Case	Breast-feeding Control	Intrauterine X-ray Exposure Case	Intrauterine X-ray Exposure Control
1	25	32	Yes	2/4	No	0/4	Yes	1/4	Yes	0/4	No	0/4	No	1/4
2	30	30	Yes	3/4	No	0/4	Yes	1/4	Yes	0/4	No	1/4	No	0/4
3	22	31	Yes	1/4	Yes	0/4	No	1/4	Yes	0/4	Yes	0/4	No	0/4
4	33	30	Yes	3/4	Yes	0/4	Yes	0/4	Yes	0/4	Yes	2/4	No	0/4
5	22	27	Yes	3/4	No	1/4	No	1/4	No	0/4	No	0/4	No	0/4
6	21	29	Yes	3/4	Yes	0/4	Yes	0/4	Yes	0/4	No	0/4	No	1/4
7	30	27	No	3/4	No	0/4	Yes	1/4	Yes	0/4	Yes	0/4	No	1/4
8	26	28	Yes	3/4	No	0/4	Yes	0/4	Yes	0/4	No	0/4	Yes	1/4
Total			7/8	21/32	3/8	1/32	6/8	5/32	7/8	0/32	3/8	3/32	1/8	4/32
Mean	26.1	29.3												
Chi Square (1 df)[a]	4.52		4.52		4.52		7.16		23.22		2.35		0	
P value	0.53		0.53		< 0.05		< 0.01		< 0.00001		0.20		(N.S.)	
	(N.S.)†		(N.S.)								(N.S.)			

[a]Matched control chi-square test used is described by Pike & Morrow.

†Standard error of difference 1.7 yr (paired *t*-test); N.S. = not statistically signficant.

Reproduced from: Herbst AL, Ulfelder H, Poskanzer DC. Adenocarcinoma of the vagina. Association of maternal stilbestrol therapy with tumor appearance in young women. *N Engl J Med* 1971;284:878–81. Copyright © 1971. Massachusetts Medical Society. All rights reserved.

intervention and, thus, prevent confounding. Moreover, randomized controlled trials, when properly conducted, will also achieve the other two "comparabilities," that is, comparability of extraneous effects and comparability of observations, which are necessary to prove that the intervention is "guilty," to return to the courtroom analogy. However, there are several reasons why this paradigm for assessing causality in intervention research is less suitable when the aim is to establish unintended intervention effects.

Typical circumstances under which randomized trials are not suited for the study of unintended effects are situations where case-control studies are particularly efficient—when the outcome is rare and when the time between exposure to the intervention and the development of the outcome is very long. There is no doubt that a randomized trial to estimate the risk of vaginal carcinoma in daughters of mothers exposed to DES during pregnancy is not feasible because it would be an unrealistically large trial with an unachievably long follow-up period. Also, when the time from exposure to the side effect is unknown, randomized trials are of limited value. In fact, one of the major strengths of observational studies on unintended effects is that they can determine the influence of the duration of the exposure on the occurrence of the effect [Miettinen, 1989].

Table 6–2 shows that the number of patients required in each of the two arms of a randomized trial to detect a relative risk of 2 (with a type 1 error of 0.05, and type 2 error of 0.20) increases dramatically when the incidence of the outcome effect becomes rare.

Type B unintended effects are especially difficult to detect in a randomized trial because the frequency of the outcome, such as anaphylactic shock in those not receiving the drug under study or an alternative intervention, is usually lower than 0.1% or even 0.01%.

TABLE 6–2   Risk of the Outcome in the Control Group and the Number of Participants Required in Each Group of a Randomized Trial

Risk of Outcome in Control Group	Number Required in Each Group
50%	8
25%	55
10%	198
5%	435
1.0%	2,331
0.1%	23,661
0.01%	236,961

There are also ethical constraints in conducting randomized trials to quantify the occurrence of unintended effects, most notably when the assessment of side effects that are burdensome to patients is the primary aim of the trial and suspicion has been raised. For some interventions, random allocation is downright impossible. One cannot envision a trial involving random allocation of patients smoking 40 cigarettes a day for 40 years to quantify the increased lung cancer risk or a trial randomly allocating participants to a sedentary life to estimate its deleterious effects on cardiovascular health. Moreover, imagine an investigator asking potential participants whether they would be willing to participate in a study designed to determine if Metoo-coxib increases the risk of myocardial infarction and relaying that their probability of being randomly allocated to receive the drug for a couple of years is 50%. Few patients would sign an informed consent for that study. Whether an ethics committee would permit such a trial to be launched clearly depends on the magnitude of the beneficial effects of Metoo-coxib relative to its comparator substance (a placebo, or another analgesic). When an intervention has proven efficacy, placebo-controlled trials will often be considered unethical and active comparators will have to be included [Wangge et al., 2013a]. Obviously, side effects should be recorded in all randomized trials primarily aimed at assessing the beneficial effects of interventions, notably in the case of drug trials performed to apply for marketing authorization. Certainly premarketing (Phase 2 and 3) trials, however, will often lack statistical power to detect less common side effects [Duijnhoven et al., 2013]. A postmarketing (Phase 4) trial is an important tool in drug risk assessment because these trials are larger than premarketing trials. With the combination of multiple similar trials in meta-analyses, the power can be further increased, sometimes even allowing the detection of rare type B side effects [Makani et al., 2012].

An example of a randomized trial that was designed to also quantify the occurrence of side effects of an intervention is shown in **Table 6–3**. A large placebo-controlled randomized trial was performed to assess both the intended and unintended effects of influenza vaccination in the elderly. The rationale for the study was provided by the alleged low efficacy and the existing fear of systemic adverse effects that were believed to underlie the low vaccination rate in older adults at that time. A separate article [Govaert et al., 1993] was devoted to the unintended effects of influenza vaccination; its main results are summarized in Table 6–3.

Although local side effects, such as swelling and itching, were much more common in the influenza group than in the placebo group, the frequencies of systemic reactions did not differ appreciably, in particular among those older adults at potential risk. The power in this latter group

TABLE 6–3 Numbers (Percentages) of All Patients and of Patients at Potential Risk* in the Influenza Vaccine and in the Placebo Group who Reported Local or Systemic Adverse Reactions

Reactions	Vaccine Group		Placebo Group		P Value	
	All patients (n = 904)	Patients at potential risk (n = 246)	All patients (n = 902)	Patients at potential risk (n = 234)	All patients	Patients at potential risk
Local Reactions:	158 (17.5)	52 (21.1)	66 (7.3)	20 (8.5)	< 0.001	< 0.001
Swelling	66 (7.3)	25 (10.2)	8 (0.9)	2 (0.9)	< 0.001	< 0.001
Itching	41 (4.5)	18 (7.3)	13 (1.4)	6 (2.6)	< 0.001	0.02
Warm feeling	43 (4.8)	17 (6.9)	14 (1.6)	4 (1.7)	< 0.001	0.01
Pain when touched	94 (10.4)	30 (12.2)	29 (3.2)	10 (4.3)	< 0.001	0.00
Constant pain	17 (1.9)	6 (2.4)	8 (0.9)	3 (1.3)	0.07	0.50
Discomfort	23 (2.5)	4 (1.6)	19 (2.1)	4 (1.7)	0.53	1.00
Systemic Reactions:	99 (11.0)	27 (11.0)	85 (9.4)	28 (12.0)	0.34	0.73
Fever	12 (1.3)	2 (0.8)	6 (0.7)	2 (0.9)	0.15	1.00
Headache	44 (4.9)	13 (5.3)	35 (3.9)	15 (6.4)	0.30	0.60
Malaise	58 (6.4)	14 (5.7)	50 (5.5)	17 (7.3)	0.45	0.50
Other complaints	33 (3.7)	8 (3.3)	31 (3.4)	11 (4.7)	0.82	0.56
All reactions	210 (23.2)	61 (24.8)	127 (14.1)	38 (16.2)	< 0.001	0.02

* Patients at potential risk were patients with heart disease, pulmonary disease, or metabolic disease.

Thirty-two subjects were excluded because of incomplete data, 10 of whom were at potential risk.

Reproduced from: Govaert TM, Dinant GJ, Aretz K, Masurel N, Sprenger MJ, Knottnerus JA. Adverse reactions to influenza vaccine in elderly people: Randomised double blind placebo controlled trial. *BMJ* 1993;307:988–90 with permission from BMJ Publishing Group Ltd.

was too low, however, to detect small differences between the groups. The comforting results of this Dutch study have probably significantly contributed to the currently high (> 80%) vaccination coverage rate among the elderly in the Netherlands.

A final disadvantage of randomized trials is their tendency to include highly selected patient populations. Although this bears on the generalizability of the findings and not on the validity of the study, it may seriously hamper the applicability of the findings, in particular with regard to side effects of interventions. Restriction of study populations (e.g., men within a certain age range) may increase the feasibility and validity of a study and, as long as the research findings can be expected to be similar in groups of patients not included (e.g., men of other ages and women), this will not restrict the applicability of the findings. There is ample evidence that for many interventions, the intended effects are not modified by age and gender, particularly when these effects are measured as a relative risk reduction. For example, treatment with cholesterol-lowering statins reduces the incidence of cardiovascular disease by approximately 30% across a wide age range of persons, irrespective of gender and prior cardiovascular disease [LaRosa & Vupputuri, 1999].

Unintended effects, however, tend to occur more often in certain patient categories, typically older patients with comorbidities who are taking multiple drugs. Pregnant women also are a particularly vulnerable group. Thus, excluding these "real-life" patients from the study population will produce unbiased results for the patient population included in the study, but these unbiased findings may underestimate the association between the intervention and the unintended effect in daily practice and will limit the generalizability and clinical relevance of the findings. To learn whether and to what extent an intervention causes an unintended effect in clinical practice requires the inclusion of patients using the drug in daily practice. Consequently, randomized trials including highly restricted patient populations often are of limited value in addressing the risk of unintended effects. Trials on the effect of anticoagulant treatments in patients with atrial fibrillation are an example. Most of these trials were primarily conducted to assess the beneficial (e.g., cerebrovascular event-reducing) effects of these drugs, and patients were selected such that their risk of bleeding (a type A unintended effect) was minimized [Koefoed et al., 1995]. For example, patients with conditions requiring permanent NSAID therapy and regular alcohol users were excluded. Consequently, the observed (and unbiased) risk in many of those trials was lower than the risk observed in daily practice. **Box 6–6** describes an example of the exclusion criteria from one of these studies, the AFASAK-2 study.

BOX 6–6   Exclusion Criteria for the AFASAK-2 Study

Systolic blood pressure > 180 mm Hg
Diastolic blood pressure > 100 mm Hg
Mitral stenosis
Alcoholism
Dementia
Psychiatric disease
Lone atrial fibrillation in patients < 60 years of age
Contraindications for warfarin therapy
Contraindications for aspirin therapy
Warfarin therapy based on other medical conditions
Thromboembolic event in the preceding 6 months
Foreign language
Pregnancy and breastfeeding
Chronic nonsteroidal anti-inflammatory drug therapy

Although multiple exclusion criteria can be very helpful and may be justified to optimize the safety of participants in an efficacy trial, they also may lead to inadequate estimates of the unintended effects occurring in daily practice where patients will be treated outside the domain of the study.

In a randomized study specifically designed to compare gastrointestinal side effects in those receiving rofecoxib and the NSAID naproxen, recipients of the COX-2 inhibitor experienced a 50% lower risk of gastrointestinal side effects (see **Table 6–4**) [Bombardier et al., 2000].

This trial among patients with rheumatoid arthritis shows the strength of randomized trials in estimating the risk of relatively frequent unintended effects (e.g., four upper gastrointestinal events per 100 patient years in the naproxen group). It also exemplifies that when trials are large enough, they may be instrumental in detecting even relatively rare effects. In this study including 8,076 randomized patients, the risk of myocardial infarction was lower in the naproxen group (0.1%) than in the rofecoxib group (0.4%; relative risk 0.2; 95% confidence interval [CI], 0.1–0.7). It took several more years, however, before another trial, this one in patients with colorectal adenoma, confirmed the increased risk of cardiovascular events among rofecoxib users, urging the firm to withdraw the drug from the market [Bresalier et al., 2005].

TABLE 6-4 Incidence of Gastrointestinal Events in Patients Using Different Types of COX-2 Inhibitors or NSAIDs

Type of Event	Rofecoxib Group (N = 4047)	Naproxen Group (N = 4029)	Rofecoxib Group (N = 4047)	Naproxen Group (N = 4029)	Relative Risk (95% CI)*	P Value
	no. with event		rate/100 patient-yr			
Confirmed upper gastrointestinal events	56	121	2.1	4.5	0.5 (0.3–0.6)	< 0.001
Complicated confirmed upper gastrointestinal events	16	37	0.6	1.4	0.4 (0.2–0.8)	0.005
Confirmed and unconfirmed upper gastrointestinal events†	58	132	2.2	4.9	0.4 (0.3–0.6)	< 0.001
Complicated confirmed and unconfirmed upper gastrointestinal events‡	17	42	0.6	1.6	0.4 (0.2–0.7)	0.002
All episodes of gastrointestinal bleeding	31	82	1.1	3.0	0.4 (0.3–0.6)	< 0.001

*CI denotes confidence interval.

†The analysis includes 13 events that were reported by investigators but were considered to be unconfirmed by the end-point committee.

‡The analysis includes six events that were reported by investigators but were considered to be unconfirmed by the end-point committee.

Reproduced from Bombardier C, and VIGOR Study Group et al. Comparison of upper gastrointestinal toxicity of rofecoxib and naproxen in patients with rheumatoid arthritis. VIGOR Study Group, *N Engl J Med* 2000;343:1520–8.

Given the limitations of randomized trials to detect unintended effects of interventions, notably when these are rare, observational (i.e., nonexperimental) studies provide an important alternative. An advantage of performing observational studies to assess unintended effects is that by definition "real" patients receiving the intervention in everyday clinical practice will be included. To allow for valid conclusions regarding the causal relationship between the intervention and the unintended effect, however, these observational studies should be designed such that comparability of natural history, observations, and extraneous factors is ensured. Notably, achieving comparability of natural history, that is, preventing confounding, is often very difficult. In this process a thought experiment, taking the randomized trial as a paradigm for observational research, can be very useful [Miettinen, 1989]. In the following section, different approaches to prevent or limit incomparability of observations, extraneous effects, and natural history will be discussed in some detail.

COMPARABILITY IN OBSERVATIONAL RESEARCH ON UNINTENDED EFFECTS

Comparability of Observations

Blinding is the generally accepted method for achieving comparability of observations between those receiving the intervention and the comparison group. In a randomized trial, tools are available to keep all those involved in measuring the outcome (the observer, but possibly also the patients and doctors or other healthcare workers when they can influence the measurements) blinded to treatment allocation, notably by the use of a placebo. In observational research, usually only part of the observations can be blinded. In a cohort study examining the effect of Metoo-coxib on the risk of myocardial infarction, for example, one could blind the researchers involved in adjudication of the outcome by deleting all information pertaining to the medication used by the patients from the data forwarded to them. If, however, the use of COX-2 inhibitors urges healthcare workers and patients to be more perceptive of signs of possible myocardial infarction, leading more often to ordering tests to establish or rule out the disease, incomparability of observations may artificially inflate the drug's risk. Alternatively, one could choose the technique of measuring the outcome such that observer bias is minimized. For example, automated biochemical measurements do not require blinding, although in daily practice routine ordering of such tests may very well be influenced by the intervention the patient receives. Finally, a hard outcome, such as death, will increase comparability of observations.

Comparability of Extraneous Effects

As in research on intended effects of interventions, one should first establish which part of the intervention is considered extraneous to the occurrence relation before the design of data collection is determined. When the goal is to quantify the causal relationship between the pharmacologic substrate of a drug and an unintended outcome, as will often be the case in drug risk assessment, all other effects of receiving a drug (such as the extra time spent by the prescribing physician and accompanying lifestyle changes) are extraneous and should be accounted for in the design of the study, typically in the design of data collection. As discussed earlier, the main tool used to achieve comparability of extraneous effects in randomized trials—a placebo or "sham" intervention—is unattainable in observational research. The observational counterpart of placebo treatment is selectivity in the choice of the intervention and reference categories of the determinant to be studied. Ideally, the extraneous effects of these two categories should be comparable (or absent). This is more likely to be achieved by comparing two drug interventions (one is the intervention and one is the reference category of the determinant) with similar indications, for example, two individual COX-2 inhibitors, then by contrasting the use of Metoo-coxib to non-use of a COX-2 inhibitor. Comparison of those receiving the intervention under study with those not receiving this or an alternative intervention may lead to considerable incomparability. Obviously, comparison of Metoo-coxib–treated patients to patients not receiving any analgesics may affect validity because of incomparability of extraneous effects, when those receiving Metoo-coxib are more likely to comply with healthy lifestyle habits influencing the risk of myocardial infarction or are more likely to visit their treating physician regularly. The choice of an appropriate reference category for the determinant is also important to deal with the major threat to the validity of observational studies on the effects of interventions: incomparability of natural history. How to prevent such confounding in research on unintended effects will be discussed in the next section.

Comparability of Natural History

Incomparability of natural history (i.e., confounding) is the most critical threat to the validity of most observational studies on the effects of interventions. Fortunately, several methods, both in the design of data collection and the design of data analysis, are available to limit or even prevent confounding. However, before embarking on a crusade of measures to reduce confounding in an observational study, one should first decide whether confounding is indeed likely. As explained earlier, the probability of confounding depends on the association between the reasons (including patient characteristics) to prescribe (or refrain from prescribing) a certain intervention with the outcome involved, that is, on the existence of the right arrow in the "confounder triangle" (see Figure 6–1). When such an association is nonexistent, as will be the case in typical type B unintended effects such as anaphylactic shock or angioedema, confounding is a non-issue.

Consider once again the example of the use of DES in mothers and the occurrence of vaginal carcinoma in their daughters. The "confounder triangle" of the occurrence relation is shown in **Figure 6–4**.

The patient characteristics influencing the physician to initiate or refrain from prescribing the drug, including habitual abortion (the indication for the drug) or age, by definition, will be related to the probability of receiving the intervention (i.e., the left arrow exists). These or other patient characteristics related to the initiation of the drug are very unlikely to also determine the occurrence of vaginal carcinoma in their daughters (i.e., the right arrow is absent). Consequently, there is no confounding. In type A unintended effects and intended effects of an intervention, the right arrow is much more likely to exist, so confounding should be dealt with appropriately. Also then, however, a detailed discussion of the probability of confounding can be very helpful.

Deep vein thrombosis (DVT) as an unintended effect of second- versus third-generation oral contraceptives serves as an example. DVT could be considered a type A unintended effect because the underlying mechanism is understood [Kemmeren et al., 2004] and the unintended effect may be

FIGURE 6–4   Potential confounding in a study on the causal role of DES prescription in the occurrence of vaginal carcinoma in daughters.

predicted to a certain extent. As third-generation oral contraceptives were initially expected to be safer, they could preferentially have been prescribed to women who had an increased risk for vascular effects of oral contraceptives, for example, those with a history of thrombosis. Nevertheless, confounding need not be an issue as long as the reasons to prescribe a second- or third-generation oral contraceptive are not related to the risk for venous thrombosis (i.e., the right arrow does not exist). To confidently exclude such a relationship is a difficult task, however, and requires detailed knowledge about the determinants of DVT and the distribution of these characteristics among women receiving second- or third-generation oral contraceptives in daily practice. Often, showing that measures to limit confounding do not materially influence the observed risk of the unintended effect is the only way to convince the readership that confounding indeed did not occur [Lidegaard et al., 2002].

METHODS USED TO LIMIT CONFOUNDING

Observational Studies on Unintended Effects of Interventions

When confounding cannot be excluded beforehand, for example, by means of a random allocation of the intervention, multiple methods can be applied to establish or approach comparability of natural history. Most observational studies assessing unintended effects of interventions apply multiple methods simultaneously to achieve comparability of natural history. Some of these methods are summarized in **Box 6–7**. The same methods also can be used to limit confounding in observational studies on intended effects of interventions, although major confounding may remain present there because the reasons to initiate an intervention are, by definition, almost always related to the outcome (i.e., its intended effect) and many may be implicit or unmeasured [Hak et al., 2002]. Such massive confounding often poses insurmountable validity problems [Vandenbroucke, 2004].

Limiting Confounding in the Design of Data Collection

Restriction of the Study Population

An important tool to prevent confounding is to choose the study population such that the baseline risk of the outcome (here, unintended effect) is more or less similar in all participants. This could be achieved, at least in part, by restricting the study population to those patients with a similar

BOX 6–7   Means to Limit Confounding by Indication in Observational Studies on Side Effects of Interventions

In the design of data collection:

1. Restriction of the study population
2. Selectivity in reference categories of determinant
3. Matching of those with and without the determinants
4. Instrumental variables*

In the design of data analysis:

1. Multivariable analyses
2. Propensity scores*

Instrumental variables and propensity scores can be applied both in the design of data collection and in the design of data analysis.

indication but without contraindications for the intervention under study. The former restriction is obvious; it primarily reflects the typical domain of a study on the effects of interventions. It will be difficult to get around the fact that some of the reasons to start an intervention, for example, the severity of the disease, are related to the risk of experiencing the unintended effect. Restriction to those without contraindications (specifically, those contraindications related to the unintended effect under study) seems straightforward, but the operationalization of this may be rather difficult. The essence of the latter restriction is that in the remainder of the study population, the reasons to refrain from prescribing the intervention will not be based on the risk for the unintended effect [Jick & Vessey, 1978]. It should be emphasized that not all reasons to initiate or refrain from an intervention in daily practice are known and measurable, let alone that their possible association with the occurrence of the unintended effect has been established. Consequently, residual confounding can never be excluded. Those receiving or not receiving the intervention in the restricted study population may still differ in characteristics that may be related to both the prescription of the intervention and the outcome, and thus act as confounders. In addition, too much restriction may limit the generalizability of the findings of the study.

In a nested case-control study with the objective of quantifying the risk of myocardial infarction or sudden cardiac death of COX-2 inhibitors, the study population was a cohort comprised of patients who filled at least one prescription of a COX-2 inhibitor or NSAID [Graham et al., 2005]. Thus, all participants had (or had in the past) an indication for a painkiller and did not have a clear contraindication for NSAIDs. Nevertheless, there may be reasons to choose a specific NSAID within the indicated population, and if these reasons are related to the risk of myocardial infarction or sudden cardiac death, confounding will result. Although restriction can be a powerful means to limit confounding, additional methods are usually required to preclude residual confounding.

Selectivity in the Reference Categories of the Determinant

The determinant of the occurrence relation for the example introduced in the beginning of this chapter is the use of Metoo-coxib. In other words, exposure is defined as the use of this drug. The definition of the reference category is less straightforward, however. Simply including patients not receiving the intervention (non-use of Metoo-coxib) carries the danger of including many patients outside the relevant domain, that is, those who do not even have an indication for analgesics (see the previous section on restriction). Even when the indications are not related to the unintended effect (and therefore are not confounders), the generalizability of the findings to the relevant patient domain may become problematic. When designing the data collection, this domain (in this case patients with rheumatoid arthritis with an indication for analgesics) should be carefully considered. Although theoretically, non-use of analgesics within this domain could be taken as the reference category when calculating the risk of myocardial infarction with Metoo-coxib use, non-users of analgesics remain an atypical, small subgroup among the domain of those indicated for these drugs. When the reasons to refrain from prescribing analgesics in this group (i.e., a history of peptic ulcer) are associated with the risk of the unintended effect, confounding will occur. Choosing another drug with similar indications and contraindications (and preferably even within the same drug class) as the reference category of the determinants is an attractive approach to prevent confounding; patients receiving Metoo-coxib are likely to be quite comparable to patients receiving an alternative COX-2 inhibitor, and one may even assume that the decision to prescribe one of the two will not be related to patient characteristics but rather is influenced by other factors (e.g., a visit by the company representative or pricing of the drug) unrelated to the risk of the unintended effect. Even when comparing individual drugs with similar indications and contraindications, however, some confounding could occur and residual confounding should be considered.

In the earlier nested case-control study, the risk of myocardial infarction or sudden cardiac death in recipients of rofecoxib was compared to those receiving celecoxib, another COX-2 inhibitor. Patient characteristics of rofecoxib and celecoxib users were expected to be similar, and a relationship between preferential prescription of one of these drugs and cardiovascular risk (i.e., the unintended effect) was considered unlikely. Close comparison of the control patients within this case-control study, however, revealed that celecoxib was prescribed more often to patients with relatively high cardiovascular risks, indicating that confounding exists and should be accounted for applying additional methodology (see **Table 6–5**).

Interestingly, tables comparing characteristics among determinant categories are not often presented in case-control studies, despite the fact that these data can be very helpful in identifying potential confounding. Table 6–5 shows that, for unknown reasons, celecoxib was prescribed to older patients and those with more unfavorable cardiovascular risk profiles. The unadjusted analysis therefore yielded a lower odds ratio (OR; as an approximation of the relative risk) of myocardial infarction or sudden cardiac death in rofecoxib versus celecoxib users (OR = 1.32) than after adjustment for confounders applying multivariable analyses (OR = 1.59).

In many studies on unintended effects, ex-users of the intervention are taken as the reference exposure category. The rationale behind this approach is the ease with which a cohort of patients receiving the intervention (often a drug) in the past can be identified (e.g., by using routinely available clinical, insurance, or pharmacy data) and the notion that these patients have (or have had) an indication (and not an important contraindication) for the intervention under study. It should be emphasized, however, that ex-users of an intervention represent a rather specific group of patients. For example, cessation of an intervention could have been related to the occurrence of the unintended effect or ineffectiveness of the therapy. In addition, the severity of the disease is likely to be less in ex-recipients of the intervention. Therefore, we do not recommend including ex-users as the reference category in research on unintended effects because of the potential for confounding.

In the nested case-control study, ex-users were treated as a separate reference group. Table 6–5 clearly shows, however, that these ex-users ("remote use") differ considerably from the current users of analgesics. Cardiovascular risk and the prevalence of comorbidity were lowest among ex-users, indicating the larger potential for confounding in the comparison with this reference group.

Matching Those With and Without the Determinants

Matching patients receiving the intervention with those in the reference group of the determinant/exposure is another option to limit confounding.

TABLE 6-5 Selected Characteristics of Controls from the Case-Control Study Receiving Different COX-2 Inhibitors or NSAIDs and Ex-users ("Remote Use") of These Drugs

	Celecoxib (n = 491)	Ibuprofen (n = 2573)	Naproxen (n = 1409)	Rofecoxib (n = 196)	Remote Use (n = 18,720)
Age (years)	73.4 (8.5)	66.9 (11.3)	68.4 (10.9)	72.1 (9.9)	66.4 (11.7)
Men	245 (50%)	1591 (62%)	801 (57%)	91 (46%)	11,807 (63%)
Cardiovascular risk score	4.21 (3.24)	3.11 (3.14)	3.22 (3.15)	3.14 (3.16)	2.91 (3.16)
Cardiovascular admissions in past year	31 (6%)	59 (2%)	51 (4%)	5 (3%)	581 (3%)
Cardiovascular drug use in past year	373 (76%)	1535 (60%)	876 (62%)	129 (656%)	10,388 (55%)
Angiotensin-converting-enzyme inhibitor	140 (29%)	512 (20%)	301 (21%)	43 (22%)	3555 (19%)
Angiotensin-receptor blocker	29 (6%)	33 (1%)	28 (2%)	2 (1%)	348 (2%)

Reproduced from *The Lancet*, Vol. 365; Graham DJ et al. Risk of acute myocardial infarction and sudden cardiac death in patients treated with cyclo-oxygenase 2 selective and non-selective non-steroidal anti-inflammatory drugs: Nested-case-control study. 475–81. © 2005, reprinted with permission from Elsevier.

Usually, for each patient exposed to the determinant, a patient in the reference category is sought who has similar values for one or more characteristics (i.e., matching factors) considered to act as important confounders. This will result in equal distribution of these confounders among the two comparison groups. Intuitively, this is an attractive approach because it seems to mimic the randomization procedure in a trial. The matching procedure, however, will only be able to achieve comparability for known and adequately measurable confounders, while randomization will prevent any known and unknown confounding. Moreover, matching may pose logistic problems, particularly when multiple matching factors are involved. Matching on more than two patient characteristics is therefore generally not feasible. Alternatively, one could match those receiving the intervention and those in the reference category according to a composite score (i.e., the propensity score), encompassing multiple potential confounders. It should be emphasized that matching of patients exposed to the intervention with patients in the reference category of the determinant (which is usually done in a cohort study) is completely different from matching of cases and controls in a case-control study. Matching of cases and controls is counterintuitive because those developing the outcome (i.e., the cases) should naturally differ from those not experiencing the outcome (controls) in all risk factors for the outcome.

Instrumental Variables

Another method is believed to not only limit (or even prevent) known, but also *unknown* confounding in observational causal research: the use of instrumental variables. An *instrumental variable* (IV) is strongly related to exposure (here, the intervention), is not related to the confounders, and is not related to the outcome (except through its relation to the intervention). Categorizing study participants according to an instrumental variable implies that, if indeed the instrumental variable is not associated with the probability of developing the outcome (other than through its strong association with the intervention), all potential confounders are equally distributed among the categories of the instrumental variable [Martens et al., 2006]. Instrumental variables that have been applied include regional preferences for the intervention (e.g., drug therapy) or the distance to a clinic. A study on the effects of more intensified treatment (including cardiac catheterization) on mortality in patients with myocardial infarction was one of the first to apply this method [McClellan, McNeill, & Newhouse, 1994]. Distance to the hospital was used as an instrumental variable as it was considered to be closely related to the chance of the intervention (i.e., intensified treatment is more likely to be initiated when the distance to the hospital is shorter), while the IV (distance to the hospital) itself was judged not to be related to the confounders or to the outcome (mortality). Theoretically, comparison of patients living close to a hospital with those living farther away would provide for an unconfounded estimate of the effect of more intensified treatment of myocardial infarction on mortality.

The IV method is increasingly being applied in research on side effects of interventions [Huybrechts et al., 2011]. Brookhart et al. [2006] used the physician's preference of COX-2 inhibitors or other NSAIDs as an IV to compare the risk of gastrointestinal side effects of these drugs. The abstract of this study is presented in **Box 6–8**; it illustrates both the potential strength and the uncertainties of the method.

BOX 6–8   The Instrumental Variable Method

Background: Postmarketing observational studies of the safety and effectiveness of prescription medications are critically important but fraught with methodological problems. The data sources available for such research often lack information on indications and other important confounders for the drug exposure under study. Instrumental variable methods have been proposed as a potential approach to control confounding by indication in nonexperimental studies of treatment effects; however, good instruments are hard to find.

Methods: We propose an instrument for use in pharmacoepidemiology that is based on a time-varying estimate of the prescribing physician's preference for one drug relative to a competing therapy. The use of this instrument is illustrated in a study comparing the effect of exposure to COX-2 inhibitors with nonselective, nonsteroidal anti-inflammatory medications on gastrointestinal complications.

Results: Using conventional multivariable regression adjusting for 17 potential confounders, we found no protective effect due to COX-2 use within 120 days from the initial exposure (risk difference = −0.06 per 100 patients; 95% confidence interval = −0.26 to 0.14). However, the proposed instrumental variable method attributed a protective effect to COX-2 exposure (−1.31 per 100 patients; −2.42 to −0.20) compatible with randomized trial results (−0.65 per 100 patients; −1.08 to −0.22).

Conclusions: The instrumental variable method that we have proposed appears to have substantially reduced the bias due to unobserved confounding. However, more work needs to be done to understand the sensitivity of this approach to possible violations of the instrumental variable assumptions.

Although IVs appear to offer a rather ideal solution to the danger of known and even unknown confounding in observational causal research, they may be hard to find in a particular study. Most notably, it is difficult to prove that the main assumptions underlying this method hold [Groenwold et al., 2010].

Limiting Confounding in the Design of Data Analyses

Multivariable Analyses

The essence of adjusting for confounders is that potential confounders should be identified in advance and measured appropriately, and then the observed crude association of the intervention and the outcome (here, unintended effect) is adjusted using available statistical techniques. There is no consensus about the way to select confounders and how to build a multivariable model. The decision to adjust for a potential confounder can be based on a close examination of its relationship with both the determinant and the outcome in the database of the study. To measure and include those potential confounders in the analysis that are, based on the available literature, known to confound the association between the intervention and the unintended effect is a more pragmatic and safe approach to limit confounding [Groenwold et al., 2011]. Often, all confounders are included in a multiple regression model all at once or researchers develop computer models to build the multivariable model using statistical reasons to include or exclude a potential confounder. However, we recommend that confounders be included one at a time, starting with the strongest confounder based on clinical expertise, earlier studies, and the univariable analysis of the confounder with the outcome. Then the effect of each included potential confounder on the risk estimate can be evaluated. When this effect is large enough, arbitrarily a change of 5% or 10% in the measure of association, for example the odds ratio, between the intervention and the outcome is sometimes chosen, confounding by this included variable is considered present. The methodical single inclusion of potential confounders may also indicate the potential for residual confounding. If, for example, the risk estimate remains stable after inclusion of the first major confounders and even after inclusion of additional potential confounders, one may argue that any unmeasured or unknown confounder is unlikely to result in a major change in the risk estimate. The advantage of subsequent inclusion of individual confounders in a multiple regression model is illustrated in our case-control study on the risk of sudden death in hypertensive patients using non-potassium-sparing diuretics compared to other antihypertensives (see **Table 6–6**).

TABLE 6–6   Risk of Sudden Cardiac Death Among Patients with Hypertension Receiving Non-Potassium-Sparing Diuretics (NPSD) Compared to Other Antihypertensive Drugs.

Results of multivariable logistic regression analysis. Subsequent inclusion of the first (strongest) confounders yielded the expected changes in the risk estimate. Inclusion of additional confounders hardly changed the odds ratio, indicating that residual confounding may be limited.

Potential Confounders Included in the Model	Odds Ratio (95%) of Sudden Cardiac Death for NPSD Versus Other Antihypertensives
Crude	1.7 (0.9–3.1)
+ Prior myocardial infarction	2.0 (1.1–3.8)
+ Heart failure	2.0 (1.0–3.9)
+ Angina	2.1 (1.1–4.1)
+ Stroke	2.1 (1.0–4.1)
+ Arrhythmias	2.1 (1.1–4.1)
+ Claudication	2.1 (1.1–4.2)
+ Diabetes	2.1 (1.0–4.1)
+ Obstructive pulmonary disease	2.2 (1.1–4.6)
+ Cigarette smoking	2.2 (1.1–4.4)
+ Hypercholesterolemia	2.2 (1.1–4.5)
+ Mean blood pressure prior 5 years	2.2 (1.1–4.6)

Data from Hoes AW, Grobbee DE, Lubsen J, Man in 't Veld AJ, van der Does E, Hofman A. Diuretics, beta-blockers, and the risk for sudden cardiac death in hypertensive patients. *Ann Intern Med* 1995a;123:481–7.

It should be noted that when adjustment for many potential confounders is anticipated, both matching and multivariable regression techniques may become problematic, the latter because the assumptions underlying the regression model often become untenable. Use of a single score summarizing patient characteristics that may act as confounders has been advocated as a better alternative [Jick et al., 1973; Miettinen, 1976a]. In particular, the use of so-called propensity scores has increased in recent years.

Propensity Scores

The propensity score represents the probability of receiving the intervention. It often (for example in the case of a dichotomous intervention variable) results from a multiple logistic regression analysis including patient and other characteristics believed to be related to initiation of the intervention as independent variables and exposure to the intervention as the dependent variable. Thus, the propensity score focuses on the left arrow of the confounding triangle and summarizes information from all potential confounders. In patients with a similar propensity score the prognosis will then be the same in the absence of the intervention. Rosenbaum and Rubin [1984] were the first to summarize all characteristics related to the initiation or non-initiation of the intervention in a propensity score. In the Metoo-coxib example, this would imply that a score predicting the use of Metoo-coxib instead of the reference exposure (e.g., other NSAIDS) would first be derived. After a propensity score is calculated for each participant, one can match those who are receiving and not receiving the intervention according to their propensity score or include the score in a multivariable regression analysis [Rubin, 1997]. The popularity of the propensity score in observational studies on intended and unintended effects of drugs has increased rapidly in recent years [Rutten et al., 2010; Yasunaga et al., 2013]. The method, however, has its inherent limitations. These include the complexity of developing appropriate propensity scores (in fact, many studies fail to report in detail how the score was derived) and the fact that only known and measurable patient characteristics can be accounted for [Belitser et al., 2011; Heinze & Jüni, 2011].

Table 6–7 compares several available methods to limit confounding in observational studies assessing the effects of interventions. The example is taken from a study on the intended effect of influenza vaccination on influenza-related complications, including death [Hak et al., 2002]. The methods compared include restriction (separate analyses in the elderly and in younger subjects are presented), individual matching ("quasi-experiment," which requires a conditional analysis to account for the matching), one-by-one inclusion of individual confounders in a multivariable regression analysis, and the propensity score method. Because influenza vaccination is expected to reduce complications, the crude odds ratio of 1.14 indicates confounding by indication.

Restriction of the study population to certain age categories and inclusion of a few confounders in a multiple regression model reduced confounding dramatically (OR < 1.0). Also, individual matching according to different confounders (quasi-experiment) or on the propensity score clearly reduced confounding, while subsequent inclusion of additional potential confounders did not change the effect estimate.

TABLE 6–7   Methods to Limit Confounding in an Observational Study on the Effect of Influenza Vaccination

Study Population and Analysis	Adjusted For	Odds Ratio (95% CI)
Adult patients		
(18–102 y, n = 1,696)	Crude value	1.14 (0.84 to 1.55)
Conventional control: MLR*		
	+ Age (in years)	0.87 (0.64 to 1.20)
	+ Disease (asthma/COPD)	0.82 (0.59 to 1.13)
	+ GP visits (in number)	0.76 (0.54 to 1.05)
	+ Remaining factors	0.76 (0.54 to 1.06)
Elderly patients		
(65–102 y, n = 630)	Crude value	0.57 (0.35 to 0.93)
Conventional control: MLR*		
	+ Age (in years)	0.56 (0.35 to 0.92)
	+ Disease (asthma/COPD)	0.53 (0.32 to 0.87)
	+ GP visits (in number)	0.50 (0.30 to 0.83)
	+ Remaining factors	0.50 (0.29 to 0.83)
Younger patients		
(18–64 y, n = 1,066)	Crude value	1.27 (0.84 to 1.94)
Conventional control: MLR*		
	+ Age (in years)	1.11 (0.73 to 1.70)
	+ Disease (asthma/COPD)	1.08 (0.70 to 1.66)
	+ GP visits (in number)	0.94 (0.61 to 1.47)
	+ Remaining factors	0.94 (0.60 to 1.45)
Quasi-experiment		
(18–64 y, n = 676)	Matched crude value	0.90 (0.63 to 1.52)
Conventional control: MCLR†		
	+ Age/disease/GP visits	0.89 (0.52 to 1.54)
Younger patients		
(18–64 y, n = 1,066)	Matched crude value	0.87 (0.56 to 1.35)
Propensity score: MCLR†		
	+ Age/disease/GP visits	0.86 (0.55 to 1.35)

*MLR, multivariable logistic regression analysis; †MCLR, multivariable conditional logistic regression analysis.

Reproduced from Hak E, Verheij TJ, Grobbee DE, Nichol KL, Hoes AW. Confounding by indication in non-experimental evaluation of vaccine effectiveness: the example of prevention of influenza complications. *J Epidemiol Community Health* 2002;56:951–5, with permission from BMJ Publishing Group Ltd.

HEALTHCARE DATABASES AS A FRAMEWORK FOR RESEARCH ON UNINTENDED EFFECTS OF INTERVENTIONS

As discussed in this chapter, most studies on unintended effects of interventions are observational, require very large sample sizes and long follow-up periods, and include identification and valid measurements of confounders to ensure their validity. The fact that the availability of many large-scale, longitudinal, computerized healthcare databases (including routinely collected data on interventions received, patient characteristics, and patient outcomes) has greatly facilitated the conduct of research on unintended effects of interventions is, therefore, hardly surprising. Several healthcare databases have proven to be invaluable in quantifying risks of interventions, particularly of drugs. These include (1) health maintenance organizations (HMOs), such as the Kaiser Permanente Medical Care Program and Group Health Cooperative (GHC) of Puget Sound, Seattle, in the United States; (2) general practice research databases, for example in the United Kingdom (CPRD) and the Netherlands (IPCI); and (3) pharmacy databases combined with hospital discharge diagnoses, such as the Institute for Drug Outcome Research (PHARMO), also located in the Netherlands. Linkage of such databases can further increase the applicability of these data to quantify unintended effects of interventions [Smeets et al., 2011]. Examples from these databases include studies on the unintended effects of COX-2 inhibitors [Graham et al., 2005], estrogen replacement therapy [Heckbert et al., 1997], statins [van de Garde et al., 2006], biphosphonates [Vinogradova et al., 2013], and quinolones [Erkens et al., 2002].

In **Box 6–9**, some characteristics of the Kaiser Permanente Medical Care Program, which started in 1961, are shown [Selby et al., 2005].

Obviously, the suitability of these databases critically depends on the quality of the (usually routinely collected) relevant data. In particular, the use of the intervention (including, in the case of drug interventions, dosage, and duration), the outcome, and potential confounders, including comedication, comorbidity, and other relevant patient characteristics, should be assessed validly. The availability of prescription-filling data from pharmacies is crucial as are high-quality coding systems for relevant diagnoses. The latter is much more problematic; one simply cannot expect that all diagnoses are coded correctly by treating physicians in daily practice and selectivity in the diagnoses used (i.e., restriction to those requiring additional diagnostic testing or the more severe outcomes) is important. The main advantages of HMO databases are that enrollees will typically visit those

BOX 6–9   Kaiser Permanente Medical Care Program

Total number of enrollees	8.2 million
Enrollees in Northern California	3.2 million
Initiation of the program	1961
Selected databases available:	Information includes:
Membership database	Enrollment status, source of insurance
Demographic database	Name, birthdate, sex, address, physical disabilities
Hospitalizations	ICD-coded hospital discharge diagnoses
Outpatient visits	Date, ICD-coded diagnoses, provider
Laboratory results	Chemistry, hematology, microbiology, pathology, etc.
Prescriptions	Name, drug code, dosage, dispensing, costs
Disease registries	Cancer, diabetes, AIDS, ICD cause of death registries

ICD = International Classification of Diseases

physicians, hospitals, and pharmacists affiliated with the organization and that complete coverage of all available health care information of its members can be ensured. The healthcare system in some European countries, such as Great Britain and the Netherlands, greatly increases the value of general practice databases. In these countries, all inhabitants are enlisted with one computerized general practice, fill their prescriptions at one computerized pharmacy, and the general practitioner has a gate-keeping function where referral to hospital specialists is initiated by the general practitioner and all relevant information (including hospital discharge letters) are available in the general practice database [van der Lei et al., 1993]. Despite the value of these databases, some information, such as more subjective diagnoses (e.g., dyspepsia, depression), lifestyle parameters (e.g., smoking, alcohol use), ethnicity, and socioeconomic status is notoriously difficult to obtain validly, if available at all. If such information is required to limit confounding, the validity of the study is at stake. Consequently, these databases are particularly suited to assess type B unintended effects, where confounding generally does not play a role.

Part 3

Tools for Clinical Research

Chapter 7

Design of Data Collection

INTRODUCTION

The design of data collection is an element of critical importance in the successful design of clinical epidemiologic studies. The prime consideration in choosing from different options to collect data is the expected quality of the results of the data analyses in terms of relevance, validity, and precision. The relevance is first and foremost determined by the research question, with the type of subjects from whom data are collected adequately reflecting the domain. A number of other issues are important as well. Time constraints and budgetary aspects of a study may impact the choice of study population and type of data collection. For example, when a widely used drug is suspected of causing a serious side effect, it is usually impossible to postpone action for a number of years until a study yields results. Also, lack of money may force an investigator to limit the number of measurements or the size of the group of patients studied. Sometimes ethical limitations apply, for example when an investigator wants to examine whether particularly high doses of radiotherapy induce secondary tumors in patients treated for a primary cancer. The investigator should preferably use the data at hand rather than wait until another group of patients is exposed.

There is no unique optimal way to collect data for any research question. Despite the sometimes fiercely voiced belief that the most reliable results are obtained in a randomized trial, there are many examples of bad trials and many of much better "non-trials," and there are obvious instances where a trial is not feasible or otherwise not justified. This chapter discusses some general aspects of the design of data collection, with the goal of offering a consistent and comprehensive taxonomy without confusing terminology.

In clinical epidemiology, all studies can be classified according to three characteristics: time, census or sampling, and experimental or observational.

TIME

Time is an essential aspect of data collection. The time between collection of determinant and outcome information can be zero or larger than zero. When data on determinant and outcome are measured simultaneously, the time axis of the study is zero and the study is called *cross-sectional*. In all other study types the time axis is larger than zero. Furthermore, both determinant and outcome data already may or may not be available at the start of the study. If the data have been recorded in the past (i.e., have been collected retrospectively), the study is termed *retrospective*. When the data are yet to be collected and recorded for both outcome and determinants when the study is started, the data are collected prospectively and the study is termed *prospective*. Combinations of retrospective and prospective data collection can occur.

There are no inherent implications for the validity of a study when data are not prospectively collected. Still, frequently authors as well as readers use and interpret the term retrospective as a negative qualification. Retrospective data should only be viewed with caution if a similar study with a prospective data collection would provide results that are more valid, precise, and/or clinically relevant. For example, in an etiologic study, the available retrospective data may lack information on certain confounders or have confounder information that is less precise than necessary for full adjustment. Results from such a study may be biased or contain residual confounding that would not apply if data had been collected prospectively.

Alternatively, data on certain outcomes may be lacking. The results would then necessarily be restricted to inferences made from the outcomes that are in the data. While restricted, the research may still be valid and relevant. In descriptive research, the lack of particular data may create even fewer problems because there is not a need for full confounder information. Consider, for example, a study on the value of exercise testing in the diagnostic workup of patients suspected of ischemic coronary disease. An available database may not include results from troponin measurements, which are being used to assist the diagnosis in these patients. Consequently, the added value of exercise testing in the presence of troponin measurements cannot be studied. Still, the results may be useful to position exercise testing for those settings in which there is no access to troponin measurements in these patients.

Retrospective data collection may suffer more from missing data than data that are purposely collected prospectively. Missing data, for example, are a typical problem for routine clinical data that were stored before they were used for research. Here, the size of the problem depends on the importance of the variables that are missing and the proportion of subjects with missing data. Depending on the size of the overall study and the completeness of other data, the problem of missing data may be reduced or overcome by estimating the value of the missing data points using, for example, multiple imputation. The *principle of imputation* is based on the view that if sufficient information on a certain subject, or comparable subjects, is available the value of unobserved variables may be estimated with confidence. For example, suppose that in an existing database the data on body weight is missing for some individuals. With the use of available data on height, age, gender, and ethnicity, a reliable estimate of an individual's body weight may be obtained through regression modeling. Provided that the number of missing data is not too high, say less than 10% for a few variables, valid analyses may be done on all subjects.

It is important to realize that the time dimension of a study is not necessarily the same as the time dimension of the object of research. With the exception of diagnostic research, where diagnostic determinants and the outcome occur at the same time, all determinant outcome relationships are longitudinal by nature. Take, for example, a study on the relationship between the BCR-ABL gene and leukemia that is conducted with a time axis of zero (i.e., cross-sectionally). Genes are measured in all patients. While in this study determinant and outcome information were collected at the same point in time (and thus time is zero), the inference of an increased risk of leukemia in those with the p210 BCR-ABL gene points at a longitudinal relationship: Those with the gene have an increased risk of acquiring the disease in the future.

The terms retrospective and prospective thus refer to the timing of data collection, that is, before or after the study is initiated. *Historical cohort study* would be a better name than retrospective cohort study because it more directly speaks to the operational aspects of the study. However, the term retrospective is much more commonly used.

CENSUS OR SAMPLING

When the determinant(s) and outcome (and, when relevant, confounders or effect modifiers) are measured in *all* members of a population that is studied (such as in a cohort study) a "census" approach is taken. The cohort study is the paradigm of epidemiologic research. A *cohort* is a group of subjects from whom data are collected over a certain time period. The word cohort is derived from Roman antiquity, where a cohort was a body of about 300 to 600 soldiers, the tenth part of a legion. Once part of the cohort, there was no escape; you always remained a member. Now that you are reading this text, you are part of the cohort of readers who read the text. You will never get rid of that qualifying event.

In epidemiologic research, the qualifying event for becoming member of a cohort is typically that a subject is selected together with a smaller or larger group of other individuals to become part of a study population that is then followed over time. Sometimes, subjects can enter and leave a study population, as for example the population of a town that is followed over time. As the months and years go by, people will move into the town and become part of the study population while others will leave. Such a study population is best called a *dynamic population*. The membership of a cohort is fixed (in essence, once a member, always a member until you die) while dynamic populations change over time. The term dynamic cohort is an oxymoron. For reasons of simplicity we will use the term *cohort studies* for all studies taking a census approach and with time between the measurement of the determinant and outcome being larger than zero. Thus, both conventional cohort studies and dynamic population studies will be referred to as cohort studies.

In studies of cohorts and dynamic populations, epidemiologic analyses will compare the development of disease outcomes across categories of a determinant. For example, if the risk of heart disease is elevated among those with high blood homocysteine levels, the rates of disease will be higher in those with a high baseline homocysteine level compared to those with a low baseline homocysteine level. This is epidemiologic research in its most basic form. Clearly, when the causal role of high homocysteine in the occurrence of heart disease needs to be clarified, a number of confounders must be taken into account simultaneously.

Sometimes investigators may face the need to follow a large population to be able to address particular rare outcomes, for example, in the study of the gene–environment interaction and the occurrence of Hodgkin's lymphoma. To determine genetic abnormalities in the whole population would create insurmountable expenses. An alternative is to wait until cases of lymphoma occur ("cases") and perform genetic analyses only in those with the disease and in a random sample of the remainder of the population ("controls"). The purpose of such a sampling approach is straightforward. If a valid sample is taken and the sample is sufficiently large, the distribution of determinants (and, in causal studies, confounders) in the sample will reliably reflect the distributions in the population experience from whom the sample was drawn. In other words, the sample provides the same information as the much larger full population would. Across categories of the determinant in the combined samples of diseased subjects and controls, relative rates and risks can now be calculated with adjustments for confounders where appropriate. In this approach, rather than examining the entire population (census), an equally informative subgroup of the population is studied (sampling). Such a study is called a *case-control study*.

There is no innate reason why the results of a case-control study should be different than when the whole population is analyzed, as long as the researcher adheres to some fundamental principles. The main principle in sampling is that determinants are sampled without any relationship to outcomes, and that outcomes are sampled without relationship to the determinant. If not, then the relationships may be biased. Suppose, for example, that only cases of Hodgkin's disease are sampled that are known to have the oncogene BCL11A. It will come as no surprise that this gene will show an increased risk even though it may not play a role in reality. In a case-control study, biased inclusion of cases or biased sampling of controls should be prevented. For example, in some situations, cases may only become known to the investigator when they have certain determinants; a physician may be less suspicious of gastrointestinal bleeding problems in patients using a new nonsteroidal anti-inflammatory drug (NSAID) that is marketed as much safer than another, older brand. In contrast, when examining patients using the older drugs the same physician may be more suspicious and thus discover more cases of minor bleeding. If a case-control study were to be conducted using the cases noted in this physician's practice over a period of time, it would show that a relationship had been introduced in favor of the newer drug, although this is not necessarily an accurate reflection.

Another issue in case-control studies compared to full cohort analyses is that the number of controls sampled needs to be sufficiently large to obtain adequate precision. There is no general rule about how large a control sample needs to be. Given that all cases that arise in a population are included in the research, this will depend on the strength of the relationship being studied and the frequency with which particular determinants of interest occur in the population. Generally, one to four times the size of the case series is drawn.

Frequently, in a case-control study the actual size of the population from which cases and controls are drawn is not exactly known. For example, in a well-known case-control study on the risk of vaginal cancer in female daughters of mothers exposed to diethylstilboestrol (DES), a case series was collected and a number of controls without any reference to the size of the population from which the cases and controls originated (see **Figure 7–1**). If the population size is not known, a limitation of the study is that no estimates of absolute risk can be obtained, such as for example, rate differences. Then, only relative measures of risk, notably odds ratios,

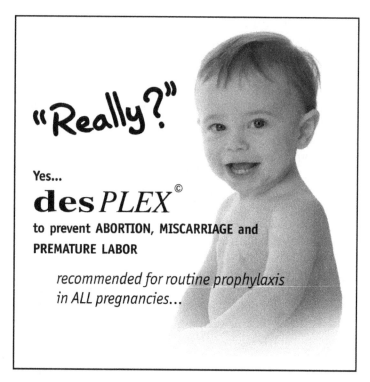

FIGURE 7–1   Advertisement for the drug diethylstilbestrol (DES).

may be obtained. However, in those instances where cases and controls are sampled from a population of known size, the same absolute and relative measures of disease risk can be calculated as in a regular full cohort analysis (i.e., using the census approach).

Case-control studies are best known for their role in etiologic research on relationships between determinants and rare outcomes. However, case-control studies also may be fruitfully employed in descriptive research, such as in diagnostic and prognostic studies.

EXPERIMENTAL OR OBSERVATIONAL STUDIES

The world is full of data, most of which are waiting to be studied. Indeed, most published clinical epidemiologic research is based on data that were previously collected from available sources, such as data in patient records of clinical files, or on data that were collected in groups of subjects for the purpose of research. To take the paradigmatic cohort study again, investigators typically start with a goal of relating a particular determinant to an outcome, as for example in a study on breast cancer risk among women using long-term estrogen-progestin treatment. Researchers would start by collecting data on hormone use plus relevant confounders and then follow the population over time to relate baseline drug information to future occurrences of breast cancer.

Sometimes a cohort study is started from a particular research aim, but with time the data may offer many other opportunities to address questions that were not on the mind of the investigator when the research was initiated. This makes cohorts highly valuable assets to investigators. The limitations only rest in the type of population studied and the extent of determinant and outcome (and, if applicable, confounder or modifier) information collected.

Sometimes the investigator will not rely on the mere recording of determinant data that occur "naturally," but rather may wish to manipulate exposure to certain determinants or allocate patients purposely to a particular exposure, such as a drug, with the principal goal of learning about the effects of this exposure. The investigator thus conducts an experiment and such studies are called *experimental studies*, in contrast to *nonexperimental studies*, where the determinant is studied as it occurs naturally. The difference between a physician treating patients with a particular drug and an investigator allocating a patient to a particular drug is in the intention. The intention of the physician is simply to improve the condition of the patient, while the investigator wants to learn about the effect of the drug, quantify the extent of improvement, and document any safety risks. Experiments in clinical epidemiology are called *trials*.

The best-known and most widely used type of trial is the randomized trial, where patients are allocated to different treatment modalities by a random process. A randomized trial obviously differs from the deliberate prescription of drugs to patients in clinical care. However, when an investigator decides to study a new series of arthritis patients, to specifically determine the functional benefit of knee replacement surgery where he measures functional status before and after the operation, he is also engaged in a trial. Studies are either experimental or nonexperimental. The term nonexperimental, while logical, is not commonly used. Rather, nonexperimental studies in epidemiology are called *observational*. The contrast between experimental and observational is somewhat peculiar because it seems to imply that in experiments no observations are made.

TAXONOMY OF EPIDEMIOLOGIC DATA COLLECTION

Like many young scientific disciplines, epidemiology suffers from the use of confusing and inconsistent terminology. Many epidemiologists use the same wording to describe different studies or use different words for the same research approach. Particularly problematic is the naming of studies by words that seem to have a qualitative implication. As indicated in this chapter, by itself the word *observational* is a clean term that applies to any form of empirical research. Too often it is used to suggest a limitation of the research.

The word *descriptive* has a similar history of misuse. In several textbooks, a distinction between analytic and descriptive research is made, where descriptive studies supposedly do not provide definitive answers. We use the term descriptive as contrasted with causal to indicate whether the determinant–outcome relationship under study is meant to explain causality or is only meant to describe the strength of the association.

All research is analytic by nature. In our view, epidemiologic studies should be classified according to three dimensions: (1) time, referring to the time (zero or > 0) between measurement of the determinant and the outcome as well as to the prospective or retrospective nature of the data collection; (2) census or sampling; and (3) experimental or nonexperimental. We recommend that you use all three elements in the nomenclature in texts describing the nature of data collection. This removes the need to rely on vague, suggestive, and noninformative jargon such as retrospective study, prospective study, survey, follow-up study, and the like. Note that a prospective study is a study in which the data are collected after the researchers decided to address a specific research question and the term can thus refer to many types of data collection, including a cohort study, case-control study, cross-sectional study, or randomized trial. Also, the meaning of the term longitudinal study is unclear. All studies, except diagnostic studies, address longitudinal associations.

Thus, the characteristics of the main approaches to data collection in clinical epidemiology can be summarized as follows (see **Table 7–1**):

- A *cohort study* has a time dimension greater than zero; analyses are based on a census of all subjects in the study population, and the data collection can be conducted prospectively or retrospectively. The study can be observational or experimental, but if it is experimental it usually takes the form of a randomized trial.
- A *dynamic population study* has a time dimension greater than zero; analyses are based on a census of all subjects in the study population

TABLE 7–1   Taxonomy of Epidemiologic Data Collection

Type of Clinical Epidemiologic Study	Time: Time Between Measurement Determinant and Outcome	Time: Data Collection (prospective or retrospective)	Census or Sampling	Observational or Experimental
Cohort study	> 0	Can be both	Census	Observational*
Dynamic population study**	> 0	Can be both	Census	Observational
Case-control study	> 0 (usually)	Can be both	Sampling	Observational
Cross-sectional study	0	Can be both	Can be both	Observational
Randomized trial	> 0	Prospective	Census	Experimental

*If a cohort study is experimental, it is called a trial.

**Because the term *dynamic population study* is hardly ever applied in the literature, we use the term *cohort study* to indicate both studies involving dynamic populations and cohorts.

for the time they are members of the population, and the data collection can be conducted prospectively or retrospectively. Such studies are typically nonexperimental (i.e., observational). Because the term dynamic population study is hardly ever applied in the literature, we use the term cohort study to indicate both studies involving dynamic populations and cohorts.

- A *case-control study* typically has a time dimension greater than zero (although cross-sectional case-control studies, for example, diagnostic case-control studies, are sometimes performed); analyses are based on sampling of subjects from the study population and the data collection can be conducted prospectively or retrospectively. Case-control studies are observational (although theoretically they could be experimental if performed within a randomized trial).

- A *cross-sectional study* has a time dimension of zero. Analyses are usually based on the census but could also be based on sampling of the study population (cross-sectional case-control study). The data collection can be conducted prospectively or retrospectively. In principle, cross-sectional studies are observational.

- A *randomized trial* is a cohort study, is an experiment, and has a time dimension greater than zero; the analyses are based on a census of all subjects from the study population and the data collection can only be conducted prospectively.

Chapter 8

Cohort and Cross-Sectional Studies

INTRODUCTION

The classic epidemiologic approach is to collect data on a defined population (a cohort) and relate determinant distributions at baseline to the occurrence of disease during follow-up. This research approach has led to our understanding such diverse cause and disease relationships as the one between the lifetime risk of coronary heart disease by cholesterol levels and selected ages in the Framingham Heart Study [Lloyd-Jones et al., 2003], the relationship between physical activity and the risk of prostate cancer in the Health Professionals Follow-up Study [Giovannucci et al., 2005], the relationship between smoking and lung cancer during 50 years of observation in the British Doctor's Study [Doll et al., 2004], the relationship between caloric restriction during the Dutch famine of 1944–1955 and future breast cancer in the DOM (which stands for "Diagnostisch Onderzoek Mamma-carcinoom" or "Diagnostic Study on breast cancer") cohort [Elias et al., 2004], the relationship between apolipoprotein E (Apo-E) and Alzheimer's disease in the Rotterdam Study [Hofman et al., 1997], and the relationship between radiation and leukemia in atomic bomb survivors in Hiroshima [Pierce et al., 1996].

The essential characteristic of a cohort study is that data are collected from a defined group of people, which forms the *cohort*. Cohort membership is defined by being selected for inclusion according to certain characteristics. For example, in the Rotterdam Study, 7,983 subjects age 55 years and over who agreed to participate after invitation of all inhabitants in a particular neighborhood of Rotterdam formed the Rotterdam Study cohort [Hofman et al., 1991].

The typical design of data collection in a cohort study is to start to collect data at the time of the inception of the cohort. The starting point of a cohort, t = zero, is called the *baseline*. Sometimes, as in the Framingham Study, data collection is subsequently repeated at certain time intervals, but for other cohorts only a single set of baseline data is collected. After the baseline collection, a cohort is generally followed over time and disease occurrences among the members are recorded. The term *cohort study* was used for the first time in research in the 1930s.

Some of the best-known cohort studies start from a population of presumed healthy individuals, but cohort studies can equally well be conducted with groups of patients. For example, one etiologic study followed a cohort of premature neonates for chronic cerebral damage and related behavioral problems [Rademaker et al., 2004]. This same cohort was also used to study the prognostic meaning of neonatal cerebral imaging by ultrasound compared to magnetic resonance imaging (MRI) scanning [Rademaker et al., 2005]. Prognostic cohort studies are obviously conducted on cohorts of patients. In diagnostic studies, the cohort typically consists of subjects suspected of having the disease of interest in whom the value of diagnostic testing is studied.

TIMING OF THE ASSOCIATION RELATIVE TO THE TIMING OF DATA COLLECTION

Most cohort studies are planned in advance and data are collected prospectively. However, this is not a necessary condition. Sometimes, a cohort is defined retrospectively and historic data are used that are already available, such as in the studies on the Hiroshima atomic bomb survivors. This study's cohort comprised all those who survived the bomb attack and investigators used the limited available baseline data, notably age, sex, and degree of nuclear exposure, to relate the exposure to subsequent cancer occurrence. This cohort study had both a retrospective and a prospective component in the data collection. In a rather unusual approach, Vandenbroucke [1985] conducted a fully retrospective cohort study to investigate survival and life expectancy at age 25 years and older in 1,282 European noblemen who had been members of the Knighthood Order of the Golden Fleece between its founding in 1430 and the early 1960s.

In these examples, data collection took place in whole or in part in the past. Note that regardless of the timing of data collection, the associations examined in a cohort study are always prospective. Etiologic research aims to learn about causes of disease. Several criteria for causal associations have been proposed, but at the very least the cause is assumed to precede the consequence (i.e., the disease). Therefore, the causal determinant always precedes the outcome regardless of the order in which the data have been collected. All etiologic research is inherently prospective, yet the data may be collected before, during, or after the determinant–outcome relationship has materialized. Even when data are collected prospectively, they will often not be collected for all members of the cohort at the same time. Baseline data collection may take time, and during that time subsequent participants enter the cohort. This type of cohort is built up obliquely.

When the time between the collection of determinant and outcome data is zero, the cohort study is referred to as *cross-sectional*. For example, in the study on Alzheimer's disease and Apo-E genotype, Apo-E genetic polymorphisms were determined at the same time that cognitive examinations were performed to assess the presence of dementia. Data collection in this cohort was cross-sectional for this particular research question. However, even though data collection was cross-sectional, the conclusion was that the Apo-E ε4 genotype, in the presence of atherosclerosis, increased the patients' risk of dementia. The determinant–outcome relationship was interpreted prospectively. The tenable assumption was that the genetic variant had been present long before dementia developed and would not change due to the occurrence of the disease.

In the design of data collection and analysis of cohort studies, it is important to be aware of differences in the timing of data collection and the true time relationship between the determinant and outcome. In etiologic research, it is necessary to be confident that, while data may be collected in a different order, the resulting association(s) indeed may be interpreted causally. For example, in a study on dietary habits and the risk of heart disease, the collection of dietary data after symptomatic coronary disease has occurred may be problematic because patients are likely to change their diet after becoming aware of the disease. Consequently, the observed associations may be confounded.

Another problem is that when outcome data on a cohort are not recorded continuously and prospectively, but rather after a longer time interval, some subjects with the outcome may be missed. As long as the chance of being missed is random, this is no real threat to validity. However, the chance of being detected and recorded as someone who developed the outcome may somehow be related to the determinant of interest. This may apply equally to causal and descriptive studies. In a prognostic study, the prognostic meaning of a patient characteristic may be overestimated when patients with the characteristic are more likely to be followed more closely. In a diagnostic study, only certain patients may be referred for diagnostic workup, making it more likely that the outcome is eventually diagnosed. For example, in a study on exercise testing in the diagnosis of coronary disease, only those with abnormal test results will be referred for invasive imaging using coronary angiography. If not all patients undergo the same reference test, some with disease may be missed, resulting in false negatives and leading to an overestimation of the diagnostic value of the test.

CAUSAL AND DESCRIPTIVE COHORT STUDIES

The origins of cohort studies in epidemiology lie in studies initiated to address causal associations. Much of the methodology and strategies for data analyses for cohort studies have been developed with a view toward causal explanation. The cohort approach is also a highly effective data collection design for descriptive research. Diagnostic or prognostic research questions can be effectively addressed using a cohort study. Clearly, for a diagnostic study where the prevalence of the diagnosis of interest in relation to a set of diagnostic indicators is studied, the time between the occurrence of the outcome and the determinants is zero. Typically, therefore, determinant and outcome information is collected simultaneously, thus making a diagnostic study a cross-sectional cohort study (see further discussion later in the chapter). However, frequently the optimal approach to research on prognosis is through a cohort study with time exceeding zero. One or multiple prognostic factors are collected at baseline and the cohort is followed up on to record the occurrence of events. For example, in one prognostic study, levels of circulating carcinoembryonic antigen (CEA) were measured in a cohort of patients with a primary colon tumor resection who were followed for mortality to determine the prognostic value of CEA after treatment for the malignancy [Stelzner et al., 2005] (see **Box 8–1**).

The difference between data collection in causal and descriptive cohort studies is a result of the difference in objectives between causal and descriptive studies. In etiologic research, determinant information and data on confounders are collected. By nature of the aim to obtain valid estimates of the causal association between the determinant and the outcome, confounder data need to be complete and of high quality. If confounders are measured poorly or not measured at all, the results of the analyses may show an association that is quantitatively or qualitatively incorrect.

In descriptive research there is no need to worry about confounders. Rather, the variables considered determinants should be as complete as is necessary for the results of the research to be relevant and in agreement with the research question. For example, in the study on the prognosis after primary tumor resection in patients presenting with unresectable synchronous metastases from colorectal carcinoma, six independent variables with a relationship to survival were found: performance status, ASA-class, CEA level, metastatic load, extent of primary tumor, and chemotherapy. Whether this includes

BOX 8-1   Survival in Patients with Stage IV Colorectal Cancer

BACKGROUND: The prognostic impact of primary tumor resection in patients presenting with unresectable synchronous metastases from colorectal carcinoma (CRC) is not well established. In the present study, we analyzed 15 factors to define the value of primary tumor resection with regard to prognosis.

PATIENTS AND METHODS: We identified 186 consecutive patients with proven stage IV CRC from the years 1995 to 2001. Variables were tested for their relationship to survival in univariate analyses with the Kaplan-Meier method and the log rank test. Factors that showed a significant impact were included in a Cox proportional hazards model. The tests were repeated for 107 patients who had no symptoms from their primary tumor.

RESULTS: Overall there were six independent variables with a relationship to survival: performance status, ASA-class, CEA level, metastatic load, extent of primary tumor, and chemotherapy. In the asymptomatic patients we investigated 13 factors, 3 of which proved to be independent predictors of survival: performance status, CEA level, and chemotherapy. Resection of primary tumor was only predictive of survival if in-hospital mortality was excluded.

CONCLUSION: Resection of the tumor, if possible, is doubtless the best option for stage IV CRC patients with severe symptoms caused by their primary tumor. In asymptomatic patients, chemotherapy is preferable to surgery.

Reproduced from Stelzner S, Hellmich G, Koch R, Ludwig K. Factors predicting survival in stage IV colorectal carcinoma patients after palliative treatment: A multivariate analysis. *J Surg Oncol* 2005; 89:211–217.

information on all potential prognostic indicators that a reader may find useful for his or her patients depends on two factors: (1) whether the final six variables agree with the set of variables available to a clinician who wants to use the research for his or her patients; and (2) in the case where a favorite variable of the reader of the research is not included in the six predictors, whether this particular variable has been included in the research at all.

Suppose, for example, that a particular clinic routinely measures lactate dehydrogenase (LDH) in serum to set the prognosis in these patients. This made it clinically relevant to include LDH in the research, although LDH was eventually shown to have no added value over the other six variables.

According to the same principles, the mode of data collection will vary in cohort studies aiming to explain causality or with the goal of prediction. In the first case, the determinant and confounder information must be collected as accurately as possible. In the second case, the data on determinants are collected according to general clinical standards because that is the way the results will eventually be applied. For either type of cohort study, outcome data should be collected as accurately as possible.

For diagnostic and prognostic studies, timing the association relative to the timing of data collection has some specific features. For prognostic studies, the same principles apply as for etiologic studies. Whatever the timing of data collection, the association is always prospective. For a variable to be prognostic with regard to a given outcome, the prognostic factor needs to be observed before the outcome has occurred. In diagnostic studies, by definition the determinant and outcome occur at the same time. In a cohort of patients suspected of a certain diagnosis, data on putative diagnostic indicators are collected at the same time that the outcome is determined by some reference test. Next, these cross-sectional determinants and outcome data are analyzed for the strength of their association. Here, no prospective association is assumed.

There is one subtlety in data collection in some diagnostic studies. Suppose, for example, that the diagnostic value of mammography for detection of early breast cancer is being studied [Moss et al., 2005]. Data from mammography are collected and women are referred for further diagnostic workup. After mammography, it may take some time before outcome data are available in those women with abnormal mammographic findings. Once the diagnosis has been established in all those who are referred, it may take even longer before those breast cancers that were missed by the mammography become apparent. Consequently, this diagnostic study may include data collection on the cohort over a prolonged period of time. Still, the determinant–outcome relationship in this study—as in any diagnostic study—has a time interval of zero.

A classic example of the problem of an inevitable incomplete follow-up in a cohort is the study of congenital malformations caused by medication use during pregnancy. When congenital malformations are recorded at birth, the presence (i.e., prevalence) rather than the incidence is determined. Pregnancies involving congenital malformations that were terminated early may have been related to the drug exposure too, but they are not included. If this is the case, then the study's risk estimates will be too low.

EXPERIMENTAL COHORT STUDIES

Cohort studies are generally based on real-life data, that is, circumstances that occur without particular interference by the investigator. Therefore, cohort studies are typically considered to be observational (i.e., nonexperimental).

However, a randomized trial is also a cohort study, given that the study population is defined by taking part in the trial and is subsequently followed over time. Yet, trials are experimental because the exposure, such as allocation to the drug, is not taken from real-life prescriptions but rather manipulated by the investigator through randomization with the goal of improving the study's ability to show unbiased estimates of the association between the drug and the outcome.

The experimental nature of trials requires prospective collection of the data. However, even though data are collected prospectively, the collection of outcome data needs to be complete to prevent selective recording of outcome events according to allocated treatment. In trials, this rule is known as the *intention to treat* principle. The principle is, however, not different from the need for outcome assessment independent from the determinant in any cohort study.

There are good examples of cohorts that were first assembled for a trial but were continued after the randomized period as a plain cohort study. Here, the exposure is experimental during a period of the cohort study and nonexperimental thereafter. Also, patients considered for the trial but eventually not randomized may be followed up on alongside the randomized subgroup of the cohort. For example, all subjects screened for the Multiple Risk Factor Intervention Trial (MRFIT) were used to create one of the largest cohort studies on cardiovascular risk factors [Stamler et al., 1986].

CROSS-SECTIONAL STUDIES

Cross-sectional studies are cohort studies with a time interval of zero between the collection of determinant and outcome data. In other words, the determinant and outcome information are collected simultaneously. An example is a study on the relationship between certain determinants and joint bleeds in hemophilia patients, where a history of bleeding is obtained at the same time as the possible risk factors for bleeding (e.g., compliance with treatment, dosage of treatment, and engagement in sports and other activities with trauma risk).

Another example is the analysis of risk of congenital malformations after exposure to antidepressant drugs during pregnancy, where all the data are collected from women at the time of delivery of their children, who may or not may have malformations. It is important to realize that while the data collection for determinants and outcome is organized at the same time, the association being studied is longitudinal. The assumption is that drug exposure precedes the occurrence of malformations. The consequence is that the investigators need to seek assurance that no bias is introduced by this difference between the timing of data collection and the temporal sequence of the presumed cause and effect. For example, suppose that women with malformed children have a better recollection of their drug use during pregnancy; this may induce an invalid, biased association between the drug use and the congenital malformation. This problem is known as *recall bias*.

When a study is cross-sectional, it is not necessarily conducted at a single point in time. Even though data collection of determinants and outcome in an individual takes place simultaneously at a particular moment, different individuals participating in a study may be examined sequentially over a longer time period.

ECOLOGIC STUDIES

Ecologic studies are cohort studies. The cohort is assembled from the aggregate experience of several populations, for example, those living in different geographic areas. In contrast to the usual approach in cohort studies, data are collected from summary measures in populations rather than from individual members of populations. For example, a study on the proportion of alcohol intake from wine and the occurrence of coronary heart disease used the distribution of wine intake across countries and the country-specific rates of coronary heart disease to determine the possible cardioprotective effect of different levels of wine consumption. The data were from different populations, but the inference was made for individuals within populations, suggesting that rather than alcohol *per se*, it was the cardioprotective effect of wine that was particularly clear (see **Figure 8–1**) [Criqui & Ringel, 1994]. The study was etiologic, and this implies that the effect from wine on heart disease risk should be adjusted for confounders. In particular, there seem to be several aspects of lifestyle, including dietary habits, which could confound the observed crude association.

A major problem in ecologic studies is the very limited extent to which confounder information is generally available. For example, data on differences in fat intake in populations of countries with a different wine consumption may not exist, or when data are available at a population level, the distribution within a country and its relationship to the distribution of wine intake within that country may remain unknown. Even when two countries show similar overall levels of intake of fat and wine, within the countries the relationship between fat intake and wine consumption on an individual level may be different. Indeed, with regard to wine and heart

FIGURE 8–1   Example of an ecological study assessing the relationship between wine consumption and the coronary heart disease (CHD) mortality rate in men aged 44 to 64.

Reproduced from *The Lancet*, Vol. 344; Criqui MH, Ringel BL. Does diet or alcohol explain the French paradox? 1719. @ 1994, reprinted with permission fom Elsevier.

disease risk, a more extensive analysis of a number of cohort studies with ample adjustment for confounders showed that an initial ecologic observation of a higher cardiovascular protection from wine compared to other alcoholic beverages could not be confirmed [Rimm et al., 1996]. This implies that it is the alcohol, rather than its form, that conveys protection. In clinical epidemiology, an example of an ecologic comparison is that between different hospital infection rates in relation to local policies regarding infection prevention. Even though the crude association suggests that infection rates are higher in those hospitals with a less extensive prevention program, this still may be confounded by, for example, differences in the type of surgery between hospitals. Because of inherent difficulties with handling of confounding, ecologic studies generally do not provide strong evidence in favor of or against causal associations.

COHORT STUDIES USING ROUTINE CARE DATA

There are an endless number of subjects who are potentially eligible for inclusion in clinical epidemiologic research among patients who are routinely seen in clinical care. The world is one big cohort. Routinely collected patient data offer an immense and underutilized resource of knowledge for diagnostic, prognostic, intervention, and etiologic research. Routine care data from patients who present with a particular symptom or sign that makes the physician suspect that they have a particular disease can be used for diagnostic research [Moons et al., 2004a]. Routine care data from patients diagnosed with a particular disease who were clinically followed over time can be used for prognostic research [Braitman & Davidoff, 1996; Concato, 2001]. Also, follow-up data from patients routinely treated for a particular disease with a particular treatment can be used for research on intended and unintended effects of interventions [Concato et al., 2000; Ioannidis et al., 2001]. Obviously, routinely collected data must meet certain criteria to be used in clinical epidemiologic research and its potential and problems need to be well understood for the research conclusions to be valid. There are various problems with routine care data drawn from patient files, which vary based on the type of research.

To facilitate research, patients must be coded in a specific and uniform way in the hospital or general practice files. For example, diagnostic research starts with a series (cohort) of patients who are selected based on the presence of particular symptoms or signs. To select the proper patients from routine care, they must be classified uniformly according to their presented symptom or sign. Commonly, however, patients are only coded by the final diagnosis or disease, for example, using the International Classification of Disease version 10 (ICD-10) or International Classification of Primary Care (ICPC) codes.

When patients are selected on the basis of their final diagnosis as determined by a reference standard for inclusion in diagnostic research, this commonly leads to *selection bias*, which is also known as *verification, workup,* or *referral bias* [Begg, 1987; Moons et al., 2004a; Ransohoff & Feinstein, 1978]. This bias occurs because in routine care patients are commonly selectively referred for eventual disease verification based on previous test results. For example, before patients suspected of coronary heart disease are submitted to coronary angiography on which the eventual diagnosis is based, they have undergone other, less invasive testing. Thus, the disease is ruled out in many subjects before ever reaching angiography. Consequently, if patients are selected for a diagnostic study using angiographically confirmed coronary disease as a criterion (and perhaps compared with healthy subjects), the study population will not represent the full spectrum of patients suspected of having coronary disease in real life. To achieve full representation, patients should be selected on the criterion, "suspicion of coronary disease requiring further diagnostic workup." Standard and uniform coding of patients according to their main symptom or sign at presentation is unfortunately not very common, but this is likely to improve with the increasing use of electronic patient records [Oostenbrink et al., 2003].

In contrast to diagnostic research, the classification in routine care of patients according to their final diagnosis does facilitate the selection of cohorts of patients with a particular disease to be included in prognostic research. Moreover, because administered treatments are commonly documented as well, routine care data in principle also provide for research on intended and unintended effects of treatments, although sometimes this may be prohibited by insurmountable problems of confounding by indication.

Another potential problem when using routine care data is the absence of a blinded outcome assessment. Clinical epidemiologic research often requires that the presence or absence of the outcome under study be documented in each study subject without knowledge of (i.e., blinded for) the determinant(s) under study. Otherwise, knowledge of the determinant status may (partly) be used and included (or incorporated) in the assessment of the outcome. Consequently, the association between the determinant(s) and outcome will be biased, a phenomenon also known as *information, observer, assessment,* or *incorporation* bias [Guyatt et al., 1993; Laupacis et al., 1997; Moons & Grobbee, 2002b; Pocock, 1984].

Of course, in routine care the patient outcome recorded in files is commonly affected by knowledge of preceding patient information, including the determinants(s) of interest. Hence, in studies solely based on routine care data, blinded outcome assessment is commonly lacking. While sometimes acceptable, an unblinded outcome assessment in particular may pose validity problems when the assessment of the presence or absence of an outcome is sensitive to subjective (observer) interpretation, as for example in imaging tests. Suppose that the goal of a diagnostic study is to determine the value of routine chest radiographs to detect small lung tumors. Interpretation of minor abnormalities on the radiograph in routine care may be quite different if the observer has additional information (e.g., on smoking status) that would make the presence of a malignancy more or less likely. Clearly, the unblinded outcome assessment is a non-issue for unequivocal outcomes such as mortality or for measurements providing objective results such as biochemical parameters (e.g., cholesterol level or leukocyte count) or automatically measured blood pressure levels.

Finally, the problem can be circumvented when investigators use routine care data to select study subjects but reassess the outcome by approaching individual patients, disregarding previously recorded patient information.

Missing Data

Probably one of the most general and difficult problems with the use of routine care data is that certain data are missing in the files. Missing data pose a problem in all types of medical research, no matter how strict the design and protocols. But this problem is accentuated in research based on routine care data, as there is commonly no strict case-record-form or data measurement protocol in daily practice.

In epidemiologic research we distinguish three types of missing data [Rubin, 1976]. If subjects whose data are missing are a random subset of the complete sample of subjects, the missing data are called *missing completely at random* (MCAR). Typical examples of MCAR are an accidentally dropped tube containing venous blood (thus blood parameters cannot be measured) or a questionnaire that is accidentally lost. The reason for the missing data is completely random. In other words, the probability that an observation is missing is not related to any other patient characteristic.

If the probability that an observation is missing depends on information that is not observed, like the value of the observation itself, the missing data are called *missing not at random* (MNAR). For example, data on smoking habits may be more likely to be missing when subjects do not smoke.

When missing data occur in relation to observed patient characteristics, subjects with missing data are a selective rather than a random subset of the total study population. This pattern of missing data is confusingly called *missing at random* (MAR), where missing values are random conditional on other available patient information [Rubin, 1976]. Data that are missing at random are very common in routine care databases. For example, in a diagnostic study among children with neck stiffness, investigators quantified which combination of predictors from patient history and physical examination could predict the absence of bacterial meningitis (outcome), and which blood tests (e.g., C-reactive protein level) have added predictive value. Patients presenting with severe signs such as convulsions, which commonly occur among those with bacterial meningitis, often received additional blood testing before full completion of patient history and physical examination, which in turn were largely missing in the records. On the other hand, patients with very mild symptoms, who frequently had no bacterial meningitis, were more likely to have a completed history and physical but were less likely to have had additional tests, because the physician had already ruled out a serious disease. Missing data on particular tests was thus related to other observed test results and—although indirectly—to the outcome.

This mechanism of missing data is even more likely to occur in longitudinal studies based on routine care data. When following patients over time in routine care practice, loss to follow-up is a common problem and often is directly related to particular patient characteristics. Accordingly, outcomes may be only available for particular patients, the selection of whom is related to certain determinants. Consider a study to compare the prognosis of patients with minimally versus invasive cancer. Suppose that patients who were treated in a particular hospital during a certain period were followed up on over time using data from patient records. Follow-up information for subsequent morbidity may be more complete for patients with initial invasive cancer, because these patients visited the clinic more regularly and during a longer time period as part of routine procedures. One can easily check whether data are MCAR [Van der Heijden et al., 2006]. If the subset of patients with and without missing values does not differ on the other observed patient characteristics, the missing values are likely MCAR (although theoretically they might still be MNAR).

Typically, in epidemiologic research, missing data are neither MCAR nor MNAR, but rather MAR, although this cannot be tested, only assumed [Donders et al., 2006; Greenland & Finkle, 1995; Little & Rubin, 1987; Schafer, 1997; Schafer & Graham, 2002; Vach, 1994].

There are various methods for dealing with missing values in clinical epidemiologic research. The best method obviously is to conduct a more active follow-up of the patients for whom crucial information is (partly) missing in order to obtain as much as possible of this information. For example, in the previously mentioned cancer study with the selective follow-up, the researchers could conduct a more active follow-up of all patients regardless of the baseline disease condition. Similarly, in the Utrecht Health Project, routine care data are supplemented with predetermined additional data collection [Grobbee et al., 2005]. The quality of the routine care data in the Utrecht Health Project is further optimized by a dedicated training program for healthcare personnel, with ample attention given to ensure complete and adequate coding.

If a more active follow-up does not suffice or is not feasible, however, researchers usually exclude all subjects with a missing value on any of the variables from the analysis. The so-called *complete* or *available* case analysis is the most common method currently found in clinical epidemiologic studies, probably because most statistical packages implicitly exclude the subjects with a missing value on any of the variables analyzed. Obviously, simply excluding subjects with missing values affects precision. But it is commonly not appreciated that—more seriously—it produces severely biased estimates of the associations investigated when data are not missing completely at random, as shown in the examples of the diagnosis of bacterial meningitis and prognosis of cancer patients presented earlier. It is better to use other methods in the data analysis than a complete case analysis [Donders et al., 2006; Little & Rubin, 1987; Schafer, 1997; Schafer & Graham, 2002; Rubin, 1987; Vach, 1994; Vach & Blettner, 1991].

There are a variety of alternative methods to cope with missing values in the analysis. Some of these are briefly discussed next. Illustrative examples can also be found in **Boxes 8–2** and **8–3**.

1. *Conditional imputation.* This replacement is more technically called *imputation of a missing value.* In this method, a value that is based or conditional on as many as possible other patient characteristics is imputed for a missing value. To do this, one commonly uses the data from all patients without missing values on the variable to develop a multivariable prediction model using regression analysis. In such a model, the variable with missing values is the dependent or outcome variable and all other patient characteristics are the independent or predictor variables. Subsequently, this imputation or prediction model is used in the patients with missing values on that variable to predict the most likely value conditional on his/her observed characteristics. After this, a complete data set has been established and standard software can be applied to estimate the association between the determinant(s) and outcome under study. We note that in the case of missing determinant values, the outcome variable must be included in the imputation model. Similarly, when outcome values are missing, all determinants under study should be included in the imputation model. This seems like a circular process. It has been shown, empirically, however, that imputation of outcome values that are MAR, using all observed information including the determinants under study, causes less bias in the associations between these same determinants and the outcome than, for example, unconditional imputation [Crawford et al., 1995; Rubin, 1996; Unnebrink & Windeler, 2001]. Similarly, imputation of missing determinant values using the outcome eventually results in less biased associations than imputations that are not conditional on the outcome [Moons et al., 2006]. This can simply be explained by appreciating that missing data on a determinant are commonly related to other determinants and directly or indirectly to the outcome, as was also shown in the earlier examples of the diagnosis of bacterial meningitis and cancer. Conditional imputation can be done once (i.e., single imputation) or more than once (multiple imputation).

2. *Unconditional imputation.* In this method, the missing value of a particular variable is replaced or "filled in" with the mean or median of that variable as estimated from the other patients in whom that variable was observed. Because here the missing value is imputed by the overall variable mean or median irrespective (unconditional) of

any other patient information, this method is also called the *overall* or *unconditional* (mean or median) *imputation* [Donders et al., 2006; Greenland & Finkle, 1995; Little & Rubin, 1987; Schafer, 1997; Schafer & Graham, 2002; Vach, 1994].

3. *Maximum likelihood estimations.* This method (e.g., using the expectation-maximization [EM] algorithm) is used for multilevel or repeated measurement analysis in studies where determinants or outcomes are documented more than once [Little & Rubin, 1987; Schafer, 1997; Schafer & Graham, 2002; Vach, 1994]. The use of this method does not impute any data but rather uses each all available data to compute maximum likelihood estimates. The maximum likelihood estimate of a parameter is the value of the parameter that is most likely to have resulted in the observed data. The likelihood can then be computed separately for those participants with complete data on some variables and those with complete data on all variables. These two likelihoods are then maximized together to find the estimates [http://www.theanalysisfactor.com/missing-data-two-recommended-solutions/, accessed May 2013].

4. *Missing indicator method.* This method uses a dummy (0/1) variable as an indicator for missing data [Greenland & Finkle, 1995; Miettinen, 1985]. For example, if there are missing values for a particular variable, an indicator is defined with "1" if the variable value is missing and "0" otherwise. In the case of categorical variables, this is equal to treating the missing values as a separate result. For the variable, the missing values are commonly recoded as zero, although any value would suffice. The idea behind this method is that the association between the original (though recoded) variable and the outcome is always fitted in combination with the indicator variable. Accordingly, all subjects are used in the multivariable analysis, the supposed advantage of the missing indicator method. While this is true, the resulting estimates are biased even in the case of MCAR [Greenland & Finkle, 1995].

When missing data are MNAR, valuable information is lost from the data and there is no universal method of handling the missing data properly [Little & Rubin, 1987; Rubin, 1987; Schafer, 1997; Schafer & Graham, 2002; Vach, 1994]. When missing data are MCAR, the complete case analysis gives unbiased, although obviously less precise, results [Greenland & Finkle, 1995; Little & Rubin, 1987; Moons et al., 2006; Schafer, 1997; Schafer & Graham, 2002; Rubin, 1987; Vach, 1994]. However, like the missing indicator method, the unconditional mean imputation method still

BOX 8–2   Example of a Simulated Diagnostic Study with Missing Data

Consider a diagnostic study with only one continuous diagnostic test and a true disease status (present/absent).

We simulated 1,000 samples of 500 subjects drawn from a theoretical population consisting of equal numbers of diseased and nondiseased subjects. The true regression coefficient in a logistic regression model linking the diagnostic test to the probability of disease was 1.0 (odds ratio = 2.7), with an intercept of 0. The diagnostic test was normally distributed with mean 0 and standard deviation 2. No other tests or subject characteristics were considered.

In each sample, 80% of the nondiseased subjects was assigned a missing value on the test. The diseased subjects had no missing data. Accordingly, missing data were MAR as they were based on other observed variables, here the true disease status only. Overall about 40% of the data was missing. Using the procedure mice (for details about the software we refer to the literature [Van Buuren, 1999]), 10 multiple imputed data sets were created for each sample. Then the association between the test and the disease status plus standard error was estimated in each data set using a logistic regression model. Subsequently, all associations with standard errors were analyzed within each of the 10 multiply imputed data sets. The 10 regression coefficients and standard errors were then combined using standard formulas [Rubin, 1987]. One extra data set was imputed and analyzed as a single imputed data set. Finally, the results were averaged over the 1,000 simulations. For both the single and multiple imputation procedure, the estimate of the association was indeed unbiased. The single imputation procedure appears more precise because of the smaller standard error, thus leading to smaller confidence intervals, but the 90% confidence interval does not contain the true parameter as often (only 63.6%) as it should, that is 90%.

Multiple imputation leads to a larger standard error and wider confidence intervals, but the estimated standard errors are more correct and the confidence interval has the correct coverage (i.e., 90.3%). Hence, in contrast to single imputation, multiple imputation gives sound results both with respect to bias and precision.

Method	Regression Coefficient	Standard Error	Coverage of the 90% Confidence Intervals
Single imputation	0.98904	0.090186	63.6
Multiple imputation	0.98920	0.136962	90.3

BOX 8–3   Illustration of the Problems with the Missing Indicator Method and the
Unconditional Mean Imputation, Even when Values Are Missing Completely at Random

Missing indicator method. We used the same example study as in Box 8–2 but considered a second continuous test, which is a proxy for the first test. This means that the second test is not directly related to the disease (OR = 1; regression coefficient = 0) but only to the first test. Fitting a logistic regression model to predict disease status using the first test, only a positive regression coefficient was found (case 1). When only the second test was included, we also found a positive association because of the indirect relationship between disease status and the second test (case 2). Using both tests, only a positive association for the first test was found, comparable to case 1, and a regression coefficient near 0 for the second test (case 3). Suppose there were missing values on the first test but not on the second test, and that these are MCAR, that is, equal proportion in diseased and nondiseased subjects. We defined a missing indicator variable as 1 if the result of the first test was missing and 0 otherwise. One can see that in a model used to predict the true disease status using both tests plus the missing indicator, the regression coefficient of the second test would not be 0 as it should be. For the subjects with no missing data, indeed, case 3 applied. But for the subjects with a missing value on the first test, case 2—rather than case 3—suddenly applied, as there were no observations for the first test. Hence the estimate for the regression coefficient of the second test was biased and somewhere between 0, the true estimate (case 3), and the value of case 2. Moreover, if the regression coefficient of the second test was biased, so was the regression coefficient of the first test due to the mutual adjustment in multivariable modeling.

To illustrate this, we performed a second simulation study similar to that of Box 8–2. We again simulated 1,000 samples of 500 subjects drawn from the same theoretical population, which now also included a proxy variable for the first test with a correlation of 0.75 with the first diagnostic test. For the first test, 40% missing values were assigned completely at random, that is, 20% for the diseased and nondiseased. The table shows that the regression coefficient of the diagnostic test was indeed heavily biased (as the true value was 1.0) as well as the proxy variable (as the true value was 0). Thus, although the indicator method has the appealing property that all available information and subjects are used in the analyses, the fact that it can lead to biased associations for the original variables is reason enough to discard this method even when missing data are MCAR, let alone when data are MAR.

Unconditional mean imputation. In the example study in Box 8–2 it may be obvious that the magnitude and significance of the association (regression coefficient) of the continuous test with the outcome was completely determined by the difference in overlap of the test result distributions between the diseased

(continues)

BOX 8–3   Continued.

and nondiseased subjects. The less overlap, the higher and more significant the regression coefficient was. If the two distributions completely overlapped, the regression coefficient would be 0. Consider the same simulation study as was used for the missing indicator method, with 40% missing values assigned completely at random (20% for the diseased and 20% for the nondiseased).

Imputing or replacing these missing values by the overall mean of the test result as estimated from the remaining (observed) subjects—that is, nondiseased and diseased subjects combined—would obviously increase the amount of overlap in the two test result distributions. Hence, the association between the test result and the outcome would be diluted and the regression coefficient would be biased toward 0 and insignificance. This is illustrated in the lower part of this box. The regression coefficient was not 1, but rather 0.55. Like the indicator method, the overall mean imputation of missing values should also be discarded, as it leads to biased associations, even when missing data are MCAR.

	Diagnostic Test	Proxy
	Regression Coefficient (standard error)	Regression Coefficient (standard error)
Indicator method*	0.55 (0.14)	0.51 (0.08)
Overall mean	0.55 (0.14)	Not applicable

*The logistic model included: $\ln[P(\text{disease})/(1 - P(\text{disease}))]$ = intercept + b1 × diagnostic test + b2 × proxy + b3 × indicator, where the indicator = 1 if the value for diagnostic test was missing and 0 otherwise, and where diagnostic test was set to 0 if its value was missing.

leads to biased results when data are MCAR [Donders et al., 2006; Greenland & Finkle, 1995]. In the case of MAR, which is most commonly encountered in research based on routine care data (as described earlier), a complete case analysis will result in biased associations between determinants and outcome due to selective missing data. Also, the indicator method and the unconditional mean imputation method then give biased results [Donders et al., 2006; Greenland & Finkle, 1995; Little & Rubin, 1987; Moons et al., 2006; Schafer, 1997; Schafer & Graham, 2002; Vach, 1994]. Only more sophisticated techniques, like conditional single or multiple imputation and the maximum likelihood estimation method, give less biased or rather the most valid estimations of the study associations. Although single and multiple conditional imputations both yield unbiased results, the latter is preferred as it results in correctly estimated standard errors and confidence intervals, while single imputation yields standard errors that are too small. All this is illustrated using simple simulation studies in Boxes 8–2 and 8–3. Empirically, it has been shown that even in the presence of missing values in about half of the subjects, multiple conditional imputation still yields less biased results as compared to the commonly used complete case analysis [Moons et al., 2006]. The question arises how many missing values one may accept and how many subjects can be imputed before multiple imputations will not suffice. There are yet no empirical studies showing an upper limit of missing values that can be imputed validly.

Apart from these problems, routine care data comply with two essential characteristics of determinant data in descriptive (diagnostic and prognostic) research. First, routine care data are likely to match the range of variables that are of interest to the investigator. For example, if an investigator wants to study the diagnostic value of symptoms, signs, and results from diagnostic tests in setting a diagnosis of heart failure in general practice and the need for referral to secondary care, the patient files from primary care practices will likely show those variables that lead a general practitioner to suspect that a patient has the disease. General practitioners may use electrocardiography but are unlikely to routinely have results from chest x-rays. Therefore, although chest x-rays may add diagnostic information, such data would not be relevant in view of the research question. Hence, the lack of this variable in the patient records is no problem. Second, routine data likely reflect a quality of data collection that is typical of the quality of the data in the application of the research findings in clinical practice. As an example, when the goal is to determine the diagnostic value of abdominal palpation for aortic aneurysms in patients suspected of having this vascular problem, routine records with results from palpation performed by the average physician are likely to offer a better view of the diagnostic value of this test in the diagnostic workup of these patients in daily practice than when all patients were carefully examined by a highly skilled vascular surgeon.

To conclude, the extent to which patient data from routine care may effectively and validly be used to answer research questions depends on the type of research question and the type of research. For causal research, the availability and quality of confounder data need to be carefully addressed and may often be shown to be inadequate. In descriptive research, it is important that the routine care data comprise all clinically relevant diagnostic or prognostic determinants to yield a relevant research result. For all types of research it is necessary that the patients can indeed be retrieved from the files based on uniform and unselective coding, that the outcome is assessed in each subject, and that missing data are properly dealt with.

LIMITATIONS OF COHORT STUDIES

There are no intrinsic limitations of cohort studies. They offer a highly effective approach in epidemiology. However, there are situations in which cohort studies cannot be used, and some research questions are difficult to address in a cohort study when the study is not experimental. Cohort studies in which data collection is prospective are generally time consuming and expensive. The time for a cohort study to be completed depends on the duration of follow-up, but research on common causes of chronic disease may require large numbers of subjects followed for considerable amounts of time. When a quick answer is desired, a prospective approach to data collection is less attractive.

Prospectively conducted cohort studies are expensive. They require the planned and systematic collection of data on the members of the cohort, which calls for adequate infrastructure and personnel. Time and expenses may be less of a problem when data can be used that have already been recorded in the past, so data collection can be retrospective. However, rather than from practical limitations, retrospective data collection may suffer from incomplete or low-quality data because the data were probably recorded without the current research question in mind. This may leave the investigator without important confounder data in causal research or without a highly interesting prognostic indicator in prognostic research. It should be noted that sometimes confounding cannot be sufficiently removed even when extensive data on confounders is available. This may apply when the determinant of interest is too closely linked to a confounder, as for example, the indication for drug use that can hardly be separated from the drug use itself, or when the full range of confounders is unclear or difficult to measure. An example of the latter situation is given by the highly contradictory results of observational cohort studies and trials with regard to the putative cardioprotective effect of postmenopausal hormone replacement therapy. A range of well-designed prospective cohort studies supported the view that hormone replacement therapy reduced the risk of coronary heart disease. However, these study results were not substantiated when hormone replacement therapy was studied in randomized trials. Unmeasured confounders could account for this discrepancy, and the indication for treatment in observational studies may have played a role. Also, differences in the exposure time to hormone replacement therapy between the trials and observational studies may have led to the conflicting findings.

Finally, it is important to discuss whether the randomized trials included the same women that were included in the observational research [Van der Schouw & Grobbee, 2005]. It is important to realize that for a given population, the only difference between a randomized trial and an observational cohort study lies in the fact that in the randomized trial the determinant (e.g., drug use) is randomly allocated to the members of the cohort, whereas in the observational study the participants are *naturally* exposed to the determinant. In the latter setting, exposure to the determinant is a characteristic of certain individuals, the individuals have chosen to be exposed, or the exposure is applied by someone else (such as a physician prescribing a drug). Any reason for being exposed that in itself is associated with the outcome could act as a confounder and should therefore be taken into account. If this is not possible, the cohort study will not yield valid results.

WORKED-OUT EXAMPLE: THE SMART STUDY

As a result of both aging and the impact of factors such as elevated cholesterol, diabetes, or high blood pressure, arteries may stiffen. Increased arterial stiffness amplifies the risk of future symptomatic cardiovascular events that these factors by themselves already confer. Whether arterial stiffening also increases the risk of reoccurrence of events in those who have already been diagnosed with manifest arterial disease is largely unknown.

At the University Medical Center Utrecht, a cohort is continuously being built up of patients referred with symptomatic cardiovascular disease, named the Second Manifestations of ARTerial disease (SMART) cohort. This is an example of a cohort study that is conducted with patients who are referred to a hospital as part of routine care. In the SMART cohort, we prospectively examined whether stiffer arteries put patients with diagnosed cardiovascular disease at increased risk of reoccurrence of events and of cardiovascular mortality [Dijk et al., 2005] (see **Box 8–4**).

Theoretical Design

The research question was, "Does arterial stiffness predict recurrent vascular events in patients with manifest vascular disease?" This leads to the etiologic occurrence relation: incidence of vascular events as a function of arterial stiffness conditional on confounders. The domain is patients who are

BOX 8–4   Cohort Study on the Causal Link Between Carotid Stiffness and New
Vascular Events in Patients with Manifest Cardiovascular Disease

AIMS: To study whether arterial stiffness is related to the risk of new vascular
events in patients with manifest arterial disease and to examine whether this
relation varies between patients who differ with respect to baseline vascular risk,
arterial stiffness, or systolic blood pressure (SPB).

METHODS AND RESULTS: The study was performed in the first consecutive
2183 patients with manifest arterial disease enrolled in the SMART study (Second
Manifestations of ARTerial disease), a cohort study among patients with manifest
arterial disease or cardiovascular risk factors. Common carotid distension (i.e.,
the change in carotid diameter in systole relative to diastole) was measured at
baseline by ultrasonography. With the distension, several stiffness parameters
were determined. In the entire cohort, none of the carotid artery stiffness parameters was related to the occurrence of vascular events. However, decreased stiffness was related to decreased vascular risk in subjects with low baseline SPB. The
relation of carotid stiffness with vascular events did not differ between tertiles of
baseline risk and carotid stiffness.

CONCLUSION: Carotid artery stiffness is no independent risk factor for vascular
events in patients with manifest arterial disease. However, in patients with low
SBP, decreased carotid stiffness may indicate a decreased risk of vascular events.

Reproduced from Dijk DJ, Algra A, van der Graaf Y, Grobbee DE, Bots ML on behalf of the SMART
study group. Cartoid stiffness and the risk of new vascular events in patients with manifest cardiovascular disease. The SMART study. *Eur Heart J.* 2005 Jun; 26 (12): 1213–20.

referred to the hospital and diagnosed with cardiovascular disease. The operational definition of recurrent vascular disease (the outcome) was vascular death, ischemic stroke, coronary ischemic disease, and the composite of
these vascular events. Measurement of arterial stiffness was operationalized
by measurement of distension of the left and right common carotid arteries. Measurement of several possible confounders and effect modifiers was
operationalized using questionnaires, blood chemistry, and measurement
of blood pressure.

Design of Data Collection

Data were collected from an ongoing (since September 1, 1996) prospective
single-center cohort of patients age 18–80 years with manifest arterial
disease who were referred to the University Medical Center Utrecht. More

TABLE 8–1   General Characteristics of the Study Population ($n = 2183$)

Men (%)	75
Age (years)	59.7
Systolic blood pressure (SBP) (mm Hg)	141
Diastolic blood pressure (DBP) (mm Hg)	79
Mean arterial pressure (MAP) (mm Hg)	99
Triglycerides (mmol/L)	2.0
Total cholesterol (mmol/L)	5.5

Reproduced from Dijk DJ, Algra A, van der Graaf Y, Grobbee DE, Bots ML on behalf of the SMART study group. Cartoid stiffness and the risk of new vascular events in patients with manifest cardiovascular disease. The SMART study. *Eur Heart J.* 2005 Jun; 26(12):1213–20.

than 6,000 patients were enrolled over 10 years. For the arterial stiffness substudy, data from patients collected from September 1, 1996 until March 1, 2003 were used because during that time period, the necessary vascular measurements were obtained. At baseline, a general questionnaire on cardiovascular risk factors and previously diagnosed diseases was completed (see **Table 8–1**).

At the screening visit, simple measurements such as blood pressure, height, and weight were taken and venous blood samples were taken for analysis of blood chemistry. Common carotid intima-media thickness (CIMT) was measured at the left and right common carotid arteries with an ATL Ultramark 9 (Advanced Technology Laboratories, Bethel, WA, USA) equipped with a 10 MHz linear array transducer. Duplex scanning of the carotid arteries was performed for assessment of presence of internal carotid artery stenosis. Stiffness was assessed by measurement of distension of the left and right common carotid arteries. The distension of an artery is the change in diameter in systole relative to the diastolic diameter during the cardiac cycle. The displacement of the walls of the left and right common carotid artery was measured with a Wall Track System (Scanner 200, Pie Medical, Maastricht, The Netherlands) equipped with a 7.5 MHz linear transducer. To obtain information on baseline vascular risk, the previously developed SMART risk score was used. The SMART risk score is based on baseline data of preexisting disease and risk factors. Patients receive points for gender, age, body mass index, smoking behavior, hyperlipidemia, hyperglycemia, hypertension, medication use, medical history, and prevalent vascular disease at baseline. Patients were biannually asked to fill in a questionnaire on hospitalizations and outpatient clinic visits in the preceding

6 months. Events of interest for this study were vascular death, ischemic stroke, coronary ischemic disease, and the composite of these vascular events. When a possible event was recorded by the participant, hospital discharge letters and results of relevant laboratory and radiology examinations were collected. With this information, all events were audited by three members of the SMART Study Endpoint Committee, comprising physicians from different departments.

Design of Data Analysis

The principal analysis was performed on the participants who were included from September 1, 1996 until March 1, 2003, excluding the 193 patients in whom stiffness measurements were missing due to equipment failure or logistical problems, the measurements of 94 participants in whom the intra-individual variance between stiffness measurements was considered out of range, and 6 patients in whom no follow-up information was available. The data of 2,183 participants were used in the analysis. It should be noted that missing variables were not imputed in this study, even though conditional imputation (see earlier discussion) would have been preferable.

Because the main interest was the causal relationship between arterial stiffness and new cardiovascular events, age, mean arterial pressure, sex, pack-years smoked, and use of antihypertensive medication were considered potential confounders. The modifying effect of baseline systolic blood pressure (SBP) and baseline risk was investigated by calculating separate hazard ratios for tertiles of SBP and baseline risk. First, the crude hazard ratio for arterial stiffness (per standard deviation increase in stiffness) was calculated with the Cox proportional hazard analysis (Model I in **Table 8–2**). Next, age was included in the model (Model II in the table) and, finally, an additional adjustment for potential confounders (notably mean arterial pressure, sex, pack-years smoked, and use of antihypertensive medication at baseline) was done (Model III in the table). To evaluate whether baseline risk (with the SMART score) and SBP were effect modifiers, interaction terms were included in the model and stratified analyses were performed in tertiles of baseline risk and SBP.

Implications and Relevance

The results of this study show that in patients with manifest arterial disease, increasing arterial stiffness, unadjusted, is associated with an increased risk of vascular events and vascular death. The relationship

TABLE 8–2   Relationship Between Carotid Stiffness and Vascular Events

		Hazard Ratio (95% CI)
Vascular Event (no. of events)	*Model*	*Distension/SD[a]*
All vascular events (192)	I	0.87 (0.75–1.01)
	II	0.97 (0.85–1.17)
	III	0.95 (0.79–1.13)
Vascular death (107)	I	0.74 (0.59–0.91)
	II	0.94 (0.75–1.18)
	III	0.86 (0.67–1.11)
Ischemic stroke (47)	I	1.14 (0.87–1.51)
	II	1.20 (0.89–1.61)
	III	1.20 (0.86–1.63)
Coronary ischemic event (117)	I	0.86 (0.71–1.05)
	II	0.99 (0.81–1.23)
	III	0.92 (0.73–1.16)

Model I: unadjusted
Model II: Model I additionally adjusted for age
Model III: Model II additionally adjusted for mean arterial pressure,
    sex, age, pack-years smoked, and use of antihypertensive
    medication at baseline

[a]In all models adjusted for end-diastolic diameter carotid arteries and mean arterial pressure.

Reproduced from Dijk DJ, Algra A, van der Graaf Y, Grobbee DE, Bots ML on behalf of the SMART study group. Cartoid stiffness and the risk of new vascular events in patients with manifest cardiovascular disease. The SMART study. *Eur Heart J.* 2005 Jun; 26(12):1213–20.

disappears after adjustment for age (Table 8–2). Thus, in this population as a whole, carotid stiffness is not an independent risk factor for the occurrence of vascular events. Stiffness probably reflects the long-term exposure to several of these risk factors but does not increase the risk of these patients over and above the risk conferred by the risk factors. We did find that in patients with low SBP, those with less stiff vessels had a lower vascular risk. Previous studies, largely in patients without diagnosed vascular disease and thus at a lesser developed stage of cardiovascular damage, mainly showed a direct relationship between arterial stiffness and subsequent disease, although the magnitude varied considerably. In our patient group, we found no relationship between arterial stiffness and vascular events.

As published data mainly reported on subjects with risk factors for vascular disease who generally can be considered to have a lower risk than the patients with manifest arterial disease in our study, the different reported relationship between arterial stiffness and vascular disease may be explained by an association between arterial stiffness and vascular events in low-risk patients only. However, the observation in studies on patients with end-stage renal disease who are known to be at high vascular risk that arterial stiffness was associated with vascular events does not jive with this explanation. Moreover, our finding that the association between arterial stiffness and vascular events is not modified by baseline risk does not support this hypothesis either.

Chapter 9

Case-Control Studies

INTRODUCTION

There is no doubt that of all the available approaches to data collection in epidemiology, case-control studies continue to attract the most controversy. On the one hand this is understandable, because many poorly conducted case-control studies have been reported in the literature and most textbooks in epidemiology present famous examples of case-control studies that produced biased results. Indeed, the validity of case-control studies in general is often questioned, and some epidemiologists go so far as to place case-control studies at the low end of their hierarchy of study designs, just above the case-report or case-series designs. This is illustrated by the following statement from the first edition of a textbook by one of the founders of clinical epidemiology:

> If the best you can find is a case-control study, you must recognize that this is a weak design that often has led to erroneous conclusions [Sackett et al., 1985].

On the other hand, one cannot deny that since their introduction to clinical research in 1920, case-control studies have proven their potential value, notably in causal research. Apart from identifying etiologic factors for many diseases (such as smoking as a causal determinant of lung cancer [Doll & Hill, 1950]), case-control studies have been important in identifying and quantifying risks of drugs. Examples of the latter include the association between aspirin use and Reye syndrome in children [Hurwitz et al., 1987] and between diethylstilboestrol (DES) use by pregnant women and the occurrence of clear cell vaginal carcinoma in their daughters [Herbst et al., 1971]. The potential strength of case-control studies in medicine was emphasized by Kenneth Rothman in the first edition of his textbook:

> The sophisticated use and understanding of case-control studies is the most outstanding methodological development of modern epidemiology [Rothman, 1986].

Although these opposing views on the value of case-control studies were expressed over 20 years ago, discussions regarding the validity of case-control studies continue. The reasons for the air of suspicion surrounding the results of case-control studies are difficult to fully elucidate but are no doubt related to both the complexity of their design and the prevailing misconception about their rationale and essence among both the researchers performing them and their readers and reviewers. In addition, case-control studies are often applied in causal research, and because these case-control studies are nonrandomized by definition, confounding may bias the results and must be dealt with appropriately. Of course, appropriate coping with confounding is equally important for other nonexperimental designs, such as cohort studies.

The main problem with case-control studies is that too often they are presented as "quick and dirty" epidemiologic studies involving some group of cases (those with the outcome or disease of interest) and a group (sometimes even several groups) of readily available human beings without that particular outcome (controls), often matched to the cases according to several (sometimes more than 10!) characteristics such as age, gender, and co-morbidity. Then, the determinant of interest, typically a risk factor believed to be causally implicated in the disease, as well as potential confounders, are measured in both cases and controls, producing an adjusted measure of association (usually an odds ratio) between the determinant and outcome. Too often, studies are conducted and presented without appreciation of the principles of case-control studies, and they do not provide the reader with the rationale for the choices that were made in the design of data collection: Why a case-control study? Why these particular cases? Why this control group? Why is there (no) matching of cases and controls? This leaves the reader with the difficult task of judging the validity of these choices and consequently the results (see **Box 9–1**).

In this chapter, we present the rationale (Why a case-control study?) and essence (What makes a case-control study a case-control study?) of case-control studies, provide a brief history of case-control studies in clinical research, and emphasize the methods available to identify cases and, in particular, to sample controls. In addition, several more recently developed types of case-control studies, including case-cohort and case-crossover

BOX 9–1   Warhol's "Campbell's Soup Can"

Many researchers conduct case-control studies where a group of patients with a certain disease is identified and compared with another group who does not have the disease. Selection of controls is often done as if quickly opening a "can" of non-cases, without an appreciation of the primary principle of case-control studies: Controls should be representative of the population experience from which the cases emerge. In addition, there is a tendency to match controls to the cases according to a range of characteristics (notably, potential confounders). This often results in very atypical control subjects (those with many risk factors for the disease but who manage not to develop the disease), who share more similarities with "museum exhibits" than with existing individuals. Consequently, and unfortunately, too many case-control studies could be summarized by the famous Andy Warhol canvas, "Campbell's Soup Can."

studies, are reviewed. We argue that when the principles of case-control studies are appreciated, these studies can be of great value in both causal and descriptive clinical research.

THE RATIONALE FOR CASE-CONTROL STUDIES

Why choose to do a case-control study? Case-control studies are conducted for efficiency reasons. Under certain circumstances, it may be cumbersome or even impossible to study an entire population in detail over a certain time period. When the outcome of interest (e.g., anaphylactic shock) is very rare, for example, a cohort study (or randomized trial) would require identification and long-term follow-up of many subjects with and without the determinant (e.g., use of a specific drug). Case-control studies can also be efficient when the time between exposure to the determinant and the occurrence of the outcome is very long (e.g., the use of DES by pregnant women and the occurrence of vaginal carcinoma in their daughters) or unknown, or when the measurement of the determinant(s) and other relevant variables (e.g., confounders) is time consuming, burdensome to patients, and/or expensive (e.g., when imaging techniques or genetic analyses are involved). Instead of studying the census (that is, all members of the cohort or dynamic population during the entire follow-up period) in detail, it is more efficient to study only those who develop the outcome of interest during the study period

BOX 9–2   Case-Control Studies: Semantics

One of the problems surrounding case-control studies is the large number of terms applied to indicate the case-control method or to describe its subtypes. A nonexhaustive list includes these terms:

Case-referent study   Case-cohort study
TROHOC study   Nested case-control study
Retrospective study   Case-crossover study
                             Case-only study
                             Case-specular study

The left row lists alternative terms for case-control studies that have been suggested over the years. Although the term *case-referent study* seems more appropriate, we propose using the term *case-control study* instead to ensure that both researchers and readers understand the underlying methodology. In particular, terms such as TROHOC (the reverse of cohort study) and retrospective studies should be avoided [Schulz & Grimes, 2002] because they imply a "reverse" nature of the case-control approach (from disease to determinant instead of the other way around), while the direction of the occurrence relation is in fact similar to studies using a census approach: outcome as a function of the determinant. Moreover, case-control studies can be both retrospective and prospective. In the right row several types of case-control studies are listed. These terms could be used because they do indicate several methods that can be applied in case-control studies, as long as one realizes that these studies are in fact case-control studies in that they sample controls from the study base.

(the *cases*) and a sample of the population from where the cases emerge (the *controls*). The determinant(s) and other relevant factors (typically the potential confounders in the case of causal research, but also possible modifiers when one is interested in assessing effect modification) are then measured in cases and controls only (see **Box 9–2**).

THE ESSENCE OF CASE-CONTROL STUDIES

What makes a case-control study a case-control study? In terms of the design of data collection, the essence is sampling, as opposed to census. The strength of case-control studies is that they allow the researcher to quantify the occurrence relation of interest by studying cases and only a sample of the population where the cases stem from, while still producing the same estimates as would have been obtained from a cohort or dynamic population study (i.e., using a census approach). A valid result, however, can only be guaranteed when the controls are sampled correctly from the population from which the cases emerge.

Figure 9–1 illustrates the essence of a case-control study [Hoes, 1995]. A population, being a cohort, dynamic population, or (less frequently) a cross-section of these, is identified. Although one can also imagine cross-sectional case-control studies (where the time dimension is zero), let us assume that a population is followed for a certain time period and that the aim of the study is to quantify the association of a determinant (det) with the future occurrence of a particular disease (dis). The population followed over time is often referred to as the *study base*. It equals the population experience available to perform the study. Members of the population do not yet have the disease under study when the investigation starts. Some of the population members will have the determinant or exposure of interest (det+) and others will not (det−). In addition, other characteristics or co-variables (notably confounders when the aim is to study causality) of the participants may be relevant.

In a census approach, such as in a cohort study or in a randomized trial, all members of the study population will be identified when they enter the

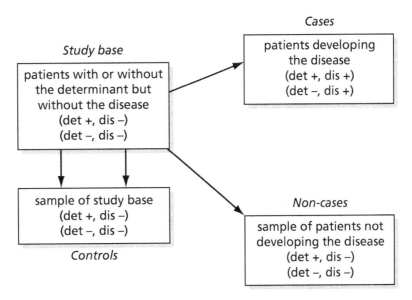

FIGURE 9–1   Case control study. Abbreviations are det, determinant; dis, disease.

study and all relevant characteristics, including the determinants and co-variables of interest, will be measured. Then, all members will be monitored over time to establish whether they do (dis+) or do not (dis−) develop the disease. At the end of the study, the incidence of the disease in those with and without the determinants can be compared, where the numerator is provided by the number of cases (cases in Figure 9–1) and the denominator either by the total number of participants with and without the determinant (when cumulative incidences are calculated) or by the number of person-years contributed to the study base by those with and without the determinant (when incidence rates are calculated).

In a case-control, and thus a sampling approach, the same study base as in the census approach is followed over time to monitor the occurrence of the disease of interest. In contrast, however, the determinants and relevant covariables are not measured in all members of the study base, but only in those developing the disease (the cases) and in a sample of the study base (controls or referents). The term *referents* is more appropriate because it clearly indicates that the sample members are referents from the study base from which the cases emerge, but we use the term *controls* because of its widespread use in the literature. By definition, the members of the control group do not have the disease of interest when they are selected as controls. It should be emphasized, however, that the controls are not a sample of the non-cases (shown in Figure 9–1), because these non-cases only represent those participants who do not develop the disease during the total follow-up period. In fact, some of the members of the control group could subsequently develop the disease. Therefore, in the likely event of changes in the population during the study period (often new people will enter and others leave the study base with or without having developed the outcome), it is wiser not to sample controls at one specific time during the study, but instead at several time points throughout the study experience, to ensure a proper representation of the study base from which the cases develop. In a later section, the methods to validly sample controls from the study base will be outlined in more detail with the introduction of the *study base* (or "swimming-pool") principle.

A BRIEF HISTORY OF CASE-CONTROL STUDIES IN CLINICAL RESEARCH

The case-control method was developed in the field of sociology. To our knowledge, the first case-control study in medicine was published in 1920 (see **Figure 9–2**) [Broders, 1920], assessing the role of smoking in

EPITHELIOMA—BRODERS

SQUAMOUS-CELL EPITHELIOMA OF THE LIP

A STUDY OF FIVE HUNDRED AND THIRTY-SEVEN CASES *

A. C. BRODERS, M.D.

ROCHESTER, MINN.

Of all the malignant neoplasms with which man is afflicted, few cause more concern and inconvenience than that of epithelioma of the lip. In the past, pathologists have been content to classify cancer of the lip as cancer, without any distinction as to the degree of malignancy. It is a well established fact that some cancers of the lip are fatal to patients and others are not. There must be a reason for this. One theory is that some persons are resistant to cancer, and this seems to be borne out in a certain percentage of cases.

Undoubtedly, a large proportion of cancer cells are destroyed by the defense cells of the body; of these, the fibrous connective tissue cell is the most important, since it cuts off nourishment from the cancer cells.

The endothelial leukocyte and lymphocyte evidently also play an important rôle in the destruction of cancer cells, for practically always they may be seen in the neighborhood of a cancerous growth. Foreign body giant cells that are most probably formed from the endothelial leukocytes are not infrequently found lying adjacent to cancer cells.

The most important factor in squamous-cell epithelioma of the lip seems to be the degree of cellular activity. The cells of some epitheliomas of the lip show a marked tendency to differentiate, that is, to produce a growth similar to the normal; the pearly body is an example. The pearly body corresponds to the horny layer of the epidermis. In other squamous-cell epitheliomas there is no differentiation whatever. In the large majority of growths whose cells show no

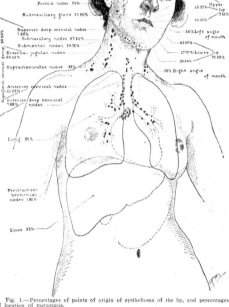

Fig. 1.—Percentages of points of origin of epithelioma of the lip, and percentages of location of metastasis.

tendency to differentiate, or at least very little, there are many mitotic figures.

In studying these epitheliomas, therefore, it occurred to me that they should be graded according to differentiation and mitosis, special stress being laid on the former. The grading was made on a basis of 1 to 4, and absolutely independent of the clinical history. If an epithelioma shows a marked tendency to differentiate, that is, if about three fourths of its structure is differentiated epithelium and one fourth undifferentiated, it is graded 1; if the differentiated and undifferentiated epithelium are about equal, it is graded 2; if the undifferentiated epithelium forms about three fourths and the differentiated about one fourth of the growth, it is graded 3; if there is no tendency of the cells to differentiate, it is graded 4. Of course the number of mitotic figures and the number of cells with single large deeply staining nucleoli (one-eyed cells) play an important part in the grading.

Some epitheliomas of the lip are very active and from the start show little or no tendency to differentiate; some grow more malignant with time, and others increase in malignancy and then retrogress. Unquestionably an epithelioma of a low grade of malignancy is made more malignant by irritation with chemicals such as hydrochloric or nitric acid, silver nitrate or arsenic paste.

Chronic ulcers of the lip, like chronic ulcers of the stomach, should be examined very closely for cancer, provided syphilis has been eliminated. MacCarty[1] has demonstrated early cancer in the epithelium at or near the edge of gastric ulcers; practically the same process is found in early cancer or ulcer of the lip. In the lip the cancer starts in the stratum germinativum of the epithelium at or near the border of the ulcer. Not all cancers of the lip are preceded by ulcers, but the majority are.

I shall present the facts in statistical form and make the deductions, not from one, but from various standpoints: (1) the duration and size of the lesion; (2) the

* From the Section on Surgical Pathology, Mayo Clinic.
* Presented before the Richmond Academy of Medicine and Surgery, Richmond ,Va., Nov. 25, 1919, and before the Roanoke Academy of Medicine, Roanoke, Va., Dec. 1, 1919.

1. MacCarty, W. C.: Pathology and Clinical Significance of Gastric Ulcer: From a Study of Material from Two Hundred and Sixteen Partial Gastrectomies for Ulcer, Ulcer and Carcinoma, and Carcinoma, Surg., Gynec. & Obst. 10: 449-462, 1910.

FIGURE 9–2   The first report of a case-control study published in the medical literature in 1920.

Reproduced from Broders AC. Squamous-cell epithelioma of the lip. A study of 537 cases. *JAMA* 1920;74:656–64.

the development of epithelioma of the lip. Smoking habits of 537 patients with epithelioma of the lip were compared to 500 patients without epithelioma. Although tobacco use was similar in both groups (79% and 80%, respectively), the proportion of pipe smokers was much higher in the cases (78%) than in the controls (38%). In this first case-control study, neither additional characteristics of the control group nor information on the way controls were sampled were provided. In addition, no formal measure of association between pipe smoking and lip carcinoma was calculated and no discussion of possible confounding was included, let alone adjustment for confounding in the analysis. These latter limitations are understandable, because it took an additional 30 years for the exposure odds ratio (the measure of association usually applied in case-control studies) to be introduced and 8 more years before a method to adjust for confounding was first described. Nevertheless, a causal association between pipe smoking and epithelioma of the lip was later confirmed in other studies.

The year 1950 heralded an important period in the acceptance of the case-control method in clinical research. In that year, four case-control studies assessing the association between tobacco consumption and the risk of lung cancer were published. Despite methodologic problems in several aspects, including the way the control group was sampled and misclassification of smoking history, these early studies clearly illustrated the potential of this study design [Doll & Hill, 1950].

In 1951, Cornfield gave a strong impulse to the further application of the case-control method by proving that, under the assumption that the outcome of interest is rare, the odds ratio resulting from a case-control study equals the incidence ratio that would result from a cohort study [Cornfield, 1951]. Another influential paper was published in 1959, in which Mantel and Haenszel described a procedure to derive odds ratios from stratified data, thus enabling adjustment for potential confounding variables. Later, Miettinen [1976a, 1976b] made several important contributions to the development of case-control studies, including landmark publications on how to appropriately sample controls from the study base so that the resulting odds ratio always (also when the outcome is not rare) provides a valid estimate of the incidence density ratio that would be observed in a cohort study.

Over recent decades, the case-control method has been applied throughout the field of clinical medicine far beyond the research on cancer etiology for which it was first developed. The method also provides important applications for the study of intended and unintended effects of interventions. Especially for the latter, case-control studies have proven their enormous potential. Examples include studies on the risk of fatal asthma in recipients of beta-agonists, cancer of the vagina in daughters of mothers receiving DES during their pregnancy, and, more recently, deep vein thrombosis resulting from the use of third-generation oral contraceptives. Thus far, the case-control method has not been widely applied in descriptive (diagnostic and prognostic) research, but its efficiency in both diagnostic and prognostic research is increasingly being recognized.

THEORETICAL DESIGN

The research question and associated occurrence relation may take any form, depending on the objective of the case-control study. Usually, case-control studies are applied when the goal is to unravel causality, and therefore the occurrence relation should include conditionality on extraneous determinants (i.e., confounders). More recently, the case-control method has also been applied in descriptive research [Biesheuvel et al., 2008].

DESIGN OF DATA COLLECTION

Sampling in Nonexperimental and (Usually) Longitudinal Studies

By definition, case-control studies take a sampling (not a census) approach and are nonexperimental. Because most case-control studies address causality, they are longitudinal, that is, there is conceptual time between the presence of a determinant and the occurrence of the outcome ($t > 0$). Diagnostic case-control studies, however, are typically cross-sectional (i.e., $t = 0$).

It should be emphasized that case-control studies can be both prospective and retrospective. If all data on determinant(s), outcome, and other factors (confounders, modifiers) are already available when the researcher initiates the study, the case-control study is retrospective. Often, however, a case-control study is prospective, so the researcher develops a method to identify cases, starting "now" and ending when enough cases have been included. The researcher samples a control group during the same time period. The common view that case-control studies are retrospective by definition (because one starts by collecting cases and controls and then looks back in time to assess earlier exposure to the determinant) is wrong.

Analogy of a Swimming Pool, Lifeguard Chair, and a Net

When designing a case-control study, it may be helpful to compare the study base from which both the cases and controls originate to a swimming pool. Researchers should then envision themselves sitting on a lifeguard chair, overlooking the water surface from a distance, while holding a net with a long handle (see **Figure 9–3**).

In the swimming pool, a changing population is present where several swimmers have the determinant(s) of interest and the remaining swimmers do not. Importantly, as in an ordinary swimming pool, people can enter and leave the study, and even possibly reenter it. Such a dynamic population closely resembles the source populations of many case-control studies,

FIGURE 9–3   A swimming pool, a lifeguard chair, and a net.

swimming pool, © Carolina/ShutterStock, Inc.; lifeguard chair, © Brett Stoltz/ShutterStock, Inc.; net, © Eyup Alp Ermis/ShutterStock, Inc.

which may include inhabitants of a certain town or region, those enlisted with a primary care practice or a health maintenance organization, or the catchment population of a certain hospital (i.e., those living in the vicinity of a hospital who would be referred to that hospital if they developed the disease of interest). New people may enter these populations when they are born, move to that particular area, and so on, and they may also leave this study base for various reasons (e.g., when they die, move away from the area, or develop the outcome under study). The role of the researcher closely resembles that of the lifeguard sitting high up in a chair, overlooking the swimming pool. Typically, the lifeguard does not know exactly how many individuals are in the pool at a certain point in time, nor their characteristics, let alone their identities. In case-control terminology, the determinant and other relevant characteristics (e.g., confounders or effect modifiers) are not measured in all individuals in the study base. The net is designed such that it will catch those fulfilling the criteria of the outcome of interest. Once a swimmer gets into trouble or is floating around in the pool (i.e., becomes a case), then the lifeguard springs into action and uses the net to capture the case. This happens each time a case occurs.

Meanwhile, the mission is to select a group of control subjects who are representative of the study base from which the cases originate. Because most populations change continuously, it is preferable to sample the controls at different points in time rather than at one specific point in time. One possibility is to sample one or a few control(s) from the pool each time a case is taken out. Then, the lifeguard who is still sitting in the chair takes the net and randomly samples other swimmers (controls) from the pool. By definition, these controls are representatives of the swimming pool from which the cases emerge. Subsequently, the lifeguard (i.e., researcher) gets out of the chair and closely examines the cases and the randomly sampled controls (in case-control terminology, the researcher measures the determinant and other relevant characteristics). Alternatives for sampling controls each time a case is identified include sampling controls at random points in time or sampling at regular intervals, for example every week or month.

The principles of identifying cases and sampling controls also apply to case-control studies that are being conducted within a cohort, that is, a particular swimming pool that is closed at some point in time and does not allow new individuals to enter. In contrast to the more typical dynamic source population outlined in the previous paragraphs, the number of swimmers included in the pool (i.e., the size of the initial cohort) is generally known. Just as in other case-control studies, however, the researcher obtains information on the determinant and other relevant characteristics in the cases and the sampled controls only. The methods available to validly sample controls within a cohort study, as well as from a dynamic population, are discussed later in this chapter.

Identification of Cases

As in any other type of study, the definition of the outcome is crucial. The challenge to the researcher lies in designing a "net" that is capable of capturing all members of the study base that fulfill the case definition during the study period while ignoring those who do not meet the case criteria. In addition, a date on which the outcome occurred should be designated for each case to facilitate valid sampling of the control subjects.

Sometimes, existing registries can be applied to identify cases. Examples include cancer or death registries, hospital discharge diagnoses, or coded diagnoses in primary care or health maintenance organization databases. It should be emphasized that the number of false-positive and false-negative diagnoses in existing registries may be considerable and they clearly depend on the outcome; for example, death is much easier to diagnose than depression, benign prostatic hyperplasia, or sinusitis.

When valid registries of the case disease are not available, ad-hoc registries can be developed. For example, in a case-control study on the risk of sudden cardiac death associated with diuretics and other classes of blood pressure–lowering drugs, we developed a method to detect cases of sudden cardiac death among all treated hypertensive patients in a well-defined geographical area [Hoes at al., 1995a]. During the 2.5-year study period, all doctors signing a death certificate received a very short questionnaire, including a question about the period between the onset of symptoms and the occurrence of death and the probability of a cardiac origin. Sudden cardiac death was defined as a death occurring within 1 hour of symptom onset for which a cardiac origin could not be excluded.

Although in theory rigorous criteria to define the case disease should be applied, one should weigh the feasibility of these methods against the consequences of false-positive diagnoses and missing cases (false-negatives). Misclassification of the outcome will dilute the association between the determinant and the outcome if such misclassification occurs independent of the determinants studied. Then, false-positive diagnosis (i.e., non-cases counted as cases) may lead to a larger dilution than nonrecognition of cases; most of these false-negatives will not be sampled as controls because in many case-control studies the outcome is rare. Consequently, incompleteness of a registry does not necessarily reduce the validity of a study. Misclassification can also be differential and, thus, depend on the presence of the determinant. For example, in a case-control study on the risk for deep vein thrombosis among users of different types of oral contraceptives, such differential misclassification might occur when thrombosis is more often classified as such in women using particular oral contraceptives. The bias resulting from such misclassification may be considerable.

Prevalent or Incident Cases

In the vast majority of case-control studies (the only exceptions are cross-sectional case-control studies) the study base is followed over time, either prospectively or retrospectively. The goal of these case-control studies is to quantify the incidence of the outcome as a function of the determinants(s), and it is logical to include incident cases. This is analogous to a cohort study in which the numerator of the incidence rates will include incident disease only.

Especially when the incidence of the outcome is very low, which is one of the main reasons to choose a case-control design, inclusion of an adequate number of incident cases may be extremely difficult. Under such circumstances, one might consider including prevalent cases or combining incident and prevalent cases. However, potential major drawbacks exist for using prevalent cases. First and foremost, one should realize that the prevalence of disease reflects both its incidence and duration. Assume that a case-control study aims to quantify the relationship between radiation because of an earlier cancer and the development of leukemia as a second malignancy. A researcher could decide to include prevalent cases of leukemia being treated at several clinics in the region. This would lead to the inclusion of patients who on average have a better prognosis (survivors) than if only incident cases were considered, because the former group includes more patients with a longer survival time. In case radiation causes types of leukemia with a relatively poor prognosis, a case-control study using prevalent cases may fail to show the increased risk. Second, it is sometimes difficult to ensure that the determinant preceded the outcome and to exclude the possibility that the outcome changed the determinant when prevalent cases are used. The resulting bias obviously depends on the determinant of interest; for example, food intake poses many more potential problems here than gender or a genetic marker. In a case-control study on the association between coffee consumption and pancreatic cancer using prevalent cases, it may be difficult to rule out that an early phase of the disease changes coffee drinking habits.

However, when the determinant is unlikely to influence the duration of the case disease or survival and the "chicken or egg" dilemma (reversed causality) plays no role, the inclusion of prevalent cases may further increase the efficiency of case-control studies. Moreover, a disease is often

TABLE 9–1   Oral Contraceptive Use and the Risk of Developing Rheumatoid Arthritis

	Never Use	Ex-Use	Current Use	Ever Use
Crude	1	0.26	0.46	0.36
		(0.16–0.42)*	(0.30–0.70)	(0.25–0.52)
Adjusted	1	0.40	0.45	0.42
		(0.22–0.72)	(0.28–0.75)	(0.27–0.65)

*95% confidence interval.

Reproduced from *The Lancet*, Vol. 320; Vandenbrouke JP, Valkenburg HA, Boersma JW, Cats A, Festen JJ, Huber-Bruning O, Rasker J. Oral contraceptives and rheumatoid arthritis: further evidence for a preventive effect. 1839-42. 1982, reprinted with permission from Elsevier.

clinically diagnosed (i.e., considered incident) quite some time after the first clinical symptoms occur, for example, in diabetes mellitus or rheumatoid arthritis. Consequently, incident cases then may actually represent prevalent cases.

Vandenbroucke and coworkers [1982] examined the alleged protective effect of oral contraceptives on the development of rheumatoid arthritis. A case-control design was chosen because rheumatoid arthritis is relatively rare, and they included prevalent cases because the incidence of the disease is extremely low. The findings of the study are summarized in **Table 9–1.**

In the discussion paragraph of their article, the authors provided a further rationale for including prevalent cases: "We opted for prevalent cases because an incident case of rheumatism is hard to define when sampling from a specialist outpatient clinic: most patients will already have been treated by their general practitioner and by other specialists before coming to a particular clinic." They further stated that, "In principle, prevalent cases can yield valid rate-ratio estimates, on condition that the survival of cases and controls is not affected differentially by the exposure of interest. It is unlikely that this condition would not be met in this investigation." In their rebuttal to criticism that women with rheumatoid arthritis would tend to avoid oral contraceptives and that this may have led to a spurious protective effect, the researchers emphasized that classification of exposure was based on oral contraceptive use before or at the first visit to their general practitioner for rheumatic complaints. Consequently, the possibility of reversed causality was minimized.

When a case-control study is cross-sectional, such as in diagnostic case-control studies, the choice between prevalent or incident cases is a non-issue: Cases will be prevalent cases by definition.

Not All Those Who Develop the Disease Need to Be Included as Cases

Because case-control studies are often done when the outcome is rare, it would be unwise not to include all members of the study base who fulfill all case criteria during the study period. There are, however, circumstances under which only a sample of those with the case disease is included as a case. When the outcome is relatively common and there is enough statistical power, the cases may consist of a random sample of all those developing the outcome. An example of this approach is a study on the risk factors for hip fractures [Grisso et al., 1991]. A random sample of 174 female patients admitted with a first hip fracture to one of the 30 participating hospitals were included as cases.

In addition, a stratified sample of all subjects with the case disease may sometimes be obtained. This could be done, for example, to facilitate adjustment for confounding (or assessment of effect modification) in causal case-control studies, when it is expected that one or more of the confounder or modifier categories may be too small to allow for proper assessment in the data analysis. Consider a case-control study on pet bird keeping as a causal factor in lung cancer. It is suggested that the pollution of the domestic interior environment is a causal factor. In such a study, cigarette smoking is an important confounder, because bird keepers are known to smoke more often and smoking is the main cause of lung cancer (see **Figure 9–4**).

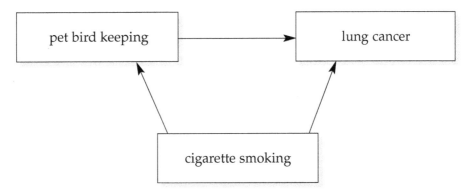

FIGURE 9–4   Confounding in a study on the causal association between pet bird keeping and lung cancer. Because pet bird keepers more often smoke cigarettes than those who do not keep birds (lower arrow to the left) and cigarette smoking strongly increases lung cancer risk (lower arrow to the right), cigarette smoking may confound the relationship between pet bird keeping and lung cancer.

Inclusion of all lung cancer patients diagnosed at several hospitals as the cases may result in very few (or even zero) cases who never smoked because of the very high prevalence of smoking among lung cancer patients, while the proportion of smokers among the controls would be much lower. Adjustment for confounding by smoking history would then be virtually impossible. One solution would be to decide to include all lung cancer patients who never smoked and a random sample (say 30%) of the lung cancer patients with a positive smoking history as cases. This stratified sampling of the cases would have important implications for the sampling of controls. In fact, the controls would need to be sampled analogously. This means that of all controls who were sampled from the study base, all controls with a negative smoking history, and a sample (again 30%) of all smoking controls would need to be included as the control group.

Interestingly, one could also imagine sampling cases in strata according to the determinant of interest, although this may seem counterintuitive. Stratified sampling should be considered when the number of cases in a certain category of the determinant is expected to be very small. Again, this implies a similar sampling strategy in the control patients.

The strengths of stratified sampling of cases are nicely illustrated in a case-control study assessing the causal role of the sex of the blood donor in the development of transfusion-related acute lung injury (TRALI) (Middelburg et al., 2010). Most TRALI cases receive blood from multiple donors from either sex and identification of the sex of the donor causing the TRALI is impossible in these cases. As a solution, the researchers restricted the analysis to "unisex" cases, that is, cases that received blood exclusively from either male or female donors. Consequently, sampling of the controls followed the same selection process; only "unisex" controls (patients without TRALI that received blood from only male or only female donors) were included to estimate the sex distribution of the donors in the study base. Thus, the researchers were able to show that plasma from female donors increased the risk of TRALI.

It is beyond the scope of this chapter to further elaborate on the specifics of stratified sampling of cases, because this approach is hardly ever used by researchers. More information can be found elsewhere [Weinberg & Sandley, 1991; Weinberg & Wacholder, 1990].

Sampling of Controls: The Study Base Principle

The strength of case-control studies lies in their capability of quantifying the occurrence relation by studying in detail only those developing the outcome and a sample of the study base (which, as explained earlier, can be viewed as a swimming pool) from which the cases originate. This efficiency gain is only acceptable when the association between the determinant and outcome can be estimated validly and is not compromised by the selection of controls. To achieve this, adequate sampling of the controls is crucial. Only then will the resulting measure of association (typically the odds ratio) be similar to the measure of association (usually an incidence rate ratio) that would be obtained from a cohort study (i.e., using a census approach). Valid sampling from the study base means taking into account the study base (or swimming pool) principle and implies that the controls should be a representative sample of the study base experience from whom the cases are drawn during the entire study period. To illustrate the methods that can be applied to provide for a valid sample of controls, we consider the two types of "swimming pools" that form the study base of virtually all case-control studies: dynamic populations and cohorts.

Control Sampling from a Dynamic Population

Most case-control studies are conducted in a *dynamic population*. These are characterized by their dynamic nature: People enter and leave the study base all the time. As mentioned in the first section of this chapter, examples of dynamic populations include inhabitants of a neighborhood, town, or region; those living in the catchment area of a hospital; and those enlisted with a health insurance company or primary care practice. **Figure 9–5** shows an example of a dynamic population (albeit unrealistically small). In this population, which is followed for a 1-year period, a case-control study is being performed. Assume that the study base represents the area around a hospital in which the cases (e.g., everyone admitted with acute appendicitis) are identified. Inhabitants of that catchment area would typically be admitted to that particular hospital when they develop the case disease.

    In total, 15 subjects are part of the study base for at least part of the study period. Subjects 1 and 3 are part of the study base when the study is initiated and remain in it without developing the outcome of interest. In subject 2, the case disease is also not diagnosed during the study period, but she enters the study base approximately 1.5 months after initiation of the study, possibly because she moves into the catchment area of the hospital. Subject 4 is in the study base from the beginning and develops the case disease after 6 months. Subject 5 enters the study base 3–4 months into the study period and leaves it again before the 11th month, possibly because he moves to another area and, if he is not followed to measure the outcome, he is considered lost to follow-up. He is not diagnosed with appendicitis during the 7 months of his membership in the study base. In

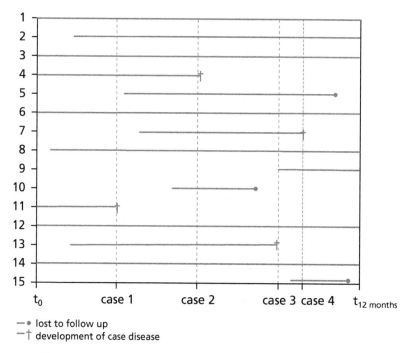

FIGURE 9–5   Dynamic population experience.

total, four cases are identified during the 12-month study period and one control subject will be sampled per case. Because of the dynamics of the population, representative samples of the study base cannot be obtained by sampling all controls at one point in time during the 12-month study period. For example, sampling at 12 months implies that subjects 5 and 10 can never be included as controls, even though they do contribute to the study base during a considerable period (and could even have become a case during that period). An attractive method for selecting controls who are representative of the study base from which the cases originate is to sample a control each time a case is identified. In this example, the first control is randomly sampled at 3 months, at which time the study base contains 10 subjects. By definition, a control does not have acute appendicitis when he is selected as a control. The same approach is taken each time a case is identified (denoted by dotted vertical lines in Figure 9–5).

A control could develop the case disease later in the study period, although this is unlikely because the studied outcome in most case-control studies is rare. Importantly, however, control subjects who later become a case do not violate the study base principle at all. Such an individual was at the time of being sampled as a control representative of the study base in which the case occurred, only later fulfilling the case definition. Consequently, this subject should be included both as a case and a control. Similarly, a control subject could again be randomly sampled as a control later in the study, for example, when subject 4 is diagnosed. Because both times this control is representative of the study base from which the cases originate, this control should be included twice. Including an individual twice during the same study period does not necessarily mean that all characteristics are the same; exposure (e.g., being prescribed a certain drug) may have changed.

Sometimes it may be difficult to sample a control each time a case occurs. An alternative is to assign each case a random date during the study period and sample controls from the members of the study base on that particular day. In addition, one could sample controls after a well-defined time period, say after each week or month.

To assess whether control subjects are indeed part of the swimming pool, the researcher should answer the following question: "Would the control subject be identified as a case should he or she develop the outcome under study during the study period?" The answer should be yes. This rule of thumb can be applied for essentially all case-control studies.

The study on the risk of sudden cardiac death associated with diuretics and other antihypertensive drug classes among treated hypertensive patients introduced earlier may serve as an example of how to sample controls each time a case develops. The study base consisted of all inhabitants of Rotterdam who were treated pharmacologically for hypertension, which clearly bears all of the characteristics of a dynamic population. Each time a case of sudden cardiac death was identified, a random control was selected as follows: A general practitioner in Rotterdam was randomly selected using a designated computer program and this general practitioner was visited at her or his surgery by one of the researchers. Then, using a computer file of all enlisted adult patients or the alphabetically ordered paper files, the first patient with the same sex and within the same 5-year age category was chosen, starting from the first name following the case's surname. If, according to the doctor, that patient was using antihypertensive drugs for hypertension on the day the corresponding case had died, that patient was included as a control. Age and gender were chosen as matching variables in this study for reasons that will be explained later in this chapter. It should be emphasized that the sampling of controls benefited from the fact that in the Netherlands all inhabitants are enlisted with one general practice and that virtually all relevant clinical information, including drugs prescribed and general practitioner and hospital diagnoses, are kept on file there. This system greatly facilitates control sampling in case-control studies.

Control Sampling from a Cohort: Case-Control Studies Nested Within a Cohort

Figure 9–6 shows a very small cohort. Although the graphic suggests that all cohort members are included on the same day ($t = 0$), this is never the case; it may take years to recruit the anticipated number of patients for a cohort. Once a member is included in the cohort, his or her follow-up time is set at $t = 0$ and the subject is followed until a certain point in time, sometimes indefinitely. In contrast to a dynamic population, at a certain point in time the cohort is complete and no additional members are allowed in. Unlike most dynamic populations, the members of a cohort are known, and at least some characteristics have been assessed. Nevertheless, it may be efficient to perform a case-control study within this cohort for a number of reasons, particularly when the assessment of the determinant is time consuming and expensive.

—• lost to follow up
—† development of case disease

FIGURE 9–6 Cohort experience.

For example, if the aim is to quantify the association between certain genetic polymorphisms and the occurrence of Alzheimer's disease, a case-control study within a cohort may be very efficient. Such studies are often termed *nested case-control* studies, but other terms are applied, sometimes depending on the method applied to sample the controls. In this case-control study, three cases of Alzheimer's disease are diagnosed among the 15 cohort members during the 12-month follow-up period. Several methods to sample controls can be applied.

Analogous to sampling controls from a dynamic population, one can randomly select a control each time a case is diagnosed. At 3 months, the first control will be sampled from the 13 remaining in the cohort: 15 minus the first case and minus individual number 10, who was lost to follow-up. Similarly, the other methods presented earlier for dynamic populations can be applied [Vandenbroucke & Pierce, 2012]. One can sample a control at a random date assigned each time a case is diagnosed or one may sample at regular time intervals, for example every week or month. Again, the control that is sampled is representative of the study base by definition, and sampling at multiple points in time during the study period will produce a valid sample. Such an approach may pose a logistical problem, however, because sampling frames including all members still in the cohort are needed each time a control is sampled randomly.

In many earlier case-control studies and sometimes even today, the controls are sampled at the end of the study period from the remainder of the cohort. This method excludes all cases as well as cohort members who are lost to follow-up. In our example, the three controls would be sampled from the eight subjects still in the cohort after the 1-year follow-up period. In contrast to the sampling methods outlined in previous sections of this chapter, this method clearly violates the study base principle because the controls are not a representative sample from the population experience during the entire study period. Especially when many cohort members are lost to follow-up and many develop the case disease (i.e., the outcome is not rare), this method will lead to biased estimates of the determinant–outcome association. For that reason, sampling of controls at the end of the follow-up period from the remainder of the cohort is discouraged.

A much better alternative is to sample the control group at the beginning of the follow-up period ($t = 0$). Although sampling at one specific point in time seems to carry the danger of violating the study base principle, sampling at $t = 0$ is an important exception. A quick look at Figure 9–6 clearly shows that a random selection of the cohort (at $t = 0$) provides a sample that is representative of the full cohort (e.g., gives full information on the determinant distribution), from which all future cases will develop during the study period. This type of nested case-control study is usually referred to as a *case-cohort study*. This term is rather confusing because it does not clearly indicate that, in essence, this study is a case-control study (because sampling from the study base is involved), not a cohort study. Because this method is increasingly being applied, a more elaborate discussion of case-cohort studies and their advantages and limitations is included in a separate paragraph in a later section.

Specific Types of Control Series

Sampling from the study base (whether a dynamic population or a cohort) is the optimal approach in case-control studies. However, sometimes this may be difficult to achieve, notably in dynamic population studies in which less is known about the members than in cohort studies [Grimes & Schulz, 2005]. To facilitate sampling of controls, specific groups of controls, such as those from the population at large (population controls), those in the hospital because of another disease than the case disease (hospital controls), and those from the same neighborhood (neighborhood controls), are often used. Although it seems attractive for logistic reasons to take neighbors, family members, or people admitted with some other diseases as controls, this may compromise the validity of the sampling of controls (and thus of the study findings) when these control group choices are made without appreciation of the study base principle. Unfortunately, the rationale for the choice of a control group is often not provided by researchers, and thus the reader is confronted with a "can" or—even worse—several "cans" of controls (see Box 9–1), leaving it to the researcher to judge whether these controls are representative of the study base. The next sections discuss several types of control series widely used in the literature.

Population Controls

In theory, population controls should be sampled when the cases included in the case-control study originate from the same population. This often is the case, notably when the domain of the occurrence relation is humanity, such as in etiologic studies examining the links between smoking and lung cancer, and physical exercise and cardiovascular disease. In case-control studies, because case identification is commonly restricted in time or region, control sampling from the population at large ideally should be restricted in a similar manner. The main advantage of sampling population controls in this manner is that these are, by definition, representative of the study base.

In a case-control study addressing the putative causal relationship between alcohol intake and acute appendicitis (the domain being all humans) in which cases are drawn from a large general hospital in a defined area during a 1-year study period, the population at large represents the source of the cases. However, control sampling, ideally, should be restricted to inhabitants of that defined area (i.e., the catchment area population of that hospital) during that time period. As outlined earlier, this may be achieved by sampling from available population registries at multiple points in time during the study period. Again, posing the question, "Would the control subject be identified as a case should he or she develop the outcome under study during the study period?" helps the researcher and reader to assess the validity of control selection. When sampling population controls from the catchment population of a hospital, one should realize that the catchment population varies with the disease studied. For example, acute appendicitis cases will originate from a much smaller area around the hospital than childhood leukemia cases in that same hospital. If, however, the distribution of the relevant characteristics in both catchment areas is similar, this has little influence on the validity of the study.

Several methods other than sampling from population registries have been proposed to efficiently draw population controls. *Random digital dialing*, where a random telephone number (usually computer generated) is dialed, may be an attractive option. It also allows for targeting a specific region using the telephone area codes. Depending on the information required from the controls, computerization in such an approach could go as far as using the computer to pose the necessary multiple-choice questions and to store the respondents' answers. The advantages of this approach are self-evident. The relatively low response rate is a major disadvantage of this method, however, especially when a potential participant is being interviewed by a computer. In addition, not all men and women have a landline telephone, some only have a cellular telephone, and many calls will remain unanswered. These phenomena are related to socioeconomic status, employment, and health status. If these factors are studied as (or related to) the determinant (or a confounder), the resulting nondifferential non-response can lead to bias. Selective non-response may threaten any method applied to sample population controls, because the motivation of members of the population at large to be involved in clinical research is usually lower than, for example, hospital controls. Random digit dialing as a means to select population controls has become less efficient now that many people mainly use mobile phones, making it difficult to cover specific areas. An example of a case-control study using population controls is given in **Box 9–3**. Controls were sampled by means of random digit dialing [Fryzek et al., 2005]. Both cases and controls were interviewed to obtain the required information.

BOX 9–3   A Case-Control Study Examining the Association of Body Mass Index with Pancreatic Cancer Using Population Controls

Increased body mass index has emerged as a potential risk factor for pancreatic cancer. The authors examined whether the association between body mass index and pancreatic cancer was modified by gender, smoking, and diabetes in residents of southeastern Michigan, 1996–1999. A total of 231 patients with newly diagnosed adenocarcinoma of the exocrine pancreas were compared with 388 general population controls. In-person interviews were conducted to ascertain information on demographic and lifestyle factors.

Unconditional logistic regression models estimated the association between body mass index and pancreatic cancer. Males' risk for pancreatic cancer significantly increased with increasing body mass index ($p_{trend} = 0.048$), while no relation was found for women ($p_{trend} = 0.37$). Among nonsmokers, those in the highest category of body mass index were 3.3 times (95% confidence interval: 1.2, 9.2) more likely to have pancreatic cancer compared with those with low body mass index. In contrast, no relation was found for smokers ($p_{trend} = 0.94$). While body mass index was not associated with pancreatic cancer risk among insulin users ($p_{trend} = 0.11$), a significant increase in risk was seen in non-insulin users ($p_{trend} = 0.039$). This well designed, population-based study offered further evidence that increased body mass index is related to pancreatic cancer risk, especially for men and nonsmokers. In addition, body mass index may play a role in the etiology of pancreatic cancer even in the absence of diabetes.

Reproduced from Fryzek JP, Schenk M, Kinnaid M, Greenson JK, Garabrant DH. The association of body mass index and pancreatic cancer in residents of southeastern Michigan, 1996–1999. *Am J Epidemiol* 2005;162:222–8, with permission from Elsevier.

The following quotation from this study illustrates the selection process typical of population controls, although it should be emphasized that the response rate among controls (76%) was relatively high. Of all eligible cases, 92% participated. "Of the 597 general population controls eligible for the study, 19 could not be reached by phone, one died before being contacted, and 27 were not contacted because there was an overselection of controls under 45 years of age early in the study period. The remaining 550 people were invited to participate, and 420 (76 percent) agreed."

Hospital Controls

The study presented in the last section also illustrates one of the advantages of using hospital controls in case-control studies: their willingness to participate. In general, the response rate in the diseased and in particular in those being admitted to the hospital is higher than in the population at large. Moreover, selecting control subjects from the same hospital with another illness than the case disease is efficient because the researcher is collecting similar data from the cases admitted to the same hospital anyway. From the introduction of the case-control method, hospital controls have been widely applied, and their popularity continues.

Disadvantages of hospital controls are, however, considerable. In particular, the validity of the case-control study is threatened if the hospital controls are not a representative sample from the study base that produces the cases. One could think of many reasons why, in patients with an illness other than the case disease, the distribution of relevant characteristics (notably the determinant of interest and possible confounders or effect modifiers) would differ from the members of the study base. For example, smoking and other unhealthy habits, overweight, comorbidity, and medication use generally will be more common in those admitted to a hospital than in the "true" study base (i.e., the catchment area population of that hospital for the case disease). A common (but incorrect) approach to prevent bias when taking hospital controls is the use of multiple control diseases. The rationale for such a "cocktail" of diseases is simple, if not somewhat naïve; should one control disease lead to bias (e.g., because the exposure to the determinant of interest in the control disease is higher than in the true study base), this bias could be offset by other control diseases (of which some may have a lower exposure than the study base). Alternatively, control diseases known to be associated with the determinant of interest are often excluded or patients visiting the emergency room are taken as controls. The advantage of the latter control group is that the prevalence of comorbidity and unhealthy habits may be lower than in other hospital controls.

However, these methods all contribute to the complexity of using hospital controls. It is usually very difficult for the readers and the researchers alike to judge whether the essential prerequisite of a case-control study—namely, that the controls are a valid sample from the study base—has been met. Too often, the researchers only mention the control disease(s) chosen without providing a rationale and fail to discuss the potential drawbacks of this choice. They then leave it up to the readers of their work to determine whether indeed the crucial characteristics of the hospital controls are similar to those of the study base (i.e., the catchment area population for the case disease). We do not suggest a moratorium on hospital controls, but there should be no doubt that the responsibility of proving the validity of hospital control sampling lies with the researcher and no one else. In their famous case-control study published more than half a century ago, Doll

BOX 9–4   Example of a Case-Control Study Using Hospital Controls

An example of a case-control study using hospital controls is the famous paper on smoking and lung cancer by Doll and Hill. The following excerpt from the original paper highlights the way the control subjects were sampled:

"As well, however, as interviewing the notified patients with cancer of one of the specified sites, the almoners were required to make similar inquiries of a group of "non-cancer control" patients. These patients were not notified, but for each lung-carcinoma patient visited at a hospital, the almoners were instructed to interview a patient of the same sex, within the same five-year age group and in the same hospital at about the same time."

The 709 control patients had various medical conditions, including gastrointestinal and cardiovascular disease and respiratory disease other than cancer.

The authors fully recognized the importance of ensuring that the control patients were not selected based on their smoking habits, and it is worth studying the additional data provided and reading their arguments to convince the reader that:

"There is no evidence of any special bias in favour of light smokers in the selection of the control series of patients. In other words, the group of patients interviewed forms, we believe, a satisfactory control series for the lung-carcinoma patients from the point of view of comparison of smoking habits."

This study, although performed more than half a century ago, still exemplifies the potential advantage of hospital controls and the way researchers should argue the validity of their control group.

Adapted from Doll R, Hill AB. Smoking and carcinoma of the lung. *BMJ* 1950;ii:739–48.

and Hill [1950] took up this responsibility and discussed the validity of their choice of hospital controls (see **Box 9–4**).

Neighborhood Controls

Selecting controls from the same neighborhood as the cases are often drawn from is an alternative to population controls. Instead of taking a random sample of the population at large (or when hospital cases are used, from the catchment population), the researcher samples one or more individuals from the same neighborhood as the corresponding case. Inclusion of neighborhood controls is attractive for several reasons, but mostly because they, almost literally, seem to originate from the same study base as the case and often the researcher is already in the neighborhood collecting the necessary information from the cases. Another often mentioned advantage is the homogeneity of the neighborhood with regard to certain characteristics, including potential confounders such as socioeconomic status.

The latter, however, also should be viewed as a potential disadvantage. Cases and controls will be matched according to these characteristics. But matching in case-control studies (as discussed in more detail later in this chapter) carries important dangers, including the impossibility of studying these characteristics as determinants. It would be unwise, for example, to sample neighborhood controls in a case-control study quantifying the causal relationship of living near high-voltage power lines with the occurrence of childhood cancer. Other disadvantages of neighborhood controls are the relatively low response and the time and costs involved, notably when the researcher needs to travel to the neighborhood to select a neighboring household.

Box 9–5 is an excerpt from the methods section of a case-control study performed to identify lifestyle and other risk factors for thyroid cancer. It describes the way neighborhood controls can be sampled and further illustrates the enormous efforts sometimes involved [Mack et al., 2002].

One could argue that the control selection in this study was independent of the risk factors studied (such as dietary habits) and that these controls may indeed represent a valid sample from the study base also producing the cases. It is unfortunate, however, that the authors did not discuss their choice of control group.

BOX 9–5   Example of Neighborhood Controls

A single neighborhood control was sought for each interviewed patient. Using a procedure defining a housing sequence on specified blocks in the neighborhood in which the patient lived at the time of her thyroid cancer diagnosis, we attempted to interview the first female matching the case on race and birth year (within five years). For each case, up to 80 housing units were visited and three return visits made before failure to obtain a matched control was conceded. We obtained matched controls for 296 of the 302 cases. For 263 patients, the first eligible control agreed to participate. Three controls were later found to be ineligible due to a prior thyroidectomy, and one control was younger than the matched case was at diagnosis. Questionnaires on 292 case-control pairs were available for analysis. The average interval between the case and matched control interview was 0.3 years.

Reproduced from Mack WJ, Preston-Martin S, Bernstein L, Qian D. Lifestyle and other risk factors for thyroid cancer in Los Angeles County females. *Ann Epidemiol* 2002;12:395–401, reprinted with permission from Elsevier.

Other Types of Control Series: Family, Spouses, and Others

The attraction of using family members or spouses (or friends, colleagues, etc.) as control subjects is obvious: Response rates will be very high and data collection will be relatively easy. Disadvantages of these control series, however, are that this method implies matching of cases and controls according to several known or unknown characteristics, such as socioeconomic status, age, family, environment, and/or lifestyle parameters. As will be explained later in the chapter, matching of cases and controls can have significant disadvantages. Clearly, the use of very specific groups of control series deviates from the principle that controls should be representative of the study base from which the cases emerge and thus endangers the validity of control selection and consequently the study findings. For example, it is not difficult to imagine that asking the case to choose a family member, friend, or colleague as a control (a frequent approach) can lead to considerable bias, because the distribution of important characteristics in the controls will be similar to the cases instead of being representative of the study base.

Multiple Control Series

In many case-control studies, multiple control series are included. Typically, separate odds ratios are then calculated for each control group. From a theoretical point of view, the use of multiple control groups is difficult to understand. The control group serves to provide information on determinant(s) and other relevant characteristics of the study base from which the cases emerge during the study period, and one such valid sample is all that is required. So why use several groups?

In a study on the role of aspirin in the occurrence of Reye syndrome in children, no less than four different control groups were sampled: (1) children admitted to the same hospital, (2) children visiting the emergency room of the same hospital, (3) children attending the same school as the corresponding case, and (4) population controls identified by means of random digit dialing [Hurwitz et al., 1987]. The main reason for inclusion of several control groups was no doubt the uncertainty of the researchers about the appropriateness of control sampling. As such, multiple control groups can be considered a sign of weakness of the design of data collection. Nevertheless, under those circumstances where sampling from the study base is considered problematic and the validity of a control sample is not straightforward, similar results obtained for two different control groups can be reassuring. When, however, the findings differ according to the control group used in the analysis, interpretation of the study results becomes problematic. The researcher retrospectively must decide which of the control groups best meets the study base principle. Had this decision been made before the study was executed, inclusion of more than one control group would have been unnecessary.

In a case-control study on the risk factors for hip fractures, the findings resulting from the use of hospital controls (from orthopedic or surgical wards) were compared with those from community controls [Moritz et al., 1997]. As expected, the prevalence of many potential determinants was higher in the hospital controls, while the corresponding odds ratios were lower, even after adjustment for potential confounders. The authors concluded that, "Community controls were quite similar to representative samples of community-dwelling elderly women, whereas hospital controls were somewhat sicker and more likely to be current smokers" and that ". . . community controls comprise the more appropriate control group in case-control studies of hip fracture in the elderly." We believe that this conclusion can be extended far beyond this particular disease.

Matching of Cases and Controls

There is continuing controversy regarding the benefits and disadvantages of matching cases and controls. Some epidemiologists strongly advise against matching according to one or more characteristics, while others advocate close matching of cases and their corresponding control(s), usually because they believe matching will prevent confounding. In our view, matching cases and controls to prevent confounding should be avoided. Matching of cases and controls is usually not required, unless for efficiency reasons.

In essence, matching of cases and controls should be viewed as an efficiency issue. Just as it may be more efficient to study a sample of controls instead of the census (i.e., to perform a case-control study), it may be more efficient to match cases and controls than to take a larger, unmatched sample [Miettinen, 1985].

Consider an etiologic study on the association between frequent sun exposure and the occurrence of melanoma and assume that gender is considered an important potential effect modifier of this relationship. Let us further assume that in order to efficiently estimate the association between frequent sun exposure and melanoma in both males and females, inclusion of five controls per case in each gender subdomain provides optimal statistical power. Power calculations for case-control studies are not included in our text, but it is generally acknowledged that a case–control ratio exceeding 1:5

does not add appreciable statistical power and is unlikely to offset the efforts required to obtain the necessary information in additional control subjects [Miettinen, 1985]. Presume that in the study base, a dynamic population of a well-defined region where 60% of persons are female is followed over a 5-year period. During this study period, 100 cases (70 men and 30 women) of melanoma are diagnosed. A large, unmatched sample of 500 controls from the study base would include 300 women (60%) and 200 men. In the female subgroup, the case–control ratio would then be 1:10 (30 out of the 300), while the corresponding ratio among men would be 1:2.9 (70 out of the 200), thus implying excessive sampling of women from the study base. In contrast, the number of males is too small to provide optimal power. Matching cases and controls according to gender would maximize efficiency: For the 70 male and 30 female cases, respectively, 350 males and 150 females would be sampled from the study base. Thus, matching may be efficient when a large unmatched sample would generate small numbers of controls per case in subcategories of the matching variables (usually potential effect modifiers or confounders). This would make the assessment of effect modification of confounding inefficient or sometimes even impossible.

In another study examining whether head trauma is a cause of Alzheimer's disease, an unmatched sample from the population at large would generate an inefficiently large number of controls in the younger age categories, because most cases will be octogenarians or even older. In this case, matching according to age could increase the power of the study to assess the role of age as a potential confounder or modifier.

Although matching of cases and controls can be helpful in determining the role of an effect modifier or confounder, matching is not the preferred means to deal with confounding in case-control studies. Unfortunately, however, this seems to be the predominant rationale for matching according to multiple potential confounders in many case-control studies. Often, researchers perceive matching of cases and controls as a "similar" method to prevent confounding (i.e., to achieve comparability of natural history) as matching in cohort studies or randomization in randomized trials. But there is a crucial difference between these last two methods and matching in case-control studies.

Randomization in trials and matching of those with and without the determinant in cohort studies will create subgroups of individuals who are similar according to relevant covariates (typically factors related to the outcome) except, of course, for the determinant (or exposure) of interest. Then, any difference in the future occurrence of the outcome is likely to be attributable to the determinant and not to confounding caused by these covariates. Matching in case-control studies, however, will not lead to comparability of the distribution of confounders between those with and without the determinant. In contrast, matching will result in a similar distribution of potential confounders among those with (cases) and without (controls) the disease. This is counterintuitive, because cases and controls are expected to differ considerably according to all characteristics associated with the outcome (i.e., risk factors), including confounders. Consequently, the often heard criticism of case-control studies, that "cases and controls differ too much," is unjustified; one should actually be surprised and question the validity of the data if cases have similar characteristics as control subjects (see also the Worked-Out Example at the end of this chapter).

Consider a case-control study assessing the causal association between a novel marker of lipid metabolism (e.g., the ratio of apolipoprotein ApoB to ApoA1) and myocardial infarction. Many potential confounders should be taken into account in this study, most notably those established cardiovascular risk factors known or anticipated to be related to the ApoB–ApoA1 ratio. According to some, prevention of confounding in this case-control study warrants rigorous matching of a case with its corresponding control according to a large number of cardiovascular risk factors, including (apart from age and gender) other lipid parameters, blood pressure, glucose metabolism, smoking habits, family history of cardiovascular disease, etc. This would result in a control series consisting of subjects with a relatively unfavorable cardiovascular risk profile (comparable to the cases in the same study) who managed not to develop myocardial infarction. Such patients belong in a museum, rather than in the control group of a case-control study. Moreover, lipid parameters (including the ApoB–ApoA1 ratio) may well have become similar as a result of the matching procedure, because cardiovascular risk factors are known to cluster.

Although the matching of cases and controls should be taken into account in the design of data analyses (discussed later in this chapter), rigorous matching according to many potential confounders seriously complicates such an analytic approach. Other disadvantages of matching cases and controls include the time and costs involved in identifying matched controls, notably when several matching factors are used, and the consequence that the matching factor cannot be studied as a determinant of the outcome. In addition, matching according to a factor that is not a confounder but is nevertheless associated with the determinant may even decrease efficiency [Miettinen, 1985; Rothman, 1986].

Because alternative methods for dealing with confounding in case-control studies (most notably, multivariable regression techniques to adjust for confounding in the data analysis) are available, matching should be restricted to those case-control studies where it leads to an efficiency gain. As illustrated in the melanoma example presented earlier in this chapter, this is the case when a disproportionate case-control ratio in subcategories of a confounder or effect modifier is expected. If applied, matching preferably should be restricted to one or two important factors. Typically, these include age and gender. Matching of controls according to all potential confounders with the aim of preventing confounding bias is irrational and should be discouraged. The statement included in the first book devoted entirely to case-control studies and published more than 30 years ago still holds true today: "Unless one has very good reason to match, one is undoubtedly better off avoiding the inclination" [Schlesselman, 1982].

DESIGN OF DATA ANALYSIS

As in any clinical epidemiologic study, the design of data analysis in case-control studies depends on their theoretical design (notably, whether the case-control study is descriptive or aimed at unraveling causality) and the design of data collection (for example, whether the case-control study is nested within a cohort study or a dynamic population). We first explain the importance of the exposure odds ratio in case-control studies. Subsequently, a summary of the main methods to adjust for confounding in the data analysis is provided, because the vast majority of case-control studies are performed to quantify causal associations. Finally, the data analysis consequences of matching cases and controls are discussed briefly.

The Odds Ratio Equals the Incidence Rate Ratio

Table 9–2 summarizes the major results of the first case-control study performed in the medical domain [Broders, 1920]. That study compared the smoking habits of 537 cases (with squamous epithelioma of the lip) with those of 500 control subjects (without epithelioma of the lip).

When asked about the analysis of this 2 × 2 table typical of case-control studies, those who have been exposed to a course in epidemiology or an

TABLE 9–2   Case-Control Study Linking Smoking and Epithelioma of the Lip

	Patients with Lip Epithelioma	Patients Without Lip Epithelioma
Pipe smoking	421 (a)	190 (b)
No pipe smoking	116 (c)	310 (d)
Total	537 (a+c)	500 (b+d)

Data from: Broders AC. Squamous-cell epithelioma of the lip. A study of 537 cases. *JAMA* 1920;74:656–64.

epidemiology textbook will immediately calculate the odds ratio by taking the cross-product (ad/bc) and possibly also calculate a 95% confidence interval (CI). In this example, the odds ratio is $(421 \times 310)/(190 \times 116) = 5.9$ (95% CI 4.5–7.8). This odds ratio is then—correctly—interpreted as an approximation of the relative risk: In this example, the risk of squamous epithelioma of the lip in pipe smokers is six times the risk in those not smoking a pipe. It should be noted that the odds ratio in fact is the exposure odds ratio, that is, the odds of exposure in the cases (a/c) divided by the odds of exposure in the controls (b/d).

The strength of the case-control method is that if indeed the controls are a valid sample of the study base from which the cases originate, the exposure odds ratio is by definition a valid estimate of the incidence rate ratio one would obtain from a cohort study; that is, if one took a census approach. It can be shown this is true irrespective of the frequency of the outcome of interest, and, thus, any assumption about the rarity of the outcome is irrelevant.

Imagine a dynamic population, including in total $N + N'$ participants during the entire study period. Note that because this is a dynamic population, the time that a subject is part of the study base theoretically ranges from 1 second to the full study period. Assuming, for simplicity, that exposure in a subject is constant, N subjects are exposed to the determinant and N' are not (see **Table 9–3**).

To calculate the association between the determinant and the outcome in this dynamic population followed over time, incidence rates of the disease in those with and without the determinant can be calculated. Taking an average follow-up time (t) of the members in the study base, the incidence rate, or incidence density of the outcome in those with the determinant, equals $a/(N \times t)$ while the incidence rate in the unexposed equals $c/(N' \times t)$.

The incidence rate ratio can be calculated as $(a/(N \times t))/(c/(N' \times t))$ or $(a \times N' \times t)/(c \times N \times t)$ or $(a \times N')/(c \times N)$.

The major findings of a case-control study conducted within this dynamic population are summarized in **Table 9–4**.

TABLE 9–3 Dynamic Population

	Outcome	No Outcome	
Determinant +	a	$N–a$	N
Determinant −	c	$N'–c$	N'
	$a + c$		$N + N'$

TABLE 9–4   Findings from a Case-Control Study in a
Dynamic Population

	Cases	Sample from the Study Base
Determinant +	a	b
Determinant −	c	d

In such a study, and in contrast to the follow-up study shown in Table 9–3, the exact number ($N + N'$) and specifics (notably exposure/nonexposure to the determinant) of the members of the study base are not known. The relevant characteristics are only measured in the cases ($a + c$) and in a sample from the study base ($b + d$). The numerator of the incidence rate of the outcome in those with and without the determinants is provided by a and c, respectively, and, thus the case series. The denominator is now not calculated directly as in the cohort study, but provided by the controls. If indeed a valid sample from the study base is taken, b will represent an unknown proportion p of N ($b = p \times N$ and $N = b/p$) and d will represent an unknown proportion p' of N' ($d = p' \times N'$ and thus $N' = d/p'$). The incidence rate ratio ($a \times N'$)/($c \times N$) derived from the cohort study can then be rewritten as [$a \times (d/p')$]/[$c \times (b/p)$]. If, for example, 10% of all members of the study base throughout the study period are sampled, then one will sample 10% of all exposed N, 10% of all unexposed N', 10% of all left-handed subjects, 10% of all subjects with blue eyes, etc. If indeed $p = p'$, then the incidence rate ratio can be rewritten as ($a \times d$)/($b \times c$). This equals the cross-product from a case-control study and is similar to the ratio of the exposure odds in the cases (a/c) and the controls (b/d). Consequently, if a valid sample from the study base is drawn, the exposure odds ratio obtained from a case-control study is exactly the same as the incidence rate ratio that would be obtained from a follow-up study in the same study base [Knol, et al., 2008]. Note that this is always true, irrespective of the frequency of the disease. Thus, there is no need for a "rare disease" assumption [Miettinen, 1985; Rothman, 1986]. It follows from these calculations that a typical case-control study will only provide relative measures of the association between the determinant (odds ratios) and no absolute disease frequencies (incidence rates) in those with and without the determinant, unless the sampling fraction p is known. This sampling fraction is usually not known, with the important exception of case-control studies that are performed within cohort studies. If in the latter type of studies individuals are followed in detail, the fraction p will be known and incidence rates can be estimated. Case-cohort studies (see later discussion) are examples of case-control studies with a known sampling fraction.

Adjustment for Confounding

Almost all available case-control studies deal with causality and because by definition no randomization of the determinant takes place in case-control studies, adjustment for confounding is crucial, just as for other nonexperimental studies addressing causality.

Methods available to adjust for confounding in the data analysis are essentially similar for all types of clinical epidemiologic studies. As a first step, a stratified analysis that estimates the odds ratio from 2×2 tables constructed separately for the categories of the confounder is useful. When, for example, gender is considered an important confounder, the odds ratio for both men and women will be calculated. Subsequently, a pooled estimate can be obtained using a Mantel-Haenszel approach or maximum likelihood methods, for example. This gender-adjusted odds ratio can then be compared to the overall crude estimate. If these two estimates are the same, confounding by gender is a non-issue. When multiple confounders should be taken into account, stratified analyses become complicated and alternative methods such as multivariable regression analyses are usually applied. Currently, multivariable logistic regression is used in most case-control studies. For a more elaborate discussion on adjustment for confounding, we refer you to other textbooks [Rothman, 2002; Schlesselman, 1982].

Taking Matching of Cases and Controls into Account

Although we discourage matching of cases and controls, matching is occasionally justified (usually by a gain in efficiency), but it should be emphasized that matching of cases and controls has important repercussions for the design of data analysis. Through the matching procedure cases and controls are made more similar than when unmatched samples of the study base are taken. Consequently, this induced effect should be taken into account by performing conditional analyses, that is, analyses conditional on the matching factor(s).

In fact, failure to take this matching into account may bias the odds ratio. This phenomenon has been used to illustrate that matching of cases and controls can actually induce confounding, rather than facilitate its adjustment. Importantly, this bias can be prevented (unless too many matching factors are involved) by means of stratified analyses according to strata of the matching factor and conditional regression analyses.

CASE-COHORT STUDIES

Recall that a case-cohort study is a case-control study nested within a co-hort, where the controls are sampled at the beginning of the study period ($t = 0$). By definition, these controls are free from the disease at $t = 0$ and are a representative sample of all members of the cohort. Note that in contrast to sampling at multiple points in time during the study period (typically each time a case develops) from either a dynamic population or a cohort, in a case-cohort study the researcher samples once from all members of the full cohort. In other words, a representative sample of persons, instead of person-years, is obtained as if the time that each cohort member is part of the study base is not taken into consideration. As a consequence, the odds ratio from a case-cohort study should be viewed as a valid estimate of the risk (or cumulative incidence) ratio and not of the rate (or incidence rate) ratio. Note that if the number of cohort members that develop the outcome is small (and this very often applies to case-control studies), the cumulative incidence ratio approximates the incidence risk ratio. In essence, therefore, both sampling of persons (from the members of the full cohort) and of person-time (from the total number of person-years all cohort members contribute to the study) is possible in a case-cohort study. If, as is usually the case, the sampling fraction (i.e., the proportion of all persons or person-years that is sampled) is known, one can even calculate absolute cumulative incidences or incidence rates for those with and without the determinant.

The case-cohort study design is generally attributed to Prentice [1986], but Miettinen had already introduced the method in 1982. Until more recent years, however, the method often was not applied. This is partly attributable to the initial problems pertaining to the data analysis of case-cohort studies, including the difficulties in calculating confidence intervals [Schouten et al., 1993]. These problems have been solved. In the analyses of case-cohort studies (with a known sampling fraction), the full cohort is first more or less "reconstructed" by multiplying the sample of controls. Subsequently, absolute risks and rates can be estimated, but the inflation of the control sample needs to be taken into account when calculating the confidence intervals. Several methods are available to analyze case-cohort data and adjust for confounding, including the Cox proportional hazards model.

The main advantage of the case-cohort approach is its efficiency, as for all case-control studies, but the fact that the controls can be identified in the beginning of the study further adds to its attractiveness. In addition, a single control group can be applied for multiple outcomes. In effect, several case-control studies can be performed using the same control group. An advantage compared to most other case-control studies is the possibility of calculating absolute risks or incidence rates (and risk or rate differences).

Case-cohort studies are less advantageous when many cohort members are lost to follow-up, when the outcome is very common, and when the exposure changes over time. Moreover, the number of controls to be sampled in the beginning is difficult to predict, because the number of cases are unknown at $t = 0$, which may lead to some loss in efficiency (i.e., the case-control ratio may not be optimal). In addition, the data analysis is less straightforward than in most other types of case-control studies. The abstract of a case-cohort study is given in **Box 9–6** [Van der A et al., 2006].

BOX 9–6   A Case-Cohort Study on the Causal Link Between Iron and the Risk of Coronary Heart Disease

Background: Epidemiological studies aimed at correlating coronary heart disease (CHD) with serum ferritin levels have thus far yielded inconsistent results. We hypothesized that a labile iron component associated with non-transferrin-bound iron (NTBI) that appears in individuals with overt or cryptic iron overload might be more suitable for establishing correlations with CHD.

Methods and Results: We investigated the relation of NTBI, serum iron, transferrin saturation, and serum ferritin with risk of CHD and acute myocardial infarction (AMI). The cohort used comprised a population-based sample of 11,471 postmenopausal women aged 49 to 70 years at enrollment in 1993 to 1997. During a median follow-up of 4.3 years (quartile limits Q1 to Q3: 3.3 to 5.4), 185 CHD events were identified, including 66 AMI events. We conducted a case-cohort study using all CHD cases and a random sample from the baseline cohort ($n = 1134$). A weighted Cox proportional hazards model was used to estimate hazard ratios for tertiles of iron variables in relation to CHD and AMI. Adjusted hazard ratios of women in the highest NTBI tertile (range 0.38 to 3.51) compared with the lowest (range -2.06 to -0.32) were 0.84 (95% confidence interval 0.61 to 1.16) for CHD and 0.47 (95% confidence interval 0.31 to 0.71) for AMI. The results were similar for serum iron, transferrin saturation, and serum ferritin.

Conclusions: Our results show no excess risk of CHD or AMI within the highest NTBI tertile compared with the lowest but rather seem to demonstrate a decreased risk. Additional studies are warranted to confirm our findings.

Reproduced from Van der A DL, Marx JJ, Grobbee DE, Kamphuis MH, Georgiou NA, van Kats-Renaud JH, Breuer W, Cabantchik ZI, Roest M, Voorbij HA, Van der Schouw YT. Non-transferrin-bound iron and the risk of coronary heart disease in postmenopausal women. *Circulation* 2006;113:1942–9.

The following paragraph from the study of Van der A et al. describes the rationale and methodology of this case-cohort study:

> The case-cohort design consists of a subcohort randomly sampled from the full cohort at the beginning of the study and a case sample that consists of all cases that are ascertained during follow-up. With this sampling strategy, the subcohort may include incident cases of CHD that will contribute person-time as controls until the moment they experience the event. We selected a random sample of [almost equal to] 10% ($n = 1134$) from the baseline cohort to serve as the subcohort. The advantage of this design is that it enables the performance of survival analyses without the need to collect expensive laboratory data for the entire cohort.

The complexity of the data analysis is illustrated in the next few lines from the same article:

> To assess the relationship between the iron variables (i.e., NTBI, serum iron, transferrin saturation, and serum ferritin) and heart disease, we used a Cox proportional hazards model with an estimation procedure adapted for case-cohort designs. We used the unweighted method by Prentice, which is incorporated in the macro ROBPHREG made by Barlow and Ichikawa. This macro is available at http://lib.stat.cmu.edu/general/robphreg and can be implemented in the SAS statistical software package version 8.2. It computes weighted estimates together with a robust standard error, from which we calculated 95% confidence intervals.

CASE-CROSSOVER STUDIES

The case-crossover study was introduced in 1991 by Maclure. A case-crossover study bears some resemblance to a crossover randomized trial. In the latter, each participant receives all (usually two) interventions and the order in which he or she receives them in this experimental study is randomly allocated, with a short time between the two interventions, allowing for the effect of the intervention to wear off. Assumptions underlying a crossover trial include the transient effect of each intervention and that the first intervention does not exert an effect during the time period the participant receives the second intervention (i.e., there is no carryover effect).

In a case-crossover study, all participants experience periods of exposure as well as periods of nonexposure to the determinant of interest. However, a case-crossover study is nonexperimental and thus the order in which exposure or nonexposure occurs is anything but random. In fact, exposure or nonexposure may change multiple times in a participant during the study period. Importantly, the previously mentioned prerequisites for crossover trials also pertain to case-crossover studies: the exposure being transient and the lack of a carryover effect.

A case-crossover study is a case-control study because a sampling instead of a census approach is taken. Instead of comparing cases with a sample from the study base, however, the exposure is compared in the risk period preceding the outcome and the "usual exposure" in the same case. The latter may be measured by calculating the average exposure over a certain time period or measuring exposure at a random point in time or specified period, for example, 48 hours before the event. The types of transient determinants that have been evaluated in case-crossover designs include coffee drinking, physical exertion, alcohol intake, sexual activity, and cocaine consumption [Mittleman et al., 1993; Mittleman et al., 1999]. In addition, a case-crossover design is an attractive option to identify transient triggers of exacerbations in patients with chronic disease, such as multiple sclerosis or migraine [Confavreux et al., 2001; Villeneuve et al., 2006].

Let us consider the example of a study aimed at quantifying the occurrence of myocardial infarction as a function of strenuous physical exertion [Willich et al., 1993]. In the article, both a typical case-control study and a case-crossover study are presented. Both designs are shown in **Figure 9–7**.

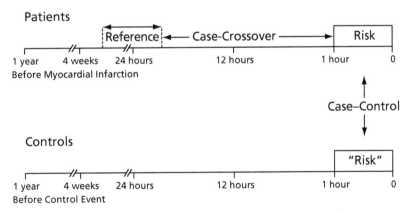

FIGURE 9–7 Comparison of a case-crossover and a case-control study examining the causal link between physical exertion and myocardial infarction.

Reproduced from Willich SN, Lewis M, Lowel H, Arntz HR, Schubert F, Schroder R. Physical exertion as a trigger of acute myocardial infarction. Triggers and mechanisms of myocardial infarction study group. *N Engl J Med* 1993;329:1684–90.

Time zero indicates the occurrence of the outcome in a member of the study base. The determinant is defined as "being engaged in physical exertion one hour before a certain point in time," and for the cases this is the time of onset of nonfatal myocardial infarction. In their case-control analysis, Willich et al. compared the prevalence of strenuous physical exertion of cases in the risk period with the prevalence in age-, sex-, and neighborhood-matched population controls. The adjusted odds ratio resulting from this analysis was 2.1 (95% CI, 1.1–3.6). In their case-crossover analysis, the authors compared the exposure during the risk period of the cases with their usual frequency of strenuous exercise. The data were obtained by interviewing the participants. In the analyses, the observed odds of strenuous exercise within the hour before the onset of myocardial infarction and the expected odds ($x{:}y$) that the case would have been engaged in exercise, based on the usual exercise frequency, were calculated. The risk ratio was calculated as the ratio of the sums of y (i.e., the probability of usually *not* being engaged in exercise) in cases who were exercising within 1 hour before the event and the sum of x (i.e., the probability of usually being engaged in exercise) in cases who did not exercise within 1 hour of symptom onset. The risk ratio resulting from this approach was similar to the case-control estimate: 2.1 (95% CI, 1.6–3.1).

The major strength of a case-crossover design is the within-person comparison, just as in crossover trials. The case and its matched control (who in fact is the same person) will be matched according to characteristics that are constant in a certain (usually short) time span (e.g., comorbidity, socio-economic status, gender). Because of this matching, these characteristics can never be studied as a determinant of the outcome event, but a case-crossover study usually focuses on one transient exposure only. The most important threat to case-crossover studies is the possibility that the determinant exerts its effect way beyond the risk period defined. This "carryover" effect cannot always be ruled out.

CASE-CONTROL STUDIES WITHOUT CONTROLS

The case-crossover study is an example of a case-control study without control subjects; in other words, the cases are the only subjects included in the analysis. Under specific circumstances, several other designs that include cases only are in use. Case-only studies are particularly useful for assessing gene–environment interactions [Khoury & Flandes, 1996; Piegorsch et al., 1994], while regular case-control studies typically lack the power to detect such interactions. In a case-only study, a 2 × 2 table is drawn comparing the single and combined exposure of the cases to the environmental and genetic determinant. Then, the case-only odds ratio is calculated as ad/bc. This odds ratio allows the researcher to assess whether there is multiplicative interaction between the two determinants or a departure from multiplicative risk ratios. A major limitation of the design is the essential assumption of independence between the two factors in the population, because only then does the case-only odds ratio equal the result that would be obtained in a regular case-control study (with enough power) [Albert et al., 2001].

When the determinant under study is the distance from a potentially harmful source, such as a power line or magnetic field, a case-specular study may be a design option. In such studies, hypothetical controls are created by reflecting the residence of the case (or reflecting the power line), for example, by mirroring the image of the case residence, taking the middle of the street as the reference [Zaffanella et al., 1998].

ADVANTAGES AND LIMITATIONS OF CASE-CONTROL STUDIES

The strengths and limitations of case-control studies follow from the particularities of the design. In **Table 9–5**, the major advantages and disadvantages are summarized.

The main advantage of a case-control study is its efficiency. Information on the determinant (and other relevant characteristics, notably confounders and effect modifiers) only needs to be obtained in the cases and a sample of the study base from which the cases originate. Thus, the costs of case-control studies are relatively low. Especially when the outcome is rare,

TABLE 9–5   Case-Control Studies: Strengths and Limitations

Strengths	Limitations
Efficiency (sampling instead of census), in particular when: —Outcomes are rare —Multiple determinants/dosages are studied —Assessment of the determinants is expensive —Duration of exposure is long or unknown	Less suited when determinant is rare Usually provides no absolute rates/risks More prone to bias than experimental studies Often performed "quick and dirty"

when measurement of the relevant (co)variates is expensive (e.g., for genetic markers), or multiple variables (including multiple exposure dosages) are involved, a sampling rather than a census approach becomes the preferred strategy in the design of data collection. Moreover, case-control studies provide ample opportunity to address the effect of determinant exposure duration on the occurrence of the outcome, for example, in the assessment of drug risks.

Several limitations inherent to a case-control design exist, such as their inefficiency when the determinant is rare. Case-control studies are often considered to be more vulnerable to bias than other designs, such as cohort studies. When one realizes that a case-control study is just a more efficient way to conduct a cohort study, the nonsense of this common myth becomes clear. Obviously, if sampling of controls depends on the determinant studied, if the cases and controls are asked retrospectively about exposure, or if confounding is not adequately addressed, bias (also termed *selection bias*, *recall bias*, and *confounding bias*, respectively) may occur in case-control studies. Bias, however, can similarly be present in any other nonexperimental study. It seems that the bad reputation of case-control studies has resulted from the "quick and dirty" manner (remember Andy Warhol's can of soup introduced in Box 9–1) in which many of them have been performed. Poor conduct of many case-control studies clearly contributes to the air of suspicion surrounding the results of case-control studies in general.

State of the art case-control studies offer an extremely powerful epidemiologic tool. Provided that the underlying principles are appreciated, case-control studies will continue to play a prominent role in providing evidence for clinical practice because of their application in both causal and descriptive clinical research.

WORKED-OUT EXAMPLE

Anesthetic care in westernized societies is of high quality and is generally considered safe. However, very rarely accidents still occur that can have serious health consequences. The Netherlands Society for Anaesthesiology decided to estimate the incidence of serious morbidity and mortality during or following anesthesia and study possible causal factors related to procedures and organization with the goal of reducing risks further. Because of the rarity of the event, large numbers of anesthetic procedures were needed for the study. This, in combination with the necessary detailed information to be obtained led to the decision to conduct a case-control study (see **Box 9–7**) [Arbous et al., 2005].

BOX 9–7   Impact of Anesthesia Management Characteristics on Severe Morbidity and Mortality

Background: Quantitative estimates of how anesthesia management impacts perioperative morbidity and mortality are limited. The authors performed a study to identify risk factors related to anesthesia management for 24-h postoperative severe morbidity and mortality.

Methods: A case-control study was performed of all patients undergoing anesthesia (1995–1997). Cases were patients who either remained comatose or died during or within 24 h of undergoing anesthesia. Controls were patients who neither remained comatose nor died during or within 24 hours of undergoing anesthesia. Data were collected by means of a questionnaire, the anesthesia and recovery form. Odds ratios were calculated for risk factors, adjusted for confounders.

Results: The cohort comprised 869,483 patients; 807 cases and 883 controls were analyzed. The incidence of 24-h postoperative death was 8.8 (95% confidence interval, 8.2–9.5) per 10,000 anesthetics. The incidence of coma was 0.5 (95% confidence interval, 0.3–0.6). Anesthesia management factors that were statistically significantly associated with a decreased risk were: equipment check with protocol and checklist (odds ratio, 0.64), documentation of the equipment check (odds ratio, 0.61), a directly available anesthesiologist (odds ratio, 0.46), no change of anesthesiologist during anesthesia (odds ratio, 0.44), presence of a full-time working anesthetic nurse (odds ratio, 0.41), two persons present at emergence (odds ratio, 0.69), reversal of anesthesia (for muscle relaxants and the combination of muscle relaxants and opiates; odds ratios, 0.10 and 0.29, respectively), and postoperative pain medication as opposed to no pain medication, particularly if administered epidurally or intramuscularly as opposed to intravenously.

Conclusions: Mortality after surgery is substantial and an association was established between perioperative coma and death and anesthesia management factors like intraoperative presence of anesthesia personnel, administration of drugs intraoperatively and postoperatively, and characteristics of delivered intraoperative and postoperative anesthetic care.

Reproduced from Arbous MS, Meursing AAE, van Kleef JW, de Lange JJ, Spoormans HHAJM, Touw P, Werner FM, Grobbee DE. Impact of anesthesia management characteristics on severe morbidity and mortality. *Anesthesiology* 2005;102:257–68.

Theoretical Design

The research question addressed was: "Which characteristics of anesthesia management are causally related to 24-hour postoperative severe morbidity and mortality?" This translates to the following occurrence relation: *severe postoperative morbidity and mortality* as a function of *factors related to anesthesia management* conditional on *confounders*. The domain was all patients given anesthesia for surgery. The operational definition of the outcome was coma or death during or within 24 hours of anesthesia administration. The determinant and confounders were operationalized by recording all relevant characteristics of anesthesia, hospital, and patients by means of a questionnaire and by scrutinizing anesthesia and recovery forms.

Design of Data Collection

The data collection was designed as a prospective case-control study. Cases were patients who either remained comatose or died during or within 24 hours of undergoing anesthesia from a cohort formed by all patients undergoing anesthesia (general, regional, or a combined technique) from January 1, 1995 to December 31, 1996, in three of the 12 provinces in the Netherlands. The number of anesthetics in the study area and study period was 869,483. Controls were obtained by taking a random patient from the remainder of the cohort immediately after a case was identified. Note that cases were in no way defined as *a priori* related to anesthesia management (the determinant of interest). Consequently, most of the cases were likely to have become comatose or have died because of other reasons, notably severity of the health condition for which surgery was needed or because of the risks associated with the surgery.

Design of Data Analysis

The principal analysis was performed on controls ($n = 883$) and all cases ($n = 807$) jointly. Crude rate ratios and 95% confidence intervals (CIs) of all preoperative, intraoperative, and postoperative risk factors for perioperative morbidity or mortality, estimated as odds ratios, were calculated by univariate logistic regression.

Because the main interest was in the causal relationship between anesthesia management and perioperative coma and death, anesthesia management–related preoperative, intraoperative, and postoperative risk factors were considered to be potential determinants of the outcome. Patient-, surgery-, and hospital-related factors were treated as potential confounders of this relationship of interest. Potential determinants were considered in the analyses if, in the univariate analysis, two-sided P values were less than 0.25 or if the variable seemed relevant from a biologic or anesthesia management point of view. To adjust risk estimates of the determinants for confounders, multivariable logistic regression was used. Patient-, surgery-, and hospital-related factors were considered as possible confounders if they were statistically significantly related to the determinant or were judged to be biologically relevant. While for the study as a whole, multiple possible causal determinants were considered, the causal role of each determinant was analyzed separately. For each determinant that was significantly related to the outcome in the univariate analysis, a set of possible confounders were tested by multivariable logistic regression. A unique regression model was considered for each individual determinant, because particular variables could act as a confounder for one determinant but not necessarily for others.

The importance of each potential confounder included in the model was verified by the likelihood ratio test and a comparison of the estimated odds ratio of the determinant from models containing and not containing the potential confounder. A significant likelihood ratio test with a change of the estimated odds ratio was taken as evidence that a biologically plausible factor was a confounder and, therefore, it was included in the model. Adjusted risks for anesthesia management factors were calculated, controlling for confounders. Patients with more than 10% missing values were excluded. Missing data are a common problem in research using data that as a whole or in part are based on routine clinical records. If the proportion of missing data is not too large, the data may be imputed using various regression-based techniques. For this study, data were analyzed both with and without imputation of variables showing up to 10% missing values. Results were virtually the same.

Implications and Relevance

The results of the study showed that in spite of the high-quality level of current anesthetic practice, several characteristics of anesthesia management could be related to risk of mortality (taking confounding variables into account). These findings point to a causal role of these characteristics. During the review process of this manuscript and after publication, a comment (common in response to case-control studies) was made by several reviewers/readers regarding the large differences between cases and controls. Here is a part of one of the critical responses [Robertson, 2006]:

> When one looks at baseline characteristics of the study and control groups, there are, as the authors note, huge differences in the categories of urgent/emergent nature, time of day procedure performed, and ASA physical status. In fact, 40% of the study cases were rated ASA V—not expected to survive for 24 hours, with or without surgery (regardless of anesthetic management). If we accept that a very large proportion of the study cases carry

greater risk by virtue of their physical status and the emergent nature of the injury or disease process, and that urgent/emergent cases generally account for all the outside working hour cases, then differences in anesthetic management processes between the two groups appear more coincidentally associated than causative.

The point made by this author is illustrated in the baseline table from the original report, a section of which is shown in **Table 9–6** [Arbous et al., 2005].

The observation of marked differences in risk between cases and controls is correct, but the inference is erroneous [Arbous et al., 2006]. Cases and controls should be inescapably different if cases are the ones who experience problems and controls are randomly sampled from the remainder of

TABLE 9–6   Baseline Characteristics of Participants in the Anesthesia Management Study

Characteristic	Cases (n = 807)	Controls (n = 883)	Two-Sided P Value
Mean age, years	64.4 (62.8–65.0)*	63.6 (62.1–65.2)*	0.53
Sex, % women	38.5	42.9	0.06
ASA physical status, %			< 0.01
I	2.2	30.6	
II	6.2	47.8	
III	21.8	19.9	
IV	30.3	1.5	
V	39.5	0.2	
Urgency of procedure, %			< 0.01
Elective	21.5	87.4	
Nonelective	15.1	10.5	
Urgent	63.4	2.0	
Time of procedure, %			< 0.01
During working hours (08:00–16:00 h)	50.7	96	
Outside working hours (< 23:00 h)	32.3	3.4	
Outside working hours (> 23:00 h)	17.1	0.6	
Duration of procedure, h	2.7 (2.5–2.9)*	1.5 (1.4–1.6)*	< 0.01

*95% confidence interval.

Reproduced from Arbous MS, Meursing AAE, van Kleef JW, de Lange JJ, Spoormans HHAJM, Touw P, Werner FM, Grobbee DE. Impact of anesthesia management characteristics on severe morbidity and mortality. *Anesthesiology* 2005;102:257–68.

the cohort. In particular, they should be different in factors that reflect known mortality risks such as age, ASA physical status, or urgency of the procedure. The question is whether these prognostic factors are also related to characteristics of anesthetic management.

To address this question, extensive confounder information was collected, including those variables so dramatically different between cases and controls, and multivariate adjustments were made. Some reviewers would have rather seen controls that were closely matched to cases on as many risk factors as possible. However, this would violate the study base principle that controls in a case-control study should be representative of the population experience from which the cases originate. While matching may sometimes be needed for efficiency reasons, this procedure has major disadvantages, as explained earlier. Most individuals in a group of controls resulting from closely matching controls to the cases according to multiple potential confounders belong in a museum for surviving the anesthesia and the operation and should not be included in the control group of a case-control study.

Chapter 10

Randomized Trials

INTRODUCTION

Trials are cohort studies in which allocation to the determinant is initiated by the investigator. Moreover, in randomized trials the allocation is made at random by some algorithm. Because the determinant is allocated with the purpose of learning about its effect on the outcome, randomized trials are experiments. The determinant that is allocated is typically a treatment such as a drug or another intervention, for example, a surgical procedure or lifestyle advice intended to provide relief, cure, or prevention of disease. In this chapter, the term *treatment* will be used for all interventions studied in randomized trials.

Randomized trials have an important role in determining the efficacy and safety of treatments. A trial can be viewed as a measurement of the effect of a treatment. It should provide a quantitative and precise estimate of the benefits or risks that can be expected when a treatment is given to patients with an indication for it.

Randomized trials can be distinguished according to the phase of development of a treatment. This distinction is most frequently applied in drug trials. *Phase I trials* are usually carried out after satisfactory findings have been reported in animal experiments. They primarily aim to determine the pharmacologic and metabolic effects of the drug in humans, and to detect the most common side effects. Study subjects in phase I trials usually are healthy volunteers who typically undergo dose escalating studies, first in single doses and later in multiple ones, to identify the safe dosage range. Also in this phase, the effects of the drug on physiologic measures may be determined, for example, on the aggregation of platelets in studies of platelet inhibitors. Usually the number of participants in a phase I trial is no more than 100.

In *phase II trials*, the new treatment is studied for the first time in the type of patients for whom the treatment is intended. Emphasis is again on safety but also on intermediate outcomes (see later discussion of types of outcomes) that broaden insight into the pathophysiologic effects and possible benefits of the treatment. Drug studies often test several doses in order to find the optimal dose for a large-scale study. For example, a trial group sought to determine whether and at what dose recombinant activated factor VII can reduce hematoma growth after intracerebral hemorrhage [Mayer et al., 2005]. The investigators randomized 399 patients with intracerebral hemorrhage within 3 hours of disease onset to either a placebo or three different doses of the drug. The primary outcome was the percent change in volume of the hemorrhage from admission to 24 hours. Clinical status was determined after 3 months as a secondary outcome.

In *phase III trials*, the treatments are brought to a "real-life" situation with outcomes that are considered to be clinically relevant in patients who are diagnosed with the indication for the treatment. Phase III trials are large (often 1,000 or more patients) and hence costly. Much of the practical aspects of clinical trials discussed in this chapter pertain specifically to phase III trials.

Phase IV trials, also termed postmarketing (surveillance) trials, may concentrate on the study of rare side effects after a treatment has been allowed access to the market. Phase IV trials can also be conducted to assess possibly new, beneficial effects of registered drugs. Phase IV trials frequently are also used for the promotion of a newly registered treatment, which is an understandable approach from the perspective of the industry but less attractive from a scientific point of view (these are referred to as *seeding trials*). There is currently ample discussion on how to best monitor the total (both beneficial and untoward) effects of a drug once it has entered the market. Sometimes, conditional approvals are considered, where the pharmaceutical industry is required to provide updated information on the effects of a drug during the first period of real-life use. This could include the continuation of specifically designed randomized comparisons to quantify side effects. However, there are several other research approaches to address the study of side effects once a treatment has come to the market.

When designing the data collection and organizational aspects of a clinical trial, it is useful for the researcher to have conceptualized the structure of the written manuscript about the study. A guideline on what to report and how to do it was issued in 2001. This document, the Consolidated Standards of Reporting Trials (CONSORT), has been revised and adopted as an obligatory format by major medical journals and was most recently updated in 2010 [Moher et al., 2001b; Moher et al., 2010]. The website of the CONSORT organization (www.consort-statement.org) also provides several extensions of the statement, including information about non-inferiority trials.

However, even before a report on the trial results is written, or even before the study has started, the International Committee of Medical Journal Editors (ICMJE) currently requires all trials (including phase III trials) that assess efficacy to be registered [De Angelis et al., 2005]. Registration must occur before the first patient is enrolled and the registry must be electronically searchable and accessible to the public at no charge. If no such registration is created, the manuscript on the results of the trial will not be accepted for publication by the journals that adhere to the ICMJE statement, which include all major general medical journals. The rationale for a trial registry is the responsibility of investigators to present the design of the study and give an account of the results of the trial, irrespective of the nature of the findings. In the past, too often the design features of a trial were changed during the study or so-called negative trials were not published, leaving the international scientific community with mainly the positive trials, thus creating publication bias.

"REGULAR" PARALLEL, FACTORIAL, CROSSOVER, NON-INFERIORITY, AND CLUSTER TRIALS

In a so-called *regular* randomized trial, two or sometimes more parallel treatments are directly compared between the patients who form the treatment groups. In a *parallel* group trial, the patient is the unit of randomization and there is no intent to switch the allocated treatment within a patient.

Sometimes, however, there are several treatment modalities to be compared for the same group of patients. In a *factorial* design, two treatments may be studied simultaneously, with the patients being randomized twice. A typical prerequisite for such a factorial design is that there is no pharmacologic interaction between the two treatment regimens, unless one wants to study that specifically. For example, in the Dutch TIA Trial [1991, 1993], the investigators simultaneously studied the effects of two different aspirin dosages (30 mg vs. 283 mg daily) and that of the beta-blocker atenolol (50 mg daily vs. matching placebo) on the occurrence of new vascular events in patients who had had a transient ischemic attack or minor ischemic stroke. Patients were randomized twice: once to allocate the dosage of aspirin and again to allocate the use of atenolol or the placebo. A factorial design has the advantage of efficiency. It basically gives the results of two trials for the price of one, because there is no need to increase the number of patients beyond that which would have been required for a single treatment comparison. A factorial design may be particularly favorable when it is difficult to recruit a sufficiently large number of patients with more or less rare diseases or conditions. Sometimes, an interaction between treatments is assumed to be likely rather than presumed absent. By nature of its design, the factorial study offers the opportunity to explicitly examine interaction. In the ADVANCE trial, two treatments of diabetic patients were compared to decide the optimal treatment for preventing vascular events. Patients were first randomized to intensified versus usual glucose control, and next to the usual treatment of hypertension versus blood pressure reduction irrespective of blood pressure level, for example, also in normotensive diabetic patients [ADVANCE 2001, 2007, 2008]. Four groups resulted: (1) usual blood pressure treatment plus intensive glucose control, (2) usual blood pressure treatment with usual glucose control, (3) blood pressure treatment irrespective of blood pressure level plus intensive glucose control, and (4) blood pressure treatment irrespective of blood pressure level with usual glucose control (see **Figure 10–1**). The four groups allowed for a comparison of the benefit of intensive glucose control and blood pressure reduction irrespective of blood pressure level, but also of the effect of the two treatments combined (versus usual care), which may well be more than

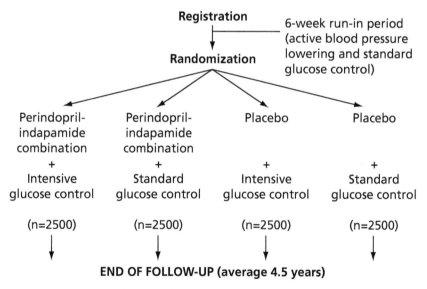

FIGURE 10–1   Flow chart showing the design of the ADVANCE study.

With kind permission from Springer Science+Business Media: *Diabetologia*. Study rationale and design of ADVANCE: Action in diabetes and vascular disease-preterax and diamicron MR controlled evaluation. *Diabetologia* 2001;44:1118–20.

the sum of either effect (indicating interaction). The latter, however, can only be done with sufficient precision if the numbers of participants in these comparison groups are sufficiently large. Typically this is not the case in a trial with a factorial design, where sample size is calculated for the two separate, yet combined, trials [Zoungas et al., 2009].

In a trial with a *crossover* design, the primary comparison of treatment effects is within a single patient. For this purpose, one-half of the patients first receive treatment A and then treatment B with the possibility of a washout period between the two treatment periods. The other half of the patients is randomized to receive treatments in the reverse order (first B, then A). The number of treatment periods may be larger than two, for example, allowing the comparison of the schemes ABAB and BABA.

A major advantage of the crossover design is that it removes between-patient variability and hence offers a more efficient approach (fewer patients are needed) to measure a treatment effect than a conventional parallel group trial when the between-patient variability of the outcome is high relative to the within-patient variability. However, not all research questions can be validly addressed with a crossover design. First, the disease must return to its "baseline" level once treatment is removed and last sufficiently long to have two disease episodes with comparable severity. Second, there must be an outcome measure that can be obtained after a limited period of observation. Third, the effects of the treatment given during the first period must not carry over to the second period. If the first condition is not met, a so-called *period effect* will be present; if the third condition is not fulfilled, a *carry-over effect* will occur. In an example of a crossover trial, the effects of azithromycin on forced expiratory volume in 1 second (FEV_1) was assessed in 41 children diagnosed with cystic fibrosis and reduced FEV_1 [Equi et al., 2002]. Half of the children first received azithromycin for 6 months, subsequently had a washout of 2 months, and then continued with 6 months of placebo. The other half received placebo first and then active treatment. In both treatment periods, there was a consistent difference between the effects of azithromycin and placebo on FEV_1; thus on the basis of this small trial, the investigators concluded that 4–6 months of treatment with azithromycin is justified in children with cystic fibrosis who do not respond to conventional treatment. Crossover trials are particularly well suited for treatment effects that occur relatively quickly and are reversible after cessation in more or less stable chronic disease. Outcomes typically are intermediate endpoints such as biochemical or physiologic measurements. For details on the design and interpretation of crossover trials, the reader is referred to the book by Senn [1993].

In a *non-inferiority* trial, the aim is not to determine whether a specific treatment is superior to an alternative treatment, but rather to show that a treatment is not worse than the comparator. When the aim is to show that the effect of the new treatment is similar, the term *equivalence trial* is often applied. Typically, in a non-inferiority (NI) trial, a new treatment is compared to currently available ("standard") treatment. This is usually done because the use of placebo is considered unethical; that is, the currently available treatment has been demonstrated to be more effective than placebo. When the NI trial indeed shows that the new treatment is not inferior to this active control treatment, one also assumes that the new treatment is effective (i.e., it is better than the placebo) [D'Agostino et al., 2003]. The design and interpretation of NI trials are not as straightforward as trials assessing whether one treatment is better than a comparator (*superiority* trial). Notably, the choice of the NI margin is a challenge. The *NI margin* is the threshold at which one still concludes that the new treatment is not worse than the active control treatment. It must also account for some uncertainty in the effect of the active control versus placebo. This is to ensure that the new treatment is also more effective than the placebo and that this effect size is clinically relevant, even though in an NI trial no placebo arm is included. There is some guidance on how to determine the NI margin [Center for Drug Evaluation and Research and Center for Biologics Evaluation and Research, 2010], One could, for example, take 50% of the effect of the active control compared to the placebo (known from previous placebo-controlled trials reported in the literature) to determine the NI margin, assuming that this boundary still signifies a clinically relevant effect compared to the placebo [Wangge et al., 2013a, 2013b]. There are several other typical features of NI trials, such as the need to report both intention to treat and per protocol analyses (see the section "Design of Data Analysis" later in the chapter), because, in contrast to superiority trials, the former may lead to the spurious conclusion that the new treatment is indeed non-inferior.

In addition, the interpretation of the findings of NI trials can be complicated. This is illustrated in **Figure 10–2**. From the results of the studies of type A, B, and C it can be concluded that the test drug is non-inferior to the comparator because the lower limit of the confidence interval of the effect estimate, (that is, the ratio or difference between the incidence of the outcome in the test drug and its active comparator) does not cross the NI margin. Findings from studies depicted by D, E, and F do not show that the test drug is non-inferior, because the 95% confidence interval of the effect estimate includes the NI margin. Some of the findings could also be interpreted differently; for example, C indicates that the test treatment might be superior to the active treatment, while A, and perhaps also D and even E, suggest

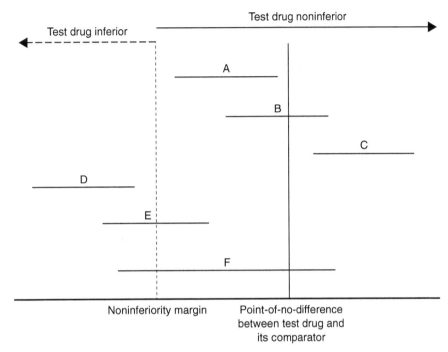

FIGURE 10-2 Confidence intervals and non-inferiority (NI) interpretation of the treatment difference between a test drug and an active comparator drug. The dashed vertical line represents the NI margin, the solid vertical line is the point-of-no-difference line, and the horizontal lines represent the confidence intervals. The point-of-no-difference is the point at which the estimated treatment difference between the new drug and comparator is neutral: zero for a difference in outcome or one for a ratio. Studies A, B, and C show that the new drug is non-inferior to its comparator. While non-inferiority is not shown for studies D, E, and F.

Reproduced from Wangge G, Klungel OH, Roes KC, de Boer A, Hoes AW, Knol MJ. Interpretation and inference in noninferiority randomized controlled trials in drug research. *Clin Pharmacol Ther* 2010;88:420–3.

that the test treatment might be worse, because the 95% confidence interval does not include the point of no difference between the two treatments. One should be cautious about making additional claims in this situation, however, because the aim was to assess whether the test drug was non-inferior, yes (A, B, C) or no (D, E, F), to the active control treatment.

The complexities surrounding non-inferiority studies have made some researchers strongly argue against their conduct [Garattini & Bertele, 2007]. For daily practice, however, such studies are becoming increasingly important, especially when a new active drug is considered to be at least as effective as the currently available treatment and also may have certain advantages, such as an easier mode of administration or fewer side effects [Wangge et al., 2013a]. The development of new classes of oral anticoagulants serves as an example. An advantage of these anticoagulants compared to the vitamin K antagonists, the "standard" treatment, is that no laboratory monitoring is required. In recent years, many NI trials comparing these novel anticoagulants with vitamin K antagonists have been published to determine whether these novel drugs were at least as effective as vitamin K antagonists in preventing thrombotic events, while the incidence of major bleedings was not higher than among those receiving vitamin K antagonists [Wangge et al., 2013b].

Sometimes it is preferable or only possible to randomize groups of patients to different interventions. Take, for example, the study of a minimal intervention strategy aimed at assessment and modification of psychosocial prognostic factors in the treatment of low back pain in general practice [Jellema et al., 2005]. It would be very difficult to randomize the patients within the practice of a single general practitioner, because the general practitioner would have to switch back and forth between two treatment strategies: the new minimal intervention strategy and the usual care strategy. It also could create dilemmas in the randomization. Moreover, it would be difficult to fully separate the strategies in patients who are in frequent contact with each other, and contamination (of the two strategies to be compared) could occur. Hence, randomization at the level of the practices of the general practitioner is the obvious solution; this method was chosen in what is termed a *cluster randomized trial*, with 30 general practitioners randomized to the minimal intervention strategy and 32 to usual care. A total of 314 patients were enrolled, that is, about five patients per practice. Because data in a cluster, here a general practice, are related, the sample size calculated on the basis of individual patient data should be increased by a factor that depends on the degree of correlation of data within a cluster. Design and data analysis features of cluster randomized trials require careful consideration, and an extension of the CONSORT statement may be helpful in addressing the issues faced by the researcher [Campbell et al., 2004, Campbell et al., 2012]. A specific type of cluster randomized trial is the *stepped wedge design trial*. In a stepped wedge cluster randomized trial, all clusters (e.g., hospitals) undergo both interventions of the trial (e.g., a new strategy and the usual care strategy). First, in all hospitals the same strategy will be followed (typically the usual care strategy) in all new patients. After a prespecified time period (e.g., each month) one hospital will change to the new strategy, and it will stick to that strategy until the end of the trial for all new patients. The next month, another hospital will change to the new strategy, etcetera. During the last period, all hospitals will apply the novel strategy. Thus, some hospitals will follow the usual care strategy while others will follow the new strategy during most of the study period, but all hospitals will experience both strategies. The point at which a hospital changes from one strategy to the other is determined through a randomization procedure. Thus, a stepped wedge cluster randomized trial combines features of a crossover trial and a before–after study. Stepped wedge trials are increasingly being applied to compare two treatment or diagnostic strategies. Advantages in comparison to a before–after study are that both strategies are applied throughout the entire study period (and thus the influence of time is reduced) and an advantage compared to a "classical" cluster randomized trial is that between-hospital differences are less likely to distort the findings because each hospital applies both strategies. The latter will also increase the participation rate when the new strategy seems to be an attractive option. For a more elaborate discussion on stepped wedge cluster randomized trials, see Brown and Lilford [2006] and Hussqy and Hughes [2007].

In the remainder of this chapter, we follow global categories of items that need to be addressed in a report of any clinical trial. These guide us along the most important practical items in the preparation and conduct of trials (see **Table 10–1**).

TABLE 10–1   Important Items for Reporting on Randomized Trials

Global Category	Items to Be Addressed
Patients	Eligibility criteria
	Setting and location
Intervention	Details on the treatments
	Methods of random allocation
Outcome	Well-defined primary and secondary outcome measures
	Outcome assessment blinded?
Data analysis	Sample size: How calculated?
	Interim analyses?
	Methods for comparison of primary outcome between groups
	Absolute risks

Reproduced from: Moher D, Hopewell S, Schulz KF, Montori V, Gotzsche PC, Devereaux PJ, Elbourne D, Egger M, Altman DG. CONSORT 2010 explanation and elaboration: updated guidelines for reporting parallel group randomised trials. *BMJ*. 2010;340:c869.

PARTICIPANTS

Trials are conducted to measure the benefits and risks of treatment in particular groups of patients. The study population in a trial should reflect these future patients in relevant aspects. The first step, therefore, is to define clearly to which future patients the findings of the trial should apply; this is referred to as the *domain*. The domain determines the generalizability of the trial findings, sometimes also called the *external validity*, of the trial. The more immediately the results of interventions need to be implemented in clinical practice, the more closely a trial population needs to resemble the population for whom the treatment is intended. Consequently, a phase I trial may well be conducted in healthy volunteers, but a phase III trial, just before registration, should be performed in patients who are very similar to the patients to whom the drug will be marketed. First and foremost, the domain of a phase III trial is defined by the presence of a treatment indication and the absence of known contraindications.

Domain characteristics are operationalized by specifying eligibility criteria. Typical selection criteria for a study population in a trial may relate to age, sex, clinical diagnosis, and comorbid conditions; exclusion criteria are often used to ensure patient safety. Eligibility criteria should be explicitly defined. The conventional distinction between inclusion and exclusion criteria is unnecessary; the same criterion can be phrased to include or exclude participants [Moher et al., 2010]. There are many additional characteristics of the population eventually included in a trial that may further restrict the domain and thus affect generalizability. Examples are the setting of the trial (country, healthcare system, primary vs. tertiary care), run-in periods of trial medication, and stage of the disease [Rothwell, 2005].

The CONSORT statement recommends using a diagram to delineate the flow of patients through the trial (see **Figure 10–3**) [Moher et al., 2010]. Its upper part describes the enrollment of patients in the trial and their subsequent allocation to the trial treatments. In fact, this part still could be expanded with the stages that precede the actual randomization, for example, identification of affected patients in primary care, referral to secondary care (typically a hospital that participates in the trial), under care of a physician taking part in the trial, meeting the eligibility criteria, and giving informed consent [Rothwell, 2005]. **Figure 10–4** shows the patient flow in the ASPECT-2 trial [Van Es et al., 2002].

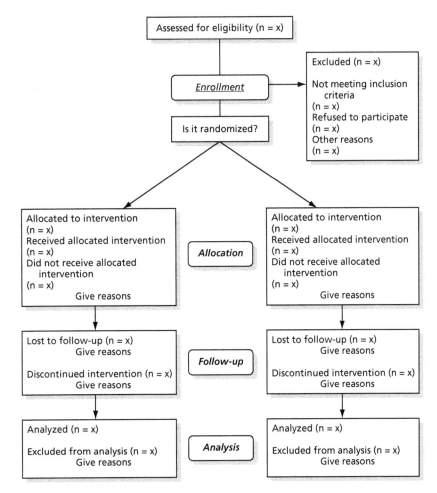

FIGURE 10–3   CONSORT algorithm.

Reproduced from *The Lancet* Vol. 357; Moher D, Schulz KF, Altman DG for the CONSORT Group. The CONSORT statement: revised recommendations for improving the quality of reports of parallel-group randomized trials 2001. *The Lancet* 2001;357:1191–4, reprinted with permission from Elsevier.

TREATMENT ALLOCATION AND RANDOMIZATION

Three comparability issues govern the design of a clinical trial: (1) natural history (or prognosis), (2) extraneous effects, and (3) observer effects. In the design of data collection in trials, comparability of extraneous effects

FIGURE 10-4   Patient algorithm for the ASPECT II study trial.

Reproduced from The Lancet Vol. 360; Van Es RF, Jonker JJ, Verheugt FW, Deckers JW, Grobbee DE. Antithrombotics in the secondary prevention of events in coronary thrombosis-2 (ASPECT-2) research group. Aspirin and coumadin after acute coronary syndromes (the ASPECT-2 study): a randomized controlled trial. *The Lancet* 2002;360:109–13, reprinted with permission from Elsevier.

and comparability of observer effects go hand in hand. Comparability of extraneous effects is achieved by the use of placebo treatment and comparability of observer effects by blinding. It is inherent to the nature of placebo treatment, even if intended to simply remove extraneous effects, that the patient and treating physician are not informed about the precise treatment that is being given; consequently, they are blinded and observer effects originating from the patient or physician are removed simultaneously.

Randomization is used to create two or more groups with equal prognosis. There are many methods to perform randomization, one of the simplest being the toss of a coin. Although acceptable from a statistical perspective, this technique is vulnerable with regard to its actual performance, because doctors may have an implicit or explicit preference for one of the treatments that are being randomized. Thus, if the patient has "bad luck" and does not draw the doctor's favorite treatment, why not flip the coin once more? Perhaps you may be "luckier" next time. Such behavior, however, would completely distort the process of creating two groups with equal prognoses. Hence, the randomization process should be designed such that the randomizing doctor has no influence on the outcome of the randomization once the patient and doctor agree to participate in the trial. Opaque, sealed, numbered envelopes may seem a reasonable alternative; however, envelopes can be manipulated as well. Sir Richard Peto, a well-known trialist from Oxford, warned that such envelopes may sometimes be unsealed before the next patient is entered [Peto, 1999]. That information could influence the decision to ask a next potential candidate to participate, again harming the aim of balanced prognosis. These problems may be circumvented by centralized randomization. This can be done by means of a telephone call with a central trial office that determines the treatment allocation in exchange for a basic set of data on the patient. If randomization does not need to be done acutely, faxes or emails may be used for communication as well. In trials examining acute diseases, 24-hour access should be available, a possibility that can be provided with Internet-based computer programs. When trials use blinded drug treatments, numbered boxes with trial medication may be shipped in advance to the participating hospitals; the boxes contain the study treatments in a random order. Then, whenever a patient agrees to participate, the next box of trial medication can be used.

The simplest approach to randomization is to have one computer list generated with random numbers from which a random allocation scheme for a trial is made. In small trials, however, this still may lead to imbalance in important prognostic factors. This can be solved with *stratified randomization*, that is, randomization within groups with a more or less homogeneous prognosis (e.g., separately for young and old patients). To make stratified randomization practical, the number of stratification factors should not be too large, probably no more than three or four.

In multicenter clinical trials, the hospital is often chosen as one of the factors for stratified randomization. This prevents small numbers of patients in a particular hospital from all receiving, by chance, the same treatment. For small trials, it may be important to have about equal numbers of patients in the treatment groups. This can be realized by means of random permuted blocks in the strata. For example, within each block of six patients in a two-treatment trial, both treatments are allocated three times; the random order differs per block. To prevent the next treatment being known at the end of a block (in this example after five patients), block size should not be made public or, even better, its size should vary.

With the help of computer programs, the prognosis and number of patients across the randomized groups may be more thoroughly balanced by a so-called *minimization procedure*. Basically, with minimization the probability of the next treatment depends on the number of patients with a specific treatment already randomized into a certain risk stratum. Assume, for example, that in a certain risk stratum 10 patients were already allocated to treatment A and eight to treatment B. Then, for the next patient the probability of treatment B could be increased to, say, 60%, rather than the standard 50%, to achieve balance in the number of patients in the treatment arms.

INFORMED CONSENT

An essential part of the randomization process is the step that precedes the actual randomization: the discussion with the patient or his or her family about participation in the trial. Ideally, this discussion is led by a physician who is not the treating physician in order to avoid a conflict of interest. The potential benefits and harms of the study treatments need to be explained, as well as all practicalities of the trial, including the fact that the patient will be randomized. All information also should be given in a patient information document. In trials with nonacute treatments, the patient should have some time to decide about participating, and only after written informed consent has been obtained will the patient be randomized.

BLINDING

The need to blind patients and doctors for the actual treatment given depends on the type of research question (pragmatic or explanatory) and the trial's primary type of outcome event (hard or soft). If the trial has an *explanatory* nature, there should be full comparability of extraneous effects and preferably, extraneous effects should be eliminated: A placebo is required, which implies that treatment needs to be given in a blinded fashion. If, however, a *pragmatic* design is preferred, the need for blinding depends on the type of outcome event and, here, comparability of observer effects is considered. If an objective measure is chosen, such as death, blinding is not mandatory. If quality of life is the primary outcome, blinding is definitely needed because of the subjective nature of this outcome. In an open trial, outcome assessment can still be blinded by using an independent assessor who does not know which study treatment has been given. For example, records on potential outcome events may be sent to a central trial office where all information on treatment allocation is removed. The blinded outcome data are then classified by members of an adjudication committee [Algra & van Gijn, 1994].

Placebos should be made such that they cannot be distinguished from the active treatment. They should be similar in appearance and, in the event of oral administration, taste the same. Even with capsules that are meant to be swallowed at once, one should be careful, as "de-blinding" has been reported when patients first bit the capsule and then tasted its content. Even with the most careful preparation of placebos, the effects or side effects of the treatment may give the allocation code away. For example, the effect on the need to urinate of a diuretic drug may be so obvious that this cannot be concealed from the patient.

When a trial aims to assess patients' perception of outcomes, blinding may be complicated. To solve this problem investigators developed a modified consent procedure in which consent was asked from the patient to collect follow-up data and that states that information on the details of the study will be provided at the end of the study [Boter et al., 2003]. In a study of an outreach nursing care program for patients discharged home after stroke that measured self-reported quality of life and satisfaction, thus two problems related to incomparability of observations could be avoided. First, patients allocated to usual care (i.e., no outreach program) might be dissatisfied because they did not receive the active intervention. Second, patients allocated to the outreach program would not feel obliged to answer more positively than they really felt because of loyalty to the staff providing the intervention. An alternative solution might be to use so-called *prerandomization* [Zelen, 1979]. Patients fulfilling the eligibility criteria of the trial are randomized before consent is sought. Subsequently, only those patients allocated to the intervention group are asked for informed consent. This design also avoids incomparability of observations; however, it comes at the price of the drop-out of the nonconsenters from the intervention group and hence compromise in the comparability of the patients receiving the intervention and those not. This design was used in a trial on risk factor reduction in patients with symptomatic vascular disease [Goessens, 2006]. Patients were prerandomized to receive treatment by a nurse practitioner plus usual care versus usual care alone.

ADHERENCE TO ALLOCATED TREATMENT

When the allocation and blinding of trial treatment is finally organized, it is also important to monitor to what extent the allocated treatments are actually used. In the eventual publication, that information on adherence may be given in the trial flowchart, as discussed earlier, for example, by the number of patients allocated to surgery who actually had the operation and the number of patients who were allocated to receive medical treatment but still underwent surgery. In drug trials, adherence to study treatment may be monitored by pill counts, defined as the count of tablets remaining in the blisters that were distributed during the previous contact with the patient. Of course, such a system is not perfect, but it may guide in the detection of overt nonadherence. Registration of adherence may be viewed as less important in pragmatic trials because nonadherence with a treatment is part of "real life." If unequivocal measurement of adherence is deemed necessary, one may consider measuring plasma levels of the study drugs or levels of its metabolites in urine, or even add a more easily measured tracer to the study medication.

OUTCOME

The choice of a particular outcome, its definition, and measurement completely depend on the goal of the trial. If, for example, the researcher wants an answer that has immediate relevance for clinical practice another outcome may be chosen than if the primary aim is to show that an intervention exerts the anticipated pathophysiologic effect. In phase II trials, the emphasis is on safety and pathophysiology. In the example of recombinant activated factor VII, the primary outcome was the percent change in volume of the hemorrhage from admission to 24 hours, which is important for a "proof of concept" but less relevant from the perspective of a patient. In phase III clinical trials with a primary explanatory design, pathophysiology driven or clinical outcomes may be chosen, whereas in pragmatic trials, investigators tend to concentrate particularly on those outcomes that are most relevant for patients.

Sometimes investigators disagree on what they deem is important for patients. For example, a recent debate addressed the question of whether in stroke prevention studies one should take only strokes as outcome [Albers, 2000] or use all vascular events because of the atherosclerotic nature of cerebrovascular disease [Algra & van Gijn, 2000]. The latter outcome is a so-called *composite outcome* because it consists of several contributing outcomes (in this example, death due to vascular diseases, nonfatal stroke, and nonfatal myocardial infarction). The composite outcome is reached as soon as one of the contributing outcomes has occurred.

Phase II and initial phase III trials often use *intermediate* (or *surrogate*) *outcomes*; that is, outcomes that on the basis of pathophysiologic reasoning will proceed to the occurrence of the clinically relevant outcome event. The validity of an intermediate outcome as a proxy for the real outcome relies heavily on the extent to which the intermediate outcome truly reflects the risk of the outcome of interest. For example, ventricular arrhythmias were chosen as an intermediate outcome for sudden death in patients with cardiac disease. In the early assessment of the effects of anti-arrhythmic drugs, the reduction of the number of ventricular premature complexes at a 24-hour electrocardiogram from baseline to follow-up was used. With this outcome, several anti-arrhythmic drugs appeared promising. However, these promising effects were completely negated in a phase III trial that used the final outcome of sudden death [CAST Investigators, 1989]. The anti-arrhythmic drugs in fact proved to be dangerous! Clearly, one should always be careful in accepting findings from trials with an intermediate outcome as proof of the effect on the outcome of interest.

Still, a major advantage of the use of an intermediate outcome is that it may produce results sooner because these outcomes occur more frequently or are continuous rather than dichotomous variables. Moreover, an intermediate outcome may effectively be used to establish the effect of a treatment by a presumed pathophysiologic pathway and thus may demonstrate the primary mode of action. Sometimes the consequence of the intermediate outcome on disease is assumed to be so clear that the measure itself suffices as an indicator of treatment effect, as for example with blood pressure–lowering drugs; although the clinically relevant outcome in trials on antihypertensive drugs would be the incidence of cardiovascular events, phase III trials typically use blood pressure level as the intermediate outcome and blood pressure level is accepted as a surrogate outcome for cardiovascular events by regulatory agencies such as the FDA. A well-established example of a proxy measure that is generally accepted as a continuous measure of atherosclerotic vascular disease is the thickness of the combined intima and media of the carotid arteries (see **Figure 10–5**) [Bots et al., 1997]. When continuous outcome measures are used, such as carotid wall thickness or blood pressure, it is possible to increase precision by taking the mean of multiple measurements, thus reducing measurement error.

FIGURE 10–5   Measurement of the thickness of the combined intima and media of the carotid arteries.

DESIGN OF DATA ANALYSIS (INCLUDING SAMPLE SIZE CALCULATION)

When a trial is still on the drawing board, one should already be thinking about the design of the data analysis. It is very helpful to "think 2 × 2" and to envision what the main 2 × 2 table of the trial would look like. But one can only do so after having thought about the precise treatments that are being compared and the definition of the primary outcome. Here we will show how to calculate the outcome of a hypothetical trial.

Suppose mortality is studied in 1,000 patients with new treatment A and 1,000 patients with standard treatment B. Assume that from an observational study it is known that 15% of the patients with standard treatment die after a follow-up of 2 years, and also that treatment A is supposed to reduce that percentage to 13%. **Table 10–2** summarizes the data. The absolute risk difference between the two groups would be 15 − 13 = 2%; the precision of that estimate is described by its 95% confidence interval (CI) that ranges from –1% (the old treatment is 1% better than the new one) to +5% (the new treatment is 5% better than the old one). The ratio of the two risks, the risk ratio, is 13/15 = 0.87, with a 95% CI from 0.70 to 1.08.

TABLE 10–2   Data from a Hypothetical Trial

	Treatment A	Treatment B
Death	130	150
Survivor	870	850
At risk	1,000	1,000
Risk (%)	13	15
Risk difference (%)	2.0	reference
95% CI RD	−1.0 to 5.0	—
Risk ratio	0.87	reference
95% CI RR	0.70 to 1.08	—

Legend: CI = confidence interval; RD = risk difference; RR = risk ratio

Note that the absolute risk difference could be presented differently as the number needed to treat to prevent one death. The latter is the reciprocal of the absolute risk difference: $1/0.02 = 50$.

Because the confidence intervals are wide, the data in this example are not sufficiently precise to infer that new treatment A is better than old treatment B; the trial was too small. Thus, before one embarks on a trial, a sample size calculation needs to be done. With a fairly simple formula one can calculate the number of participants required. Advanced methods for calculating the power of a study and the required sample size may seem attractive, but the numbers that follow from any calculation are highly dependent upon the assumptions that are being made. By definition the researcher is uncertain and subjective about the size of the expected treatment effect. Here, not only the plausible size but also the clinical relevance of this estimate matters.

A parameter that one needs to estimate or assume is the percentage of outcome events in the patients who receive standard treatment (denoted as p_0), which is 15% in the given example. This is also called the background rate. The expected percentage in the treated group (p_1) would be 13%. The sample size per treatment group needed would then be:

$$f(\alpha,\beta) * [p_0 * (100 - p_0) + p_1 * (100 - p_1)] / (p_1 - p_0)^2$$

where $f(\alpha,\beta)$ is a statistical constant. It depends on the type I error (α) and the type II error (β) that one accepts. The *type I error* is the probability that one incorrectly would infer that there is a difference between the two treatments when there is no such difference. The *type II error* is the probability that one would incorrectly conclude that there is no difference between the two treatments when in fact there is a difference. The constant $f(\alpha,\beta)$ is calculated as $(Z_\alpha + Z_\beta)^2$. Conventional values for a and b are 0.05 and 0.20, respectively, with $Z_\alpha = 1.96$ and $Z_\beta = 0.84$. With these values $f(\alpha,\beta)$ is equal to 7.84. In our example, we now calculate that 4,750 patients are required for each treatment group. With the anticipated values of p_1 and p_0, the 95% CI of the risk ratio would then range from 0.78 to 0.96. The confidence interval no longer contains the neutral value of 1 (no difference) for the risk ratio and the data now are sufficiently precise to conclude that the new treatment is better. The sample size can be further refined by estimating the percentage of patients that will drop out of a trial and the percentage of patients that will cross over from one arm of the trial to the other.

Before the analyses of a trial can start, several steps need to be taken. Again, the CONSORT flow diagram (see Figure 10–3) can be used as a guide. The lower panels of the figure describe the numbers of patients who were lost to follow-up, those who discontinued the intervention, and finally the numbers of patients included in and excluded from the data analyses. Inclusion of these numbers allows the reader to judge whether the authors have done an intention-to-treat analysis. In the *intention-to-treat analysis*, all patients who were randomized should be analyzed irrespective of whether they received the complete treatment, only part of it, or none at all. Thus, the intention of a treatment strategy in a realistic clinical situation is evaluated.

Take, for example, a trial comparing the effects of coronary angioplasty and coronary artery bypass surgery in patients with angina pectoris and narrowed coronaries [RITA Trial Participants, 1993]. After randomization, the procedures could not be performed instantaneously and some primary outcome events (death or myocardial infarction) occurred before revascularization was done. Still, in an intention-to-treat analysis these events should be counted in the treatment arm the patient was allocated to, an approach that matches real-life clinical practice. The alternative of an intention-to-treat analysis is the *on-treatment* or *per-protocol analysis*. This is typically done in the setting of an explanatory trial where only those patients who, in retrospect, fulfilled all eligibility criteria and also received the allocated trial treatment are included in the analysis. The resulting effect size is likely to be higher than in real life.

Another problem in per-protocol analyses is that noncompliance with the allocated treatment is generally not random, and the resulting selection may induce prognostic imbalances between groups. In other words, the beneficial effect of the randomization process (achievement of comparability of prognosis) is, at least partly, counteracted. As a rule, one should always perform an intention-to-treat analysis. An on-treatment analysis cannot be interpreted without knowledge of the intention-to-treat results. Often it is possible to perform both types of analyses. For example, in the Dutch TIA Trial [1991], the primary analysis was on an intention-to-treat basis:

All 3,131 patients randomized to either low- or medium-dose aspirin were analyzed, and the resulting hazard ratio for the primary outcome of vascular death, myocardial infarction, or stroke was 0.95. In the on-treatment analysis, the 23 patients who in retrospect appeared to have been enrolled inappropriately (14 had a brain tumor, 4 an intracerebral hemorrhage, and 5 other diseases) were excluded from the analysis [Dutch TIA Trial Study Group, 1991]. Moreover, patients were only counted in the intervention arm for the time that they were on the trial medication and the 28 days after discontinuation of such medication to allow for a washout effect. That analysis resulted in a hazard ratio of 0.92. The larger effect in the on-treatment analysis supports the view that the treatment in the indicated patients is indeed effective, because one would assume that with a better indication and higher compliance, a greater benefit results.

To be able to conduct an intention-to-treat analysis, it is of paramount importance to obtain a follow-up that is as complete as possible. Without complete follow-up, the comparability between the randomized treatment groups may be compromised. Therefore, the extent to which follow-up is complete is often viewed as a quality marker of a trial. To minimize loss to follow-up, it is very helpful to ask the trial patient to provide the address and telephone number of a contact person, for example, a brother, sister, or a neighbor who lives at a different address than the patient. This will help to trace the patient if contact is lost.

Another important step that needs to be taken before a reliable analysis can be done is quality control of the data. If done properly, this will have been an ongoing process since the start of the trial, conducted on the basis of feedback provided by the central trial office. For all forms that are sent to the office, a check needs to be done on the completeness and actual values of the data. For example, a value of 510 mm Hg for systolic blood pressure should not be accepted automatically, because it most likely was a reporting error for a value of 150 mm Hg. Missing and potentially erroneous values may be resolved by sending queries from the central trial office to the local investigators. This entire process can be sped up considerably when electronic data forms are being used with built-in error checks and checks for consistency.

By means of interim analyses, an external data monitoring committee (DMC) may evaluate whether such large benefits or harms already are present in an early phase of the trial, where it is no longer ethically justifiable to continue with the study. For this purpose, so-called *stopping rules* have been developed that assist the DMC in deciding whether to recommend early termination of a trial. Interim analyses force the investigators to periodically generate a report on their data, and this stimulates the collection of good quality data early on. There are also downsides to interim analyses. Especially when done frequently, they carry the risk of stopping trials when the benefit (or harm) of the intervention first becomes apparent. A randomized controlled trial that is stopped prematurely because of a striking benefit or a strong untoward effect is most probably suffering from a "random high." With premature stopping, the conclusions often will be either too optimistic or too pessimistic. In the early phases of an investigation, the intermediate results show wider fluctuations around the hypothetical "truth" than in the later phases because of small numbers and thus lack of precision. For these reasons, the timing of interim analyses and conservative stopping rules should be prespecified in the study protocol.

The next step in the data analysis is to generate the baseline table, which in most published papers will be the well-known "Table 1." This table describes the baseline characteristics of the patients according to the allocated treatment. Use of the table for its readers is twofold: (1) to assess whether randomization achieved comparability of prognosis between the treatment groups and (2) to describe the patients who were enrolled in the trial to the reader. The latter allows the readers to decide on the domain of the trial results, which is typically defined by the presence of an indication and absence of a contraindication for the treatment, but other restrictions may apply. The description of the patients by means of the baseline table will give a good notion of the domain and thereby of the generalizability of the trial findings. However, for this purpose, one also should keep in mind the process by which the patients were actually recruited into the trial and which selections were made along the way [Rothwell, 2005].

In large trials, there hardly ever is important prognostic incomparability between the treatment groups, because of the large numbers. However, in small trials and/or inadequate randomization procedures (described earlier in the chapter) imbalance may occur. It may be repaired in the analyses by means of the calculation of adjusted effect estimates using regression analysis. Sometimes, investigators provide P values to judge the difference in baseline characteristics of a randomized trial. This makes no sense, because in the case of adequate randomization, any difference is the result of the play of chance, by definition, and P values have no meaning [Knol et al., 2012]. Rather, qualified judgment about the size of the differences, the extent to which they may have created differences in prognosis, and the size of the treatment effect are needed to decide whether the crude results can be interpreted validly.

A second major table describes the occurrence of outcome events in relation to allocated treatment with measures of the size and precision of the treatment effects. Often the table contains both data on the primary outcome event as well as on the secondary outcome event. It is important to realize that a hierarchy among the outcome events may need to be taken into account. For example, in a cardiovascular outcome trial, it may be quite misleading to only analyze the occurrence of nonfatal myocardial infarction, because a favorable trend for this outcome may be offset by an increase in fatal events. Hence, nonfatal outcomes should never be analyzed in isolation.

Often, a trial protocol specifies that the treatment effects will also be determined in specific subgroups of patients, for example, in men and women. It is very important to keep in mind that such subgroups are likely to be too small to estimate the treatment effect with sufficient precision. After all, the size of the trial was determined for the main outcome in the entire study and not for the subgroups. This being said, it may nevertheless be worthwhile to study treatment effects in a limited number of subgroups.

Note that studying the effects of treatment according to subgroups with a certain characteristic, such as age or gender, implies an analysis of the modification of treatment effects by these characteristics. Be aware of the risks of so-called "fishing expeditions" when analyses are pursued on the basis of curiosity. One certainly might "catch a fish," but such a fish is not suited for consumption. Take, for example, the Dutch TIA Trial discussed earlier in this chapter. In an analysis by month according to the start of their trial medication, it appeared that the 207 August starters experienced a tremendous benefit with the 30 mg dose of aspirin in comparison to those on the dose of 283 mg; the hazard ratio was 0.38 (95% CI 0.16–0.89), whereas when all participants were included in the analysis, there was no difference. This finding clearly is implausible and the "fish" should be thrown back immediately (and not have been caught in the first place). Note that this example is a variant on the famous example on the effects of aspirin according to birth sign in the ISIS-2 [ISIS-2, 1988]. Again, sensible judgment, biologic plausibility, or definition of subgroups in advance (thus in the study protocol, before data are available) may help to prevent spurious results.

Chapter 11

Meta-Analyses

INTRODUCTION

The decision to apply findings from research to clinical practice is rarely based on a single study. Trust in the validity of research findings grows after results are replicated by similar studies in different settings. Moreover, the results of a single study are often not sufficiently precise and thus leave room for doubt about the exact magnitude of the association between the determinant(s) and outcome(s) of interest, such as, for example, the effects of a certain treatment. This is particularly important when the magnitude of the expected benefits of an intervention must be balanced against the possible risks. For this purpose, the evidence that a treatment works may be valid but too imprecise or too general. What works in a high-risk patient may be counterproductive in a low-risk patient because the balance between benefits and risks differs. The contribution that meta-analysis can make is to summarize the findings from several relevant studies and improve the precision of the estimate of the treatment effect, thereby increasing confidence in the true effect of a treatment.

Meta-analysis is a method of locating, appraising, and summarizing similar studies; assessing similar determinants and comparable outcomes in similar populations; and synthesizing their results into a single quantitative estimate of associations or effect. The magnitude of the "average" association between the determinant and outcome can be used in decisions in clinical practice or in making healthcare policy. Meta-analysis may reduce or resolve uncertainty when individual studies provide conflicting results, which often leads to disagreement in traditional (narrative) reviews.

Traditional reviews typically only offer a qualitative assessment of the kind, "This treatment seems to work and appears to be safe." In addition to providing a quantitative effect estimate across studies, meta-analysis uses a transparent approach to the retrieval of evidence from all relevant studies, employs explicit methods aimed at reducing bias, and uses formal statistical methods to synthesize evidence. Unless individual patient data from the studies included are available, a meta-analysis treats the summary result of each study (e.g., the number of events and the number of patients randomized by treatment group) as a unit of information.

Meta-analysis originated in psychological research and was introduced in medicine around 1980. With the rapid adoption of evidence-based medicine and the increasing emphasis on the use of quantitative evidence as a basis for patient management, meta-analysis has become popular. Today, meta-analysis has an indispensable role in medicine, in general, and in clinical epidemiologic research in particular.

This chapter introduces the design and methods of meta-analysis aimed at summarizing the results from randomized trials comparing an intervention arm to a control arm. Meta-analysis of etiologic, diagnostic, and prognostic studies is increasingly common, but it is beyond the scope of this chapter.

RATIONALE

Meta-analysis helps to answer questions such as these: "What is the best treatment for this patient?" "How large is the expected effect?" "How sure are we about the magnitude of this effect?" Definite answers are rarely provided by the results of a single study and are difficult to give when several studies have produced results that seem conflicting. Traditionally, decisions about the preferred treatment for a disease or health condition have largely relied on expert opinion and narrative reviews in medical textbooks. These may be based on a biased selection of only part of the evidence, frequently only the largest studies, studies with "positive" results (i.e., those reporting P values less than 0.05), or—even worse—only studies with results that support the expert's personal opinion. Clearly, such studies are not necessarily the most valid. Moreover, due to the rapid accumulation of evidence from clinical research, expert opinion and medical textbooks can quickly become outdated.

Access to up-to-date evidence on treatment effects is needed to make informed decisions about patient management and health policy. For instance, several authors have shown convincingly that medical textbooks lag behind medical journals in presenting the evidence for important treatments in cardiology [Antman et al., 1992; Lau et al., 1992]. Often, investigators perform a meta-analysis before starting a new study. From studying previous trials, they learn which questions remain unanswered, what pitfalls exist in the design and conduct of the anticipated research, and which common errors must be avoided. Meta-analyses may provide valuable assistance in deciding on the best and most relevant research questions and in improving the design of new clinical studies. In addition, the results of meta-analyses are increasingly being incorporated into clinical guidelines.

An example of the value of meta-analysis is the research on the putative benefits of minimally invasive coronary artery bypass surgery. Minimally invasive coronary bypass surgery is a type of surgery on the beating heart that uses a number of technologies and procedures without the need for a heart–lung machine. After the introduction of this procedure, the results of the first randomized trial were published in 1995 [Vural et al., 1995]; four years later the initial results of a second randomized trial were published [Angelini et al., 2002]. Subsequently, 12 trials were published up to January 2003, 12 more trials were published between January 1 and December 31, 2003, and another 10 were published in the first 4 months of 2004 [Van der Heijden et al., 2004]. Meta-analysis is extremely helpful in summarizing the evidence provided by studies conducted in this field. In particular, it may support timely decisions about the need for more evidence and prevent the conduct of additional trials when precise effect estimates are available.

PRINCIPLES

The direction and size of the estimate of a treatment effect observed in a trial, commonly expressed as a *ratio of*, or a difference between, two measures of occurrence, indicates the strength of the effect of an index treatment relative to that of a reference treatment. The validity of the estimate of the treatment effect depends on the quality of the study. In research on treatment effects, validity depends in particular on the use of randomization to achieve comparability with regard to the initial prognostic status, and potentially the use of blinding and placebo to achieve comparability of extraneous effects and observations. In addition, the validity of the observed treatment effect depends on the completeness of follow-up data and whether the data were analyzed correctly.

The precision of an estimate of a treatment effect from a study is reflected in the confidence interval (CI) of the effect estimate. This denotes the probabilistic boundaries for the true effect of a treatment. That is, if a study was repeated again and again, the 95% CI would contain the true effect in 95% of the repetitions. The width of the confidence interval is determined by the number of the outcome events of interest during the period of follow-up observation, which in turn depends on the sample size, the risk or rate of the outcome of interest in the trial population, and the duration of follow-up. In general, a large study with many events yields a result with a narrow confidence interval. Inconsistent results of multiple randomized trials lead to uncertainty regarding the effect of a treatment. Contradictory results, such as a different magnitude or even a different direction of the effect, may be reported by different trials. In addition, some trials may be inconclusive, for example, when the point estimate of effect clearly deviates from "no effect" even though its confidence interval includes "no effect." Uncertainty about the true treatment effect can be overcome by combining the results of trials through meta-analysis.

It should be emphasized, however, that differences in findings between studies may be the result of factors other than a lack of precision. Diversity in the way trials are conducted and in the type of study populations may lead to different trial results. To maintain validity when different studies are combined in a meta-analysis, aggregation of data is usually restricted to trials considered combinable with respect to patients, treatments, endpoints, and measures of effect. To ensure adequate selection of trials, their designs need to be systematically reviewed and they must be grouped according to their similarity. Contradictory results may also reflect problems in the study design or data analysis that may have biased the findings of some trials. Because the results of meta-analyses cannot be trusted when flawed trials are included, it is important to make an explicit effort to limit such bias. Hence, the study design needs to be critically appraised with regard to the randomization procedure and concealment of treatment allocation, blinding of outcome assessments, deviation from the allocation scheme, contamination of the treatment contrast (e.g., unequal provision of care apart from the allocated treatment), and completeness of follow-up, as well as the statistical analysis.

Small trials often lack statistical power. In a meta-analysis, statistical power is enhanced by pooling data abstracted from original trial publications to determine a single combined effect estimate, using statistical methods that have specifically been developed for this purpose. Many such methods exist, and their appropriateness depends on underlying assumptions and practical considerations. Unfortunately, quite often the possibilities for pooling are restricted by poor data reporting of individual studies.

Adherence to fundamental design principles of meta-analyses can prevent misleading results and conclusions. These should be articulated in a protocol to be used as a reference in conducting the meta-analysis and writing the methods section of the report. Guidelines and manuals for writing a protocol for meta-analyses are available [Higgins, 2006; Khan et al., 2003]

BOX 11–1   Internet Resources for Writing a Protocol for Meta-Analysis (accessed May 7, 2013)

The Cochrane Handbook for Systematic Review of Interventions, from the Cochrane Collaboration: http://www.cochrane.org/training/cochrane-handbook

Systematic Reviews: CRD's guidance for undertaking systematic reviews in health care, from the Centre for Reviews and Dissemination, University of York, UK: http://www.york.ac.uk/inst/crd/report4.htm

(see **Box 11–1**). As for clinical epidemiologic studies in general, the design of a meta-analysis involves:

1. The theoretical design of the research question, including the specification of the determinant–outcome relation of interest
2. The design of data collection, comprising the retrieval of publications, the selection and critical appraisal of trials, and the data extraction
3. The design of data analysis and the reporting of the results

THEORETICAL DESIGN

As in any research, a meta-analysis should start with a clear, relevant, and unambiguous research question. The design of the occurrence relation includes three components: (1) the determinant contrast (typically, the treatments or exposures compared), (2) the outcome of interest, and (3) the domain. All need to be explicitly defined to frame the search and selection strategy for eligible trial publications. By using unambiguous definitions of these components, the scope and objective of the meta-analysis are narrowed. This directly impacts the applicability of the results.

To illustrate, there are similarities between the following questions: "What is the effect of intermittent lumbar traction on the severity of pain in patients with low back pain and sciatica?" and "What is the effect of spinal traction on the recovery of patients with back pain?" [Clarke et al., 2006]. Despite the similarities, these questions have a completely different scope that would result in different criteria for selection of trials and subsequently different estimates of treatment effect and applicability of findings. Due to its more detailed wording, the first question may provide a more informative summary of the evidence for a particular type of patient management, while the more general wording of the domain, determinant, and outcome in the second question may serve public health policy more generally. Although it is not the primary objective of a meta-analysis to formulate recommendations for patient management, but rather to quantitatively summarize the evidence on a particular mode of treatment, meta-analyses are often used in the development of clinical guidelines.

Just as in the design of any epidemiologic study, it is necessary to carefully decide on the *domain*, that is, the type of patients or subjects to whom the results of the meta-analysis will apply. Definition of the domain determines how the study populations to be considered will be collected and thus assists in obtaining relevant summaries of evidence from published trials.

DESIGN OF DATA COLLECTION

The challenge in the retrieval and selection of publications is to identify all relevant and valid evidence from previous research. The rapid growth of electronic publications, as well as the improved accessibility of electronic bibliographic databases and complete journal content on the Internet, has facilitated the retrieval and filtering of pertinent evidence, in particular from reports on the results of clinical trials. To comprehensively locate all available evidence requires skills in the design of search strategies, however. With proper library and information technology skills, information retrieval becomes less time consuming and searches become more comprehensive.

Bibliographic Databases

For a comprehensive search, several medically oriented electronic bibliographic databases are available. These include:

- PubMed (National Library of Medicine and National Institutes of Health) [Dickersin et al., 1985; Gallagher et al., 1990]
- EMBASE (Elsevier, Inc.) [Haynes et al., 2005; Wong et al., 2006a], Web of Science (Thompson Scientific), PsycINFO (American Psychological Association) [Watson & Richardson, 1999a; Watson & Richardson, 1999b]
- CINAHL (Cumulative Index to Nursing and Allied Health Literature, EBSCO Industries) [Wong et al., 2006b]; LILACS (Literatura Americana e do Caribe em Ciências da Saúde) [Clark, 2002]
- Cochrane Database of Randomized Trials (Wiley Interscience)

A listing of bibliographic databases is available from the University of York Centre for Reviews and Dissemination (http://www.york.ac.uk/inst/crd/finding_studies_systematic_reviews.htm).

The coverage of subject matter and the list of scientific journals included in these databases are different, and the highest yield is likely to depend on the topic that is studied [McDonald et al., 1999; Minozzi et al., 2000; Suarez-Almazor et al., 2000; Watson & Richardson, 1999a].

Search Filters

Search filters are command syntax strings in the database language for retrieving relevant records. Most electronic bibliographic databases provide indexing services and search facilities, which make it easy to create and use search filters. For every research question, a reproducible subject-specific search filter must be defined. There is no standard for building a subject-specific search filter, and they need to be customized for each database. The art of building a subject-specific search filter comes down to reducing the "numbers-needed-to-read" to find a single pertinent record for an original trial publication [Bachmann et al., 2002].

Building a Search Filter

Building a subject-specific search filter starts with breaking down the defined research question into parts: the subjects or patients (the domain), the treatments (the determinant contrast), and the outcomes of interest. Candidate terms and relevant synonyms should be listed for each part of the question. To accomplish this, medical dictionaries, medical textbooks, and the thesaurus and index of bibliographic databases can be used. After selecting the search terms for the domain, these terms are usually combined with the Boolean operator "OR." The same is done with the selected search terms for the determinant contrast and the outcome. These three separate search queries are then combined by the Boolean operator "AND." Depending on the focus of the research question, limits such as age categories and publication date can be used to restrict the number of retrieved records to more manageable proportions. This is not recommended in the context of meta-analysis, however, because it can easily result in the exclusion of relevant records of publications. Moreover, language restrictions should be avoided, as the aim is to retrieve all relevant evidence, including evidence from publications in languages other than English.

Thesaurus and Index

The thesaurus and index of bibliographic databases may assist with the identification and selection of candidate search terms for the domain, determinant contrast, and outcome. A *thesaurus* is a systematic list, or database, of hierarchically arranged related standardized subject headings, referred to as the *controlled vocabulary*. The hierarchy of a thesaurus (that is, the more specific narrower terms that are arranged beneath more general broader terms) provides a context for topical search keywords. Standardized subject headings are available and may be helpful when exploring and identifying relevant candidate retrieval terms for well-defined and generally accepted medical concepts. In general, about 10 standardized subject headings are assigned to each record contained in electronic bibliographic databases (this is called the *tagging* of articles).

One should be aware of the drawbacks to using the thesaurus database in the exploration and identification of relevant candidate retrieval terms. First, while searching with subject terms in the thesaurus database, for example, in the PubMed MeSH (Medical Subject Headings; NIH and NLM) database, the *explosion function* (which occurs when a default automatically includes all hierarchical lower subject heading terms in the search) dramatically increases the number of retrieved records. This increase in number of retrieved records invariably includes many irrelevant records, which always reduces the retrieval efficiency by an increase in the "number-needed-to-read." Second, it takes time before a term is included in the thesaurus as a standardized subject heading. Research that was published before its appropriate medical subject heading was added to the thesaurus will be indexed under different headings. The first studies that defined a new research field may not be found under the subject heading concerned when the heading was added to the thesaurus at a later stage. This is because indexing of records is static; subject terms attached to older records are not updated when the thesaurus is changed. Hence, records indexed according to the previous version of the thesaurus may not be retrieved when newer standardized subject headings are used in a search filter. Third, one should be aware of the time lag between publication dates and tagging. The most recent pertinent records will always be missed in a search that uses only standardized subject headings. Finally, a thesaurus grows over time, and so it is subject to change. This means that the context of and relationship between subject heading terms is subject to change, which may result in misspecification of retrieval terms and, consequently, omission of pertinent records.

An *index* is a detailed list, or database, of alphabetically arranged search keywords, which, for example, is found under the PubMed Preview/Index tab. The index of a bibliographic database contains search keywords from different indexed record fields, such as author, title, abstract, keywords, publication type and date, and author affiliation. An index is not subject to the obvious drawbacks of a thesaurus, which as mentioned include time lags in standardized tagging, term misspecification, and explosion of attached lower terms. Using index databases facilitates exploration and identification of relevant candidate retrieval terms because the frequency of occurrence of words per field is usually listed. Authors of original publications will use terms and synonyms relating to the domain, treatment contrast, and outcomes in both the title and the abstract. One should make use of this and explore relevant candidate search terms and synonyms, in particular in the title and abstract fields, to retrieve pertinent records.

A drawback to this approach is that one must always include several different synonyms for the same concepts and take into account differences in U.K. and U.S. spellings. A well-designed search string increases the efficiency of the search and notably decreases the total number of records retrieved while increasing the number of pertinent records. Using the thesaurus database may help to identify candidate search terms that can be explored for their relevance in the title and abstract fields.

In building a search filter, one should always avoid the pitfalls of *automatic term mapping*, where search terms without a field specification are automatically translated to, for example, MeSH terms. To see if this has happened in PubMed, check the Details tab. For example, when in PubMed, the term "blind" without field specification is used to identify trials with blind outcome assessment; this word is translated to the MeSH term "visually impaired." This leads to misspecification of the context and the records to be retrieved, and thus a large number of irrelevant records and a dramatic increase in the numbers of records that must be read. Therefore, we advise always using a field specification, in particular the title and abstract field ("tab" in PubMed syntax). Under the PubMed Index/Preview tab, the frequency of tagged search terms can be explored for each field, and this will automatically provide the adequate syntax for the fields of the search terms.

Clinical Queries

PubMed includes *clinical queries*; these can be found in the blue sidebar on the PubMed home page. The therapy query, using the Boolean operator "AND," can be combined with the constructed subject-specific search filter in order to retain records about treatment effects and type of study while reducing the search yield to a more manageable number of records.

Several other methods filters that allow searching for a type of study are available for different bibliographic databases [Watson et al., 1999b; Wong et al., 2006a; Wong et al., 2006b; Zhang et al., 2006]. Some of these have been tested intensively [Jadad & McQuay, 1993; Montori et al., 2005;

Shojania & Bero, 2001; Wilczynski et al., 1994; Wilczynski & Haynes, 2002; Wilczynski et al., 2005], but none are perfect, and often certain relevant articles will be missed. The added value of methods filters, in terms of accuracy of their yield, may depend on the medical field or research question of interest [Sampson et al., 2006a]. For PubMed clinical queries, a broad (i.e., sensitive or inclusive) or a narrow (i.e., specific or restrictive) pre-specified search methodology filter is available. While a broad methods search filter is more comprehensive, the number-needed-to-read will always be higher. With a narrow methods filter, the number of records retrieved will be smaller, but the likelihood of excluding pertinent records is higher. Therefore, using narrow methods filters in the context of meta-analyses is not advised.

Complementary Searches

Publications are not always properly included or indexed in electronic bibliographic databases. Sometimes, relevant studies identified by other means turn out to be included in electronic bibliographic databases but are inappropriately indexed because of changes in the thesaurus, for example. Therefore, searching for lateral references is always necessary to supplement initial retrieval of relevant publications and to optimize a search filter.

Additional relevant publications can be found by screening the reference lists of available systematic reviews, meta-analyses, expert reviews, and editorials on your topic, for publications not retrieved by your search filter. Web of Science, the bibliographic database of the Institute of Scientific Information, facilitates such cross-reference searching by providing links to publications cited in the identified paper and links to publications citing the identified paper. PubMed facilitates such cross-reference searching by providing a link to related articles. It is advisable to use cross-reference searching for all pertinent records selected by the initial search and to use the Boolean operator "OR" to combine them all. To avoid duplication of work, records already retrieved by the initial search filter can be excluded by combining an additional filter for the collection of related articles and the initial search filter using the Boolean operator "NOT." Then, the remainder of the related articles is screened for relevant additional records.

When cross-reference searching yields additional relevant publications, these should be scrutinized for new relevant search terms related to the domain, determinants, and outcomes in the title and abstract. These should always be added to update the initial subject-specific search filter. Again, the

Boolean operator "NOT" should be used to exclude the records already retrieved by the initial search filter (plus the combined related articles). Then the remaining records are screened for other additional relevant records and new search terms. Thus, building a subject-specific search filter becomes a systematic iterative process. Still, the total number of original studies published on a topic of a particular meta-analysis always remains unknown. Therefore, it may be useful to write to experts, researchers, and authors, including a list of the retrieved trial publications, and ask them to add studies not yet on the list.

Most electronic bibliographic databases only include citations for studies published as full-text articles. To retrieve studies without full publication it is useful to write to researchers, authors, and experts for preliminary reports, and search in Web of Science or on the Internet (e.g., websites of conferences and professional societies) for abstracts of meetings and conference proceedings. The recently initiated registries for clinical trials [Couser et al., 2005; De Angelis et al., 2004] promise a better view on all studies started, some of which may never be published in full (see **Box 11–2**). Some authors have suggested that journal hand searching, which is a manual page by page examination of contents of relevant journals, may reveal additional relevant publications [Hopewell et al., 2002; Jefferson & Jefferson, 1996; McDonald et al., 2002; Sampson et al., 2006b]. In addition, Internet search engines, in particular, Google Scholar (http://scholar.google.com), may prove useful in the retrieval of citations [Eysenbach et al., 2001] and, in particular, full-text articles that somehow have not made it to other databases.

BOX 11–2   Internet Resources for Trial Registries (accessed May 17, 2013)

The U.S. National Library of Medicine: http://www.clinicaltrials.gov

The International Standard Randomized Controlled Trial Number Registry, Bio Med Central: http://www.controlled-trials.com

The National (UK) Health Service: http://www.nhs.uk/Conditions/Clinical-trials/Pages/clinical-trial.aspx and http://www.nihr.ac.uk/Pages/NRRArchive.aspx

The European Clinical Trials Database: https://www.clinicaltrialsregister.eu

Screening and Selection

Aggregation of data in a meta-analysis is restricted to studies judged to be combinable with respect to subjects, determinants, methodology, and outcomes. For studies that differ considerably in these aspects, it may not be appropriate to combine the results.

Titles and abstracts of all records for clinical trials should be screened using prespecified and explicit selection criteria that relate to the combinability of studies. These include:

- *Domain*: Types of patients, disease or health problem, specific subgroups, and setting (e.g., primary or secondary care)
- *Treatments*: Characteristics of treatment, type of comparator (placebo, active, add-on)
- *Outcomes*: Types of endpoints, scales, dimensions, and follow-up time
- *Design of data collection and analysis, and reporting of data*: Randomization, double blinding, concealment of treatment allocation, blinded endpoint assessment, reporting of absolute risks

Based on the results of the selection process, combinable studies can be identified or grouped for separate or stratified analysis. In our experience, any physician familiar with the subject but untrained in library information can handle the scanning of titles at a pace of about 250 per hour, provided that abstracts are read only when the title does not provide sufficient information (e.g. when the term "randomized" is not mentioned in the title). For this, it is convenient and advisable to store titles and abstracts of all retrieved electronic records in a citation management program (see **Box 11–3**). When doubts remain about the appropriateness of the selection of a particular study after reading the abstract, the full publication must be scrutinized.

BOX 11–3   Internet Resources for Bibliographic and Citation Management Software Programs

Endnote (Thomson ResearchSoft, Thomson Scientific):
http://www.endnote.com

Reference manager (Thomson ResearchSoft, Thomson Scientific):
http://www.refman.com

Refworks (Bethesda, MD, USA): http://www.refworks.com

Avoiding Bias

Retrieval and selection of original studies should be based on a comprehensive search and explicit selection criteria. Relevant publications can be easily missed by a not fully comprehensive or even flawed retrieval and selection procedure. Selection of studies must be based on criteria related to study design, rather than on results or a study's purported appropriateness and relevance. Holes in a methodology filter as well as searching in a limited number of bibliographic databases may lead to serious omissions. When a search is not comprehensive or selection is flawed, the results of the meta-analysis may be biased; this type of bias is known as *retrieval and reviewer bias*.

To prevent reviewer bias, the selection of material should preferably be based on the consensus of at least two independent researchers [Edwards et al., 2002; Jadad et al. 1996; Moher et al., 1999a]. Still, any comprehensive strategy for the retrieval and selection of relevant original studies can be frustrated by flaws in the reporting of individual trials [Sutton et al., 2002].

Trials with positive and significant results are more likely to be reported and are published faster, particularly when they are published in English (i.e., *publication bias*) [Jüni et al., 2002; Sterne et al., 2002]. Furthermore, such positive trials are cited more often (i.e., *citation bias*), which makes them easier to locate, so only a comprehensive search can prevent such retrieval bias [Ravnskov, 1992]. Multiple reporting of a single trial (for example, separate reporting of initial and final results, different follow-up times or endpoints in subsequent publications) and preferential reporting of positive results cause *dissemination bias* that may be difficult to detect. There is no complete remedy against these types of bias in the reporting and dissemination of trial results.

Omission of pertinent studies and inclusion of multiple publications may change the results of a meta-analysis dramatically [Simes, 1987; Stern & Simes, 1997]. For example, from around 2,000 eligible titles that were retrieved in a meta-analysis assessing the effect of off-pump coronary surgery, only 66 publications remained after exclusion of publications of non-randomized trials and randomized trials with another treatment comparison or endpoint. After assessing the 66 reports, seven conference abstracts of trials not fully published were further excluded. There were 17 duplicate publications relating to three trials, leaving only 42 full trial publications for further analysis [Van der Heijden et al., 2004].

Before critically appraising the studies selected for inclusion, it is important to ensure that errata that were published later have been traced, as these may contain errors in the data initially reported. It is also recommended to ensure that design papers (available for many large multicenter trials) have been traced and are available for critical appraisal together with the results report(s). One may encounter a report that is based on a smaller number of subjects than was planned according to the design paper. This may suggest publication bias, unless the reasons for this are explained in the results report.

CRITICAL APPRAISAL

Randomized trials are the cornerstone of evaluation of treatment effects. They frequently offer the best possibility for valid and precise effect estimations, but many aspects of their design and conduct require careful handling for their results to be valid. Hence, critical appraisal of all elements of a study design is an important part of meta-analysis. *Critical appraisal* concentrates on aspects of a study design that impact the validity of the study, notably randomization techniques and concealment of treatment allocation, blinded endpoint assessment, adherence to the allocation scheme, contamination of treatment contrast, postrandomization attrition, and statistical techniques applied. This requires information regarding inclusion and exclusion criteria, treatment regimens, and mode of administration, as well as the type of endpoints, their measurement scale, and the duration of follow-up and the time points of follow-up assessments. Each aspect of the study design needs to be documented on a predesigned critical appraisal checklist to decide whether the publication provides sufficient information and, if so, whether the applied methods were adequate and bias is considered likely or not. Based on this critical appraisal, studies can be grouped by the type and number of design flaws, as well as by the level of omitted information. Accordingly, decisions about which studies are combinable in a pooled or a stratified analysis can be made.

Although the requirements for reporting the methods of clinical trials are well defined and have been generally accepted [CONSORT, 2010; Chalmers et al., 1987a, 1987b; Moher et al., 2005; Plint et al., 2006], information on important design features cannot be found in the published report of many studies. For example, only 11 of 42 trials comparing coronary bypass surgery with or without a cardiopulmonary bypass pump that are reported as a "randomized trial" provided information on the methods of randomization and concealment of treatment allocation, while only 14 reported on blinding of outcome assessment or standardized postsurgical care, and only 30 gave details on deviations from the protocol that occurred [Van der Heijden et al., 2004]. The unavailability of this information hampers a complete and critical appraisal of such studies and raises questions about the validity of their results.

Blinding for the journal source, the authors, their affiliation, and the study results during critical appraisal by editing copies of the articles requires ample time and resources. Therefore, this should only be considered when reviewer bias as an important threat to the validity of the meta-analysis needs to be excluded [Jadad et al., 1996; Verhagen et al., 1998]. To avoid errors in the assessment of trials, critical appraisal should be standardized using a checklist that is preferably completed independently by two reviewers as they read the selected publications. In the event of disagreement between these two reviewers, the eventual data analyzed can be based on a consensus meeting or a third reviewer may provide a decisive assessment.

Studies that are the same with respect to the outcome, including scales used and follow-up times, can be pooled by conventional statistical procedures. Similarity can be judged by the information that is derived during data extraction. Data extraction entails documentation of relevant data for each study on a standardized data registry form and should include the number of patients randomized per group and their baseline characteristics, notably relevant prognostic markers (i.e., potential confounders). The follow-up data to be recorded for each treatment group should, for each outcome and follow-up time, include the point effect estimates and their variance, and the number of patients analyzed, with accrued person-time "at risk." Using these data, trials can be grouped by outcome, follow-up time, or even risk status at baseline. Accordingly, this gives a further quantitative basis for decisions about which studies are combinable in the pooled or stratified analysis. Unfortunately, details about follow-up are frequently omitted. Inadequate or incomplete reporting of outcome parameters precludes statistical pooling in a meta-analysis. For example, only 4 of 42 trials comparing coronary bypass surgery with or without a cardiopulmonary bypass pump reported data that allowed calculating a composite endpoint for death, stroke, and myocardial infarction [Van der Heijden et al., 2004].

DESIGN OF DATA ANALYSIS

The ultimate goal of a meta-analysis, while maintaining validity, is to obtain a more precise estimate of a treatment effect. The confidence interval of the combined estimate of the effect should be narrow relative to the confidence interval of the individual studies included. Thus, a meta-analysis increases statistical power. But sophisticated statistical procedures cannot compensate for inclusion of flawed data. There is an analogy between individual studies included in a meta-analysis and the analysis of subgroups in a single trial. Subgroup analyses are suspected of producing spurious results due to their limited statistical power and repeated testing of statistical significance. The best estimate of effect for a particular subgroup may be the overall estimate for the total population. The principle behind this so-called *Stein's paradox* is the "shrinkage" of individual subgroup results toward the grand mean (also known as *regression toward the mean*). The extent of the potential shrinkage of an observed value depends on the precision of the observed value. Based on the principle of shrinkage, combined analysis of studies included in a meta-analysis will improve statistical power of the estimate of effect and reduce chance findings. The principle of shrinkage is also used in a *cumulative meta-analysis*, where in a Bayesian approach information from a new trial is incorporated in the complete evidence provided by earlier trials. For example, thrombolytic treatment (streptokinase) was shown by clinical trials to provide a clinically important and statistically significant survival benefit in patients with suspected acute myocardial infarction long before this treatment was widely accepted as being effective. Similarly, corticosteroids were shown to accelerate fetal lung maturity long before they were widely accepted as being effective [Antman et al., 1992; Berkey et al., 1996; Lau et al., 1992; Lau & Chalmers, 1995; Whitehead, 1997].

Measures of Occurrence and Effect

The most common meta-analyses found in the medical literature concern clinical trials. Trials compare the occurrence of the outcome(s) of interest between randomly allocated treatment groups. Effects of treatment are usually expressed as a ratio, such as a risk ratio, an odds ratio, or a rate (hazard) ratio, calculated from an appropriate measure of occurrence for treated subjects and controls respectively. Alternatively, "difference" measures of effect may be used, or measures that are based on the latter, such as *"number-needed-to-treat."* Calculated as 1/risk difference, this is a popular way to express the results of a trial and is often interpreted as the number of patients that have to be treated to prevent one outcome from occurring.

A measure of effect can only be understood if the definition of the occurrence measure on which the effect measure concerned is based is properly appreciated. Occurrence measures have a *numerator* and a *denominator*. The numerator is usually the number of subjects with a certain event (e.g., the number of deaths due to any cause, the number of subjects sustaining a first myocardial infarction, etc.), or a certain combined event, such as the combination of cardiovascular death due to any cause (e.g., myocardial infarction and stroke) "taken together." Note that such a combined event also either occurs, or does not occur, in any trial subject, and that the combined event is considered to have occurred when the first component event occurs. Exceptionally, the total number of events, such as the total number of myocardial infarctions that occurred during follow-up, may be used as the numerator [Poole-Wilson et al., 2007]. We stress that the use of the total number of events as the numerator requires the use of a person-time denominator (see later discussion) and special statistical methods that are beyond the scope of this chapter.

Whether an occurrence measure with the number of subjects with the event in the numerator is a risk, an odds, or a rate (hazard) depends on the choice of the denominator. When the denominator is taken as the number of subjects for whom follow-up was started (and who were all "at risk" at that moment), the occurrence measure is called a *risk* in this chapter, and is denoted by R. When the denominator is taken as the number of subjects who completed follow-up without the occurrence of the event concerned, the occurrence measure is commonly called a risk odds, or *odds*, denoted here by O. On the other hand, when the denominator is taken as the total person-time "at risk" for the event concerned, the occurrence measure is called a *rate* in this chapter, and denoted by the letter h (from *hazard*).

A risk or odds on the one hand, and a rate (hazard) on the other, differ importantly in the way time is accounted for. A risk and the derived measure odds (which is equal to the corresponding risk divided by one minus this risk) are dimensionless quantities that at first sight do not involve time. Nonetheless, a risk or odds can only be interpreted when the duration of the time interval over which the risk or odds was taken is specified. It is meaningless to say that a certain subject has a risk of 10% of death unless one also specifies the time interval (1 year, 2 years, 5 years, etc.) to which the 10% risk applies. It follows that a risk can only be determined when all subjects have been followed for at least the time interval chosen. Risks are therefore a first-choice measure of occurrence only when all subjects in a study have been followed without loss to follow-up for at least the same fixed time interval. This is generally possible only for acute conditions, such as suspected acute myocardial infarction, as for such conditions the outcome of interest can be captured during a relatively short follow-up period that is the same for all subjects.

A rate, on the other hand, has the dimension $1/(time)$ due to its person-time denominator. A rate of, say, 10 deaths per 100 person-years of follow-up "at risk" for death does not imply a particular duration of follow-up. As long as the rate is constant over time, it does not matter whether a large group of subjects was followed for a short time, or a smaller group for a long time. Because the contribution of each subject to the total person-time "at risk" in a rate's denominator is determined separately for each subject, rates can also deal with within-study variability in the duration of follow-up. As we shall see in further discussion, rates are therefore the occurrence measure of choice for studies with a variable duration of follow-up, as is commonly the case for stable (chronic) conditions. This is particularly so when the rate can be assumed to be essentially constant over the *time span* of the trial (taken as the time interval between start of enrollment and the end of follow-up for all subjects enrolled).

As will be illustrated in the following discussion, there is a well-known and simple exponential relationship between a risk and a rate when the latter is constant over time, a relationship that can help us in understanding which measure of effect to use in a meta-analysis.

Unfortunately, risk ratios (denoted by *RR*), odds ratios (*OR*) and rate (hazard) ratios (*HR*) are often considered somehow equivalent and therefore interchangeable concepts. Nonetheless, the choice is not trivial [Deeks & Altman, 2001]. Furthermore, despite attempts to standardize the format of trial reports in major medical journals, consistency in terminology is still lacking. Thus, a risk as defined earlier may also be called an incidence, incidence rate, or rate. Conversely, a rate as defined here may in a report be called a risk (how confusing!). What is meant exactly by "risk reduction" in a report can often only be inferred from the statistical methods that were used. The terms *hazard* and *cumulative hazard* (as defined later) are rarely used in reports in medical journals and have an unequivocal meaning only in the statistical literature.

Before considering the relative merits of using RRs, ORs, or HRs in meta-analysis, we will first define these concepts based on an example taken from the literature. One purpose of this is to show the relevance of treatment-specific person-time denominators and to explain how these can be obtained from data that could be abstracted from a report that did not state absolute rates, or give data on treatment-specific durations of follow-up "at risk."

Occurrence and Effect Measures in Study Reports: A Detailed Example

The SOLVD treatment trial [SOLVD Investigators, 1991] compared the ACE-inhibitor enalapril ($n = 1,285$) to a placebo ($n = 1,284$) in patients with chronic heart failure.

SOLVD is an example of a common type of trial in subjects with a chronic condition and a follow-up duration that differs by design between subjects. Patients were enrolled during a 34-month period. Scheduled follow-up was terminated for all patients on a so-called *common stopping date*. This resulted in a follow-up duration that ranged, as stated in the report, from 22 to 55 months.

There were 452 deaths in patients assigned to enalapril, as opposed to 510 deaths in those assigned to the placebo. According to the abstract, this corresponded to a "reduction in risk" of 16% (95% CI 5–26%, $P = 0.0036$).

Although the SOLVD report was published more than 20 years ago, its format is fairly typical for how this type of trial is reported today.

The authors state that "the percentage reduction in mortality was reported as $(1 - RR) \times 100$, where RR is the estimated relative risk of an event in the enalapril group as compared with the placebo group estimated from life tables." That the RR mentioned in the SOLVD report was neither taken as the risk ratio nor as the odds ratio based on the corresponding definitions given earlier can be verified readily from the SOLVD data already given. When the risks of death are taken as 452/1,285 for enalapril and 510/1,284 for the placebo (note that, strictly speaking, these are not risks as defined earlier because of the variable follow-up duration), it follows that the risk ratio is equal to (452/1,285)/(510/1,284), or 0.89, which corresponds to a "reduction in risk" of $(1 - 0.89) \times 100$, or 11%. Similarly, the odds ratio can be taken as [452/(1,285 – 452)]/[(510/(1,284 – 510)] or 0.82, which corresponds to an 18% reduction (always have a calculator or a spreadsheet program on hand while reading a report). How then might the SOLVD authors have arrived at the stated 16% reduction based on risks "estimated from life tables"?

The report states that groups were compared by the log-rank test. This test (or the equivalent Cox proportional hazards analysis with treatment allocation as the only covariate) is commonly used to compare treatment groups for trials with a variable follow-up duration. This is not understood by all readers, however; it is obvious only to those who are aware of the fact that the two analysis methods mentioned return *the rate (hazard) ratio—* assumed constant over time—as a *relative measure of treatment effect,* which is calculated from the rates for treated subjects and controls respectively, each with a person-time "at risk" denominator determined separately for the treatment concerned. It follows that in all likelihood the 16% reduction in death reported by SOLVD corresponds to a *rate ratio* of 0.84. But can this be verified from the data given in the report?

Treatment-specific person-time "at risk" data are rarely given in trial reports, SOLVD being no exception. Most reports give *Kaplan-Meier (KM) curves* for the outcomes considered. The KM curve for total mortality shown in the SOLVD report is reproduced here as **Figure 11–1**.

Placebo 1284 1159 1085 1005   939   819   669   487   299
Enalapril 1285 1195 1127 1069 1010   891   667   526   333

FIGURE 11–1   Mortality curves in the placebo and enalapril groups. The numbers of patients alive in each group at the end of each period are shown at the bottom of the figure. P = 0.0036 for the comparison between groups by the log-rank test.

Reproduced from *The New England Journal of Medicine*. The SOLVD investigators. Effect of enalapril on survival in patients with reduced left ventricular ejection fractions and congestive heart failure. *N Eng J Med* 1991;325:293–302.

When the numbers of patients still "at risk" for the outcome concerned are given under a KM curve (as is often the case), the total person-time "at risk" can be calculated for each treatment. This is not just true for death as outcome. For any other outcome considered in a KM curve, person-times "at risk" can be calculated, even when the outcome concerned is subject to competition from other outcomes. When (exceptionally, and the reason for using SOLVD as an example) data are also given on how the number of subjects with the outcome concerned (death in this case) evolves over time, one can also determine how the corresponding rates evolve over time.

The calculations required are illustrated in **Table 11–1** and are explained here. For the time points given in column (1), the numbers of patients still "at risk" for death (as shown in Figure 11–1) appear in columns (2) and (6) for the enalapril and the placebo group, respectively. Columns (4) and (8) give the corresponding number of deaths by interval as derived from Table 3 in the report. For example, there were 118 deaths in the enalapril arm in the interval 12–24 months.

TABLE 11-1 Mortality Data Extracted from the SOLVD Trial Report

	Enalapril				Placebo				
(1)	(2)	(3)	(4)	(5)	(6)	(7)	(8)	(9)	(10)
		Months of		Rate/100		Months of		Rate/100	
Months	N "at risk"	follow-up	New deaths*	person-years	N "at risk"	follow-up	New deaths*	person-years	Hazard ratio
0	1,285		0		1,284		0		
6	1,195	7,440	91**	14.7	1,159	7,329	126**	20.6	0.71
12	1,127	6,966	68	11.7	1,085	6,732	75	13.4	0.88
18	1,069	6,588			1,005	6,270			
24	1,010	6,237	118	11.0	939	5,832	143	14.2	0.78
30	891	5,703			819	5,274			
36	697	4,764	119	13.6	669	4,464	106	13.1	1.04
42	526	3,669			487	3,468			
48	333	2,577	47	9.0	299	2,358	54	11.1	0.81
>48		999	9			897	6		
Total		44,943	452	12.1		42,624	510	14.4	0.84
Mean		35.0				33.2			

*Derived from the cumulative numbers of deaths in Table 3 of the report.
**Inconsistent with Figure 11–1, which suggests that 1,285–1,195, or 90, enalapril subjects and 1,284 – 1,159, or 125, placebo subjects did not complete the first 6 months of follow-up. This does not affect the calculations.

Columns (3) and (7) give the interval number of patient-months of follow-up for those "at risk" for death by treatment group and by interval as calculated using Excel from the data given in columns (2) and (6). For example, it follows from the data in column (2) that during the first 6 months, follow-up was terminated in 1,285–1,195, or 90 enalapril patients either because of death or an early end to follow-up. Assuming that this occurred on average halfway the interval (which is equivalent to approximating the mortality curve for the interval 0–6 months by a straight line), these 90 patients have contributed 90 × 3, or 270 patient-months of follow-up to the total. In the same treatment group, 1,195 patients were still alive at 6 months. These have contributed at that time point another 1,195 × 6, or 7,170 patients-months of follow-up to the total for enalapril. Adding 7,170 to 270 gives the 7,440 months shown in column (3) for the interval 0–6 months.

The same calculation can be repeated for each subsequent time interval and for each treatment. At 48 months, 333 enalapril and 299 placebo patients were still alive and were followed further. According to the report, the maximum duration of follow-up was 55 months, that is, another 7 months beyond 48. The calculations in columns (3) and (7) assume an average of 3 months of follow-up beyond 48 months. This explains the last entries in columns (3) and (7): 333 × 3 = 999 for enalapril and 299 × 3 = 897 for placebo. Note that the total follow-up time does not critically depend on the assumption made concerning the additional follow-up duration beyond 48 months in the 333 and 299 patients concerned, as their number is small.

One can now calculate the mortality rates in SOLVD. The numerator for enalapril is 452 deaths. The corresponding denominator is the sum of the interval durations in column (3) of Table 11–1, and is equal to 44,943 patient-months. This is equivalent to 44,943/12, or 3,745.25 patient-years. Hence, the mortality rate for enalapril is (452/3,745.25) × 100, or 12.1 deaths per 100 patient-years "at risk" for death. Similarly, the mortality rate for placebo is 510/42,624, which corresponds to 14.4 deaths per 100 patient-years "at risk" after conversion of months to years, and multiplying by 100.

Based on these rates, one can now also calculate the rate (hazard) ratio comparing enalapril to placebo, which is 12.1/14.4, or 0.84. As (1 – 0.84) × 100 = 16, note that this corresponds exactly to the "reduction in risk" of death of 16% as stated in the SOLVD report.

The number of subjects still "at risk" as shown for SOLVD in Figure 11–1 is today a fairly common feature of trial reports in major journals, but the number of subjects with event by time interval, as presented in Table 11–1, is rarely given. That these numbers were reported for SOLVD allows us to determine how the rates of death and the rate (hazard) ratios evolve over time. In Table 11–1, interval rates were calculated as the number of deaths for the interval concerned, divided by the corresponding patient-time of follow-up. For example, the rate of death for enalapril in the interval 12–24 months in column (5) of Table 11–1 is $\{118/[(6588 + 6237)/12]\} \times 100$, or 11.0 deaths per 100 patient-years. When follow-up is partitioned by time intervals in this manner, one would expect that the time interval rates vary. What matters here is whether there is a trend over time. Note that the rates for enalapril given in column (5) are essentially stable over time. For the placebo, the rate appears high in the first 6 months and is then also essentially stable. Why this is so cannot be answered from the data given. What matters for meta-analysis is that the overall rates of 12.1 per 100 patient-years for enalapril and 14.4 for the placebo are convenient and credible *summary occurrence measures* for SOLVD that can often easily be calculated even if they are not given and that can be taken as essentially constant over time for the chronic disease condition concerned. As we shall see later, as long as the rates can be assumed constant over time, the particular duration of follow-up in each trial or study included in a meta-analysis no longer matters. The same cannot be said for the risk or the odds ratio and for the "number-needed-to-treat" as commonly calculated [Lubsen et al., 2000].

In column (10) of Table 11–1, the rate (hazard) ratios are also given by time interval. As is true for the rates, these vary but are essentially constant over time. Both the log-rank test and Cox proportional hazard analysis with treatment as the only covariate assume that the rate (hazard) ratio is constant over time. In the case of SOLVD, the data do not clearly violate this assumption. We emphasize that these methods of comparing rates do not assume that the rates themselves are also constant. Few trial reports address the question of whether the rates are constant over time, or whether the data support the assumption made in the analysis that the rate (hazard) ratio is constant.

Because the time "at risk" for death is the same for all causes, cause-specific death rates can be calculated when a breakdown by cause is reported and the subject time of follow-up by treatment is given or can be calculated. As we shall see later, this is essential when a meta-analysis is performed for specific causes of death, or for nonfatal events that are subject to competitive censoring.

Treatment-specific subject times of follow-up also suggest an alternative measure of treatment effect that may be easier to understand for patients than the statement—based on SOLVD— "if you take enalapril for your heart failure, your mortality rate will go down by 16 percent." Note that in Table 11–1 the mean follow-up is calculated as 35.0 months for enalapril, as opposed to 33.2 for the placebo. Based on this, a physician could say to a patient: "After you have taken enalapril for 35 months, you will have gained 1.8 months of life." Of course, this is only true on average. Nonetheless, it puts the effect of treatment in a different perspective. An extra 1.8 months may be worthwhile if enalapril does not cause any side effects and reduces the symptoms of heart failure. On the other hand, if the treatment has quality of life decreasing side effects, the perspective may be different. Few if any meta-analyses have thus far considered effects on duration of life.

When numbers "at risk" are not given under a KM curve one can obtain treatment-specific follow-up durations if the mean follow-up duration until death or end of study for both treatments combined and the rate (hazard) ratio for all-cause death are given in a report. This involves solving the following two equations with two unknowns:

$$(N_1 + N_0) \times MFUP_C = N_1 \times MFUP_1 + N_0 \times MFUP_0$$
$$HR = [e_1/(N_1 \times MFUP_1)]/[e_0/(N_0 \times MFUP_0)]$$

In these equations, N_1 and N_0 respectively denote the number of subjects allocated to each of the two treatments compared. Similarly, e_1 and e_0 denote the corresponding number of deaths. HR denotes the rate (hazard) ratio, and $MFUP_C$ the mean duration of follow-up for both treatments combined.

The two unknowns are $MFUP_1$ and $MFUP_0$ respectively, that is, the two treatment-specific mean follow-up durations to be determined. Solving the two equations for $MFUP_1$ and $MFUP_0$ by algebra is tedious and is not necessary when the Solver function of Excel is used.

A note of caution is in order here. From Table 11–1, the $MFUP_C$ for SOLVD is (44,943 + 42,624)/(1,285 + 1,284), or 34.1 months. This is much less than the 41.4 months stated in the report. Based on the calendar dates given for inclusion and the common stopping date, the likely explanation is that the average duration of follow-up stated in the report is in fact the mean time span between entry into the trial and the common stopping date. This shows that a uniform definition of terms used in study reports has yet to be agreed upon and illustrates that abstracting data from a report for inclusion in a meta-analysis can be challenging because of confusion about the exact meaning of the terms used.

Further methods of estimating person-time denominators based on data abstracted from published reports may be found elsewhere [Skali et al., 2006].

Risk, Odds, or Rate (Hazard) Ratios?

The choice of the measure of effect to be used in a meta-analysis must be carefully considered and depends both on the purpose of the meta-analysis and the data that are available for each study considered.

Meta-analyses that rely on a ratio rather than difference measures of effect predominate in the medical literature. The odds ratio has been used most often, unfortunately without much consideration for whether this measure is appropriate given the purpose of the analysis. Also, the measure used in an analysis is not necessarily the same as the measure reported for the studies considered. To illustrate, in a meta-analysis by Garg and Yusuf [1995] of ACE-inhibitor trials in heart failure, the SOLVD trial discussed earlier is represented by the odds ratio of 0.82 rather than the rate (hazard) ratio of 0.84. More recently, Sattar et al. [2010] reported a meta-analysis of 13 trials with a total of 91,140 participants comparing a statin to a placebo that focused on the question of whether statins may cause diabetes mellitus. In the report, the authors state: "Because the effect estimates for incident diabetes were directly reported as hazard ratios (HRs) in only three of the six published trials, we adopted a standard approach across all trials, in which we calculated odds ratios (ORs) and their 95% CIs from the abstracted data for the number of patients who did not have diabetes at baseline and those developing incident diabetes."

It appears that both Garg and Yusuf [1995] and Sattar et al. [2010] consider the odds ratio an appropriate proxy for the rate (hazard) ratio. Undoubtedly, the reason for this is primarily practical. Rate (hazard) ratios cannot always be found in reports, let alone absolute rates or person-times of follow-up by treatment. On the other hand, risk or odds ratios can always be calculated.

For acute conditions with a fixed follow-up duration, a meta-analysis based on risks or odds may be appropriate, in particular when the fixed follow-up duration is the same for all studies included or can be made the same by only considering events up to the same time point for all studies. In such instances, the risk ratio or risk difference is preferred, as these are more understandable measures of effect than the odds ratio.

What is true for acute conditions does not apply to chronic conditions and meta-analyses of studies with durations of follow-up that vary both within and between studies. Here, the basic measure of occurrence is the rate, not the risk. The reason is that for a constant rate, the risk depends on the duration of the time interval over which the risk is taken. That this has consequences for commonly used effect measures based on risks can be shown as follows.

Consider, for example, a death rate of 14/100 for treated subjects and 20/100 person-years for comparable controls. For a constant rate, the relationship between the risk of death and the rate is given by the well-known exponential relationship $R(t) = 1 - exp(-h \times t)$, where $R(t)$ stands for the risk over a time interval of duration t, exp for the base of the natural logarithm (e) to the power to (in this case to the power $-h \times t$), and h for the rate. Based on this formula, **Table 11–2** shows how the risks of death and several risk-based effect measures evolve over time for constant rates of 14/100 and 20/100 person-years respectively.

Note that the relative risk reduction derived from the risk ratio underestimates the risk reduction derived from the constant hazard ratio of 0.7 in a time-dependent manner and that the opposite is the case for the relative risk reduction derived from the odds ratio. It follows that both the risk and the odds ratio are biased estimators of the rate (hazard) ratio. Note also that the risk difference, and therefore the "number-needed-to-treat" depends markedly on the duration of follow-up. This implies that a study with, for example, 3 years of follow-up cannot be compared to a study with 5 years of follow-up based on risk-based effect measures. Duration of follow-up is a "nuisance factor" when comparing studies with different follow-up durations and increases the heterogeneity when risk-based rather than rate (hazard)-based effect measures are used in a meta-analysis.

Ideally, estimators of effects should be as unbiased as possible. Nonetheless, one may argue that the time-dependent bias in either the risk or the odds ratio when used to estimate the hazard ratio (see Table 11–2) is too small to be relevant, in particular when the rates are low. Whether this argument always holds is another matter.

TABLE 11–2   Risk of Death and Risk-Based Treatment Effects by Duration of Follow-up for Constant Rates of 14/100 and 20/100 Subject-Years of Follow-up "At Risk" for Death for Treated and Control Subjects Respectively (Hazard Ratio = 0.7)

Follow-up (years)	Risk Treated	Risk Control	Risk Ratio	Odds Ratio	Risk Difference	NNT*
1	0.13	0.18	0.72	0.68	−0.05	19.8
2	0.24	0.33	0.74	0.66	−0.09	11.7
3	0.34	0.45	0.76	0.63	−0.11	9.2
4	0.43	0.55	0.78	0.61	−0.12	8.2
5	0.50	0.63	0.80	0.59	−0.13	7.8
6	0.57	0.70	0.81	0.57	−0.13	7.7

*NNT = "number-needed-to-treat," commonly taken as 1/ | Risk difference |.

Meta-analysis may reliably detect effects of treatment on outcomes for which individual studies have inadequate statistical power. To be useful in this regard, the effect measure chosen must be such that the analysis will show "no effect" when there is no difference between treated and control subjects. For all-cause death, this requirement is met no matter which effect measure is chosen. Had Table 11–2 been made for the same rate for treated subjects and controls respectively, all effect measures shown would indicate "no effect" for all time points. However, for any outcome other than all-cause death, this requirement is not met by risk-based measures of effect.

That this must be so can be clarified based on the imaginary trial data for cardiovascular (CV) death and noncardiovascular (NCV) death, respectively, as two mutually exclusive outcomes given in **Table 11–3**.

Note that because the mean duration of follow-up "at risk" for death is given by treatment (rather than for both treatments combined, as is usually the case in reports), and all rates and measures of effect shown can be readily verified. For example, the rates of CVD are by definition 196/(2.445 × 2,000), or 4/100, for treated subjects, and 451/(2.256 × 2,000), or 10/100 person-years, for controls. The corresponding hazard ratio for CVD is equal to 0.4, etc.

There is a lesson in Table 11–3 that has been overlooked thus far in several published meta-analyses. Imagine that a meta-analysis is undertaken to answer the very relevant question of whether a cardiovascular drug

TABLE 11–3   Occurrence of Death by Cause in a Simulated Trial with 2000 Treated Subjects and 2000 Controls

	Treated (N = 2,000)	Controls (N = 2,000)	Hazard Ratio	Risk Ratio	Odds Ratio
Mean duration of follow-up (years)	2.445	2.256			
All-cause death (rate/100 person-years)	686 (14)	902 (20)	0.7	0.76	0.64
CV death (rate/100 person-years)	196 (4)	451 (10)	0.4	0.43	0.37
NCV death (rate/100 person-years)	490 (10)	451 (10)	1.0	1.08	1.11

CV, cardiovascular; NCV, noncardiovascular

Numbers of all-cause deaths taken as 2000 × R(t), with $R(t) = \{1 - exp[-(h_{CVD} + h_{NCVD})] \times t\}$ for $t = 3$, and CV and NCV death rates (h_{CVD} and h_{NCVD} respectively) for mutually exclusive causes of death as shown. Number of CV deaths taken as $[h_{CVD}/(h_{CVD} + h_{NCVD})]$ × number of all-cause deaths. Mean duration of follow-up taken as $R(t)/(h_{CVD} + h_{NCVD})$, with $R(t)$ = risk of all-cause death, $t = 3$, and the rates shown. Hazard, risk, and odds ratios calculated from the data given.

(such as a statin, for example), has an effect on NCV death. Table 11–3 shows convincingly that such a meta-analysis must focus on the rate (hazard) ratio for NCV death, as both the risk and the odds ratio suggest an untoward effect on this cause of death, although there is none because the corresponding rate (hazard) ratio is 1.0. The reason for this is that treated subjects live longer (mean follow-up = 2.445 years) due to the markedly reduced CV death rate compared to controls (mean follow-up is 2.256 years; see Table 11–3). In a *closed cohort* (i.e., a population with a membership defined once at the start of follow-up) of treated subjects, this results in a higher number of NCV deaths (490) because of the increased mean duration of follow-up "at risk" relative to controls (451; see Table 11–3) although the rate (hazard) of NCV death is the same for both treatments. This phenomenon has been called *cause-of-death competition.*

Obviously, both the risk and the odds ratio for NCV death in Table 11–3 do not take cause-of-death competition into account. The reason for this is not that the numerators used in calculating the risks or the odds of NCV death are any different from those used in calculating the rates. Rather, the reason is that the denominators (number of participants allocated to the treatment in the case of risks, number of participants with no event in the case of odds) do not take the increased person-time "at risk" for treated subjects in comparison to controls into account. On the other hand, rates have by definition person-time "at risk" as the denominator, and are therefore sensitive to effects of treatment on the person-time "at risk."

The hazard ratios for all death, CV death, and NCV death shown in Table 11–3 follow directly from the corresponding rates for treated and controls that were the basis of the calculations, as explained in the table's legend. The same hazard ratios can also be obtained from the familiar log-rank statistic (O/E) for treated subjects, divided by (O/E) for controls, with O denoting the observed numbers of deaths for the cause concerned, and E the expected number. The expected numbers of deaths by cause must be obtained by first calculating the rates for both groups combined. For example, the CV death rate for both groups combined is $(196 + 451)/(2,000 \times 2.445 + 2,000 \times 2.256)$, or 6.9 per 100 person-years. By applying this rate to the total person-years of follow-up for treated and controls respectively, the corresponding expected numbers of CV deaths are 336.9 and 310.1, respectively. Hence, the log-rank statistic estimate of the rate (hazard) ratio for CV death is $(196/336.9)/(451/310.1)$, or 0.4, which corresponds to the value calculated directly from the data in Table 11–3. This shows that in calculating the log-rank statistic for CV death, it does not matter whether follow-up "at risk" is terminated by competing NCV death or by the end of follow-up. Contrary to the risk and the odds ratio, the rate (hazard) ratio from the log-rank statistic is also an unbiased estimator of treatment effect when the event concerned is subject to competition from other event(s).

Trials always compare closed cohorts of differently treated subjects. Hence competition between events will always occur. A subject who, for example, dies in a car accident is no longer "at risk" for acute myocardial infarction. A comparison between treatments for the occurrence of myocardial infarction cannot ignore events that terminated follow-up "at risk" for infarction.

Because of this, the already mentioned odds ratio–based meta-analysis by Sattar et al. [2010] of statins and new diabetes is difficult to interpret. In the report, the authors have tabulated for each included trial a proxy of the rates of new diabetes for statins and controls, respectively, using the mean or median duration of follow-up until death or the end of study for statin and control subjects combined in calculating the denominators. These "rates" are useful as an indicator of the frequency of new diabetes, which ranged from 4.5 to 34.8 per 1,000 person-years. However, these are not true rates according to its definition because the denominators were not taken as the person-time "at risk" for new diabetes for statin and control subjects. This data was obviously not available to the authors. It would have been of interest to know whether the authors attempted to obtain such data from the investigators concerned, but failed (our experience in this regard is not good).

In the studies considered by Sattar et al. [2010], there were 2,226 cases of new diabetes for statin users as opposed to 2,052 for control subjects. This represents an increase of 8.5%. The overall odds ratio for new diabetes comparing statin to control subjects was 1.09 (95% CI, 1.02–1.17). The authors conclude that "statin therapy is associated with a slightly increased risk of development of diabetes, but the risk is low both in absolute terms and when compared with the reduction in coronary events." In the discussion, the authors note that "improved survival with statin treatment" may be "a residual confounding factor," and then, quoting a meta-analysis of statins by the Cholesterol Treatment Trialists' Collaborators [2005], state that "overall survival with statins is very similar to survival with control therapy (about 1.4% absolute difference), suggesting that survival bias does not explain the variation."

Sattar et al. [2010] do not define survival bias or explain how this relates to a 1.4% absolute difference. A definition of survival bias that follows from Table 11–3 is the difference in mean follow-up "at risk" for death (which may also be called mean survival) between statin users and controls. Hence, the question is whether an estimate of the difference in mean survival can be derived from the report of the Cholesterol Treatment Trialists' Collaborators [2005].

The Cholesterol Treatment Trialists' meta-analysis used a sophisticated extension of the log-rank statistic to estimate rate (hazard) ratios for all-cause death and for major CV events. The mean duration of follow-up for survivors for the trials included in this meta-analysis was given in the report as 4.7 years. This quantity cannot be used to determine the mean survival for statin users and controls by the method of solving two equations with two unknowns given previously. Hence, another method is required to determine how large the difference in mean survival might be.

The method concerned assumes that the mean duration of follow-up for survivors is the same for treated and controls, which is reasonable. The absolute rate (assumed constant) of all-cause death h is equal to $-ln[S(t)]/t$, where $S(t)$ denotes the survival probability at time t, and ln the natural logarithm. The Cholesterol Treatment Trialists' meta-analysis concerned 45,054 subjects assigned statins and 45,002 assigned the control treatment. The corresponding numbers of deaths were 3,832 and 4,354, respectively. It follows that there were (45,054 − 3,832), or 41,222, survivors among statin users and (45,002 − 4,354), or 40,648, for controls. Hence, the approximate (approximate because a fixed follow-up of 4.7 years is assumed) rates of death were $-ln(41,222/45,054)/4.7$, or 1.891 deaths per 100 person-years for the statin group, and $-ln(40,648/45,002)/4.7$, or 2.165 deaths per 100 person-years for controls. The rate ratio from this is 1.891/2.165, or 0.87, which reassuringly is the same as the overall rate ratio for all-cause death stated in the Cholesterol Treatment Trialists' meta-analysis. From an equation for mean duration of follow-up "at risk" for death used earlier to determine the data given in Table 11–3, it follows that the mean survival is (3,832/45,054)/(1.891/100), or 4.50 years, for the statin group, and (4,354/45,002)/(2.165/100), or 4.47 years, for controls. The "survival bias" is thus 0.03 years, which is equivalent to less than 1% of the mean survival for controls. This small increase in survival cannot explain the 8.5% increase in new diabetes reported by Sattar et al. [2010]. The conclusion is that the bias that can be attributed to increased survival by statin treatment in the effect measure for new diabetes reported by these authors is indeed irrelevant (that there may be other biases is an entirely different matter).

In the case of the meta-analysis by Sattar et al. [2010] it did not matter that a theoretically biased estimator of treatment effect was used. This is not always the case.

Koller et al. [2008] performed a meta-analysis of nonarrhythmic death for nine trials comparing an implantable cardiac defibrillator (ICD) to control treatment. Deaths were classified as either due to arrhythmia or not.

The overall odds ratio for nonarrhythmic death was 1.11 (95% CI 0.84–1.45). Although not convincingly so because of the wide confidence interval, this suggests that ICD implantation may have an untoward effect on nonarrhythmic death. Because of cause-of-death competition, the odds ratio for nonarrhythmic death is potentially biased. The authors also calculated an overall rate (hazard) ratio for this outcome, using person-time denominators calculated from the data given in each report. The overall rate (hazard) ratio for nonarrhythmic death obtained was 1.03 (95% CI 0.80–1.32).

The meta-analysis by Koller et al. [2008] shows that an odds ratio–based analysis can be seriously biased and potentially result in a spurious conclusion. As shown in Table 11–3, the same applies to a risk ratio–based analysis. There are therefore compelling reasons to use rate (hazard) ratios in meta-analysis unless the studies included all have the same fixed duration of follow-up. In practice, this can be difficult because the rate ratio data required for the outcome(s) of interest cannot be abstracted in a consistent manner for all studies included.

Occurrence Measures and Kaplan-Meier Curves

Competition between events also affects the interpretation of Kaplan-Meier (KM) curves, which must be taken into account when estimating risks from published KM curves. A KM curve for all-cause mortality shows the risk of death and the proportion of subjects still alive over time irrespective of censoring, but assuming that the censoring was non-informative. It is important to understand what is meant here by *non-informative*. When subjects are followed over time for any death, follow-up is either terminated (censored) because of death, or because the subject is still alive and also still "at risk" for death when the study ends. Note that there are only two ways that follow-up for any death can be censored.

Now, suppose that a KM curve is derived for CV death. In that case, there are three different reasons for censoring: (1) A CV death has occurred and is counted as an event, (2) an NCV death has occurred (not counted as an event!), after which the subject concerned is no longer "at risk" of CV death, and (3) follow-up is terminated in a subject who is still alive and "at risk" for any death. A conventional KM analysis for CV death will treat censoring because of the second and the third reason as equivalent, although the second reason is by no means non-informative because a subject who died of NCV death is no longer "at risk" for CV death. It follows that a KM curve for CV death can only be interpreted as showing the risk of CV death when there are no competing deaths due to an NCV cause. By the same token, a KM curve for the combined outcome of any death, myocardial infarction, or stroke can be interpreted as showing event-free survival as there is no informative censoring due to competing events. The same cannot be said about a KM curve for the combined outcome CV death, myocardial infarction, or stroke. This KM curve will be subject to informative censoring due to competing NCV death. Hence, the curve for this combined outcome does not show event-free survival unless there are no NCV deaths that precede CV death, myocardial infarction, or stroke.

The error of interpretation made when taking, for example, a risk of CV death from a KM curve for CV death is avoided by considering the rate of CV death rather than the risk. The latter can only be obtained, however, when person-time "at risk" for death data are available or can be calculated. KM curves in study reports are of little use, other than showing how the events considered "spread out" during follow-up.

A KM curve for an event that has a constant rate will have the well-known exponential shape. A more useful way to determine whether rates are constant can be understood based on the exponential relationship between the risk and the rate of death $R(t) = 1 - exp(-h \times t)$, which is equivalent to $S(t) = exp(-h \times t)$. If one were to plot $-ln[S(t)]$ in lieu of $S(t)$, the plot would be determined by $h \times t$, or by a straight line when h is constant. In the statistical literature, the quantity $-ln[S(t)]$ is called the *cumulative hazard*. Cumulative hazard plots are much more informative than conventional KM curves and less prone to misinterpretation in the case of competing events. However, they are rarely found in trial reports. An example may be found in Connolly et al. [2011].

Pooling Effects Across Studies

Once the studies to be included, the outcome(s), and the effect measure (or measure of association) of interest have been chosen, the next steps in a meta-analysis are to abstract the data and determine combined (pooled) estimate(s) of effect or association.

In general, the data abstracted for each study have the form of a 2×2 table. Rate data require person-time denominators for each treatment. Occasionally, only effect estimates and their P values or confidence intervals are available.

Effect estimates from small studies are more subject to the play of chance than large studies and will therefore be less precise with wider confidence intervals. In a simple arithmetic average of the effect estimates for each study, smaller and larger studies are considered equally important. This is inappropriate, as the difference in information contributed by the various studies included in the analysis is not taken into account.

Adding up the 2×2 tables for each study to derive one summary 2×2 table of totals across all studies gives an adequate summary of the result for all studies combined that does justice to the size of each study included. The combined effect estimates obtained directly from the totals are usually close to the results obtained by any of the statistical methods developed for meta-analysis. Nonetheless, this method should not be used as a basis for calculating an overall estimate of effect, as the information contained in each study may not be represented correctly. Importantly, the differences in effect estimates between studies (heterogeneity) cannot be assessed in this manner.

Representing each study in a combined effect estimate according to the amount of information contained is achieved by calculating a *weighted average* across all studies, which has the following general form:

$$E_C = (weight_1 \times E_1 + weight_2 \times E_2 \ldots)/(weight_1 + weight_2 \ldots)$$

where E_C denotes the combined effect estimate; $E_1, E_2 \ldots$ the effect estimate for each study considered; and $weight_1, weight_2 \ldots$ the corresponding weight given to each study. In other words, the weighted average is equal to the sum of the study-specific weights multiplied by the corresponding value of the effect estimate, divided by the sum of the weights. Note that the arithmetic average is a special case of a weighted average, with weights all equal to 1.

The various Mantel-Haenszel–type methods that use 2×2 table cell counts to calculate combined risk-based effect measures can be thought of as using the size of each study as weights in calculating weighted combined effect estimates. The *generalized* or *inverse variance procedure* for combining effect estimates uses 1/(variance of effect estimate) for each study as weights. Weights that depend on the variance of effect estimates in this manner will be smaller for small studies (large variance) in comparison to those for larger studies (small variance). As for Mantel-Haenszel–type methods, this implies that large studies have more impact on the combined estimate than smaller ones.

The computationally simple calculations required by the inverse variance method for ratio measures of effect can conveniently be performed by using a spreadsheet program (Excel or similar) and are explained in detail in **Table 11–4** using data on the occurrence of stroke in six trials as an example.

The method for risk ratios is illustrated in Table 11–4. For odds ratios and rate (hazard) ratios, the denominators entered have to be adapted accordingly. Note that the calculations are performed for a natural logarithmic transformation of the relative effect measure concerned. The formula for the corresponding standard error is slightly different for risk ratios, odds

TABLE 11-4 Example of Combining Relative Effect Measures by the Inverse-Variance Method, Using Stroke Data from Six Trials

Study	Treated Events (a_i)	Treated Deno-minator (b_i)	Control Events (c_i)	Control Deno-minator (d_i)	RE_i	$ln(RE_i)$	Se of $ln(RE_i)$	95% CI of RE LL_i	95% CI of RE UL_i	W_i	$W_i \times ln(RE_i)$	Q_i
HOPE[1]	156	4645	226	4,652	0.69	−0.36917	0.10200	0.57	0.84	96.10959	−35.48108	0.06290
PART 2[2]	7	308	4	309	1.76	0.56286	0.62159	0.52	5.94	2.58816	1.45677	2.37340
QUIET[3]	1	878	1	872	0.99	−0.00686	1.41341	0.06	15.85	0.50057	−0.00343	0.07532
SCAT[4]	2	229	9	231	0.22	−1.49538	0.77615	0.05	1.03	1.65998	−2.48231	2.01087
PREVENT[5]	5	417	5	408	0.98	−0.02182	0.62861	0.29	3.35	2.53068	−0.05522	0.35197
SYSTEUR[6]	47	2,398	77	2,297	0.58	−0.53669	0.18279	0.41	0.84	29.93004	−16.06312	0.60295
Sums	218	8,875	322	8,769						133.31904	−52.62840	5.47741

$ln(RE_C)$: −0.39476
RE_C: 0.67

0.57   0.80

Cochran's Q has Chi-squared distribution with 6 − 1 degrees of freedom   **p = 0.36**

(1) The Heart Outcomes Prevention Evaluation Study Investigators, *N Engl J Med*. 2000;342:145–153.

(2) MacMahon S et al., *J Am Coll Cardiol*. 2000;36:438–343.

(3) Pitt B et al., *Am J Cardiol*. 2001;87:1058–1063.

(4) Teo KK et al., *Circulation*. 2000;102:1748–1754.

(5) Pitt B et al., *Circulation*. 2000;102:1503–1510.

(6) Staessen JA et al., *Lancet*. 1997;350:757–764.

a_i, c_i	= Number of subjects with event for treated and controls.
b_i, d_i	= Denominators of occurrence measures compared. Totals allocated for risk ratio (as in this example), totals of subjects without event for odds ratio, person-time "at-risk" for rate (hazard) ratio.
RE_i	= Relative effect = $(a_i/b_i)/(c_i/d_i)$ = risk ratio in this example. *May be entered directly when combining rate (hazard) ratios.*
$ln(RE_i)$	= Natural logarithm of relative effect RE_i.
Se of $ln(RE_i)$	= Standard error of natural logarithm of RE_i. For risk ratio (as in this example) = square root of $(1/a_i − 1/b_i + 1/c_i − 1/d_i)$. For odds ratio (with b_i and d_i equal to subjects without event) = square root of $(1/a_i + 1/b_i + 1/c_i + 1/d_i)$. For rate (hazard) ratio (with b_i and d_i equal to person-time "at risk") = square root of $(1/a_i + 1/c_i)$.
95% CI of RE_i	= 95% confidence interval of RE_i = exponent $[ln(RE_i) − 1.96 \times$ standard error of $ln(RE_i)]$ for lower limit (LL_i), exponent $[ln(RE_i) + 1.96 \times$ standard error of $ln(RE_i)]$ for upper limit (UL_i).
W_i	= Weight = inverse of variance = $1/[se$ of $ln(RE_i)]^2$. The sum of the weights appears below the bottom study-specific weight.
$W_i \times ln(RE_i)$	= Weight × natural logarithm of relative effect. The sum of these appears below the bottom study-specific entry for this quantity.
$ln(RE_C)$	= Natural logarithm of combined relative effect RE_C = (sum of weights × natural logarithm of relative effects) / (sum of weights)
RE_C	= Combined relative effect = exponent of $ln(RE_C)$, with lower and upper limits of 95% confidence interval given by exponent $[(ln(RE_C) \pm 1.96 \times$ square root of $(1/$sum of weights)]$.
Q_i	= Contribution to Cochran's Q test for heterogeneity, taken as $W_i \times [ln(RE_i) − ln(RE_C)]^2$.
Cochran's Q	= Sum of Q_i. Follows chi-squared distribution with k−1 degrees of freedom, where k is the number of studies. P value shown is the P value for Cochran's Q test.

ratios, and rate (hazard) ratios (see legend for Table 11–4) and must therefore be adapted in the spreadsheet as appropriate. Note also that calculating the combined effect estimate directly from the sums gives the same result, as $(218/8,875)/(322/8,769) = 0.67$. Starting from the natural logarithm of this and by using the formula for its variance as given in the legend of Table 11–4, one can readily verify that the 95% CI calculated from the sums has a lower limit of 0.56 and an upper limit of 0.79, which corresponds closely to the values obtained by the inverse variance pooling procedure.

Theoretically, the inverse variance method requires only that the effect estimates for each study be included, along with their standard errors. When the latter are not given, a standard error can be derived from either the P value or the confidence interval. The cell count data necessary for risk ratios and odds ratios will generally be available. This is not so for person-time denominators required to calculate rate (hazard) ratios. When combining the hazard ratios for studies that have all reported a hazard ratio value for the outcome of interest, the standard error of its natural logarithm can be obtained from the number of subjects with an event for treated and controls (see legend for Table 11–4). In that case, person-time denominator data are not required. The inverse variance method can also be used to combine odds ratio data from one study and hazard ratio data from another. It follows from what has been said earlier about competition between events that this may give results that are difficult to interpret. Hence, whether it is reasonable to combine odds ratios and hazard ratios must be considered carefully.

When the number of events is zero for any treatment in a particular study, the study concerned cannot be included as such in calculating an overall measure of effect by the inverse variance, as is obvious from the formula for the standard error given in Table 11–4 ($1/0 = $ infinity). In such cases, a Mantel-Haenszel–type method may be a better choice. For odds ratios, Sweeting et al. [2004] compared different methods for sparse data and concluded that the inverse invariance procedure with a *continuity correction for zero cell counts* (i.e., replacing a zero with 0.5, for example) gives biased results. The same applies to risk difference [Tang, 2000].

Heterogeneity

As is evident from Table 11–4, effect estimates may vary in magnitude and direction across studies. This poses the question of whether this reflects genuine differences between studies or chance. Assessment of consistency of effects across studies is an essential part of meta-analysis, as inconsistent results are not generalizable [Higgins et al., 2003].

A test for *heterogeneity* examines whether the variability in effect estimates between studies exceeds the variability that can be attributed to chance alone. There are essentially two underlying assumptions for this test that differ in the way variability across studies is considered. The *fixed-effects model* assumes that variability between studies is entirely random around one true value of the effect estimate concerned. The *random-effects model*, on the other hand, assumes that true effects differ randomly between trials [DerSimonian & Laird, 1986]. The random-effects model implies the use of a larger study-specific variance of the effect estimate than the fixed-effects model. Hence, the confidence interval obtained for the combined effect estimate will in general be wider for the random- than for the fixed-effects model.

Higgins et al. [2003] reviewed various approaches to the assessment of inconsistencies in meta-analyses that have been proposed. The usual heterogeneity test statistic known as Cochran's Q assumes a fixed-effects model, has a Chi-squared distribution, and is computed as shown in Table 11–4. A value that exceeds the number of degrees of freedom (rather than the corresponding P value) is generally interpreted as evidence of heterogeneity.

Heterogeneity tests pose subtle problems of interpretation. First, absence of "significant" heterogeneity is not proof of homogeneity. Cochran's Q test is known to be poor at detecting true heterogeneity among studies as significant, in particular when the number of studies included is limited. An alternative test statistic called I^2 does not depend on the number of studies included [Higgins et al., 2003]. Second, when clinically relevant (which is something other than "statistically significant") heterogeneity is observed across studies, one may question whether these studies can be combined by the chosen effect measure in the first place. Conventionally, a random-effects or other model is assumed when one of the available tests for a fixed-effects model suggests "significant" heterogeneity [Berry, 1998]. But this may mask the existence of a credible explanation for the heterogeneity that was observed. To illustrate, suppose that the studies considered in Table 11–4 had been ranked according to the mean age of the subjects in each study, and that the effect estimates showed a relationship between mean age and effect estimate across studies, indicating that age is an effect modifier. The value of Cochran's Q statistic is the same, regardless of whether age is an effect modifier. Another reason for effect modification that could explain heterogeneity is difference in study design, such as choice of treatment and type of treatment comparison (e.g., add-on treatment or replacement, comparisons between two active treatments, double-blind, or open comparison, etc.).

Taking lack of significance of a test of heterogeneity as proof of homogeneity forces the data to fit a preconceived model that assumes that the true effect estimate of interest is either the same (fixed effect), or varies at random (random effect) across studies. This may result in conclusions about effects of treatment that are not generalizable. Therefore, the possible causes of the heterogeneity must always be explored, whether or not the heterogeneity observed is statistically significant.

L'Abbé Plots: Fitting a Model to the Data

A particularly relevant effect modifier that may be overlooked by forcing the data into a preconceived model based on an insignificant heterogeneity test may be the absolute event risk or rate among the controls in the studies considered. A useful way to examine whether this is the case is to first plot the absolute occurrence measures for treatment and control in a so-called *L'Abbé plot* [L'Abbé et al., 1987]. This allows us to determine which effect model seems to best fit the data, as is shown in **Figure 11–2**.

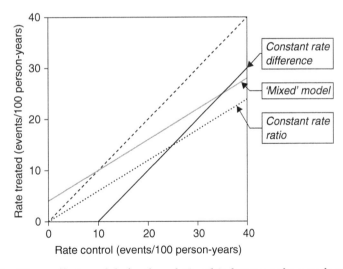

FIGURE 11–2   Three effect models for the relationship between the rate for treated and the rate for controls respectively. The dotted line is given by y = x, which indicates that treatment has no effect, relative to controls, across the range of risks for controls. The constant rate ratio line is given by y = HR × x, and the constant rate difference line by y = y − RD. The 'mixed' model is given by y = a × x + b (with constant a and b).

Figure 11–2 shows three possible relationships between the rates for treated and control subjects. The constant rate (hazard) ratio model assumes that treatment reduces the rate on a ratio scale to the same extent for any value of the control rate. The same applies to the constant rate difference model on the absolute difference scale. For low rates neither model is credible. The mixed model, on the other hand, allows for the possibility that a treatment may be highly effective in high-risk subjects while having no effect at all (or even an untoward effect) in low-risk subjects, as will often be the case in clinical practice.

Of course the data points plotted will never fall exactly on any line shown in Figure 11–2 due to random variability and other factors. Nonetheless, a L'Abbé plot can be helpful in determining whether any effect model illustrated in Figure 11–2 seems to fit the data, and therefore in determining whether heterogeneity between studies can perhaps be explained by a mixed-model relationship that implies by definition that there will be heterogeneity both for ratio and for difference measures of effect.

An example given by Hoes et al. [1995b] is reproduced here as **Figure 11–3**. Based on a weighted least-squares regression analysis that assumes a mixed model as shown in Figure 11–2, Hoes et al. [1995b] concluded that the rate (hazard) ratio for all-cause death cannot be assumed constant over the range of absolute rates across the trial subgroups considered and that there is no evidence that drug treatment improves survival when the death rate for control is below 6/1,000 person-years. The mixed-model result obtained by Hoes et al. [1995b], as shown in Figure 11–3, has been criticized by Egger & Smith [1995], who contended that regression bias is a more likely explanation for the relationship shown. Arends et al. [2000] have reanalyzed the data used by Hoes et al. [1995b] using a Bayesian approach and they came to a similar conclusion about the existence of a cut-off point for efficacy at a death rate of 6/1,000 person-years.

Effect models as shown in Figure 11–2 can also be explored by plotting the effect measure concerned on the vertical axis and the absolute occurrence measure for treated and controls combined in the horizontal axis. Further details may be found in Van Houwelingen et al. [2002].

Meta-Regression

Staessen et al. [2001] plotted treatment effects on clinical events expressed as odds ratios on a vertical axis against the difference in mean on treatment blood pressure levels between treatment and control on the horizontal axis (see **Figure 11–4**). This is an example of *meta-regression*.

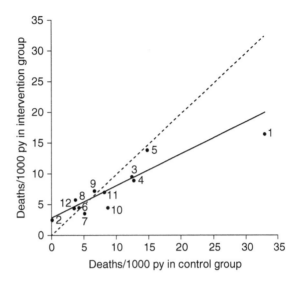

FIGURE 11–3   All-cause mortality rates (deaths/1000 patient-years [py]) in the intervention and control groups of 12 sub-groups from 7 trials in mild-to-moderate hypertension. The dotted 'no-effect' line indicates that the rates are the same for the intervention and control groups. The continuous weighted least-squares regression line is given by $y = 0.53 \times x + 0.0029$ and describes the estimated intervention death rate as a function of the control rate. The 95% confidence interval of the regression coefficient is 0.33–0.73. The no-effect line and the regression line intersect at a control rate of 6/1000 patient-years.

Reproduced with permission from the *Journal of Hypertension*. Hoes AW, et al. Does drug treatment improve survival? Reconciling the trials in mild-to-moderate hypertension. *J Hypertens* 1995;13:805–811.

Meta-regression may help to explore possible sources of heterogeneity and effect modification across trials. Meta-regression may also be performed to examine the relevance of the potential bias of individual studies, that is, flaws in the study design [Bjelakovic et al., 2007; Sterne et al., 2002], or to determine whether characteristics of a study population such as mean age and cholesterol level act as effect modifiers. The use of such mean covariates in meta-regression, however, may reduce power and can even lead to bias [Berlin et al. 2002; Lambert et al. 2002; Thompson & Higgins 2002].

Meta-regression must be distinguished from meta-analysis for subgroups. The latter is based on data from individual studies that have been stratified for specific characteristics of the study populations, such as gender. As with any subgroup analysis, meta-analysis to determine treatment effects

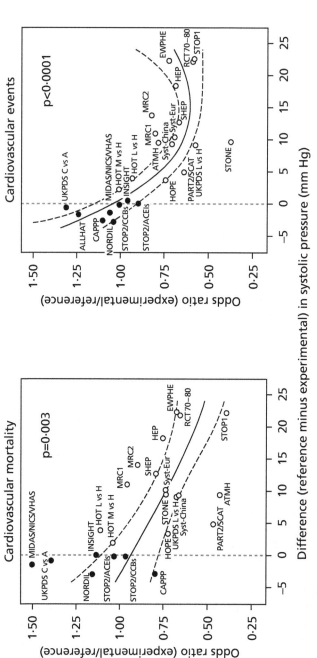

Relation between odds ratios for cardiovascular mortality and all cardiovascular events, and corresponding differences in systolic blood pressure.

Odds ratios were calculated for experimental versus reference treatment. Blood pressure differences were calculated by subtracting achieved levels in experimental groups from those in reference groups. Negative differences indicate tighter blood pressure control on reference treatment. Regression lines were plotted with 95% CI and were weighted for the inverse of the variance of individual odds ratios. Closed symbols denote trials that compared new with old drugs.

FIGURE 11-4   Example of a meta-regression analysis [Staessen, 2001]. On the horizontal axis the difference in systolic blood pressure (mm Hg) is depicted. The vertical axis shows the odds ratio for cardiovascular mortality (left panel) and cardiovascular events (right panel) of the trials considered.

Reproduced from *The Lancet* Vol. 358; Staessen JA, Whang J, Thijs L. Cardiovascular protection and blood pressure reduction: a meta-analysis. *The Lancet* 2001;358:1305–1315, with permission from Elsevier.

by subgroup should be based on sound reasoning and, preferably, a plausible biomedical reason for the existence of a difference in effect between subgroups. Because stratified data for exactly the same subgroups are rarely reported for all studies chosen for inclusion in a meta-analysis, subgroup meta-analyses are rarely feasible. In subgroup meta-analysis using stratified data, Berger et al. [2006] showed that aspirin reduced the risk of cardiovascular events in both men and women, albeit by a different mechanism: reduction of ischemic stroke in women, as opposed to reduction of myocardial infarction in men. This apparent difference in cardiovascular protection between men and women may also be attributable to other factors, however, such as gender differences in absolute risk for controls in the studies considered or differences in other risk factors.

Individual Patient Data Meta-Analysis: Unfulfilled Promise?

Meta-analyses based on pooled raw data for individual subjects, also called *individual patient data (IPD) meta-analyses*, are considered a more reliable alternative to meta-regression and meta-analysis for subgroups [Clarke & Stewart, 2001; Oxman et al., 1995; Stewart & Tierney, 2002].

Two approaches can be used. First, pooled raw data from individual studies can be merged into one database and then analyzed as if the data came from one (multicenter) study. For example, Rovers et al. [2006] performed an IPD meta-analysis of six randomized trials on the efficacy of antibiotics in children with acute otitis media. Discharge from the ear (otorrhea), age younger than 2 years, and bilateral acute otitis media were shown to modify the effect of antibiotics. Children younger than 2 years of age with bilateral acute otitis media and children in whom acute otitis media was accompanied by otorrhea benefited most from antibiotics as judged from pain, fever, or both at 3–7 days follow-up.

In an analysis of pooled data, dummy variables for individual studies are often included in regression models to adjust for possible residual confounding or to determine whether differences between studies can explain the heterogeneity of effect estimates.

Alternatively, a two-stage approach can be used. Summary results are obtained by reanalyzing the raw data of individual studies separately, which are then used as the basis for a conventional meta-analysis.

Although many IPD meta-analyses have been published, most emphasize the overall treatment effect without addressing subgroup effects, although examining treatment effects for subgroups is the main strength of IPD meta-analysis. Moreover, the two-stage approach, rather than the statistically more efficient direct modeling approach [Koopman et al., 2007], appears to be used more frequently.

Subgroup analyses often lack a clear rationale, are unreliable because of false-positive statistical tests of significance, and are of limited value in deciding on treatment in clinical practice because patients do not come in subgroups, but rather as individuals characterized by multiple unique attributes (such as age, gender, symptoms, prior history, etc.). As noted by Pocock and Lubsen [2008], univariate subgroup analysis must be distinguished from risk stratification based on a multiattribute prognostic model. Based on the latter, subjects are categorized into several ordered risk groups. Then the absolute risk or rate reductions in each risk group are obtained. Note that this has undeniable *a priori* rationale, as zero risk can only be increased by treatment, not reduced further.

An early but still relevant example can be found in the report on the MIAMI trial [MIAMI Trial Research Group, 1985], which compared 2,877 subjects with suspected acute myocardial infarction assigned to metoprolol (a beta-blocker) to 2,901 subjects assigned to a placebo. The 15-day risk of death was 123 deaths (4.3/100) for metoprolol, as opposed to 142 (4.9/100) for the placebo. The difference was not statistically significant ($P = 0.3$). Can one decide that metoprolol has little effect, if any, on mortality on this basis?

This question could not be answered without risk stratification. In the protocol, the MIAMI investigators predefined eight simple binary baseline risk factors such as age > 60 years (no/yes). Subjects were stratified according to the total number of risk factors (which is equivalent to a multiple logistic regression score, with equal coefficients for all variables). The advantage of this is that the investigators could not be accused of data dredging in defining the risk stratification procedure post-hoc. The absolute 15-day risk of death was steeply related to the number of risk factors and ranged in the placebo group from 0.0/100 for subjects without risk factors to 11.6/100 for those with five or more risk factors. The corresponding risks for metoprolol were 0.0 and 5.8/100, respectively. Metoprolol had no apparent effect on the low-mortality risk group (3,740, two-thirds of the trial population), but was associated with a 29% statistically significant lower mortality rate in the high-mortality risk group (2,038 patients).

It should be emphasized that statistical analysis of this type of data is slightly more complex than determining the statistical significance of the effect estimate for each of two strata for one binary characteristic (such as gender, for example). What is needed for data stratified as described for MIAMI is a test for interaction, with one P value for the test of the null hypothesis that there is no interaction between the number of risk factors and the magnitude of effect. Subgroup analyses for three or more strata (such as for three categories of age) that can be found in the literature are often inappropriate in this regard (any treatment effect can be rendered insignificant by using a large number of age categories and calculating a *P* value for each category separately).

The MIAMI trial example shows that risk stratification based on a multiattribute risk score is potentially much more clinically relevant than the ubiquitous univariate subgroup analyses found in the literature, as it may identify those subjects in clinical practice who really benefit and those who do not benefit at all. Currently, few if any such analyses have been reported for single trials, let alone for meta-analyses. IPD meta-analysis aimed at assessing effects for strata of multiattribute risk has considerable, but as of yet, ill understood potential. The practical difficulties should not be overlooked, however, the most important being that raw data bases from industry-sponsored trials are rarely in the public domain.

REPORTING RESULTS FROM A META-ANALYSIS

A report on a meta-analysis should clearly describe the methods of retrieval, selection, critical appraisal, data extraction, and data analysis so that others can repeat the analysis if desired. Decisions and comments on the completeness and combinability of evidence should be transparent and supported by clear tabulations and graphic presentation of data. Evidence from data analysis should be separated from value judgments. Guidelines may be found in the Preferred Reporting Items for Systematic Reviews and Meta-Analyses (PRISMA) statement [PRISMA, n.d.], which has replaced the earlier Quality of Reporting of Meta-Analyses (QUOROM) statement [Moher et al., 1999b].

Flowchart

The strategy for retrieval and selection of the publications and results must be stated clearly. The search filter syntax per bibliographic source with the subsequent number of retrieved publications, the number and reasons for exclusion of publications, the final number of publications included, and the number of studies concerned should be reported, preferably as a *flowchart* (see **Figure 11–5**).

Funnel Plot

A *funnel plot* is a scatter plot of the treatment effect estimates from individual studies against a measure of its precision, which can be the sample

FIGURE 11–5 Example of a flow diagram representing the search and selection of trials.

Reproduced from Cappuccio FP, Kerry SM, Forbes L, Donald A. Blood pressure control by home monitoring: meta-analysis of randomized trials. *BMJ* 2004;329:145.

size or the inverse of its variance. Its proponents suggest that a funnel plot can be used to explore the presence of publication and retrieval bias. Effect estimates from small studies will scatter more widely around the true value than estimates from larger studies because the precision of the treatment effect estimate increases when the sample size increases. Conventionally, a skewed (asymmetrical) funnel plot is considered to indicate bias in publication, retrieval, and selection of trials [Sterne et al., 2000]. If smaller trials with a beneficial treatment effect (see the upper left part of **Figure 11–6**) are

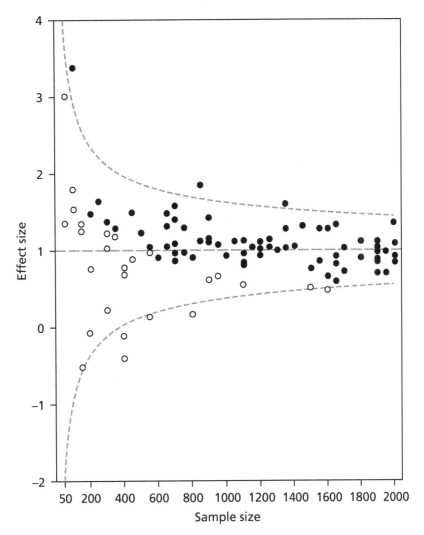

FIGURE 11–6   Example of a funnel plot based on simulated data. Simulated funnel plot, created by randomly drawing 100 samples of size varying from 50 to 2000 from an underlying normal distribution with a mean of 1 unit and standard deviation of 10 units. The curves indicate the region within which 95% of samples of a given size are expected to fall. Closed circles indicate samples where the mean is significantly increased (above zero) at $P < 0.05$, open circles samples where it is not. For the full sample, the funnel shape is evident, but this would not be so if the open circles (or a proportion of them) were not included due to publication bias.

Reproduced from Thornton A, Lee P. Publication bias in meta-analysis: its causes and consequences. *J Clin Epidemiol* 2000;53:207–216, with permission from Elsevier.

preferentially published and more likely to be retrieved and selected than smaller studies with no or even a harmful effect of treatment (see the lower left part of the figure), the plot will be asymmetric.

Many other reasons for funnel plot asymmetry have been suggested, but a rigorous simulation study exploring the impact of several explanations on the impact of funnel plot asymmetry is lacking. Hence, the relevance of funnel plots for evaluating completeness of the studies included in a meta-analysis remains questionable.

Tables

The results of the critical appraisal and data extraction should be reported in *tables*. These tables should account for the validity of trials and their combinability. Notably, this includes the relevant characteristics of the participating patients, the compared treatments, and reported endpoints. The occurrence measures per treatment group should be tabulated with the effect estimate and its confidence interval for each trial. Examples are given in **Table 11–5** and **Table 11–6**.

Forest Plot

The results from the data analysis are preferably displayed as a *Forest plot* showing the effect estimates for each included study with its confidence interval and the pooled effect estimate with its confidence interval (see **Figure 11–7**). The treatment effect estimate of each trial is represented by a black square with a size that is proportional to the weight attached to the trial, while the horizontal line represents the confidence interval.

The 95% CIs would contain the true underlying effect in 95% of the repetitions if the study were redone. The solid vertical line corresponds to "no effect." If the 95% CI crosses this solid line, the effect measure concerned is not statistically significant at the conventional level of (two-sided) $P \le 0.05$. The diamond represents the combined treatment effect. The horizontal width of the diamond represents its confidence interval.

The dashed line is plotted vertically through the combined treatment effect. When all confidence intervals cross this plotted line, the trials are rather homogeneous. Ratio measures (e.g., risk, odds or rate [hazard] ratios) of effect are typically plotted on a logarithmic scale, the reason being that in that case confidence intervals are displayed symmetrically around the point estimate. An example is given in **Figure 11–8**.

TABLE 11-5 Example of Table for Reporting Results of Critical Appraisal of the Methodology of Individual Studies from a Meta-Analysis of Trials Comparing Off-Pump and On-Pump Coronary Bypass Surgery (ordered by the number of items satisfied)

Trial ID	Concealed treatment allocation	Standardized post-surgical care	Blinding of outcome assessment	Intention to treat analysis	Contamination	Attrition
Zamvar	●	●	●	●	●	●
Ascione	●	●	●	●	●	●
Puskas	●	●	●	●	●	●
Octopus	●	○	●	●	●	●
Lee	●	●	●	○	●	●
Gulielmos (1999)	○	●	○	●	●	●
Parolari	●	●	○	●	●	●
Gulielmos (2000)	○	●	○	●	●	●
Diegeler	○	○	○	●	●	●
Matata	○	○	○	●	●	●
Velissaris	○	○	○	●	●	●
Tang	○	○	○	●	●	●
Guler	○	○	○	●	○	●
Al-Ruzzeh	○	○	○	●	○	●
Vural	○	●	○	●	○	●
Baker	○	●	○	○	●	∞
Wandschneider	○	○	○	∞	●	●
Czerny	○	○	○	∞	●	●
Malheiros	○	●	○	∞	●	●
Penttilä	○	○	○	○	○	○
Krejca	○	○	○	○	○	○
Wildhirt	○	○	○	○	○	○
Czerny	○	○	○	○	∞	○
Covino	○	∞	○	○	○	○

Meaning of item ratings:

Contamination: ● ≤ 10% crossover, ∞ > 10% crossover

All other items:
- ● = bias unlikely (yes, adequate design or method)
- ∞ = bias likely (no, inadequate design or method)
- ○ = unclear (insufficient information available)

Reproduced from Nathoe HM, Coronary revascularization: stent-implantation, on pump or off pump bypass surgery? PhD thesis; Utrecht University (2004) 90-393-3739-X.

TABLE 11–6 Example of Table for Reporting Results of Data Extraction from a Meta-Analysis of the Effect of Lipid Lowering Treatment

First Author or Study	Intervention	Follow-Up (years)	Coronary Heart Disease* (%)	Mean Age (years)	Men (%)	Diabetes* (%)	Hypertension* (%)	Baseline Cholesterol (mmol/L) (%)†	Randomization (treatment/ control)	Nonfatal/ Fatal Stroke (treatment/ control)	Nonfatal/ Fatal Myocardial Infarction (treatment/ control)
Pravastatin multinational study	Pravastatin	0.5	75	55	77	0	48	6.8 (18)	530/532	0/3	0/8
Sacks	Pravastatin	5	100	59	86	15	43	5.4 (20)	2081/2078	54/78	159/211
Bertrand	Pravastatin	0.5	100	58	84	7	31	5.9 (18)	347/348	1/0	5/4
Bradford	Lovastatin	0.9	33	56	59	1	40	6.7 (24)	6582/1663	10/1	63/20
4S	Simvastatin	5.4	100	58	82	5	26	6.8 (26)	2221/2223	56/78	464/491
Athyros	Atorvastatin	3	100	59	79	20	43	6.6 (32)	800/800	9/17	41/89
Blankenhorn	Lovastatin	2	100	58	91	0	46	6.0 (31)	123/124	0/3	4/5
Heart protection study	Simvastatin	5	65	64	75	25	31	5.9 (24)	10,269/10,267	444/585	944/1281
Holdaas	Fluvastatin	5.1	11	50	66	19	75	6.5 (14)	1050/1052	74/63‡	82/120

*Percentage of subjects per trial with the established diagnosis.
†Relative reduction of total cholesterol levels in the treatment group.
‡Includes transient ischemic attacks.

Reproduced from Briel M, Studer M, Glass TR, Bucher HC. Effects of statins on stroke prevention in patients with and without coronary heart disease: a meta-analysis of randomised controlled trials. *Am J Med* 2004;117:596–606, with permission from Elsevier.

Studies with SBP>130 mm Hg

Bak (1), 1998	1.9 (−4.78, 8.58)
Bak (2), 1998	−2.30 (−8.81, 4.21)
Balletshofer, 2005	−10.00 (−21.78, 1.78)
De Rosa (1), 2003	−2.00 (−9.50, 5.50)
De Rosa (2), 2003	−3.00 (−10.36, 4.36)
Ferrier, 2002	−6.00 (−11.11, −0.89)
Glorioso, 1999	−7.00 (−10.03, −3.97)
Hommel, 1992	−8.00 (−25.49, 9.49)
Ideda, 2004	−4.90 (−7.16, −2.64)
McDowell, 1991	−4.00 (−19.12, 11.12)
O'Callaghan, 1994	0.00 (−14.71, 14.71)
Straznicky, 1995	0.50 (−4.04, 5.04)
Subtotal	**−4.00 (−5.81, −2.18)**

Studies with SBP<=130 mm Hg

Jenkins, 2003	5.20 (−2.67, 13.07)
Kool, 1995	3.00 (−4.34, 10.34)
Lee, 2002	−1.00 (−6.52, 4.52)
Nakamura, 2001	−6.00 (−12.97, 0.97)
Shige, 2001	1.00 (−5.55, 7.55)
Tonolo, 1997	0.00 (−2.02, 2.02)
Subtotal	**0.03 (−1.91, 1.96)**

AHT Rx started at same time as statin

Foari, 2004	−4.20 (−7.27, −1.13)
Koh, 2004	5.00 (0.15, 9.85)
Subtotal	**0.20 (−8.81, 9.21)**
Overall	**−1.94 (−3.77, 0.12)**

−25   0   25

Intervention effect

FIGURE 11-7 Example of a Forest plot from a meta-analysis examining the relationship between use of statins and change in blood pressure level. Mean differences and 95% CIs in systolic blood pressure (SBP) achieved in patients who took statins compared with those who took placebo or other control treatment are shown. Separate evaluations were made for studies in which the baseline SBP was > 130 or <= 130 mm Hg. Symbols are (box) treatment effect estimate of each trial, with a size proportional to its weight; (—) CI of the treatment effect estimate of each trial (the treatment effect with 95% CI is also displayed on the right of the plot); (I) no effect on treatment; (vertical dashes) combined treatment effect; (diamond) width of the diamonds represents the CI of the combined treatment effect.

Reproduced from Strazzullo P, Kerry SM, Barbato A, Versiero M, D'Elia L, Cappuccio FP. Do statins reduce blood pressure? A meta-analysis of randomised, controlled trials. *Hypertension* 2007;49:792–8.

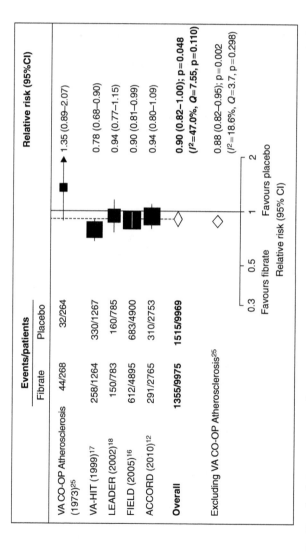

FIGURE 11–8 Results from a meta-analysis to investigate the effects of fibrates on major cardiovascular outcomes (Jun et al., 2010).

BOX 11–4   Internet Resources for Computer Software and Programs for Meta-Analysis (accessed May 17, 2013)

Cochrane Review Manager (RevMan) Information Management System (IMS): http://ims.cochrane.org/revman

Comprehensive Meta-Analysis, Biostat: http://www.meta-analysis.com

Meta-Analyst Software (download): http://www.meta-analysis-made-easy.com/index.html

EasyMA, Department of Clinical Pharmacology, Lyon, France: http://www.spc.univ-lyon1.fr/easyma.dos

StatsDirect Ltd., Cheshire, England, UK: http://www.statsdirect.com

STATA Data Analysis and Statistical Software, College Station, Texas: http://www.stata.com

MetaWin software: http://www.metawinsoft.com

DATA ANALYSIS SOFTWARE

There are many computer programs and software for meta-analyses, which usually include various methods of data analysis and allow different output in tables and graphs. A selection is given in **Box 11–4**.

INFERENCE FROM META-ANALYSIS

The decision of whether or not to apply findings from research to clinical practice is rarely based on a single study. Therefore, meta-analyses have an increasing influence on the translation and implementation of research findings to routine clinical care.

Conclusions from meta-analysis should not only concern the magnitude, direction, and precision of the summary effect estimate. The consistency of effect across trials should be related to potential sources of bias, while sources of heterogeneity between studies should be described and possibly explained.

Meta-analyses summarize the evidence from available original trials. Meta-analyses, with the exception of some IPD meta-analyses, are not designed to provide specific practice guidance for selecting patients for particular treatments. Their relevance for such guidance may be smaller than the relevance of the original data [Moses et al., 2002]. In addition, many subjective decisions are made when performing a meta-analysis. It is therefore important that value judgments are separated from reproducible methods and transparent decisions.

Meta-analyses have been criticized because they may not yield clear answers to relevant questions. The results and conclusions of many meta-analyses are considered confusing, and they are unable to provide specific guidance for practice in selecting patients for certain interventions. Still, it is important that trial results are put in the appropriate scientific and clinical context, and meta-analyses help researchers and readers do this. Without incorporating appropriate contextual information and results from other sources of evidence, there may be problems with the implementation and dissemination of the results of a meta-analysis.

Therefore, based on a transparent meta-analysis, the following categorization may be helpful in arriving at valid clinical recommendations:

- *Strong evidence*: A solid summary effect of clinically relevant magnitude, without apparent heterogeneity across a large number of exclusively high-quality trials, that is, the direction and size of effect is consistent across trials. Clinical recommendation: Treatment should be considered in all patients; effects in subgroups could still be of interest.
- *Moderate evidence*: A summary effect of clinically relevant magnitude, without apparent heterogeneity across multiple high- to moderate-quality trials, that is, the direction and size of effect is consistent across trials. Clinical recommendation: Treatment may be considered for all patients, but different subgroups effects could be of interest. Clinical consensus may be helpful.
- *Weak evidence*: A summary effect with statistical significance of clinically relevant magnitude, that is, the direction of effect is consistent across trials of moderate to low quality. Exploration for sources of heterogeneity across trials at the patient level (i.e., subgroups) or study design level appears justified. Clinical recommendation: Treatment may be considered for most patients, and different subgroup effects may be of interest. Clinical consensus could be helpful.
- *Inconsistent evidence*: The magnitude and direction of effect varies across moderate- to low-quality trials. Exploration for sources of heterogeneity across trials at the patient level (i.e., subgroups) or study design level appears justified. Clinical recommendation: Treatment may be considered for patients, but clinical consensus will be helpful.

- *Little or no evidence*: Limited number of trials of low quality. Clinical consensus is needed; research is warranted.

Evidently, these categories all pertain to beneficial effects of an intervention. If, for example, a meta-analysis reveals strong evidence that an intervention has no effect or is even harmful, then the ensuing clinical recommendations will be equally strong but clearly opposite. In this case, treatment should not be considered.

The *stainless steel law* of research on treatment effects states that trials with a more rigorous design show less evidence favoring the effect of the treatment evaluated than earlier trials, if only by regression toward the mean. The same may be true for meta-analysis: The more fastidious its design, the less marked its outcome. Because original trials may be insufficient in number or their design may be flawed, clear evidence may not exist and uncertainty remains. However, a well-designed and well-executed meta-analysis effectively maps the sources of uncertainty. Although meta-analysis includes an explicit approach to the critical appraisal of a study design, it is not a formal method of criticizing existing research. Nonetheless, meta-analysis can be extremely helpful when establishing the research agenda, thereby directing the design of new studies.

Chapter 12

Clinical Epidemiologic Data Analysis

INTRODUCTION

The critically essential stages of designing clinical epidemiologic research are over when the occurrence relation and the mode of data collection have been established. Design of data analysis is important because it will determine the utility of the result and should maintain the relevance and validity achieved so far. Yet, in general, there are only a few appropriate and feasible ways to analyze the data of a given study. Ideally, the design of data analysis follows naturally from the nature of the occurrence relation and the type of data collected. Similar to the design of the occurrence relation and the design of data collection, the design of data analysis in diagnostic, etiologic, prognostic, and intervention research each have their particular characteristics.

This chapter deals with elementary techniques used in data analysis. Often these techniques are sufficient to answer the research question. For more extensive information on data analysis, the reader must consult textbooks that are specifically dedicated to data analysis [Altman, 1991; Kleinbaum & Kupper, 1982] or the referred literature in the chapters on diagnostic, etiologic, prognostic, and intervention research. A simple statistical calculator, "WhatStat," can be found in Apple® iTunes® digital store.

A typical data analysis begins with a description of the population; key characteristics are provided in the first, so-called baseline table. Its format depends on the type of research that is performed. In a randomized trial, the baseline table summarizes the frequencies and levels of important prognostic variables in the randomized groups. This table is important because the reviewers and readers of the eventual publication learn about the study population and can judge the quality of the randomization. In etiologic research, the frequencies and levels of relevant characteristics (in particular potential confounders) will be summarized by categories of the determinant, while in diagnostic and prognostic research, predictors according to the disease or outcome will be shown. In the first step of data analysis, the data are reduced by giving summary estimates (e.g., mean, range, standard deviation, frequencies). Next, measures of association between the determinant(s) and the outcome of interest are calculated with corresponding 95% confidence levels. In etiologic research, the crude association measure will generally be adjusted by one or more confounding variables.

Before we deal with the data analysis steps that are performed in nearly every clinical epidemiologic study, we focus attention on how to calculate prevalence and incidence measures. Next, we cover the concept of variability in research and the way uncertainty is reflected in the description of the data. Finally, adjustment for confounding with several techniques such as stratified analysis (Mantel-Haenszel, 1959), linear, logistic, and Cox regression is explained.

MEASURES OF DISEASE FREQUENCY: INCIDENCE AND PREVALENCE

Measurement is a central issue in epidemiology. The simplest way to measure the occurrence of disease in a population is by giving the prevalence (P). The *prevalence* estimates the presence of a disease in a given population by means of a proportion. For example, the prevalence of obesity in U.S. adults participating in a particular study could be 40%. This proportion is calculated by dividing the number of subjects with a particular feature by the total number of subjects in the study. Prevalence applies only to a particular point in time and can change when time passes. To appreciate the estimate, we have to be informed about its precision. If we repeat the study, will the estimate have the same value? The 95% confidence interval (CI) of prevalence is calculated with the formula,

$$95\% \, \text{CI} \, P = P \pm 1.96\sqrt{\left[P(1-P)/N\right]} \qquad \text{(Eq. 1)}$$

where CI is the confidence interval, P is probability, and N is the total number of study participants.

This formula can be used for all estimates that have a binomial distribution (yes/no) and that are based on large numbers. A disadvantage of this method is that it does not perform well when zeros or small numbers

BOX 12–1   Calculating the Prevalence (and Confidence Interval) of Metabolic Syndrome in 1,000 Patients with Coronary Ischemia

---

In a study population of 1,000 patients with coronary ischemia the proportion (prevalence) of patients with the metabolic syndrome is 40% (400 patients).

The 95% CI can be calculated with the traditional method of formula (1):

$$95\% \text{ CI} = 40\% \pm 1.96\sqrt{[40 \times 60/1000]} = 37\% - 43\%.$$

In comparable populations, the prevalence of diabetes will be found in the range between 37% and 43%. With the method proposed by Altman, the following calculations need to be done: P = 400/1000 = 0.40, q = 600/1000 = 0.60, and r = 400 [Altman et al., 2000b].

$A = (2 \times 400) + 1.96^2 = 803.84$

$B = 1.96\sqrt{(1.96^2 + 4 \times 400 \times 0.6)} = 60.8)$

$C = 2(1000 + 1.96^2) = 2007.68$

The 95% CI of the 40% = (A − B)/C to (A + B)/C
                      (803.84 − 60.8)/2007.68 to (803.84 + 60.8)/2007.68
                      0.37 to 0.43
                      37% to 43%

Data from Altman D, Machin D, Bryant TN, Gardner MJ. *Statistics with Confidence.* 2nd edition. BMJ Books, 2000b.

are involved. In that case, other methods have to be used that are less easy to understand but that perform much better irrespective of the numbers involved [Altman et al., 2000b]. Altman and coworkers recommended a method by which the first three quantities (A, B, and C) can be calculated (**Box 12–1**):

$$A = 2r + z^2; B = z\sqrt{(z^2 + 4rq)}; C = 2(n + z^2)$$

where r is the number of participants that has the feature, q is the proportion that does not have it, n is the total number of participants, and z (usually) is 1.96. The confidence interval for the population prevalence P is now calculated by:

(A − B)/C to (A + B)/C

Software such as Confidence Interval Analysis (CIA) [Altman et al., 2000b] dedicated to the estimation of confidence intervals is available and easy to use.

To estimate the *incidence*, two measures are commonly used: *cumulative incidence* and *incidence rate*. The cumulative incidence is the number of subjects developing the disease during a particular time period divided by the number of subjects followed for the time period. The incidence rate estimates the occurrence of disease per unit of time. The incidence rate is also called force of morbidity. The cumulative incidence is a proportion, binomially distributed, and the 95% CI can be calculated with Equation 1 or the alternative method as explained in the earlier calculations. The cumulative incidence is often interpreted as the "risk."

The incidence rate is the number of cases occurring per unit of follow-up time and can be expressed as the number of cases (I) per 1,000 (or 10,000) person-years (PY). For the prevalence and the cumulative incidence, the number of cases cannot become larger than the denominator, but in the formula of the incidence rate (IR = I/PY), the denominator has no fixed relationship with the numerator. Confidence intervals for this type of distribution can be calculated by assuming that the incidence rate has a Poisson distribution (see **Box 12–2**) [Altman, 1991]. The 95% CI of incidence rates can be easily read from a table that can be found in most statistics textbooks or on the Internet (Health Data, 2012).

BOX 12–2   Calculation of the Incidence Rate of Myocardial Infarction

In a population with a mean follow-up of 2.3 years cumulating in 9,300 person-years (PY) of follow-up, 35 patients experience a myocardial infarction.

Incidence rate (IR) = I/PY = 35/9,300 PY = 37.6/10,000 PY

In the confidence limits table for variables that have a Poisson distribution, we find that the lower border of the incidence rate (95% CI) is 24.379 and the upper border is 48.677. These are absolute numbers and have to be expressed per 10,000 PY:

24.379/9,300 PY to 48.677/9,300 PY = 26.2/10,000 PY to 52.3/10,000 PY

Data from Washington State Department of Health (2012). *Guidelines for Using Confidence Intervals for Public Health Assessment.* http://www.doh.wa.gov/Portals/1/Documents/5500/ ConfIntGuide.pdf. Accessed June 20, 2013.

DATA ANALYSIS STRATEGIES IN CLINICAL EPIDEMIOLOGIC RESEARCH

Baseline Table

In the methods section of an article, the researchers meticulously describe the study population so the readers can get acquainted with this population and judge the domain to which the results of the study pertain. In the first part of the results section, the authors describe the key characteristics in the *baseline table*. In **Box 12–3**, a baseline table is given from a study in which investigators examined the relationship between the presence of the metabolic syndrome in patients with symptomatic vascular disease and the extent of atherosclerosis [Olijhoek et al., 2004].

The baseline table provides an overview of the most important characteristics of the study population. In this example, the relationship between metabolic syndrome and the extent of vascular disease was the subject of research. For patients with and without metabolic syndrome, the relevant characteristics are summarized in the first table of the report [Olijhoek et al., 2004].

For each characteristic, either the *mean* (with standard deviation) or *frequency* is given. *Variability* is a key concept in clinical research. People differ in their characteristics and their responses to tests and treatment, so there are many sources of variability. To reduce the amount of available information, the data need to be summarized. A continuous variable (e.g., age, blood pressure) is summarized by a central measure (the mean) and a measure of variability (the standard deviation), or a *median* with an interquartile range.

The *standard deviation* (SD) characterizes the distribution of the variable and can be calculated by taking the square root of the variance. The mean ± 2 SD includes 95% of the observation distributions that are approximately normally distributed, but in non-normal and even skewed distributions at least 75% of the observations are within this range. If variables have a skewed distribution, the median will likely be a more relevant summary measure than the mean and in that event, the distribution is characterized by giving the interquartile ranges, that is, the range from the 25th (P_{25}) to the 75th (P_{75}) percentile. Interquartile values are typically more useful than the full range, as the extremes of a distribution may comprise erroneous or unlikely data (see **Figure 12–1**).

Categorical variables are summarized by giving their frequencies. For example, 70% of the population is male. Data of this type with only two possibilities (i.e., dichotomous variables) have a binomial distribution and are very common in medical research. If sample sizes are large enough, the

BOX 12–3   Baseline Characteristics of the Study Population from a Study in which the Relationship Between Metabolic Syndrome and the Extent of Vascular Disease is Determined

	Metabolic Syndrome		
	No (n = 576)	Yes (n = 469)	P value
Male gender	84	74	< 0.001
Age (years)	59 ± 10	60 ± 10	0.4
Body mass index (kg/m²)[1]	25 ± 3	28 ± 4	< 0.001
Smoking[a]	82	81	0.8
History of other vascular disease[b]	16	21	0.02
Total cholesterol (mmol/l)[2]	5.2 (4.5–5.9)	5.6 (4.8–6.2)	< 0.001
Homocysteine (μmol/l)[1]	14 ± 6	15 ± 7	0.2
Serum creatinine (μmol/l)[1]	93 ± 37	95 ± 46	0.4
Creatinine clearance (Cockcroft) ml/min[1]	76 ± 19	79 ± 22	0.01
Diabetes mellitus[c]	7	33	< 0.001
Glucose lowering agents	4	18	< 0.001
Antihypertensive drugs	25	45	< 0.001
Lipid lowering agents	38	38	0.4
Components of metabolic syndrome			
Waist circumference (cm)[1]	92 ± 9	10 ± 10	< 0.001
Blood pressure systolic (mm Hg)[1]	134 ± 21	143 ± 20	< 0.001
Blood pressure diastolic (mm Hg)[1]	78 ± 11	81 ± 10	< 0.001
HDL cholesterol (mmol/l)[2]	1.21 (1.04–1.42)	0.96 (0.83–1.11)	< 0.001
Triglycerides (mmol/l)[2]	1.33 (1.05–1.65)	2.12 (1.72–2.78)	< 0.001
Fasting serum glucose (mmol/l)[2]	5.6 (5.2–5.9)	6.2 (5.6–7.2)	< 0.001

All data in percentages, or as indicated: 1 mean ± standard deviation or 2 median with interquartiles range.
HDL: high-density lipoprotein.
[a]Still smoking, recently stopped smoking, or previously smoking.
[b]History of vascular disease other than qualifying diagnosis.
[c]Fasting serum glucose ≥ 7.0mmol/l or self-reported diabetes.

Reproduced from Olijhoek JK, van der Graaf Y, Banga JD, Algra A, Rabelink TJ, Visseren FL. The SMART study group. The metabolic syndrome is associated with advanced vascular damage in patients with coronary heart disease, stroke, peripheral arterial disease or abdominal aortic aneurysm. *Eur Heart J* 2004;25:342–8.

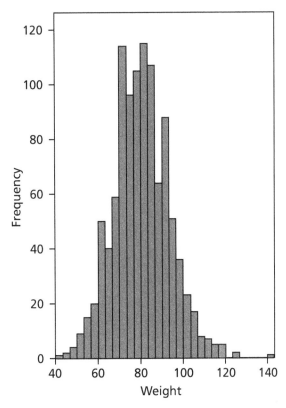

FIGURE 12–1   Plot of weight of the 1045 patients with symptomatic atherosclerosis: mean 80.25 k; SD 13.0; SEM (standard error of the mean) 0.40; median 80.0 k; interquartile range 17; P_{25} is 72 k and P_{75} is 89 k; range 42–143 k.

Reproduced from Olijoek JK, van der Graaf Y, Banga JD, Algra A, Rabelink TJ, Visseren FL; the SMART study group. The metabolic syndrome is associated with advanced vascular damage in patients with coronary heart disease, stroke, peripheral arterial disease or abdominal aortic aneurysm. *Eur Heart J* 2004;25:342–8, by permission of Oxford University Press.

binomial distribution approaches the normal distribution with the same mean and standard deviation.

Variability is not only present between subjects but also between studies. The variability of the sample is expressed by the standard error (SE) and can be calculated by dividing the population standard deviation by the square root of the number of observations.

In research, inferences about populations are made from samples. We cannot include all patients with a myocardial infarction in our study; instead we want to generalize the findings from our sample to all patients with myocardial infarction. Thus, we sample and estimate. The way we sample determines to what extent we may generalize. Generally, the results from a sample are valid for the study population from whom the sample was drawn and may be generalized to other patients or populations that are similar to the domain that is represented by the study population.

Extrapolations of inference from one population to other populations are not "hard science" but rather a matter of knowledge and reasoning and, consequently, they are subjective. Variability of the sample mean is expressed with the 95% CI of that mean that can be calculated from the SE. If the mean weight in the example given previously is 80.25 kilograms and the SE of the mean is 0.40, the upper and lower limits of the 95% CI can be calculated as $80.25 - (1.96 \times 0.40)$ and to $80.25 + (1.96 \times 0.40)$, respectively. This infers that the real population mean will be somewhere between 79.5 and 81.0 kilograms.

The 95% CI (or the precision of a study result) indicates the reproducibility of measurements and reflects the range of values that estimates can have when studies are repeated. If a study was repeated again and again, the 95% CI would contain the true effect in 95% of the repetitions. A confidence interval for an estimated mean extends either side of the mean by a multiple of the standard error. The 95% CI is the range of values from mean $- 1.96$ SE to mean $+ 1.96$ SE. SEs can also be used to test the statistical significance of a difference between groups.

A common statistical test for continuous variables is the *unpaired* t-*test*, for example, to estimate the significance of a difference in age between patients with and without the metabolic syndrome. When a continuous variable is compared before and after the intervention, a paired *t*-test is done. Paired and unpaired *t*-tests assume that the difference (paired or between groups) represents a simple shift in mean, with the variation remaining the same (same standard deviation). Under these assumptions, the *t*-tests are approximately valid as long as the sample size is sufficiently large, even for a skewed distribution. However, in the case of skewed distributions, the difference between groups is typically reflected in a shift in mean as well as a change in standard deviation: Often the standard deviation then increases with increasing mean. The most appropriate solution in most cases is to apply a transformation, for example, to analyze the data on logarithmically transformed values. Then results can be represented in relative instead of absolute changes. In the event that normality is very unlikely, nonparametric variants of the paired and unpaired *t*-tests can be chosen, such as the Mann-Whitney U-test. Note, however, that for this test too the assumption is that the difference represents a simple shift in mean, with the variation remaining the same. To compare categorical variables, cross-tables with corresponding chi-square analyses are chosen. In general, however, epidemiologists prefer an estimation of a particular parameter and description of its precision with a 95% CI instead of performing tests. We return to this issue later in this chapter.

In a randomized clinical trial the baseline table presents the most important prognostic factors according to the treatment arm. Here, differences should not be tested for statistical significance and P values should not be calculated, as differences in distributions between treatments reflect chance by definition [Knol et al., 2012].

THE RELATIONSHIP BETWEEN DETERMINANT AND OUTCOME

Continuous Outcome

In many studies, the outcome is a continuous variable such as blood pressure or body weight. In the previously mentioned example in which the relationship between the presence of metabolic syndrome and the extent of vascular disease in patients with symptomatic atherosclerosis was investigated, the extent of vascular damage was measured by ultrasound scanning of the carotid artery intima media thickness (IMT), the percentage of patients with a decreased ankle-brachial blood pressure index, and the percentage of patients with albuminuria. As a first step in the comparison of the IMT of the patients with and without the metabolic syndrome, the mean IMT and its standard deviation and standard error are calculated for both groups. The mean IMT in patients with the metabolic syndrome was 0.98 mm and in patients without the syndrome 0.92 mm (see **Table 12–1**).

The standard deviation gives an impression of the underlying distribution in the two groups. The mean $\pm$ 2 SD covers 95% of the observations in that population. The mean $\pm$ 1.96 SE reflects the variability of the population mean, as shown in the SPSS® (SPSS, Inc., Chicago, IL) output in **Table 12–2**.

TABLE 12–1 Intima Media Thickness (in mm) Data for Metabolic Syndrome

Metabolic Syndrome	N	Mean	Standard Deviation	Standard Error of the Mean
No	576	.9159	.33258	.01386
Yes	469	.9754	.34362	.01587
Total	1,045	.9426	.33871	.01048

TABLE 12-2   Independent Samples Test: Intima Media Thickness in Patients With and Without Metabolic Syndrome

		Levene's Test for Equality of Variances		t-Test for Equality of Means					95% Confidence Interval of the Difference	
		F	Significance	t	df	Significance (2-tailed)	Mean difference	Standard error difference	Lower	Upper
Mean intima media thickness (mm)	Equal variances assumed	4.242	0.040	2.831	1043	0.005	0.05944	0.02100	0.01824	0.10063
	Equal variances not assumed			2.821	986,901	0.005	0.05944	0.02107	0.01810	0.10078

The *t*-test for unpaired samples estimates the likelihood that the means are really different from each other, rather than the difference being due chance. From the SPSS output in Table 12–2, we can read that there are two possible answers. The first line gives the results if we assume the variance to be equal and the second line if variances are not assumed to be equal. Whatever we assume here, although the variances are not equal in this situation, the conclusion is that the IMTs are different and that the mean difference of 0.059 mm is statistically significantly and different from zero. Whether this also reflects a clinically relevant difference is an entirely different matter.

If we need to adjust our result for confounding variables (e.g., age and sex), there are several possibilities. We can adjust the mean IMT in both groups for age and sex with a general linear model procedure (PlanetMath, 2012a). It will provide us with adjusted mean IMTs in both groups that cannot be explained by differences in age and sex between the patients with and without the metabolic syndrome (see **Table 12–3**).

If we want to quantify the differences between the two groups (with and without metabolic syndrome), we can also perform a linear regression in which we define IMT as a dependent variable and the metabolic syndrome as a "yes/no" (1/0) independent variable (PlanetMath, 2012b).

The regression coefficient of metabolic syndrome is 0.059 (see **Table 12–4**), which means that in patients with the metabolic syndrome the mean IMT is 0.059 mm thicker. Exactly the same number is obtained when subtracting the mean IMT in patients with and without the metabolic syndrome. Using the same approach, we can now adjust for confounders such as gender and sex and directly obtain an adjusted difference (see **Table 12–5**).

The regression coefficient changed after adjusting for age and gender from 0.059 to 0.061. This means that in patients with the metabolic syndrome, the mean IMT is 0.061 mm thicker when differences in age and

TABLE 12–3   Intima Media Thickness (in mm) According to Metabolic Syndrome, Taking Gender and Age into Account as Possible Confounders, Using a General Linear Model Procedure

Metabolic syndrome	Mean	Standard error	95% Confidence Interval Lower boundary	Upper boundary
No	0.915[a]	0.013	0.890	0.941
Yes	0.976[a]	0.014	0.948	1.005

[a]Covariates appearing in the model are evaluated at the following values: gender = 1.21, age = 59.66.

TABLE 12–4 Relationship Between Metabolic Syndrome and Intima Media Thickness, Using Linear Regression Analysis

Model		Unstandardized Coefficients[a]		Standardized Coefficients[a]	t	Significance	95% Confidence Interval for Beta	
		B	Standard Error	Beta			Lower boundary	Upper boundary
1	Constant	0.916	0.014		65.118	0.000	0.888	0.944
	Metabolic syndrome	0.059	0.021	0.087	2.831	0.005	0.018	0.101

[a]Dependent variable: mean intima media thickness (mm).

TABLE 12–5 Relationship Between Metabolic Syndrome and Intima Media Thickness, Taking Confounding by Age and Gender into Account, Using Linear Regression

Model		Unstandardized Coefficients[a]		Standardized Coefficients[a]	t	Significance	95% Confidence Interval for Beta	
		B	Standard Error	Beta			Lower boundary	Upper boundary
1	Constant	0.290	0.064		4.526	0.000	0.164	0.416
	Metabolic Syndrome	0.061	0.020	0.090	3.114	0.002	0.023	0.099
	Gender	-0.089	0.024	-0.106	-3.693	0.000	-0.136	-0.042
	Age	0.012	0.001	0.367	12.838	0.000	0.010	0.014

[a]Dependent variable: mean intima media thickness (mm).

gender are taken into account. The section on linear regression later in this chapter explains the principles of this type of analysis. The SPSS output presents the unstandardized coefficient and the standardized coefficients. The latter refers to how many standard deviations a dependent variable will change per standard deviation increase in the predictor. Standardization of the coefficient is usually done to determine which of the independent variables have a greater effect on the dependent variable in a multiple regression analysis, when the variables are measured in different units of measurement. However, the validity of this interpretation is subject to debate, if only because the coefficients are unitless [Simon, 2010].

Discrete Outcome

In medicine, often the outcome of interest is a simple "yes/no" event or continuous data are categorized in a structure that permits a "yes/no" outcome. Instead of calculating the difference in blood pressure levels between two groups, we can compare the percentage of patients above or below a particular cut-off level. The study design dictates the data analysis "recipe." In a longitudinal study, such as a cohort study, absolute risks and relative risks can be calculated, while in most case-control studies the odds ratios should be calculated.

Relative risks can be easily calculated with a hand-held calculator. The simplest layout for data obtained in a cohort study is summarized in **Table 12–6**, if we assume there is no differential follow-up time.

The absolute risk (cumulative incidence) for disease in the people with the determinant is $R_+ = a/(a + b)$, while the absolute risk in people without the determinant is $R_- = c/(c + d)$.

From these absolute risks, the relative risk (RR) can be calculated by dividing both absolute risks:

$$RR = \frac{a/(a+b)}{c/(c+d)}$$

TABLE 12–6   Data Layout in a Cohort Study

Determinant	Disease During Follow-Up	
	Yes	*No*
Present	a	b
Not present	c	d

The formula for the standard error is given here, and the 95% CI of the relative risk is calculated from Equation 2:

$$SE_{lnRR} = \sqrt{b/a(a+b) + d/c(c+d)}$$

$$95\% \text{ CI RR} = e^{lnRR \pm 1.96\sqrt{[b/a(a+b)+d/c(c+d)]}} \tag{Eq. 2}$$

An example of a cohort study examining the association between previous myocardial infarction and future vascular events including calculation of the relative risk with confidence interval is shown in **Box 12–4**. The sampling in a typical case-control study conducted in a dynamic population of unknown size permits no direct calculation of absolute risks. Instead, the odds ratio can be calculated. The odds ratio is the ratio of exposure to nonexposure in cases and controls (**Table 12–7**). The odds ratio obtained in case-

---

BOX 12–4   Example of a Cohort Study on Prior Myocardial Infarction and Future Vascular Events

In a cohort study (N = 3288) in which patients with vascular disease are included 218 patients experienced a vascular event within 3 years. In the table, the occurrence of the event according to a history of previous myocardial infarction (MI) is summarized.

Previous MI	Event Within 3 years		Total
	Yes	No	
Present	95	763	858
Not present	123	2307	2430

The cumulative incidence in 3 years in patients with a previous MI 95/858 = 11%, the cumulative incidence in patients without previous MI is 123/2430 is 5%. The relative risk (RR) is the ratio of both risks ($R_{previousMI}$ = 95/858 divided by $R_{nopreviousMI}$ = 123/2430) = 2.1874. The

$SE_{lnRR} = \sqrt{[763/95(95+763) + 2307/123(123+2307)]}$ is 0.13 and the 95%

CI RR = $e^{ln2.2 \pm 1.96\sqrt{[763/95(95+763)+2307/123(123+2307)]}}$ = $e^{0.78845 \pm 0.25607}$ = e 1.7 – 2.8. The relative risk in the underlying population will be between 1.7 – 2.8. Patients with symptomatic vascular disease and a previous MI have 2.19 times the risk compared with patients with symptomatic disease without previous MI.

TABLE 12–7   Data Layout in a Case-Control Study

Determinant	Cases	Controls
Present	a	b
Not present	c	d

control studies is a valid estimate of the incidence rate ratio one would obtain from a cohort study, provided that the controls are appropriately sampled. However, in cohort studies and randomized clinical trials, odds ratios are often also interpreted as risk ratios. This is problematic because an odds ratio always overestimates the risk ratio, and this overestimation becomes larger with increasing incidence of the outcome [Knol et al., 2012].

The odds ratio for being exposed versus nonexposed is a/c in the cases and b/d in the controls (Box 12–4). The odds ratio (OR) is the ratio of the two odds:

$$OR = \frac{a/c}{b/d} = ad/bc$$

The formulas for the standard error of the odds ratio and the 95% CI (Equation 3) are given here. Note that a logarithmic transformation is needed just like when calculating the SE of the relative risk.

$$SE_{\ln OR} = \sqrt{[1/a + 1/b + 1/c + 1/d]}$$

$$95\% \, CI_{OR} = e^{\ln OR \, \pm \, 1.96\sqrt{[1/a+1/b+1/c+1/d]}} \tag{Eq. 3}$$

An example of a case-control study assessing the relationship between the use of oral contraceptives and the occurrence of peripheral arterial disease, including calculations of the odds ratio with confidence interval, is shown in **Box 12–5**.

PROBABILITY VALUES OR 95% CONFIDENCE INTERVALS

Epidemiologists generally prefer to estimate the magnitude of a difference in a variable between populations and obtain a measure of the precision of this estimate, as opposed to merely conducting significance testing. This view contrasts with that of those who are in favor of hypothesis testing. In *hypothesis testing*, the researcher ascertains whether the observed difference could have occurred purely by chance. This probability is given

BOX 12–5   Example of a Case-Control Study on Oral Contraceptive and Peripheral
Arterial Disease

The following data are taken from a study that investigated the relationship
between oral contraceptive use and the occurrence of peripheral arterial disease
[Van den Bosch, et al., 2003]. Of the women with peripheral arterial disease
(n = 39), 18 (46%) used oral contraceptives, while of the 170 women without
peripheral arterial disease only 45 (26%) used oral contraceptives. The layout of
the data table is as follows:

Oral Contraceptive Use	Peripheral Arterial Disease		
	Yes	No	
Yes	18	45	
No	21	125	OR = 2.4

The odds ratio for having peripheral arterial disease is

$(18 \times 125)/(21 \times 45) = 2.4$. The $SE_{ln2.4} = \sqrt{[1/18 + 1/45 + 1/21 + 1/125]}$

$95\%\ CI_{OR} = e^{ln2.4 \pm 1.96\sqrt{[1/18 + 1/45 + 1/21 + 1/125]}} = 1.17 - 4.90$. The odds ratio of 2.4
means that women who use oral contraceptives have 2.4 times the risk to
develop peripheral arterial disease compared to women who do not use oral
contraceptives. If we repeat the study 100 times, the odds ratio will have a value
of between 1.17 and 4.90 in 95 out of 100 studies.

Adapted from Van den Bosch MA, Kemmeren JM, Tanis BC, Mali WP, Helmerhorst FM, Rosendaal
FR, Algra A, van der Graaf Y. The RATIO Study: oral contraceptives and the risk of peripheral
arterial disease in young women. *J Thromb Haemost* 2003;1: 439–444.

by the *P* value. Hypothesis testing starts from the assumption that the
observed difference is not a real difference, but rather produced by chance;
this is called the *null hypothesis*. Subsequently, one calculates the probability of the observed difference being due to chance. If the *P* value is lower
than the predetermined value (typically 0.05), the inference is that the
observed difference is real and is not explained by chance, and thus the
null hypothesis is rejected.

Authors of current epidemiologic and statistical studies favor the use of
confidence intervals rather than *P* values [Gardner & Altman, 1987; Goodman, 1999]. Many journals (but in our view still too few) discourage the use
of *P* values [Lang et al., 1998]. The *P* value tells us only whether there is a
statistically significant difference or not and provides little information
about the size of the difference. For the same clinically relevant difference

and standard deviation, the *P* value can be very low if the populations are large or high if the populations are small. Similarly, a difference can be highly statistically significant but clinically irrelevant if the size of the study is large. The 95% CIs present a range of values that tell us about the size of difference in outcomes between two groups and allow us to draw our own conclusions about the relevance and utility of the study result. Most importantly, confidence intervals retain information on the scale of the measurement itself.

ADJUSTMENT FOR CONFOUNDING

Detecting the presence and effect of possible extraneous determinants (i.e., confounders) is critical to obtaining valid results in etiologic studies. In this section, a simple method to deal with confounding in the analysis phase is introduced. However, in real life, the situation is often much more complicated than in the examples provided in this chapter. Generally, several confounders must be taken into account that can only be handled with modeling techniques, so the use of statistical software is necessary. The Mantel-Haenszel procedure (explained in this section) can be used without a computer and can provide a great deal of insight into the process of adjustment for confounding.

Stratified Analysis

One way to address confounding is to do a *stratified analysis*, where the data are analyzed in strata of the confounding variable. Consequently, in each stratum, the effect of the confounder is removed and the determinant–outcome relationship is estimated conditional on the confounder. The effect estimates for the relationship between determinant and outcome are calculated in each stratum. Next, the investigator compares the magnitude of the strata-specific estimates before they are pooled in one summary estimate. Strata-specific estimates can only be pooled when they are more or less comparable and have the same direction and magnitude. If not, effect modification is likely to be present. Then, the relationship has to be expressed for each stratum of the effect modifier, and calculation of a single overall summary estimate may be of limited use. Note that in that situation, confounding may still need to be removed from each stratum.

   To estimate the degree of confounding, the crude effect estimate is calculated and compared with the pooled estimate adjusted for the confounding variable. The pooled estimate, according to Mantel-Haenszel method, is calculated with the following formula:

$$OR_{MH} = \Sigma(a_i d_i / N_i) / \Sigma(b_i c_i / N_i) \tag{Eq. 4}$$

In **Box 12–6**, the Mantel-Haenszel procedure is applied in the same case-control study on oral contraceptives and peripheral arterial disease risk presented earlier, to adjust for the confounder age.

Typically, the presence and extent of confounding is best detected by comparing crude to adjusted estimates of the relation (Box 12–6). Similarly, the Mantel-Haenszel Risk Ratio and the Mantel-Haenszel Risk Difference can be calculated in randomized trials and cohort studies. With the spreadsheet made available by Rothman [2012], the different Mantel-Haenszel effect

---

BOX 12–6   Adjustment for the Confounder Age, Using the Mantel-Haenszel Approach in a Case-Control Study on Oral Contraceptive Use and the Occurrence of Peripheral Arterial Disease

---

Mantel-Haenszel odds ratio for peripheral arterial disease (PAD) in relation to oral contraceptive use in women [Van den Bosch et al., 2003].

Age (years)	Oral Contraceptive Use	PAD Patients	Control Subjects	
< 40	Yes	25	249	
	No	7	223	$OR_{<40} = 3.0$
40–44	Yes	18	45	
	No	21	125	$OR_{40-44} = 2.4$
> 45	Yes	35	54	
	No	36	220	$OR_{>45} = 3.9$
All	Yes	78	348	
	No	64	568	$OR_{crude} = 2.0$

The odds ratios in the different age strata for age are 3.0, 2.4, and 3.9 respectively. The age-adjusted odds ratio (3.2) is quite different from the crude (2.0) odds ratio. This implies that age confounds the relationship between oral contraceptive use and the occurrence of peripheral arterial disease.

$$OR_{MH} = \frac{(25 \times 223)/504 + (18 \times 125)/209 + (35 \times 220)/345}{(7 \times 249)/504 + (21 \times 45)/209 + (36 \times 54)/345} = 3.2$$

Adapted from Van den Bosch MA, Kemmeren JM, Tanis BC, Mali WP, Helmerhorst FM, Rosendaal FR, Algra A, van der Graaf Y. The RATIO Study: oral contraceptives and the risk of peripheral arterial disease in young women. *J Thromb Haemost* 2003;1: 439–444.

measures can be easily calculated. There are other ways to adjust for confounding. Health statistics make use of so-called direct or indirect *standardization techniques* to control for differences in, for example, the age distribution, but in clinical epidemiology, direct and indirect standardization techniques are hardly ever used. A good description of the technique can be found in the work of Hennekes and Buring [1987].

Regression Analysis

In the event of one or two confounding variables and sufficient data, the Mantel-Haenszel technique is suitable for adjustment for confounding. If there are more confounders involved, the database quickly will not be of sufficient size to perform a stratified analysis. To overcome this problem, a regression technique such as linear regression, logistic regression, and Cox regression can be used (PlanetMath, 2007). The occurrence relation and the type of the outcome variable largely determine the choice of the technique. If the outcome is measured on a continuous scale (blood pressure, weight, etc.), linear regression analysis will be the first choice. If the outcome is dichotomous (yes/no), logistic regression is usually chosen, while if time-to-event is the outcome (survival), a Cox model will be used to estimate the effect measure. When logistic regression is chosen, the effect measure is expressed as an odds ratio. Odds ratios can be interpreted as risk ratios if the outcome occurs in less than 10% of the participants. If the incidence of the outcome is higher than 10%, other methods have to be used to estimate risk ratios such as log-binomial regression or Poisson regression [Knol et al., 2012]. Both methods are available in SPSS, SAS, R, and Stata [Lumley et al., 2006, Spiegelman & Hertzmark, 2005].

Linear Regression

Techniques for fitting lines to data and checking how well the line describes the data are called *linear regression methods*. With linear regression, we can examine the relationship between a change in the value of one variable (X) and the corresponding change in the outcome variable (Y).

The simple linear regression model assumes that the relationship between outcome and determinant can be summarized as a straight line. The line itself is represented by two numbers, the intercept (where the line crosses the *y*-axis) and the slope. The values of intercept and slope are estimated from the data.

Outcome (Y) = intercept + $b_1 X_1$ (Eq. 5)

In the observed relationship between IMT and age (**Box 12–7**) several confounders that differ in subjects with different ages and also have a

BOX 12–7   Age and Intima Media Thickness in Patients with Symptomatic
Atherosclerosis

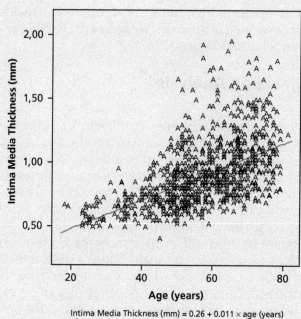

Intima Media Thickness (mm) = 0.26 + 0.011 × age (years)
$R^2 = 0.29$

In 1000 patients with symptomatic atherosclerosis the relationship between intima
media thickness (IMT) of the carotid artery and age (in years) is investigated. The
intercept is 0.26 and the coefficient of age is 0.01. The interpretation of the coefficient is that with each year increase in age the mean IMT increases 0.01 mm. The
R^2 is a measure for the variation in Y (IMT) that is explained by X (age). The precision of the coefficient is expressed with the 95% CI. The lower limit of the 95% CI
(0.010) means that if we repeat this study generally the coefficient for age will not
be below 0.010 (in 95 out of 100 studies).

Coefficients[a]

Model		Unstandardized Coefficients		Standardized Coefficients			95% Confidence Interval for B	
		B	Standard error	Beta	t	Signi-ficance	Lower boundary	Upper boundary
1	Constant	0.260	0.034		7.700	0.000	0.193	0.326
	Age (years)	0.011	0.001	0.542	19.458	0.000	0.010	0.012

[a]Dependent variable: intima media thickness (mm).

relationship with IMT can play a role, for example, sex. With regression analysis we can control for confounding in an easy way by including the confounder in the regression model. Assuming that we have enough data, we can extend Equation 5 with several confounders.

$$\text{Outcome (Y)} = \text{intercept} + b_1X_1 + b_2X_2 + b_3X_3 + \cdots \qquad \text{(Eq. 6)}$$

We have extended our analysis by including sex in the regression model. In this example, the coefficient of age does not materially change, which means that sex is not a confounder in the relationship between IMT and age (**Table 12–8**).

The first step in fitting a regression line is always inspection of the data. Just plot Y and X; the shape of the plot may suggest whether or not a straight-line equation is appropriate. Rather than linear, the most likely line may be log-linear. In that case, log transformation of the variables can be a solution. A plot also gives insight in outlying data points. Generally, it is not desirable for one or two outliers to determine the fitted regression line and after carefully examining the possible reasons for the deviant data points, removal of the outliers may be preferred. An impression of the variability of the outcome can be obtained by looking at the confidence interval curves of the fitted line.

When reporting results, the author should give the reader enough information and report the regression equation, the variances of the coefficients, and the residual variance of the regression model in diagnostic and prognostic studies. In etiologic studies the beta coefficient and the variance of the coefficient are reported.

In the relationship between IMT and age, we deal with two continuous variables, and the coefficient is the unit change of Y when X changes with one unit. In the event of a dichotomous variable, the coefficient represents the difference in Y in the two categories of the variable. For example, if we are interested in the relationship between IMT and gender, we can estimate the regression coefficient for sex (**Table 12–9**). The coefficient is -0.096 for sex, meaning that the mean IMT in women is 0.096 mm smaller than the mean IMT value in males. This value is exactly the same as when the mean of the IMT value for males and females would have been simply subtracted. The advantage of calculating this mean by regression modeling is that the model can be expanded by adding confounders, the result being an adjusted mean. Note that the value may become different from simple subtraction once other variables have been added to the regression model to adjust for confounding.

Logistic Regression

Linear regression is indicated when the outcome parameter of interest is continuous. The dependent variable can either be continuous or dichotomous. When the outcome is discrete (e.g., diseased/nondiseased), *logistic*

TABLE 12–8 Relationship Between Age and Intima Media Thickness in Patients with Atherosclerosis, Adjusting for Sex

Model		Unstandardized Coefficients[a]		Standardized Coefficients[a]				95% Confidence Interval for Beta	
		B	Standard error	Beta	t	Significance		Lower boundary	Upper boundary
1	Constant	0.247	0.034		7.269	0.000		0.180	0.313
	Age (years)	0.011	0.001	0.528	18.730	0.000		0.010	0.012
	Sex	0.044	0.016	0.078	2.766	0.006		0.013	0.074

[a]Dependent variable: intima media thickness (mm).

TABLE 12–9 Relationship Between Sex and Intima Media Thickness

Model		Unstandardized Coefficients[a]		Standardized Coefficients[a]				95% Confidence Interval for Beta	
		B	Standard error	Beta	t	Significance		Lower boundary	Upper boundary
1	Constant	0.836	0.015		55.831	0.000		0.806	0.865
	Sex	0.096	0.018	0.172	5.255	0.000		0.060	0.132

[a]Dependent variable: intima media thickness (mm).

regression analysis is suitable. Logistic regression is very popular because in medicine the outcome variable of interest is often the presence or absence of disease or can be transformed into a "yes" or "no" variable. A regression model in this situation does not predict the value Y for a subject with a particular set of characteristics (as in linear regression), but rather predicts the proportion of subjects with the outcome for any combination of characteristics. The difference between linear regression and logistic regression is that instead of predicting the exact value of the dependent variable, a transformation of the dependent variable is predicted. The transformation used is the logit transformation. The formula of the logistic model is:

$$\ln [Y/(1 - Y)] = b_0 + b_1 X_1 \tag{Eq. 7}$$

where Y is the proportion of subjects with the outcome (e.g., the probability of disease); $(1 - Y)$ is the probability that they do not have the disease, $\ln [Y/(1 - Y)]$ is the logit or log (odds) of disease, b_0 is the intercept, and X_1 is one of the independent variables.

From the regression model, we can directly obtain the odds ratio because the coefficient (b_1) in the regression model is the natural logarithm of the odds ratio. This is a major reason for the popularity of the logistic regression model. Computer packages not only give the coefficients but also the odds ratios and corresponding confidence limits. The 95% CI in the output in **Box 12–8** shows that 1 is not included in the interval, meaning that the relationship between smoking and the presence of cardiovascular disease is significant at the 5% level. Odds ratios are generally expressed in literature by giving the value and corresponding 95% CIs, for example, OR is 1.9 (95% CI 1.5–2.3). In the example in Box 12–8, the independent variable is entered as a discrete variable (yes/no), but variables with more categories or continuous variables can also be included in a logistic regression model.

In the example in **Table 12–10**, smoking has three categories—present smoker, former smoker, never smoker; the never-smoker is chosen as reference category. The outcome is coronary disease.

Some computer packages (e.g., the SPSS statistical software program) create so-called *dummies* when variables have more categories. In other packages, the user has to define the dummies before the variables can be included in the model. If a variable has three categories, two new variables are needed to translate that variable into a "yes/no" variable. If categorical variables are entered without recoding dummies in the model, the model will consider the covariate as if it was a continuous variable. Now the regression coefficient applies to a unit change, for example, from never smoking (0) to former smoker (1), or from former smoker (1) to present smoker

BOX 12–8 Smoking Link with Cardiac Disease, Logistic Regression Analysis

In a cross-sectional study of 3,000 subjects, we estimated the relationship between smoking and the presence of coronary disease with logistic regression analysis.

Variables in the equation

		B	Standard Error	Wald	df	Significance	Exp (B)	95% CI for Exp (B) Lower	Upper
Step	Smoking	0.641	0.105	37.641	1	0.000	1.899	1.547	2.330
	Constant	−1.550	0.095	267.521	1	0.000	0.212		

Variable(s) entered on step 1: smoking.

The regression equation for the model with one variable (smoking) is:
Logit (coronary disease) = −1.150 + 0.641 (smoking)
With this equation we can calculate the odds of coronary disease for smokers and for nonsmokers:
For smokers: logit (coronary disease) = −1.150 + 0.641
For nonsmokers: logit (coronary disease) = −1.150
$Logit_{(smokers)} - logit_{(nonsmokers)} = 0.641$
$Odds\ ratio_{(smokers)} = e^{0.641}\ 5\ 1.89$

(2). Such a single coefficient, however, makes no sense. Creating dummies is more useful and is also simpler. Two new variables can be defined as smoking1 and smoking2, where smoking1 is 0 except when the subject is a former smoker and smoking2 is 0 except when the subject is a present smoker. The following possibilities appear:

- Smoking1 (dummy former smoker) = 0 and Smoking2 (dummy present smoker) = 0: the subject is a never smoker
- Smoking1 (dummy former smoker) = 1 and Smoking2 (dummy present smoker) = 0: the subject is a former smoker
- Smoking1 (dummy former smoker) = 0 and Smoking2 (dummy present smoker) = 1: the subject is a present smoker

Many dependent variables are continuous and generally it is not preferable to categorize a variable that is measured on a continuous scale because information will be lost. For example, if we determine the association

TABLE 12–10 Smoking (in Three Categories) and Coronary Artery Disease

	B	Standard Error	Wald	df	Significance	Exp (B)	95.0% CI for Exp (B)	
							Lower	Upper
Step 1[a]								
Smoking			72.118	2	0.000			
Former smoker	0.332	0.122	7.365	1	0.007	1.394	1.097	1.772
Present smoker	0.861	0.110	61.021	1	0.000	2.366	1.906	2.936
Constant	−1.550	0.095	267.521	1	0.000	0.212		

[a]Variables entered on step 1: smoking

For former smokers: logit (coronary disease) = −1.150 + 0.332

For present smokers: logit (coronary disease) = −1.150 + 0.861

For nonsmokers: logit (coronary disease) = −1.150

$\text{Logit}_{(former\ smokers)} - \text{logit}_{(nonsmokers)} = 0.332$ $\text{Odds ratio}_{(former\ smokers)} = e^{0.332} = 1.39$

$\text{Logit}_{(present\ smokers)} - \text{logit}_{(nonsmokers)} = 0.861$ $\text{Odds ratio}_{(present\ smokers)} = e^{0.861} = 2.36$

TABLE 12–11   Weight and the Risk of Coronary Disease

	Beta	Standard error	Wald	df	Significance	Exp (Beta)	95.0% CI for Exp (Beta) Lower	Upper
Step 1ᵃ Weight	0.008	0.003	08.554	1	0.003	1.008	1.003	1.013
Constant	−1.676	0.223	56.317	1	0.000	0.187		

ᵃVariable(s) entered on step 1: weight

between weight (in kilograms) and coronary disease (yes/no), the output is shown in **Table 12–11**.

The coefficient of weight is 0.008 and the odds ratio (Exp B) is 1.008. This means that for each kilogram increase in weight, the risk for coronary ischemia increases by 0.8%. Often age is treated as a continuous variable as well. In **Table 12–12**, the risk increases by 3.8% each year of increase in age.

The absolute probability (or risk) of the outcome for each subject can be directly calculated from the logistic model by substituting the determinants X1, X2, etcetera by the values measured in these patients, according to the following formula (see also **Box 12–9**):

$$P = \frac{1}{1 + e^{-(\beta_0 + \beta_1 X_1 + \beta_2 X_2 + \ldots)}}$$

Cox Regression

In many studies, not only the event but also the time to event is of interest. This event may or may not have occurred during the observation period. If an event did occur, it will have occurred at different intervals for each subject. For these type of data, linear and logistic regression techniques are not sufficient because it is not possible to include the time to event in the

TABLE 12–12   Age and the Risk of Coronary Disease

	Beta	Standard error	Wald	df	Significance	Exp (Beta)	95.0% CI for Exp (Beta) Lower	Upper
Step 1ᵃ Age	0.037	0.003	116.355	1	0.000	1.038	1.031	1.045
Constant	−3.199	0.209	234.707	1	0.000	0.041		

ᵃVariable(s) entered on step 1: age.

BOX 12–9   Age, Gender, and Cardiac Ischemia

With logistic regression, the relationship between the risk of cardiac ischemia and age and gender was examined. With each year increase in age the risk of the outcome increases 1.036 times, while males have 2.38 times the risk of women (output below). For each patient the absolute risk in the observed follow-up time for the presence of myocardial infarction can be calculated with the following formula:

$$P = \frac{1}{1 + e^{-(\beta_0 + \beta_1 X_1 + \beta_2 X_2 + \dots)}}$$

Variables in the equation

	B	Standard error	Wald	df	Significance	Exp (B)	95% CI for Exp (B) Lower	Upper
Step 1[a] Age	0.035	0.004	100.899	1	0.000	1.036	1.029	1.043
Sex	0.868	0.101	73.396	1	0.000	2.383	1.954	2.907
Constant	−3.739	0.225	275.748	1	0.000	0.024		

[a]Variable(s) entered on step 1: smoking.

The coefficients are given in the printed output. β_0 is the intercept, β_1 is the age coefficient, and β_2 is the coefficient for gender for a 60-year-old male. The risk of cardiac ischemia in the observed follow-up time is:

$$P = \frac{1}{1 + e^{-(-3.739 + 60 \times 0.035 + 0.868)}} = 31.6\%$$

model [Steenland et al., 1986]. Generally, these types of data are referred to as *survival data*, but apart from death as an outcome, all kinds of "yes/no" events (e.g., disease progression, discharge from hospital, the occurrence of an adverse event or a disease) can be analyzed with survival techniques. If only one independent variable is investigated, the Kaplan-Meier method of estimating a survival distribution can be used. If more variables have to be included in the analysis, the Cox proportional hazards regression model is needed.

A *time-to-event analysis* requires a well-defined starting point. This point, often referred to as T_0, may be (chronologically) different for all participants and is precisely defined by the researcher. Often it is the date of the baseline screening in a cohort study or the day of randomization in a clinical trial. Some participants will subsequently experience the outcome of interest and others will not. The survival function S_t describes the proportion of subjects (S) who survive beyond time (t). If death is not the outcome, the survival curve describes the proportion of subjects free from the defined outcome at t.

Censoring is a typical phenomenon that pertains to survival analysis. Subjects who do not experience the outcome during the follow-up period are censored at the end of the study period. Subjects who beyond a certain point of time are lost to follow-up (e.g., because they move to another part of the country) are also censored. Censoring should be uninformative. This means that for all subjects, the risk of being censored is independent of the risk for the event. If subjects who are going to die are more likely to be lost, censoring is not uninformative and the results of survival analysis will be biased. In the example in **Figure 12–2**, the event-free survival is plotted for patients with symptomatic atherosclerosis. Here, the event is defined as the occurrence of nonfatal myocardial infarction, nonfatal stroke, or cardiovascular death. From Figure 12–2, we can see that, for example, after 3 years the event-free survival S is 95%. The 95% CI of this proportion can be calculated from the output [SE 4.6%; 95% CI = S ± (1.96 × SE)]. If we want to investigate whether the risk of the outcome in this example is determined by sex, we make two survival plots.

In males, the 5-year event-free survival rate is 83.7%, while in females it is 92.1% (exact estimates can be read from the output). If we want to test whether event-free survival is different between the two groups, we use the log-rank test. With this test, we compare the survival distributions of males and females. In this example, the *P* value of the log-rank test was 0.0001.

Often we are interested in the simultaneous and independent effects of different variables on the survival function, for example, when we want to adjust one variable for another (see **Table 12–13**). The most common

TABLE 12–13   Sex, Age, and the Risk of Cardiovascular Events: Results from Cox Regression

	Beta	Standard error	Wald	df	Significance	Exp (Beta)	95.0% CI for Exp (Beta) Lower	Upper
Sex	0.572	0.169	11.502	1	0.001	1.772	1.273	2.466
Age > 60	1.043	0.144	52.768	1	0.000	2.839	2.142	3.762

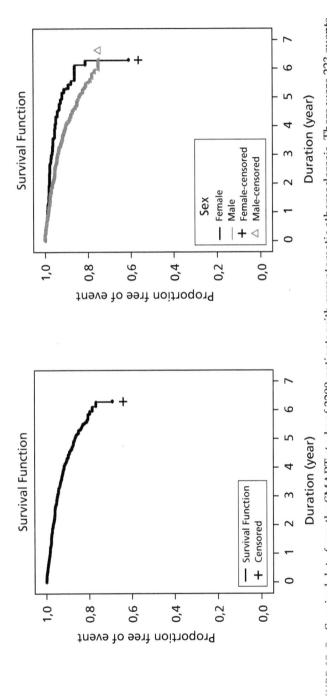

FIGURE 12–2 Survival data from the SMART study of 3200 patients with symptomatic atherosclerosis. There were 223 events.

With kind permission from Springer Science+Business Media: Simons PC, Algra A, van de Laak MF, Grobbee DE, van der Graaf Y. Second Manifestations of ARTerial disease (SMART) study: rationale and design. *Eur J Epidemiol* 1999;15:773–81.

approach for this type of analysis is the Cox proportional hazards analysis. In the Cox model it is assumed that the independent variables are related to survival time by a multiplicative effect on the hazard function. If we want to simultaneously analyze the effect of age and sex on the event-free outcome in the previously mentioned example, the Cox model assumes that the hazard function of a subject has the following expression:

$$h_0(t) \times e^{b_1 X_1 + b_2 X_2}$$

(Eq. 8)

where $h_0(t)$ is the underlying hazard; this is the proportion of subjects who fail at time t among those who have not failed previously; β_1 and β_2 are the unknown regression coefficients (for age and sex, respectively) that can be estimated from the data, and x_1 and x_2 are the values of the two variables age and sex in an individual. The hazard functions for the different subjects would have the following form if we assume a female younger than age 60 as the reference:

Female below age 60 $h_0(t)$
Female over age 60 $h_0(t) \times e^{b_2}$
Male below age 60 $h_0(t) \times e^{b_1}$
Male over age 60 $h_0(t) \times e^{b_1 + b_2}$

These hazard functions are proportional to each other, and it is not necessary to know the underlying hazard $h_0(t)$ in order to compare the four groups. From the Cox model, coefficients and their standard errors can be estimated and several computer packages generate the hazard ratios, a type of relative risk, as well.

In the computer output in Table 12–13, the results of a Cox regression are shown. An event was defined as a combined outcome of a nonfatal myocardial infarction, a nonfatal stroke, or cardiovascular death. Data were collected in a cohort of patients with elevated risk for cardiovascular disease. In this analysis, gender and age are investigated as determinants of the outcome. Females younger than age 60 are the reference group. A female older than age 60 has a hazard ratio of 2.8 (b_2, coefficient of age). This hazard ratio can be interpreted as a relative risk, meaning that, compared to women younger than 60 years of age, women older than 60 years have 2.8 times the risk for a cardiovascular event. A male younger than age 60 (b_1, coefficient of gender) has 1.7 times the risk compared to a female younger than age 60. A male older than age 60 has the coefficient of sex and age ($e^{0.572 + 1.043}$) leading to a hazard ratio of 5.0.

FREQUENTISTS AND BAYESIANS

Frequentist analysis is the most common statistical approach [Bland & Altman, 1998] and the approach to data analysis in this chapter is frequentist. Classic statistical data analysis rests on *P* values and hypothesis testing, which is rooted in the work of Fisher, Neyman, Pearson, and others in the early 19th century, building upon randomized experiments and random sampling, where random error provides the reference and hypothetical infinite replications of the experiment offer a distribution against which the observed data needs to be judged. The inference is a verdict on one assumed true parameter in real life, such as a difference in effect between treatments. Either the hypothesis (e.g., a new drug is better than a placebo) is true, for example, sufficiently certain in view of the data, or it is not. Likewise, the "verdict" is one estimate of that true parameter with a confidence interval; this too is a frequentist approach, and for most problems confidence intervals and hypothesis testing are fully consistent and lead to the same conclusions.

In general, we intuitively tend to think in the "probability" of the superiority of a particular treatment given the outcome of our experiment. Very likely, we will build our research upon previous findings or plausible mechanisms, and, as a consequence, there will be expectations (rooted in data) about the results the research will yield even before the data are available. When a difference is observed, it may not be statistically significant but yet very plausible and in agreement with findings in other research and therefore confirms our expectations. The observed difference is credible, and, despite the lack of frequentist statistical significance that may reflect the small sample or large variance, we "believe" it to be true because we merge it with prior data and expectation.

One area in which the importance of plausibility (or prior beliefs) is particularly important in judging the meaning of subsequent findings is in diagnosis.

Clinicians have prior beliefs about the benefits of treatment and these prior beliefs could influence the posterior probabilities. This way of reasoning is called Bayesian, named after the mathematician and Presbyterian minister, Thomas Bayes (1702–1761; see **Figure 12–3**) and predominantly known from the Bayes theorem published in 1764 [Bayes, 1764]. In a Bayesian statistical approach, prior beliefs are made explicit (**Box 12–10**) through a probability distribution on unknown parameters (e.g., true treatment effects).

It is not only the results of a particular study but also the already available knowledge (for example, summarized in meta-analyses) that determines the credibility or superiority of a particular treatment strategy. Importantly, as elegantly argued by Greenland [2006], frequentist as well as

The Reverend Thomas Bayes, F.R.S. — 1701?–1761
Who is this gentleman? When and where was he born?

The first correct (or most plausible) answer received in the Bulletin Editorial office in Montreal will win a prize!

This challenge was made in *The IMS Bulletin*, Vol. **17**, No. 1, January/February 1988, page 49. The photograph is reproduced, with permission, from the page facing December of the *Springer Statistics Calendar 1981* by Stephen M. Stigler (pub. Springer-Verlag, New York, 1980). It is noted there that "the date of his birth is not known: Bayes's posterior is better known than his prior. This is the only known portrait of him; it is taken from the 1936 History of Life Insurance (by Terence O'Donnell, American Conservation Co., Chicago). As no source is given, the authenticity of even this portrait is open to question". The original source of this photograph still remains unknown. The photo appears on page 335 with the caption "Rev. T. Bayes: Improver of the Columnar Method developed by Barrett. [There is a photo of George Barrett (1752-1821) on the facing page 334: "Mathematical genius and originator of Commutation Tables: Ignored by the august Royal Society in its *Transactions* because he had never gone to school." – See also comments by Stephen M. Stigler on page 278.]

The most plausible answer received in the Bulletin Editorial office is from Professor David R. Bellhouse, University of Western Ontario, London, Ontario, Canada. A prize is on its way to Professor Bellhouse, who wrote:

FIGURE 12–3   British mathematician, Reverend Thomas Bayes, whose solution to "inverse probability" was published posthumously.

Courtesy of the MacTutor History of Mathematics Archive, University of St. Andrews, Scotland, United Kingdom. Available at http://www-history.mcs.st-andrews.ac.uk/history/Biographies/ Bayes.html. Accessed July 11, 2007.

BOX 12–10   Probability

Statistics as a discipline remains sharply divided, even on the fundamental definition of "probability."

The frequentist's definition sees probability as the long-run expected frequency of occurrence. $P(A) = n/N$, where n is the number of times event A occurs in N opportunities. The Bayesian view of probability is related to degree of belief. It is a measure of the plausibility of an event given incomplete knowledge. A frequentist believes that a population mean is real, but unknown, and unknowable, and is one unique value that needs to be estimated from the data. Knowing the distribution for the sample mean, he constructs a confidence interval, centered at the sample mean.

Here it gets tricky. Either the true mean is in the interval or it is not. Thus, the frequentist cannot say there is a 95% probability that the true mean is in this interval, because it is either already in, or it is not. And that is because to a frequentist the true mean, being a single fixed value, does not have a distribution. The sample mean does. Thus, the frequentist must use circumlocutions like "95% of similar intervals would contain the true mean, if each interval were constructed from a different random sample like this one." Graphically this is illustrated here:

Bayesians have an altogether different worldview. They say that only the data are real. The population mean is an abstraction, and as such some values are more believable than others based on the data and their prior beliefs. (Sometimes the prior belief is very non-informative, however.) The Bayesian constructs a credible interval, centered near the sample mean, but tempered by "prior" beliefs concerning the mean. Now the Bayesian can say what the frequentist cannot: "There is a 95% probability that this interval contains the mean."

In summary, probability according to a frequentist can be defined as the long-run fraction having a characteristic, while according to a Bayesian it can be considered a degree of believability.

In caricature, a frequentist is a person whose long-run ambition is to be wrong 5% of the time, while a Bayesian is one who, vaguely expecting a horse, and catching a glimpse of a donkey, strongly believes he has seen a mule.

Courtesy of Charles Annis, P.E./Statistical Engineering. Available at: http://www.statisticalengineering. com/frequentists_and_bayesians.htm.

Bayesian techniques are based on models and assumptions that are subjective. Without a model and assumptions, any set of data is meaningless.

The Bayesian approach makes the subjective and arbitrary elements shared by all statistical methods explicit through a prior probability distribution. Bayesian analysis thus requires that these prior beliefs be explicitly specified. This could be done using empirical evidence available before the next study is conducted, insights into mechanisms that make the presence of an association likely, or any other belief or knowledge obtained without the data generated by the new study. One clear consequence is that Bayesian results can only be interpreted conditional on the prior belief. Hence, if there is no universal agreement on the prior belief, the same data will necessarily lead to different estimates, different credibility intervals, and different conclusions among groups that have different prior beliefs. To put it in another way, before you believe the results of a Bayesian analysis as presented in a paper you first have to commit yourself to the prior belief that was used as a basis. This problem is often avoided by using "vague" or noninformative priors, but then in fact the advantage of using directed and real prior data or belief is lost.

It has been argued that Bayesian statistical techniques are difficult, but they are not necessarily more complicated than frequentist techniques. They do require more intensive computation, even in cases that can be approximated in the frequentist setting. This is due to the fact that combining the prior distribution with the data can only be done in a straightforward analytical way under restrictive assumptions that do not allow the flexibility for prior beliefs that is needed in practice. Most current statistical computer packages are implicitly based on the frequentist's way of thinking about hypothesis testing, P values, and confidence intervals. However, even with standard frequentist software, it is possible to approximate Bayesian analyses and incorporate prior distributions of the data, for example, by inverse variance weighting of the prior information with the frequentist estimate [Greenland, 2006]. In the statistical data analysis of clinical epidemiologic data there is room for both frequentist and Bayesian approaches, with the Bayesian approach being perhaps more natural to medical reasoning [Brophy & Joseph, 1995]. To promote the use of Bayesian analyses, however, both the understanding of Bayesian concepts and analyses and the accessibility of Bayesian statistics in data analysis software packages need to be improved.

References

ADVANCE Collaborative Group. Study rationale and design of ADVANCE: Action in diabetes and vascular disease—preterax and diamicron MR controlled evaluation. *Diabetologia*. 2001;44:1118–1120.

ADVANCE Collaborative Group. Effects of a fixed combination of perindopril and indapamide on macrovascular and microvascular outcomes in patients with type 2 diabetes mellitus (the ADVANCE trial): A randomised controlled trial. *Lancet*. 2007;370:829–840.

ADVANCE Collaborative Group. Intensive blood glucose control and vascular outcomes in patients with type 2 diabetes. *N Engl J Med*. 2008;358:2560–2572.

Ahlbom A, Alfredsson L. Interaction: a word with two meanings creates confusion. *Eur J Epidemiol*. 2005;20:563–564.

Albers GW. Choice of endpoints in antiplatelet trials: Which outcomes are most relevant to stroke patients? *Neurology*. 2000;54:1022–1028.

Albert PS, Ratnasinghe D, Tangrea J, Wacholder S. Limitations of the case-only design for identifying gene-environment interactions. *Am J Epidemiol*. 2001;154:687–693.

Algra A, van Gijn J. Science unblinded [letter]. *Lancet*. 1994;343:1040.

Algra A, van Gijn J. Is clopidogrel superior to aspirin in secondary prevention of vascular disease? *Curr Control Trials Cardiovasc Med*. 2000;1:143–145.

Allain P. *Hallucinogens et Société*. Paris: Payot; 1973:184. http://www.druglibrary.org/Schaffer/hemp/history/first12000/8.htm. Accessed October 2013.

Altman DG, Andersen PK. Bootstrap investigation of the stability of a Cox regression model. *Stat Med*. 1989;8:771–783.

Altman DG. *Practical Statistics for Medical Research. Monographs on Statistics and Applied Probability* (first ed.). London, Chapman & Hall, 1991.

Altman DG, Royston P. What do we mean by validating a prognostic model? *Stat Med*. 2000a;19:453–473.

Altman DG, Machin D, Bryant TN, Gardner MJ. *Statistics with Confidence*. 2nd ed. London: BMJ Books; 2000b.

Altman DG, Vergouwe Y, Royston P, Moons KG. Prognosis and prognostic research: Validating a prognostic model. *BMJ*. 2009;338:b605. doi: 10.1136/bmj.b605.

Altman DG, McShane LM, Sauerbrei W, Taube SE. Reporting recommendations for tumor marker prognostic studies (REMARK): explanation and elaboration. *BMC Med* 2012;10:51.

Andersohn F, Suissa S, Garbe E. Use of first- and second-generation cyclooxygenase-2-selective nonsteroidal antiinflammatory drugs and risk of acute myocardial infarction. *Circulation*. 2006; 25;113:1950–1957.

Angelini GD, Taylor FC, Reeves BC, Ascione R. Early and midterm outcome after off-pump and on-pump surgery in Beating Heart Against Cardioplegic Arrest Studies (BHACAS 1 and 2): A pooled analysis of two randomised controlled trials. *Lancet.* 2002;359:1194–1199.

Antman EM, Lau J, Kupelnick B, Mosteller F, Chalmers TC. A comparison of results of meta-analyses of randomised control trials and recommendations of clinical experts. Treatments for myocardial infarction. *JAMA.* 1992;268:240–248.

Apgar V. A proposal for a new method of evaluation of the newborn infant. *Curr Res Anesth Analg.* 1953;32:260–267.

Arbous MS, Meursing AEE, van Kleef JW, et al. Impact of anesthesia management characteristics on severe morbidity and mortality. *Anesthesiology.* 2005;102:257–268.

Arbous MS, Meursing AE, van Kleef JW, Grobbee DE. Impact of anesthesia management characteristics on severe morbidity and mortality: Are we convinced? (letter). *Anesthesiology.* 2006;104:205–206.

Arends LR, Hoes AW, Lubsen J, Grobbee DE, Stijnen T. Baseline risk as predictor of treatment benefit: Three clinical meta-re-analyses. *Stat Med.* 2000;19:3497–3518.

Asch, DA, Patton JP, Hershey JC. Knowing for the sake of knowing: the value of prognostic information. *Med Decis Making.* 1990;10:47–57.

Bachmann LM, Coray R, Estermann P, Ter Riet G. Identifying diagnostic studies in MEDLINE: Reducing the number needed to read. *J Am Med Inform Assoc.* 2002;9:653–658.

Bak AA, Grobbee DE. The effect on serum cholesterol levels of coffee brewed by filtering or boiling. *N Engl J Med.*1989;321:1432–1437.

Bayes T. An essay towards solving a problem in the doctrine of chances. *Philos Trans R Soc Lond.* 1764;53:370–418.

Begg CB. Biases in the assessment of diagnostic tests. *Stat Med.* 1987;6:411–423.

Begg CB, Metz CE. Consensus diagnoses and "gold standards." *Med Decis Making.* 1990;10:29–30.

Belitser SV, Martens EP, Pestman WR, Groenwold RH, de Boer A, Klungel OH. Measuring balance and model selection in propensity score methods. *Pharmacoepidemiol Drug Saf* 2011;20:1115–29.

Berger JS, Roncaglioni MC, Avanzini F, Pangrazzi I, Tognoni G, Brown DL. Aspirin for the primary prevention of cardiovascular events in women and men: A sex-specific meta-analysis of randomised controlled trials. *JAMA.* 2006;295:306–313.

Berkey CS, Mosteller F, Lau J, Antman EM. Uncertainty of the time of first significance in random effects cumulative meta-analysis. *Control Clin Trials.* 1996;17:357–371.

Berlin JA, Santanna J, Schmid CH, Szczech LA, Feldman HI. Individual patient-versus group-level data meta-regressions for the investigation of treatment effect modifiers: Ecological bias rears its ugly head. *Stat Med.* 2002;21:371–387.

Berry SM. Understanding and testing for heterogeneity across 2 x 2 tables: Application to meta-analysis. *Stat Med.* 1998;17:2353–2369.

Biesheuvel CJ, Grobbee DE, Moons KG. Distraction from randomization in diagnostic research. *Ann Epidemiol.* 2006;16:540–544.

Biesheuvel CJ, Vergouwe Y, Oudega R, Hoes AW, Grobbee DE, Moons KG. Advantages of the nested case-control design in diagnostic research. *BMC Med Res Methodol.* 2008a;8:48.

Biesheuvel CJ, Vergouwe Y, Steyerberg EW, Grobbee DE, Moons KG. Polytomous logistic regression analysis could be applied more often in diagnostic research. *J Clin Epidemiol.* 2008b;61:125–134.

Bjelakovic G, Nikolova D, Gluud LL, Simonetti RG, Gluud C. Mortality in randomised trials of antioxidant supplements for primary and secondary prevention: Systematic review and meta-analysis. *JAMA*. 2007;297:842–857.

Bland JM, Altman DG. Statistics notes: Regression towards the mean. *BMJ*. 1994;308:1499.

Bland JM, Altman DG. Statistics notes: Bayesians and frequentists. *BMJ*. 1998;317:1151–1560.

Bleeker SE, Moll HA, Steyerberg EW, et al. External validation is necessary in prediction research: A clinical example. *J Clin Epidemiol*. 2003;56:826–832.

Boersma E, Simoons ML. Reperfusion strategies in acute myocardial infarction. *Eur Heart J*. 1997;18:1703–1711.

Bombardier C, Laine L, Reicin A, et al. VIGOR Study Group. Comparison of upper gastrointestinal toxicity of rofecoxib and naproxen in patients with rheumatoid arthritis. VIGOR Study Group. *N Engl J Med*. 2000;343:1520–1528.

Bossuyt PPM, Lijmer JG, Mol BW. Randomised comparisons of medical tests: Sometimes invalid, not always efficient. *Lancet*. 2000;356:1844–1847.

Bossuyt PM, Reitsma JB, Bruns DE, et al. Towards complete and accurate reporting of studies of diagnostic accuracy: The STARD initiative. Standards for Reporting of Diagnostic Accuracy. *Clin Chem*. 2003a;49:1–6.

Bossuyt PM, Reitsma JB, Bruns DE, et al. The STARD statement for reporting studies of diagnostic accuracy: explanation and elaboration. *Clin Chem*. 2003b;49:7–18.

Bossuyt PM, Reitsma JB, Linnet K, Moons KG. Beyond diagnostic accuracy: The clinical utility of diagnostic tests. *Clin Chem*. 2012;58:1636–1643.

Boter H, van Delden JJ, de Haan RJ, Rinkel GJ. Modified informed consent procedure: Consent to postponed information. *BMJ*. 2003;327:284–285.

Bouwmeester W, Zuithoff NP, Mallett S, Geerlings MI, Vergouwe Y, Steyerberg EW. Reporting and methods in clinical prediction research: a systematic review. *PLoS Med* 2012;9(5):1–12.

Bots ML, Hoes AW, Koudstaal PJ, Hofman A, Grobbee DE. Common carotid intima-media thickness and risk of stroke and myocardial infarction: The Rotterdam Study. *Circulation*. 1997;96:1432–1437.

Bouwmeester W, Zuithoff NP, Mallett S, at al. Reporting and methods in clinical prediction research: a systematic review. *PLoS Med*. 2012;9:1–12.

Braitman LE, Davidoff F. Predicting clinical states in individual patients. *Ann Intern Med*. 1996;125:406–412.

Bresalier RS, Sandler RS, Quan H, et al. Adenomatous Polyp Prevention on Vioxx (APPROVe) Trial Investigators. Cardiovascular events associated with rofecoxib in a colorectal adenoma chemoprevention trial. *N Engl J Med*. 2005;352:1092–1102.

Briel M, Studer M, Glass TR, Bucher HC. Effects of statins on stroke prevention in patients with and without coronary heart disease: A meta-analysis of randomised controlled trials. *Am J Med*. 2004;117:596–606.

Broders AC. Squamous-cell epithelioma of the lip. A study of 537 cases. *JAMA*. 1920;74:656–664.

Brookhart MA, Wang PS, Solomon DH, Schneeweiss S. Evaluating short-term drug effects using a physician-specific prescribing preference as an instrumental variable. *Epidemiology*. 2006;17:268–275.

Brophy JM, Joseph L. Placing trials in context using Bayesian analysis. GUSTO revisited by Reverend Bayes. *JAMA*. 1995;273:871–875.

Brotman, DJ, Walker E, Lauer MS, O'Brien RG. In search of fewer independent risk factors. *Arch Intern Med* 2005;165:138–45.

Brown CA, Lilford RJ. The stepped wedge trial design: A systematic review. *BMC Med Res Methodol.* 2006;6:54.

Bruins Slot MH, Rutten FH, van der Heijden GJ, et al. Diagnostic value of a heart-type fatty acid-binding protein (H-FABP) bedside test in suspected acute coronary syndrome in primary care. *Int J Cardiol.* 2013. doi:pii: S0167-5273(12)01679-8. 10.1016/j.ijcard.2012.12.050. [Epub ahead of print]

Büller HR, Ten Cate-Hoek AJ, Hoes AW, et al. AMUSE (Amsterdam Maastricht Utrecht Study on thromboEmbolism) Investigators. Safely ruling out deep venous thrombosis in primary care. *Ann Intern Med.* 2009;150:229–235.

Burger H, de Laet CE, Weel AE, Hofman A, Pols HA. Added value of bone mineral density in hip fracture risk scores. *Bone.* 1999;25:369–374.

Burton A, Altman DG. Missing covariate data within cancer prognostic studies: A review of current reporting and proposed guidelines. *Br J Cancer.* 2004;91:4–8.

Campbell MK, Machin D. *Medical Statistics. A Commonsense Approach.* Chichester: John Wiley and Sons; 1990.

Campbell MK, Elbourne DR, Altman DG, for the CONSORT Group. CONSORT statement: Extension to cluster randomised trials. *BMJ.* 2004;328:702–708.

Campbell MK, Piaggio G, Elbourne DR, Altman DG. Consort 2010 statement: Extension to cluster randomised trials. *BMJ.* 2012;345:e5661

Cappuccio FP, Kerry SM, Forbes L, Donald A. Blood pressure control by home monitoring: Meta-analysis of randomised trials. *BMJ.* 2004;329:145. (Errata: *BMJ.* 2004;329:499.)

Cardiac Arrhythmia Suppression Trial (CAST) Investigators. Preliminary report: Effect of encainide and flecainide on mortality in a randomized trial of arrhythmia suppression after myocardial infarction. *N Engl J Med.* 1989;321:406–412.

Casey BM, McIntire DD, Leveno KJ. The continuing value of the Apgar score for the assessment of newborn infants. *N Engl J Med.* 2001;344:467–471.

Center for Drug Evaluation and Research and Center for Biologics Evaluation and Research. 2010 Draft guidance: Guidance for industry non-inferiority trials. http://www.fda.gov/downloads/Drugs/GuidanceComplianceRegulatoryInformation/Guidances/UCM202140.pdf. Accessed April 21, 2013.

Chalmers TC, Levin H, Sacks HS, Reitman D, Berrier J, Nagalingam R. Meta-analysis of clinical trials as a scientific discipline. I: Control of bias and comparison with large co-operative trials. *Stat Med.* 1987a;6:315–28.

Chalmers TC, Berrier J, Sacks HS, Levin H, Reitman D, Nagalingam R. Meta-analysis of clinical trials as a scientific discipline. II: Replicate variability and comparison of studies that agree and disagree. *Stat Med.* 1987b;6:733–744.

Cholesterol Treatment Trialists' Collaborators. Efficacy and safety of cholesterol-lowering treatment: Prospective meta-analysis of data from 90,056 participants in 14 randomised trials of statins. *Lancet.* 2005;366:1267–1278. (Errata: *Lancet.* 2005;366:1358; *Lancet.* 2008;371:2084.)

Christensen E. Prognostic models including the Child-Pugh, MELD and Mayo risk scores—where are we and where should we go? *J Hepatol.* 2004;41:344–350.

Clark OA, Castro AA. Searching the Literatura Latino Americana e do Caribe em Ciencias da Saude (LILACS) database improves systematic reviews. *Int J Epidemiol.* 2002;31:112–114.

Clarke J, van Tulder M, Blomberg S, de Vet H, van der Heijden G, Bronfort G. Traction for low back pain with or without sciatica: An updated systematic review within the framework of the Cochrane collaboration. *Spine*. 2006;31:1591–1599.

Clarke MJ, Stewart LA. Obtaining individual patient data from randomised controlled trials. In: Egger M, Smith GD, Altman DG, eds. *Systematic Reviews in Health Care: Meta-Analysis in Context*. 2nd ed. London: BMJ Publishing Group; 2001.

Concato J. Challenges in prognostic analysis. *Cancer*. 2001;91(suppl 8):1607–1614.

Concato J, Feinstein AR, Holford TR. The risk of determining risk with multivariable models. *Ann Intern Med*. 1993;118:201–210.

Concato J, Peduzzi P, Holford TR, Feinstein AR. Importance of events per independent variable in proportional hazards analysis. I. Background, goals, and general strategy. *J Clin Epidemiol*. 1995;48:1495–1501.

Concato J, Shah N, Horwitz RI. Randomized, controlled trials, observational studies, and the hierarchy of research designs. *N Engl J Med*. 2000;342:18871–892.

Confavreux C, Suissa S, Saddier P, Bourdès V, Vukusic S; Vaccines in Multiple Sclerosis Study Group. Vaccinations and the risk of relapse in multiple sclerosis. *N Engl J Med*. 2001;344:319–326.

Connolly SJ, Eikelboom J, Joyner C, et al. AVERROES Steering Committee and Investigators. Apixaban in patients with atrial fibrillation. *N Engl J Med*. 2011;364:806–817.

Conroy RM, Pyörälä K, Fitzgerald AP, et al. Estimation of ten-year risk of fatal cardiovascular disease in Europe: the SCORE project. *Eur Heart J*. 2003;24:987–1003.

CONSORT. http://www.consort-statement.org. Updated 2010. Accessed on May 17, 2013.

Copas JB. Regression, prediction and shrinkage. *J R Stat Soc B*. 1983;45:311–354.

Cornfield JA. A method of estimating comparative rates from clinical data. Applications to cancer of the lung, breast and cervix. *J Natl Cancer Inst*. 1951;11:1269–1275.

Costantino JP, Gail MH, Pee D, et al. Validation studies for models projecting the risk of invasive and total breast cancer incidence. *J Natl Cancer Inst*. 1999;91:1541–1548.

Couser W, Drueke T, Halloran P, Kasiske B, Klahr S, Morris P. Trial registry policy. *Nephrol Dial Transplant*. 2005;20:691.

Cowling BJ, Muller MP, Wong IO, et al. Clinical prognostic rules for severe acute respiratory syndrome in low- and high-resource settings. *Arch Intern Med*. 2006;166:1505–1511.

Crawford SL, Tennstedt SL, McKinlay KB. A comparison of analytic methods for non-random missingness of outcome data. *J Clin Epidemiol*. 1995;48:209–219.

Cremer OL, Moons KG, van Dijk GW, van Balen P, Kalkman CJ. Prognosis following severe head injury: Development and validation of a model for prediction of death, disability, and functional recovery. *J Trauma*. 2006;61:1484–1491.

Criqui MH, Ringel BL. Does diet or alcohol explain the French paradox? *Lancet*. 1994;344:1719–1723.

D'Agostino RB Sr, Massaro JM, Sullivan LM. Non-inferiority trials: Design concepts and issues—the encounters of academic consultants in statistics. *Stat Med*. 2003; 22:169–186.

De Angelis C, Drazen JM, Frizelle FA, et al. International Committee of Medical Journal Editors. Clinical trial registration: A statement from the International Committee of Medical Journal Editors. *Ann Intern Med*. 2004;141:477–478.

De Angelis CD, Drazen JM, Frizelle FA, et al. International Committee of Medical Journal Editors. Is this clinical trial fully registered?—A statement from the International Committee of Medical Journal Editors. *N Engl J Med*. 2005;352:2436–2438.

Deeks JJ, Altman DG. Effect measures for meta-analysis of trials with binary outcomes. In: Egger M, Davey Smith G, Altman DG (eds), *Systematic Reviews in Health Care. Meta-Analysis in Context*. London: BMJ Publishing Group; 2001.

de Groot JA, Janssen KJ, Zwinderman AH, Moons KG, Reitsma JB. Multiple imputation to correct for partial verification bias revisited. *Stat Med*. 2008;27:5880–5889.

de Groot JA, Bossuyt PM, Reitsma JB, et al. Verification problems in diagnostic accuracy studies: Consequences and solutions. *BMJ*. 2011a;343:d4770. doi: 10.1136/bmj.d4770.

de Groot JA, Janssen KJ, Zwinderman AH, Bossuyt PM, Reitsma JB, Moons KG. Correcting for partial verification bias: A comparison of methods. *Ann Epidemiol*. 2011b;21:139–148.

de Groot JA, Dendukuri N, Janssen KJ, Reitsma JB, Bossuyt PM, Moons KG. Adjusting for differential-verification bias in diagnostic-accuracy studies: A Bayesian approach. *Epidemiology*. 2011c;22:234–241.

Denys D, Burger H, van Megen H, de Geus F, Westenberg H. A score for predicting response to pharmacotherapy in obsessive-compulsive disorder. *Int Clin Psychopharmacol*. 2003;18:315–322.vb.

Den Ruijter H, Peters SA, Anderson TJ, et al. Common carotid intima-media thickness measurements in cardiovascular risk prediction. A Meta-analysis. *JAMA*. 2012;308(8):796–803.

DerSimonian R, Laird N. Meta-analysis in clinical trials. *Control Clin Trials*. 1986;7:177–188.

Detrano R, Janosi A, Lyons KP, Marcondes G, Abbassi N, Froelicher VF. Factors affecting sensitivity and specificity of a diagnostic test: The exercise thallium scintigram. *Am J Med*. 1988;84:699–710.

Diamond GA. Off Bayes: Effect of verification bias on posterior probabilities calculated using Bayes' theorem. *Med Decis Making*. 1992;12:22–31.

Dickersin K, Hewitt P, Mutch L, Chalmers I, Chalmers TC. Perusing the literature: Comparison of MEDLINE searching with a perinatal trials database. *Control Clin Trials*. 1985;6:306–317.

Dieren van S, Beulens JW, Kengne AP, et al. Prediction models for the risk of cardiovascular disease in patients with type 2 diabetes: a systematic review. *Heart*. 2012;98:360–369.

Dijk JM, Algra A, van der Graaf Y, Grobbee DE, Bots ML: SMART study group. Carotid stiffness and the risk of new vascular events in patients with manifest cardiovascular disease. The SMART study. *Eur Heart J*. 2005;26:1213–1220.

Doll R, Hill AB. Smoking and carcinoma of the lung. *BMJ*. 1950;ii:739–748.

Doll R, Peto R, Boreham J, Sutherland I. Mortality in relation to smoking: 50 years' observations on male British doctors. *BMJ*. 2004;328:1519.

Donders AR, Heijden van der GJ, Stijnen T, Moons KG. A gentle introduction to imputation of missing values. *J Clin Epidemiol*. 2006;59:1087–1091.

Doran MF, Crowson CS, Pond GR, O'Fallon WM, Gabriel SE. Predictors of infection in rheumatoid arthritis. *Arthritis Rheum*. 2002;46:2294–300.

Dorresteijn JA, Visseren FL, Ridker PM, et al. Estimating treatment effects for individual patients based on the results of randomised clinical trials. *BMJ*. 2011;343:d5888.

Duggan AE, Logan RP, Knifton A, Logan RF. Accuracy of near-patient blood tests for Helicobacter pylori (Letter). *Lancet*. 1996;348:617.

Duggan AE, Elliott C, Logan RF. Testing for Helicobacter pylori infection: Validation and diagnostic yield of a near patient test in primary care. *BMJ*. 1999;319:1236–1239.

Duijnhoven RG, Straus SM, Raine JM, de Boer A, Hoes AW, De Bruin ML. Number of patients studied prior to approval of new medicines: a database analysis. *PLoS Med.* 2013;10:e1001407. doi: 10.1371/journal.pmed.1001407. Epub 2013 Mar 19.

Dupont WD, Plummer WD Jr. Power and sample size calculations for studies involving linear regression. *Control Clin Trials.* 1998;19:589–601.

Dutch TIA Trial Study Group. A comparison of two doses of aspirin (30 mg vs. 283 mg a day) in patients after a transient ischemic attack or minor ischemic stroke. *N Engl J Med.* 1991;325:1261–1266.

Dutch TIA Trial Study Group. Trial of secondary prevention with atenolol after transient ischemic attack or nondisabling ischemic stroke. *Stroke.* 1993;24:543–548.

Edwards P, Clarke M, DiGuiseppi C, Pratap S, Roberts I, Wentz R. Identification of randomised controlled trials in systematic reviews: Accuracy and reliability of screening records. *Stat Med.* 2002;21:1635–1640.

Efron B, Tibshirani R. *An Introduction to the Bootstrap. Monographs on Statistics and Applied Probability.* New York, NY: Chapman & Hall; 1993.

Egger M, Smith GD. Risks and benefits of treating mild hypertension: A misleading meta-analysis? *J Hypertens.* 1995;13:813–815.

Elias SG, Peeters PH, Grobbee DE, van Noord PA. Breast cancer risk after caloric restriction during the 1944–1945 Dutch famine. *J Natl Cancer Inst.* 2004;96:539–546.

El-Metwally A, Salminen JJ, Auvinen A, Kautiainen H, Mikkelsson M. Lower limb pain in a preadolescent population: prognosis and risk factors for chronicity—a prospective 1- and 4-year follow-up study. *Pediatrics.* 2005;116:673–681.

Elwood P. Shattuck lecture. *N Engl J Med.* 1988;318:1549–1556.

Equi A, Balfour-Lynn IM, Bush A, Rosenthal M. Long term azithromycin in children with cystic fibrosis: A randomised, placebo-controlled crossover trial. *Lancet.* 2002;360:978–984.

Erkens JA, Klungel OH, Herings RM, et al. Use of fluorquinolones is associated with a reduced risk of coronary heart disease in diabetes mellitus type 2 patients. *Eur Heart J.* 2002;23:1575–1579.

Eysenbach G, Tuische J, Diepgen TL. Evaluation of the usefulness of Internet searches to identify unpublished clinical trials for systematic reviews. *Med Inform Internet Med.* 2001;26:203–218.

Fang MC, Go AS, Hylek EM, Chang Y, Henault LE, Jensvold NG, Singer DE. Age and the risk of warfarin-associated hemorrhage: The anticoagulation and risk factors in atrial fibrillation study. *J Am Geriatr Soc.* 2006;54:1231–1236.

Feenstra H, Grobbee DE, in 't Veld BA, Stricker, BH. Confounding by contraindication in a nationwide study of risk for death in patients taking Ibopamine. *Ann Int Med.* 2001;134:56–72.

Feenstra J, Lubsen J, Grobbee DE, Stricker BH. Heart failure treatments: Issues of safety versus issues of quality of life. *Drug Saf.* 1999;20:1–7.

Feinstein AR. "Clinical Judgment" revisited: The distraction of quantitative models. *Ann Intern Med.* 1994;120:799–805.

Ferrante di Ruffano L, Hyde CJ, McCaffery KJ, Bossuyt PM, Deeks JJ. Assessing the value of diagnostic tests: A framework for designing and evaluating trials. *BMJ.* 2012;344:e686. doi: 10.1136/bmj.e686.

Ferry SA, Holm SE, Stenlund H, Lundholm R, Monsen TJ. The natural course of uncomplicated lower urinary tract infection in women illustrated by a randomized placebo controlled study. *Scand J Infect Dis*. 2004;36:296–301.

Fields HL, Price DD. Toward a neurobiology of placebo analgesia. In: Harrington A, ed. *The Placebo Effect: An Interdisciplinary Exploration*. Cambridge, MA: Harvard University Press; 1997.

Fijten GH, Starmans R, Muris JW, Schouten HJ, Blijham GH, Knottnerus JA. Predictive value of signs and symptoms for colorectal cancer in patients with rectal bleeding in general practice. *Fam Pract*. 1995;12:279–286.

Fisher RA. Theory of statistical estimation. *Proc Camb Philol Soc*. 1925;22:700–725.

Fisher RA. *The Design of Experiments*. Edinburgh: Oliver & Boyd; 1935.

Fryback D, Thornbury J. The efficacy of diagnostic imaging. *Med Decis Making*. 1991;11:88–94.

Fryzek JP, Schenk M, Kinnaid M, Greenson JK, Garabrant DH. The association of body mass index and pancreatic cancer in residents of southeastern Michigan, 1996–1999. *Am J Epidemiol*. 2005;162:222–228.

Galea MH, Blamey RW, Elston CE, Ellis IO. The Nottingham Prognostic Index in primary breast cancer. *Breast Cancer Res Treat*. 1992;22:207–219.

Gallagher KE, Hulbert LA, Sullivan CP. Full-text and bibliographic database searching in the health sciences: An exploratory study comparing CCML and MEDLINE. *Med Ref Serv Q*. 1990;9:17–25.

Galton F. Regression towards mediocrity in hereditary stature. *J Anthr Inst*. 1886;15:246–263.

Ganna A, Reilly M, de Faire U, Pedersen N, Magnusson P, Ingelsson E. Risk prediction measures for case-cohort and nested case-control designs: an application to cardiovascular disease. *Am J Epidemiol*. 2012;175:715–724.

Garattini S, Bertele V. Non-inferiority trials are unethical because they disregard patients' interests. *Lancet*. 2007;370:1875–1877.

Garbe E, Suissa S. Hormone replacement therapy and acute coronary outcomes: Methodological issues between randomized and observational studies. *Hum Reprod*. 2004;19:8–13.

Garcia-Closas M, Malats N, Silverman D, et al. NAT2 slow acetylation, GSTM1 null genotype, and risk of bladder cancer: results from the Spanish Bladder Cancer Study and meta-analyses. *Lancet*. 2005;366:649–659.

Garcia Rodriguez LA, Jick H. Risk of gyneacomastia associated with cimetidine, omeprazole, and other antiulcer drugs. *BMJ*. 1994;308:503–506.

Gardner MJ, Altman DG. Using confidence intervals. (Letter) *Lancet*. 1987;1:746.

Garg R, Yusuf S. Overview of randomized trials of angiotensin-converting enzyme inhibitors on mortality and morbidity in patients with heart failure. Collaborative Group on ACE Inhibitor Trials. *JAMA*. 1995;273:1450–1456.

Giovannucci EL, Liu Y, Leitzmann MF, Stampfer MJ, Willett WC. A prospective study of physical activity and incident and fatal prostate cancer. *Arch Intern Med*. 2005;165:1005–1010.

Goessens BM, Visseren FL, Sol BG, de Man-van Ginkel JM, van der Graaf Y. A randomized, controlled trial for risk factor reduction in patients with symptomatic vascular disease: The multidisciplinary Vascular Prevention by Nurses Study (VENUS). *Eur J Cardiovasc Prev Rehabil*. 2006;13:996–1003.

Goodman SN. Toward evidence-based medical statistics. 1: The P-value fallacy. *Ann Intern Med*. 1999;130:995–1004.

Govaert TM, Dinant GJ, Aretz K, Masurel N, Sprenger MJ, Knottnerus JA. Adverse reactions to influenza vaccine in elderly people: Randomised double blind placebo controlled trial. *BMJ.* 1993;307:988–990.

Graham DJ, Campen D, Hui R, et al. Risk of acute myocardial infarction and sudden cardiac death in patients treated with cyclo-oxygenase 2 selective and non-selective non-steroidal anti-inflammatory drugs: nested-case-control study. *Lancet.* 2005;365:475–481.

Greenland S. Bayesian perspectives for epidemiological research: I. Foundations and basic methods. *Int J Epidemiol.* 2006;35:765–776.

Greenland S, Finkle WD. A critical look at methods for handling missing covariates in epidemiologic regression analyses. *Am J Epidemiol.* 1995;142:1255–1264.

Grimes DA, Schulz KF. Compared to what? Findings controls for case-control studies. *Lancet.* 2005;365:1429–1433.

Grisso JA, Kelsey JL, Strom BL, et al. Risk factors for falls as a cause of hip fracture in women. The Northeast Hip Fracture Study Group. *N Engl J Med.* 1991;324:1326–1331.

Grobbee DE. Epidemiology in the right direction: The importance of descriptive research. *Eur J Epidemiol.* 2004;19:741–744.

Grobbee DE, Hoes AW. Confounding and indication for treatment in evaluation of drug treatment for hypertension. *BMJ.* 1997; 315:1151–1154.

Grobbee DE, Hoes AW, Verheij TJ, Schrijvers AJ, van Ameijden EJ, Numans ME. The Utrecht Health Project: Optimization of routine healthcare data for research. *Eur J Epidemiol.* 2005;20:285–287.

Grobbee DE, Miettinen OS. Clinical epidemiology: Introduction to the discipline. *Neth J Med.* 1995;47:2–5.

Grobbee DE, Rimm EB, Giovannucci E, Colditz G, Stampfer M, Willett W. Coffee, caffeine, and cardiovascular disease in men. *N Engl J Med.* 1990;323:1026–1332.

Groenwold RH, Hak E, Klungel OH, Hoes AW. Instrumental variables in influenza vaccination studies: Mission impossible?! *Value Health.* 2010;13:132–137.

Groenwold RH, Klungel OH, Grobbee DE, Hoes AW. Selection of confounding variables should not be based on observed associations with exposure. *Eur J Epidemiol.* 2011;26:589–593.

Grundy SM, Balady GJ, Criqui MH, et al. Primary prevention of coronary heart disease: Guidance from Framingham: A statement for healthcare professionals from the AHA Task Force on Risk Reduction. American Heart Association. *Circulation.* 1998;97:1876–1887.

Guyatt GH, Sackett DL, Cook DJ. Users' guides to the medical literature. II. How to use an article about therapy or prevention. A. Are the results of the study valid? Evidence-Based Medicine Working Group. *JAMA.* 1993;270:2598–2601.

Hahn RA. The Nocebo Phenomenon: Scope and foundations. In: Harrington A, ed. *The Placebo Effect: An Interdisciplinary Exploration.* Cambridge, MA: Harvard University Press; 1997.

Hak E, Buskens E, van Essen GA, et al. Clinical effectiveness of influenza vaccination in persons younger than 65 years with high-risk medical conditions: The PRISMA study. *Arch Intern Med.* 2005;165:1921–1922.

Hak E, Verheij TJ, Grobbee DE, Nichol KL, Hoes AW. Confounding by indication in non-experimental evaluation of vaccine effectiveness: The example of prevention of influenza complications. *J Epidemiol Community Health.* 2002;56:951–955.

Hanley JA, McNeil BJ. The meaning and use of the area under a receiver operating characteristic (ROC) curve. *Radiology.* 1982;143:29–36.

Hanley JA, McNeil BJ. A method of comparing the areas under receiver operating characteristic curves derived from the same cases. *Radiology.* 1983;148:839–843.

Harrell FE, Califf RM, Pryor DB, Lee KL, Rosati RA. Evaluating the yield of medical tests. *JAMA.* 1982;247:2543–2546.

Harrell FE, Lee KL, Mark DB. Multivariable prognostic models: Issues in developing models, evaluating assumptions and adequacy, and measuring and reducing errors. *Stat Med.* 1996;15:361–387.

Harrell FE, Margolis PA, Gove S, et al. Development of a clinical prediction model for an ordinal outcome. *Stat Med.* 1998;17:909–944.

Harrell FE. *Regression Modeling Strategies.* New York, NY: Springer-Verlag; 2001.

Hayden JA, Cote P, Bombardier C. Evaluation of the quality of prognosis studies in systematic reviews. *Ann Intern Med.* 2006;144:427–437.

Haynes RB, Kastner M, Wilczynski NL. Developing optimal search strategies for detecting clinically sound and relevant causation studies in EMBASE. *BMC Med Inform Decis Mak.* 2005;5:8.

Heart Outcomes Prevention Evaluation Study Investigators. Effects of an angiotensin-converting-enzyme inhibitor, ramipril, on cardiovascular events in high-risk patients. *N Engl J Med.* 2000;342:145–153.

Heckbert SR, Weiss NS, Koepsell TD, et al. Duration of estrogen replacement therapy in relation to the risk of incident myocardial infarction in postmenopausal women. *Arch Intern Med.* 1997;157:1330–1336.

Heinze G, Jüni P. An overview of the objectives of and the approaches to propensity score analyses. *Eur Heart J.*2011;32:1704–1708.

Hennekens CH, Buring JE. *Epidemiology in Medicine.* Boston, MA: Little, Brown; 1987.

Hennekens CH, Drolette ME, Jesse MJ, Davies JE, Hutchison GB. Coffee drinking and death due to coronary heart disease. *N Engl J Med.* 1976;294:633–636.

Herbst AL, Ulfelder H, Poskanzer DC. Adenocarcinoma of the vagina. Association of maternal stilbestrol therapy with tumor appearance in young women. *N Engl J Med.* 1971;284:878–881.

Higgins PT, Thompson SG, Deeks JJ, Altman DG. Measuring inconsistency in meta-analysis. *BMJ.* 2003;327:557–560.

Higgins JPT, Green S. *Cochrane Handbook for Systematic Reviews of Interventions 4.2.6* (updated September 2006). In: The Cochrane Library, Issue 4, 2006. Chichester, UK: John Wiley & Sons, Ltd.

Hilden J, Habbema JDF. Prognosis in medicine: An analysis of its meaning and roles. *Theor Med.* 1987;8:349–365.

Hill AB. The clinical trial. *Br Med Bull.* 1951;7:278–282.

Hill AB. The environment and disease: Association or causation? *Proc R Soc Med.* 1965;58:295–300.

Hlatky MA, Pryor DB, Harrell FE, Califf RM, Mark DB, Rosati RA. Factors affecting sensitivity and specificity of exercise electrocardiography. Multivariable analysis. *Am J Med.* 1984;77:64–71.

Hlatky MA, Greenland P, Arnett DK, et al. American Heart Association Expert Panel on Subclinical Atherosclerotic Diseases and Emerging Risk Factors and the Stroke Council. Criteria for evaluation of novel markers of cardiovascular risk: a scientific statement from the American Heart Association. *Circulation.* 2009;119:2408–2416.

Hobbs FD, Davis RC, Roalfe AK, Hare R, Davies MK, Kenkre JE. Reliability of N-terminal pro-brain natriuretic peptide assay in diagnosis of heart failure: Cohort study in representative and high risk community populations. *BMJ*. 2002;324:1498.

Hoehler FK, Mantel N, Gehan E, Kahana E, Alter M. Medical registers as historical controls: Analysis of an open clinical trial of inosiplex in subacute sclerosing panencephalitis. *Stat Med*. 1984;3:225–237.

Hoes AW. Case-control studies. *Neth J Med*. 1995;47:36–42.

Hoes AW, Grobbee DE, Lubsen J, Man in 't Veld AJ, van der Does E, Hofman A. Diuretics, beta-blockers, and the risk for sudden cardiac death in hypertensive patients. *Ann Intern Med*. 1995a;123:481–487.

Hoes AW, Grobbee DE, Lubsen J. Does drug treatment improve survival? Reconciling the trials in mild-to-moderate hypertension. *J Hypertens*. 1995b;13:805–811.

Hofman A, Grobbee DE, de Jong PT, van den Ouweland FA. Determinants of disease and disability in the elderly: The Rotterdam Elderly Study. *Eur J Epidemiol*. 1991;7:403–422.

Hofman A, Ott A, Breteler MM, et al. Atherosclerosis, apolipoprotein E, and prevalence of dementia and Alzheimer's disease in the Rotterdam Study. *Lancet*. 1997;349:151–154.

Hopewell S, Clarke M, Lusher A, Lefebvre C, Westby M. A comparison of handsearching versus MEDLINE searching to identify reports of randomised controlled trials. *Stat Med*. 2002;21:1625–1634.

Hosmer D, Lemeshow S. *Applied Logistic Regression*. New York, NY: John Wiley & Sons; 1989.

Hróbjartsson A. The uncontrollable placebo effect. *Eur J Clin Pharmacol*. 1996;50:345–348.

Hung RJ, Boffetta P, Canzian F, et al. Sequence variants in cell cycle control pathway, x-ray exposure, and lung cancer risk: A multicenter case-control study in Central Europe. *Cancer Res*. 2006;66:8280–8286.

Hurwitz ES, Barrett MJ, Bregman D, et al. Public Health Service study of Reye's syndrome and medications. Report of the main study. *JAMA*. 1987;257:1905–1911. (Errata in *JAMA*. 1987;257:3366.)

Hussey MA, Hughes JP. Design and analysis of stepped wedge cluster randomized trials. *Cont Clin Trials*. 2007;28:182–191.

Huybrechts KF, Brookhart MA, Rothman KJ, et al. Comparison of different approaches to confounding adjustment in a study on the association of antipsychotic medication with mortality in older nusing home patients. *Am J Epidemiol*. 2011:174:1089–1099.

Iglesias del Sol A, Moons KGM, Hollander M, et al. Is carotid intima-media thickness useful in cardiovascular disease risk assessment? The Rotterdam Study. *Stroke*. 2001;32:1532–1538.

Ingenito EP, Evans RB, Loring SH, et al. Relation between preoperative inspiratory lung resistance and the outcome of lung-volume-reduction surgery for emphysema. *N Engl J Med*. 1998;338:1181–1185.

International Neonatal Network. The CRIB (clinical risk index for babies) score: A tool for assessing initial neonatal risk and comparing performance of neonatal intensive care units. *Lancet*. 1993; 324:193–198.

Ioannidis JP, Haidich AB, Pappa M, et al. Comparison of evidence of treatment effects in randomized and nonrandomized studies. *JAMA*. 2001;286:821–830.

ISIS-2 (Second International Study of Infarct Survival) Collaborative Group. Randomised trial of intravenous streptokinase, oral aspirin, both, or neither among 17,187 cases of suspected acute myocardial infarction. *Lancet*. 1988;2:349–360.

Jadad AR, McQuay HJ. A high-yield strategy to identify randomised controlled trials for systematic reviews. *Online J Curr Clin Trials*. 1993;33:3973.

Jadad AR, Moore RA, Carroll D, et al. Assessing the quality of reports of randomised clinical trials: Is blinding necessary? *Control Clin Trials*. 1996;17:1–12.

Janssen KJ, Moons KGM, Kalkman CJ, Grobbee DE, Vergouwe Y. Updating methods improved the performance of a clinical prediction model in new patients. *J Clin Epidemiol*. 2008;61:76–86.

Janssen KJ, Vergouwe Y, Kalkman CJ, Grobbee DE, Moons KG. A simple method to adjust clinical prediction models to local circumstances. *Can J Anaesth*. 2009; 56:194–201.

Jefferson T, Jefferson V. The quest for trials on the efficacy of human vaccines. Results of the handsearch of vaccine. *Vaccine*. 1996;14:461–464.

Jellema P, van der Windt DA, van der Horst HE, Twisk JW, Stalman WA, Bouter LM. Should treatment of (sub)acute low back pain be aimed at psychosocial prognostic factors? Cluster randomised clinical trial in general practice. *BMJ*. 2005;331:84.

Jick H, Miettinen OS, Neff RK, Shapiro S, Heinonen OP, Slone D. Coffee and myocardial infarction. *N Engl J Med*. 1973;289:63–67.

Jick H, Vessey MP. Case-control studies of drug induced illness. *Am J Epidemiol*. 1978;107:1–7.

Joensuu H, Lehtimaki T, Holli K, et al. Risk for distant recurrence of breast cancer detected by mammography screening or other methods. *JAMA*. 2004;292:1064–1073.

Jones CE, Dijken PR, Huttenlocher PR, Jabborn JT, Maxwell KN. Inosiplex (isoprinosine) therapy in subacute sclerosing panencephalitis (sspe): A multicentre non-randomised study in 98 patients. *Lancet*. 1982;i:1034–1037.

Jun M, Foote C, Lv J, et al. Effects of fibrates on cardiovascular outcomes: A systematic review and meta-analysis. *Lancet*. 2010;375(9729):1875–1884.

Jüni P, Holenstein F, Sterne J, Bartlett C, Egger M. Direction and impact of language bias in meta-analyses of controlled trials: Empirical study. *Int J Epidemiol*. 2002;31:115–123.

Justice AC, Covinsky KE, Berlin JA. Assessing the generalizability of prognostic information. *Ann Intern Med*. 1999;130:515–524.

Kalkman CJ, Visser K, Moen J, Bonsel GJ, Grobbee DE, Moons KG. Preoperative prediction of severe postoperative pain. *Pain*. 2003;105:415–423.

Kalow W, Staron N. On distribution and inheritance of atypical forms of human serum cholinesterase, as indicated by dibucaine number. *Can J Biochem*. 1957;35:1306–1317.

Kelder JC, Cramer MJ, van Wijngaarden J, et al. The diagnostic value of physical examination and additional testing in primary care patients with suspected heart failure. *Circulation*. 2011;124:2865–2873.

Kemmeren JM, Algra A, Meijers JCM, et al. Effect of second- and third-generation oral contraceptives on the protein C system in the absence or presence of the factor V-Leiden mutation: A randomized trial. *Blood*. 2004;103:927–933.

Khan KS, Kunz R, Kleijnen J, Antes G. *Systematic Reviews to Support Evidence-Based Medicine: How to Review and Apply Findings of Healthcare Research*. Oxford: Royal Society of Medicine Press; 2003.

Khoury MJ, Flandes WD. Nontraditional epidemiological approaches in the analysis of gene-environment interaction. Case-control studies with no controls! *Am J Epidemiol*. 1996;144:207–213.

Kiemeney LA, Verbeek AL, van Houwelingen JC. Prognostic assessment from studies with non-randomized treatment assignment. *J Clin Epidemiol.* 1994;47:241–247.

Kleinbaum DG, Kupper LL, Morgenstern H. *Epidemiologic Research. Principles and Quantitative Methods.* New York, NY: Van Nostrand Reinhold Company Inc.; 1982.

Klungel OH, Martens EP, Psaty BM, et al. Methods to assess intended effects of drug treatment in observational studies are reviewed. *J Clin Epidemiol.* 2004;57:1223–1231.

Knaus WA, Wagner DP, Draper EA, et al. The APACHE III prognostic system. Risk prediction of hospital mortality for critically ill hospitalized adults. *Chest.* 1991;100:1619–1636.

Knol MJ, Groenwold RH, Grobbee DE. P-values in baseline tables of randomised controlled trials are inappropriate but still common in high impact journals. *Eur J Prev Cardiol.* 2012;19(2):231–232.

Knol MJ, Vandenbroucke JP, Scott P, Egger M. What do case-control studies estimate? Survey of methods and assumptions in published case-control studies. *Am J Epidemiol.* 2008;168:1073–1081.

Knottnerus JA. Between iatrotropic stimulus and interiatric referral: The domain of primary care research. *J Clin Epidemiol.* 2002a;55:1201–1206.

Knottnerus JA. *The Evidence Base of Clinical Diagnosis. How to Do Diagnostic Research.* London: BMJ Publishing Group; 2002b.

Koefoed BG, Gulløv AL, Petersen P. The Second Copenhagen Atrial Fibrillation, Aspirin and Anti-coagulant Trial (AFASAK 2): Methods and design. *J Thromb Thrombolys.* 1995;2:125–130.

Koffijberg H, van Zaane B, Moons KG. From accuracy to patient outcome and cost-effectiveness evaluations of diagnostic tests and biomarkers: An exemplary modelling study. *BMC Med Res Methodol.* 2013;13:12. [Epub ahead of print]

Koller MT, Stijnen T, Steyerberg EW, Lubsen J. Meta-analyses of chronic disease trials with competing causes of death may yield biased odds ratios. *J Clin Epidemiol.* 2008;61:365–372.

Koopman L, Van der Heijden GJ, Glasziou PP, Grobbee DE, Rovers MM. A systematic review of analytical methods used to study subgroups in (individual patient data) meta-analyses. *J Clin Epidemiol.* 2007;60:1002–1009.

Kyzas PA, Denaxa-Kyza D, Ioannidis JP. Quality of reporting of cancer prognostic marker studies: association with reported prognostic effect. *J Natl Cancer Inst.* 2007;99:236–243.

L'Abbé KA, Detsky AS, O'Rourke K. Meta-analysis in clinical research. *Ann Intern Med.* 1987;107:224–233.

Lambert PC, Sutton AJ, Abrams KR, Jones DR. A comparison of summary patient-level covariates in meta-regression with individual patient data meta-analysis. *J Clin Epidemiol.* 2002;55:86–94.

Lang JM, Rothman KJ, Cann CI. That confounded P-value. *Epidemiology.* 1998;9:7–8.

LaRosa JC, He J, Vupputuri S. Effect of statins on risk of coronary disease: A meta-analysis of randomized controlled trials. *JAMA.* 1999;282:2340–2346.

Lau J, Antman EM, Jimenez-Silva J, Kupelnick B, Mosteller F, Chalmers TC. Cumulative meta-analysis of therapeutic trials for myocardial infarction. *N Engl J Med.* 1992;327:248–254.

Lau J, Chalmers TC. The rational use of therapeutic drugs in the 21st century. Important lessons from cumulative meta-analyses of randomised control trials. *Int J Technol Assess Health Care.* 1995;11:509–522.

Laupacis A, Sekar N, Stiell IG. Clinical prediction rules. A review and suggested modifications of methodological standards. *JAMA.* 1997;277:488–494.

Leeflang MM, Deeks JJ, Rutjes AW, Reitsma JB, Bossuyt PM. Bivariate meta-analysis of predictive values of diagnostic tests can be an alternative to bivariate meta-analysis of sensitivity and specificity. *J Clin Epidemiol.* 2012;65:1088–1097.

Le Gall JR, Lemeshow S, Saulnier F. A new Simplified Acute Physiology Score (SAPS II) based on a European/North American multicenter study. *JAMA.* 1993;270:2957–2963.

Leserman J, Petitto JM, Golden RN, et al. Impact of stressful life events, depression, social support, coping, and cortisol on progression to AIDS. *Am J Psychiatry.* 2000;157:1221–1228.

Leslie WD, Tsang JF, Caetano PA, Lix LM. Effectiveness of bone density measurement for predicting osteoporotic fractures in clinical practice. *J Clin Endocrinol Metab.* 2007;92:77–81.

Lidegaard Ø, Edström B, Kreiner S. Oral contraceptives and venous thromboembolism: A five-year national case-control study. *Contraception.* 2002;65:187–196.

Lijmer JG, Bossuyt PM. Various randomized designs can be used to evaluate medical tests. *J Clin Epidemiol.* 2009;62:364–373.

Lijmer JG, Mol BW, Heisterkamp S, et al. Empirical evidence of design-related bias in studies of diagnostic tests. *JAMA.* 1999;282:1061–1066.

Little RA, Rubin DB. *Statistical Analysis with Missing Data.* New York, NY: Wiley; 1987.

Lloyd-Jones DM, Hlatky PW, Larson MG, et al. Lifetime risk of coronary heart disease by cholesterol levels at selected ages. *Arch Intern Med.* 2003;163:1966–1972.

Lord SJ, Irwig L, Simes RJ. When is measuring sensitivity and specificity sufficient to evaluate a diagnostic test, and when do we need randomized trials? *Ann Intern Med.* 2006;144:850–855.

Loy CT, Irwig L. Accuracy of diagnostic tests read with and without clinical information: A systematic review. *JAMA.* 2004;292:1602–1609.

Lubsen J, de Lang R. *Klinisch geneesmiddelen onderzoek.* Utrecht: Bunge; 1987.

Lubsen J, Hoes A, Grobbee D. Implications of trial results: The potentially misleading notions of number needed to treat and average duration of life gained. *Lancet.* 2000;356:1757–1759.

Lumley T, Kronmal R, Ma S. *Relative Risk Regression in Medical Research: Models, Contrasts, Estimators, and Algorithms.* UW Biostatistics Working Paper Series. Paper 293. Washington, DC: The Berkeley Electronic Press; 2006.

Mack WJ, Preston-Martin S, Bernstein L, Qian D. Lifestyle and other risk factors for thyroid cancer in Los Angeles County females. *Ann Epidemiol.* 2002;12:395–401.

Maclure M. The case-crossover design: A method for studying transient effects on the risk of acute events. *Am J Epidemiol.* 1991;133:144–153.

MacMahon S, Sharpe N, Gamble G, et al. Randomised, placebo-controlled trial of the angiotensin-converting enzyme inhibitor, ramipril, in patients with coronary or other occlusive arterial disease. PART-2 Collaborative Research Group. Prevention of atherosclerosis with ramipril. *J Am Coll Cardiol.* 2000;36:438–443.

MacMahon B, Yen S, Trichopoulos D, Warren K, Nardi G. Coffee and cancer of the pancreas. *N Engl J Med.* 1981;304:630–633.

Makani H, Messerli FH, Romero J, et al. Meta-analysis of randomized trials of angioedema as an adverse event of renin-angiotensin system inhibitors. *Am J Cardiol.* 2012;110:383–391.

Mantel N, Haenszel W. Statistical aspects of the analysis of data from retrospective studies of disease. *J Natl Cancer Inst.* 1959;22:719–748.

Marsh S, Kwok P, McLeod HL. SNP databases and pharmacogenetics: Great start, but a long way to go. *Hum Mutat.* 2002;20(3):174–179.

Marsoni S, Valsecchi MG. Prognostic factors analysis in clinical oncology: Handle with care. *Ann Oncol*. 1991;2:245–247.

Martens EP, Pestman WR, de Boer A, Belitser SV, Klungel OH. Instrumental variables: Application and limitations. *Epidemiology*. 2006;17:260–267.

Mayer SA, Brun NC, Begtrup K, et al. Recombinant Activated Factor VII Intracerebral Hemorrhage Trial Investigators. Recombinant activated factor VII for acute intracerebral hemorrhage. *N Engl J Med*. 2005;352:777–785.

McClellan M, McNeill BJ, Newhouse JP. Does more intensive treatment of acute myocardial infarction in the elderly reduce mortality? Analysis using instrumental variables. *JAMA*. 1994;272:859–866.

McColl KE, Murray LS, Gillen D, et al. Randomised trial of endoscopy with testing for Helicobacter pylori compared with non-invasive H pylori testing alone in the management of dyspepsia. *BMJ*. 2002;324:999–1002.

McDonald S, Lefebvre C, Antes G, et al. The contribution of handsearching European general health care journals to the Cochrane Controlled Trials Register. *Eval Health Prof*. 2002;25:65–75.

McDonald S, Taylor L, Adams C. Searching the right database. A comparison of four databases for psychiatry journals. *Health Libr Rev*. 1999;16:151–156.

Medical Research Council Streptomycin in Tuberculosis Trials Committee. Streptomycin treatment for pulmonary tuberculosis. *BMJ*. 1948;2:769–782.

Mennen LI, de Maat MP, Meijer G, et al. Postprandial response of activated factor VII in elderly women depends on the R353Q polymorphism. *Am J Clin Nutr*. 1999;70:435–438.

MIAMI Trial Research Group. Metoprolol in acute myocardial infarction (MIAMI). A randomised placebo-controlled international trial. *Eur Heart J*. 1985;6:199–226.

Middelburg RA, Van Stein D, Zupanska B, et al. Female donors and transfusion-related acute lung injury: A case-referent study from the International TRALI Unisex Research Group. *Transfusion*. 2010;50:2447–2454.

Miettinen OS. Estimability and estimation in case-referent studies. *Am J Epidemiol* 1976a;103:226–235.

Miettinen OS. Stratification by a multivariate confounder score. *Am J Epidemiol*. 1976b104:609–620.

Miettinen OS. Design options in epidemiology research. An update. *Scand J Work Environ Health*. 1982;8(suppl 1):7–14.

Miettinen OS. The need for randomization in the study of intended effects. *Stat Med*. 1983;2:267–271.

Miettinen OS. *Theoretical Epidemiology: Principles of Occurrence Research in Medicine*. New York, NY: John Wiley and Sons; 1985.

Miettinen OS. The clinical trial as a paradigm for epidemiologic research. *J Clin Epidemiol*. 1989;42:491–496.

Miettinen OS. Epidemiology: Quo vadis? *Eur J Epidemiol*. 2004;19:713–718.

Minozzi S, Pistotti V, Forni M. Searching for rehabilitation articles on MEDLINE and EMBASE. An example with cross-over design. *Arch Phys Med Rehabil*. 2000;81:720–722.

Mittleman MA, Maclure M, Tofler GH, Sherwood JB, Goldberg RJ, Muller JE, for The Determinants of Myocardial Infarction Onset Study Investigators. Triggering of acute myocardial infarction by heavy physical exertion. Protection against triggering by regular exertion. *N Engl J Med*. 1993;329:1677–1683.

Mittleman MA, Mintzer D, Maclure M, Tofler GH, Sherwood JB, Muller JE. Triggering of myocardial infarction by cocaine. *Circulation*. 1999;99:2737–2741.

Moher D, Cook DJ, Eastwood S, Olkin I, Rennie D, Stroup DF. Improving the quality of reports of meta-analyses of randomised controlled trials: The QUOROM statement. Quality of Reporting of Meta-analyses. *Lancet.* 1999a;354:1896–1900.

Moher D, Cook DJ, Jadad AR, et al. Assessing the quality of reports of randomised trials: Implications for the conduct of meta-analyses. *Health Technol Assess.* 1999b;3:98.

Moher D, Hopewell S, Schulz KF, et al. CONSORT 2010 explanation and elaboration: Updated guidelines for reporting parallel group randomised trials. *BMJ.* 2010;340:c869.

Moher D, Schulz KF, Altman DG; CONSORT Group (Consolidated Standards of Reporting Trials). The CONSORT statement: Revised recommendations for improving the quality of reports of parallel-group randomized trials. *J Am Podiatr Med Assoc.* 2001a;91:437–442.

Moher D, Schulz KF, Altman DG, Lepage L. The CONSORT statement: Revised recommendations for improving the quality of reports of parallel-group randomised trials. *Lancet.* 2001b;357:1191–1194.

Moher D, Schulz KF, Altman D. The CONSORT statement: Revised recommendations for improving the quality of reports of parallel-group randomised trials 2001. *Explore (NY).* 2005;1:40–45.

Montori VM, Wilczynski NL, Morgan D, Haynes RB. Optimal search strategies for retrieving systematic reviews from Medline: Analytical survey. *BMJ.* 2005;330:68. (Comment in *BMJ.* 2005;330:1162–1163.)

Moons KG. Criteria for scientific evaluation of novel markers: A perspective. *Clin Chem.* 2010;56:537–541.

Moons KG, Bots ML, Salonen JT, et al. Prediction of stroke in the general population in Europe (EUROSTROKE): Is there a role for fibrinogen and electrocardiography? *J Epidemiol Community Health.* 2002c;56(suppl 1):i30–i36.

Moons KG, Biesheuvel CJ, Grobbee DE. Test research versus diagnostic research. *Clin Chem.* 2004a;59:213–215.

Moons KG, de Groot JA, Linnet K, Reitsma JB, Bossuyt PM. Quantifying the added value of a diagnostic test or marker. *Clin Chem.* 2012c;58:1408–1417.

Moons KG, Donders ART, Steyerberg EW, Harrell FE. Penalized maximum likelihood estimation to directly adjust diagnostic and prognostic prediction models for overoptimism: A clinical example. *J Clin Epidemiol.* 2004b;57:1262–1270.

Moons KG, Donders ART, Stijnen T, Harrell FE Jr. Using the outcome variable to impute missing values of predictor variables: A self-fulfilling prophecy? *J Clin Epidemiol.* 2006;59:1092–1101.

Moons KGM, Grobbee DE. Diagnostic studies as multivariable prediction research. *J Epidemiol Comm Health.* 2002a;56:337–338.

Moons KG, Grobbee DE. When should we remain blind and when should our eyes remain open in diagnostic research? *J Clin Epidemiol.* 2002b;55:633–636.

Moons KG, Grobbee DE. Clinical epidemiology: An introduction. In: Vaccaro AR, ed. *Orthopedic Knowledge Update: 8.* Rosemont, IL: American Academy of Orthopedic Surgeons; 2005.

Moons KG, Harrell FE. Sensitivity and specificity should be deemphasized in diagnostic accuracy studies. *Acad Radiol.* 2003;10:670–672.

Moons KG, Kengne AP, Woodward M, et al. Risk prediction models: I. Development, internal validation, and assessing the incremental value of a new (bio)marker. *Heart.* 2012a;98:683–690.

Moons KG, Kengne AP, Grobbee DE, et al. Risk prediction models: II. External validation, model updating, and impact assessment. *Heart.* 2012b;98:691–698.

Moons KG, van Es GA, Deckers JW, Habbema JD, Grobbee DE. Limitations of sensitivity, specificity, likelihood ratio, and Bayes' theorem in assessing diagnostic probabilities: A clinical example. *Epidemiology*. 1997;8:12–17.

Moons KG, van Es GA, Michel BC, Buller HR, Habbema JD, Grobbee DE. Redundancy of single diagnostic test evaluation. *Epidemiology*. 1999;10:276–281.

Moritz DJ, Kelsey JL, Grisso JA. Hospital controls versus community controls: Differences in inferences regarding risk factors for hip fracture. *Am J Epidemiol*. 1997;145:653–660.

Moses LE, Mosteller F, Buehler JH. Comparing results of large clinical trials to those of meta-analyses. *Stat Med*. 2002;21:793–800.

Moss S, Thomas I, Evans A, Thomas B, Johns L. Trial Management Group. Randomised controlled trial of mammographic screening in women from age 40: Results of screening in the first 10 years. *Br J Cancer*. 2005;92:949–954.

Neaton JD, Grimm RH Jr, Cutler JA. Recruitment of participants for the multiple risk factor intervention trial (MRFIT). *Control Clin Trials*. 1987;8(suppl 4):41S–53S.

Nicholas J. Commentary: What is a propensity score? *Br J Gen Pract*. 2008;58:687.

O'Leary D, Costello F. Personality and outcome in depression: An 18-month prospective follow-up study. *J Affect Disord*. 2001;63:67–78.

Olijhoek JK, van der Graaf Y, Banga JD, Algra A, Rabelink TJ, Visseren FL. The SMART Study Group. The metabolic syndrome is associated with advanced vascular damage in patients with coronary heart disease, stroke, peripheral arterial disease or abdominal aortic aneurysm. *Eur Heart J*. 2004;25:342–348.

Oostenbrink R, Moons KGM, Bleeker SE, Moll HA, Grobbee DE. Diagnostic research on routine care data: Prospects and problems. *J Clin Epidemiol*. 2003;56:501–506.

Oostenbrink R, Moons KG, Donders AR, Grobbee DE, Moll HA. Prediction of bacterial meningitis in children with meningeal signs: Reduction of lumbar punctures. *Acta Paediatr*. 2001;90:611–617.

Oostenbrink R, Moons KG, Derksen-Lubsen G, Grobbee DE, Moll HA. Early prediction of neurological sequelae or death after bacterial meningitis. *Acta Paediatr*. 2002;91:391–398.

Ottervanger JP, Paalman HJA, Boxma GL, Stricker BHCh. Transmural myocardial infarction with sumatriptan. *Lancet*. 1993;341:861–862.

Oudega R, Hoes AW, Moons KG. The Wells rule does not adequately rule out deep venous thrombosis in primary care patients. *Ann Intern Med*. 2005a;143:100–107.

Oudega R, Moons KGM, Hoes AW. A simple diagnostic rule to exclude deep vein thrombosis in primary care. *Thromb Haemost*. 2005b;94:200–205.

Oxman AD, Clarke MJ, Stewart LA. From science to practice: Meta-analyses using individual patient data are needed. *JAMA*. 1995;274:845–846.

Patino LR, Selten JP, Van Engeland H, Duyx JH, Kahn RS, Burger H. Migration, family dysfunction and psychotic symptoms in children and adolescents. *Br J Psychiatry*. 2005;186:442–443.

Peduzzi P, Concato J, Feinstein AR, Holford TR. Importance of events per independent variable in proportional hazards regression analysis. II. Accuracy and precision of regression estimates. *J Clin Epidemiol*. 1995;48:1503–1510.

Peduzzi P, Concato J, Kemper E, Holford TR, Feinstein AR. A simulation study of the number of events per variable in logistic regression analysis. *J Clin Epidemiol*. 1996;49:1373–1379.

Pencina MJ, D'Agostino RB Sr, D'Agostino RB Jr, Vasan RS. Evaluating the added predictive ability of a new marker: From area under the ROC curve to reclassification and beyond. *Stat Med.* 2008;27:157–172; discussion 207–212.

Peters SA, den Ruijter HM, Bots ML, Moons KG. Improvements in risk stratification for the occurrence of cardiovascular disease by imaging subclinical atherosclerosis: a systematic review. *Heart.* 2012;98:177–184.

Peto R. Failure of randomisation by "sealed" envelope. *Lancet.* 1999;354:73.

Piegorsch WW, Weinberg CR, Taylor JA. Non-hierarchical logistic models and case-only designs for assessing susceptibility in population-based case-control studies. *Stat Med.* 1994;13:153–162.

Pierce DA, Shimizu Y, Preston DL, Vaeth M, Mabuchi K. Studies of the mortality of atomic bomb survivors. Report 12, Part I. Cancer: 1950–1990. *Radiat Res.* 1996;146:1–27.

Pitt B, Byington RP, Furberg CD, et al. Effect of amlodipine on the progression of atherosclerosis and the occurrence of clinical events. PREVENT Investigators. *Circulation.* 2000;102:1503–1510.

Pitt B, O'Neill B, Feldman R, et al. QUIET Study Group. The QUinapril Ischemic Event Trial (QUIET): Evaluation of chronic ACE inhibitor therapy in patients with ischemic heart disease and preserved left ventricular function. *Am J Cardiol.* 2001;87:1058–1063.

PlanetMath. Probit. http://planetmath.org/encyclopedia/Probit.html. Accessed January 24, 2007.

PlanetMath. General Linear Model. http://planetmath.org/encyclopedia/GeneralLinearModel.html. Accessed December 31, 2012.

PlanetMath. Regression Model. http://planetmath.org/encyclopedia/RegressionModel.html. Accessed December 31, 2012.

Plint AC, Moher D, Morrison A, et al. Does the CONSORT checklist improve the quality of reports of randomised controlled trials? A systematic review. *Med J Aust.* 2006;185:263–267.

Pocock SJ. *Clinical Trials: A Practical Approach.* New York, NY: John Wiley & Sons; 1984.

Pocock SJ, Lubsen J. More on subgroup analyses in clinical trials. *N Engl J Med.* 2008;358:2076.

Poole-Wilson PA, Kirwan BA, Vokó Z, et al. ACTION (A Coronary disease Trial Investigating Outcome with Nifedipine GITS) investigators. Resource utilization implications of treatment were able to be assessed from appropriately reported clinical trial data. *J Clin Epidemiol.* 2007;60:727–733.

Prandoni P, Villalta S, Bagatella P, et al. The clinical course of deep-vein thrombosis. Prospective long-term follow-up of 528 symptomatic patients. *Haematologica.* 1997;82:423–428.

Prentice RL. A case-cohort design for epidemiologic cohort studies and disease prevention trials. *Biometrika.* 1986;73:1–11.

PRISMA. http://www.prisma-statement.org. Accessed January 6, 2014.

Psaty BM, Heckbert SR, Koepsell TD, et al. The risk of myocardial infarction associated with antihypertensive drug therapies. *JAMA.* 1995;274:620–625.

Rademaker KJ, Lam JN, Van Haastert IC, et al. Larger corpus callosum size with better motor performance in prematurely born children. *Semin Perinatol.* 2004;28:279–287.

Rademaker KJ, Uiterwaal CS, Beek FJ, et al. Neonatal cranial ultrasound versus MRI and neurodevelopmental outcome at school age in preterm born children. *Arch Dis Child Fetal Neonatal Ed.* 2005;90:F489–F493.

Randolph AG, Guyatt GH, Calvin JE, Doig DVM, Richardson WS. Understanding articles describing clinical prediction tools. *Crit Care Med.* 1998;26:1603–1612.

Ransohoff DF, Feinstein AR. Problems of spectrum and bias in evaluating the efficacy of diagnostic tests. *N Engl J Med.* 1978;299:926–930.

Rasanen P, Roine E, Sintonen H, Semberg-Konttinen V, Ryynanen OP, Roine R. Use of quality-adjusted life years for the estimation of effectiveness of health care: A systematic literature review. *Int J Technol Assess Health Care*. 2006;22:235–241.

Ravnskov U. Frequency of citation and outcome of cholesterol lowering trials. *BMJ*. 1992;305:717.

Rawlins MD, Thompson JW. Pathogenesis of adverse drug reactions. In: Davies DM, ed. *Textbook of Adverse Drug Reactions*. Oxford: Oxford University Press, 1977.

Reilly BM, Evans AT. Translating clinical research into clinical practice: Impact of using prediction rules to make decisions. *Ann Intern Med*. 2006;144:201–209.

Reitsma JB, Moons KG, Bossuyt PM, Linnet K. Systematic reviews of studies quantifying the accuracy of diagnostic tests and markers. *Clin Chem*. 2012;58:1534–1545.

Reitsma JB, Rutjes AW, Khan KS, Coomarasamy A, Bossuyt PM. A review of solutions for diagnostic accuracy studies with an imperfect or missing reference standard. *J Clin Epidemiol*. 2009;62:797–806.

Riegelman R. *Studying a Study and Testing a Test*. Boston, MA: Little, Brown; 1990.

Rietveld RP, ter Riet G, Bindels PJ, Sloos JH, van Weert HC. Predicting bacterial cause in infectious conjunctivitis: Cohort study on informativeness of combinations of signs and symptoms. *BMJ*. 2004;329:206–210.

Riley RD, Abrams KR, Sutton AJ, et al. Reporting of prognostic markers: Current problems and development of guidelines for evidence-based practice in the future. *Br J Cancer*. 2003;88:1191–1198.

Riley DG. *Practical Statistics for Medical Research*. New York, NY: Chapman & Hall/CRC; 1991.

Rimm EB, Klatsky A, Grobbee D, Stampfer MJ. Review of moderate alcohol consumption and reduced risk of coronary heart disease: Is the effect due to beer, wine, or spirits? *BMJ*. 1996;312:731–736.

RITA Trial Participants. Coronary angioplasty versus coronary artery bypass surgery: The Randomized Intervention Treatment of Angina (RITA) trial. *Lancet*. 1993;341:573–580.

Robertson BC. Lies, damn lies, and statistics (letter). *Anesthesiology*. 2006;104:202.

Roest M, van der Schouw YT, de Valk B, et al. Heterozygosity for a hereditary hemochromatosis gene is associated with cardiovascular death in women. *Circulation*. 1999;100:1268–1273.

Roland M, Torgerson DJ. Understanding controlled trials: What are pragmatic trials? *BMJ*. 1998;316:285.

Roldán V, Marín F, Fernández H, et al. Predictive value of the HAS-BLED and ATRIA bleeding scores for the risk of serious bleeding in a "real-world" population with atrial fibrillation receiving anticoagulant therapy. *Chest*. 2013;143:179–184.

Rosenbaum PR, Rubin DB. Reducing bias in observational studies using subclassification on the propensity score. *J Am Stat Assoc*. 1984;79:516–524.

Rothman KJ. *Modern Epidemiology*. Boston, MA: Little & Brown; 1986.

Rothman KJ. *Epidemiology. An Introduction*. New York, NY: Oxford University Press; 2002.

Rothman KJ, Greenland S. Causation and causal inference in epidemiology. *Am J Public Health*. 2005;95(suppl 1):S144–S150.

Rothman KJ. Episheet: Spreadsheets for the analysis of epidemiologic data. krothman.hostbyet2.com/Episheet.xls. Updated October 4, 2012. Accessed January 1, 2013.

Rothwell PM. External validity of randomised controlled trials: "To whom do the results of this trial apply?" *Lancet*. 2005;365:82–93.

Roukema J, Loenhout van RB, Steyerberg EW, Moons KGM, Bleeker SE, Moll HA. Polytomous logistic regression did not outperform dichotomous logistic regression in diagnosing serious bacterial infections in febrile children. *J Clin Epidemiol*. 2008;61:135–141.

Rovers MM, Glasziou P, Appelman CL, et al. Antibiotics for acute otitis media: A meta-analysis with individual patient data. *Lancet.* 2006;368:1429–1435.

Rovers MM, Glasziou P, Appelman CL, et al. Predictors of a prolonged course in children with acute otitis media: An individual patient data meta-analysis. *Pediatrics.* 2007;119:579–585.

Royston P, Altman DG, Sauerbrei W. Dichotomizing continuous predictors in multiple regression: A bad idea. *Stat Med.* 2006;25:127–141.

Rubin DB. Inferences and missing data. *Biometrika.* 1976;63:581–590.

Rubin DB. *Multiple Imputation for Nonresponse in Surveys.* New York: Wiley; 1987.

Rubin DB. Multiple imputation after 18+ years. *J Am Stat Assoc.* 1996;91:473–489.

Rubin DB. Estimating causal effects from large data sets using propensity scores. *Ann Intern Med.* 1997;127:757–763.

Rudakis T, Thomas M, Gaskin Z, et al. Sequences associated with human iris pigmentation. *Genetics.* 2003;165:2071–2083.

Rutjes AW, Reitsma JB, Vandenbroucke JP, Glas AS, Bossuyt PM. Case-control and two-gate designs in diagnostic accuracy studies. *Clin Chem.* 2005;51:1335–1341.

Rutjes AW, Reitsma JB, Di Nisio M, Smidt N, van Rijn JC, Bossuyt PM. Evidence of bias and variation in diagnostic accuracy studies. *CMAJ.* 2006;174:469–476.

Rutjes AW, Reitsma JB, Coomarasamy A, Khan KS, Bossuyt PM. Evaluation of diagnostic tests when there is no gold standard. A review of methods. *Health Technol Assess.* 2007;11:iii, ix–51.

Rutten FH, Cramer MJ, Grobbee DE, et al. Unrecognized heart failure in elderly patients with stable chronic obstructive pulmonary disease. *Eur Heart J.* 2005a;26:1887–1894.

Rutten FH, Hoes AW. Chronic obstructive pulmonary disease: A slowly progressive cardiovascular disease masked by its pulmonary effects? *Eur J Heart Fail.* 2012;14:348–350.

Rutten FH, Moons KG, Cramer MJ, et al. Recognising heart failure in elderly patients with stable chronic obstructive pulmonary disease in primary care: Cross sectional diagnostic study. *BMJ.* 2005b;331:1379.

Rutten FH, Moons KGM, Hoes AW. Improving the quality and clinical relevance of diagnostic studies. *BMJ.* 2006;332:1129–1130.

Rutten FH, Vonken EJ, Cramer MJ, et al. Cardiovascular magnetic resonance imaging to identify left-sided chronic heart failure in stable patients with chronic obstructive pulmonary disease. *Am Heart J.* 2008;156:506–512.

Rutten FH, Zuithoff NP, Hak E, Grobbee DE, Hoes AW. Beta-blockers may reduce mortality and risk of exacerbations in patients with chronic obstructive pulmonary disease. *Arch Intern Med.* 2010;170:880–887.

Ryan CM, Schoenfeld DA, Thorpe WP, Sheridan RL, Cassem EH, Tompkins RG. Objective estimates of the probability of death from burn injuries. *N Engl J Med.* 1998;338:362–366.

Sackett DL, Haynes RB, Tugwell P. *Clinical Epidemiology: A Basic Science for Clinical Medicine.* Boston, Toronto: Little, Brown; 1985.

Sampson M, Barrowman NJ, Moher D, et al. Can electronic search engines optimize screening of search results in systematic reviews: An empirical study. *BMC Med Res Methodol.* 2006a;6:7.

Sampson M, Zhang L, Morrison A, et al. An alternative to the hand searching gold standard: Validating methodological search filters using relative recall. *BMC Med Res Methodol.* 2006b;6:33.

Sargeant JK, Bruce ML, Florio LP, Weissmann MM. Factors associated with 1-year outcome of major depression in the community. *Arch Gen Psychiatry.* 1990;47:519–526.

Sattar N, Preiss D, Murray HM, et al. Statins and risk of incident diabetes: A collaborative meta-analysis of randomised statin trials. *Lancet*. 2010;375:735–742.

Schafer JL. *Analysis of Incomplete Multivariate Data*. London: Chapman & Hill; 1997.

Schafer JL, Graham JW. Missing data: Our view of the state of the art. *Psychol Methods*. 2002;7:147–177.

Schlesselman JJ. *Case Control Studies. Design Conduct, Analysis*. New York, Oxford: Oxford University Press; 1982.

Schouten EG, Dekker JM, Kok FJ, et al. Risk ratio and rate ratio estimation in case-cohort designs: Hypertension and cardiovascular mortality. *Stat Med*. 1993;12:1733–1745.

Schulz KF, Grimes DA. Case-control studies: research in reverse. *Lancet*. 2002;359:431–434.

Schwartz D, Lellouch J. Explanatory and pragmatic attitudes in therapeutic trials. *J Chron Dis*. 1967;20:637–648.

Selby JV, Smith DH, Johnson ES, Raebel MA, Friedman GD, McFarland BH. Kaiser Permanente Medical Care Program. In: Strom BL, ed. *Pharmacoepidemiology*. 4th ed. Chichester: John Wiley & Sons; 2005.

Senn SJ. *Cross-Over Trials in Clinical Research*. Chichester: John Wiley; 1993.

Shojania KG, Bero LA. Taking advantage of the explosion of systematic reviews: An efficient MEDLINE search strategy. *Eff Clin Pract*. 2001;4:157–162.

Sierksma A, van der Gaag MS, Kluft C, Hendriks HF. Moderate alcohol consumption reduces plasma C-reactive protein and fibrinogen levels: A randomized, diet-controlled intervention study. *Eur J Clin Nutr*. 2002;56:1130–1136.

Silverman W. The schizophrenic career of a monster drug. *Pediatrics*. 2002;110:404–406.

Simel DL, Samsa GP, Matchar DB. Likelihood ratios with confidence: Sample size estimation for diagnostic test studies. *J Clin Epidemiol*. 1991;44:763–770.

Simes RJ. Confronting publication bias: A cohort design for meta-analysis. *Stat Med*. 1987;6:11–29.

Simon R, Altman DG. Statistical aspects of prognostic factor studies in oncology. *Br J Cancer*. 1994;69:979–985.

Simon S. P. Mean: The controversy over standardized beta coefficients. http://www.pmean.com/09/StandardizedBetas.html. Updated April 12, 2010. Accessed January 6, 2014.

Simons PC, Algra A, van de Laak MF, Grobbee DE, van der Graaf Y. Second Manifestations of ARTerial disease (SMART) study: Rationale and design. *Eur J Epidemiol*. 1999;15:773–781.

Skali H, Pfeffer MA, Lubsen J, Solomon SD. Variable impact of combining fatal and nonfatal end points in heart failure trials. *Circulation*. 2006;114:2298–2303.

Smeets HM, de Wit NJ, Hoes AW. Routine health insurance data for scientific research: potential and limitations of the Agis Health Database. *J Clin Epidemiol*. 2011;64:424–430.

Smith GC, Pell JP. Parachute use to prevent death and major trauma related to gravitational challenge: Systematic review of randomised controlled trials. *BMJ*. 2003;327(7429):1459–1461.

Smith GD, Timpson N, Ebrahim S. Strengthening causal inference in cardiovascular epidemiology through Mendelian randomization. *Ann Med*. 2008;40:524–541.

Snow J. *On the Mode of Communication of Cholera*. 2nd ed. London: John Churchill; 1855.

SOLVD Investigators. Effect of enalapril on survival in patients with reduced left ventricular ejection fractions and congestive heart failure. *N Engl J Med*. 1991;325:29–302.

Spiegelman D, Hertzmark E. Easy SAS calculations for risk or prevalence ratios and differences. *Am J Epidemiol*. 2005;162:199–200.

Spijker J, de Graaf R, Ormel J, Nolen WA, Grobbee DE, Burger H. The persistence of depression score. *Acta Psychiatr Scand.* 2006;114:411–416.

Staessen JA, Fagard R, Thijs L, et al. Randomised double-blind comparison of placebo and active treatment for older patients with isolated systolic hypertension. The Systolic Hypertension in Europe (Syst-Eur) Trial Investigators. *Lancet.* 1997;350:757–764.

Staessen JA, Wang JG, Thijs L. Cardiovascular protection and blood pressure reduction: A meta-analysis. *Lancet.* 2001;358:1305–1315.

Stamler J, Wentworth D, Neaton JD. Is relationship between serum cholesterol and risk of premature death from coronary heart disease continuous and graded? Findings in 356,222 primary screenees of the Multiple Risk Factor Intervention Trial (MRFIT). *JAMA.* 1986;256:2823–2838.

Starr JR, McKnight B. Assessing interaction in case-control studies: Type I errors when using both additive and multiplicative scales. *Epidemiology.* 2004;15:422–427.

Steenland K, Beaumont J, Hornung R. The use of regression analyses in a cohort mortality study of welders. *J Chronic Dis.* 1986;39:287–294.

Stelzner S, Hellmich G, Koch R, Ludwig K. Factors predicting survival in stage IV colorectal carcinoma patients after palliative treatment: A multivariate analysis. *J Surg Oncol* 2005;89:211–217.

Stern JM, Simes RJ. Publication bias: Evidence of delayed publication in a cohort study of clinical research projects. *BMJ.* 1997;315:640–645.

Sterne JA, Gavaghan D, Egger M. Publication and related bias in meta-analysis: Power of statistical tests and prevalence in the literature. *J Clin Epidemiol.*2000;53:1119–1129.

Sterne JA, Jüni P, Schulz KF, Altman DG, Bartlett C, Egger M. Statistical methods for assessing the influence of study characteristics on treatment effects in "meta-epidemiological" research. *Stat Med.* 2002;21:1513–1524.

Stewart LA, Tierney JF. To IPD or not to IPD? Advantages and disadvantages of systematic reviews using individual patient data. *Eval Health Prof.* 2002;25:76–97.

Steyerberg EW. *Clinical Prediction Models: A Practical Approach to Development, Validation, and Updating.* New York, NY: Springer Science+Business Media; 2009.

Steyerberg EW, Bleeker SE, Moll HA, Grobbee DE, Moons KGM. Internal and external validation of predictive models: A simulation study of bias and precision in small samples. *J Clin Epidemiol.* 2003;56:441–447.

Steyerberg EW, Borsboom GJ, van Houwelingen HC, Eijkemans MJ, Habbema JD. Validation and updating of predictive logistic regression models: A study on sample size and shrinkage. *Stat Med.* 2004;23:256–2586.

Steyerberg EW, Eijkemans MJ, Harrell FE, Habbema JD. Prognostic modelling with logistic regression analysis: a comparison of selection and estimation methods in small data sets. *Stat Med.* 2000;19:1059–1079.

Steyerberg EW, Harrell FE Jr., Borsboom GJ, Eijkemans MJ, Vergouwe Y, Habbema JD. Internal validation of predictive models: efficiency of some procedures for logistic regression analysis. *J Clin Epidemiol.* 2001;54:774–781.

Steyerberg EW, Neville BA, Koppert LB, et al. Surgical mortality in patients with esophageal cancer: Development and validation of a simple risk score. *J Clin Oncol.* 2006;24:4277–4284.

Steyerberg EW, Pencina MJ, Lingsma HF, Kattan MW, Vickers AJ, Van Calster B. Assessing the incremental value of diagnostic and prognostic markers: A review and illustration. *Eur J Clin Invest.* 2012;42:216–228.

Stiell I, Wells G, Laupacis A, et al. Multicentre trial to introduce the Ottawa ankle rules for use of radiography in acute ankle injuries. Multicentre Ankle Rule Study Group. *BMJ.* 1995;311:594–597.

Strom BL, ed. *Pharmacoepidemiology.* 4th ed. Chicester: John Wiley; 2005.

Suarez-Almazor ME, Belseck E, Homik J, Dorgan M, Ramos-Remus C. Identifying clinical trials in the medical literature with electronic databases: MEDLINE alone is not enough. *Control Clin Trials.* 2000;21:476–487.

Sullivan JL. Iron and the sex difference in heart disease risk. *Lancet.* 1981;1:1293–1294.

Sun GW, Shook TL, Kay GL. Inappropriate use of bivariable analysis to screen risk factors for use in multivariable analysis. *J Clin Epidemiol.* 1996;49:907–916.

Sutton AJ, Abrams KR, Jones DR. Generalized synthesis of evidence and the threat of dissemination bias. The example of electronic fetal heart rate monitoring (EFM). *J Clin Epidemiol.* 2002;55:1013–1024.

Swartzman LC, Burkell J. Expectations and the placebo effect in clinical drug trials: Why we should not turn a blind eye to unblinding, and other cautionary notes. *Clin Pharmacol Ther.* 1998;64:1–7.

Sweeting MJ, Sutton AJ, Lambert PC. What to add to nothing? Use and avoidance of continuity corrections in meta-analysis of sparse data. *Stat Med.* 2004;23:1351–1375.

Swets JA. Measuring the accuracy of diagnostic systems. *Science.* 1988;240:1285–1293.

Tang JL. Weighting bias in meta-analysis of binary outcomes. *J Clin Epidemiol.* 2000;53:1130–1136.

Taubes G. Epidemiology faces its limits. *Science.* 1995;269:164–169.

ten Have M, Oldehinkel A, Vollebergh W, Ormel J. Does neuroticism explain variations in care service use for mental health problems in the general population? Results from the Netherlands Mental Health Survey and Incidence Study (NEMESIS). *Soc Psychiatry Psychiatr Epidemiol.* 2005;40:425–431.

Teo KK, Burton JR, Buller CE, et al. Long-term effects of cholesterol lowering and angiotensin-converting enzyme inhibition on coronary atherosclerosis: The Simvastatin/Enalapril Coronary Atherosclerosis Trial (SCAT). *Circulation.* 2000;102:1748–1754.

Thompson JF, Man M, Johnson KJ, et al. An association study of 43 SNPs in 16 candidate genes with atorvastatin response. *Pharmacogenomics J.* 2005;5:352–358.

Thompson SG, Higgins JP. How should meta-regression analyses be undertaken and interpreted? *Stat Med.* 2002;21:1559–1573.

Thornton A, Lee P. Publication bias in meta-analysis: Its causes and consequences. *J Clin Epidemiol.* 2000;53:207–216.

Toll DB, Janssen KJ, Vergouwe Y, Moons KG. Validation, updating and impact of clinical prediction rules: a review. *J Clin Epidemiol.* 2008;61:1085–1094.

Tu JV. Advantages and disadvantages of using artificial neural networks versus logistic regression for predicting medical outcomes. *J Clin Epidemiol.* 1996;49:1225–1231.

Tzoulaki I, Liberopoulos G, Ioannidis JP, Assessment of claims of improved prediction beyond the Framingham risk score. *JAMA.* 2009;302:2345–2352.

Unnebrink K, Windeler J. Intention-to-treat: Methods for dealing with missing values in clinical trials of progressively deteriorating diseases. *Stat Med.* 2001;20:3931–3946.

Urquhart, 2001, quoted at *www.pharmacoepi.org/publications/scribe_spring01.pdf.* Accessed May 9, 2013.

Vach W. *Logistic Regression with Missing Values in the Covariates.* New York, NY: Springer; 1994.

Vach W, Blettner M. Biased estimates of the odds ratio in case-control studies due to the use of ad hoc methods of correcting for missing values for confounding variables. *Am J Epidemiol.* 1991;134:895–907.

Van Berkum FN, Birkenhager JC, Grobbee DE, Stijnen T, Pols HA. Erasmus University Medical Center, Rotterdam, The Netherlands. Personal communication of unpublished data, Van Buuren S, Oudshoorn K. Flexible multivariate imputation by mice. Technical report. Leiden, The Netherlands: TNO prevention and Health, 1999. http://www.stefvanbuuren.nl/publications/ Flexible%20multivariate%20-%20TNO99054%201999.pdf. Accessed November 17, 2013.

Van Calster B, Van Belle V, Vergouwe Y, Timmerman D, Van Huffel S, Steyerberg EW. Extending the c-statistic to nominal polytomous outcomes: The Polytomous Discrimination Index. *Stat Med.* 2012;31:2610–2626.

Van den Brink RH, Ormel J, Tiemens BG, et al. Accuracy of general practitioner's prognosis of the 1-year course of depression and generalised anxiety. *Br J Psychiatry.* 2001;179:18–22. (Comment in *Br J Psychiatry.* 2001;179:177–178.)

Van de Garde EM, Hak E, Souverein PC, Hoes AW, van den Bosch JM, Leufkens HG. Statin treatment and reduced risk of pneumonia in patients with diabetes. *Thorax.* 2006;61:957–961.

Van den Bosch JE, Moons KGM, Bonsel GJ, Kalkman CJ. Does measurement of preoperative anxiety have added value in the prediction of postoperative nausea and vomiting? *Anesth Analg.* 2005;100:1525–1532.

Van den Bosch MA, Kemmeren JM, Tanis BC, et al. The RATIO study: Oral contraceptives and the risk of peripheral arterial disease in young women. *J Thromb Haemost.* 2003;1:439–444.

Van der A DL, Marx JJ, Grobbee DE, et al. Non-transferrin-bound iron and risk of coronary heart disease in postmenopausal women. *Circulation.* 2006;113:1942–1949.

van der Graaf R, van Delden JJ. Equipoise should be amended, not abandoned. *Clin Trials.* 2011;8(4):408–416.

Van der Heijden GJ, Donders AR, Stijnen T, Moons KGM. Handling missing data in multivariate diagnostic accuracy research: A clinical example. *J Clin Epidemiol.* 2006;59:1102–1109.

Van der Heijden GJ, Nathoe HM, Jansen EW, Grobbee DE. Meta-analysis on the effect of off-pump coronary bypass surgery. *Eur J Cardiothorac Surg.* 2004;26:81–84.

Van der Lei J, Duisterhout JS, Westerhoff HP, et al. The introduction of computer-based patient records in the Netherlands. *Ann Intern Med.* 1993;119:1036–1041.

Van der Schouw YT, Grobbee DE. Menopausal complaints, oestrogens, and heart disease risk: An explanation for discrepant findings on the benefits of post-menopausal hormone therapy. *Eur Heart J.* 2005;26:1358–1361.

Van Dijk D, Jansen EW, Hijman R, et al. Octopus Study Group. Cognitive outcome after off-pump and on-pump coronary artery bypass graft surgery: A randomized trial. *JAMA.* 2002;287:1405–1412.

Van Es RF, Jonker JJ, Verheugt FW, Deckers JW, Grobbee DE. Antithrombotics in the Secondary Prevention of Events in Coronary Thrombosis-2 (ASPECT-2) Research Group. Aspirin and coumadin after acute coronary syndromes (the ASPECT-2 study): A randomised controlled trial. *Lancet.* 2002;360:109–113.

Van Houwelingen JC. Shrinkage and penalized likelihood methods to improve diagnostic accuracy. *Stat Neerl.* 2001;55:17–34.

Van Houwelingen HC, Arends LR, Stijnen T. Advanced methods in meta-analysis: Multivariate approach and meta-regression. *Stat Med.* 2002;21:589–624.

Van Houwelingen JC, Le Cessie S. Predictive value of statistical models. *Stat Med.* 1990;9:1303–1325.

Vandenbroucke JP. Survival and expectation of life from the 1400s to the present. A study of the Knighthood Order of the Golden Fleece. *Am J Epidemiol.* 1985;122:1007–1016.

Vandenbroucke JP. When are observational studies as credible as randomised trials? *Lancet.* 2004;363:1728–1731.

Vandenbroucke JP. What is the best evidence for determining harms of medical treatment? *CMAJ.* 2006;174:645–646.

Vandenbroucke JP, Pierce N. Case-control studies: Basic concepts. *Int J Epidemiol.* 2012;41:1480–1489.

Vandenbroucke JP, Valkenburg HA, Boersma JW, et al. Oral contraceptives and rheumatoid arthritis: Further evidence for a preventive effect. *Lancet.* 1982;320:1839–1842.

Vergouwe Y, Steyerberg EW, Eijkemans MJ, Habbema JD. Validity of prognostic models: When is a model clinically useful? *Semin Urol Oncol.* 2002;20:96–107.

Verhagen AP, de Vet HC, de Bie RA, Kessels AG, Boers M, Knipschild PG. Balneotherapy and quality assessment: Interobserver reliability of the Maastricht criteria list and the need for blinded quality assessment. *J Clin Epidemiol.* 1998;51:335–341.

Vickers AJ, Elkin EB. Decision curve analysis: A novel method for evaluating prediction models. *Med Decis Making.* 2006;26:565–574.

Villeneuve PJ, Szyszkowicz M, Stieb D, Bourque DA. Weather and emergency room visits for migraine headaches in Ottawa, Canada. *Headache.* 2006;46:64–72.

Vinogradova Y, Coupland C, Hippisley-Cox J. Exposure to bisphosphonates and risk of gastrointestinal cancers: series of nested case-control studies with QResearch and CPRD data. *BMJ.* 2013;346:f114. doi: 10.1136/bmj.f114.

Voight BF, Peloso GM, Orho-Melander M. Plasma HDL cholesterol and risk of myocardial infarction: A mendelian randomisation study. *Lancet.* 2012;380:572–580.

Vural KM, Tasdemir O, Karagoz H, Emir M, Tarcan O, Bayazit K. Comparison of the early results of coronary artery bypass grafting with and without extracorporeal circulation. *Thorac Cardiovasc Surg.* 1995;43:320–325.

Wangge G, Klungel OH, Roes KC, de Boer A, Hoes AW, Knol MJ. Interpretation and inference in noninferiority randomized controlled trials in drug research. *Clin Pharmacol Ther.* 2010;88:420–423.

Wangge G, Klungel OH, Roes KC, de Boer A, Hoes AW, Knol MJ. Should non-inferiority drug trials be banned altogether? *Drug Discov Today.* 2013a. pii: S1359-6446(13)00005-6. doi: 10.1016/j.drudis.2013.01.003. [Epub ahead of print].

Wangge G, Roes KC, de Boer A, Hoes AW, Knol MJ. The challenges of determining noninferiority margins: A case study of noninferiority randomized controlled trials of novel oral anticoagulants. *CMAJ.* 2013b;185:222–227.

Watson RJ, Richardson PH. Accessing the literature on outcome studies in group psychotherapy: The sensitivity and precision of MEDLINE and PsycINFO bibliographic database searching. *Br J Med Psychol.* 1999a;72(Pt 1):127–134.

Watson RJ, Richardson PH. Identifying randomised controlled trials of cognitive therapy for depression: Comparing the efficiency of EMBASE, MEDLINE and PsycINFO bibliographic databases. *Br J Med Psychol.* 1999b;72(Pt 4):535–542.

Weijnen CF, Hendriks HA, Hoes AW, Verweij WM, Verheij TJ, de Wit NJ. New immunoassay for the detection of Helicobacter pylori infection compared with urease test, 13C breath test and histology: Validation in the primary care setting. *J Microbiol Methods.* 2001;46:235–240.

Weinberg C, Wacholder S. The design and analysis of case-control studies with biased sampling. *Biometrics.* 1990;46:963–975.

Weinberg CR, Sandler DP. Randomized recruitment in case-control studies. *Am J Epidemiol.* 1991;134:421–432.

Wells PS, Anderson DR, Bormanis J, et al. Value of assessment of pretest probability of deep-vein thrombosis in clinical management. *Lancet.* 1997;350:1795–1758.

Whang Y, Klein JG, Zhang Y, et al. Gene-expression profiles to predict distant metastasis of lymph-node-negative primary breast cancer. *Lancet.* 2005;365:671–679.

Whitehead A. A prospectively planned cumulative meta-analysis applied to a series of concurrent clinical trials. *Stat Med.* 1997;16:2901–2913.

Whiting PF, Rutjes AW, Westwood ME, et al. QUADAS-2 Group. QUADAS-2: A revised tool for the quality assessment of diagnostic accuracy studies. *Ann Intern Med.* 2011;155:529–536.

Wilczynski NL, Haynes RB. Robustness of empirical search strategies for clinical content in MEDLINE. *Proc AMIA Symp.* 2002;904–908.

Wilczynski NL, Morgan D, Haynes RB. An overview of the design and methods for retrieving high-quality studies for clinical care. *BMC Med Inform Decis Mak.* 2005;5:20.

Wilczynski NL, Walker CJ, McKibbon KA, Haynes RB. Quantitative comparison of pre-explosions and subheadings with methodologic search terms in MEDLINE. *Proc Annu Symp Comput Appl Med Care.* 1994;905–909.

Willich SN, Lewis M, Lowel H, Arntz HR, Schubert F, Schroder R. Physical exertion as a trigger of acute myocardial infarction. Triggers and Mechanisms of Myocardial Infarction Study Group. *N Engl J Med.* 1993;329:1684–1690.

Wilson PW, D'Agostino RB, Levy D, Belanger AM, Silbershatz H, Kannel WB. Prediction of coronary heart disease using risk factor categories. *Circulation.* 1998;97:1837–1847.

Wong SS, Wilczynski NL, Haynes RB. Comparison of top-performing search strategies for detecting clinically sound treatment studies and systematic reviews in MEDLINE and EMBASE. *J Med Libr Assoc.* 2006a;94:451–455.

Wong SS, Wilczynski NL, Haynes RB. Optimal CINAHL search strategies for identifying therapy studies and review articles. *J Nurs Scholarsh.* 2006b;38:194–199.

Yasunaga H, Horiguchi H, Kuwabara K, et al. Outcomes after laparoscopic or open distal gastrectomy for early-stage gastric cancer: a propensity-matched analysis. *Ann Surg.* 2013;257:640–646.

Zaffanella LE, Savitz DA, Greenland S, Ebi KL. The residential case-specular method to study wire codes, magnetic fields, and disease. *Epidemiology.* 1998;9:16–20.

Zelen M. A new design for randomized clinical trials. *N Engl J Med.* 1979;300:1242–1245.

Zhang L, Ajiferuke I, Sampson M. Optimizing search strategies to identify randomised controlled trials in MEDLINE. *BMC Med Res Methodol.* 2006;6:23.

Zoungas S, de Galan BE, Ninomiya T, et al. Combined effects of routine blood pressure lowering and intensive glucose control on macrovascular and microvascular outcomes in patients with type 2 diabetes: New results from the ADVANCE trial. *Diabetes Care.* 2009;32:2068–2074.

Index

Note: Page numbers followed by *b*, *f*, or *t* indicate material in boxes, figures, or tables, respectively.

CPSIA information can be obtained
at www.ICGtesting.com
Printed in the USA
FSHW021709240321
79796FS